TAXES, LIBERTY AND PROPERTY

Ve·roche sanctissie
nobili natus sã
guine? euas sig
nans stēmate: si
nistro tuo latere: Roche przegre
prosectus: pestifere mortis tact

FERDINAND H. M. GRAPPERHAUS

TAXES, LIBERTY AND PROPERTY

the role of taxation in democratization and national unity 511-1787

MEIJBURG & CO.

After centuries of a "Naturalwirtschaft", a monetary economy slowly began to emerge in the 11th century. Initially, only silver and bronze coins were issued. It was not until the 13th century that gold gradually began to come into circulation. The "écu", a coin depicting a shield (French: écu), was minted in France in the first half of the 14th century. The print depicted here was taken from the Book of Hours of Albrecht of Brandenburg (1522-1523). It shows St. Rochus of Montpellier distributing the possessions of his wealthy and recently deceased parents to the poor, an act symbolized by the stream of gold and silver coins. Rochus then became a beggar and pilgrim. During his travels in Italy, he healed many plague victims with his prayers. Stricken with the plague in Piacenza, Rochus went into seclusion and was cared for by an angel. Every day, his faithful dog brought him bread and licked his sores clean. He died around 1327.

Translated from the Dutch by Susan Massotty.

Taxes, Liberty and Property has been published to observe the 50th anniversary of the founding of Meijburg & Co., Tax Consultants in Amsterdam.

© 1989 F. H. M. Grapperhaus, Amsterdam

Published by: De Walburg Pers/Kluwer

Publication and design: De Walburg Pers, Zutphen
Jacket design: Ferdinand H. M. Grapperhaus

CIP / ISBN 906011.665.8

Contents

Preface   9

1   **Verdun**   15

Striding through the history of the Merovingians and Carolingians in seven-league boots   15

Gregory of Tours' "History of the Franks"   22

Stories of Gregory of Tours in which taxation plays a role   29

Fredegund and Brunhild   34

Taxes in the Merovingian age: head tax and land tax   38

A free Frank does not (or should not?) have to pay taxes   42

The Treasury   43

The Edict of Paris of 614   46

The Carolingian state   47

The feudal system   52

The imposition of tolls   55

Voluntary donations   56

The dissolution of the Carolingian state and the disappearance of taxation   57

2   **Cologne**   61

Bishops as administrators in the Eastern Frankish Kingdom   61

From feudalism to sovereignty   64

Taxation: a prerogative of the holders of the powers of low justice   69

The four cases in which subjects were obliged to pay taxes to the sovereign ruler   71

Taxation of the clergy   74

Both the Archbishop and the city gain power and prestige   75

The unsuccessful rebellion against Archbishop Anno   80

The city begins to organize   84

Taxation and the Large Council   87

The city and its Archbishop: a marriage of convenience turns sour   88

The struggle between the Staufers and the Welfs   89

Engelbrecht of Berg: the city is no match for the Archbishop   92

Conrad of Hochstadt: constant strife between the city and the Archbishop   96

Siegfried of Westerburg: the city gains virtual independence   101

The guilds struggle to obtain more influence over the municipal
government   104

Diedrich of Moers, an ambitious potentate in the Archbishop's chair   113

Poor government sows the seeds of financial troubles   114

The successes and failures of Diedrich of Moers' political objectives   115

The estates in *Kurköln*   120

Diedrich of Moers finds it increasingly difficult to obtain the approval
of the estates for his taxes   121

3   Utrecht   129

The Netherlands on the threshold of the revolt against Spain   129

The need for tax reform   136

The events in the decade prior to the outbreak of the revolt
against Spain   137

Alva proposes new taxes   146

Utrecht: a special case   151

The adoption of Alva's tax program   153

A temporary outright grant of two million florins a year replaces
the Tenth and Twentieth Pennies   159

The placard of July 31, 1571 immediately implementing the Tenth
and Twentieth Pennies   168

The growing opposition to the Tenth Penny   174

Increasing resistance to the Tenth Penny   176

Alva fails to collect the Tenth Penny   181

The last resort: deputations to the King   185

Suspension and abolition of the Tenth and Twentieth Pennies   187

Replacing the Tenth Penny with other taxes also fails   191

The significance of the Tenth Penny   195

The failure of the Tenth Penny and the struggle against
the reinforcement of absolutist royal authority   200

Convoys and licenses, the only common taxation under the
Union of Utrecht   203

4   Westminster   217

England under James I, the first Stuart king   217

Foreign relations   223

The leaven of religion   229

The first Parliament under Charles I (1625)   230

The second Parliament under Charles I (1626)   238

The third Parliament under Charles I (1628 - 1629)   243

The Petition of Right   247

Tonnage and poundage: the right to impose taxes   251

A peaceful interlude   257

The ship money affair   260

The case of Rex versus Hampden   267

The Short Parliament   275

The Long Parliament   280

5   **Boston**   291

The thirteen American colonies   291

Relations with the Mother Country   300

Tea   305

The Stamp Act   307

The Townshend Acts   318

Incidents   329

The East India Company starts shipping tea to America   334

The situation in Boston   337

The Boston Tea Party   341

British sanctions   353

The colonies join forces and rise in revolt   358

The Articles of Confederation   363

The new Constitution   371

Maps

The Frankish Kingdom in the Merovingian period   376

The division of the Frankish Kingdom by the Treaty of Verdun (843)   377

Cologne and the surrounding area at the end of the 13th century   378

The Low Countries in 1559   380

The thirteen American colonies on the eve of the Revolution   381

Index of Persons   383

Bibliography   393

List of illustrations   405

THE EUROPEAN DILIGENCE.

An engraving made in 1779, when the American colonies were in full revolt against Great Britain. Each European country meddled in the War of Independence according to its own self-interest. Despite its treaty with England, Holland profited from the smuggling of weapons via the island of St. Eustatius. Holland, represented as a crude farmer pushing a wheelbarrow over fallen England, steps on the Memorial to Sir Joseph Yorke and asks: "What's treatise to gilt?" (What is a treaty compared to money?) France, seated in the wheelbarrow, says to England: "O Madame 'tis de fine Politique." America adds: "My good and great Ally, strike home," while Spain calls out: "Now Brother of Portugal join the Confederacy and Agrandize our Family." Poor England cries: "Ah Cruil Neighbours thus to assist Rebellious Children." On the wheelbarrow is written: "De Jonge Johan Petronella Cornelis Dirk Vandermeulen for Eustatia," evidently a reference to a ship and a well-known Dutch merchant. The farmer is blocked by an English soldier saying: "My Mistress is determined to Chastise Yr HOGEN MOGEN for Yr Ingratitude and Duplicity and Oblidge you to Assist that Power that first Assisted you." Although the print was primarily intended to express English resentment at the apparent perfidy of the Dutch, in a broader perspective, it can also be said to depict the disunity among the countries, extending across the Atlantic Ocean. As one of the themes of this book is that common taxation can promote national unity, the print serves as a suitable introduction to this work.

Preface

This book owes its existence to an initiative of Meijburg & Co., Tax Consultants, with offices in Amsterdam, Rotterdam, The Hague, Utrecht and other locations in The Netherlands as well as in Brussels (Belgium) and Willemstad (Curaçao). With 55 partners and approximately 350 employees, Meijburg & Co. is an independent and autonomous organization affiliated with the KPMG Group, an international organization of accountants, tax consultants and organizational consultants, totaling 5,050 partners and 63,700 employees in 105 countries.

Founded in 1939, Meijburg & Co. is one of the oldest established companies of its kind in Europe. Meijburg & Co. decided to celebrate its 50th anniversary in 1989 with the publication of a jubilee book, examining the social implications of taxation in the broadest sense of the term. The author, an independent consultant affiliated with Meijburg & Co., narrowed this theme to the influence of taxation on the political emancipation of Western Europe and North America, which can be summarized as follows: by voluntarily agreeing to taxation, certain groups in society obtained the right to participate in discussions about revenue expenditures, enabling them to exert some influence on national government. In time, this participation assumed the form of a popular assembly elected by general franchise. When politically fragmented territorial units started sharing financial burdens with other regions, a modern unified state began to evolve.

The author was entrusted with writing a book of interest to the general reader rather than a textbook and was charged with achieving a balance between scholarship and anecdote, text and illustration, seriousness and entertainment, factual accounts and descriptive sketches. The author has thus confined himself to a narrative of events and has only occasionally delved into the underlying questions of cause and effect. The author has assumed that the reader will want to determine whether the events described here are relevant to today's world. The reader is free to choose between two basic options: there is nothing new under the sun or the past cannot be compared to the present.

Given these aims, exact references to sources have been omitted; instead, a bibliography of each chapter has been included at the end of the book. For the reader's convenience, an index of the characters appearing in the book, a set of maps and a genealogical chart of the Merovingian kings (page 26) has also been provided. In resolving orthographical problems, preference has been given to historical convention and the use of terms familiar to the general reader. The author felt fully justified in Chapter 3 in borrowing from two of his earlier Dutch-language publications, ''Alva and the Tenth Penny'' (1984) and ''Convoys and Licenses'' (1986), which describe fiscal developments in The Netherlands in the sixteenth century.

The book has been divided into five independent chapters. The chapters deal with the events of five chronologically ordered periods in five different geographical areas. This number appeared to be a workable compromise between having too little material to weave the various threads together and having too much material, so that the reader would no longer be able to see the wood for the trees.

Chapter 1 describes the centuries-long disintegration of the tax system that the Frankish conquerors had adopted (starting in c. 500) from the Gallo-Roman system of government. This disintegration occurred in conjunction with the erosion of central government and the rise of regional and local centers of power. Because of the key role played by the Treaty of Verdun (843) in this process of dissolution, this chapter is entitled ''Verdun.''

Chapter 2 first recounts the many conflicts over taxation between the city of Cologne and its secular ruler, the Archbishop of Cologne (in the period from 953 - 1463). The city ultimately gained control of the revenue and thus became a free imperial city, independent of the Archbishop. The chapter then goes on to describe the guilds' struggle to wrest the right to impose taxes (and assume power) from the city's patricians. Lastly, the Archbishop's attempts to extend his *external* power by purchasing or capturing fortresses, cities and regions are outlined. To finance his ambitious expansionist policies, the Archbishop sacrificed *internal* power to the representatives of the three estates, i.e. the clergy, the nobility and the cities. Once the estates held the purse strings, they gained a voice in government. Consequently, this chapter plays a pivotal role in the book, as it illustrates how the flower of democratization blossomed under the influence of taxation.

Chapter 3 concentrates on the Duke of Alva, who was sent by King Philip II of Spain to govern the Low Countries. In 1569, Alva introduced a tax, the so-called Tenth Penny. As a step toward political unity between the provinces, Alva wished to establish a *uniform* tax applicable to all provinces. He also hoped to make the Tenth Penny a *permanent* tax, so that the King would not have to continually request the approval of the provincial assembly, the States-General, for a tax known as an ''aid.'' As the King would have no further use for the States-General, he would be able to become an absolute ruler. The ensuing Dutch Revolt foiled Alva's twofold design. The seven Northern provinces eventually united in the Union of Utrecht in 1579. Their attempts to set up a common system of taxation failed. As a result, the Dutch Republic long remained a mere confederation of states rather than a federal state. This chapter owes its title ''Utrecht'' to the Union of Utrecht and to the fact that the province of Utrecht was the only province to reject Alva's Tenth Penny.

Chapter 4 narrates Charles I's attempt to set himself up as an absolute ruler in England. As the King wished to govern without consulting Parliament, he resorted to various extra-parliamentary means to obtain income for the Crown. An account is also given of the trial of John Hampden (1637), who refused to pay ship money because permission for this levy had not been previously obtained from Parliament. Although the Crown won the case, it was a Pyrrhic victory, for it awakened many minds to the danger of absolute monarchy. Charles' tax troubles were therefore a harbinger of the Civil War, which led to his execution in 1649. Because of the key role played by Parliament, this chapter is entitled ''Westminster.''

Chapter 5 takes the reader to Boston, in English eyes the most troublesome of the cities in the thirteen American colonies. The import duties levied on the colonies by the English Parliament led to serious unrest, for the colonists resisted the concept of "taxation without representation." Their opposition culminated in the Boston Tea Party (1773), in which the residents of Boston threw tea subject to an English tax into the harbor. The bumbling reactions of the English government encouraged the colonies to rally together, and the American Revolution ensued. The newborn confederation of states was hampered by the fact that the government could not levy taxes on its citizens. The new Constitution of the United States, which was drawn up in 1787, empowered the federal government to impose taxes. Only when common taxes were imposed was the foundation for a unified state laid and was the United States able to develop into a world power. Although other American cities were imbued with patriotic fervor, Boston was a prominent center of colonial resistance, sufficient reason to confer its name on the last chapter.

At this point, it might be useful to put some meat on the bones of this outline by sketching the relationship between taxation and the process of democratization and national unity. The Merovingian kings failed to maintain the Gallo-Roman system of taxation. The central government eroded, until feudal lords held sway over territorial units of various sizes. After the decline of feudalism, Western Europe had to be politically restructured from these fragmented territories. For centuries, the relationship between a feudal lord and vassal or a ruler and his subjects was dominated by the principle of mutual aid. The ruler provided shelter and protection, and in return received the subjects' aid and advice.

The imposition of taxes in Europe grew out of this mutual obligation. The subjects gradually began offering their ruler an impersonal monetary payment in lieu of personal services. This development occurred in conjunction with a return to a monetary economy, the rise of cities and the creation of mercenary armies. The general decline in the mutual obligation inherent in the ruler-subject relationship gave rise to greater cooperation and solidarity among various groups in society. The estates which eventually came to represent these groups voluntarily decided to contribute financial aid to the sovereign ruler in exchange for a greater voice in government affairs. Initially, the estates' interest did not extend any further than their own group. Later, it was expanded to encompass their own city, their own province and eventually their own country, a process spanning several centuries. In theory, it is an ongoing process, as today countries are cooperating on an increasingly broader scale.

The evolution of popular representation from the concept of mutual obligation (described in Chapter 2) was a long and eventful process. Initially, only the clergy, the nobility and the cities had a voice in government affairs. The fiction that these groups represented the people gained in truth as the active and passive right to vote (to borrow some old-fashioned terms) was expanded to broader segments of society. Citizens can personally give their fiat to government decisions, as still happens in some small cantons in Switzerland, or they can elect representatives to govern in their name. The process of political enfranchisement is exemplified by the conflict over taxation between England and the thirteen American colonies (Chapter 5), which can be summed up in four words: "no taxation without representation."

Through the ages, emphasis has always been placed on the voluntary nature of taxation, even though the representative assemblies approving tax levies in the name of the people were initially elitist and centuries passed before broad layers of society were represented. Indeed, the term "aid" used to describe a medieval tax (Chapter 1) underscores this voluntary aspect. The pamphlets opposing the Stamp Act and William Pitt's speeches in favor of its repeal (Chapter 5) paid more than lip service to the concept that taxation was based on a voluntary act.

Occasionally, the representative bodies placed restrictions on these voluntary contributions. For example, the seventeen Dutch provinces (Chapter 3) were able to set conditions on tax revenue expenditures, trade and foreign policy, and thus gain a certain amount of political clout. Alva attempted to make the Tenth Penny a permanent tax so that the King would not be dependent on the States-General and could become a *señor assoluto*. Three quarters of a century later, the same process took place under the first two Stuart kings (Chapter 4). Charles I's attempts to levy ship money were also motivated by his desire to become an absolute ruler.

As a holdover from the system of mutual aid, the estates initially only granted taxes when the revenues were spent on their own regions. For instance, the residents of the province of Brabant had no desire to help pay for something that only benefitted the province of Holland. On a broader level, the people in the Low Countries had no vested interest in Spain's conflicts and did not wish to help finance Spanish wars (Chapter 3). The attempts of Alva and the Union of Utrecht to create a common system of taxation and thus forge unity in The Netherlands failed miserably. In contrast, unity was achieved in America, shortly after the colonies had achieved independence (Chapter 5). Common sense and common taxation were the foundation for the voluntary cooperation between the individual states and thus for their union.

Voluntary rather than obligatory cooperation between peoples and societies presupposes a higher plane of civilization. The concept of political emancipation must be viewed in this context. In this sense, it can be said that, through the ages, taxation has acted as a lubricant smoothing the way toward a democratic unified state, the main theme of this book.

At this point, a word on the title of the book seems appropriate. For individual citizen, *taxes* constitute a compulsory payment (in cash or in kind) to the government, for which he or she receives no individual benefit in return. Although taxes are compulsory, in a democratic society the citizens as a whole have consented in *liberty* (via their popularly elected assemblies) to curtail their power over finances and therefore their own *property* by means of taxation.

One last remark. To those who feel the book's title, "TAXES, LIBERTY AND PROPERTY," gives too materialistic a view of politics, the author would like to point out that taxation is frequently a driving force in the achievement of political, social and religious freedom. Freedom is at the center of this book's title, just as it is at the center of this process!

The author would like to extend his thanks to Drs. Wouter Kotte of Utrecht, Dr. Giselle de Nie of Schalkwijk, Prof. Dr. Bernhard Diestelkamp of Frankfurt am Main, Dr. Simon Groenveld of Hoofddorp and Prof. Dr. Wim Schulte Nordholt of Wassenaar, who read earlier versions of respectively the entire manuscript, Chapter 1, Chapter 2, Chapter 4 and Chapter 5 and offered critical and instructive comments. Naturally, the author is ultimately accountable for the final text.

Further, the author would like to express his appreciation for the assistance received from various library staff members, including those of the Vrije Universiteit in Amsterdam, the Rijksuniversiteit in Leiden, the Bibliotheca Philosophica Hermetica in Amsterdam, the Bibliothèque Municipal in Laon, the Bibliothèque National in Paris, the British Library in London, the libraries of the Universities of Cologne, Bamberg and Kansas and the library of the University of Florida, College of Law, in Gainesville, as well as the Print Room of the Rijksmuseum in Amsterdam, the Museum of Fine Arts in Boston, the Print Room of the Rijksuniversiteit in Leiden, The Print and Drawing Room of the British Museum in London, the Archives Nationals in Paris, the Rijksmuseum Het Catharijneconvent in Utrecht, the Städtisches Museum in Ingelheim, the Musée Condé in Chantilly, the Musée des Antiquités Nationales in Saint-Germain-en-Laye, the Musée d'Art et d'Histoire de la Ville de St. Denis, the Musée Nationale des Art et Traditions Populaires, the Erzbischöfliches Diözesan-Museum in Cologne, the Schnütgen Museum in Cologne, the Graphische Sammlung des Walraff-Richartz-Museum in Cologne, the Centraal Museum in Utrecht, the Topografisch-Historische Atlas in Utrecht, the Abdij Saint Maurice in Saint-Maurice, the Mary Evans Picture Library in London, the Mansell Collection in London, the Rheinische Bildarchiv in Cologne and the Photographie Giraudon in Paris. Moreover, the author would like to express his gratitude to Her Majesty, Queen Elizabeth of Great Britain, for permission to reproduce the portraits in her possession as well as to the City of Boston and the Francis Bartlett Foundation.

The author is indebted to the many who helped obtain suitable illustrations, but would particularly like to single out the efforts of Christa Kämper, Prof. Anton Legner and Clemens Sandmann of Cologne, Suzanne Martinet of Laon, Prof. Dr. Pieter Obbema of Leiden, Prof. Dr. F. A. Jansen of Amsterdam, Theo Laurentius of Voorschoten, Nico Israël of Amsterdam, H. Kettlitz of Utrecht, Janet Hennessy and Leslie Keller of Boston, Melitta Zimmer of Ingelheim, Francis Duncals and Paul Dove of London, Marguérite La Porte of Noyon and Johann Kumpf of Siegburg.

Ria van den Akker, with her word processor, helped immeasurably with the preparation of the manuscript and also arbitrated on the use of the Dutch language. Karin Gouveneur provided a large portion of the references, Kees Slager put together the Index of Persons and the maps and Susan Massotty worked diligently for months on the translation, with the editorial assistance of Gordon Watson, Nicholas Webb, Susan Lyons and Frances Corbett. The author is deeply grateful for the assistance of all of these individuals.

Baptism of Clovis in 496 (?) (from a 14th century manuscript).

1 Verdun

Striding through the history of the Merovingians and Carolingians in seven-league boots

For centuries, Germanic tribes had been chipping away at the northern regions which the Romans had managed to bring under their rule. Gaul, the fertile territory which Julius Caesar had conquered in the first century B.C. and which, fully Romanized, formed an integral part of the Roman Empire, had made a virtue of necessity by including the invaders in their mercenary armies and thus fighting Germans with Germans. When the pressure of the tribes drifting from Middle Europe became too great, this system began, in the second half of the fourth century, to burst at its seams, until it collapsed in the course of the fifth century under the repeated waves of onrushing Vandals, Visigoths, Avars and Franks. When in 476 the German Odoacer deposed the last Emperor, Romulus Augustulus, this set the seal on a process of disintegration that had been going on for decades, much as the walls of a blazing house suddenly cave in because the wooden supports have collapsed.

This chapter will illustrate how the Gallo-Roman system of taxation, which was adopted by the Franks, disappeared in the course of a few centuries as the Frankish Kingdom fell into decline. Before going into this topic further, it will be useful to give a rough indication of how the Franks fared in Gaul.

The Franks — a collective term later used to describe several tribes, the most important of which were the Ripuarians and the Salians — broke through the collapsing Roman lines of defense around the middle of the fifth century and began to fan out over the Belgian provinces and Northern Gaul. The dynasty of the Merovingians was founded by a legendary king supposedly named Merovech, head of the largest tribe, the Salians. The first of the Merovingians to emerge into the full light of history was Chlodovech,[1] better known as Clovis, who expanded his sphere of influence considerably during his reign. Working from the center — the area between the Rhine and the Meuse, along the Seine and between the Somme and the Loire — he built up a large empire by successively defeating the Alamans in the Southeast and the Visigoths in the Southwest. The territories and tribes which could not be overcome by force of arms were annexed by none too fastidious methods; the king did not balk at deceit, breach of promise or even murder. A typical example is the story of how Sigibert, a Frankish king headquartered in Cologne and ruling over the Frankish tribe inhabiting the area to the left of the Rhine, met his end. Sigibert was already old when he was crippled in the Battle of Zülpich in 497, fighting side by side with Clovis against the Alamans. In this condition, he was unfit to lead his warriors to victory. In 508 Clovis sent a message to Chloderic, Sigibert's son, acknowledging that if the father were to die, his kingdom should by right pass to his son. Chloderic understood this to mean that Clovis would recognize him as king after his father's death and had his father killed during a hunting party in the forest. He sent word of this to Clovis and invited him to come select a few jewels from his late father's treasure chest. Clovis sent two servants to Chloderic, and they killed him while he was bending over his father's treasure chest. Clovis then appeared before the assembled soldiers, washed his hands of guilt and accused Chloderic

1. The French form of his name, Clovis, is more familiar to us. In German his name is Chlodwig, from which Ludwig was derived by omitting the ch. This ultimately led to Louis.

*Clovis is raised on a shield
and thus proclaimed king
(19th century print).*

of patricide. And so Clovis was lifted on his shield and proclaimed king of this tribe as well.

Although Clovis' conversion to Christianity (c. 496?) may have been prompted by political expedience rather than religious zeal, the subsequent Christianization of the Franks did create a common basis for the coexistence of the Frankish rulers and the Gallo-Roman inhabitants, who still constituted the overwhelming majority of the population. Christianization also gained Clovis the approval of the Emperor of the East Roman Empire — at that time still a force to be reckoned with — and laid the foundation for his collaboration with the Church, which was gradually growing in power and prestige. A significant point is the fact that the metropolitan bishops, who were generally descended from Gallo-Roman senatorial circles, were by and large able administrators and capable, when necessary, of defending with force the interests of the people against the excesses of what will be referred to here (for lack of a better word) as the Frankish government. That Clovis opted for the Orthodox variant of the Christianity of that time rather than the Arian one, which was already in retreat and had been declared heretical, can be attributed to his search for support against the Arian Visigoths. He also undoubtedly heeded the promptings of his wife Clotild, the daughter of a Burgundian king and a Catholic.

The Franks realized that it would be better to leave the Gallo-Roman structure of government intact (although it did erode) and were prepared to allow their new subjects to live under the existing laws, usages and customs. The existing civilization did not die out; instead, a gradual assimilation process was set in motion. The feuds, vendettas and civil wars the Franks inflicted upon each other contrasted sharply with their peaceful coexistence with the original Gallo-Roman population. Mixed marriages, shared habitation in cities and joint trade and real-estate transactions were facts of everyday life. The dividing line between the two population groups faded as time went by. The most persistent distinction was that the Salian Franks lived according to the *Lex Salica* (c. 510) and the Ripuarian Franks according to the *Lex Ripuaria* (beginning of the 7th century), while the old Roman legislation remained in force for the Gallo-Romans. In later times, when other peoples — Burgundians, Bretons, Basks, Goths, Slavs and Thuringians — were subjected to Frankish rule, they were allowed to keep their own tribal structure. In fact, the Frankish Kingdom, with its many peoples, was only held together by the monarchy.

Clovis shifted his residence from Tournai to Paris, which he turned into a genuine capital. Additional residences were added in Soissons, Rheims and Orléans. This novel development for the Franks, who were more or less nomads, clearly resulted from their striving toward territorial power. Nevertheless, the king continued to move around, preferring to hold court on his estates.

When he died, Clovis left behind four sons and a daughter. The oldest, Theuderic,[2] was the result of an unlawful union, while the three remaining sons, Childebert, Chlodomer and Lothar,[3] were products of his marriage with Clotild. Because Clovis himself had been the only son, his succession from his father, Childeric, had posed no problems. Nothing is known about inheritance matters prior to Clovis.

The situation was totally different in 511, when Clovis left behind him a large and established kingdom that stretched from Flanders to the Provence and from Normandy to the Rhine. The succession which took place in that year has turned out to be of great significance for the development of Europe. The kingdom that Clovis and his father had built up was divided among Clovis' four sons. As three of them were still minors, it is likely that Clovis himself roughly outlined his succession. This is not inconsistent with the fact that the sons later had the division confirmed in a treaty. It did not matter that the oldest, Theuderic, was illegitimate. The four portions were neither equal nor contiguous. For example, the youngest son, Lothar, received the smallest portion, the region known today as Flanders, Picardy and Artois, as well as the region between the Pyrenees and Toulouse. This division into separate sub-kingdoms did not mean that four entirely separate, independent states were created. There was still a strong degree of cohesiveness, which was buttressed by the fact that the brothers conferred with each other as kings of the sub-kingdoms and sometimes took common action, even though they waged wars or conspired against each other from time to time. Their internecine feuds did not prevent them from extending the Frankish Kingdom even further by subjecting the Thuringians and the Burgundians to their rule and advancing beyond the Alps and annexing Northern Italy.

In the Frankish view, both the kingdom and the estates denoted as "crown domains" belonged to the royal family in its entirety. This blood right probably dates back to the beliefs of German paganism and explains the division among the four sons. The Franks were not familiar with the right of primogeniture, in which only the eldest son inherited the crown. The burning question that arose soon was whether, when one of the brothers died, the other three could divide up the deceased's portion or whether the dead king's own children should be eligible for succession. In the latter case, the lack of a right of primogeniture would create an increasingly fragmented kingdom. Such disintegration was held in check for several centuries in a row, thanks to a series of strong personalities,

2. Theodore. In German, Diedrich and in French, Thierry.
3. As with Clovis, his name was originally spelled with a ch: Chlotachar.

first under the Merovingians and then under the Carolingians, each of whom became ruler over the entire kingdom by means of deception, murder or some other act of violence, or simply because a rival died in battle or in his sleep, although the latter was a rarity. It was only in 843 that the kingdom, which in the meantime had grown considerably and now covered the greater part of what is currently continental Western Europe, was divided into three parts by the Treaty of Verdun. This event ultimately led to the division of Western Europe into independent states.

The tripartite division into a Western Kingdom, a Middle Kingdom and an Eastern Kingdom was replaced in 925 by a bipartite division when the northern part of the Lotharian Middle Kingdom was acquired by the Eastern Kingdom after the rest of the Middle Kingdom had broken up into a number of small territories. In the centuries that followed, a further fragmentation into small, or even minute, territorial units took place, first in the Western Kingdom and later in the Eastern Kingdom. By an extremely laborious process, the nations of France and Germany were built up from these fragments. The foundation for these two countries, and therefore for the differences between them which have so long held sway over the European stage, can be traced back to the first division which took place in 511. Even though the kingdom was then divided into four parts, the embryo of the bipartite division was already present, for the most important parts were Neustria (in the region north of Paris) and Austrasia (on the left bank of the Rhine).

But let us return to the division of 511. The problem was whether the share of a brother who died would be passed on to the remaining brothers through accretion or to his descendants through inheritance. This problem cropped up shortly after Clovis' death when one of the sons, Chlodomer, was killed in action in 524 in the battle against the Burgundians. The youngest brother, Lothar, who had been dealt the poorest hand, saw his opportunity. After hearing of his brother's demise, Lothar rushed to his brother's palace and married the widow, thus laying claim to the royal treasury. The significance of this treasury (consisting of jewels, gold, horses and even warehouses full of grain and barrels of wine) will be dealt with later. Chlodomer left behind three sons, who were taken into protective custody by their grandmother, Clotild. Her aim was to safeguard the interests of her grandsons and to have them succeed to Chlodomer's kingdom. Her son Lothar now stood in the way of this endeavor. He had two of the three sons murdered. The third escaped by the skin of his teeth by cutting off his long hair − a characteristic of the Frankish kings − as a sign that he was taking clerical orders. He then went into hiding in a monastery. This cleared the way for the other brothers to divide up Chlodomer's kingdom. To unfold all the machinations of the remaining brothers with respect to each other − these ranged from innocent adoption to less innocent assassination attempts − would be to stray too far from the subject at hand. To cut a long story short, in 559 Lothar was the sole survivor; his brother Childebert died childless and the children of the other brother, Theuderic, were dead. Consequently, the reins of the kingdom were once again in one hand. Two years later, Lothar died as well, and the merry-go-round was set spinning again, for he also left behind four sons: Charibert, Guntram, Sigibert and Chilperic.

The story is unfortunately all too repetitive, for hatred and malice, murder and fraternal strife, deceit and betrayal predominated among Lothar's four sons as

Wooden bucket found in Cologne in a 6th century grave of a young boy.

Helmet found in Cologne in a 6th century grave of a young boy.

well. At the end of it all, Lothar II, the son of Chilperic, remained and proceeded in 613 to unite the entire kingdom under his blood-stained scepter. His son, Dagobert, who ruled from 629 to 639, was the last of the mighty Merovingian kings. How this dynasty continued after that, feuding and slaughtering each other, is not so important, for a new dynasty, later dubbed the Carolingians, presented itself at about this time. In the eastern part of the Frankish Kingdom, called Austrasia, the founder of the Carolingian dynasty had risen to the position of major-domo or mayor of the palace. As manager of the royal household, the holder of this office was the most important servant in the king's court. In 687, one of the members of this dynasty, Pepin of Heristal, got control of the office of the mayor of the palace in the three sub-kingdoms and made the office hereditary. Thus the power of the Carolingians rose as the significance of the Merovingians declined.

One of the best-known mayors of the palace was Pepin's son, Charles Martel, who at the Battle of Poitiers (732) was able to repel the persistent attacks of the Moslems and to keep Islam at bay, even though it would plague large parts of Southern France, Sicily and the Italian peninsula for centuries. In 751 the current mayor of the palace, Pepin the Short, deposed the last Merovingian king with papal approval. Putting an end to the Merovingian monarchy which had ruled for centuries, ever since the great Clovis, was no small matter, and Pepin was wise enough to obtain the consent of the kingdom's magnates. Three years later, the Pope consecrated and anointed him as king of the Frankish Kingdom. The king's wife and sons were likewise anointed. An alliance was thus forged between the Pope and the Carolingians. While the papal consecration and anointment of Pepin added a religious dimension to the kingship, it sowed the seeds of the king's subordination to the Church. In time, this led to discord between the Church and the monarchy.

In former times, the king had been invested amid an assembled army. The king was raised three times on a shield, and the soldiers approved his elevation by brandishing their swords. Later, in the tenth century, the royal custom of riding horseback through the entire kingdom, the so-called *Umritt* or *Umfahrt*, arose as a condition for investiture.

A brief look at the political map of Europe at the beginning of the Carolingian period would not be out of place at this juncture. The Pope was increasingly threatened by the Lombards, a tribe that had overrun Italy a few centuries earlier. The Emperor of the East Roman Empire was no longer able or prepared to support the papacy. One reason for this was that Islam had driven Byzantium into a tight corner and was in the process of conquering more and more territory around the Mediterranean coast. Ultimately, the Carolingian support of the Pope was sufficient not only to drive away the Lombards, but in 756 to subjugate them and in 779 even annex them to the Frankish Kingdom. This tie between the Frankish king and the papacy, which was politically significant for centuries, prompted Pepin to give part of Middle Italy that had been conquered by the Lombards to the Pope, the so-called Donation of Pepin. A side-effect of this development was the creation of the Papal states, the Pope's sovereign territory, which de facto divided Italy into three parts and remained in existence until 1870. The Carolingians continued the practice of dividing the kingdom among several sons. Still, up to the Treaty of Verdun in 843, they continued to be faced with only one successor.

Since the Carolingian Age, the king was elected by the magnates. To safeguard his dynastic interests, the king often had his son crowned as (co-) king during his lifetime (from a 12th century manuscript).

After Pepin, the imposing figure of Charles the Great or Charlemagne arrived on the scene. Ruling from 768 to 814, Charlemagne's major achievements were to substantially expand the kingdom, create a new basis for the political structure and improve relations with the Pope. This led to Pope Leo III's celebrated coronation of Charlemagne as Emperor in St. Peter's in Rome on Christmas Day in the year 800. The question of whether the Pope thus also set the crown on a policy designed to make the mighty Frankish ruler dance to the papal tune or whether Charlemagne himself wanted to be crowned as Emperor is a moot point. Contemporary chronicles appear to conflict with the latter theory, as they report how surprised the newly crowned Emperor was by his coronation. Other sources nevertheless make it clear that it was a consummate piece of theater, whose influence has been felt for more than a thousand years. The truth is probably that Charlemagne did wish to become Emperor, but only with the consent and active participation of the Emperor of the East Roman Empire. This would have restored the state of affairs to what it had been a few centuries earlier, when there was one Emperor for the West and one for the East. It was not until 812, however, that Charlemagne achieved this distinction. As he feared that an imperial coronation initiated by the Pope would make the Frankish king too dependent on the papacy, he had his son, Louis the Pious (who reigned from 814 to 840) crowned as Emperor in 813 while he was still alive. The Pope retaliated with a second coronation of Louis in 816. This power game was repeated a year later when Louis the Pious had his son Lothair crowned in Aachen. In turn, the Pope held another coronation for Lothair in 823. The Pope emerged as the ultimate victor, making the right to crown an emperor a papal prerogative. Three years after Louis' death, his three feuding sons concluded the Treaty of Verdun, in which Lothair received the Middle realm (and the imperial crown!), Charles the Bald got the Western realm and the Eastern realm was meted out to Louis the German.

Charlemagne's coronation on Christmas Day by Pope Leo III (from a 14th century manuscript).

Gregory of Tours' ''History of the Franks''

In telling this story of taxation in the Merovingian and Carolingian periods, generous use has been made of a chronicle dating from the second half of the sixth century. Written by Gregory of Tours, this chronicle is known as the ''History of the Franks.'' A descendant of the Gallo-Roman senatorial class, Gregory was born in 539 and was appointed Bishop of Tours in 573, where he died in 594. His chronicle is replete with personal experiences and eyewitness accounts of contemporary events. His prominent ecclesiastical position, combined with his great erudition (at least for his day and age), his towering moral authority and his engaging manners, made him an eminently suitable defender of the people and confidant of the Merovingian kings. As will appear from the narrative, the latter were barely better than brigand chiefs. The Merovingians not only believed in blood feuds and the concept of ''might makes right,'' but frequently put them into practice.

Gregory, as a Gallo-Roman patrician and a prince of the Church, was not always an unbiased observer. He despised paganism and looked down upon the half-civilized Franks who had conquered the land a few generations earlier. Although Gregory was sometimes prone to exaggeration, his ''History of the Franks'' is widely regarded as the most important source of information on Merovingian society. Historians consider Gregory to be reasonably reliable and accept the core of his stories as true.

Gregory not only chronicled the history of his time, but made history himself. We repeatedly see him in the role of mediator between the various Merovingian kings. For example, he once acted as the representative of Queen Brunhild and her underage son Childebert II. Gregory was highly respected by King Guntram, who involved him in many weighty matters. Gregory always stood up for the people of his diocese and defended refugees seeking asylum from King Chilperic in his church. In short, he was a courageous person, whose outstanding character and intellectual talents were equal to the challenges of his era.

Because of his lively and penetrating narrative style, Gregory has been quoted liberally. A clarification has sometimes been added in brackets to the quoted material. Let us begin by painting a picture of the age in which Gregory lived.

Lothar died in 561 and had hardly been buried by his four sons in Soissons with a great deal of pomp and circumstance before the youngest of them, Chilperic, reached out his greedy hand toward his father's treasury, bought off a number of the kingdom's magnates with gifts and made his entry into Paris. But his virtual coup d'état was foiled by his three brothers. Finally, the four brothers divided the kingdom as Clovis had done half a century earlier. The kingdom was apportioned in such a way that each brother received a few widespread territories he could call his own, with Paris shared in common. As the grass always looked greener on another brother's territory, this division sparked off constant fraternal strife.

One of the four, Sigibert, was disgusted by the mesalliances of his brothers, who thought nothing of marrying slaves. In 566 he requested the hand of a woman from distant Spain, Brunhild, the daughter of Athanagild, the King of the Visigoths. As Gregory recounts it: ''This young woman was elegant in all that

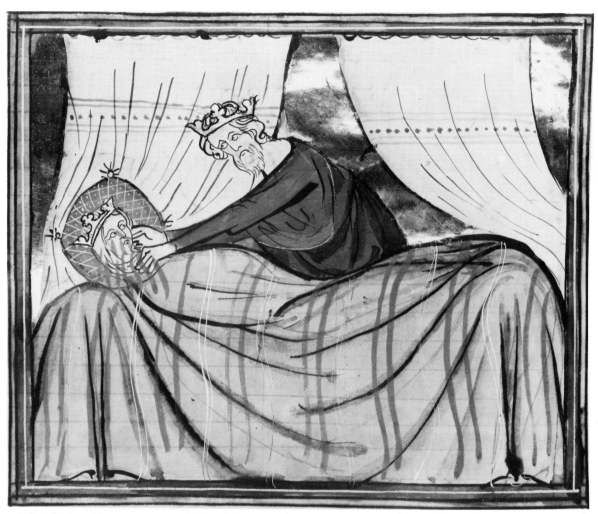

According to Gregory of Tours, King Chilperic had a servant garrotte his wife Galswinth. In this print, "Les Grandes Chroniques de France jusqu'en 1321" (a manuscript from Brabant dating somewhere between 1321 and 1340), it is the King himself who carries out the heinous deed.

she did, lovely to look at, chaste and decorous in her behavior, wise in her genera- tion and of good address." Her father granted the request and sent her with a large dowry to Sigibert. "When he saw this [the following year], King Chilperic [one of the other brothers] sent messengers to ask for the hand of Galswinth, the sister of Brunhild, although he already had a number of wives. He told the messengers to say that he promised to dismiss all the others, if only he were con- sidered worthy of marrying a King's daughter of a rank equal to his own. Galswinth's father believed what he said and sent his daughter to him with a large dowry, just as he had sent Brunhild to Sigibert. Galswinth was older than Brunhild. When she reached the court of King Chilperic, he welcomed her with great honor and made her his wife. He loved her very dearly, for she had brought a large dowry with her. A great quarrel soon ensued between the two of them, however, because he also loved Fredegund, whom he had married before he mar- ried Galswinth. Galswinth [originally Arian] was converted to the Catholic faith and baptized with the chrism. She never stopped complaining to the King about the insults which she had to endure. According to her he showed no respect for her at all, and she begged that she might be permitted to go back home, even if it meant leaving behind all the treasures which she had brought with her. Chilperic did his best to pacify her with smooth excuses and by denying the truth as convincingly as he could. In the end he had her garrotted by one of his servants

Chilperic, Galswinth and Fredegund on horseback (from a 14th century manuscript).

and so found her dead in bed... King Chilperic wept for the death of Galswinth, but within a few days he had asked Fredegund to sleep with him again. His brothers had a strong suspicion that he had connived at the murder of the Queen and they drove him out of his kingdom.''

Gregory's last remark deserves some explanation. According to Germanic law, the relatives of murder victims could seek revenge through a blood feud. Although this did not apply to royalty, Sigibert and Brunhild, the brother-in-law and sister of Galswinth, were bent on blood and riches. They therefore took upon themselves the blood-feud rights of ordinary citizens, and Sigibert waged war against his brother Chilperic. One of the other brothers, Guntram, mediated a compromise. By way of atonement, Brunhild received part of Chilperic's possessions in the South, namely the cities of Bordeaux, Limoges, Cahors and Béarn, which he had granted Galswinth as *Morgengabe*.[4] Galswinth's murder began a vendetta which would poison Frankish society for decades and expressed the bitter hate between Brunhild and Fredegund. When Charibert died in that same year, Guntram hastened to enter into marriage negotiations with Charibert's widow, which he used as an excuse to take control of her treasure. Breaking his matrimonial promises, Guntram then shipped the widow off to a cloister. Years

4. The Merovingian kings were in the habit of making over the income from certain of their cities to their queens the morning after their first night together. Appropriately enough, this is called the *morgengabe* or ''morning gift.''

of feuds, wars, and robbery among the three remaining brothers followed, even though they had divided up Charibert's kingdom in equal portions. Chilperic, who was inwardly chafing because he had had to relinquish so much land in the South as a peace offering, attacked Sigibert in 573. Two years later, Sigibert almost succeeded in dislodging Chilperic from his throne. Chilperic's army had already partly defected to Sigibert and proclaimed him king by lifting him on a shield when two young men — apparently put up to it by Queen Fredegund — stabbed him to death with daggers smeared with poison for good measure.

At the time of Sigibert's death in Vitry, Queen Brunhild was living with her children in Paris. Filled with fear and grief, she was at her wit's end. Duke Gundovald — one of Sigibert's faithful followers — secretly kidnapped her five-year old son Childebert, thereby rescuing him from almost certain death, and even had him proclaimed king. But the tables were now turned, and Chilperic advanced on Paris, where he took Brunhild and her two daughters prisoner. They were banished to Rouen, and Chilperic took possession of the treasure Brunhild had brought to Paris upon her marriage.

Chilperic was soon confronted with a fresh dilemma. He had sent his son Merovech, the product of an earlier union, with an army to Poitiers. Because

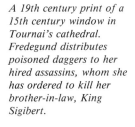

A 19th century print of a 15th century window in Tournai's cathedral. Fredegund distributes poisoned daggers to her hired assassins, whom she has ordered to kill her brother-in-law, King Sigibert.

Genealogical chart of the Merovingians (up to 657)

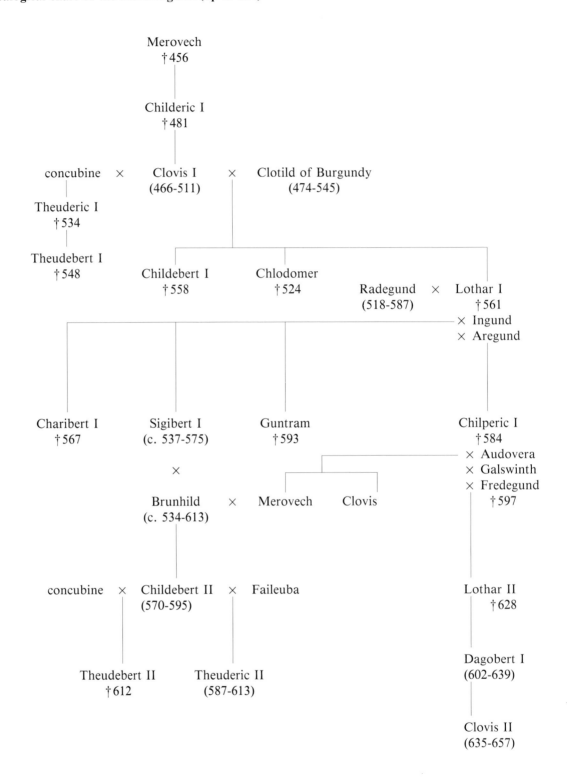

A Merovingian buckle, depicting Daniel in the lion's den. The prophet Habakkuk is bringing him food (6th century).

Merovech was afraid that his stepmother Fredegund would somehow arrange matters so as to exclude him in favor of her own sons, he decided to stage a kind of coup d'état. In a surprise move, he made for Rouen, where he entered into marriage with his aunt Brunhild, hoping to scoop up Sigibert's kingdom with the aid of Sigibert's widow. But his father would not hear of this arrangement and had the bride and groom separated. Merovech was thrown into detention, from which he made an abortive attempt to escape.

The drama ended when Merovech had his closest servant kill him with a sword in order to escape what might have been a more painful end at the hands of his enemies.

These feuds within the royal family − brother against brother, father against son and uncle against nephew − are mirrored in the strife between cities and regions. Gregory provides us with extremely graphic reports of the violence that was so prevalent in his time. Nonetheless, all this bloodshed should be seen in the light of the contemporary belief in "an eye for an eye and a tooth for a tooth." Ruthlessness seems to have been a requirement for survival. The Church's moral code as well as the mores adopted from the Gallo-Romans formed an extremely thin patina of civilization.

The main judicial instrument for maintaining law and order, particularly for preventing mutual bloodbaths, was a fine. A fine consisted of two payments. The first was a compensatory payment paid to the victim or the victim's relatives. This was actually the price paid to buy off the revenge, which is why it was known as *faidus* (vendetta). For example, the fine to be paid in the case of murder was "wergild," the price of a man. The second part of the fine was the *fredus*, or "peace money," which was paid to the king as compensation for disturbing the peace.

There were seemingly also kings with more appealing characters than Chilperic's, for Gregory praises the king's brother Guntram more than once for his benevolence and tolerance. But even Guntram was occasionally overwhelmed by the treachery. For political reasons, Guntram continued to receive Fredegund's representatives, even though she had more than once sent men to kill him. Yet when she failed three times to come at the agreed time to the baptismal ceremony of her young son Lothar, where Guntram was to act as godfather, even Guntram's patience was exhausted. He cast doubts upon the legitimacy of Lothar's birth, which led to serious political conflict. Years passed before Guntram, normally so conciliatory in family affairs, again made his peace with Fredegund.

However reprehensible their behavior may seem in our eyes, the Merovingians did have a culture, in which poetry and a striving after theological knowledge played a role. Venantius Fortunatus, an Italian and the last poet to have a thorough command of Latin, produced numerous ecclesiastical poems, two of

Carolingian boat from a 9th century manuscript (see page 56).

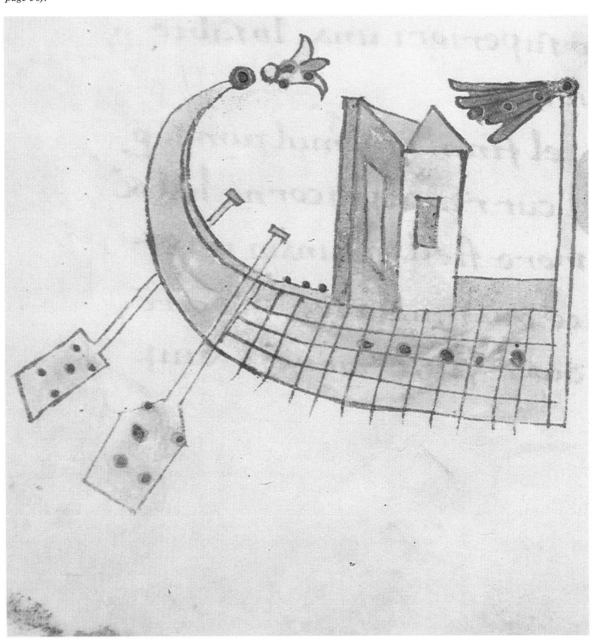

which are still recited in the Roman Catholic Church: the *Pange lingua* and the *Vexilla regis prodeunt*. He also wrote poems for special occasions, including the wedding song to mark the marriage of Sigibert and Brunhild. Even Chilperic, someone from whom you would least expect it, had intellectual interests and literary ambitions. He wrote a theological treatise, invented four new letters for sounds in the Frankish language and authored two books of poems. Gregory, to be sure, disparaged the meter of the verses. But this is scarcely surprising, as in his eyes nothing Chilperic did was of any value, including his poetry.

The Frankish kings maintained international contacts, although they were hardly extensive. For example, King Charibert sent his daughter Bertha to England to marry Aethelbert, the King of Kent. Liudhard, her chaplain, set about converting the Anglo-Saxons so zealously and with such apparent success that the Pope asked the Frankish kings Theuderic II and Theudebert II to lend support to the mission in Kent. Chilperic maintained contacts with Byzantium and had no scruples about accepting financial support from the Emperor of the East Roman Empire. This aid came in the form of gold, which the Merovingians coveted greatly. As a result, Emperor Justinian got a foot in the door of the barbarian West and subsequently reconquered part of the lost West Roman Empire. To accomplish his goal, the Emperor was allowed to recruit Frankish soldiers in Austrasia, although he was made to pay dearly for this privilege.

Stories of Gregory of Tours in which taxation plays a role

Let us pick up the story in 579 and once again listen to what Gregory of Tours has to report. "King Chilperic decreed that a new series of taxes should be levied throughout the kingdom, and these were extremely heavy. As a result a great number of people emigrated from their native cities or from whatever bits of land they occupied and sought refuge elsewhere, for they preferred to go into exile rather than endure such punitive taxation. The new tax laws laid it down that a landowner must pay five gallons of wine for every half-acre which he possessed.[5] Many other taxes were levied, not only on land but also on the number of workmen employed, until it became quite impossible to meet them. When they realized how they were to be mulcted by this taxation, the people of Limoges called a meeting on 1 March [since the time of the Romans the day new taxes were to begin] and decided to kill Mark, the tax collector who had been ordered to put the new laws into effect. They would have carried out their threat, too, had not Bishop Ferreolus saved Mark from the danger which threatened him. A mob gathered; the people seized the tax collector's demand books and burned them to ashes. The King was furious. He sent his officials to Limoges and inflicted terrible punishments on the populace, having them tortured and even put to death out of hand. It is said that these officials sent from the King's court falsely accused the abbots and priests of having incited the people to burn demands during the riot, and that they had them staked to the ground and then submitted them to all sorts of torture. Then they demanded even more punitive payments."

5. This tax should be roughly estimated as 10%. It is difficult, if not impossible, to measure how oppressive the tax burden was. Judged according to present criteria, the taxes were not very high. But given the small spending capacity of the population, the taxes must have been onerous.

The year after this episode, a very serious epidemic broke out. "While the Kings were quarreling with each other again and once more making preparations for civil war, dysentery spread throughout the whole of Gaul. Those who caught it had a high temperature, with vomiting and severe pains in the small of the back: their heads ached and so did their necks. The matter they vomited up was yellow or even green." Gregory continues: "The epidemic began in the month of

August. It attacked young children first of all and to them it was fatal: and so we lost our little ones, who were so dear to us and sweet, whom we had cherished in our bosoms and dandled in our arms, whom we had fed and nurtured with such loving care. As I write I wipe away my tears and I repeat once more the words of Job the blessed: 'The Lord gave, and the Lord hath taken away; as it hath pleased the Lord, so is it come to pass. Blessed be the name of the Lord, world without end'.''

Gregory goes on further to say: ''In these days King Chilperic [also] fell ill. When he recovered, his younger son, who had not yet been baptized in the name of the Holy Ghost, was attacked in his turn. They saw that he was dying and so they baptized him. He made a momentary recovery, but then his older brother caught the disease. When their mother Fredegund realized that he, too, was at death's door, she repented of her sins, rather late in the day, it is true, and said to the King: 'God in his mercy has endured our evil goings-on long enough. Time and time again He has sent us warnings through high fevers and other indispositions, but we have never mended our ways. Now we are going to lose our children. It is the tears of paupers which are the cause of their death, the sighs of orphans, the widows' lament. Yet we still keep on amassing wealth, with no possible end in view. We still lay up treasures, we who have no one to whom we can leave them. Our riches live on after us, the fruits of rapine, hated and accursed, with no one left to possess them once we are gone. Were our cellars not already overflowing with wine? Were our granaries not stuffed to the roof with corn? Were our treasure houses not already full enough with gold, silver, precious stones, necklaces and every regal adornment one could dream of? Now we are losing the most beautiful of our possessions! Come, then, I beg you! Let us set light to all these iniquitous tax demands! What sufficed for King Lothar, your father, should be plenty enough for our exchequer, too.' As she said this, the Queen beat her breast with her fists. She ordered to be placed before her the tax demands which had been brought back by Mark from her own cities, and she put them on the fire. She spoke to the King a second time. 'What are you waiting for?' she asked. 'Do what you see me doing! We may still lose our children, but we shall at least escape eternal damnation.' King Chilperic was deeply moved. He tossed all the files of tax demands into the fire. As soon as they were burned, he sent messengers to ensure that no such assessments should ever be made again.'' However, both sons died and, lamented by the entire population, were carried to their graves.

A few years after these events, the royal couple was belatedly blessed with another son. As Lothar II, he would again unite the entire kingdom under one scepter in 613. Shortly after his son's birth, King Chilperic met his end at the hand of an assassin (584). According to the testimony of the usually rather gentle Gregory, Chilperic was a cross between Nero and Herod.

There are numerous stories relating the strong aversion of the Franks to paying taxes. Their rage was frequently vented on the persons charged with collecting the tax. Gregory describes how the population sought revenge on a tax collector after the death of King Theudebert I in 548: ''The Franks hated Parthenius bitterly, for in the time of the late King it was he who had levied the taxes. Now was their moment to take vengeance. Seeing what danger he was in, he fled from the city and begged two bishops to help him. He asked them to escort him to the town of Trier and to quell the riot of the enraged citizens by their sermons... The

Tombstone of a Jewish man named Peleger, found in the French department of Auch (7th century). Many Jews were merchants during the Merovingian and Carolingian periods, and were well thought of and respected.

two bishops reached Trier [with him], but they could do nothing to quell the riot of the howling mob, and they had to hide Parthenius in a church. They put him in a chest and covered him over with church vestments. The people rushed in and poked about in every corner of the church. They found nothing and left again in a fury. Then one man more perspicacious than the others said: 'What about the chest? What about the chest? We haven't looked in the chest yet, to see if our enemy is there!' The churchwardens maintained that the chest contained nothing but church vestments. The people demanded the key. 'Open it quickly,' they bellowed, 'or we will break it open ourselves!' The chest was unlocked, and when they had moved the vestments to one side they discovered Parthenius and dragged him out. They clapped their hands and shouted: 'The Lord God has delivered our enemy into our hands!' They struck him with their fists and spat at him. Then they bound his hands behind his back, tied him to a pillar and stoned him to death.''

The following story of Gregory's illustrates the fate which sometimes befell tax farmers and indicates how difficult it was to obtain justice: ''In this same year [584] a Jew called Armentarius [presumably a tax farmer], accompanied by a man of his own religion and two Christians, came to Tours to collect payment on some bonds which had been given to him on the security of public taxes by Injuriosus, who had been Vice-Count at the time, and by Eunonius, who had then been Count. Armentarius had an interview with the two men and they agreed to repay the money with the accrued interest. They told him that they would go on ahead. 'If you follow us to our house,' they said, 'we will pay you what we owe, and in addition we have some gifts to give to you, as is only right in the circumstances.' Armentarius made his way there and was received by Injuriosus. He sat down to dinner. When the meal was over and night had begun to fall, they moved from this house to another. Then, so they say, the Jews and

the two Christians were killed by the servants of Injuriosus and their bodies were
thrown into a well which was near the house. Their relations heard what had happened and travelled to Tours. From information received from certain persons,
they identified the well and recovered the bodies. Injuriosus hotly denied that he
had played any part in the crime. He was prosecuted; but, as I have said, he
denied his guilt vehemently, and the plaintiffs had no evidence on which he could
be convicted. He was sentenced to clear himself by oath. The dead men's relations were not satisfied with this, and they demanded that the case should be
brought before King Childebert's court. The money and the bonds of the dead
Jew were never found. Many said that Medard, the assistant of Injuriosus, was
mixed up in this crime, for he, too, had borrowed money from the Jew. Injuriosus attended the court before King Childebert, and sat there waiting three
days in succession until the setting of the sun. The plaintiffs never came and no
one put in an appearance to prosecute Injuriosus, so he returned home."

Gregory also describes the fierce resentment against tax farmers in his account
of Queen Fredegund, who was obliged to seek asylum in the Paris cathedral after
the death of her husband, King Chilperic, as people sought their revenge on her.

Illustration of an evangelist from the Gospel of Xanten, believed to date from the 6th century. Gregory of Tours might have looked like this.

As Gregory observes: ''Fredegund had no fear of God, in whose house she had sought sanctuary, and she was the prime mover in many outrages. At this time she had with her the judge Audo, who, during the lifetime of King Chilperic, had been her accomplice in much evildoing. With the support of the prefect Mummolus, this Audo had, in the time of King Childebert, exacted taxes from many Franks who had been free men. When that King died, these men stripped and despoiled Audo of everything, so that nothing remained to him except the clothes that he stood up in. They burned his house to the ground; and they would have killed him too, had he not sought sanctuary with the Queen in the cathedral.''

Fredegund and Brunhild

While Fredegund remained in the cathedral under the protection of the Bishop of Paris, the young King Childebert II advanced on the city, but his troops were denied entry. Childebert begged his uncle Guntram, who held sway in Paris at that time, to hand over his father Sigibert's assassins along with those responsible for the death of his aunt Galswinth and his cousins. Guntram refused. Finally, Fredegund, pleading that she was once again with child, was granted a safe-conduct for herself and her young son Lothar.

As the events of Fredegund's life show, she learned little from the death of her two sons during the plague epidemic. The catalog of ghastly deeds began when she sent Chilperic's grown son, Clovis (at that time his only remaining son), to an area where the dysentery epidemic was raging, in the hope that he would catch the disease and die. When that failed to work, she had Clovis accused of using magic to cause the death of her own sons. Finally, she had him murdered and his retinue cruelly put to death, all of which was a matter of total indifference to King Chilperic. Nor did her period of sanctuary in the Paris cathedral persuade Fredegund to mend her ways. She had barely regained her freedom before she had sent out hirelings to murder her sister-in-law Brunhild, although without success. The attempt of priest-assassins to kill Brunhild's son, the young King Childebert, with poisoned daggers also failed; the poor men trembled like leaves even before the planned assassination and their terror gave them away. After their capture, they were deprived first of their limbs and then of their lives. A summary of Fredegund's evil deeds, as recorded by Gregory of Tours, would form a long list. And to think that she outlived Gregory by three years! But perhaps we should not judge Fredegund too harshly. For a woman to hold her own in the cruel world of that time — in which it was considered improper for a woman to wield a sword and dagger herself — the use of hired assassins, preferably equipped with poison-tipped swords and other assorted weapons of destruction, was a form of self-defense. It could be said to her credit that by her skillful intrigues she succeeded in protecting her son Lothar, first against her brother-in-law Guntram and later against her still young nephew by marriage, Childebert II. Inevitably, both Guntram and Childebert would have seized any opportunity to gain control of the kingdom of the late Chilperic. Guntram, who left no sons as heirs, had to content himself in 592 with leaving his Burgundian sub-kingdom to his nephew Childebert. Immediately after Childebert's death in 596, Fredegund attempted, with her grown son Lothar II, to appropriate both sub-kingdoms from Childebert's two sons, but to no avail.

Fredegund's death marked the dawning of a great age for Brunhild. She was to dominate Frankish history for the next eighteen years, first as guardian and then

*Door knocker from the
Merovingian period (5th to
6th century).*

*Door knocker from the
Merovingian period (5th to
6th century).*

as advisor of Childebert's two sons. One of them, Theuderic II, was the
legitimate son of Childebert's marriage with Queen Faileuba. From his youth,
Theuderic was destined to become king of the sub-kingdom of Burgundy. The
other son, Theudebert II, was born to a concubine and was designated by his
father to be king of the sub-kingdom of Austrasia. Both children came of age
in 599.

Brunhild's misdeeds almost rivaled those of her sister-in-law Fredegund. In the
Chronicles of Fredegar, we find the following statement: "So that Berthold
would die all the more quickly, they sent him to certain cities and *gaus*[6] in the
kingdom for the purpose of collecting taxes." The background to this statement
is as follows: in 604, Theudebert II was King of Burgundy, one of the sub-
kingdoms of the Frankish Kingdom. His grandmother, Brunhild, who had partly
raised him and still exercised a great deal of influence over him, induced
Theudebert to dispatch the mayor of the palace, Berthold, with whom she had
a quarrel, to collect taxes. After all, there was only a slight chance that Berthold
would come back from this dangerous mission alive! As the plot thickens, it appears that the author of the chronicle was guilty of some exaggeration. But we
should bear in mind that the chronicler belonged to the camp of Lothar II,
Fredegund's son, and was therefore hostile to Brunhild. However, the story does
highlight the risks involved in being a tax collector. The chronicle relates
elsewhere that Berthold marched out to collect taxes in the company of three
hundred armed men. This makes one wonder whether this was more of a raid
than an orderly, legal tax levy. And indeed, in the course of the seventh century,
as the Merovingian Kingdom declined, it became increasingly more difficult to
distinguish between the two.

6. A *gau* was an
administrative district.

The elderly Queen Brunhild was tortured for three days and then dragged to death by wild horses (from the chronicle ''Cas des nobles hommes et femmes'' (Boccace, 1465).

A "close-up" of the same scene (from a 15th century manuscript; miniature attributed to the master of the Champion des Dames).

Several years later, Brunhild became embroiled in the struggle for power between her two grandsons, Theuderic and Theudebert. Each of the half-brothers coveted the other's kingdom, and war broke out in 612 when both of them were about twenty-five years old. Theuderic concluded a treaty with Lothar II and won the Battles of Toul and Zülpich. His brother then fled to Cologne, and the city was put under siege. The residents surrendered, thus betraying their own king, Theudebert, who was taken prisoner. Brunhild had allowed this grandson to fall for the simple reason that she had always preferred the legitimately born Theuderic. The defeated Theudebert was first stripped of his royal garments, his horse and his royal saddle. The loss of these symbols signified the end of his rule. He was then shorn of his long hair and tucked away in a monastery, where he was finally murdered. Theuderic took possession of his brother's treasury, including the entire Austrasian Kingdom, and had himself invested in the Basilica of St. Gereon in Cologne.

Brunhild's hand in these events is unmistakable. Matters, however, turned out badly for her. In 613, Lothar, with the help of the great lords in Austrasia, who had defected to his side, defeated Theuderic at Metz. Theuderic was felled in the battle, and Brunhild, by now advanced in years, took his four sons under her protection. She made a desperate attempt to hoist the oldest onto his father's throne. She sent the five or six year old boy off to head an army against Lothar, but Lothar won this unevenly matched battle. Two of the children were slaughtered, one managed to escape and the last was spared because he was Lothar's godchild. Brunhild, well into her seventies, was also taken prisoner by Lothar. In an apparent act of revenge for his mother, Fredegund, Lothar had Brunhild tortured for three days and then dragged to death by wild horses.

The *Nibelungenlied*, created in about 1200, contains an echo of the conflict between Fredegund and Brunhild, neither of whom hesitate to use any means to harm the other, wield power and wreak vengeance. In the poem, it is the royal sisters-in-law, Kriemhild and Brunhild, who are locked in a struggle for power and revenge. The treasury is also a bone of contention, but I'll return to this point in a moment.

Leaving aside Gregory's moralizing, his account makes it clear that levying taxes was exceedingly difficult, dangerous and immoral. A king and a queen who did not shrink from any act of ignominy as long as it served their own interests apparently only considered levying taxes an actual crime if they were new or exceeded the time-honored levies. At this stage, it may be useful to explore the position occupied by taxation in the Merovingian and Carolingian Kingdoms. Furthermore, the texts cited below will help clarify the significance of the treasury.

Taxes in the Merovingian age: head tax and land tax

As we have seen, the Merovingian kings preserved the Gallo-Roman system of government as much as possible. This included the tax system as well as its administrative organization. There were two main types of taxes: head tax and land tax. Head tax was levied on those who owned no property and therefore did not have to pay any land tax. The payment of a head tax was an indication of low social status. To the Franks, paying head tax meant surrendering part of one's freedom to the king. This restriction in freedom was expressed in various contexts. For example, head tax payers were not allowed to enter a clerical order, unless granted permission by the king or a royal magistrate. The Franks reasoned that without this regulation, the king's tax revenues would suffer, for the clergy were exempt from head taxes.

The head tax was either paid by the subject himself or by someone with whom he shared a particular bond. For example, a father paid for his dependent children, even though the children were liable for the tax. This practice could conceivably have led to infanticide, but accounts of this from one of the sources should be taken with a grain of salt. Similarly, a landowner paid for the laborers who worked on his estate. Although French and German historians differ greatly in their opinions about the contradictions contained in the scanty texts handed down to us, it can be assumed that head tax did not have to be paid by the Frankish soldiers. Attempts to subject them to this tax foundered on extremely strong opposition. When Montesquieu stated that a free Frank did not have to pay a tax, he was referring to head tax only. A chronicler from the Merovingian era articulated this concept even more clearly: a man is only free if his name does not appear in a tax register.

Land tax was imposed on land that was owned, leased or worked. It was tied to the land rather than to its owner. When a Gallo-Roman transferred his land to a Frank, it was the Frank who had to pay the tax. The aversion of the Franks to taxation, attested to by many sources, was not usually directed at land tax. The land-linked nature of the land tax is also apparent from the fact that a subject of the king ruling over the Burgundian sub-kingdom had to pay land tax to the Neustrian king for his estates in the Neustrian sub-kingdom.

Land tax was sometimes paid in money and sometimes in kind. Even though trade and consequently the circulation of money decreased considerably after the Frankish conquest, there was still a lot of money around. Economic stagnation had not prevented new gold coins from being minted. The trade with Byzantium, in the hands of Jewish and Syrian merchants, did not wane until Islam gained control of the western shores of the Mediterranean in Carolingian times. Frankish soldiers sometimes returned from their campaigns of conquest laden with enemy booty and ransom money. In an economy in which trade had decreased sharply, goods were scarce, and the soldiers were unable to buy much with their money. They accordingly preferred to pay their land tax in gold rather than in kind.

It is impossible to ascertain how heavily head and land taxes weighed on the population. The general moaning and groaning about taxes which has been going on since time immemorial is a poor yardstick. Initially, only the king's property was exempt from land tax. This exemption remained intact, even when the lands were given away by the king as a reward for services rendered. Those in the king's immediate circle understandably attempted to wangle an exemption for their own estates. They often succeeded, either because they exploited their connections or because the king wished to reward them for their services. This practice naturally ate away at the heart of the tax system, which was further eroded by the success of the Gallo-Roman bishops in gaining tax exemptions for lands bestowed on the Church.

On the other hand, it sometime happened that the Church was dealt with particularly harshly. Through the centuries, rulers have always cast a greedy eye at the Church's possessions. As we shall see, in the eighth century this led to outright confiscations. A seemingly more subtle approach was to impose exceptionally high taxes on the Church. Gregory cites an example: ''King Lothar [Clovis' youngest son] had ordained [c. 544] that all the churches in his kingdom should pay a third part of their revenues to the treasury. All the other bishops had agreed to this and had signed documents saying so, with the greatest unwillingness, let it be admitted, but Saint Injuriosus [the Bishop of Tours] would not sign and had the courage to refuse to pay. 'If you have made up your mind to seize what belongs to God, then the Lord will soon take your kingdom away from you,' he said [to the king], 'for it is criminal for you, who should be feeding the poor from your own granary, to fill your coffers with the alms which others give to them.' Injuriosus was so angry with the King that he went off without saying goodbye. Lothar was disturbed by this, for he was afraid that Saint Martin [the first Bishop of Tours] would punish him for what he had done. He sent messengers laden with presents after Injuriosus, to beg his pardon, cancel what he had done and beg that he would pray to Saint Martin for help.'' Lothar, who normally did not shrink at any piece of villainy, apparently came to the conclusion that hampering the Church in its task of caring for the infirm and the needy was an unforgivable crime even he was unwilling to commit. It is not clear whether Tours was the only place where this extra tax was abolished.

This illustration in the Stuttgart Psalter (from the beginning of the 9th century) depicts plowing and sowing. The scene was painted before the 10th century agrarian revolution. The grain harvest was then increased nearly tenfold in a short amount of time by the invention of the iron plow (which allowed the farmer to make furrows, unlike the above-depicted wooden plow, which only turned the soil) and the introduction of three-course rotation (in which the land lay fallow for one year every second year so that it could be revitalized). The land could therefore sustain more people, who sought refuge in the towns which were arising partly as a result of this development.

Land tax revenues declined with the passage of time, not only because the exemptions increased in number and magnitude, but also because the tax registers were no longer maintained accurately. The existing land register had lost its significance since changes in ownership resulting from sale or inheritance were no longer being recorded on a regular basis. As a consequence, many landowners could not be traced and were able to get off scot-free. The government made occasionally successful attempts to arrange for an entire district, a *gau* or an abbey to pay a set sum for all its lands. However, this was merely a stop-gap. The shortcomings of the land tax registers also affected the imposition of head taxes. Initially, the names of head tax payers were recorded on special lists by estate. But as time went on, the names of those who died were not crossed out and those who fiscally came of age were not entered in the registers. In order to arrive at a previously determined fixed number of taxpayers residing on each estate, the authorities resorted to registering people formerly exempted from head tax, namely widows, orphans and the infirm. This is the background to the above-quoted passage, in which Queen Fredegund says to King Chilperic: "It is the tears of paupers which are the cause of their death, the sighs of orphans, the widows' lament." Clearly, the queen was aware of the apparently accepted practice of exacting head tax from society's oppressed and ignoring the exemptions they had formerly enjoyed.

From time to time, a major overhaul of the head tax registers was ordered. Of course, this was primarily in the interest of the tax farmers. Gregory of Tours describes just such a revision of the registers in Poitiers, involving his fellow bishop Maroveus, and the registers in Tours, where he himself played a part. The bishop of Poitiers informed King Childebert II that the tax registers, with the exception of those in Touraine, had not been revised since the death of his father Sigibert fourteen years earlier (in 575), and that the poor had been left to foot the bill. Names had only been recorded randomly anyway! The bishop asked the king to send "descriptores" (i.e. tax collectors) to Poitou, the region around Poitiers. In response, the king dispatched the mayor of the queen's palace, Florentianus, along with one of the counts of his own palace, Romulf. "Their orders were to prepare new tax lists and to instruct the people to pay the taxes which had been levied from them in the time of Childebert's father. Many of those who were on the lists had died, and, as a result, widows, orphans and infirm folk had to meet a heavy assessment. The inspectors looked into each case in turn: they granted relief to the poor and infirm, and assessed for taxation all who were justly liable."

Gregory continues: "After this they came to Tours. When they announced that they were about to tax the townsfolk, and that they had in their possession tax lists showing how the people had been assessed in the time of earlier kings, I [Gregory] gave them this answer: 'It is undeniable that the town of Tours was assessed in the days of King Lothar. The books were taken off to be submitted to the King. Lothar had them thrown into the fire, for he was greatly overawed by our Bishop, Saint Martin. When Lothar died, my people swore an oath of loyalty to King Charibert, and he swore in his turn that he would not make any new laws or customs, but would secure to them the conditions under which they had lived in his father's reign. He promised that he would not inflict upon them any new tax laws which would be to their disadvantage. Gaiso, who was Count at that time, took the tax lists, which, as I have said, had been drawn up by earlier tax inspectors, and began to exact payment. He was opposed by Bishop Eufronius, but he went off to the King with the money which he had collected illegally and showed to him the tax lists in which the assessment was set down. King Charibert sighed, for he feared the miraculous power of Saint Martin, and he threw the lists into the fire. The money which had been collected he sent back to Saint Martin's Church, swearing that no public taxation should ever again be forced upon the people of Tours. King Sigibert held this city after Charibert's death, but he did not burden it with taxation. In the same way Childebert has made no demands in the fourteen years during which he has reigned since his father's death.[7] The city has not had to face any tax assessment at all. It lies in your power to decide whether or not tax should be collected; but beware of the harm which you will do if you act contrary to the King's sworn agreement.' When I had finished speaking, they made the following reply: 'You see that we hold in our hands the book which lists the tax assessment for your people.' 'That book was not issued by the King's treasury,' I answered. 'For all these long years it has been in abeyance. I would not be at all surprised if it had been kept carefully in someone's house out of hatred for these townsfolk of mine. God will surely punish the individuals who have produced it after such a long passage of time, just to despoil my citizens.' That very day the son of Audinus, the man who had produced the inventory, caught a fever. He died three days later. We then sent representatives to the King, to ask that he send instructions and make clear just what his orders were. An official letter came back almost immediately, confirming the immunity from taxation of the people of Tours, out of respect for Saint Martin. As soon as they had read it,[8] the men who had been sent on the mission returned home."

7. As we have previously seen, Childebert II was five years old when his father was killed in 575. Gregory means to say that Fredegund, ruling in Childebert's name, did not demand any taxes.

8. The tax collectors could therefore read!

We can only speculate on the reason for this. It may have had something to do with their particular veneration and fear of Saint Martin, the patron saint of Tours. Or perhaps the residents had insisted on the exemption when swearing their oath of loyalty to Lothar. One thing is clear: the many incidental exemptions increasingly eroded the general tax base. Nor was canceling outstanding debts, as King Childebert II did for Clermont-Ferrand (c. 595?), conducive to regulated taxation.

As an absolute ruler, the Merovingian king could control taxation arbitrarily. He granted exemptions and high-handedly raised taxes as he deemed fit. Tax increases did not require the consent of the great lords or the abbots and bishops who, in a sense, may be thought of as representing the people, or at any rate as being concerned with their interests. As no one was consulted, tax hikes met with widespread resistance. Only the extent of the king's power determined whether and for how long he was able to enforce his will.

A free Frank does not (or should not?) have to pay taxes

Although Gregory probably exaggerated the Franks' antipathy to taxation because he felt that the Church was also hard pressed, other texts also tell of the Franks' bitter resentment to taxes raised from long-established levels. In one tale, Wiomad, the friend of the banished king Childeric (the father of Clovis), advised Aegidius, a Roman who served as commander of the Franks, to levy a head tax. Wiomad's intention was for the Franks to rebel against Aegidius in disgust at the head tax and recall Childeric to the throne. This is a saga, but it does typify the Franks' distaste for taxes.

Although land tax and head tax were by far the most important, there were other taxes as well. In the Rhine area, taxes were imposed in kind (honey, apparel, lambs, chickens, eggs, timber and grain) on produce from the land. These taxes can be seen as the counterpart of the land tax that was levied in the Western — formerly Gallo-Roman — part of the kingdom. In addition, tolls were levied in many places, usually in the form of a portion of the goods being transported. These tolls were located in places through which travelers were obliged to pass: harbors, bridges, river fords, canals, mountain passes, city gates and fortresses. These tolls somewhat resembled what we would refer to today as appropriated taxes. Toll revenues were primarily allocated to local maintenance projects and security measures to protect the travelers. Port dues and tolls on market stalls were also levied, but were only of marginal significance because trade was stagnating.

To what can we attribute the Franks' great aversion to taxation? In the Merovingian age, the centralized Gallo-Roman form of government, with its formal hierarchical structure, slowly broke down, leaving several loosely knit tribes. The tasks for which the state had assumed responsibility were quite uncomplicated and could be performed by the subjects themselves, or in the case of communal services (such as caring for the poor and recording births, deaths and marriages) by the Church. Consequently, the government's authority dwindled and taxes lost their importance as an integral part of governmental structure. The revenues from taxes that were still in existence (e.g. tolls) were earmarked for local use. As we shall see, national taxes, particularly head tax and land tax, disappeared in the Carolingian age and were replaced by obligatory services on the part of the general populace.

By far the most important obligation placed on the subjects was military service. The Frankish soldier had to appear in the field every year, ready to follow the king in his campaigns of conquest, usually outside the Frankish Kingdom. Both the king and his warriors benefitted from victory. The king rose in respect and increased the number of his subjects and the dimensions of his territory. He could enrich his own treasury by exacting a tribute from the vanquished peoples and ransom from his captives. His subjects shared in the booty. In Merovingian times in particular, warriors were rewarded with gold and military equipment. Merovingians set great store by being buried in their splendid gold jewelry and in full military dress. Grave robbery was the order of the day. Much of the stolen gold was then melted down and brought back into circulation. The soldiers were also often rewarded with a parcel of land in the conquered territory. Partly as a result of the decreasing circulation of money, these land grants predominated in the Carolingian era. As colonizers, the land-grant recipients allowed the Frankish Kingdom to gain a firmer foothold on what was formerly enemy soil. In the expansionist Frankish Kingdom, the subjects were quite prepared to assume the expense of the campaign (they were required to bear the costs of their own weapons and upkeep) with the prospect of later profit.

Military service was increasingly complemented in the Frankish state by other public services, such as constructing and maintaining roads and bridges. In the collective mind, the payment of head and land taxes became less and less acceptable. The general populace particularly balked at taxes that were higher or more extensive than those paid in the past. Tax hikes were considered unjust and in many cases led to tax rebellions and riots. Depending on his place in the prevailing power structure, a Merovingian king sometimes managed to exact new or higher taxes. But such rudimentary tax systems inevitably collapsed immediately after the king's death or defeat.

The ire of the populace manifested itself most clearly when the king attempted to extend the head tax that was levied on the unpropertied Gallo-Roman population (and thus not on those who paid land tax) to his Frankish subjects. In terms of fiscal equity, there was probably something to be said for this approach in cases involving unpropertied citizens not subject to compulsory military service. But of course it was precisely these subjects who saw the tax as a step down the social ladder, as it would lower them to the status of the unfree. Whenever they could, the people put up a fierce resistance. In Gregory's stories of popular wrath against taxes, we must assume that he was referring to head tax, even though the texts themselves only mention the word "tax." When reading Gregory's narrative, we should also bear in mind that the bishops not only threw themselves into the breach to protect their flocks from the king, but also to relieve the Church from the burden of taxation. With its vast estates, the Church incessantly strove to have its property exempted from land tax, claiming that it would then be in a better position to care for the poor.

The Treasury

The king was not entitled to employ tax levies as a means of enlarging the royal treasury. The treasury was an integral part of the governmental structure, without which the king would have been severely hamstrung. It was filled with the king's share of the spoils of war, tributes from subjected peoples, goods confiscated from (suspected) lawbreakers, plunder from the churches, gifts from

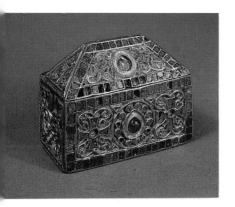

Gilded brass reliquary from the 8th century.

foreign rulers honoring the king and more or less voluntary gifts from subjects who wanted to win the king's favor or − as was quite customary − felt compelled to contribute to the prestige and dignity of their king. The treasury was an outward sign of the king's excellence. It not only symbolized the extent and magnitude of the king's power and worth, but it was also a material indication of accumulated wealth. As such, it was a tool the king could use in the exercise of his power and a pool into which he could dip when he wished to hand out rewards or curry favor with foreign rulers. Indeed, the treasury formed the fulcrum of the king's domestic and foreign policies.

The treasury contained many movable items which reflected its nomadic origins. These included minted and non-minted gold and silver, valuable armlets, jewels, precious stones, pearls, kitchenware, wagons, costly embellished weapons and other tools, silks, robes, furniture, horses with magnificent harnesses and even religious paraphernalia such as crosses, books and relics. King Chilperic and Queen Fredegund also had warehouses packed with grain and barrels of wine. Even though most of these supplies were mainly reserved for the use of the whole court, they were considered to be part of the treasury. Chests and objects of that sort contained in the treasury were used to store documents and tax registers.

The significance of the treasury emerges on a number of occasions. We have already seen that after Chlodomer's death, his youngest brother Lothar immediately married his widow in a kind of coup d'état in order to take possession of the treasury and that Guntram did much the same thing half a century later, although he did not marry the widow, but shut her up in a cloister. It appears from these stories that the treasury, often mentioned in surviving texts in the same breath as the kingdom, was important because it was inherited or divided up in the same way as the kingdom. In the Merovingian age, the site of the king's palace, where he maintained his entourage and kept the treasury, was the capital of the sub-kingdom. Bereft of its treasury, a city lost its status as capital. Cologne, for example, ceased to be a capital when the treasury was carried off after Sigibert and his son Chloderic were murdered in 508.

Pitcher from the time of Charlemagne.

Weapons and gold, the two main components of the treasury, were the Franks' most treasured goods. There are frequent reports of the ever-warlike spirit and insatiable ostentation of the Germanic tribes, and the Franks were no exception. Weapons and decorative artefacts, marking the status of the buried person, have been found in Merovingian graves. Some brief financial data will now be given about the composition of the treasury and its relation to the cost of living. To get an impression of the treasury's value, let us take the solidus, the monetary unit of the Roman and Frankish monetary system. This was a gold coin weighing 4.55 grams. In the later period of the Roman Empire, 1 solidus was enough to buy provisions for a year, while the annual salary of a soldier was 4 − 5 solidi. The cost of living amounted to a total of 6 − 7 solidi per year. The *Lex Ripuaria* mentions the following prices: a helmet cost 6 solidi, a sheath and sword 7 solidi, a lance and shield 2 solidi, a horse 10 solidi and a cow 2 solidi. A complete set of military equipment − a helmet, a sheathed sword and a lance and shield − would therefore cost a soldier 8 cows; if he omitted the helmet, he was adequately equipped as a soldier for only 5 cows, at any rate provided the enemy did not get too close, for that could cost him his head instead of 3 cows.

A lady of some distinction is buried under the chancel in Cologne's cathedral.

Golden chalice from c. 500.

Was she related to the defeated Sigibert? Was she one of King Lothar's women? Or was she Wisigard, Theudebert's Lombardian wife? Whoever she was, she was wearing in her grave a gold bracelet weighing 66 grams, the equivalent of a full set of military equipment. More than 100 gold coins were found in the grave of King Childeric, Clovis' father, who died in 482. This would have been sufficient to equip a retinue of ten warriors. When King Childebert proclaimed his nephew Theudebert as his heir in 535, he provided him in advance with six swords, six helmets and six sets of military equipment from his treasury, or in other words enough to equip a small retinue of six men. Gregory of Tours informs us that Emperor Maurice sent 50,000 gold solidi to Childebert as remuneration for his help in fighting the Lombards. Gregory also mentions the gold medallions, each weighing 500 grams (i.e. 72 solidi), that Emperor Tiberius Constantine (578 – 582) supposedly sent to King Chilperic. This same king also had in his treasury a jewel-encrusted basin reportedly weighing 500 Roman pounds, or 36,400 solidi, which was enough gold to equip an army of 1,000 warriors.

Like a pump, the king's treasury sucked up gold and recirculated it in the form of dowries for his daughters, rewards to faithful followers, alms to the poor and donations to the Church. For example, Saint Amandus received money to convert the Franks to Christianity. Dagobert (the last important Merovingian king) made a donation so that the apse of the Basilica of St. Denis could be covered in silver. Brunhild dipped into the treasury to bribe the barbarians who were threatening to attack. Private individuals also had their own treasuries. The prefect Mummolus – presumably a Gallo-Roman, who has been mentioned earlier – bequeathed 250 pounds of silver and 30 pounds of gold. After his death, during an internal power struggle, these precious metals were carried off to the royal treasury.

Left: ring, bracelet and pendant and right: earrings, rosette-shaped buckles and clasps, found in the grave of a prominent lady buried under the chancel of Cologne's cathedral (6th century).

In the *Nibelungenlied*, Siegfried had to divide King Nibelung's treasury between his two sons. Dissatisfied with Siegfried's mediation, the two sons and their retinues attacked him. Siegfried fended off all his assailants and won the treasury, which included Kriemhild, the Burgundian king's daughter. When

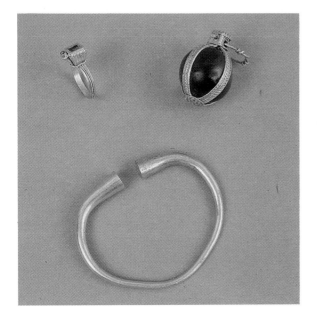

Siegfried was treacherously murdered, Kriemhild was left with the treasury, which had to be transported to a conveniently waiting ship in twelve wagons. As might be expected, Kriemhild's brother King Gunther then determined to deprive his sister of the treasury by any fair or foul means. Thus, the *Nibelungenlied* poetically reflects the Merovingian reality.

The Edict of Paris of 614

Although the Franks were prepared to help their king augment his treasury by serving as soldiers, the thought that they should do so by paying taxes did not enter their heads. This emerges clearly in the Edict of Paris of 614. We have frequently encountered Brunhild in these pages, and watched her scheming and plotting to secure the throne for her grandchildren and greatgrandchildren. Protadius, one of Brunhild's protégés, had supplemented the queen's treasury by exacting illegal taxes and confiscating goods. That, at least, was what her adversaries claimed. According to her defenders, she had updated the registers to modernize the land tax system. The magnates in the Austrasian Kingdom had rebelled against these fiscal measures and sided with Lothar II in his struggle against her grandson Theuderic II. The Edict of Paris concluded on October 18, 614 served as a kind of peace treaty between Lothar and the Austrasians and arranged for a large national assembly to reorganize the kingdom. It also promised that: "Everywhere where a new tax has been wickedly introduced and has incited the people to resistance, the matter will be investigated and the tax mercifully abolished." Significantly, this same Edict stated that henceforth the provincial administrators would have to be selected from among the local population. This departure from previous practice inevitably weakened central government, for the great lords were inclined to put local interests (which usually coincided with their own interests) above those of the kingdom. This erosion of central government continued under the Carolingians. Having been recruited from the local population, the counts (the administrators of the *gaus*) gradually parted company with royal authority. Slowly but surely, they turned into quasi-independent potentates. After the reign of Louis the Pious (814 − 840), it was increasingly difficult for the king to exercise his power to appoint and dismiss counts. In the Western and Middle Kingdoms, the office of count rapidly became virtually hereditary. The prevalence of the custom prompted Charles the Bald, who ruled over the Western Kingdom, to note in 877 that this inheritance was based on an existing and legally enforceable practice.

The Edict of 614 has been compared to the *Magna Carta*, the famous document of 1215 in which King John of England declared that he would no longer levy taxes without the consent of the barons, the bishops and the gentry. However, the comparison has been grossly exaggerated. It is true that the magnates had left Theuderic II in the lurch and more or less handed the kingdom over to Lothar II because of tax grievances. And it was also because of grievances that the Edict of 614 restricted taxes to those which had been levied in olden times. But this was the only similarity between the Edict and the *Magna Carta*. The crucial difference was that the Edict of Paris did not arrange for new taxes to be levied with the consent of the magnates, which meant, in fact, that no new taxes could be introduced.

At the same time, the existing tax structure was being gradually dismantled. The administrators, now recruited from the local population, became increasingly reluctant to collect taxes for the central government. If they levied any taxes at all, they preferred to spend them at a local level. The situation was exacerbated by the government's neglect of the Gallo-Roman tax system; the head and land tax registers had been allowed to become grossly outdated with the passage of time. The incessant feuds, bordering on civil war, between Sigibert and Chilperic and their descendants had made matters worse. The arbitrary levies which had replaced the customary taxes and which often had to be collected by brute force – an act greatly resembling robbery – had created disorder in the tax system and discredited it even further. Examples of tax levies can be found in the seventh century, when the power of the Merovingian kings was on the wane. But these can sometimes barely be distinguished from brazen confiscation. The year 614 is regarded as a watershed in the erosion of the tax system. The disappearance of the phenomenon of taxation was facilitated by the fact that, as of the seventh century, local tax revenues were frequently bestowed on previously tax-exempt churches and monasteries. In this way, the land tax was transformed into a kind of ground rent collected for the benefit of the Church. Later still, the "ground rent" merged with the so-called religious tithes.

Twenty-five years after the Edict of Paris, King Dagobert once again ventured to impose taxes, if we are to believe the hagiography of Saint Sulpicius, the Bishop of Bourges. This biography of a saint gives the following account: "In these days, King Dagobert, motivated by greed, ordered Lallon, a ruffian who had done much wickedness, to levy taxes. Without an ounce of mercy, he began to impose head taxes on the inhabitants of Bourges, a measure that was contrary to custom, under the protection of the king's authority. The inhabitants, filled with repugnance, hurried in a great multitude to the man of God, begging him with lamentations and confused cries to please help them. Moved by pity, but not able to act on their sobs and tears, Sulpicius commanded a three-day fast and begged divine Providence to help his oppressed people. Then he sent one of his clerks, Ebargisilus, to King Clovis [Dagobert had died in the meantime] to ask his royal grace in all humbleness, with tears and lamentations, to render his assistance against the wicked deeds. Horrified, the king ordered the levy to be discontinued and the already-compiled tax books to be abolished immediately. And the people of Bourges, relieved of this assessment, still live today in their former freedom."

Naturally, as this is the biography of a saint, the story is biased. But it is the last we hear of taxation in the Merovingian period. Although sporadic traces of land and head taxes can be found up to the ninth century, for all practical purposes, the phenomenon of taxation had ceased to exist. Nothing more is heard of it in the Carolingian age. Instead, the Franks, though unwilling to honor compulsory tax levies, were quite prepared to offer donations, provided they were on a voluntary basis. I will return to this subject shortly.

The Carolingian state

It would be a misconception to view the Carolingian Empire as merely a religiously oriented continuation of the more secular Merovingian state. Merovingian organization had been crude, as were the behavior and opinions of its leaders. Yet the former Gallo-Roman governmental structure had been formally maintained. Despite their many internecine feuds and wars, the Merovingian kings did rule according to a certain concept of government. Internally and exter-

Oldest-known illustration of the twelve months of the year, with agriculture as the main theme (Salzburg Calendar, 818).

Golden coin of Dagobert I (629-639), minted for the city of Paris.

Silver denier of Charlemagne (769-814), minted in Mayence.

Charlemagne as depicted by the Nürenburg Chronicle (1493).

nally, the state continued to show a certain cohesiveness: some trade was being conducted, cities still existed, taxes were being imposed − albeit sporadically − and the king's power was still absolute. All this applied to a lesser degree in the Carolingian period. Charlemagne had stretched the borders of his realm to encompass almost the entire Christian West; only Southern and Middle Italy, Spain and the British Isles lay outside it. As a result, the Carolingian Empire became a vast patchwork of peoples, all with their own cultures and ambitions. The more land Charlemagne conquered, the more the internal cohesion of the state was weakened. An even greater danger was that the Carolingian mayors of the palace, aided and abetted by the magnates, had usurped the power formerly held by the Merovingian kings. The king by no means became a puppet of the aristocracy. But it is significant that at the annual assembly with the magnates, the king requested their consent for many royal ordinances and decisions. We may assume that this consent was essentially formal in character and that the annual assembly was also designed to make it absolutely clear to those present which of the king's measures they were to support. Yet a certain interdependence was being created between the sovereign, who professed to be an absolute ruler, and the magnates, who presumed to represent the people. This presumption was not entirely unfounded, for the majority of the population worked on their estates, either as serfs or as freemen. Without the magnates, the sovereign could not maintain the Empire or extend its boundaries. And to extend their personal power and their own territory, the magnates were in turn dependent on the king, particularly on his success in battle.

As long as powerful figures such as Pepin the Short or Charlemagne ruled over the Frankish Kingdom, the central government and the magnates held each other in balance. However, disintegration set in after Charlemagne's death. His son, Louis the Pious, lacked his father's brilliance and authority, and as discord spread among the Carolingians, the power of the local potentates increased.

There was another reason for the weakness of the Carolingian Empire: the continuing decline in trade. Significantly, the gold that had formed the basis of the Merovingian monetary system was replaced with silver by the Carolingians. Charlemagne decreed that a pound of silver was to be divided into twenty shillings, which were, in turn, subdivided into twelve pennies. The decrease in trade that had begun in the Merovingian period accelerated at the beginning of the eighth century when Islam gained control of the western shores of the Mediterranean, effectively blocking maritime trade. Although trade did not disappear entirely, particularly in the North, it did taper off. The result was that cities, which in Roman times had been the centers of trade, commerce, government and culture, either disappeared or withered away into small, insignificant communities. Characteristically, the Frankish Kingdom had no cities to match Constantinople, Baghdad or Cordoba, huge metropolises which radiated a magnetic charisma. In short, under the Franks, civilization had reverted to a purely agrarian society, in which regular trade or a system of credit was not necessary to maintain a social organization. Only the North Sea − Baltic trade route was of any significance.

Charlemagne − the mightiest and most prominent of the Carolingians − governed his vast kingdom with the help of several hundred counts who were responsible for all administrative functions at a local level. The king often dispatched his trusted representatives to inspect their work. These representatives, called *missi*, were commonly recruited from the ranks of the bishops. The counts were entrusted with numerous duties. They were required to issue and implement capitularies (imperial laws), collect tolls, direct public works such as the construction and maintenance of bridges and roads and oversee the construction of large buildings. When, for example, a Carolingian king wished to erect a church or a palace[9] or construct a road or a bridge, he customarily contracted the work out to the local magnates, who employed their own resources and workmen to realize the project. In the case of smaller construction projects, the regional count decided who was to carry out the work. The workmen could not refuse and were obliged to follow his instructions. The king did not necessarily pay the counts for their efforts. Instead, he could grant them a third of the revenues from fines. The counts who supervised regions known as *gaus* were responsible for maintaining law and order and administering justice, and they also had a military function. As the counts were usually selected from the local population (initially by custom and later by law) and had managed to make their office hereditary, the office of count was another factor which severely undermined central government.

The duty to house the king and his retinue was a different matter altogether. As the royal entourage could easily swell to one thousand people, this was not a task to be taken lightly. As a rule, however, the subjects were not required to bear the burden of the king's upkeep. According to the Roman custom adopted by the Franks, the king commanded public domains in order to meet his own needs. While the Merovingian kings had sometimes stayed in the old Roman municipal palaces, Carolingian rulers preferred to erect their palaces on the crown domains and to travel restlessly from one base to another, meting out justice, dealing with administrative problems and maintaining contacts with the local administrators and magnates. To support themselves, the sovereign and his entourage received supplies from the royal estates. These were large farms located on the crown domains, designed to satisfy the court's food and lodging requirements. The subjects' only legal obligation in this respect, of which they were frequently reminded, was to provide food and lodging for representatives of the king and others under his protection passing through their locality. The amount of provisions which had to be made available was regulated down to the last detail. For example, a bishop had to be furnished with forty loaves of bread, an abbot or a count with thirty loaves, and a simple vassal of the king with seventeen loaves. The royal estates served as a model for the organization of other large manors. During the Carolingian period, in particular, this manorial system developed rapidly in conjunction with feudalism, which will be discussed further below. The peasants were forced into large agricultural complexes as serfs. The dissolution of governmental authority meant that the lord of the manor gradually obtained jurisdiction over the serfs who were bound to his land and obliged to supply him with services and goods in kind.

9. This is derived from the Latin *palatium*. We should not think of them in the light of today's palaces. Instead, they were fortified regional centers of royal power located near an abbey. They contained storehouses and accommodations for the king and his retinue. The palace in Ingelheim is an example.

Responsibility for the care of society's poor and needy, specifically widows, orphans and the infirm, lay initially with the Church. Its work was made possible by means of gifts. Although these donations came mainly from the king (from the public domains), prominent Franks also donated gifts, stipulating in return that Church buildings were to be erected so that prayers might be offered for their souls. The kings had similar concerns, but their objectives went further than their own spiritual well-being. By binding the Church to the monarchy, they secured the cooperation of the bishops, most of whom originated from the Gallo-

Carolingian warriors in various actions (from a 9th century manuscript).

Roman senatorial class, and with it that of an administratively able and loyal corps of officials. As an extension of the tax exemption granted earlier, the king also bestowed the right of immunity on certain religious communities. This immunity not only exempted the religious communities from all tax obligations and forbade royal office-holders to enter immune property, but also entitled the bishop or abbot to act as the highest magistrate over his subordinates, to impose fines and, in fact, to exercise public control in the area of immunity. Needless to say, this further undermined royal power, especially in Carolingian times when these immunities increased in number and scope.

From this time on, the Church was able to extend the welfare services it had taken upon itself as a result of the development of religious tithes (based on the Biblical injunction commanding people to give the Levites a tenth part for God). King Pepin the Short was the first to decree (in 750) that the clergy should be paid tithes to cover the costs of their upkeep in order to enable them to provide education, care for the sick and the poor, etc. Oddly enough, despite its sweeping effects, the introduction of religious tithes never elicited so much as a murmur. The explanation lies in the fact that the tithes were transformed into an indemnification for the large-scale confiscations of Church property made by Pepin's predecessor, Charles Martel, and passed on to his vassals. This will be explained below in the discussion of the feudal system. Later, Charlemagne not only upheld the tithe introduced by Pepin, but also extended it to include all real estate. In their final form, these religious tithes resembled tax levies, although there is a distinct difference between the two. Because the tithes were tied to the land, they later developed into a form of private law, a process facilitated by the fact that the rights to the tithes were transferable. However, this stage was not reached in the Carolingian age.

One important task entrusted to the counts was administering the subjects' oath of obedience to the sovereign. All males over the age of twelve had to take this oath, which made them entirely subject to the will of the Emperor. Every act of disobedience or (attempted) deception was seen as a violation of this oath. Military service was by far the heaviest obligation weighing on the subjects as a result of the oath of loyalty. In the nearly fifty years of his reign (from 768 to 814), Charlemagne only missed the annual campaign three times. His subjects had to be ready, year after year, to make their way to designated assembly points at a moment's notice. If they received their orders in the morning, they had to be on their way that evening; if they got their orders at the end of the day, they had to leave early the next morning. They set out with weapons, provisions for three months, clothes, carts and other pieces of equipment, all of which they were obliged to pay for themselves. No soldier would have considered wearing less than full battledress, as this would have reduced his chances of survival. It was also in every soldier's interest to have sufficient provisions, so as not to risk starving to death. Although a note of protest was sounded in the later Carolingian period, the oath of fealty was generally sufficient to mobilize the subjects year after year. It is true that only those who lived more or less in the vicinity of the hostilities were called to arms, but the subjects had to be prepared to go to war at all times. This obligation did not extend to the elderly, the infirm, the clergy, the unfree or certain of the counts' assistants. In 806, it was decreed that no one could become a priest or a monk without the consent of the court, for experience had shown that this was frequently a ploy to escape military service. Capitularies from 807 and 808 show that only the owners of several farms, as freemen, were liable for military service. Those not included in that category were obliged to contribute to the expenses of those who went off to battle. This brings us to the phenomenon of vassalage.

The feudal system

For centuries, every great lord in the Frankish Kingdom, whether descended from the Gallo-Romans or the Franks, had been surrounded by a retinue, which was dependent on him, worked his land, served him and stood by him in feuds and battles. This social phenomenon was partially derived from old German customs, in which mutual aid and loyalty governed the relationship between lord and retinue, and partially from the perilous times of the decline of the Roman Empire, when self-defense against the roving and plundering Germanic tribes was the order of the day.

It had long been customary for the lords to provide for the upkeep of those in their service and to allocate a parcel of land to provide for their living expenses and military equipment. The relationship between the lord and his servants, which sprang from their mutual oath of fealty, was based on the lord's offering shelter and protection, in return for which the servants offered him advice and service. As of the eighth century, the latter were called "vassals." This term was derived from the Celtic word "gwas," which meant "boy" or "servant."

The system of vassalage was given further impetus in the first half of the eighth century by Pepin of Heristal and his illegitimate son, Charles Martel, also mayor of the palace. During their numerous wars, both father and son had been compelled to grant land to their vassals in order to secure their loyalty. In 717, Charles Martel took possession of his father's treasury in Austrasia, which he used as a power base to became master of Neustria as well. To reinforce his position and bind his vassals to him, he confiscated the Church's vast estates and gave them to his powerful servants, who in turn doled out portions of their newly acquired estates to their own underlings. The Church had been stripped of its source of income to such an extent that it could no longer adequately perform its welfare and religious services. Pepin the Short realized that this indirectly undermined the state, but refused to consider returning the confiscated possessions to the Church. The solution to his dilemma was to have the vassals give back the confiscated lands to the king. The king then restored the lands as fiefs on one condition: that their holders bestow a tenth of the proceeds from the land to the monastery or abbey which had originally owned it. In return, they were discharged of their obligations except for the usual advice and service entailed in the vassalage relationship.

This practice gave birth not only to religious tithes, but also to the feudal system. While they spring from a joint source, tithes and feudalism are two distinct concepts. The tithes rode piggyback on the feudal system, but they did not constitute feudal rights. Indeed, centuries later, during the French Revolution, the tithes were abolished, but not because they were considered to be feudal in character.

Thus, Pepin the Short laid the foundation for a network of vassal and sub-vassal obligations. The system was expanded further under the Carolingians, who not only gave away Church possessions as fiefs, but also their own estates and conquered territories.

After the eighth century, feudalism spread like an oil slick over all of Western Europe. Free noblemen, unencumbered by feudal obligations, had virtually become extinct in France by the year 1000 A.D. The impact of feudalism was less pervasive in Germany, where some families still owned land inherited from their forebears, which was known as *allodium*. Yet even in Germany, the *feodum*, the property given as fiefs, was the most common form of land control. In the agrarian society of the time, land was by far the most coveted possession. As we have already seen, the lands were by and large worked by serfs. The mutual obligations of the vassalage system were interwoven with those of the land fiefs. Together, they gave rise to feudalism, a singular but colorful system of legal relationships that dominated Western European society for centuries.

The feudal system weakened the state, particularly when Charlemagne began to grant not only landed estates but also public offices as fiefs. Though intended to create a stronger tie between officials and the central government and thus shore up the weak governmental structure, the practice backfired. Before long, the counts and other public officials were able to make these offices hereditary and thus beyond royal control.

Many historians believe that the Frankish army's evolution from a rabble of foot soldiers into an elite force of cavalrymen can be attributed to feudalism. Another thought-provoking theory concerning this change in battle tactics has been expounded by Lynn White, Jr. According to White, "The horse has always given his master an advantage over the footman in battle, and each improvement in its military use has been related to far-reaching social and cultural changes." He argues that the stirrup was one such change. Introduced after the Battle of Poitiers (732), it helped the Frankish army to switch from foot to horseback. The stirrup, in White's opinion, gave the mounted soldier the decisive advantage over the foot soldier, for it enabled him to throw a spear, thrust a lance and wield a sword with much greater force by adding the combined weight of his own body and that of his horse to his own muscle power. Henceforth, the hand of the combatant did not propel but merely guided the instrument of death. The stirrup – probably invented by the Chinese centuries earlier – replaced human energy with horse power and significantly increased the chance of mortally wounding the enemy. This development also led to a change in weapons. The battle-axe disappeared, the sword was made longer for mounted warriors and the spear was reinforced and provided with barbs. The barbs could not be too large, as this made it difficult to withdraw the spear from the body of the dead or dying victim.

Needless to say, this new way of fighting meant greater expense for the combatants, who, as we know, had to pay for their own weapons. A cavalryman's equipment cost no less than twenty oxen, and this does not take into account the cost of at least one extra horse and the huge amounts of costly and scarce grain these animals devoured. Even though every freeman in the Frankish Kingdom was duty-bound to bear arms, regardless of his financial situation, only a minority of substantial landholders could afford to purchase horses and the necessary weapons. Charles Martel, as we saw, solved this problem by confiscating ecclesiastical estates and parceling them out to members of his entourage. Toward the end of his reign, Charlemagne blazed another trail: he ordered less prosperous freemen to form groups based on the size of the plots they cultivated and to jointly finance one of their number to go to war as a cavalryman. This freed them of any further military obligations. Before long, the general conscription

*A Carolingian horseman.
Note the stirrup and the
barbed lance. The print has
been taken from "The
gentium migrationibus" of
Wolfgang Lazins
(1514-1565).*

*Warrior from a 9th century
manuscript.*

of all freemen had disappeared entirely. This created a gap in society between the huge mass of farmers who made their contribution in cash or − as was more frequent − in kind and a small select group of warriors later called "knights." Charlemagne's earlier-mentioned capitularies of 807 and 808 reflected this development.

Loyalty and courage on the battlefield, so the new class felt, were the outstanding virtues which should distinguish them from the rest of society. Lynn White, Jr. traces the roots of feudalism to the advent of this new equestrian class, which largely shaped the social structure of the late Carolingian Empire. According to White, the monumental effect of the technological advance sparked by the stirrup was embodied in the Battle of Hastings (1066), in which William the Conqueror conquered the English with his superior cavalry from the shores of Normandy. Although the stirrup had already been introduced to the Anglo-Saxons, it had not led to the socially dominant elite class of mounted soldiers that characterized feudal society. As it turned out, William consolidated his military success by grafting the feudal fabric onto Anglo-Saxon society. Such "modernization" was not achieved until after William had won the battle, the country and the crown.

Two groups of horsemen in a manuscript dating from the second half of the 9th century. Note that the stirrup was already part of the horse's equipment. The light cavalry at the top of the picture do not have shields. Those on the bottom are better equipped. The one in front is carrying a pole with a banner in the form of a dragon. The banner-carrier and one of the horsemen are wearing coats of armor, consisting of tiny, overlapping iron plates attached to a linen or leather undergarment. The armor shown here is in a more advanced stage of development, as the upper arms and legs are protected as well as the chest. The coat of armor was the soldier's most valuable piece of equipment. It was of such military significance that it was strictly forbidden to export armor from the Frankish Kingdom.

As is usually the case when an attempt is made to explain a historical development on the basis of a single fact, White's explanation has encountered heavy opposition. We will sidestep the question of cause and effect and simply say that considering the paucity of the sources available to us one thousand years after the event, such theorizing is mostly guesswork anyway. It must be admitted, however, that White's theory has shed new light on an intriguing phenomenon: the creation, in a fairly short span of time, of a military aristocracy that was to form one of the main pillars of society in the High Middle Ages.

The imposition of tolls

Military service dwarfed the other obligations of subjects. The only real taxes known in the Carolingian age, a carry-over from the Merovingian age, were tolls, especially those levied on rivers, bridges and sluices. Abbeys and monasteries (like pilgrims and soldiers) were often exempted from these levies. Toll revenues, or *teloneum*, granted to the Church represented one of the clergy's most important sources of income. But as the counts received an honorarium of one third of the toll revenues, they were naturally not so keen to bestow them on churches and abbeys. Nor were they overjoyed at the granting of exemptions from tolls.

The following story will shed some more light on toll exemptions. It has been taken from the *Miracula Sancti Benedicti* (The Miracles of Saint Benedict), written in c. 875 by Adrevald, a monk at the Abbey of Fleury. "This very sacred monastery [Fleury] had received from the Frankish kings the right, written in a formal deed, to have four boats sail on the Loire every year, exempt from whatever taxes were to be given to the treasury. At the time of the above-mentioned count [Raho], one of these boats had sailed as far as Nantes to take on a load of salt. On the way back it had called in at the cities and harbors that lay on his travel route and, thanks to the protection of the royal charter, had not encountered any trouble. It finally reached Orléans. The toll collectors of this city detained the vessel and demanded that the captain pay the toll. The captain referred him to the exemption granted by the king. However, the toll collector took no notice of the royal charter and, as payment to the treasury, impounded the boat and its load of salt and entrusted it to the harbor master so that it would be put under embargo along with other vessels. This happened on a Sunday. However, at the third hour of the day when everyone was attending mass, our boat, under guard along with the other impounded boats in the harbor, suddenly lay outside the harbor, without the intervention of a human oarsman; it reached the middle of the Loire, where the current is the strongest. And sailing upstream, it reached the water gate that is still called 'The Gate of Saint Benedict' and berthed there." The townspeople came running to see it and to rejoice at the miracle. The passage ends with the words: "The tax officials were thus brought to shame for their boldness; from then on they avoided giving evidence of their foolishness."

There was a frequent misuse of tolls. I am referring less to English merchants disguising themselves as pilgrims in order to obtain free passage than to the toll collectors who pocketed the tolls themselves and even created their own tolls to line those pockets; after all, it was easy enough to chain off a road or a bridge. The Carolingian kings did everything they could to clamp down on toll abuses, but to no avail, for royal authority was already well into its decline. Another shortcoming in the system was the government's neglect of the *quid pro quo* that it offered in exchange for the tolls: the construction of a bridge, a ferry, a ford or a road through marshy ground. These projects were supposed to be financed from the toll revenues, but little could be done in the face of the government's neglect.

Voluntary donations

The gifts which were offered annually to the sovereign by the clergy and the aristocracy formed one of the cornerstones of the royal and later imperial finances. Dignitaries who held the reins of government, such as bishops, abbots, high-ranking officials and great lords, appeared annually before the king in a kind of general assembly and offered him presents in coin or kind. We can safely assume that this was not a spontaneous gesture. The gift was more or less compulsory and thus closely resembled a tax. Still, there were differences. The gift was not based on an exact assessment of the donor's property; moreover, the donor personally handed over his contribution to the king without the intervention of a tax collector or other intermediary and without being subjected to an audit. The donor parted with gift upon gift until he had struck a fine balance between love for the king and love of personal wealth. The custom of giving gifts can be traced back to the Merovingian period. Under the Carolingians, the annual gift became more widespread and institutionalized. In a similar fashion, the ecclesiastical and secular dignitaries received compulsory but ostensibly voluntary support from their subjects. This procedure laid the foundation for the feudal system. A case in point is Einhard, the lay abbot of St. Baafs in Ghent, who in 833 ordered his steward to pass the gift he received as abbot to Emperor Lothair in Compiègne, but not before recording what each of the inhabitants of the abbey's estates had donated.

This type of gift giving was clearly of German origin. Apart from the practical aspect of replenishing the royal coffers, its primary function was to embody the solidarity between the sovereign and his representatives. The gift was the visual manifestation of the fact that Frankish kingship did not rest on abstract rules and institutions, but on a network of personal allegiances between liege lord and vassal, vassal and sub-vassal, etc. The donor was undoubtedly acutely aware when presenting his sovereign with a gift that his predecessors had done likewise.

Those players caught up in the ritual of power saw the gift as a voluntary gesture, even though the legal relationship of personal fealty had made it more or less compulsory. It is customarily referred to as an "aid" (or the French aide), a term which captures the symbolic essence of the contribution in the Frankish era. After Charles the Bald (d. 877), no more traces of this custom are found in the Western Frankish Kingdom, and it sank into oblivion. This is not to say, however, that the gift system did not continue to exist for a long time after that.

After the death of this grandson of Charlemagne, the Western Frankish Kingdom rapidly disintegrated. By the time the Carolingian dynasty died out in 987 and Hugh Capet was made king, his sole territory was the Île de France, the region around Paris. The remainder of the Western Kingdom was ruled by magnates, dukes and counts. In the absence of a strong monarchy, their power was almost unlimited. For three long centuries, we hear nothing more about royal finances. The Capetians were fully occupied in expanding their territory, the Île de France, into the powerful kingdom which formed the basis for today's France. The financial development from gift to aid and from aid to tax is easier to follow in the eastern part of the Frankish Empire, which also encompassed the northern part of the Lotharian Middle Kingdom. But we will leave this to the next chapter.

The dissolution of the Carolingian state and the disappearance of taxation

The seeds of the division that was to fragment continental Western Europe into a number of states had already been sown in the Treaty of Verdun, and even earlier in Clovis' design to divide his kingdom among his four sons. This process was accelerated by the many centrifugal forces tearing the Frankish Kingdom apart, several of which have been cited above: conquered peoples were allowed to maintain their own laws and customs, so that there was a constant leaning towards autonomy, though not independence; vast estates were bestowed on the Church and the magnates as a reward for their services, and this was later followed by the rise of feudalism; immunities were granted to religious communities and this practice, like the rule of large landowners, promoted the breakdown of central government; and lastly, counts who should have owed their primary loyalty to the king were recruited from the local population, a decentralizing factor that was reinforced by the tendency to make the office hereditary. In addition, the state, already weakened by continuous vendettas and civil wars, was threatened in the North by the Vikings, in the South by Islam and in the East by the Magyars. All of these destabilizing forces and the rise of regional centers of power might have propelled events in the opposite direction had a general tax been levied throughout the kingdom. However, as we have seen, in the period between the death of Clovis in 511 and the Treaty of Verdun in 843, general taxation disappeared almost entirely. This was partly due to the forces of dissolution referred to above, partly to the fact that the earlier monetary economy had made way for a barter economy, and partly to the Edict of Paris (614), which had made the imposition of new taxes virtually impossible. The mortar of taxation which had held the bricks of state together had been washed away, and the walls of the structure slowly but surely crumbled under their own weight.

According to legend, Archbishop Kunibert of Cologne (c. 626-648) founded the hospital of St. Lupus and laid down alms for the poor. In return for their care, they were to hold a wake upon the death of an archbishop. This picture (from 1248) shows Archbishop Kunibert entrusting the care of the poor to the head of his chapel.

St. Bruno, Archbishop of Cologne (953-965). Various rulers are depicted in the medallons. The defeated Duke of Lorraine, Conrad, is lying at Bruno's feet. In his hand, Bruno is holding the Abbey of Pantaleon, which he founded.

2 Cologne

Bishops as administrators in the Eastern Frankish Kingdom

The Western world at the end of the Carolingian era was falling apart: the former monetary economy had all but passed out of existence, and governmental authority was in shreds. Legislation was gradually replaced by unwritten laws, and power relations came to be embedded in the feudal system. Aided by the hierarchical structure of feudalism, based on the relationship between liege lord and vassal, vassal and sub-vassal, etc., feudal society was set the task of maintaining a rudimentary form of law and order and providing protection against outside foes. Feudalism could ill accommodate a system of general taxation as a binding force between the government and its subjects.

Central authority had been dealt the worst blows in the Western and Middle Frankish Kingdoms, which had been created by the Treaty of Verdun in 843. Although the Eastern Frankish Kingdom developed differently, the hereditary monarchy of the Carolingians was replaced here as well by elected kingship. Needless to say, the position of an elected king was much weaker. Moreover, as the ninth century moved into the tenth century, several so-called tribal or stem duchies were created. As warrior chieftains, the dukes in these duchies attempted to arrogate royal prerogatives and to make their ducal title hereditary. In 919, following a period of disorder, Henry the Fowler, the Stem Duke of Saxony, was elected king. He brought the various centrifugal forces under control and reestablished royal authority in the stem duchies. In 925, he even acquired the northern part of the Frankish Middle Kingdom and incorporated it into the Eastern Frankish Kingdom as the Duchy of Lorraine.

His son, Otto the Great, who had already been named as co-regent during Henry the Fowler's lifetime to facilitate succession, was again faced with the Stem Dukes' thirst for independence. In 953, his son-in-law, Conrad, whom he had appointed as Duke of Lorraine, even rose in rebellion against him. That same year, Otto ousted Conrad from his duchy at the Imperial Diet in Fritzlar. He then appointed his youngest brother, Bruno, to administer Lorraine. Shortly before, Bruno had been chosen Archbishop of Cologne with his brother's consent. Bruno was thus the first of a long series of ecclesiastics to hold positions of secular power in certain parts of the Eastern Frankish Kingdom. Ever since the pact between Pepin the Short and the Pope in 754, the king had decisively influenced the selection of the bishop. This allowed Otto and his successors to have their own trusted representatives rule over large territories. Yet it placed the bishop in an ambiguous position. On the one hand, he was the spiritual leader of his diocese and, on the other, he was the highest secular authority. In the century to follow, the bishops even became sovereign rulers. The bishops' worldly authority did not always extend over the same territory as their bishoprics. In fact, their secular power was often more limited. But the bishops went to great lengths to remedy that situation and passionately strove to enlarge their worldly territory so that it at least coincided with their diocese. They were not restrained in these endeavors by moral or other scruples, seizing secular authority over parts of another diocese wherever possible.

Emperor Otto I. Miniature from the "Emperor Chronicle," a manuscript dating from the beginning of the 12th century.

1. The Holy Roman Empire of the German nation was headed by a king elected by the most powerful of his vassals, known as of the thirteenth century as Electoral Princes. He bore the title of King of the Holy Roman Empire. The right to wear the imperial crown was first conferred by the Archbishop of Cologne in coronation ceremonies held in the imperial city of Aachen. From Otto's coronation in 962 until the end of the Middle Ages, the Pope normally crowned the kings of the Eastern Frankish Kingdom as Emperors and successors of Charlemagne. In this book, the term "king" refers to the actual office-holder and "emperor" to the titular holder of the office.

In line with the feudal practice of granting offices as fiefs, the Emperor[1] had enfeoffed some of his royal authority to the bishops. The Emperor benefitted from this arrangement because the bishops could not make these enfeoffed offices hereditary. After all, their vow of celibacy prevented them from fathering legitimate children. Any power delegated to the bishops was eventually returned to the Emperor, who could then pass it on as a fief to the next bishop. No rules required the rights and territory to be identical each time, so that the Emperor was free to rearrange matters as he deemed fit.

Initially, this system worked splendidly, at least from the Emperor's point of view. He had a number of loyal assistants at his command, the bishoprics were located in strategically important areas and when a certain dynasty died out, he could fill the empty slot by enfeoffing it to a bishop, thereby reinforcing his own position. Using the universal church as a front, he was able to call a halt to the stem dukes' aspirations toward autonomy. A drawback to this system was that it posed a serious threat to the Church. Although canon law required the bishops to be chosen by the clergy and the people, in practice they were appointed by the Emperor. He selected candidates for their loyalty and military prowess rather than for their spiritual qualities. As a result, his choice often fell upon ruffians, who were only ordained after they had been appointed bishop. In time, the Emperor's political machinations gnawed away at the Church's credibility as spiritual leader.

During the tenth century, the Abbey of Cluny in France (founded in 910) instigated a reform movement, designed to purge the Church of secular elements and bring it back to its intended spiritual values. The spirit of Cluny spread throughout the kingdom, also conquering Rome. It culminated in the appointment of the monk Hildebrand, an ardent and powerful supporter of the reform movement, as Pope Gregory VII. Shortly thereafter, a conflict with the Emperor flared up over the appointment of bishops, the so-called Investiture Controversy. The Investiture Controversy dominated the last quarter of the eleventh century and the first quarter of the twelfth century and left an indelible impression on medieval thinking about the ostensibly inextricable tie between the Emperor and the Pope. The conflict between the two powers continued to divide Western Christianity well into the next century.

This controversy left the scars of discord throughout all of the then known Christian world. The Concordat of Worms (1122) decreed that both the clergy and the people were to elect the bishops, but the choice was soon left to local cathedral chapters. As far as the Church was concerned, this was going from the frying pan into the fire, since the election of bishops became a matter of fierce local rivalry. To extend their power radius, neighboring rulers flexed their diplomatic muscles in attempts to obtain ecclesiastical offices, especially episcopal sees, for their sons who were not in line for succession.

The bishops, solely concerned with extending and consolidating their own power, gradually gained secular power over territories that nominally belonged to the Emperor according to feudal law, but were virtually independent of his rule. The bishops steered their own course, occasionally opposing the Emperor and undermining his authority. Even after the Concordat of Worms, we frequently encounter bishops who preferred wielding the sword to preaching the Sermon on the Mount.

Several of Cologne's Archbishops in the tenth and eleventh centuries were able to keep the helmet and the miter in equilibrium: they shepherded their flocks in times of peace as effectively as they commanded their armies in times of war. Archbishops Bruno I, Anno II (both of whom will be discussed below) and Heribert were even canonized by the Church. It should be borne in mind that canonization was sometimes politically motivated and that occasionally an Archbishop of Cologne who died in the odor of sanctity had been instrumental in scenting the eau de cologne himself.

In the twelfth and thirteenth centuries, following the Concordat of Worms, an increasing number of bishops swapped the staff for the sword, even though the Church forbade ecclesiastics to bear arms, let alone use them. A Parisian Scholastic (a clergymen schooled in philosophy and theology) of that period vented his disgust at this development: "I can believe anything, but I cannot believe that one of the German bishops will ever be vindicated for the way he holds down his ecclesiastical office." Abbess Hildegard of Bingen also hurled

This harmoniously carved and beautifully decorated ivory comb dates from the second half of the 9th century in Metz. It was later presented to St. Heribert, Archbishop of Cologne (999-1021), and was used in the coronation and anointment of the kings as well as in the consecration of the bishops. In symbolic terms, the comb meant that the thoughts of the one being consecrated could be put in order and directed toward heaven.

*Abbess Hildegard of
Bingen (1098-1179).*

reproaches at the bishops for setting a bad example, citing their neglect of ecclesiastical duties, parsimony, greed and insatiable craving for power. Surprisingly — or perhaps significantly — the bishops' immorality apparently raised few eyebrows. The only comment on that score is the confession of Archbishop Henry of Molenark that as a young cleric sowing his wild oats he had not even passed up a married woman.

The archbishops in Cologne during these centuries were mainly descendants of the great noble families of that area: Are, Hochstadt and Berg. Serving family interests was their uppermost priority, and they frequently benefitted from their powerful family connections. In the fourteenth and fifteenth centuries, Cologne's archbishops were sometimes chosen by and sometimes from the cathedral chapter, a body which likewise largely consisted of great nobles. Johannes Gerson painted a black picture of these ecclesiastics in his *Bishop's Mirror*. He perceived them as shepherds who had changed into wolves and now devoured their sheep. In his eyes, their most obvious failings were *avaria* (avarice) and *luxuria* (ostentation). One of the worst offenders was no doubt Archbishop Diedrich of Moers, who will be described in detail later in this chapter.

Three themes are dealt with in this chapter. The first examines the power struggle between the city of Cologne and its Archbishop. Their conflict revolved around the question of who was entitled to levy taxes and spend the revenues. This chapter further describes how in the tenth century Archbishop Bruno gained control of the city, how in the eleventh century Archbishop Anno exercised this control and how in the thirteenth century the city was at loggerheads with successively Archbishops Engelbrecht of Berg, Conrad of Hochstadt and Siegfried of Westerburg. At the end of the thirteenth century, the city ultimately prevailed and became a free imperial city.

The second theme tackles the power struggle between the patricians and the guilds in the fourteenth century, in which taxation again played a key role. This gave birth to a rudimentary form of democracy in Cologne's city government. Pressured by the guilds, the patricians controlling the municipal government were compelled in 1396 to accept a document called the *Verbundbrief*. As a result, governmental bodies elected by the citizens were granted the power to decide on taxation.

The third theme demonstrates how the Archbishop of Cologne had to sacrifice internal power in order to achieve external territorial expansion. To finance his expansionist aspirations, he needed the consent of the estates — the clergy, the nobility and the cities — to levy taxes. In turn, the estates demanded and received influence on the government.

From feudalism to sovereignty

To gain a better understanding of the relationship between the Archbishop and the city of Cologne, i.e. between the estates, it is necessary to devote a few words to the visible disintegration of the feudal system in the twelfth century. The origins of feudalism, which reached full maturity in the tenth century, can be traced back to the Carolingian Age, described in the previous chapter. Feudalism was a system in which freemen bound themselves as vassals to powerful lords, to whom they owed homage and fealty. In exchange for their aid and advice, the vassals were protected and maintained by the liege lord. In turn, these lords pledged themselves to even more powerful figures. Society was thus a hierarchical network of feudal relationships between liege lords and vassals, vassals and sub-vassals, etc., with the king at the top of the hierarchy. Property granted as fiefs to vassals was at the heart of this system. In later times, offices, tolls and administrative rights were likewise enfeoffed. In theory, a vassal obligation could be of limited duration. In practice, a vassalage relationship was usually only terminated by misconduct or death. The vassal did his utmost to maintain the relationship and make it hereditary. By recognizing an inherited position, a liege lord accepted the fact that the enfeoffed property had been de facto passed to the vassal.

In Merovingian times, the monarchy had been hereditary and the king had appointed his own counts and advisers. In the age of feudalism, the roles were reversed: the king was elected by magnates with hereditary positions. The kings naturally attempted to make the monarchy hereditary as well. To achieve this objective and remain firmly ensconced in the royal saddle, the kings were obliged to secure the loyalty of a host of vassals by endowing them with large parcels of crown lands or sometimes even entire regions as fiefs. Bound by their oath of loyalty to the king as sovereign ruler, the vassals provided help and military assistance. The early medieval notion that land ownership also involved governing those living on the land implied that the king's vassals were turned into administrators, a process that was further reinforced by the king's habit of occasionally delegating certain royal prerogatives, the so-called regalia, to his own vassals. His vassals in turn delegated land and power to their vassals. In this way, the costly armies of knights could be financed by means of land ownership, or to be more accurate, by payments in kind. Thus a feudal society evolved, rooted in the personal relationships between a liege lord and his vassals and sub-vassals. The system as a whole covered the empire like a giant tapestry of interwoven power relationships.

Initially, the king was the sovereign ruler and as such was charged with maintaining peace and administering justice. Later, the dukes, who originally functioned as the king's deputies in certain territories, developed into sovereign rulers, a process that was accelerated by the fact that these public offices had become hereditary. The dukes were eventually eclipsed by their vassals, counts and other nobles who assumed the tasks of protecting the populace from marauders and maintaining law and order within gradually shrinking territories. The counts, who were originally officials appointed by the Carolingian kings to govern in certain regions on their behalf, were incorporated in the feudal system when their offices became hereditary. This continual fragmentation of power, a process so characteristic of feudalism, was not arrested until the formation of territories which were virtually autonomous. These lands were headed by a duke, a count or a bishop, in short by a sovereign ruler, who acknowledged the king's supremacy while taking little notice of him. By 1100, feudal society had been transformed into a motley patchwork of independent territories, regions and cities governed by a local sovereign ruler or municipal government.

Just how did this transformation come about? It started with a growing awareness among the dukes, counts and bishops that the entire administrative system had become entangled in a web of inherited feudal relationships. Vassalage had degenerated from an instrument of cohesion into an instrument

Archbishop Frederick of Schwartzenburg (1100-1131) offers Lothar III the imperial crown (from Vincent de Beauvais, "Le Miroir Historial," vol. 4, Southern Netherlands, fourth quarter of the 15th century).

2. The *Erzstift* was the area over which the Archbishop exercised his secular authority. After 1356, this area was referred to as *Kurköln*, a name change associated with the Golden Bull issued in that year, which specified that the German Emperor would henceforth be elected by seven Electoral Princes, including the Archbishop of Cologne. Because of the difficulty of finding a suitable English equivalent, both *Erzstift* and *Kurköln* have been left untranslated.

of fragmentation. The remedy designed by the ruling figures was to create a group of dependent officeholders whom they could dismiss at will. Only then was it possible to check the fragmentation of power and form self-contained territorial units. Examples of such independent petty principalities in this narrative are the *Erzstift*[2] and the Duchy of Westphalia (governed by the Archbishop of Cologne), the Duchies of Brabant and Gelre and the Counties of Berg and Cleves. It would be unfair to compare these principalities to the sovereign states familiar to us since the nineteenth century. Instead, the territorial "state" of the later Middle Ages is best seen as a compact between a sovereign prince and freemen.

Chapter 1 has already described how the military use of the horse had led, since the Carolingian age, to a small but dominant knighthood. Unlike the great mass of peasants, knights had the right as freemen to bear arms to defend themselves and their communities. While free subjects had initially provided direct military aid, in later years this was usually replaced by financial assistance.

Thomas Aquinas instructs an emperor, a king, a chancellor and several nobles (from ''Le Livre de l'information,'' Paris, 1453).

The need to finance this elite force in battle revived taxation, which had virtually disappeared in the Carolingian age. The introduction of taxes did not proceed smoothly. The subjects had to drastically revise their entire philosophy to accept the idea that the limitation on private ownership inherent in the concept of taxation was legitimate and therefore acceptable. Even such a clear thinker as Thomas Aquinas struggled in his *Summa Theologica* with the right to levy taxes. Asking whether it was possible for a robbery to take place without being a sin, Aquinas concluded that this was only possible when the sovereign ruler requested or imposed quasi-voluntary contributions known as ''aids.'' These aids, he wrote, had to accord with the demands for justice and equity before the law and promote the general welfare. As Aquinas later explained in a letter to the Duchess of Brabant, anything beyond that was unlawful. Therefore even Aquinas, who lived in Cologne between 1248 and 1252 and who therefore must have witnessed the city's attempt to abrogate the Archbishop's right to impose taxes, regarded taxation with a wary eye. He could not place the concept in an appropriate context and therefore described it as a kind of robbery. Even today, we jokingly describe taxes we feel to be excessive (particularly those coming out of our own pockets) as "highway robbery."

In 1151, the Archbishop of Cologne was enfeoffed with the ducal power over Lorraine. This laid the foundation for his progress from Church prelate into sovereign ruler over a territory. As the feudal system eroded, large territories broke up into small autonomous units (e.g. the Counties of Berg, Jülich and Cleves). To expound on this process would be to stray from the subject at hand. Suffice it to say that the Archbishop of Cologne was able to mold the *Erzstift* and the Duchy of Westphalia, which had been enfeoffed to him since 1180, into a pair of separate territorial states. The tools he used to accomplish this feat were the powers of high and low justice, which I will briefly discuss below.

In the *Erzstift*, as elsewhere, the owners of large real estate complexes – sometimes as many as one hundred farms – exercised a certain sovereignty over the people working their land that dated from Frankish times. This manorial system or *Grundherrschaft* (which basically means mastery over lands and people) not only obligated the inhabitants of the manor to work the land, but even put their very lives in the hands of the landowners. In the twelfth century, this state of serfdom gradually began to be modified, until in most areas, serfs were only obliged to supply goods and services. This process of emancipation was partly prompted by the regeneration of towns and cities, which owed their rise to the change from a barter economy to a monetary economy. The attendant increase in trade created markets, where peasants could sell their wares and where they were no longer fettered by the shackles of manorial self-sufficiency. A bourgeois awareness of liberty (*Stadtluft macht frei*) manifested itself in the countryside. The peasants loosened their ties with the manors and gradually became tenants in their own right, first paying their rent in kind and then in coin. Now they were free to come and go as they pleased. They had shed their personal bondage to a landowner and had become independent subjects of whoever ruled over their local territorial unit. Landowners therefore evolved into lords and thus administrators and magistrates over specific territories. Many knights also gained this status on the strength of their assistance on the battlefield or administrative and other rights received as a fief.

Two types of jurisdictional powers were granted to a lord: the powers of high justice and the powers of low justice. Armed with the powers of high justice in a certain area, a lord could exercise blood justice, meaning he could adjudicate cases involving capital punishment and life imprisonment. The powers of low justice enabled him to hear less serious criminal cases and civil suits. The lord's jurisdiction did not confine itself to judicial cases, but encompassed legislative and administrative responsibilities as well. Any person or official body empowered to exercise high justice was also automatically empowered to exercise low justice, unless the latter had been granted to someone else. As will appear shortly, the distinction between these two types of justice was particularly important for taxation.

The Archbishop regarded anyone exercising the powers of high and/or low justice over the motley territories in the *Erzstift* and the Duchy of Westphalia to be encroaching on his sovereign power. He therefore continually strove to extend his own power by purchasing or otherwise acquiring the powers of high and/or low justice.

The monasteries and abbeys dotting the countryside often had vast immune properties, where the abbot or dean maintained legal order himself. As canon law forbade the clergy to try capital offenses, these religious communities engaged laymen called "advocates" to handle legal and military matters. These advocates seized every opportunity to make their office hereditary. Moreover, they identified themselves with their interests and the property they were supposed to protect to such an extent that they simply took possession of the property. Some advocates even succeeded in usurping the powers of high justice.

What was happening at this time in the *Erzstift* and the Duchy of Westphalia, the two territories over which the Archbishop held sway? The Archbishop often bought up castles and the surrounding lands, only to return them to the sellers as fiefs in order to reserve for themselves the powers of low justice. Frequently, monasteries and abbeys bound themselves to the Archbishop to protect themselves against their advocates, for which he received the powers of low justice. Any Archbishop who had used this method to obtain low justice in a certain area was in possession of high justice as well, because of his position as sovereign ruler. In the *Erzstift*, to which we will limit ourselves, some nobles possessed the powers of low justice, although a few had also acquired the powers of high justice in certain areas. There are also examples of a territory in which one noble had the powers of low justice while another had high justice. But occasionally the Archbishop had high justice and someone else low justice. In short, the Archbishop was always entitled to the powers of high justice in his territory by virtue of his being sovereign ruler, unless someone else had already been granted this power. Anyone having the powers of high justice was automatically entitled to the powers of low justice, unless someone else had been granted low justice first.

In the Middle Ages, it was normal practice for land to be enfeoffed, bought, sold and used as collateral, etc. The same held for intangible rights, such as administrative rights, the right to mint coins and hold markets, etc. Lands and rights usually changed ownership through sale or inheritance. But someone could also voluntarily renounce his rights, or in cases of criminal behavior, a person's rights were declared null and void. Lands or rights pledged as security on a loan could often not be redeemed. For secular rulers, marriage was an efficacious means of expanding one's territory or enhancing one's legal position. Ecclesiastical rulers, such as the Archbishop of Cologne, had no such arrows in their quivers. But they had another weapon at their disposal: they could exercise their ecclesiastical powers over persons who belonged to the diocese but were not residents of the *Erzstift* or the Duchy of Westphalia. In addition to the clerics who were part of the Archbishop's hierarchy, this included laymen who for one reason or another were obliged to answer to the ecclesiastical court. For example, the disputes between Diedrich of Moers and the Duchy of Cleves (which will be discussed later) arose as a result of the Archbishop's attempt to impose taxes on the clerics in that duchy.

Taxation: a prerogative of the holders of the powers of low justice

Let us now turn to the phenomenon of taxation. Basically, taxation means subjects are forced to surrender part of their cash (or in former times, also a payment in kind) without receiving any tangible benefit in return. When the payment involves a *quid pro quo* arrangement with an individual, it is referred to as a

*Seal of Archbishop
Engelbrecht of Berg
(1182-1225).*

"tribute". A case in point is the tolls collected by the Archbishop along the Rhine. A merchant would pay these tolls with a portion of his wares and receive the Archbishop's shelter and protection in return. This was then said to be a tribute.

Although toll revenues were part of the Archbishop's total budget, he used the bulk of the revenues to maintain and reward his local officials. In time, the tolls evolved into a monetary payment, in which merchants were required to pay a percentage of the value or weight of the goods they transported over the Rhine to the Archbishop. By this time, the tribute had developed into a full-fledged tax.

An "aid," another form of taxation, also underwent a similar evolution. According to medieval thought, the relationship between the king or lord and his subjects was governed by the principle of *do ut des*: "I give so that you may give.'' The lord offered his subject shelter and protection and received aid and advice in return. Initially, the relationship was one of mutual obligation, of the type we encountered in the tribute. In time, this system of mutual ties evolved into taxation.

Generally speaking, only lords possessing the powers of low justice were entitled to impose taxes. They did this on their own initiative, without obtaining the consent of their subjects. It is likely that the right to impose taxes developed along the lines sketched below.

Initially, the holder of the powers of low justice requested the assistance and support of his subjects, a request the subjects could not refuse because they were obliged to assist the lord in return for the protection he offered them. As some subjects were incapable of providing military assistance, the obligation was often transformed into a demand for goods, particularly provisions for soldiers in the field. In time, this payment in kind was replaced by a monetary payment. As money began to dominate the economy, all subjects were asked, in lieu of military service, to make a financial contribution towards the upkeep of the mercenaries now making up the bulk of the fighting forces. Although formally a request, this contribution was hardly voluntary, particularly when it was demanded at regular intervals. This practice eventually developed into a regularly recurring tax, similar to today's local taxes. Since the taxpayers could see where their money was going, a regular, recurrent tax evolved without too much grumbling on the part of the taxpayers.

An Archbishop could only impose an aid in those areas of the *Erzstift* where he possessed the powers of low justice. His dual role as holder of the power of low justice and sovereign ruler gave rise to the misconception (to be discussed below) that he requested the aid throughout the *Erzstift* in his role of sovereign ruler. In the fifteenth century, the aid in the *Erzstift* (known at the time as *Kurköln*) had developed into a tax on cultivated and uncultivated land, in which the house and the *morgen*[3] functioned as measurement units. The tariff was fixed. This usually put the cities in a privileged position, since they themselves were allowed to determine the aid at a fixed amount for their own territory. It is worth noting that the tax revenues did not always flow into the Archbishop's coffers: it was quite customary for the salaries of the Archbishop's officials to be paid directly from the tax revenues.

The four cases in which subjects were obliged to pay taxes to the sovereign ruler

From time to time, a sovereign ruler was confronted with extraordinary situations involving such enormous expenses that the normal tax levy to which he was entitled by his powers of low justice was inadequate. In four specific cases, the ruler could compel all subjects, including the holders of the powers of low justice, to make an extra contribution. No one could refuse. The principle of four cases (sometimes three cases) is found throughout Western Europe, albeit in different forms according to region.

Just what were these four cases? To begin with, there was the case of national emergency. This was a fairly elastic notion. Even though it implied defense against an outside enemy, a national emergency could easily arise from the

3. A unit of land measurement, customarily equal to about two acres.

sovereign ruler's own hostilities against a neighboring territory. Where the sovereign ruler was himself the cause of the conflict, his right to impose additional taxes was debatable, to say the least. In such situations, the de facto balance of power was the deciding factor. A weak count or bishop — even though such individuals do not often set out to conquer other lands — would have to tread carefully, while a strong one would sweep his subjects as well as his enemy right off their feet.

The second case was when the sovereign ruler fell into enemy hands and had to be ransomed.

The third case occurred when he married off his daughter. Even though this involved huge expenses — the dowry alone was often staggering — it could also enhance the prestige of the ruler's dynasty and thus indirectly serve the public interest. I note as an example of medieval emancipation that the marriage of a son was also sometimes counted as one of the four cases.

Finally, the fourth case occurred when money had to be raised to purchase land from a neighboring lord. In some regions, the fourth case involved covering the lord's costs when he was knighted or when he joined the imperial army for one of the many Italian campaigns of the time.

While the sovereign ruler normally held the powers of both high and low justice throughout his territory, it sometimes happened that someone else possessed the powers of low justice. Regarding this as an encroachment on his power, the sovereign ruler strove to acquire low justice as well. For this reason, it was long thought that the sovereign ruler derived his right to impose taxes from his capacity as holder of the powers of high justice; the powers of low justice not in his possession were viewed as exceptions, like islands in a sea of overlapping jurisdictions. According to this theory, the lords having the powers of low justice enjoyed the privilege of tax exemption in return for their compulsory military service. In turn, they were entitled to levy taxes.

Today, thanks to the German historian Georg Droege, this interpretation is increasingly being rejected. It is now widely assumed that the nobility and clergy were exempted from taxes not as a form of privilege, but simply on account of their powers of low justice and the authority to levy taxes in their own territory without the consent of the sovereign ruler. The nobility and the clergy were regarded as separate estates because they possessed the powers of low justice. They could only be involved in the sovereign ruler's tax levy if one of the four cases occurred or if they themselves approved the levy. Thus, taxation planted the seeds for representation by the estates. Ultimately, only one of the four cases really carried weight: national emergency. In the later Middle Ages, the significance of the other three cases declined, and they survived only in folklore. But, as has already been noted, the concept of national emergency was open to many interpretations. In time, the boundary between an *obligatory* tax (justified by a national emergency) and a *voluntary* contribution blurred. This development clearly resulted from the estates' desire to exchange voluntary consent to taxation for a voice in governmental affairs.

The formation of territorial states and mini-states, whose power was only restricted by the gradually decreasing supreme authority of the king, ran parallel with mounting tension between the prince and the estates, which represented certain groups of subjects. The word "state" (which came into vogue later) is derived from this. Initially, the estates consisted of freemen who usually possessed at least the powers of low justice. These men had been charged by the king with maintaining public order, a responsibility they shared with the sovereign ruler. This cooperation between the sovereign ruler and the estates gave birth to the concept of a country with clear territorial boundaries, an army to defend it from internal and external enemies and a judicial system. Later, the estates evolved into separate but equal factions, each with laws and regulations which its members had to obey. The cities also began to be included in the delegations the estates sent to deliberate with the sovereign ruler. The composition of the estates differed from country to country. The clergy, the nobility and the cities were normally represented; occasionally one group dominated, and sometimes one group was absent. This largely depended on whether the country was ruled by a secular or an ecclesiastical ruler and on whether it was predominantly agrarian with few cities or whether trade and industry thrived and its cities were large and influential.

The tension between the prince and the estates led to centuries of power struggles. Where the prince was victorious, as in France and Spain, absolutism prevailed. In Chapter 4, we shall follow Charles I of England's unsuccessful attempts to become an absolute ruler by, among other things, imposing taxes without the consent of Parliament. Sometimes the cities were able to free themselves from the prince's grip. The cities of Cologne and Soest, as we shall see later, are notable examples. The next chapter describes how in The Netherlands, the estates of several distinct regions joined together to form a States-General. In the absence of the sovereign ruler, this governmental body assumed power, an act that ultimately led to the founding of the Dutch Republic. In all of these processes, taxation played an important – and sometimes decisive – role.

However, there are also examples in which the power struggle between the prince and the estates did not culminate in an outright victor. Sometimes, as in *Kurköln*, power was divided between the two contending factions. The prince (or in this example the Archbishop of Cologne) was frequently obliged to request financial assistance from the estates. This dependence on the estates inexorably led to the ruler conceding part of his power.

One final question remains: why did the municipal government, unlike the holders of the powers of low justice, need the consent of the sovereign ruler to levy taxes on its citizens? The explanation is fairly simple. The cities were generally granted their charters from the sovereign ruler, who reserved the right to levy taxes. Alternatively, a *Stadtherr* (or "municipal lord") had the right to impose taxes. In Cologne, this was the Archbishop. He was particularly keen on appropriating the municipal excise taxes levied on the use of certain commodities such as wine, flour, beer and meat. Municipal governments paid the Archbishop handsomely for the right to impose certain taxes. But even that did not always satisfy him. He often tried – for example, in the case of Conrad of Hochstadt in 1239 – to seize a portion of the tax revenues in the bargain.

The taxes submitted by the sovereign ruler for approval by the estates resembled the aids requested and imposed by the holders of the powers of low justice; they were even initially designated as such. Both taxes were imposed in times of crises

or unusual circumstances, when the sovereign ruler could no longer manage with
the normal sources of income. They both eventually developed into periodical
(usually annual) taxes; the legal basis for this development was the *quid pro quo*
arrangement with the sovereign ruler. The difference between the two forms of
tax lay in the nature of the estates. The estates were not the sovereign ruler's subjects; instead, they gave their consent in tax matters as equal partners under the
law. Admittedly, the sovereign ruler proposed a tax levy, determined its nature
and decided how it was to be spent. But over the years, the dialogue between the
prince and the estates was broadened, in the sense that the estates gained a voice
in the imposition of taxes and the allocation of tax revenue. The rise of the
estates, which came to represent increasingly larger segments of the population
– although that only took place on the European continent after the French
Revolution – gave birth to our present-day form of representative democracy.
Once the estates assumed joint responsibility for taxation, the seal was set on the
formation of the territorial state.

In a certain sense, there is a paradox: the liege lord had to raise money to consolidate his position as a sovereign ruler. To achieve this objective, he relinquished rights, and this undermined his power. As we shall see, this paradox played
a role in the history of the disputes between the Archbishop and the city of Cologne. It likewise colored his relations with the clergy, nobility and cities in the
territories under his secular rule.

Taxation of the clergy

Before turning to the central conflict in Cologne, a few words must be said about
the taxation of the clergy. The relationship of the clerical orders to the bishop
was twofold: on the one hand, he was their leader and shepherd in spiritual matters, and on the other hand, he was their secular prince. From time to time, the
Archbishop used his spiritual leadership to impose taxes on the clergy subordinate to him in accordance with canon law. This took him beyond the boundaries of his own secular territory into his entire diocese, leading, as we shall see,
to strained relations with neighboring princes. Though the Archbishop levied
taxes on his diocesan clergy, the revenues went directly into his secular coffers.
The Archbishop also imposed taxes on the clergy as an estate, in exactly the same
way as he taxed the other estates.

The taxation on the clergy was based on two legal principles. The first, based on
Roman law, was rooted in the clergy's subordinate position in relation to the
Archbishop. The second, derived from German law, held that the Archbishop
as a secular prince and the clergy as an estate were bound in a relationship of
mutual obligation. As sovereign ruler, the Archbishop was obliged to grant his
subjects protection, and the subjects, represented by the estates, were obliged to
provide him aid and advice. The latter relationship implied that the clergy and
the Archbishop were equal partners under the law, so that the clergy only needed
to pay taxes that it had approved. The frequent non-payment of taxes can be
ascribed to the fact that monasteries and chapters enjoyed tax exemptions
granted for a variety of reasons in former times. Another limiting factor was that
the secular princes needed the Pope's consent to levy taxes on the clergy. In the
time of Diedrich of Moers, the Pope frequently granted his permission to impose
a so-called *subsidium charitativum* on the clergy of Cologne. This "charitable
grant" was, in reality, nothing more than a tax on church possessions.

Seal of Archbishop Conrad of Hochstadt (d. 1261).

Both the Archbishop and the city gain power and prestige

The transfer of administrative power in Lorraine to Archbishop Bruno in 953 ensured that he would become a secular ruler over a significant portion of the German Empire. A number of royal rights, the so-called regalia, were passed on to him, enabling him to administer justice, organize markets and grant permission to certain communities to fortify their cities with walls. In practice, the latter usually went hand in hand with the granting of a municipal charter. It was thus, we may assume, that Bruno became the municipal lord of Cologne and acquired the powers of high and low justice within the city. In return for having been enfeoffed with the regalia, the Archbishop had to maintain the king, who had no fixed residence, when he and his entourage were staying in the Archbishop's territory. In addition, the Archbishop was required to place a number of fighting men at the Emperor's disposal in case of war. For example, Otto II, the son of Otto the Great, was able to demand one hundred armored cavalrymen from the Archbishop of Cologne when he set off on his Italian campaign. Bruno never disappointed his brother, the Emperor, remaining loyal to him throughout his life. After establishing peace and order in Lorraine, Bruno divided it in 959 into

Detail of a 1531 woodcut of Cologne by Anton Woelman, illustrating the activity in the harbor, the ships plying the Rhine and part of the monastery of St. Heribert. Cologne owed its trade primarily to its favorable location on the Rhine, which had not yet been regulated in the Middle Ages, so that there were different widths, depths and currents. Cologne − located on the boundary between the Middle Rhine and the Lower Rhine (each part of the river required different types of ships) − had so-called staple rights, which meant that commodities had to be unloaded in Cologne. For three days, these wares were on sale to Cologne's citizens, who either bought them for their personal use, for further processing or for transshipment via the warehouses of the great merchants. Consequently, those who were not citizens of Cologne could not immediately purchase the wares. The staple rights were also politically and militarily significant because in the Frankish era, Cologne was a royal residence and therefore always had to be ready to meet the needs of the court and the army. In time, the staple rights ensured that Cologne became an economic crossroads. The goods unloaded in Cologne were subjected to strict supervision by the crafts guilds. If they passed inspection, they were packed with Cologne's coat of arms on the new packing. They then made their way into the world as Cologne wares, making Cologne's name synonymous with quality. The most important commodities were various kinds of textiles, fish, butter, cheese, oil, honey, cod-liver oil, sea salt, tar and, last but not least, wine.

Upper and Lower Lorraine, appointing dependents as dukes to govern these duchies.

Bruno and his successors could draw on various sources of finance. They received revenue from the tolls levied on the Rhine as well as tributes from markets (in return for granting permission to organize the market and promising to protect the traveling merchants). In addition, the Jews were required to pay a kind of head tax which also put them under the special protection of the Archbishop. His successors in the episcopal see gained the right to mint coins in 1027. These regalia were part of public law. Nevertheless, the regalia could be transferred as if they belonged to the domain of private law. Consequently, as we shall see, the Archbishop, who was almost always pressed for funds, periodically used certain regalia as collateral to borrow money from the city. If he was unable to pay off the debt, the right was transferred to the city. To help exercise his secular power, the Archbishop recruited functionaries, a practice which in later centuries was to spawn a kind of noble class of officials. As early as 1032, the Archbishop of Cologne appointed a viscount to handle administrative affairs and administer justice. In 1061, the Archbishop expanded his corps of officials by appointing a number of aldermen and an advocate to administer justice.

In 1151, King Conrad III enfeoffed to Cologne's Archbishop, Arnold II, not only the regalia, but also the ducal rule over a vast territory stretching southward almost to Trier, westward to the Meuse, northward to the County of Cleves and eastward to the County of Berg. The purpose of this exceptional enfeoffment was to make the Archbishop, whose diocese largely coincided with this territory, responsible for restoring and maintaining the peace throughout the area. He was particularly expected to ensure the safety of traffic on all the highways and waterways crisscrossing the region. This gave the Archbishop the right to collect tolls from travelers at certain points to pay for their safe passage. This enfeoffment, unprecedented in scale, endowed the Archbishop with sovereignty over the *Erzstift*, as the territory then came to be called.

The Archbishop continued to reinforce his position as a prince within the German Empire. Significantly, starting in 1028, the Archbishop of Cologne crowned the kings in the city of Aachen, which lay within his diocese. Another sign of the Archbishop's ascendancy was the fact that he was granted the office of Chancellor of Italy. In 1180, the Archbishop's territory was further expanded when the famous Emperor Frederick Barbarossa enfeoffed a large portion of the Duchy of Westphalia to Archbishop Philip of Heinsberg, in gratitude for his loyal support during the Emperor's protracted power struggle with Henry the Lion, the Duke of Saxony, whose fiefs were all declared invalid. The Duchy of Westphalia bordered on the Archbishops's territory and encompassed almost the entire Bishopric of Paderborn. Later, the Archbishop of Cologne also became the secular prince of the region around Recklinghausen, the so-called Recklinghausen Fortress.

In Bruno's time, the city of Cologne underwent a period of revival after centuries of decline. Founded around 40 B.C., the city had been named "Colonia Claudia Ara Agrippinensum" in 50 A.D. It grew steadily in Roman times until the population was roughly 40,000. The incursions of the Franks had put an end to this prosperity. By the time of King Sigibert, whose reign was so grimly ended by Clovis, no more than a few hundred inhabitants remained. But during the

*Picture of Anno (from the
"Vita Annonis," a manu-
script from around 1183).
He is encircled by the
churches he founded.*

Canon Hillinus of Cologne presents the Gospels to the Apostle Peter, who is seated in Cologne's cathedral. This is the only known portrayal of the Carolingian cathedral (from a manuscript dating from c. 1020-1030).

twelfth century, the city's population rose to over 20,000, and by the first half of the fourteenth century, it had shot up to roughly 40,000. The population then did not increase significantly until the French Revolution.

The rise of Cologne began after the final retreat of the Vikings, who had laid waste to the city in 881. It was reportedly reconstructed within ten years. The position of Cologne, initially situated on the periphery of the Frankish Middle Kingdom, was considerably enhanced when it was drawn into the Eastern Kingdom in 925. The road links between the Rhine, the Meuse and the Scheldt were repaired, and after a period of stagnation, shipping along the Rhine increased. As the Archbishop received the lion's share of the Rhine tolls, he stood to benefit substantially from this economic revival. Although the toll collectors were usually prominent citizens of Cologne, they continued to be functionaries of the Archbishop. Cologne also prospered, as its phenomenal growth indicates. Traditionally, the Jews and the Frisians had dominated the city's trade. Each had its own neighborhood, although neither was very large by today's standards. But Bruno realized that Cologne could be restored to its former prosperity by opening the gates to merchants from all over the world. Consequently, the old Roman wall was torn down, allowing the city to extend its boundaries to the banks of the Rhine. Thus, Cologne opened its arms in a gesture of welcome to the influx of foreign merchants who were largely responsible for the city's later prosperity and prestige.

Cologne's development mirrored that of Europe as a whole. As we have seen, the Western world underwent an economic revival starting in the tenth century. Barter gradually lost ground as money came back into circulation. Towns began to take shape, first as market places and later as independent centers of commerce. Cologne was at the forefront of the revival and soon developed into the largest city and most important trading center in the German Empire. At first, the Archbishop was the driving force behind the city's revival. While he initially held the reins of power, events soon hurtled out of his control. The Archbishop was bound to clash with a city populated by increasingly self-confident merchants. But he temporarily kept the aspiring merchants at bay.

The unsuccessful rebellion against Archbishop Anno

The first clash came in 1074 when Archbishop Anno was in power. Anno was descended from a family of Swabian knights and owed his appointment in 1056 to Emperor Henry III, in whose chancery he had worked for some time. Anno did not stem from the highest nobility and for this reason was initially held in some contempt in Cologne. Their contempt was quite unjustifiable, as events were to prove. The Emperor died in that same year (1056). Although his six year old son, the later Henry IV, had previously been crowned co-king, in reality, Henry III's widow, Agnes of Poitou, ruled as regent. Anno and the other princes were dissatisfied with the vacillating Agnes. With the princes' approval, Anno absconded with the child in 1062, the first move toward assuming the regency. The medieval historian Lambert of Hersfeld described the scene as follows: In the first days of April, the empress-mother was with her son on the island of Kaiserswerth, located in the Rhine near Düsseldorf. Anno invited the cheerful and uninhibited eleven year old youngster to view his beautifully decorated ship. Soon after boarding, Henry was surrounded by the Archbishop's henchmen; rowing furiously, the oarsmen steered the ship to the middle of the river. Panick-

This romantic print, drawn from a painting of M. von Schwind, shows King Henry IV being kidnapped by Archbishop Anno at the moment the panicked young King jumped overboard.

ing, the boy jumped overboard, in the middle of the river's powerful current. He would have met a watery grave except that some of the conspirators, endangering their own lives, rescued him. For a while, a crowd of people followed the ship from the river bank, cursing at the top of their lungs about the lese majesty committed before their very eyes.

After this coup d'état, Anno dominated the conspiring magnates, and eventually acquired the de facto position of regent in the Empire. He suffered a temporary setback in 1065 when one of his rivals, Archbishop Adalbert of Bremen, gained control over the young king. Not surprisingly, this struggle over his person left an indelible mark on the king.

For his part, Anno was iron-willed and fanatic, but fair and deeply religious. His unbounded religious zeal inspired him to found and support many churches and abbeys. Surpassing even contemporary standards of nepotism, Anno appointed numerous friends and relatives to high ecclesiastical offices. Sometimes these appointments backfired. For example, in 1066, Anno persuaded the king to appoint his cousin Conrad, the former Dean of Cologne's Cathedral, as Archbishop of Trier. Angered by not being consulted on the appointment, the clergy and the common people murdered Conrad as he was making his entrance into the city.

At the end of his career, the harsh and inflexible Anno clashed painfully with Cologne's rising citizenry. The crisis flared up on the Wednesday after Easter in 1074. During Cologne's annual market, a throng of merchants from all corners of the earth flocked to the city. The Bishop of Münster, one of Anno's suffragan bishops, had been Anno's guest during Easter. He indicated that he wished to make the first part of his return journey by boat via the Rhine, and Anno ordered his servants to commandeer a boat in the harbor. It is doubtful whether the Archbishop himself had the right to demand free travel on board a ship. However, his servants certainly had no right to order − under threat of violence − the captain of a fully loaded ship to unload the cargo and prepare to set off with the Bishop of Münster. But this is precisely what happened. The son of the wealthy Cologne merchant who owned the ship was alerted immediately. He and a handful of friends flew to the rescue and, after a brief scuffle, drove off the Archbishop's servants. A tense atmosphere permeated the city when the residents took the young man's side.

The following day, Anno preached fire and brimstone at mass, berating the people for their rebellious attitude. This sermon inflamed the unrest, which had initially showed signs of abating, and that evening the windows of the Bishop's residence were pelted with stones. Anno was forced to take refuge, along with a few trusted servants, behind the Cathedral's barricaded doors. Meanwhile, the crowd plundered his palace and sought the fugitive. In their fury, they killed an innocent bystander, whom they mistook for the Archbishop. The Cathedral was under siege for days. On the fifth day, the obstinate Anno was finally prevailed upon to escape. He and the Bishop took an underground passage to the house of one of the canons, passing from there to a house near the city wall. As luck would have it, Anno had recently granted the owner of this house permission to construct a gate in the city wall.

And so he and the Bishop of Münster were able to make their escape under cloak of darkness. In a bid for time, Anno's supporters pretended that he was still in the Cathedral. When it was deemed safe, they opened the doors and announced to the rebellious crowd that the Archbishop had escaped and was returning with a military force. The crowd quickly came to its senses. The citizens made preparations for a siege, and in desperation sent a messenger to King Henry to request his assistance.

Four days later, Anno, livid with rage about the slander directed at him, arrived before the city walls with an army hastily scraped together in Neuss. He demanded − and obtained − the city's surrender. Anno promised to spare the lives of the rebels, but excommunicated them all and ordered them to appear barefoot before his seat of justice to do penance. As the story has it, six hundred of the wealthiest merchants fled to the King in the dark of night, and not a soul appeared in the Cathedral at the set time. Against his wishes, Anno's embittered functionaries took ruthless revenge. The merchant's son, the instigator of the riot, and his companions had their eyes gouged out, and many citizens were beaten and robbed of their worldly possessions. With customary exaggeration, a contemporary chronicler described Cologne after the uprising as follows: "And so the city, which had recently been so populous and which was, next to Maintz, the jewel in the Gallic crown, was suddenly turned into a wilderness; its streets, which could formerly hardly contain the thick swarms of pedestrians, seldom sported a living soul."

The top print depicts a reconstruction of the cathedral in Cologne as it probably appeared at the time of its consecration in 870. The bottom print shows the route Archbishop Anno took in 1074 when he fled the cathedral and escaped through the city wall. For an illustration of this cathedral, see also page 79.

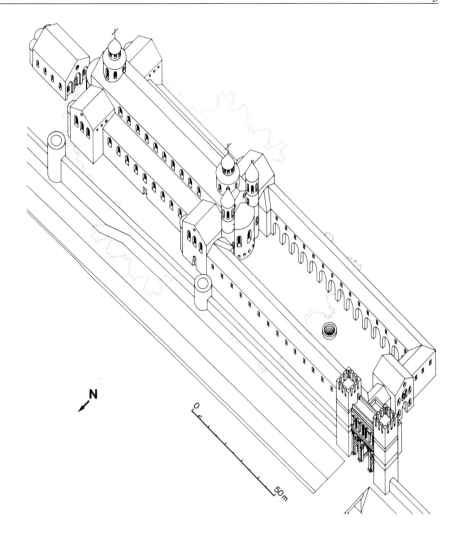

N

0   50 m

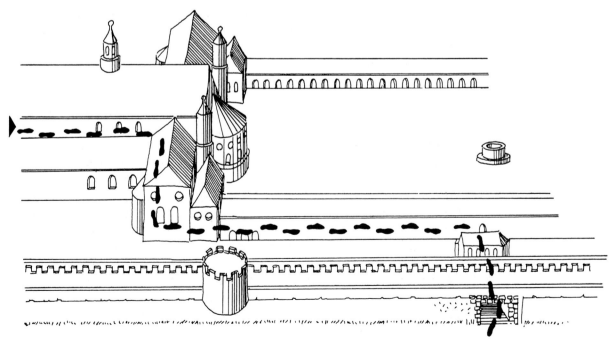

*Emperor Henry IV.
Miniature from the
anonymous "Emperor
Chronicle," a manuscript
dating from the beginning
of the 12th century.*

Thus, the merchants' first act of opposition against the regime of the Archbishop came to naught. They had matched wills with an extremely powerful Archbishop. More importantly, they had not been well-organized, as evidenced by their desperation and helplessness after Anno's flight. Anno's death a year later coincided with the beginning of the Investiture Controversy, which immediately flared up with a great deal of violence.

Nearly a hundred years later (in 1183), Anno was canonized, largely owing to two biographies, written shortly after his death by monks of the Abbey of Siegburg (which he had founded and favored in many ways). These biographies depict him as a person who regularly did penance, subjected himself to mortifications and fasts and was charitable to the poor. In addition to these descriptions of his virtues, there are faint echoes of his domineering behavior. Without a doubt, Anno's canonization was furthered by the *Annolied*, a glorification of Anno's ecclesiastical virtues written in verse around 1100 by another Siegburg monk. Shortly thereafter, the skillful hands of Master Nicholas of Verdun created the Anno shrine, which can still be admired today in the Michael Chapel of the Abbey of Siegburg.

The city begins to organize

When the Emperor and the Pope clashed during the Investiture Controversy over the appointment of bishops, Cologne and its Archbishops sided with Emperor Henry IV. But when the Emperor came in conflict with his son, the later Henry V, the city chose the Emperor's side, while the Archbishop sided with the son. The citizens, seemingly more organized than their forbears, drove the Archbishop and his followers out of the city. In preparation for the impending battle, the city constructed a new wall, a moat and city gates, which gave the city room to expand. The right the citizens had obtained from the Emperor to defend their city (which meant they could construct city walls and form a citizens' militia) weakened the Archbishop's hold over the city. The citizens retained this right, even after Henry IV died that year. When his successor, Henry V, marched on Cologne, the city paid the new king 6,000 pounds of silver to retreat. This testifies to the fact that, even at this early stage, some form of municipal organization existed. Not only was the city powerful enough to organize its defense and build a city wall, but it was also dynamic enough to raise a large amount of money from its citizenry to serve the common good.

Several years later (1112), the citizens of Cologne took an oath to guard their freedom, which is described in the Pantaleon Chronicle as: *Coniuratio coloniae facta est pro libertate*. It is unclear whether the oath bound the affiliated parishes into one administrative entity, so that the municipality became a stronger faction, or whether, as is more likely, it referred to the rebellion of 1114 on the Lower Rhine, in which the Archbishop, various other princes and the citizens of Cologne participated. Whichever theory is accepted, the oath bears witness to the growing self-awareness of the citizens of Cologne. Shortly afterwards, the Archbishop granted the municipality the use of his own seal, a privilege for which the residents of Cologne no doubt paid dearly.

The power-craving Archbishops were permanently pressed for funds. Their aspirations to expand their sphere of influence and reinforce their own power base were accompanied not only by the clanging of armor, but also by the chink of coins. By that time mercenary armies had made their appearance, making the use of armed force frightfully expensive. The days in which unpaid vassals followed their liege lords into battle on the strength of their oath of fealty were gradually drawing to a close. Anyone wishing to wage war – and that was just about everyone – was obliged to use mercenary armies.

The clashes between the city and the Archbishops in the thirteenth century eventually led, after the Battle of Worringen in 1288, to the city's virtual independence. But before going into this further, let us first take a look at the city's government structure and its embryonic tax system. The rise of the city's own governing body in the twelfth century may partially account for the fact that Archbishops rarely resided in the city. As imperial Chancellors, they were constantly on the move, on behalf of the Emperor. As a result, the administration of the *Erzstift*, and the city of Cologne in particular, often fell by the wayside.

Presumably not long after Cologne was granted the right to use the seal, the appearance of two mayors signaled the very first beginnings of the city's voice in its own government. The mayors were elected for a period of one year by a council known as the *Richerzeche*, which, as the name implies, was an assembly of the rich. All of its members came from patrician families, in those days referred to collectively as the "Families." The *Richerzeche* created in the second quarter of the twelfth century was a kind of club of like-minded people from similar backgrounds who were dedicated to the city, but who wished to control municipal matters in accordance with their own views, if not to their own advantage. The members of the *Richerzeche* claimed to be descendants of the ancient Roman civilization, but this was, of course, pure propaganda, designed to induce the people to accept their oligarchical leadership.

The *Richerzeche* developed into an independent council alongside the Aldermen's Board. The Aldermen, functionaries in the Archbishop's service and bound to him by loyalty oaths, lived in the city and were accepted as fellow citizens. In time, they came to be elected from the same patrician families as the *Richerzeche*. In the thirteenth century, the Aldermen formed a separate Board, consisting of twenty-five persons. They divided up among themselves the administrative and judicial activities as well as the monies collected. As they were appointed for life, both the Aldermen and the *Richerzeche* continued to receive their shares of the revenues until they died. The members of the *Richerzeche* were not only charged with appointing the two mayors (one of whom had to be an Alderman), but also with granting citizenship and supervising tax collection, trade and the guilds. The Aldermen and the *Richerzeche* were exclusively chosen from the Families and consequently held an unassailable position. Frequently, an individual was a member of both the Aldermen's Board and the *Richerzeche*.

The Small Council, a fifteen-member council that was first appointed in 1216, recruited its members from the same group of patricians. In the thirteenth century, this Small Council succeeded in curbing the powers of the *Richerzeche* and the Aldermen and replacing them as the most important governing body. The members of the Small Council, like its predecessors, had to be elected every year. Departing Councilmen could nominate their own successors and were only eligible for re-election two years later.

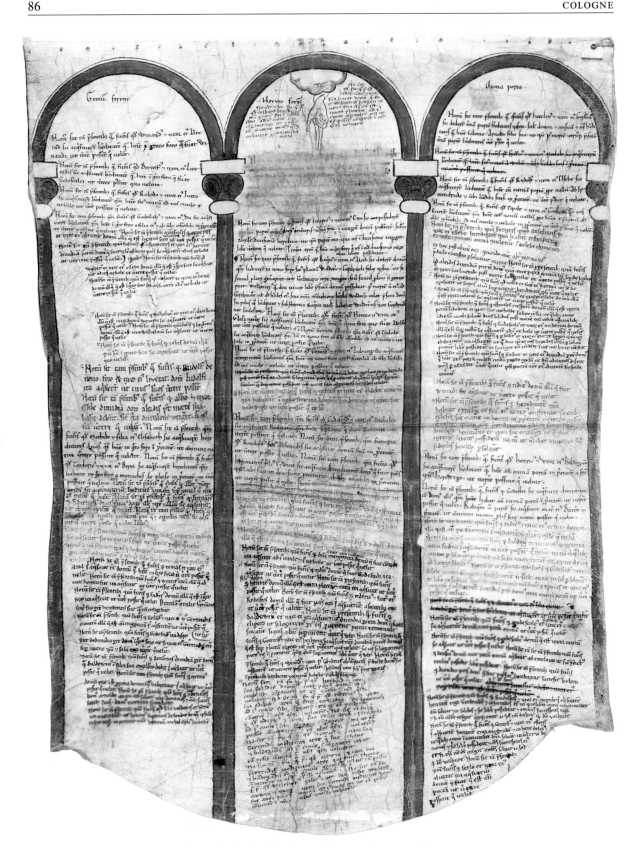

"Schreins" cards from 1186-1196 from the parish of St. Aposteln.

This method of rotating the members of the Small Council therefore constituted the very first (albeit modest) step toward the democratization of the municipal government.

Taxation and the Large Council

Taxation acted as a catalyst in the formation of the Large Council, which was first cited in surviving texts in 1318. The members of the Large Council were chosen from the ranks of the prominent citizens living in the city's boroughs, which for the most part coincided with the parishes. Here, too, a system of cooptation applied, in which sitting members designated their successors. More than one third of the members of the Large Council originated from the patrician families. The remainder were leading citizens to whom the patricians had to concede a measure of influence in the municipal government. This concession of power was partly based on the fact that, as early as the twelfth century, when taxation first made its appearance, these citizens had been responsible for collecting direct taxes in their capacity as church wardens.

The city, or at any rate the small group of patricians who held the reins of municipal government, adopted the viewpoint that the city itself should assume responsibility for taxes imposed by the Emperor and the sovereign ruler and apportion the assessments over the citizens. We find the first signs of taxes in the few sporadic reports which survive from the twelfth century. The *Richerzeche* played a role in collecting these taxes as well as the excise taxes which appeared later in the thirteenth century. The first taxes were wealth taxes, based on land registers known as *Schreinsbücher*. Around 1135, the church wardens began to record the real-estate transactions in their parishes. These transactions were initially noted on individual cards, which were stored in a cupboard (*Schrein*), but before long they were recorded in books containing accurate data about all parcels of land, houses and owners; these books thus formed an excellent point of departure for taxation. The *Schreinsbücher* were maintained without interruption from 1135 onwards, and have been fully preserved until the present day.

In fact, this property tax was confined to the revenues from cultivated and uncultivated land. The tax was apportioned over the parishes according to a fixed ratio. Within the parishes, the leading parishioners (the church wardens) were responsible for determining the taxes per lot and per taxpayer. This created a modest form of self-government at a parochial level. The property tax was structured to include even those who held property in the city but did not live there.

Initially, the clergy were exempt from the tax on account of the immunity rights granted by earlier emperors. But Cologne succeeded in limiting the tax exemption to property that traditionally belonged to the abbeys, chapters, etc., and ensuring that newly acquired property fell outside the scope of the exemption. Those without property were unaffected by the property tax. The poor, however, did suffer from the excise taxes which were imposed by the rapidly expanding city in the thirteenth century. Obviously, indirect taxes such as excise taxes were more advantageous to the propertied than property taxes. Therefore, under their influence, the significance of property taxes dwindled during the fourteenth century, while that of excise taxes gradually rose, so much so that the municipal accounts from the first quarter of 1370 do not mention a single instance of property taxes. This development can probably also be attributed to the fact that in 1349

Emperor Charles IV exempted Cologne from its contribution to the Empire.

The transition from direct to indirect taxation deprived the parishes of a basis for joint financial decision-making. The creation of the Large Council, composed of prominent parishioners, can be seen as a method of allowing the parishes to retain some financial influence, however marginal.

The city and its Archbishop: a marriage of convenience turns sour

Throughout the thirteenth century, Cologne attempted to wrest itself from the Archbishop's grip, and the Archbishop did his utmost to thwart the city's ambition. The Archbishop vigorously sought to exchange his role as a vassal of the German Emperor for that of sovereign prince in his own right. The composition and size of the Archbishop's territories largely depended on his military and political successes.

The Archbishop's episcopacy, which was considerably larger than the territories he governed as secular ruler, included the later Duchies of Cleves, Berg, Jülich and Mark, several manors and, of course, the city of Cologne and its surrounding territory. The Archbishop's goal was to create more unity, order and cohesion in his secular territories, and it never entered his mitered head that the city of Cologne might not be willing to be an integral part of his scheme.

In fact, Cologne and its citizenry had other plans. They were eager to free themselves from the Archbishop's oppressive grip in order to gain economic and political independence. This would permit the city to step up its trade, mainly with England and The Netherlands, in order to sell the products of its numerous and industrious guilds. The Archbishop's tolls along the Rhine were frequent bones of contention to the city's commercial aristocracy. But even when the toll issue is ignored, there were numerous other areas of dispute. Most of the disagreements concerned finances. The city needed to be able to levy taxes in order to stand financially on its own two feet. The struggle was therefore concentrated on the question of whether the city should have the power to impose taxes on its citizens and if so, whether the revenue from these taxes should go completely or partially to the Archbishop or whether the municipal government could use the revenue as it deemed fit to benefit the city and its citizens.

The events of the thirteenth century, which were decisive for the rise of Cologne, will be described below in terms of the conflicts between the city and the three great Archbishops who left their mark on the era: Engelbrecht of Berg, Conrad of Hochstadt and Siegfried of Westerburg.

The first half of the thirteenth century was dominated by the construction of a large city wall to protect Cologne's newly developed areas. The residents actually began construction in 1180, initially against the wishes of Philip of Heinsberg. After being paid 2,000 marks in compensation for the infringement on his supremacy as Archbishop, Philip acquiesced in the construction and even lent his support. Building the city wall, with its nine huge gates and fifty half towers, was a massive task, which took fifty to sixty years to complete. But the result was well worth the effort, for it doubled Cologne's area to roughly one thousand acres.

The struggle between the Staufers and the Welfs

Central to Cologne's development was the struggle between the Welfs (also spelled Guelphs) and the Staufers (sometimes also referred to as the Hohenstaufers or the Ghibellines), two princely dynasties competing for power in Germany. From the middle of the twelfth century, the Emperor was usually a Staufer. As the Pope and the Emperor were almost always at loggerheads, the Pope as a rule took sides with the Welfs. For this reason, the Welfs were seen as the papal party and the Staufers as the imperial party. Their differences had significant international repercussions, as the Welfs were allied with England and the Staufers with France. The conflict came to a head at the beginning of the thirteenth century with the appointment of two Emperors. When a Staufer, Philip of Swabia, became king in 1198, the Welfs retaliated by installing one of their number, Otto IV of Brunswick as anti-king. At a lower level, the Staufer-oriented Archbishop, Adolf of Altena, was removed from office by the Pope, after which the Welf-oriented Archbishop, Bruno of Sayn, who had been chosen shortly afterwards, was taken prisoner by the opposite party. Needless to say, the conflict was accompanied by much bloodshed and destruction.

The 1206 fight in Cologne between the Welf Otto IV and the Staufer Philip of Swabia (from the Koelhoff Chronicle of 1499).

Cologne therefore had good grounds for hastening the construction of the city wall. The city's expansion was aided by the fact that the monastery churches of

St. Severin, St. Pantaleon, St. Mauritius and St. Gereon had a vested interest in ensuring that their establishments lay safely within the city walls, and these churches made generous donations. The wall's construction required vast sums of money, more than the municipal government could afford. Not surprisingly, the city decided to expand its tax policy, which until then had been very limited. The time was propitious. Cologne, the most powerful city in the German Empire, had progressed sufficiently from a barter economy to a monetary economy to risk imposing taxes on certain commodities. As country people who came to the city to make their purchases were also hit by these taxes, the complaints poured in. The Emperor and the Archbishop were sensitive to the complaints and made attempts to lower the levies, but their measures were ineffectual. It was not until the end of the thirteenth century, after decades of conflict which alternately flared up and died down, that the city succeeded in gaining the right to levy taxes as an inviolable and indisputable prerogative; partly thanks to this, Cologne became a free imperial city.

Before this, in the struggle between Otto IV and Philip of Swabia, Cologne had aligned itself with Otto, because he was related by marriage to King Richard the Lion-Hearted of England, one of its closest trading partners. Very likely, at around the turn of the century, Otto permitted the city to impose taxes on wine and salt. However, as the fortunes of war would have it, the city later felt compelled to side with Philip of Swabia, who had previously (unsuccessfully) laid siege to the city on several occasions. Philip of Swabia arrived in the city in 1206. He confirmed all its rights and exemptions in a letter which – in an unprecedented step – he addressed to the city itself rather than the Archbishop. The letter explicitly declared that the people of Cologne were entitled to continue building their city wall. Philip did, however, impose one restriction, namely that the city abolish the tax on wine and salt. According to Philip, the city had encroached on the Archbishop's supremacy by imposing these taxes on its own authority. Philip's murder in 1208 ushered in another shift in power. Philip's imperial counterpart, Otto IV, again exempted the residents of Cologne from paying tolls to the Archbishop. More importantly, in 1212 he granted the citizens permission to work on their city wall and allowed them to finance the construction by imposing an excise tax on beer and flour for three years. This tax deeply affected the daily life of the city. In addition, it created a precedent, one to which the city would repeatedly refer in years to come. Although Cologne formally required the Emperor's permission to renew existing levies or introduce new ones, it did not always take the trouble to obtain it. An arrangement was made in which the Archbishop agreed to support Cologne against the Emperor. Needless to say, the city was obliged to fork out a hefty sum for this assistance.

In the struggle between the Welfs and the Staufers, the city and the Archbishop had usually found themselves in opposite camps. As the Archbishop did not hesitate to demand oppressive taxes from his own clergy in order to bear the cost of his war efforts, the municipal clergymen were driven into the arms of the city. As a result, Cologne's position in its struggle with the Archbishop was strengthened.

The Battle of Bouvines took place in 1214. The French King Philip II Augustus and his allies, the Staufers, won a resounding victory over the English and their allies, the Welfs, whose side the city of Cologne had joined. The combined French-Staufer victory had widespread repercussions. The Welfs disappeared

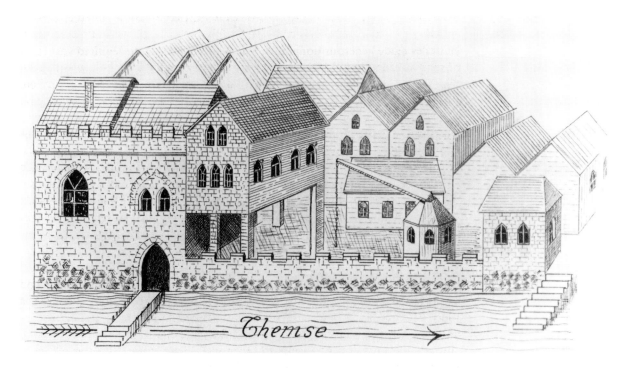

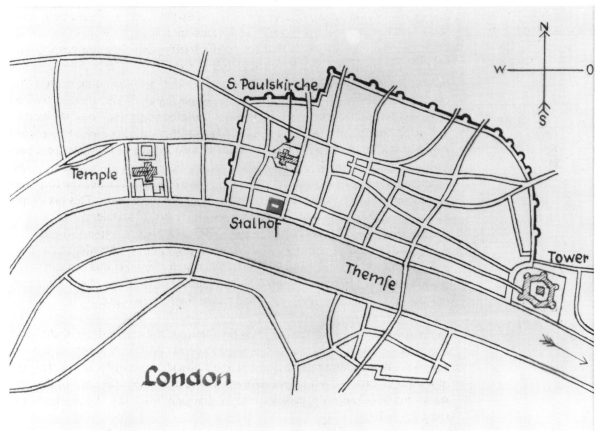

Cologne's Syndics' Hall in London, located on the Thames. This warehouse complex, built in 1423, was the place where Cologne's goods (particularly linen) were stored and inspected.

as a political force, and the Staufer Frederick II was generally recognized as king.

England was temporarily compelled to abandon its hope of dominating France. The defeat greatly undermined the position of England's King John I. His arbitrary measures, especially with regard to taxation, had already aroused resentment among the barons and bishops. Taking advantage of the king's weak position, they compelled him, after lengthy negotiations, to sign the *Magna Carta Libertatum* in 1215. Better known as the *Magna Carta*, this document guaranteed the liberties of English subjects. The famous charter also contained a few clauses pertaining to taxation. Section 12 stated that: "No scutage or aid is to be levied in our realm except by the common consent of our realm, unless it is for the ransom of our person, the knighting of our eldest son, or the first marriage of our eldest daughter; and for these only a reasonable aid is to be levied...." This section therefore cited three of the four earlier-mentioned cases in which a subject was obliged to pay taxes. A novel concept for its day and age was that the subjects had the right to offer opposition if the *Magna Carta* was not complied with.

The *Magna Carta* was the first step toward the dialogue between a ruler and his subjects that ultimately led to parliamentary democracy. In light of the central role this dialogue plays in this book, the narrative has been interrupted to sketch the origins of the *Magna Carta*.

Engelbrecht of Berg: the city is no match for the Archbishop

In accordance with his vision of social order, Frederick II attempted to curb the rising power of the cities in favor of the princes. But the Emperor was not Cologne's only antagonist. In 1216 the Dean of the Cathedral, Engelbrecht of Berg, one of the best-known and most famous (or perhaps notorious?) of Cologne's prelates, was chosen Archbishop. Given the opportunity, he would have liked nothing better than to have stripped the city of its privileges to which — in his eyes — it had no right. For the time being, Engelbrecht had to content himself with restraining the Small Council (which first appeared in 1216) and keeping the nascent guilds in check. The city's desire to levy taxes was one of the biggest thorns in his side, and Engelbrecht did his utmost to prevent the city from developing its tax policies. Although the citizens were obliged to acquiesce in his restrictive measures, legend has it that the gnashing of their teeth could be heard all the way to Aachen!

Engelbrecht, a younger son from the Berg family of counts, was born in 1185 and was already Dean of St. Gereon at the age of fourteen. At the age of eighteen, he was chosen by a majority of the cathedral chapter to be its Dean. A fierce election campaign was fought between Engelbrecht, a young and ambitious clergyman, and his opponent. Faced with disqualification because he had only received minor orders, Engelbrecht obtained papal dispensation and won the election. He scarcely had time to celebrate his triumph before the episcopal see of Münster was vacant. In order not to ruin his chances of eventually becoming Archbishop of Cologne, Engelbrecht let this opportunity to climb higher up the career ladder pass him by. Shortly afterwards, the conflict between the Welfs and the Staufers burst forth in all its intensity. For the sum of 9,000 marks and a handful of rights and wares, Archbishop Adolf of Altena, Engelbrecht's uncle, switched his allegiance from the party of Emperor Otto to the party of the anti-king Philip of Swabia. Consequently, Adolf was removed from office and a new Archbishop was chosen. During the conflict, Engelbrecht had aligned himself with his uncle. As a follower of the anti-papal Staufer party, he and an army of his cohorts so thoroughly ravaged the *Erzstift* that the canons and the Archbishop were no longer able to maintain a minimum standard of living.

After Philip of Swabia was murdered in 1208, the tables were turned. Engelbrecht made peace with the new Archbishop, Bruno of Sayn, who obliged him to pay for his sins by embarking on a crusade against the unbelievers. As this included heretics within the Church, in 1212, Engelbrecht battled the Albigensians and Waldensians in far-off Southern France. The Battle of Bouvines in 1214 heralded the downfall of the Welf party. A year later, Engelbrecht, now one of the most zealous disciples of the new Emperor, the young Frederick II, conquered the Castle of Kaiserswerth for the Emperor and subjected the city of Cologne to his rule. His services did not go unrewarded. On February 29, 1216, Engelbrecht was appointed Archbishop of Cologne, only to find himself confronted with the damage he had wrought during his earlier devastations. Engelbrecht's task was now to put the city's totally neglected finances in order and restore Cologne to its pre-war prominence. With great dedication and at considerable personal expense, he succeeded in reviving the city and replenishing its depleted coffers. Naturally, Engelbrecht did not bear the entire financial burden by himself. An additional compulsory tax (also paid by the prosperous monasteries) produced 22,000 marks, a large sum in those days. Indeed, the *Erzstift* alone had been obliged to pay 16,000 marks to Rome toward the fees and legal costs incurred by the endless procession of archbishops in the previous decades. In order to justify the tax and exonerate himself of any blame, Engelbrecht inserted the following words in the introduction to the tax decree: *sine pecuniis pacem se non posse facere in terris*: "without money, it's impossible to make peace on earth."

These words sound cynical in view of Engelbrecht's past. After all, during his adventurous but fairly typical career, he had been a robber baron, land ravager and persecutor of heretics before becoming a church prelate. Nor was this the end of Engelbrecht's career. When Frederick II, like so many German Emperors before him, felt the urge to seek his salvation in Italy and took up permanent residence there, Engelbrecht was appointed (in 1221) *Reichsverweser*, i.e. regent over the German Empire. He and his fellow bishops had been officially recognized as sovereign rulers in an imperial edict issued the year before.

When considered in the light of Engelbrecht's future, the expression *sine pecuniis pacem se non posse facere in terris* has a decidedly hypocritical ring. Most sovereign rulers used their subjects' money to satisfy their craving for territorial expansion rather than to promote peace. But when measured by the standards of the day, these words clearly reflect the reality of the time. For Engelbrecht forcefully restrained the many robber barons who roamed the countryside after the war. Many a noble freebooter learned through bitter experience that he could not sow the seeds of war without reaping the consequences. Engelbrecht broke the pride of reckless vassals and kept them under his thumb by having fortifications constructed. He also kept an eye on his own County of Berg, soon acquiring an excellent reputation as an upholder of law and order and protector of the poor. And he indeed needed a lot of money to accomplish that!

According to one tale, a merchant went to the bishop of a certain region to request a military escort for a large transport of goods. The bishop refused, but Engelbrecht, who happened to be the bishop's guest at that time, simply handed the merchant his glove and instructed him to show the glove to any rapacious waylayers he encountered en route. This was evidently security enough for the merchant, for he embarked forthwith on his journey.

Considering Engelbrecht's reputation, it is not surprising that the citizens of Cologne failed to undermine his rights. Cologne's clergy had likewise ultimately submitted to his yoke. The city's immensely wealthy monasteries and bishoprics took a dim view of the rising Franciscan and Dominican mendicant orders preaching the ideal of poverty. But Engelbrecht's perseverance prevailed over the protests of the established clergy, and in time the two new monastic communities were able to settle in Cologne.

Engelbrecht, however, was to come to a sorry end. The events leading up to his death were as follows: The advocates appointed to protect monasteries and abbeys frequently resorted to violence in order to appropriate these interests for themselves. Pope Honorius III decided to call a halt to the advocates' acquisitiveness and instructed the bishops to proceed against any advocates guilty of such abuses. One of Engelbrecht's distant relations, Frederick of Altena and Isenburg, advocate of a convent in Essen, was allegedly guilty of these practices. After some hesitation, the Archbishop decided to take action against him. Engelbrecht no doubt also reasoned that if he could take possession of the convent's vast territory, which cut a deep wedge into the Duchy of Westphalia, he could make his ducal territory complete. Instead, Frederick decided to kidnap the Archbishop in hopes of consolidating his bargaining position. His plan did not take quite the turn he had expected: when the Archbishop and his retinue were attacked, the Archbishop was unexpectedly struck dead. The day after the attack, Engelbrecht's companions hauled the dead Archbishop on a dung cart to the family castle, Burg on the Wupper, but nobody dared let them enter. The corpse was then transported to the abbey church of Altenberg, where the internal organs were buried, and his body was subsequently conveyed to Cologne. It was decided that Engelbrecht would not be buried before the murderers were apprehended. The body was boiled in order to separate the flesh from the bones, and for the time being the bones remained above ground. Frederick was excommunicated and lived as a fugitive for a year, hunted by everyone, until he was finally caught and brutally put to death.

Engelbrecht's premature death in 1225 was undoubtedly lamented throughout the Empire. Yet it is difficult to make an accurate assessment of his true merits. To highlight the ambiguities surrounding his personality, let us turn to one of his biographers, the Cistercian monk Cesarius of Heisterbach. During Engelbrecht's lifetime, Cesarius had not written a word of praise of Engelbrecht. One month after the murder, Cesarius preached a sermon which touched on the heinous event. In this sermon, Cesarius depicted Engelbrecht as neither a saint in life nor a martyr in death. Cesarius considered the Archbishop's atrocious death as a terrible, but not necessarily unjust, penance for his worldly life. God had been merciful, for Engelbrecht had fallen in defense of the Church, i.e. over the advocacy of the monastery of Essen. Engelbrecht emerged from Cesarius's sermon as a sinner who had atoned for the dereliction of his ecclesiastical duties and his excessive attention to secular matters by dying in the service of the

The corpse of Engelbrecht of Berg is transported to the castle of Burg on the Wupper (mural of Prof. Claus Meyer in Castle Burg).

Church. In contrast, Cesarius the biographer struck an entirely different note, presumably acting on orders from on high (i.e. Engelbrecht's successor). Suddenly Engelbrecht was presented as a saint and a kind of German version of Thomas Becket (d. 1170). Formerly seen as a penance, the murder was now viewed as a sacrifice, and Engelbrecht was adorned with all kinds of human and spiritual virtues. Before long, Engelbrecht was venerated as a martyr and saint by the people whose devotion, verging on hysteria, was fomented by such beautified and cloyingly sentimental descriptions of his life. Even though he was never canonized, he has been known ever since as St. Engelbrecht, a title which surely marked the final and most brilliant pinnacle of his career.

Engelbrecht has been described at length to show what a formidable opponent Cologne had to contend with all those years. He succeeded in pruning the city's budding independence inch by inch. After his death, the people of Cologne hastened to publicly burn all of Engelbrecht's decrees which had hampered their quest for independent rule, including the right to levy municipal taxes. While his death sent waves of shock through the Empire, his passing created only a ripple in his own city. The people of Cologne breathed a sign of relief at being delivered from an obdurate opponent. Luckily for Cologne, Engelbrecht's rule had been too brief to reverse the city's rise to power.

Engelbrecht's successor, Henry of Molenark, was cut of lesser cloth. Not surprisingly, indirect taxes reappeared under his rule. The city considered these levies one of its normal privileges. As there is no report of the city's requesting permission from the Emperor or Archbishop to levy excise taxes on beer, it would appear that this privilege was already well established. Engelbrecht's successor helped the city advance its cause in other ways as well. In 1226, Henry gave the Aldermen a free hand in running Cologne's affairs, although he delicately reminded them of their oath of fealty to him. Five years later, at the assembly in Worms, the citizens of Cologne took a momentous step forward when, apparently without any opposition from the Archbishop, they managed to put an end to their obligation to guarantee the Archbishop's debts. Under contemporary law, the subjects were required to cover debts incurred by the sovereign ruler. This debt weighted heavily on those Cologne residents engaging in international trade. The Concordat of Worms, signed by the Emperor in 1236, confirmed that the citizens of Cologne were in a different legal position than the other residents of the *Erzstift*.

Conrad of Hochstadt: constant strife between the city and the Archbishop

While the Pope and the Emperor continued to quarrel, in 1238 Conrad of Hochstadt, another powerful potentate, was chosen as Archbishop. Conrad was initially a follower of the Staufers, but secretly joined the papal party a year later. The city backed the Emperor. In the 1240's, the dispute between the Pope and the Emperor reached its zenith. At a council held in Lyon (1245), which Conrad attended as a papal follower, the Emperor was deposed and the Electoral Princes were summoned to elect a new king. Their choice fell a year later on Henry Raspe of Thuringia. Not long afterwards, when Henry had fallen in battle, Conrad and the Pope engineered the appointment of one of Conrad's protégés, the young Count William of Holland, as anti-king. The Archbishop and William remained on good terms as long as William, who had little power, danced to Conrad's tune. Both of them made an appearance, along with the Dukes of Brabant and Limburg, the Counts of Gelre, Berg and Cleves, the Bishop of Liège and many other secular and ecclesiastical dignitaries from the Lower Rhine region, at the 1248 solemn laying of the first stone of the Gothic Cathedral in Cologne, which still stands as one of the mightiest edifices in Germany.

The following story shows how Conrad's contemporaries viewed him. In October 1254, King William of Holland, the papal legate Petrus Capocci and Archbishop Conrad of Hochstadt assembled to consider the possibility of releasing the Bishop of Paderborn, whom Conrad had captured when he and his army attacked the *Erzstift*. The negotiations had reached a deadlock when a fire broke out and reduced the building which housed the king and the legate to ashes; the two narrowly escaped death. The suspicion that the Archbishop had plotted an assassination attempt was immediately on everyone's lips. The legate apparently shared this suspicion, for Conrad excommunicated him soon afterwards. Years later, Petrus Capocci claimed compensation for the damage he suffered on this occasion. Although Conrad's guilt was never proved, the fact that the finger of suspicion immediately pointed in his direction is significant in itself. Anyone wanting to demonstrate the plausibility of Conrad's responsibility for the event would not have far to look. Conrad's notorious insolence and extraordinary lack of scruples made him a likely candidate. He was a warmongering and competent military commander, and his salient features were a relentless drive and cold calculation. These characteristics, acceptable in a secular ruler, were considered, even in those days, dubious in an archbishop, who was supposedly the spiritual leader of his flock. Conrad's rule did little to inspire the faithful to obey the Ten Commandments. Despite the growing power of the cities and their leagues, Conrad founded a number of new towns, especially in the Duchy of Westphalia. He was thus able to expand and strengthen his own territories and take firm action against marauders and invaders. Not surprisingly, the tension between the autocratic Archbishop and the city's patricians, who were rapidly gaining in importance, led to a confrontation. The city's quest for self-government and its wish to impose taxes and monitor expenditures set it on a collision course with the Archbishop.

*Ancient Cologne from the
Chronicle of Rolevinck
(1485).*

In the beginning, all was sweetness and light between Cologne and the Archbishop, thanks in no small measure to the influential role of the city in his election. Two months later, just before receiving imperial and papal recognition, Conrad granted the city permission to continue imposing the excise tax on beer. He even went so far as to promise that he would shoulder the blame if the Emperor castigated the city for failing to obtain imperial consent. For this, the city obviously paid him a handsome sum, money Conrad desperately needed to finance his expensive trip to Rome to obtain papal recognition of his election. As early as 1239, Conrad recognized the city's right to try any citizen who had committed a crime within its boundaries. In a manner of speaking, a legal wall was thus also built around the city.

However, relations quickly cooled when Conrad betrayed Cologne in Rome. Like his predecessors, Conrad had received the regalia from Emperor Frederick II, the customary gift of a liege lord to his vassal. The Emperor, averse to the idea of promoting the autonomy of the cities, had conceded Conrad the right to levy excise taxes on beer and wine. Armed with this imperial privilege, the Archbishop set off to negotiate with the city. Claiming half of the revenues from the excise tax on beer for himself, he permitted the city the other half ''out of love for the citizens and so as not to encroach upon their rights and liberties.'' No wonder the city felt it had been hoodwinked! Cologne took its revenge at the first opportunity, when the Archbishop was obliged to call on the city to supply soldiers. On March 17, 1240, the city compelled him to declare that ''we [Conrad] do not now and shall not in the future have any right to the penny on beer by imperial consent.'' In the statement, the Archbishop declared that any future privileges granted to him or to his successors in the area of excise tax on beer were null and void. However, he did not relinquish his right to half of the revenues from the excise tax on beer. Shortly thereafter, on July 27, 1240, Conrad assured the city, by way of thanks for their assistance on the battlefield, that he would henceforth relinquish the revenues from the excise tax on wine. In effect, Conrad implicitly recognized the municipality's right to impose taxes. Clearly, all this squabbling over the taxes in 1239 and 1240 considerably cooled the good relations between the city and the Archbishop. In the years that followed, the temperature quickly dropped to freezing.

Conrad attempted to outmaneuver the city by minting his own coins. That tactic would not have been so bad, if the coins, minted outside Cologne, had been sufficiently heavy. But as these light coins did not differ externally from the coins the city itself minted, Conrad's minting posed a serious threat to Cologne's trade. In his chronicle of the year 1252, Godefrit Hagen writes that Archbishop Conrad "wanted to mint a new coin, [which] would do so much damage to both the rich and the poor." Conrad also established tolls at Neuss and other places, thus seriously impeding the free flow of trade. Before long, an actual war broke out between the city and the Archbishop. It was the first time ever that the city had taken up arms against the Archbishop. Coming to their senses, the two parties decided to submit their dispute to arbitration. The arbitrators were the Cardinal Legate, Hugo of St. Sabina, and the Dominican teacher in Cologne, Albertus Magnus, who was exalted after his death as a Doctor of the Church. Their judgement, known as the *kleinen Schied*, was pronounced on April 17, 1252 and was clearly sympathetic to the city. Although Conrad's right to mint his own coins was acknowledged, he was obliged to abandon the illegally established tolls in Neuss and elsewhere. Significantly, the city's hard-won privileges formed the basis for the arbitrators' rulings.

Despite the settlement, the dispute between the city and the Archbishop continued, leading to renewed hostilities. The Archbishop again laid siege to the city, which then concluded an alliance with his rival, the Count of Berg. Within a few years, both parties again requested arbitration. Once more, the arbiter was Albertus Magnus, together with four clergymen, who were probably in league with the Archbishop. Against numerical odds, Albertus negotiated a reasonably favorable compromise for the city. The ruling, put into effect on May 20, 1258, is known as the *groszen Schied*. The bulky document, its size swelled by numerous letters of protest written by both parties, recognized the Archbishop as the highest judge in spiritual and secular matters of state, and condemned the rampant abuses (mainly corruption) in the Aldermen's administration. But of more lasting importance was the fact that the citizens' institutions of self-government − such as the election of the mayors by the *Richerzeche* and the autonomy of Cologne's boroughs and guilds − were recognized and confirmed. Unlike Engelbrecht, Conrad had failed to ban the Small Council from the city.

One of the minor points of dispute settled in the *groszen Schied* was the excise tax on wine for clergymen. When the Archbishop relinquished his right to this excise tax, the city imposed the tax itself. Tolerating the clergy's tax exemption was one matter, but seeing some monasteries unabashedly fitted out as wine bars tested the city's endurance. Its measures brooked no argument. Municipal inspectors raided the monasteries and smashed all the wine barrels to pieces. The adjudicators considered this line of action rather drastic, because it flagrantly violated the immunity rights of the monasteries. Nonetheless, the monasteries were henceforth forbidden to sell wine.

Albertus Magnus
(1193-1280).

Indirectly, the *groszen Schied* also confirmed the city's right to impose other taxes. One example is the tax on livestock brought to the slaughterhouse. Originally, the right to impose tolls on livestock transports was part of the Archbishop's regalia. However, being perennially pressed for funds, the Archbishop had borrowed money from the city, putting up this right as security. When he was unable to pay off his debt, this right passed into the city's hands. Another example is the tax which Conrad claimed the city was levying on all manner of goods without his consent. Not only did the tax drive away foreign merchants, but it also laid a disproportionately heavy burden on the poor. The latter was a sore point, for the ruling classes had continued to force up taxes on basic commodities, which cut deepest into the pockets of the poor. Conrad's ploy was designed to create disunity between the guilds and the patricians. His scheme failed, however, as the adjudicators arrived at a compromise: the city was allowed

Archbishop Siegfried of Westerburg lays siege to Aachen (from Jan van Boendale, "Brabantsche Yeesten," Southern Netherlands, 15th century).

to impose these taxes provided the clergy was exempt and the poor were entitled to appeal to the Archbishop for help. Conrad had triumphed on one point before the *groszen Schied* was drawn up: in 1258, for a period of ten years, he regained control of half of the excise revenue on beer, a lucrative source of income which the city had prudently kept to itself during the hostilities.

Even though the *groszen Schied* was primarily a victory for the city, the Archbishop made a strong comeback. Before the year was out, he had driven a wedge between the merchants and the guilds. The guilds and the common people were dissatisfied with the mismanagement and nepotism of the leading patrician families. Conrad knew how to turn this to his advantage, so much so that he was able to instigate a kind of "revolution from above," in which the patricians were forced to yield their power to the guilds, who entered into a *Schwurverband* (or "sworn alliance") with Conrad. The patricians toppled from power were imprisoned in castles in the *Erzstift*, where they were utterly at the Archbishop's mercy. Conrad was so embittered that even on his deathbed, in 1261, he categorically declined every request to release his captives.

Conrad appeared to have reduced the city to subservience. But the restrictive policies of his successor, Engelbrecht II, alienated his former allies, the guilds. Engelbrecht II then proceeded to take the city by force, appropriating all tax revenues and removing the elected Aldermen from office. Enraged, the guilds and merchants joined forces and in 1262 drove the Archbishop out of the city, after holding him captive for three weeks. Their dogged resistance forced Engelbrecht II to recognize the *groszen Schied*. By way of compensation for missing his half of the beer tax revenues, he was granted 6,000 marks. The city wanted to buy out his share at the price of 16 marks a week, but this proposal collapsed.

Inwardly chafing and unwilling to let bygones be bygones, Engelbrecht II began the struggle anew. The city and the Archbishop concluded a peace no less than six times, but each time the latter broke his word. Finally, the parties called on the elderly Albertus Magnus to arbitrate. The conflict was only resolved three years later: the earlier-mentioned 6,000 marks were to be made over to Engelbrecht II, the city received the right to impose excise taxes until its debt was repaid — a meaningless condition — and the clergy retained its exemption. Evidently, the Archbishop's half share of the beer tax had vanished into the alcohol-laden air, for no more traces of it are to be found in the documents of the time. But this hardly made a dent in the Archbishop's ample financial resources. According to a description from the second half of the thirteenth century, the Archbishop of Cologne had an annual sum of 50,000 marks in silver at his disposal, a tidy sum compared to the Archbishops of Mainz and Trier, who had to content themselves with respectively 7,000 and 3,000 marks.

Siegfried of Westerburg: the city gains virtual independence

In November 1273, the new King Rudolf of Hapsburg renewed the toll privileges (in Boppard and Kaiserswerth) of the ''noble citizens'' of Cologne. He reaffirmed that they were not liable for the Archbishop's debts and could not be prosecuted outside the city's walls. A few months later, Rudolf took matters a step further. On March 2, 1274, he confirmed the city's right to impose taxes independently, without requiring the consent of the Emperor or the Archbishop. To all intents and purposes, this made the city financially independent. No longer were taxes restricted to fixed periods of time (typically three to ten years). When the third great Archbishop of that century, Siegfried of Westerburg, came to power in the same year (1274), there was one final tug-of-war, with the city's total emancipation at stake.

Once again, relations between the city and Siegfried (who was every bit as harsh and inflexible as his two great predecessors, Engelbrecht of Berg and Conrad of Hochstadt) were initially harmonious. One of the Archbishop's first acts of office was to guarantee the citizens all their existing rights, liberties and customs. In an unprecedented step that expressed the strength of its position, the city replied (as if it were his equal) that it would in turn respect the rights and customs of the *Erzstift*.

In the years that followed, Siegfried pursued an extensive expansionist policy, using the *Erzstift* and the Duchy of Westphalia as stepping stones to expand his power. The feudal age was drawing to a close. Power was no longer channeled through the feudal system but was exercised by autonomous princes ruling over their own territories. One of these rulers, William, Count of Jülich, whose castle was located in Worringen, posed a continuous threat to Siegfried. In order to cope with this threat, Siegfried erected his own castle, promising the distrustful citizens of Cologne that he would demolish both castles once he had defeated Count William. As he was in straightened circumstances at the time, Siegfried did not hesitate in 1276 to hock the German royal crown (which the Archbishops of Cologne used for the coronation of the German kings) for 1,050 marks. In 1277, he invaded Jülich's territory and soon triumphed over his adversary with the practical assistance of the citizens of Cologne. When Siegfried received word on March 17, 1278 that Count William of Jülich and his oldest son had been beaten to death by a citizen of Aachen, he promptly ordered Holy Mass to be held in Cologne's Cathedral. This mass, normally celebrated later on the feast of St. Peter in Chains, includes the passage: "Now I truly know that the Lord has sent his angel, who has freed me from the vengeance of the lion." This was a reference that Siegfried's contemporaries would have understood, for a lion was emblazoned on the coat of arms of the slain Count of Jülich!

Although Siegfried failed to keep his promise to demolish the castles in Worringen, a decade later the city was once again prepared to enter into an alliance with him. This was prompted by the war that had broken out as a result of a quarrel between the Counts of Berg — who had been the *Erzstift*'s bitter enemy since St. Engelbrecht's death — and the Counts of Gelre over the succession to the Duchy of Limburg. The Archbishop was in danger of being drawn into the conflict when Count Adolf of Berg transferred his claims to Limburg to Duke John of Brabant, whose objective was to extend his territory to the Rhine. Duke John of Brabant felt he had a rightful claim to the Duchy of Lorraine, the northern part of the Carolingian Middle Kingdom that had been incorporated in the German Empire three centuries earlier in 925. As Lorraine was many times larger than the Duchy of Brabant, the stakes were high. John of Brabant used several dramatic and symbolic gestures to substantiate his claim to the disputed territory. In one such instance, he rode to the Rhine to let his horse drink its waters. In another gesture of defiance, clearly aimed at provoking the Archbishop, he held an elaborate hunting party in the Archbishop's game reserve in Brühl. If Duke John's ambition were to be realized, the Archbishop would lose the position of power that his predecessors had built up on both sides of the Rhine. Consequently, Siegfried allied himself with, among others, the Count of Gelre, who had transferred his claim to Limburg to the Count of Luxembourg. Duke John likewise sought to ally himself with powerful nobles. Thus, the battle lines between the two parties were gradually drawn.

To finance the impending war, the Archbishop had created tolls in several places. In 1287, he entered into an alliance with Cologne, agreeing to abolish the tolls when the war was over. Both parties took a solemn oath that they would not enter into an alliance against the other party. Before the year was out, the city violated its oath by joining with Duke John of Brabant, who had penetrated as far as Bonn, and allowing his army inside the city walls. In the political arena of the day, such power shifts were commonplace. For his part, Siegfried had succeeded in winning over Nassau, neutralizing Paderborn and Heinsberg and effecting a reconciliation with his nephew Siegfried of Runkel, who until then had aligned himself with John of Brabant. The city's decision to switch sides had mainly been prompted by economic and political considerations. Economically speaking, the trade routes to Brabant and Flanders were vital to Cologne's commerce and had

The Battle of Worringen on July 5, 1288 (from the Koelhoff Chronicle of 1499).

to be kept open at all costs. Politically speaking, Cologne wanted to prevent itself from being hemmed in and threatened by the Archbishop and his new (and old!) allies. To protect its trade interests, the city had since 1263 courted the friendship of the lords of neighboring castles with bribes and flattery. As a result, the city had gained a string of footholds along the busiest trade routes. The lords of the castles were made burghers of the city and were called *Edelbürger* (or "noble citizens"). Their friendship was purchased at a heavy price but offered no guarantee, because an *Edelbürger* was quite prepared to defect to the city's enemies for a generous price. Cologne could afford this type of expense, thanks to the fact that the city had complete and unlimited control over its own taxes. Naturally, the revenues kept pace with the city's prosperity.

The long-expected war finally broke out in the summer of 1288. A drove of Cologne's citizens joined Duke John and his allies as they marched on Archbishop Siegfried's castle in Worringen with the firm intention of capturing it and razing it to the ground. The battle, fought on the Fühlinger Heath in Worringen on July 5, 1288, was one of the largest and bloodiest battles in the Middle Ages. Siegfried and his allies suffered a crushing defeat, in which the citizens of Cologne and the peasants of the County of Berg played a decisive role. By vanquishing the Archbishop, the Duke of Brabant had finally realized his ambition of becoming the Duke of Limburg. But the Archbishop had put up a good and courageous fight. In eyewitness Jan van Heelu's epic poem about the Battle of Worringen (dedicated to the Duke of Brabant), he wrote: "I am convinced that a more courageous cleric than Bishop Siegfried has never girded his sword, for when he entered into battle no one, except those who knew him, could see that he wore the tonsure or could detect even a trace of the ecclesiastical or spiritual in him, as he proved himself to be a praiseworthy knight, in offence as well as defense." Notwithstanding his staunch resistance, Siegfried was captured and held in captivity for more than a year by the Count of Berg.

After the battle, the citizens of Cologne laid waste to the Archbishop's castles in Worringen, Neuenburg and Zons and used the stones for their own city walls. The Archbishop was stripped of a large part of his territory, destroying his dream of a large state stretching between the Meuse and the Weser under his leadership. More importantly, the city of Cologne had at last freed itself from his grip and achieved its virtual independence. The city did not even feel it was necessary to ask Siegfried for written confirmation of its independent status, a clear indication of the new power relations. It was not until 1475 that Cologne officially received its freedom, when Emperor Frederick III raised it to the status of a free imperial city.

The guilds struggle to obtain more influence over the municipal government

At last, the city had won its independence. In its struggle, taxation had played a central role, both as an objective and as a means of obtaining that objective. Taxation remained a bone of contention even after independence had been achieved. The patrician families had succeeded in reducing direct taxes, which affected the rich rather than the poor, and in creating a system of excise taxes. These taxes were paid by everyone, rich and poor alike, and considerably increased the cost of living. Another source of conflict was the tight grip that the patricians held on trade and industry through the *Richerzeche*. This situation generated discontent among the guilds, who represented large segments of the population. But the ruling class obdurately clung to its power and took no steps to defuse the rising tension. Fourteenth-century Cologne was dominated by the struggle of the crafts guilds to secure a legitimate share in the municipal government. Taxes often constituted a point of friction between these two parties. The merchants, who were a less homogeneous group and consequently less tightly organized, generally observed the struggle from the sidelines.

Politically, the guilds and the *Gaffeln*,[4] often lumped together in the sources as "the people," wanted a voice in the city's financial affairs. This could only be achieved by gaining a foothold in the Large Council and trying to extend its powers. Just how little financial influence the Large Council had in relation to the Small Council is reflected in the "Book of Oaths," dated 1341. This book shows that the Large Council's role in tax matters was confined to granting its consent to the introduction of new taxes to cover debts. The Large Council clearly did not have an active say in the running of the city's affairs.

In 1348, a revolt broke out, which demonstrated the unequal distribution of power in the city. The immediate cause of the trouble was that the butchers were required to sell their meat according to weight (in the consumer's favor, I might add) and not "by hand." The butchers' rebellion was nipped in the bud and quashed with summary justice: the butchers' guild was abolished and anyone was allowed to sell meat. These harsh measures effectively blighted the political aspirations of a middle-class group that held considerable power in many other cities. The ease with which the *Richerzeche* eliminated this troublesome guild testifies to the patricians' power during this period.

However, several decades later, the tables were turned. In the interim, some of the guilds, such as the weavers and the goldsmiths, had achieved great prosperity. In the 1350's, merchants who were not related to one of the all-powerful Families had started organizing religious brotherhoods. These organizations soon set their sights on acquiring political power. One prominent brotherhood was the Eisenmarkt *Gaffel*, which played a central role in the following incident. In 1362, the Small Council took advantage of a ten-month vacancy in the Archbishop's chair to arrange a "deal" with the Emperor. He granted the city permission to levy an extra toll, in return for which he would receive a gratuity of 2,000 marks. To imbue this novel transaction with a semblance of legality, matters were arranged so that the four existing Rhine tolls were first transferred to the Emperor, who subsequently pledged the revenues from these tolls to the municipality for 2,000 marks. This roundabout route was to be the city's undoing. When the naive citizens arrived at the Bavarian tower, on the South side of the city (on the banks of the Rhine), they discovered that a new toll had been created. The toll primarily affected merchants transporting their wares upstream or from the Upper and Middle Rhine to Cologne. The merchants of the Eisenmarkt *Gaffel* immediately joined forces with the weavers' guild and demanded the abolition of the toll. The Small Council was evidently no match for their passive resistance, since it was soon abolished.

What is worse, it cost the municipality a fortune to wind up the toll affair. To receive full control over the four other Rhine tolls, the city had to pay the Emperor 14,000 marks. Add to this the 2,000 marks, and it appears that the city had lost half of its usual income in one fell swoop! This affair triggered "hate and malice between the council and the people," and almost culminated in an

4. In the second half of the fourteenth century, *Gaffeln* were founded in Cologne as religiously oriented social clubs. Before long, their area of interest had expanded to include politics. The original members were mainly merchants and other related professionals. The word *Gaffel* (the singular form) has been left in the text because of the difficulty of finding an exact equivalent in English.

armed clash between the weavers' guild and the patricians. However, thanks to the intervention of outsiders (including the Count of Mark), a civil war was averted, at least for the time being.

Shortly thereafter, in 1363, an extremely unpopular excise tax on wine-tapping was introduced. As rich and poor alike engaged in this practice, the Small Council failed to exact compliance.

The coalition of the Eisenmarkt *Gaffel* and the weavers' guild next attacked corruption among the ruling clique, an evil to which Conrad of Hochstadt had already pointed a century earlier. To finance municipal expenses, the city issued annuities via an Annuity Board for a lump sum. In 1367, rumor had it that Rutger Hirzelin von Grin, the head of the Annuity Board, had embezzled monies belonging to the city. Neither Rutger, the other members of the Annuity Board nor the assessors (all members of the Families) were able to prove that the annuity transactions were above suspicion. At the coalition's insistence, a committee of three senior statesmen, consisting of two non-patrician members of the Large Council and one member of the Small Council, audited the Annuity Board's books. Fraud was quickly detected, and the steward Rutger was tried and executed. This scandal was a further blow to the prestige of the ruling class. Significantly, the committee of auditors remained in existence. This marked an important step forward for the opposition.

Two years later, events escalated once again. It occurred to one of the mayors that immune monasteries were forbidden to sell bottles of wine. The municipality was responsible for ensuring that the clergy did not abuse its wine tax exemption all too blatantly. Suddenly a tempest in a wine cup blew up over a minor incident. The event itself was insignificant. What was more important was that, in the face of stormy protests from the ecclesiastical world, the Small Council stood squarely behind its mayor. The upshot of the matter was that the municipality was excommunicated and many of the clergymen moved away. The quarrel was presumably patched up later, but once again, the Small Council's authority had suffered a painful, if not mortal, blow.

Before the year was out, a more serious incident occurred, following the arrest of a street thief. Before the Council could try the thief, a howling mob, mainly members of the weavers' guild, gathered in front of City Hall, demanding that he be handed over to them. The municipal government was already so weakened that it had to yield to this demand, and the man was brutally murdered by the mob on that very spot. The exact cause of this outburst of violence is unclear, but there seems to have been growing dissatisfaction among the citizens over the exercise of criminal justice. Trials were frequently postponed without justification and there were even cases of confirmed criminals being set free.

The association formed by the weavers' guild and the merchants of the Eisenmarkt *Gaffel* rose in significance as more and more guilds joined forces with them. Cologne's motley group of artisans thus became known collectively as "the Weavers." By March 1370, the once all-powerful Families could no longer keep the Weavers at bay and were forced to give them access to municipal office. The immediate cause of this change was the municipal government's failure to take appropriate action against the knight Edmund Birkelin, who vented his animosity against the city by waylaying merchants from Cologne and robbing

The Bavarian tower (lithograph made by F. A. Mote around 1821, based on a 1531 woodcut by Anton Woelsam). A toll was introduced in 1362 and then quickly abolished (see text). Initially, toll was levied per ship. In the beginning of the 13th century, the ship toll was replaced by a toll based on the value of the goods. As wine was by far the most important item of trade on the Rhine, the value of one tun ("fuder") of wine became the basis for the toll. The price and quality of the wine was not constant, reason in the 14th century to tax the value of the goods directly. Because of commercial and political expediency, it was determined that one tun of wine was equal to 10 anker ("aam"), even though it actually equaled 6 anker. In addition, the merchants received a 10% discount off the tolls levied on ships sailing upstream of Cologne and even 15% off those sailing downstream. Cologne annually had wine sales amounting to about 12,000 tun. For every fourth tun, the merchant had to hand over four times a quarter of a liter to the toll officials and their personnel. According to an ordinance regulating tolls, the toll officials had to receive their gratuity in jugs instead of bottles, as otherwise, the ordinance continues, the unnecessary opening of bottles might give the merchants cause for complaint! The toll collectors were regularly monitored to ensure that they carried out their work properly, whether they recorded the ship and its load correctly and whether the toll monies were deposited in the chest in the presence of the bookkeeper! As the same ordinance notes, there was every reason to keep an eye on the toll collectors, since they and the captains often spent an inordinate amount of time in the alehouse and they were all too likely to accept gifts. Nevertheless, the toll officials were advised to treat the merchants with respect, to avoid violence and to bend the law, where necessary. They were also forbidden to engage in trade themselves or be a partner in a mercantile firm. The average tariff amounted to 2-10% of the value of the goods per toll.

them of their merchandise. Under pressure from the Weavers, the three persons responsible for the government's inaction (all of whom were members of the Small Council and were also either Aldermen or members of the *Richerzeche*) were thrown into prison. The following day, eight more Council members were put under house arrest in the monastery of St. Kunibert. Despite the tense atmosphere in the city, these events did not give rise to bloodshed. The power of the patricians had been severely undermined by the scandals of the previous years, and they had no alternative but to submit to the Weavers' pressure.

The Weavers were not interested primarily in overhauling the structure of municipal government. What they wanted was more control over the collection and allocation of taxes. After months of talks, a settlement was reached. Given the circumstances, the compromise was not unfavorable to the Families. The government structure was changed so that Aldermen were no longer permitted to sit in the Small Council or become mayor, thus abolishing the system of rotation which had long sustained the power of the ruling families. The *Richerzeche*, the body supervising trade and industry, which was particularly hated by the guilds, was to be phased out. The *Richerzeche* received a compensatory annual annuity from the municipality to compensate for the lack of future income; nowadays we would say that they were put on half-pay. The most drastic change concerned the composition and powers of the Large Council. The members of the Large Council were no longer to be chosen from the parishes. Instead, the new Large Council, now reduced to fifty members, was to be chosen from "the people," i.e. the guilds and boroughs. The new members were therefore drawn from the ranks of weavers, smiths, girdle-makers, armor-makers, painters, liverymen, tinsmiths, belt-cutters, goldsmiths and other craftsmen. However, the merchants in the Eisenmarkt *Gaffel* were only allocated one seat in the Large Council. The Weavers, who had otherwise conducted their affairs with moderation, committed a tactical error in not extending more influence to the *Gaffeln* of the merchants. The Weavers' reluctance to do so was presumably due to the merchants' aloof stance during the guilds' struggle to break the hegemony of the Families. Their impartiality perhaps derived from the fact that they viewed both groups primarily as customers.

Not everything changed. The city's stewards remained patricians, although they were henceforth required to submit quarterly accounts. The Councilors in the Large Council, the majority of whose fifty members were drawn from the guilds, held the keys to the chests in City Hall, which contained the municipal seal and gold bars. Under the new structure, the Large Council and the Small Council had a virtually equal voice in managing the city's finances. As a result, the Weavers were able to carry out their long-cherished wish of relieving the lower classes of their crippling tax burden.

The new Council initiated two new taxes. The first was the scutage, a tax on income from real estate. It was evidently a heavy tax, for it constituted almost half of the municipal revenues. The patrician families, who had gradually become accustomed to an aristocratic lifestyle and were now largely dependent on income from rents, leases and annuities rather than trade, were the hardest hit by this tax. But the wealthy merchants, many of whom were affiliated with the Eisenmarkt *Gaffel*, had also invested a substantial part of their profits in real estate and also felt the impact of the new tax. This threatened to drive a wedge between the Weavers and the merchants.

Stonemasons at work in Cologne (from the Koelhoff Chronicle of 1499).

The second new tax, a tax on wine imports, was even more questionable. The tax hit the wine trade, long an important pillar of Cologne's economy, by shrinking its profit margins. Another source of bitterness was that no additional export tax had been levied on blankets and other products of the wool industry, another pillar of Cologne's prosperous economy. The wine merchants of the Eisenmarkt *Gaffel* were understandably furious at this unjust tax regime that squeezed their profits while sparing their colleagues in the textile trade, who were also members of this *Gaffel*.

A further source of dissatisfaction was the reduction in the costs of becoming a burgher, which the Large Council implemented with the apparent intention of increasing their following within the city in support of municipal reforms.

The tense atmosphere in the city exploded on November 20, 1371. A member of the weavers' guild had been sentenced to death for his involvement, against the city's express wishes, in a local war between the Dukes of Brabant and Jülich. The city wished to remain neutral in this conflict and did not want to become embroiled through the individual actions of its citizens. On the way to his execution, the man was rescued by a group of fellow Weavers. Their action was mainly motivated by the fact that a few patricians who had also taken part in the conflict had got off scot-free. The patricians retaliated swiftly and mercilessly. Aided by the city's militia, which was still under the Small Council's and therefore the patricians' command, they dealt the Weavers a crushing blow. Events had happened so quickly that the smiths and tailors had been unable to hasten to their rescue. The merchants, who were barely represented in the Large Council, and a wide-ranging group of small businessmen and craftsmen looked on from the sidelines. Following the "Battle of the Weavers," the *nova ordinatio* of July 2, 1370 was rendered totally null and void. After only a year and a half, the blossoming flower of joint government was crudely trampled underfoot. The weavers' guild was abolished, its former members heavily fined, while some of its master craftsmen were banned from the city and their property and goods confiscated. The number of looms in the city was limited to two hundred, and an extra tax was imposed on Cologne's textiles. In addition, the weavers, tailors and smiths were no longer allowed to carry weapons. They were also compelled to sell their guild houses. Certain other guilds were outlawed, and all remaining guilds were placed under the supervision of the Small Council, which remained the preserve of the patriciate. From this time forward, the Large Council, reduced to thirty-three members, was to replenish its numbers through co-optation. The patricians, having learned from past mistakes, restored the *Richerzeche* to its former glory, but not its former power. Furthermore, in the future only two Aldermen were to be members of the Small Council. The merchants − who had taken no part in the weavers' battle − retained some voice in the Small Council, but their influence was marginal compared to that of the Families.

The Families hung on to their power for several decades. But discord between the two most powerful families, the Greifen and the Freunde, then led to the downfall of the patricians as a ruling class. The cause of this typically medieval vendetta was that the Freunde had gained the upper hand in both the *Richerzeche* and the Board of Aldermen. The Greifen, aided by the guilds, consequently set out to destroy the power of both the *Richerzeche* and the Aldermen. They succeeded, but at the same time unwittingly laid the foundation for far-reaching reforms. Another ordinance regulating city government was enacted in 1396. This new ordinance no longer distinguished between the Small and the Large Council. There were to be forty-nine Council members, thirty-six of whom were to be chosen directly by the twenty-two *Gaffeln*. In certain cases, the *Gaffeln* consisted of several affiliated guilds, while in other cases, the *Gaffel* and the guilds were in fact the same body. The weavers' guild was to supply four members, and the Windeck, Himmelreich, Schwartzhaus and Eisenmarkt *Gaffeln* (these apparently contained a mixed population) were to send two each. The guilds of the smiths, girdle-makers, goldsmiths, furriers and fishmongers were to send two representatives, while the brewers, painters, bakers, tailors, coopers,

The "Battle of the Weavers" between the Weavers and the Families on November 20, 1371 (from the Koelhoff Chronicle of 1499).

bricklayers, cobblers, tinsmiths and linen-weavers were to supply one representative each. The Council was to choose the remaining thirteen members at random from the citizenry. Two additional Councilors per member were to be appointed for singularly important decisions, i.e. those concerning war, alliances and exceptional expenditures. The day-to-day management of the city's affairs was the province of two mayors, both chosen by the Council for a one-year term. The Archbishop's rule was limited to appointing the Aldermen, whose function was now restricted to administering justice in important cases. To ensure that each citizen had a voice in municipal government, every burgher had to join one of the twenty-two *Gaffeln*. Membership in the Council, which could not be refused, was limited to one year.

All of these changes were set forth in a document known as the *Verbundbrief*. This document clearly was not the product of the endless disputes over taxes. However, taxes had certainly been one of the citizens' central motives for removing the Families from power. After 1396, all was quiet on the tax front in Cologne for a while. However, as the city was increasingly recognized as the center of power in the area, greater outlay was required to maintain its reputation and position, where necessary by force of arms. As a consequence, taxes continued to rise steadily to keep pace with spending. The citizens understandably balked at such tax hikes. In 1481, an increase in the consumer tax on wine and bread

The coat of arms of the Schumacher "gaffel" (around 1650).

View of a merchant house in Cologne (drawn by Augustin Braun, 1590).

sparked an insurrection. The Council only regained control after the first fury of the insurgents was spent, and many heads rolled into the executioner's basket. The insurrection undoubtedly added some momentum to the movement to amend the *Verbundbrief* of 1396. However, it was not until 1513, after yet another bloody insurrection had been suppressed, that the *Transfixbrief* came into existence. The measures in this document were designed to prevent corruption

and embezzlement of municipal funds by the Councilors. In addition, individual citizens were offered greater protection against the municipal government than anywhere else in the Western world, with the exception of England. Individual liberty was declared to be inviolable: henceforth citizens could not be arrested in their own homes unless they had been caught in the act of committing a criminal offense or their crime had been made public. Thus, from the turn of the fifteenth century up to the French Revolution, the *Verbundbrief* and the *Transfixbrief* ensured that Cologne — even by modern standards — was a reasonably democratic society.

Diedrich of Moers, an ambitious potentate in the Archbishop's chair

The struggle of Cologne's Archbishops to gain hegemony in the Rhineland persisted for several centuries, from around 1250 to 1450. The struggle reached its peak and subsequently died out during the long rule of Diedrich of Moers. The earlier-mentioned paradox, "more external power leads to less internal power," is even more applicable to the events occurring during his long episcopacy (1414 – 1463) than to the conflict between his predecessors and the city of Cologne.

Diedrich was descended from a distinguished family. His brother Henry became Bishop of Münster in 1424 and administrator of the Diocese of Osnabrück in 1441. Diedrich was clearly instrumental in obtaining these appointments for his brother and other family members. Later, Diedrich attempted to put his brother Walram in the episcopal see of Utrecht. His ultimate goal was to annex the Diocese of Paderborn to *Kurköln*,[5] which would have created a conglomerate of ecclesiastical principalities stretching from the North Sea to the Lippe River and from the mouth of the IJssel River to Hessen. However, history took a different turn.

Between 1430 and 1445, all that stood between Diedrich and the achievement of his goal was the Diocese of Utrecht. After 1450, in an attempt to set the seal on his life's work, Diedrich tried to purchase the Duchy of Berg and thus create a kind of land bridge between *Kurköln* and the Duchy of Westphalia. As we will see, these ambitious plans ultimately came to grief.

Diedrich — whose birth date is unknown — was more a man of the world than an ecclesiastic, which is hardly surprising considering what has already been said of his predecessors. His leading the troops in battle was the order of the day. But the fact that he challenged the Duke of Cleves to a duel was unusual, even in those days. According to a reliable eyewitness, when he was seventy Diedrich wielded the sword as if he were a young man. He was headstrong to the point of being domineering. He enjoyed a lavish lifestyle and held court like a renaissance prince. On more than one occasion, the Pope upbraided him for immoral and scandalous behavior. According to an account cited in the Koelhoff Chronicle, in 1416 Diedrich had two priests, including a cathedral canon who two years earlier had campaigned against his appointment as bishop, murdered in a dungeon. Clearly, Diedrich's ostentatious lifestyle and the many gifts he bestowed in order to buy people and power were expensive foibles. His political objectives, namely to consolidate and expand his own territory and control his neighbors, were even costlier. Diedrich was motivated by an insatiable urge to dominate, along with his family, the political arena of his time.

5. The name of the *Erzstift* after 1356.

Poor government sows the seeds of financial troubles

Diedrich set his power politics in motion immediately after his election as Archbishop. The 1414 election had not been without snags. Admittedly, he had been
chosen by the majority of the cathedral chapter. But there had been another
strong contender: William, the son of the Duke of Berg. At the age of sixteen
(in 1402), William had climbed his way up the career ladder to the episcopal see
of Paderborn and now set his cap at reaching yet another rung. For the allied
Duchies of Berg and Gelre, this ambition opened up the prospect of keeping
Kurköln under their combined thumbs. When the previous Archbishop died on
April 14, 1414, it took a minority of the cathedral chapter only five days to elect
William of Berg as Archbishop. Six days later, a majority chose Diedrich. As
Diedrich had the backing of King Sigismund as well as that of the Electoral
Princes, the outcome was a foregone conclusion. All the more so after Diedrich,
with lightning speed, made over (via Florentine bankers) to the Pope, who had
to approve the appointment, the usual payment of 5,000 marks plus 1,418 marks
in a papal tax. In addition, Diedrich had lavished gifts on anyone who could be
of assistance. He still had to make amends with his rival, and he did this very
elegantly. In 1416, he concluded a peace with William of Berg. Diedrich then
presented William (who had not yet been ordained) with a wife in the form of
his extraordinarily beautiful niece Adelheid of Tecklenburg and paid him 20,000
marks in the bargain. After the College of Cardinals had received its usual sum
of 5,000 marks, the bill could be drawn up. It had cost him a pretty penny, but
Diedrich was now in possession of huge sources of income, and he could apply
the money derived from these sources to realize his ambitions.

Diedrich's lavish lifestyle seems to suggest that money was no object. However,
this expression implies that money is plentiful, which was decidedly not the case
with Diedrich. His whole life revolved around obtaining sufficient funds to
quench his insatiable thirst for political power. His financial exploits had begun
with his election as archbishop. As Sigismund still had to be crowned king, he
urged the Pope to recognize the newly elected but unordained Diedrich as quickly
as possible. His wish was fulfilled. In a ceremony that lasted eight hours,
Diedrich was able to celebrate his first Holy Mass on November 8, 1414 and at
the same time crown Sigismund as king in his capacity as Archbishop of Cologne.
Immediately afterwards, Diedrich was enfeoffed with the customary regalia,
such as the tolls in Andernach, Bonn, Neuss and Rheinberg, the right to mint
coins, the patronage of the Jews and other rights. A rather complicated financial
transaction followed, involving Sigismund's mediation of a dispute between the
Archbishop and the city of Cologne. The result was that the Archbishop was to
be allowed to make a festive entrance into the city and was to receive a handsome
present of 5,000 marks. The city gave Sigismund 25,000 marks for his services
as middleman, but Diedrich promised in turn to repay this amount to the city
over a number of years, using his revenues from the toll in Bonn.

The Archbishop initially appeared to have received the short end of the financial
stick, but this was fortunately not the case. Sigismund was prepared to concede
to Diedrich the revenues from the imperial taxes on several cities in the Alsace
(Hagenau and Colmar, to name two), up to a maximum of 32,000 marks,
although this sum was also to cover the costs of Sigimund's coronation, which
the Archbishop had loaned him in advance. Nevertheless, this source could only
be tapped once the lien on these cities had lapsed. This would not happen for at

least another fifteen years, i.e. between 1428 and 1430. As a result, the last of the payments only flowed into the Archbishop's coffers in 1446. Conspiciously absent in this complex system of long- and short-term loans was any mention of interest payments.

The financial problems which plagued Diedrich throughout his decade-long period of office were partially due to his own headstrong actions. The Bishop's Council did have a financial steward. But it was exceedingly difficult for him to keep pace with the impulsive gifts and loans of the itinerant Archbishop or the bills for unexpected purchases that descended upon him out of the blue. Of course, from time to time Diedrich received a windfall. In 1435, for example, Diedrich emerged 60,000 marks richer from the conflict over the succession of Saxony's Electoral Prince, simply by defecting to the other side. Generally speaking, however, the steward was busy robbing Peter to pay Paul. His task was made more arduous by the system of allocation, whereby the Archbishop did not pay contributions directly from his treasury, but from the revenues accruing to him from specific sources, e.g. tolls. Viewed objectively, it was a practical system, for it avoided the pitfalls of unsafe roads and the spoilage of taxes paid in kind. What is more, the Archbishop had the revenues from far-off places directly at his disposal. Still, this system did not make matters any easier for the steward, particularly when, as often happened, local officials settled their accounts with the Archbishop personally, more often than not to their own advantage. Bookkeeping was still rather basic in those days. Furthermore, the steward had no knowledge of local transactions and could only record his own receipts and expenditures. Not surprisingly, Diedrich's spur-of-the-moment actions coupled with the steward's lack of control over the accounts exacerbated the problems already created by his extravagant lifestyle and ambitious policies. In this light, it was perfectly understandable that the Archbishop's financiers, particularly the cathedral chapter and the estates, tried to acquire a more influential voice in financial affairs. Diedrich, however, obstinately refused to allow this. His only concession was to establish (around 1440) an investigative committee, which included the steward. The committee was charged with looking into the financial system and drawing up proposals for improvements. Very little came of their efforts, for Diedrich thwarted any attempt to curb his power. Indeed, he had a more important matter on his mind: his ambition to gain military and political supremacy.

The successes and failures of Diedrich of Moers' political objectives

Diedrich's first objective was to annex the Bishopric of Paderborn, which William of Berg had renounced and which was part of the Archbishopric of Mainz. This, of course, was an expensive venture, as many factions had to be bribed. Paderborn was a politically sensitive area, necessitating shrewd diplomacy. In 1444, after decades of political wheeling and dealing between all parties involved, including the Pope, the Emperor, the ecclesiastical Council, the Chapter, etc., this adventure finally failed. As a consolation prize, Diedrich was allowed to govern the Bishopric of Paderborn during his lifetime.

In another ill-fated political ploy, the Archbishop attempted to reinforce his own position as sovereign ruler over *Kurköln* by extending his secular power in territories that belonged to his diocese but were ruled by secular princes. To achieve this, he tried to expand the powers of the ecclesiastical courts and impose a clerical tax on the resident clergy. In the process, he naturally offended many of his neighbors. In the decades to follow, they opposed the Archbishop's policies, with varying degrees of success. Cleves, in particular, was at daggers drawn with the Archbishop, so much so that the Duke of Cleves asked the Pope to make his territory a separate bishopric, thus detaching it from the Archbishop's diocese. Pope Eugenius IV was willing to connive with the Duke, and granted his permission in 1444. However, Diedrich refused to cooperate. Several years later, matters came to a head when the Pope removed Diedrich from office and appointed someone else in his place. A compromise was soon reached in 1448: the Pope agreed to drop the plan to make Cleves a separate bishopric, while Diedrich discontinued the taxes on the clergy in that duchy and abandoned his plans to expand his ecclesiastical jurisdiction. In short, Diedrich had once again failed to realize his political ambition.

A few years later, in 1450, the death of Henry of Moers, Diedrich's brother, sparked off a struggle for the episcopal see in Münster. Fortunately, Diedrich had another brother, Walram. Having been rejected as Bishop of Utrecht, Walram could conveniently replace his brother in Münster. At great cost, Diedrich secured the majority vote of the Münster chapter for his brother. Meanwhile, another contender had emerged in the person of Eric of Hoya, a descendent of the Hoya family of counts. Just as the Moers family had attempted to gain control over the Rhineland-Westphalia episcopacies, the Hoya family had tried to dominate Lower Saxony. As a fellow countryman, Eric of Hoya enjoyed broad popular support as well as the backing of a minority of the chapter. A protracted struggle for this episcopacy, in which the Pope was no innocent bystander, ensued. In 1452, Walram declared his willingness to renounce his claim in return for an annual allowance. The cause of his sudden withdrawal was that Archbishop Diedrich's financial well had run completely dry, preventing him from deciding the dispute with Münster in his favor by military intervention. Shortly afterwards, several of the bantams in this barnyard struggle, including Rudolf of Diepholt, the Bishop of Utrecht (who had sided with Cologne), and Walram himself died, so that within a few years the disagreement had resolved itself.

As we have already seen, the Archbishop owed his precarious financial position to his efforts to extend his power and influence beyond the borders of *Kurköln* and the Duchy of Westphalia. In the long run, his expansionist policies would deliver a mortal blow to his finances.

Kurköln was both the subject and the object of the struggle for hegemony in the Rhineland. It formed the subject of the debate in that the Archbishops, during a time in which the local balance of power in the territorial duchies and counties was being consolidated, strove to acquire control over the area and to unify or expand their possessions. The possibility of forming a land bridge to the predominantly agricultural Duchy of Westphalia, which was governed independently of *Kurköln* and also had its own institutions, played a role as well. *Kurköln* formed the object of the struggle in the sense that neighboring dukes and counts attempted to obtain control of it to provide their younger sons with a position and reinforce the power base of their own dynasties.

In the decade-long conflict that ensued, the Dukes of Cleves, Gelre, Jülich and Berg, the city of Cologne and the Archbishop exhausted each other in a trade

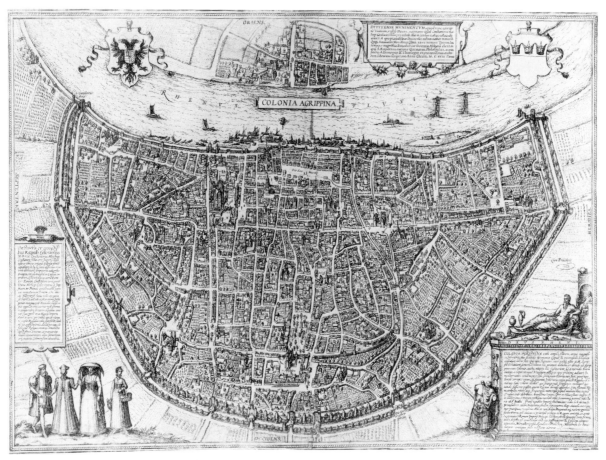

Map of Cologne and Deutz from the Braun-Hogenberg atlas (second half of the 16th century).

war and through mutual plundering and destruction. The coalition partners changed at first, but later an outright war broke out between two clearly defined factions. One of the alliances, consisting of the city of Cologne, Cleves, Jülich and Berg, was supported by the powerful Duke of Burgundy, who took a grim view of the threat to his possessions in the Low Countries. The other camp was comprised of Archbishop Diedrich, with his allies the Bishops of Münster, Hildesheim and Minden, the Dukes of Saxony, Brandenburg and Bavaria as well as several neighboring counts and lords. These allies, however, offered him scant military support. Gelre and the Count of Mark offered what little material assistance they could afford, but basically Diedrich had to battle it out with his own army.

Broadly speaking, the fight for the hegemony of the Lower Rhine area was fought between the Duke of Burgundy, who enjoyed papal support, and the Archbishop of Cologne, who could rely on French sympathy.

Diedrich won the lifelong loyalty of Gerard of Mark, the brother of Duke Adolf of Cleves, by helping him in 1437 separate the County of Mark from the Duchy of Cleves and gain control of it. As a condition of the alliance between Diedrich of Moers and Gerard of Mark, the Archbishop paid the Count 100,000 marks. In return, the Archbishop was entitled to the toll revenues in Kaiserswerth. This toll, the most important source of income for *Kurköln* until 1772, was of tremendous political and military significance. Even so, 100,000 marks was a substantial investment, requiring cash reserves that the Archbishop did not have. Conse-

quently, Diedrich was obliged to take out a loan, using several large rural districts as security. The loan payments proved to be a severe drain on his finances. Not long after, Gerard, the son of his former rival William of Berg and his niece Adelheid of Tecklenburg, gained control of the Duchies of Jülich, Gelre and Berg and the Counties of Zutphen and Ravensberg, which had been used as security for a loan. In 1442, Diedrich extended his control to include the city of Dortmund and the advocacy over the monastery of Essen, whose vast possessions had been received from Emperor Frederick III. By 1440, Diedrich was in a very strong position. Nevertheless, his chronic financial malaise was to be his downfall.

Cleves, believing that it had been passed by in the matter of Dortmund and Essen, began the hostilities in 1445. The military provocations of the previous years soon escalated into outright war. A major turning point came when the city of Soest, the former capital of the Duchy of Westphalia, decided not to tolerate

An early print of Cologne, taken from the Nürenburg Chronicle (1439).

the autocratic Archbishop's attacks on its civil liberties and threw in its lot with Cleves. The Archbishop's main financial lifeline was *Kurköln*, which had to defray the costs of the 15,000 strong army with which he attacked Soest. Vast sums of money were also spent on securing the loyalty of a motley crew of bishops, dukes, counts and cities, although they offered little more than friendly neutrality. All this warmongering depleted the financial resources of *Kurköln* to such an extent that it felt the effects for centuries.

The Archbishop's financial and military exertions were to no avail. Not only did he fail to take Soest by siege, but the city ultimately achieved independence. Thus the "Feud of Soest" ended in a severe defeat for Diedrich. Undaunted, he attempted shortly thereafter, as mentioned above, to seize the episcopal see of Münster for his brother Walram. The stiff resistance of the Archbishop's opponents probably resulted from their fear that Diedrich's purchase of the County of Berg would provide him with a land bridge between *Kurköln* and the Duchy of Westphalia, and thus further reinforce his position. However, as Diedrich lacked the funds either to take Berg by military force or purchase it outright, he had to forgo his ambition to acquire the County of Berg. Slowly but surely, he lost his hold on events. The Archbishop was obviously no match for the mighty Philip the Good of Burgundy, who supported Cleves and Hoya during the disputes over Münster. Diedrich's advanced age, the tensions in the country, his constant quarrels with the city of Cologne, his lamentable financial state and the related disputes with the estates all prevented him from pursuing his ambitions further. When Diedrich died virtually penniless on February 13, 1463, the city of Cologne had to grant a loan to give him a decent burial. The once mighty complex of states that *Kurköln* and the house of Moers had intended to acquire had dwindled to a roughly sixty-mile long and fifteen-mile wide strip of land along the Rhine. Still called *Kurköln*, it was a mere political ball in the hands of the surrounding powers.

The estates in *Kurköln*

Diedrich's actions had spawned the development he feared most: the estates gained a greater voice in government, particularly in financial matters.

The estates in *Kurköln* consisted of four groups: the cathedral chapter, the nobility, the knights and the cities. The first group, the cathedral chapter, represented the clergy. It predominated by virtue of its 1297 right to be the only official body allowed to elect the Archbishop. It also laid down the conditions under which the Archbishop exercised his ecclesiastical and secular powers. Moreover, the cathedral chapter ruled the country when the Archbishop's chair was vacant. As early as 1344, Archbishop Walram of Jülich promised not to sell or encumber any parts of the country and not to start any major wars without the consent of the chapter. The Archbishop was also obliged to include several chapter members in his Council. In return, the chapter guaranteed his large debts. Although later Archbishops did not always keep their word, these arrangements prepared the way for the later restriction on the Archbishop's freedom to rule as he pleased, in particular as manifested during Diedrich of Moers' period of rule. Diedrich's autocratic demeanor incited his subjects to opposition, and led them to organize themselves into estates.

The second group, usually small in number, consisted of the nobility. They were usually counts, having the powers of high justice over territory they owned in *Kurköln*. The counts, unlike the knights, also exercised independent territorial rule elsewhere. The counts were actually not the Archbishop of Cologne's subjects, and sometimes their interests even conflicted with those of *Kurköln*. Yet owing to their possessions in *Kurköln*, they were represented as an estate.

The next group, that of the knights, was the most numerous. As a rule, the knights only held the powers of low justice. In earlier times, knights were bound to the Archbishop as vassals. Now many were his functionaries. Some knights succeeded in climbing the social ladder and acquiring property – an indisputable sign of power and prosperity in those days – thus becoming gentry.

The fourth group was the cities. This group, very influential in other territories, was extremely weak in *Kurköln*. In Flanders, for instance, cities like Ghent, Bruges and Ypres had a powerful voice in matters, while in Brabant the cities of

Fragment (stained glass) of a deacon in Cologne around 1430.

Brussels, Antwerp, Louvain and 's-Hertogenbosch were also dominant, though to a lesser extent.

Initially, the composition of the estates in *Kurköln* was subject to constant alteration, but they ultimately came to be comprised of four prelates from the cathedral chapter, eleven members of the nobility, two hundred and twenty-seven knights and seventeen cities. In terms of size, it was the largest gathering of its kind.

Diedrich of Moers finds it increasingly difficult to obtain the approval of the estates for his taxes

The estates began to tighten their grip on *Kurköln*'s government during Diedrich of Moers' long period of rule. It was the cities, perhaps inspired by Cologne's example, which initiated and organized the opposition to the Archbishop. As we have already seen, Cologne had become virtually independent of the Archbishops after the Battle of Worringen. From time to time the Archbishops attempted to disturb the balance of power in Cologne in order to regain lost ground. Diedrich of Moers was no exception. Once he had shaken off his foes, Diedrich began in 1417 to get his hooks into Cologne. Taxation was the focal point of their disputes. The first bone of contention was the *Judenregal*, a tax the Jewish community in Cologne had to pay the Archbishop in return for his protection. Diedrich's opening move was to demand 25,000 marks from the city's Jews to cover his expenses. If they refused to pay, Diedrich would deprive the Jewish community of several of its privileges. This demand contravened the agreement the city had entered into with the previous Archbishop, in which both parties ensured the Jews that their lives and property were to be protected and their privileges left intact until 1424. In return, each Jew was to pay 70 marks annually to the Archbishop. In addition, they paid the city a head tax, more or less scaled to individual economic means. Several other payments were also levied in exceptional cases. The city presumably stood behind the Jews because it believed itself to be best equipped to tap their resources, caring little if this meant exploitation and extortion. Cologne felt little sympathy for the Jews: when the period of protection had lapsed in 1424, the city did not hesitate to drive the entire Jewish community out of Cologne and into neighboring Deutz. In fact, Jews were forbidden to live in the city of Cologne until 1798!

In addition to the conflict over the *Judenregal*, a struggle was also waged over the wine tax that the city wanted to introduce. The Archbishop felt that Cologne should request permission to impose the tax. After the customary arguments, both sides submitted to arbitration by the Archbishop of Trier. As a result, the Jews were obliged to pay the requested 25,000 marks, but their rights (sic!) were to remain intact. The city was allowed to impose a tax on wine, but the buying and selling of wine was to be exempt from taxes four weeks a year, around the feast of St. Martin (November 10th). This suggests that Diedrich did not make an issue of his dispute with Cologne, probably because he needed its financial assistance to realize his ambitious plans.

In 1435, the Archbishop was engaged in a struggle with the city of Neuss. This time, the conflict involved both taxation and the question of who was to have the powers of high justice in the city. The dispute began, as usual, over the imposition of taxes. Diedrich imposed a supposedly non-recurring general tax for the first time in 1435. A contemporary chronicler reports on this as follows: "In that same year, the Archbishop of Cologne compelled his entire people, clergy and laity, Christians and Jews and all his cities, barring no one, rich as well as poor, to pay a barbarously high tax, taking more from the people than they possessed." The chronicle also describes how Diedrich was able to impose the tax: "In that same year, the Bishop of Cologne secretly recorded the members of all the households...." It appears that the names of the people living in every city, village and hamlet were recorded, along with the number of personnel, cows, horses, pigs, sheep, household goods, etc., each resident possessed. The clergy and the Jews were registered separately. Salaries and annuities were noted, and in addition, every person had to state his means of support. This implies that registers were being compiled for the specific purpose of imposing income taxes, property taxes, capital-gains taxes and head taxes; these notes (probably of doubtful accuracy) have been lost, but similar registers of certain districts dating from 1449 have been preserved.

Because the cathedral chapter and the knights, being possessors of the powers of low justice, were exempt from paying taxes, the tax of 1435 was not really a

Sixteenth century Torah scroll from the Jewish community in Deutz. In the Middle Ages, the Church and the state had a special legal relationship with the Jews. As they did not share the Christian faith and were also not viewed as fellow citizens, the Jews were considered legally incompetent. The Emperor and the sovereign rulers granted them special protection and privileges to safeguard their lives and property and granted them special permission to engage in trade. The Jews were obliged to make steep payments in return for these concessions. Even higher payments were frequently extorted from them under the threat of a withdrawal of their privileges. Initially, the "Judenregal" was a royal privilege since the Jews were obliged to pay a so-called coronation tax when a new king was crowned. Diedrich of Moers' relationship to the Jewish community was wholly determined by fiscal considerations. The Jews in the Rhineland were mainly money changers and merchants. In 1349, Cologne's municipal government accused them of causing the Black Death and drove them out of the city. They were allowed back in Cologne in 1372, where they agreed to pay an annual sum of money to the Archbishop.

ויהי בימי אחשורוש הוא אחשורוש המלך מהדו ועד כוש שבע
ועשרים ומאה מדינה בימים ההם כשבת המלך אחשורוש על כסא
מלכותו אשר בשושן הבירה בשנת שלש למלכו עשה משתה לכל
שריו ועבדיו חיל פרס ומדי הפרתמים ושרי המדינות לפניו בהראתו
את עשר כבוד מלכותו ואת יקר תפארת גדולתו ימים רבים שמנים
ומאת יום ובמלואת הימים האלה עשה המלך לכל העם הנמצאים
בשושן הבירה למגדול ועד קטן משתה שבעת ימים בחצר גנת
ביתן המלך חור כרפס ותכלת אחוז בחבלי בוץ וארגמן על גלילי
כסף ועמודי שש מטות זהב וכסף על רצפת בהט ושש ודר וסחרת
השקות בכלי זהב וכלים מכלים שונים ויין מלכות רב כיד המלך
והשתיה כדת אין אנס כי יסד המלך על כל רב ביתו לעשות כרצון
איש ואיש גם ושתי המלכה עשתה משתה נשים בית המלכות
אשר למלך אחשורוש ביום השביעי כטוב לב המלך ביין אמר
למהומן בזתא חרבונא בגתא ואבגתא זתר וכרכס שבעת הסריסים
המשרתים את פני המלך אחשורוש להביא את ושתי המלכה לפני
המלך בכתר מלכות להראות העמים והשרים את יפיה כי טובת
מראה היא ותמאן המלכה ושתי לבוא בדבר המלך אשר ביד
הסריסים ויקצף המלך מאד וחמתו בערה בו ויאמר המלך
לחכמים ידעי העתים כי כן דבר המלך לפני כל ידעי דת ודין
והקרב אליו כרשנא שתר אדמתא תרשיש מרס מרסנא ממוכן

Starting in 1384, this contract was valid for a renewable ten-year period. Only a few years after renewing the contract, Diedrich of Moers requested an additional 25,000 marks. In 1424, the "Judenregal" was again a bone of contention between Cologne and the Archbishop. However, the city could not be forced to allow the Jews to stay within the city walls, and it drove them out en masse to Deutz, Siegburg and Mülheim. They only returned to Cologne in 1798, after the Rhineland was occupied by French Revolutionary Army troops!

general tax. Although we have no further information about the nature of this tax, the cities and regions were undoubtedly assessed a specific amount that was to be apportioned over their residents. The city of Neuss rebelled against the tax. Had not Archbishop Engelbrecht of Berg determined the city's contribution to the Archbishop's treasury two centuries ago (in 1222), stipulating that the city would never have to pay a higher tax, even in times of emergency? The conflict was exacerbated when the knight Johan of Kriekenbeke rampaged through *Kurköln* without having declared war. Diedrich had him captured and imprisoned in the city of Neuss. An argument then ensued over whether the city or the Archbishop was entitled to try him. The city closed its gates, sounded the tocsin to summon all its citizens to its aid and, threatening the Archbishop with his life, forced him to release the prisoner. The city then locked Johan up again, but set him free a few days later.

Of course Diedrich did not accept this turn of events calmly. The city was summoned to appear in court and threatened with severe punishment. Neuss then requested the intercession of the cathedral chapter, the nobility, the knights and the other cities. As a result of their mediation, Neuss was to recognize the inviolable rights and supremacy of the Archbishop, in all respects. But the municipality was let off with a fine of 10,000 marks, which it was allowed to raise by means of an excise tax.

What Cologne had achieved one hundred and fifty years earlier and Soest was to receive a decade later was not destined for Neuss. However, legally speaking, a novel event had taken place: the four estates, which could evidently already be distinguished as four individual interest groups and had organized themselves as such, had cooperated during the arbitration. Their words had apparently carried sufficient weight for the Archbishop to be forced to listen (although their financial clout was undoubtedly a factor). The Archbishop ultimately maintained the upper hand, probably because without Neuss the cities were a weak opponent and the knights and the cathedral chapter enjoyed tax exemption. Still, it would not be long before these groups would also be caught in the tax collector's net. Diedrich, with the consent of Pope Eugenius, had already included the clergy in a special tax euphemistically referred to as the *subsidia charitativa*. It was highly unusual for a Pope to grant permission for taxation of the clergy. In this case, however, it was understandable, because Diedrich had, in addition to his other military commitments, helped the Pope wage war against the Hussites, followers of the heretical Czech John Hus, who was burned at the stake in 1415. This additional war effort had made his substantial debts soar. The "charitable grant" was intended to help him cover his debts. From then on, the clergy were obliged to pay taxes on their income. The fact that Diedrich also imposed these taxes on the clergy in neighboring territories that belonged to his diocese was one of the causes of his conflict with Cleves, as has already been described above.

The extra tax on *Kurköln* in 1435 was apparently lucrative, for two years later Diedrich imposed a similar tax on the Duchy of Westphalia, which brought him into conflict with the powerful Hanse city of Soest. This dispute was identical to that with Neuss: behind the tax issue lay the question of who would ultimately gain power in the city. It was of paramount importance to Diedrich that Soest cooperate with this Westphalian tax. He had already tried to placate the city in many ways: he had transferred the seat of the Archbishop's official[6] to Soest and had granted his permission for an excise tax on imported goods. He had also

6. An "official" was the chairman of an ecclesiastical court.

Heads of some men in Cologne around 1460 (stained glass).

promised the city in 1437 one third of the tax which he wanted to impose in Westphalia. However, when the citizens stood their ground, Diedrich decided to resort to force. He soon found a pretext to take up arms against the city when it refused to hand over a notorious criminal for trial. Diedrich marched on the city with an army of knights and vassals, but soon softened his approach and agreed to let the Westphalian knights and cities mediate their dispute. The resulting peace was short-lived for, as we saw, a few years later Soest sided with Cleves and thus ultimately obtained its independence. The city's defection undoubtedly accounts for the exorbitant fine of 150,000 marks that the Archbishop subsequently demanded. However, the city never paid the fine.

In 1435, the four estates in *Kurköln* had not yet joined forces to address the Archbishop as a single body with a common cause. In 1449, the nobility and the knights consented to an extra, one-time tax to pay for the Archbishop's protection and to relieve the debt burden. This was the first real general tax in *Kurköln*, because it was paid not only by the cities, but also by freeholders and subjects on the lower manors. The clergy paid the *subsidium charitativum*. This is therefore the first tax arranged with the cooperation, if not the consent, of the estates. Four years later, another one-time tax was ordered. Again, this was ostensibly a one-time − voluntary − tax. But the writing was on the wall, and it would not be long before the regularly recurring requests for an additional tax developed into an annual − compulsory − tax. In 1455, Diedrich tried to persuade the Pope to include the clergy in an additional tax, even though a few years earlier he had solemnly promised the cathedral chapter not to address any such requests to the Pope without its consent.

These frequently repeated requests for financial assistance intensified the opposition of the four estates to the Archbishop. However, it would be a misconception to assume that the four estates did not agree with Diedrich's foreign policies. Their main grievance was that they felt they were entitled to take part in deciding the nature, amount and allocation of the taxes. In 1463, the opposition had taken such a definite form that six weeks after Diedrich's death on February 14th, it reached an agreement known as the *Erblandesvereinigung*. The preamble stated that in carrying out his wars and feuds, the Archbishop "had acted without the knowledge and consent of the Chapters, Nobles, Knights and Cities in the Archbishopric." Its wording clearly refers to Diedrich's absolutist form of government. The demands put forward by the national estates during the discussions with the cathedral chapter show that they were primarily concerned with curbing the Archbishop's fiscal authority. What they wanted was greater influence on the imposition of taxes and the spending of tax revenues. However, the definitive text of the *Erblandesvereinigung* does not contain many of their proposed regulations (such as what to do if problems arose during tax collection), probably because they were too detailed.

The leitmotif of the *Erblandesvereinigung* was that the estates owed allegiance to the lord of the land who, in turn, was to allow them their rights. The document contains a detailed description of what the sovereign ruler could and could not do in certain cases. For instance, he could not start a war without the country's knowledge and consent and could not take out loans or incur debts. Failure to abide by these agreements could result in revocation of allegiance, a clause also included in the *Magna Carta*. The agreement also applied to future Archbishops. In addition, the Archbishop was responsible for a fair and objective administration of justice and the appointment of a permanent council to manage day-to-day affairs. Besides this council, the estates were mainly interested in having a voice in the imposition and allocation of taxes. The document contains explicit provisions to this effect. The taxes approved by the estates were to be administered by a separate body, which was to be accountable only to the estates. Further, it was agreed that half of the tax revenues raised by the country, including the clergy's *subsidia charitativa*, was to go to the cathedral chapter for discharging the Archbishop's debts. As we have seen, Diedrich had operated year after year with − to borrow a modern term − huge budget deficits.

The regulations governing the election of the new Archbishop declared that he and his successors had to swear to uphold the *Erblandesvereinigung*. That same year, when the Duchy of Westphalia entered into an *Erblandesvereinigung* with the estates, the newly elected Archbishop, Ruprecht of the Palatinate, was even one of the negotiating partners. Six years later, the estates pressured him into accepting another, more elaborate, version of the *Erblandesvereinigung*, in which the section on finances, in particular, was worked out in more detail.

The *Erblandesvereinigung*, which was later improved and expanded several times, functioned as a kind of constitution for *Kurköln* and Westphalia until the end of the eighteenth century. Similar documents, namely the "Joyous Entry" of 1356 in the Duchy of Brabant, the *Landbrief* of 1375 in the Diocese of Utrecht and the *Ordonnantie* of 1448 for the Duchy of Gelre, had a comparable function.

All of these documents were inspired by the *Magna Carta*. This suggests that *Kurköln* was a latecomer rather than a front-runner. Only at the end of the seventeenth century, after a papal ban had forbidden the cathedral chapter to determine the conditions for electing a new archbishop, was the Archbishop able to expand his authority in this age of absolutism. However, the estates reserved the right to decide on their own financial matters, thus preventing the Archbishop from turning his power into absolute supremacy. It can therefore rightfully be said that taxation helped make Cologne free and that thanks to the struggles over taxation, Cologne's citizens obtained a voice in governmental affairs, and the Archbishop's power was curbed in *Kurköln* and Westphalia.

A 1770 print depicting the signing of the Union of Utrecht (1579). The Union's articles served as a kind of constitution for the Dutch Republic until 1795.

3 Utrecht

The Netherlands on the threshold of the revolt against Spain

The impetuosity with which Charles the Bold, as Duke of Burgundy and sovereign ruler of a great number of provinces in the Low Countries, attempted to subject even more cities and states to his rule and thus re-create the Lotharingian Middle Kingdom between France and the German Empire was inversely proportional to the ultimate success of his endeavor. He met his end at the Battle of Nancy, fighting against a handful of Swiss peasants prepared to stake their lives on their freedom. His body, stripped of valuables and clothes after the battle, was recovered on January 5, 1477, and could only be identified from old scars. The motley collection of duchies and counties he had built up, a jagged patchwork stretching roughly from Dijon to the North Sea coast, was robbed of its French possessions, i.e. Burgundy and Franche-Comté, by the French King Louis XI. All that remained were a dozen provinces in the Low Countries, the most important being the Duchy of Brabant and the Counties of Flanders and Holland.

Although these provinces were only united in the person of their ruler, the Burgundian princes had attempted to achieve more structure and unity in their various lands by centralizing certain governmental institutions. Consequently, under Philip the Good, Charles the Bold's father, the very first assembly of representatives from the individual provinces was held in Bruges on April 29, 1464. As this was a gathering of the Provincial Councils known as "States," the assembly was henceforth called the "States-General."

Charles the Bold also introduced several centralizing reforms, particularly in the area of finance. Taxes had skyrocketed during his administration, in order to provide the warmongering prince with sufficient funds to pay his mercenary armies and enable him to purchase those lands he was either unable or unwilling to subdue by force of arms. After his death, his twenty year old daughter, Mary of Burgundy, confronted with a rebellious people made destitute by oppressive taxation, was obliged to grant the States in most of the provinces a charter known as the "Great Privilege." This document not only outlined, in keeping with practical developments, what influence the States were to have in the various provinces, but even extended their influence, allowing them to assemble on their own initiative, both separately as provinces and collectively as the States-General. In addition, they were to be consulted on important matters, and wars could no longer be waged without their consent. An important proviso outlining the subjects' rights was adopted from a charter in Brabant known as the "Joyous Entry". Ever since 1356, the Dukes of Brabant had sworn on this charter when invested as sovereign rulers. This proviso, taken from the *Magna Carta* and included in the "Great Privilege," stated that if any ruler violated the liberties of his subjects, they were relieved of their obligations toward him. That this was not just an empty promise was to become clear less than a century later, at the onset of the revolt against King Philip II, ruler of Spain and the Low Countries.

The agreements Mary of Burgundy had been obliged to make with the individual States meant the abolition of most of the centralized institutions established by her father and grandfather. The historical pendulum has often swung to and fro between centralization and decentralization. A breakdown in power centered around a common sovereign ruler was often followed by a buildup of power as soon as opportunity presented itself. This tendency toward centralization can also be observed under Mary's successors: her husband Maximilian of Austria, her son Philip the Handsome and her grandson Charles V. In 1531, this led to the formation of three advisory councils, namely the Council of State, the Privy Council and the Council of Finance.

The most prominent of these three Councils, known collectively as the "Collateral Councils," was the Council of State, consisting of a variable number of members (normally twelve), who were for the most part high nobility. They advised on the most important matters of state, particularly those involving domestic and foreign affairs and national defense. The importance of the Council of State is evidenced by the fact that it ruled the country in the temporary absence of its Governor, Mary of Hungary, in 1547 and 1548.

The legally-schooled Councilors were seated in the Privy Council, which dealt with the issues of legislation and the maintenance of public order. The Council of Finance, the umbrella organ of the Provincial Accounting Offices, managed the crown lands, supervised the system of taxation as well as the many financial institutions and advised on all large monetary transactions.

The process of unification was reinforced by a decree handed down by the Imperial Diet held in Augsburg in 1548, taking the seventeen Dutch provinces from imperial jurisdiction and placing them in a new jurisdictional unit called the Burgundian *Kreits*. This virtually put the seal on the autonomy of these provinces, although they were, formally speaking, still part of the Holy Roman Empire. A few decades previously, Charles V had already cut the feudal ties between France and several of the provinces, such as Flanders, Artois and Walloon Flanders, compelling France to abandon any national claims. The unity of the Burgundian holdings was strengthened following the Pragmatic Sanction of November 5, 1549, which provided for identical succession in all Dutch provinces and naturally linked them closely to the Spanish-Hapsburg monarchy.

Since the 1530's, there had been a move toward uniformity in many fields, for example in the area of criminal law and judicial procedures. This process went hand in hand with a movement toward political unification. Privileges, both local and otherwise, were systematically examined. Time-honored customs that met with approval were finally set down in writing, and various administrative controls were promulgated. The Board of Aldermen also changed in composition. As a result of centralization, the monarchy became more important. The councilors and royal governmental officials, who resided in Brussels, increased in number and in influence. By the time Emperor Charles V, ruler of the Dutch provinces, abdicated his throne in favor of his son, Philip II, "Brussels" had become an indispensable power faction in its own right in the Low Countries. However, by modern standards this court was by no means large. According to reliable estimates, there could have been no more than a couple of hundred officials in Brussels at that time. Although what we would call a "national consciousness" had hardly germinated, Netherlanders abroad usually considered

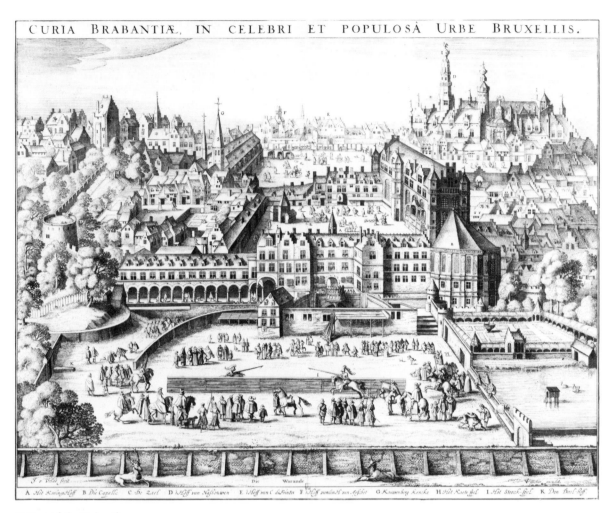

CURIA BRABANTIÆ, IN CELEBRI ET POPULOSÀ URBE BRUXELLIS.

Picture of the Duke of Brabant's palace and surrounding buildings on the Koudenberg in Brussels, which in the 16th century was the residence of the sovereign ruler or his governor as well as the seat of the government.

the provinces en bloc as their fatherland. But once they were home again, they thought in terms of their own province (say Brabant or Holland), or even in smaller units like their own city or village. The inhabitants of the patrimonial provinces, which had been under the same sovereign ruler for many decades, did not have a highly developed sense of unity. Understandably, this was even less developed in the non-patrimonial provinces which Charles V had acquired: Friesland, Utrecht, Overijssel/Drenthe, Gelre and Groningen (including the surrounding area known as the "Ommelanden").

When the ruler needed money, he requested the States-General to grant him an annual sum for a certain period of time, say six years, which was then apportioned over the provinces according to an existing formula. One advantage of this system of apportionment was that it prevented internecine quarrels over how the fixed ratio was to be determined. A disadvantage, one which became more obvious as time went on, was that it either failed to take economic fluctuations into account, or only noted them at a much later date, and then only imperfectly.

Cities that contributed less than their fair share under the traditional formula fought any proposals for change tooth and nail, making modifications to the fixed ratio a long-drawn-out affair. Even so, the ratio was revised several times, usually after repeated complaints had led to an investigation into the ability of the residents in a certain area to pay. Such inquiries were conducted in the province of Holland in 1494 and 1514 and in Flanders in 1517.

Apart from these centralized institutions, the Low Countries also had certain provincial institutions in common. The use of such terms as "provincial" and "central" are indicative of the embryonic unified state which the monarchs of the House of Burgundy and later the House of Hapsburg had so tenaciously set their sights on. Step by step, this ideal of unification came closer to realization, in spite of the opposition of local rulers who watched balefully as their say in matters was increasingly curtailed. When Charles V abdicated in 1555, the unified state had already begun to assume a vague shape. Nevertheless, the individual provinces and their representatives, the States, retained a great deal of autonomy, and their privileges and liberties greatly restricted the prince's power. When the States met, each of the seventeen provinces conducted its own individual dialogue with the sovereign ruler. Even so, the Burgundian rulers sought to maintain an equilibrium between the three estates:[1] the clergy, the nobility and the bourgeoisie. The estates were the most evenly balanced in Brabant, where the States were comprised of the abbots of the largest abbeys (such as Affligem, Averbode, Postel and Tongerlo), the representatives of the nobility and the representatives of Brabant's four main metropolises: Brussels, Antwerp, Louvain and 's-Hertogenbosch.

By contrast, the States in Flanders had little clout. Here, the role of the nobility, clergy and small cities had degenerated into a purely advisory capacity. In Flanders, the four orders[2] were comprised of the Aldermen in the three largest cities, Ghent, Bruges and Ypres, together with the representatives of the rural area between Bruges and the River Scheldt, known as the Bruges *Vrije*. As these four orders constituted the actual representation in this province, the States were obliged to assume a formal role on occasions like the investiture of a new ruler. The nobility could only give voice to its wishes and grievances through its representation in the Bruges *Vrije*.

In the province of Holland, where the clergy was not represented and the nobility only sparsely, the representatives of the cities of Dordrecht, Haarlem, Delft, Leiden, Amsterdam and Gouda predominated. Dordrecht also spoke on behalf of the southern part of the province, while the knights were assumed to represent the smaller cities and the northern part of the province.

Making decisions within the States was a laborious process. Brabant is a good example. As we saw above, the States typically consisted of three estates: the clergy, the nobility and the cities. However, the cities themselves were sometimes subdivided into three or even four orders. Brussels, for example, had three orders: the magistrates, the Large Council (the former magistrates plus the masters of the drapers' guild) and the so-called "nations" (the masters of the crafts guilds). Similarly, Antwerp and 's-Hertogenbosch had three orders, namely the magistrates, the Board (the former Aldermen) and the guilds. Louvain had four orders: the magistrates, the Families (the patricians), the masters of the drapers' guild and the guilds themselves. When the sovereign ruler brought a proposal before the States of Brabant, the municipal representatives first had to consult their own rank and file. A proposal could only be accepted by the States of Brabant after unanimity had first been reached within each of the four main cities, then among the four cities themselves, and finally together with the clergy

1. Do not confuse "estates" and "States." The estates were composed of certain groups from the general population, while the States were provincial representatives recruited from the estates; the method of recruitment varied from province to province.
2. Orders are sub-divisions of what was typically the third estate, the cities.

and nobility. The principle of unanimity provided municipal governments, in particular, with a great deal of power. But it was an unwieldy instrument, leading to interminable negotiations and an extremely slow-moving decision-making process. To break through this paralyzing principle of unanimity, at least to some extent, the sovereign ruler was able to "replace" the minority that rejected the proposal, which in effect meant having the de facto majority of votes decide the issue. However, this replacement, also known as "outvoting," was an exceptional method, theoretically applied only in emergency situations. Matters had to reach a pretty pass in Brabant before the principle of replacement was invoked. The central government only took this bold step when endless negotiations had reached absolute deadlock or when social unrest threatened. The order in the cities which represented the craftsmen and the small businessmen, who usually had to contribute the greatest financial share, could and regularly did hold up the decision-making process, which enabled the voice of the tradespeople to be heard at the highest political level. The fourth estate, the unskilled urban laborers, the farm laborers and the great mass of people who lived from hand to mouth and were lucky to have any work at all, could only express their political wishes through direct action: strikes, riots and rebellion.

It was the States who decided whether a tax known as an "aid" was to be granted and how the money to pay the aid was to be raised. In the course of the sixteenth century, some provinces gained considerable power, while the States obtained some say over the management and expenditure of the aid revenues. The States were also allowed to meet without being convened by the sovereign ruler. When they met, they discussed many subjects besides aids, appointing an official to act as secretary and spokesman.

The provinces acquired later by Charles V, i.e. Friesland, Utrecht, Overijssel/Drenthe, Gelre and Groningen/the Ommelanden, remained outside the system of apportionment. These non-patrimonial provinces paid their contributions separately and, as a rule, did not take part in the States-General. After its incorporation in 1521, Tournai was treated for many years as a part of Flanders and even sent delegates to the States-General; as a result, it soon found itself embroiled in the issue of apportionment.

It was up to the sovereign ruler to persuade the province that the aid revenues served the province's own interests and that they were being spent on defensive wars. What the provinces feared most was that the sovereign would squander their hard-earned money and fight wars that did not serve their interests. This was by no means a figment of their imagination under the Burgundians, particularly the warmongering Charles the Bold. When The Netherlands was incorporated into the Hapsburg Empire, the danger was even more real.

Charles V waged wars ceaselessly throughout most of his reign. His grandest project was the conflict with the Turks. But closer to home, he would, at the slightest provocation, take up arms against the French in Italy. In Germany, he was continually at odds with the rebellious Lutheran princes and was instrumental in quelling the Peasant's Revolt in 1525 and the earlier revolt of the *Comuneros* in Spain. The situation improved little under Philip II. The struggle against the French on the southern borders was a war of defense, but it still was not easy to pry the necessary funds loose from the States. The States were even less willing to finance the offensive wars in Italy (which lasted until 1559) or the fights against the Turks for the hegemony of the Mediterranean, which were of no concern to the residents of the Low Countries; they were constantly on the alert to ensure that the Spanish king did not use Dutch tax revenues for these wars. Ironically, exactly the reverse was to occur later, when Spain had to send huge shipments of money to the Low Countries to make up the incessant financial deficits in the Dutch provinces. The tax strategy of the Duke of Alva, the Spanish Governor in The Netherlands from 1567 to 1573, which is the major theme of this chapter, was aimed at having The Netherlands pay its own way. This strategy was in line with the prevailing Dutch and Spanish view that tax revenues were only to be spent on wars in defense of one's own country. But in a world power such as Spain was then, it was hard to distinguish between a defensive and an offensive war.

In the Burgundian-Hapsburg period, the seventeen Dutch provinces developed rapidly into one of the most prosperous and most densely populated areas in Europe. This prosperity was based on trade and navigation, fishing and various branches of industry. The indisputable affluence of the Dutch, which was also clearly perceptible to foreigners, did not prevent them from suffering the consequences of the general inflation which raged in the sixteenth century. Salaries lagged behind prices, and the real income of wage earners, self-employed artisans and small tradesmen dropped. However, the vigorous expansion of trade and industry in The Netherlands served to cushion the blow somewhat. In the sixteenth century, the rapidly growing trading metropolis of Antwerp suffered the least, and presumably the Northern Netherlands fared better than the Southern Netherlands, and the countryside better than the cities.

The majority of the population earned its living from agriculture, animal husbandry and fishing, although trade and industry were the major sources of affluence in the Dutch provinces. Industry produced a rich variety of products. In many branches of industry, there was a fairly advanced division of labor, which usually went hand in hand with an elementary form of capitalist production methods. The highly important textile industry pioneered the way. The shipbuilding industry followed suit, as did a host of other industries such as brickmaking, peat-cutting, metallurgy, coal, brewing and printing. Nevertheless, these forward-looking industries were outnumbered by the myriads of guild members, who performed their crafts primarily for the local market. The most important of these were the carpenters, cabinetmakers, coopers, tanners, smiths, tailors and cobblers.

Trade and navigation, which were initially even more important than industry, also made a major contribution to the prosperity of The Netherlands. As trade was largely conducted by water, the merchant was also often the shipowner or the owner of a share in a ship. This merchant/skipper combination, mainly encountered in the provinces of Holland and Zealand, served as the basis for the burgeoning commerce of the seventeenth century. The risk-hedging practice of taking shares in ships is a typical feature of capitalism. The size of the shares ranged from substantial half-shares down to sixty-forth shares or even smaller interests. In the bustling port of Amsterdam alone, hundreds of ships arrived annually from the Baltic laden with grain. The bulk of this grain was then shipped to France and England and later on to Spain and Portugal. Amsterdam not only acted as Western Europe's granary, but also served as its storehouse for such products as lumber, beer and salt.

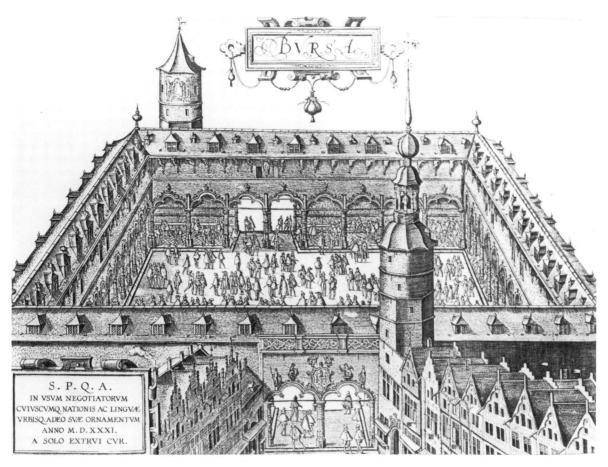

S. P. Q. A.
IN VSVM NEGOTIATORVM
CVIVSCVMQ. NATIONIS AC LINGVÆ
VRBISQ. ADEO SVÆ ORNAMENTVM
ANNO M. D. XXXI.
A SOLO EXTRVI CVR.

*Antwerp's exchange
(engraved by Pieter van der
Borcht, 1581).*

The Southern Netherlands steered a very different course. After the Zwin River had silted up, Bruges had lost its position as an international trading center to Antwerp, which soon grew into the main transfer point for Portuguese spices and produce from colonies in Africa, India and Brazil. Around this time, Antwerp's trade became more important than its shipping. Its annual trade fair was put on a permanent basis, and the city became a busy intersection of international trade. Antwerp's exchange of goods was centered on French wine, English cloth, Italian silk, woolens, oil, American silver, Mediterranean fruits and a whole host of luxury items. Merchants from Cologne arrived with Rhenish wine and linen and departed with English cloth; the Southern Germans traded fustian fibers,[3] copper and spices (transported over the Alps from Italy) for the greatly coveted English cloth. Frequently, these goods were not actually transported through Antwerp, but were only traded on paper. Naturally, important international merchants needed to keep their finger on the financial pulse. Many foreign merchants therefore established themselves in Antwerp, turning the city − by far the largest in the Low Countries and one of the largest in Europe − into a cosmopolitan center with an international allure.

The economic expansion in The Netherlands which began during the Middle Ages and continued into the 1560's clearly exhibited proto-capitalist features. The growth in the textile and metal industries, based on new production techniques, created a large urban proletariat. In some cities, such as Bruges, Dordrecht and Middelburg, the laborers in these industries outnumbered those in trade. In spite of an increase in rural affluence as a result of more intensive

3.   Fustian is a fabric having a linen warp and a cotton woof.

agricultural methods, agrarian society was not flexible enough to provide the booming population with work and a living wage. Economic necessity drove many rural residents to the city, swelling the urban population. Around 1550, about 34% of the population of Brabant lived in cities, while in Holland this was as high as 46% in 1514. For The Netherlands as a whole, this figure was about 30% around the middle of the sixteenth century. This percentage is quite staggering compared to France, where less than 10% of the population were city-dwellers. The largest city by far at this time was Antwerp, with a population of 90,000 in 1566; Brussels had around 50,000 inhabitants, Ghent 30,000, Bruges and Amsterdam 25,000 each, while Louvain and 's-Hertogenbosch had 20,000 inhabitants. Cities such as Leiden, Haarlem and Dordrecht trailed behind with about 10,000 – 15,000 residents.

The need for tax reform

As the sixteenth century drew to a close, the Dutch provinces began to realize that the tax system, which dated back to the Middle Ages, had outlived its usefulness. Exemptions for the nobility and the clergy had long ago become meaningless. While the rigid system of apportionment probably worked well enough in an economy based on agriculture and small-scale industry, it was no longer appropriate in the trade-driven economy of the sixteenth century. As time progressed, new economic relationships emerged: wholesale trade expanded enormously, a rudimentary form of capitalist industry began to take shape and capital was being invested in various kinds of public finance schemes. The loans made to princes and cities by various banking dynasties are an example. But this new-found prosperity was largely untouched by wealth taxes, as these were generally imposed only on real estate. Indeed, if anyone suffered from taxation, it was the poor, who were disproportionately burdened by the aids, all the more so since the high imposts[4] levied to raise money for the aids were imposed on the basic necessities of life. Equally unjust, the politically and economically dominant cities frequently succeeded in making the less affluent countryside cough up a comparatively larger share of the tax bill. But the central government in Brussels had a political rather than a humanitarian reason to implement tax reform. The individual provinces had to negotiate their share of the aid and were free to determine how to raise their share. A common means of taxation, equally binding on each of the provinces, would not only have broken down the inflexible and unjust system of apportionment, but would also, once it had been firmly established, have made it easier to obtain revenues for the treasury. Emperor Charles V, who was constantly on the warpath, needed the money badly; in all likelihood, his continual lack of funds was actually responsible for the tax reforms. If so, it was neither the first nor the last time that new forms of taxation sprang from the treasury's needs.

The States of each of the provinces as well as the national government set to work on improving the fiscal system. The former, reluctant to pay more money to the central government, felt it was time the nobility and clergy also paid their share. Consequently, the States launched a campaign against the exemptions granted to the second estate, and within a short time their efforts bore fruit. This was equitable, since the privileges of the nobility were basically remnants of a bygone era. With the arrival of mercenary armies, the nobility had lost its traditional role as defenders of the county. Similarly, the clergy had seen its own organization swallowed up in a larger political entity and its charitable and educational tasks

4. Nowadays we would call these "excise taxes."

slowly taken over by local governments. To compound this process, bourgeois lawyers were increasingly replacing the nobility and clergy at the top of the bureaucratic hierarchy and even occupying government posts.

The government attempted in 1542 and in 1556 to implement a more fundamental tax reform, but failed on both occasions. The second attempt, in particular, initiated by Philip II a year after Charles V had abdicated, met with dogged opposition from the provincial States.

As the government's original tax plan and even a standard aid had encountered so much resistance, particularly in Brabant and Holland, the sovereign ruler decided to follow the road of gentle persuasion rather than Draconian enforcement. He invited the States-General to convene in Valenciennes on August 3, 1557, where he explained his financial needs and requested their advice about how to attend to these needs. It would be straying too far from our subject to report the ensuing discussions. Suffice it to say that the States-General only convened several months later. It had taken the provinces that long to provide their delegates with sufficient instructions to participate meaningfully in the debate.

The delegates made use of the occasion to air their grievances against the government and to propose policies in areas only indirectly related to taxation, such as trade problems, leasing the alum monopoly (alum was a dye fixative which was crucial to the wool industry), equipping and deploying the army and lowering the interest payments on government debts.

While the States were fairly united in their criticism of the government, they were hopelessly divided when it came to advising the government about how to extricate itself from its financial impasse. Although an aid was granted for a period of nine years – hence known as the *novennale* – no agreement was reached about a uniform tax system for all of the provinces. Flanders, Zealand and Hainaut made various proposals, but Brabant and Holland (the latter invoking the principles of free trade) blocked any attempt to establish common taxation. As a result, when the meeting broke up, the old system of apportionment was still in place, leaving each province free to raise its share of the aid as it saw fit. Though the assembly in Valenciennes bore little immediate fruit, it was an important step toward broadening the dialogue between a ruler and his subjects to include topics other than finances.

In less than twenty years, the fiscal tables had been turned. The privileges of the nobility and the clergy had been curtailed, the provincial States had a larger finger in the central government's financial pie and had, in addition, carved out their own territory with respect to taxation: the rigid and thus often inequitable system of apportionment was in retreat. Still, it remained extraordinarily difficult for the central government in Brussels to get money from the provincial States.

The events in the decade prior to the outbreak of the revolt against Spain

After Charles V's abdication in 1555, his son and heir Philip II was obliged by the war with France to stay in The Netherlands for some time. As soon as the opportunity presented itself, he departed for Spain, never to leave it again until his death in 1598.

Antoine Perrenot, Cardinal
of Granvelle (1517-1586).

Antoine Perrenot, Cardinal
of Granvelle (1517-1586).

Philip appointed his half-sister, Margaret of Parma, as Governor of The Netherlands. She was assigned three experienced counselors – Granvelle, Viglius and Berlaymont – whose loyalty to the Crown was beyond dispute. These men dominated the three advisory Councils: the Council of State, the Privy Council and the Council of Finance. Granvelle, one of the King's personal confidants, was by far the most important. The great nobles, Orange and Egmond, were also appointed to the Council of State, but their role was considerably less prominent than they had hoped and expected, which immediately created bad blood in the Council.

Their discontent was aggravated when in 1561 the King and the Pope engineered a new division of the bishoprics behind their backs. It appeared that Granvelle had not only been appointed Archbishop of Mechelen and Primate of The Netherlands, but also Cardinal. As the final touch, he was made abbot of the wealthy Abbey of Afflighem in Brabant and thus the spokesman of the first estate in Brabant, the most important of the seventeen provinces. The ecclesiastical restructuring served to consolidate the government's grip on ecclesiastical affairs and therefore also on political life, for naturally the new bishops (for the most part capable, honorable and well-educated men) supported those to whom they owed their positions. As abbots of the monasteries in their dioceses, they sometimes held a seat in the States, much to the dismay of the other members of the States.

Despite the fact that the episcopal reorganization was an improvement in religious terms, it initially caused much unrest. Many clergymen justifiably feared that they would come under close scrutiny, and several large abbeys realized that they would have to surrender important sources of income to the new dioceses. Furthermore, the path to lucrative episcopal benefices, previously trod by the nobility's younger sons, was now blocked. The great nobles were also afraid that the persecution of heretics would escalate. They agitated bitterly against Granvelle, aligning themselves with his enemies in the Spanish court, until Philip recalled him in 1564 and appointed him as ambassador to Rome. Yet thanks to his network of informers in the Low Countries, the Cardinal[5] continued to give valuable advice to Philip II about matters in the Low Countries.

As time went on, unrest spread through the country, increasing the number of complaints about the placards[6] which threatened adherents of the Reformation, whether they were Lutheran, Mennonite or Calvinist, with dire punishment. Heretics were occasionally sprung from jail, and riots broke out when they were actually burned at the stake. Heretics had last been burned at the stake in Amsterdam in 1553, and only a few had met the same fate in Friesland after 1557. Brabant agitated continually and successfully against the Inquisitors.

The Council of State sent a representative to Philip II, asking him to come to The Netherlands and pacify the general unrest in the country, the combined result of economic decline, religious tensions and the need for administrative reforms.

The King rejected the Council's request, and the Council in turn refused to cooperate any longer with the Governor, Margaret of Parma. She immediately asked the King to clarify his policies. His answer, which only arrived months later, was emphatic: the placards were to be enforced, the heretics burned at the stake and the Inquisition was to carry on with its work. Furthermore, no reforms of the Council of State were to be allowed. William of Orange managed to get this exchange of letters published in December of 1565. Having helped shape the opposition to the Spanish domination in recent years, Orange realized the propaganda value of the letters as well as the boost their publication would give to his own political aspirations.

As a result of the letters, the lower nobility rose in protest. Some, confirmed Calvinists, had met during the summer to deliberate on the situation. Feeling that the time was now ripe for action, they drew up a document known as the "Compromise," which laid down their objectives of moderating the punishments announced in the placards and suspending the Inquisition. Signed by hundreds of

5. Sixteenth century usage referred so regularly to Charles V as the "Emperor," Philip II as the "King," Elizabeth I of England as the "Queen," William of Orange as the "Prince," Alva as the "Duke," Granvelle as the "Cardinal" and Leicester as the "Earl" that these functions almost became synonymous with their own names. In keeping with this practice, this chapter employs the same designations, using initial capitals when referring to these individuals.
6. Placards were governmental edicts issued for the general information of the population. The most famous of these, drawn up by Charles V and Philip II, were heresy laws designed to suppress the Reformation.

*The nobles submitting their
Request (April 5, 1566).*

lesser nobles, Calvinists and Catholics alike, this document was offered as a ''Request'' to the Governor on April 5, 1566. Margaret of Parma found herself in an awkward position and complied with the nobles' request to send a messenger to Philip, to ask him to moderate the placards and convene the States-General. On April 27th, she secretly urged the local magistrates to proceed with caution against the heretics while awaiting the King's approval. Inevitably, Margaret's secret orders soon became known, and within a short time the persecution was halted. Nevertheless, the adherents of the Reformation were forbidden to organize mass meetings, and new repressive placards against the heretics were already being promulgated.

As a result of the uncertainty surrounding government policies, the Calvinists became over-confident. Many exiles and refugees who had fled the country returned. Open-air meetings held outside the cities attracted flocks of people who had been alienated from the Church and sought relief from their troubles in the new religion. As the tension mounted, their number grew. Long summer evenings, massive unemployment and simple human curiosity ensured that first hundreds and then thousands of people all over the country went to listen to the Calvinist preachers. Before long, they went armed to these meetings. Working rapidly, the Calvinists successfully built up their internal organization, which had been set up underground years ago, in the form of a synod with elders, deacons and consistories. Philip's answer arrived on August 12th: the Papal In-

An open-air prayer meeting.

quisition could be abolished provided the Episcopal Inquisition was functioning efficiently, and the placards could be moderated provided this did not endanger the Catholic religion or Philip's authority as King. However, the States-General was not to be convened on any account. Apart from forbidding the States-General to meet, Philip had somewhat softened his attitude. But it was too late. Two days before the King's answer arrived, the Iconoclastic Fury[7] broke out in Steenvoorde in Flanders on August 10th. Though ostensibly a purely religious revolt, this outburst of iconoclasm was also rooted in economic and social factors. Increasing unemployment resulting from the trade battle with England and the closing of the Sont had been exacerbated by the severe winter of 1564-1565 and the poor harvest of 1565. The savagely cold winter of the following year only made matters worse. Exorbitant grain prices plunged the numerous poor into abject poverty. Quite understandably, the half-frozen and starving masses became increasingly disaffected.

7. In this and subsequent outbursts of iconoclasm, the adherents of the Reformation sacked numerous Catholic churches and destroyed many statues and images.

The Iconoclastic Fury fanned out over the country, occasionally creating the impression of an organized effort. Indeed, in a number of places, the iconoclasts received a normal day's wage for their work. Significantly, a wealth of religious treasures was destroyed, but little was stolen. By September 29th, the storm had died down. Not all cities were affected, but the wave of destruction had swept through the entire country, leaving traces everywhere. The political damage to the Reformers and malcontents was even greater.

*The Iconoclastic Fury
(August/September 1566).*

Though shaken, Margaret was quick to take the counter-offensive, with the help of the great nobles who had remained loyal to her. The government soon managed to suppress the resistance, defeating a Calvinist army of insurgents and forcing cities such as Valenciennes and Tournai to surrender. Catholicism was then reinstated as the only official religion. Many were killed, and those who did not fall victim to Margaret's repressive response were forced to flee the country.

In the eyes of the Governor, the three great nobles – Orange, Egmond and Horne – had failed to give her adequate support during the riots. Their efforts had been half-hearted, and they had done even less to defuse the tension among the lesser nobles prior to the uprising. Margaret's words confirmed Philip's suspicions, and, even though they were not informed, the fate of the men was sealed. Either unaware or underestimating the gravity of their position, Egmond and Horne signed an oath of unconditional loyalty to the King and remained, unsuspecting, in The Netherlands. The more politically astute Orange fled to Germany on April 21, 1567.

Margaret's reports of the Iconoclastic Fury caused great alarm at the Spanish court. Owing to the King's illness, the Spanish Council of State was not able to convene until the end of September 1566 to decide what action to take. The Council, chaired by the King, was divided into two camps: the moderate "doves," who favored an empire with a federative structure, and the hard-line "hawks," who wanted a centralized government with Spain (i.e. Castile) at its center. The former faction, led by Ruy Gómez, felt that the King should go to The Netherlands and restore order by means of his royal authority and the gentle hand of compromise. The Duke of Alva, the leader of the latter faction, argued

*Alva's entry into Brussels
(August 22, 1567).*

that only military force could bring the unruly provinces to heel. After an extensive debate, the latter faction carried the day. Alva himself was appointed to command the army. Very probably, the volatile situation in France, where the Catholics were locked in a power struggle with the Huguenots, was partly responsible for the hard line taken by the King.

Unfortunately, by the time the celebrated General Alva arrived in the Low Countries, his services were no longer necessary, as Margaret of Parma had restored order. The Duke had departed from Asti in Italy on June 18, 1567 with an army of 10,000 men — roughly 9,000 infantry and 1,000 cavalry — which mainly consisted of Spaniards, but also included Italians and Albanians. Alva's Spanish troops were exceptionally well-trained and well-equipped, particularly when judged by the standards of the day. But between his departure from Italy in 1567 and 1572, many less disciplined German and Walloon mercenaries joined his ranks. Though this considerably increased the size of Alva's army (86,000 strong in March of 1574), it also diminished its quality.

The moment Alva's soldiers set foot on Dutch soil they acted as if they were on enemy territory and each inhabitant was a heretic. Their pride, arrogance, and rapaciousness soon struck hatred as well as fear into the hearts of the population. The soldiers vacillated between expressions of religious devotion and outbursts of cruelty. Although the Spaniards were courageous in battle and willing to endure great hardship, they were often underpaid (or not paid for months on end). This may explain, but not excuse, the virulence of their behavior. In any case, it did little to promote their cause.

DUCDALF

HEER VAN MONTIGNY   MARQUIS VAN BERGHEN

Nederlantsche Gesanten in Spanien gesonden ende aldaer omcomen.

*Session of the Council of
Troubles, known popularly
as the "Council of Blood."*

Initially, Margaret of Parma was to remain as Governor, until Philip was able
to come to The Netherlands himself. As the situation in the Low Countries showed little signs of improvement, Alva advised the King to remain in Spain for the
time being. Even before the Duke's arrival, Margaret had decided to resign from
office. She rightfully regarded the Duke's arrival with such a large military force
and such broad powers as a flagrant insult, especially since she had in the meantime restored peace and gained a tighter grip on the Dutch provinces than before
the outbreak of the riots. She apparently did not fully realize that it was her
panic-stricken letters to Philip, written the year before, that had set the entire
machinery into motion. An embittered Margaret pressed the King to accept her
resignation. When he finally acquiesced, she left The Netherlands as quickly as
she could, swearing in Alva as Governor at the last moment. Alva, who had expected to complete his mission in The Netherlands within a few months, had not
bargained for this development. However, making a virtue of necessity, he and
his handful of loyal aides, largely recruited from his army officers, soon took
the government in hand. His contempt and distrust of the Netherlanders led him
to bypass the existing bureaucratic machinery whenever he could. This policy
greatly marred the efficiency of his administration. However, he could not get
around the Dutch Councilors who had not been imprisoned, like Egmond and
Horne, or had fled, like Orange and Hoogstraten. The news that Alva was on
his way to the Low Countries and his reputation for harshness had already
caused many to flee abroad.

The beheading of Egmond and Horne in Market Square in Brussels (June 5, 1568).

On September 9, 1567, five days after his arrival in The Netherlands, Alva created a special tribunal called the "Council of Troubles." This "Council of Blood," as the court soon came to be called by the populace, sentenced more than ten thousand people, according to reliable estimates. Because of the abundance of cases, dozens were tried simultaneously. Nine thousand of these were condemned *in absentia* and their property and goods confiscated. Even Orange did not escape sentence. Those who had not managed to flee in time suffered a crueler fate. Eleven hundred people were executed, including many who were captured in the 1568 campaign.

The Council of Blood's most famous victims were, without a doubt, Egmond and Horne. In spite of the repeated requests of the German Emperor Maximilian II and Queen Elizabeth I of England to spare their lives, they were beheaded on June 5, 1568 in Market Square in Brussels, an event that made a deep impression at home and abroad.

As the execution of Egmond and Horne has been well documented, we will concentrate here on the fate of Antoon van Straelen, banker and burgomaster (i.e. mayor) of Antwerp. About ten years before his arrest, together with Egmond and Horne, van Straelen had been appointed superintendent of the revenues from the *novennale*,[8] and had presumably not been made any the poorer for his pains. One of the judges in the Council of Blood pointedly remarked that van Straelen should wage war against those who had used the *novennale* to line their own pockets at the King's expense. Another member characterized the wealthy banker who had fed off the fat of the land as "une fine pièce." In prison, van Straelen's health visibly deteriorated. He was afflicted with gout and was frequently given almost nothing to drink for a week at a time. As a consequence, his interrogators, Vargas and Del Rio, had to keep postponing his torture until he had regained sufficient strength to undergo his ordeal. Vargas, not content with the customary instrument of torture, had added extra pieces which crushed poor van Straelen's bones. It was such a gruesome sight that Del Rio could stand it no longer and left the room retching. Still, van Straelen confessed nothing. Once when he was untied, he tried in desperation to smash his head against the wall, presumably in a suicide attempt. He not only recovered, but was no longer plagued with gout; according to the incorrigible cynic Morillon,[9] van Straelen presumably feared Vargas and Del Rio would attempt another cure of a similar kind! Despite the entreaties of many, including Granvelle, that his life be spared, van Straelen was beheaded on September 24, 1568, together with Bakkerzeel, Egmond's secretary, who had also been severely tortured.

At the time of these executions, Alva's army was under attack from all sides. Its assailants were the Huguenots in the South, the mercenary forces of Louis of Nassau (William of Orange's brother) in the Northeast and Orange's mercenary forces in the Southeast, commanded by William himself. Alva managed to successfully eliminate them one after the other. Louis of Nassau, initially victorious in Heiligerlee, suffered a devastating defeat in Jemmingen. No battle at all was fought against Orange. Alva had stayed out of his reach until the Prince's funds ran out. Orange was then compelled to flee the fury of his unpaid troops.

Alva proposes new taxes

In the beginning of 1569, Alva was at the height of his power. The foreign invaders had been beaten back, the internal opposition had choked in its own blood, the local officials obediently carried out his orders, the population lived in fear and almost everything was going according to his wishes. Still, there was one cloud which kept getting larger and darker until it threatened to eclipse Alva's sun completely: the constant lack of money to pay his troops on time. Since his arrival in this part of the world, he had not asked the provincial States for a new aid, but had been content with the one-year renewal of the *novennale* which was about to expire. In addition, he had asked the provincial States to lend him some money: 340,000 florins from Flanders, 300,000 florins from Brabant and 150,000 florins from Holland. Alva intended to pay off these loans with the revenues from future aids. In any event, the loans were totally inadequate for maintaining an expensive army of occupation. The Council of Troubles made vigorous attempts to confiscate the money and goods of the heretics who had fled the country and of the invaders who had been captured. Still, this source of income was too uncertain and too slow to provide a basis for government.

One of Philip's policies was that the individual countries in his vast empire should paddle their own financial canoes. But this policy was not always practicable. Since he had come to power, enormous sums of money had been sent to The Netherlands. The Spanish court balked at this lavish spending, contend-

8. The nine-years' aid approved in 1557 by the States-General.
9. Morillon was Vicar-General of the Archbishopric of Mechelen, which he continued to administer after Granvelle had renounced his Archbishop's title. He was the Cardinal's most important informer, providing him with news of the situation in The Netherlands.

The statue the Duke of Alva had erected in the Citadel of Antwerp. It was hastily pulled down after Alva's departure.

ing that the rich provinces abroad should be made to foot the bill for their own domestic security against outside attacks. So the idea of introducing a new tax system in the Low Countries began to ripen in Madrid. What Philip felt was needed was a system that would raise sufficient money and would furthermore make government financing independent of the headstrong estates.

According to Alva's own testimony, his orders were to make an example of all insurgents, regardless of their social class, to reissue and enforce the placards, to persevere with the ecclesiastical restructuring and to keep printers and bookstores under close surveillance. Further, his instructions of January 31, 1567 were to ignore or abolish the privileges of the cities; to construct, at the expense of the residents of Antwerp, Valenciennes, Flushing, Amsterdam and Maastricht, citadels which would serve to control the population and function as bases for a military occupation; to appoint royal officials in the place of municipal magistrates; and to demobilize the native troops that Margaret of Parma had recruited. To pay for all of this, a tax was to be levied without the consent of the Netherlanders. In his letter of January 6, 1568, the King added the following objective: "to restore a certain amount of order in these lands and to unite them under one and the same law and customs."

The point concerning taxation was made more explicit in a letter dated December 12, 1567. The King wrote Alva that the Netherlanders themselves were to raise the money needed to maintain the country and fulfill its obligations. Philip had adequate reasons for making this demand. In Margaret of Parma's term of office alone he had been obliged to pump more than 5.5 million florins into The Netherlands to cover its deficits, while the Duke had set off with his army in 1567 with an additional 1.65 million florins in his coffers. Philip distrusted the States and wrote his Governor to be wary of any attempts on their part to delay granting new aids. Should there not be enough time to consult Madrid, Alva was to take matters into his own hands, without obtaining the consent of the States. Although it was not stated in so many words, Alva's orders were to introduce a permanent uniform tax that did not depend on the approval of the States and applied equally to all provinces. Alva's new tax program consisted of a one-time wealth-tax levy of one percent, the so-called Hundredth Penny, a perpetual ten-percent turnover tax on the sale of movable goods, the Tenth Penny, and a five-percent transfer tax on real estate, the Twentieth Penny.

The Duke discussed the plans for a new tax system with his most important Dutch advisers in the spring of 1568. The proposals were scathingly criticized by the members of the Councils. The King, they stated, had already demanded the Hundredth Penny once before in 1556. The States had not been in a position to grant this because broad segments of the Dutch population had refused to reveal the extent and sources of their wealth to government scrutiny. The King had then agreed to commute the Hundredth Penny. If the Duke wanted to levy his Hundredth Penny, he would have to find a way around this objection. The Councilors also felt that the Tenth Penny on the sale of movable goods would be almost impossible to impose and would anyway be costly and give rise to large-scale fraud. They added that prices would be driven up, because foreign merchants would raise their prices in the face of such a heavy tax on their merchandise. Moreover, their allies would probably protest that the tax was incompatible with previous agreements allowing free trade free in the Low Countries, provided the traditional tolls were paid.

Coninck philips van spaengien doer synen raet
vanden bischop ende inquisiteurs heeft dat ganse
Neder lant laten comen in groot verdriet

Ie roy philip de spenie par la playnte des
Efeeks et inquisiteurs a delayseés le pais
bas en grand doleurs   15 7z

Twee moncken togen nae hispaengien
Ende hebben geclaecht dat ꝑ wt
Haren kercken werden veriaecht

Deus moyne se partoyent en espaenie et
Playnderent au roy a grand tritresse
Comme fusifs de leur eglises et abaie

Allegorical print showing the King of Spain with a bishop on his right and an inquisitor on his left and two monks kneeling on either side of him.

In response, Alva argued that the Tenth Penny was a fair tax that would not burden one province more than another. He considered that one of the drawbacks of the existing tax system was that the public was able to see how much was paid in taxes; with the Tenth Penny, the total revenues would ultimately only be known to insiders. In his plea in favor of the new tax structure, Alva argued that the Tenth Penny would place the heaviest burden on the merchants and artisans and the lightest burden on the countryside, the nobility and the clergy. He added that, in his opinion, the taxes on foodstuffs should be abolished as soon as the Tenth Penny was granted. Finally, Alva stated the underlying reason for his enthusiasm for this tax. He felt that the authority of the rulers was eroded to an unacceptable degree by the need to repeatedly request financial support, especially since such support was usually only granted in exchange for inordinate privileges. This then was the real reason for introducing a permanent tax. The cat had finally been let out of the bag: royal authority was to be bolstered by depriving the King's subjects of their voice in financial matters. The Councils avoided a fundamental discussion of this important point. They merely pointed out that from time immemorial taxes in these regions had only been imposed when the treasury was in need of money and that it might be unwise to ride rough-shod over such long-standing traditions. Alva did not seriously intend to discuss his tax schemes with the States, as is evident from his November 4, 1568 dispatch to the King, in which he reported that his talks with the Dutch Councilors had come to an end. This letter also included the final version of his tax proposal for the King's approval. On March 7, 1569, matters had finally reached the point where he could convene the States-General and unfold his Tenth Penny scheme. Three days later, he reported to Philip that he hoped to arrange matters in The Netherlands so that it would no longer be necessary to have money sent from Spain. He expected the new tax to enable him to pay off a large portion of the money that the King had already advanced him.

Several hundred representatives from the patrimonial provinces and from Tournai and Utrecht had complied with the request to convene on March 20th. In all likelihood, they assembled with a good share of skepticism, if not anxious foreboding as to what the future held in store for their provinces. This was the first assembly of the States-General since 1559. In the intervening period, the King had frequently been urged to convene the States-General and to attend in order to discuss grievances with his subjects in person. Now that the time had finally come, it was Alva who appeared instead of the King, and he was more interested in a monologue than in a dialogue. The Duke made no attempt to disguise the fact that he was in The Netherlands to boost royal authority and abhorred having to negotiate the aids on an equal footing with the States. He had written to Philip, telling him that his dealings with the States-General would take the form of a policy statement rather than a proposal.

At the assembly, Alva informed the States that the treasury was in great financial distress due to the numerous and costly war efforts that the country had financed since the time of Charles V. As the King was no longer able to give the Low Countries assistance from his own domains, a lump sum raised by a tax levy was needed immediately to cover financial deficits and, in addition, provide sufficient reserves against calamities such as invasions or rebellions. Having examined all the alternatives, Alva felt a Hundredth Penny wealth tax imposed on all citizens was the wisest and most just course, as it would prevent any disputes among the provinces over whether one or the other of them was being too heavily taxed.

To cover the normal annual expenses, the Duke sought to obtain a "perpetual aid and subvention" by introducing a new tax on the sale of movable goods and real estate. This type of general tax would, in particular, alleviate the disproportionately heavy burden currently being borne by rural areas, as it was his intention to abolish existing taxes on food, drink and clothing. The Tenth Penny on the sale of movable goods and the Twentieth Penny on the sale of real estate were to be levied on the vendor. Any fiscal burdens previously placed on real estate were to be absorbed by the Twentieth Penny. To keep exported goods from surreptitiously evading the tax, the export of goods produced in the Low Countries was explicitly included in the Tenth Penny. However, an exception was made for goods which were imported into the Low Countries solely for re-exportation.

The new tax would benefit the poor, because the taxes on foodstuffs and drink were to be abolished. The good news for the rich was that they would no longer have to endure those irksome visits that the tax inspectors paid to their houses and cellars.

To ensure that trade and business would not stagnate, it was decided that merchants would be exempt from the Tenth Penny on the first sale of imported goods. This would prevent the importers of Baltic grain or English cloth from blaming high prices on the Tenth Penny. To spare landowners further hardship, the first sale of their produce – whether grain, livestock or other farm produce – was to be exempt from the Tenth Penny.

Alva concluded his statement by emphasizing that he had no intention of crippling trade and industry. He claimed that, once the new taxes were in operation, he would be prepared to discuss and resolve any problems that might arise. Nor did he rule out in advance lowering the general rate, exempting certain sales transactions or employing moderation in the collection of the taxes.

Despite the conspicuous absence of the non-patrimonial provinces from the meeting of the States-General, Alva attempted to have the Tenth Penny adopted by these provinces. In his October 31, 1569 letter to the King, he wrote that the non-patrimonial provinces would also have to pay their share, even though their revenues would not amount to much. In the end, however, he had to content himself with the lump sums these provinces paid in lieu of their tax obligation.

The reason Alva did not seriously attempt to push through the Tenth Penny in the non-patrimonial provinces and was satisfied instead with accepting an outright grant of money is a matter of conjecture. The most obvious explanation is that it was difficult enough for him to get the patrimonial provinces to toe the line. As the returns from the non-patrimonial provinces were marginal, Alva apparently saw little point in doing battle with them over the question of whether he was breaking the agreement they had made with the Emperor when they had recently surrendered.

This uncharacteristic slackness on Alva's part brought him into confrontation with the patrimonial provinces, which had consented to the Tenth Penny on the condition that the tax would be imposed in all provinces. Holland, in particular, protested vehemently. As we shall see, Holland feared it would suffer from unfair competition if neighboring provinces were able to commute the tax by paying an outright grant.

Utrecht: a special case

Even though Utrecht was one of the non-patrimonial provinces, it was not allowed to take part in the tax commutation described in the previous section. By way of introduction to later events, let us now discuss the vicissitudes in the fortunes of Utrecht, which Alva treated more harshly than any other province.

As early as April 20, 1569, a month after the States-General had been confronted with the new tax structure, the States of Utrecht adopted a resolution rejecting the Tenth Penny. Utrecht remained firm in its opposition. Indeed, this province, unlike the others, never granted its permission to levy the Tenth Penny. The deed reporting the provinces' agreement to pay an outright grant instead of the tax concludes with the telling phrase: "Ceux d'Utrecht n'ont rien accordé."

In their resolution, the States of Utrecht noted that the province had suffered severe damage at the hands of the iconoclasts and the soldiers sent to restore order as well as from the economic crisis which had caused many of its residents to move elsewhere. Utrecht offered 72,000 florins − later raised to 200,000 florins − but it resolutely refused to accept the new tax. The province of Utrecht also argued that it had surrendered to Charles V on the condition that it would remain outside the system of apportionment applied to the patrimonial provinces.

Utrecht's status as a province was the subject of bitter controversy. The province of Holland had lent the Emperor the money to enable him to occupy the non-patrimonial provinces, demanding that Utrecht be annexed in return. Utrecht opposed this arrangement with all its might, and a compromise was reached in 1534: Utrecht was to remain independent, but was to share Holland's Lieutenant-Governor, known as a "Stadtholder". The two provinces were to send joint representatives to meetings in which the central government dealt with financial and defense matters. Utrecht consistently boycotted these meetings and continued to refuse to accept the apportionment, on the grounds that it was a non-patrimonial province. It preferred to pay an even larger sum rather than pay its share of the apportionment. The central government in Brussels had always turned a blind eye to Utrecht's position and thus unwittingly reinforced the province's case against the tax. Utrecht was later to refer to this precedent time and again.

The Duke was enraged by another justification which Utrecht advanced for refusing to pay the new taxes: Utrecht invoked the papal bull *In Coena Domini*, which forbade taxes to be imposed on the clergy without permission from Rome. Alva claimed that this bull was aimed at the Church's persecutors rather than its advocates. His wrath extended not only to the printer who had recently reprinted the bull, but also to the Privy Council and its chairman, Viglius, who had authorized the printing. He even went so far as to have De La Torre, the secretary who had signed the authorization, placed under house arrest and removed from office for a year.

Utrecht paid a heavy price for its fierce opposition. On August 21, 1569, after the other provinces had submitted and Utrecht alone persevered in its struggle, Alva had a regiment from Lombardy quartered in the city of Utrecht. The soldiers, brought almost to the point of mutiny by long-overdue back pay, were

Ie pape a donue ɉayne au duck cruelle   Deu pays heeft duck dalba dat sweert gedaen
Setoyent a grannelle et parma bieu leur cas   Grannelle ende die herthogin van parma weeten
Pour ruenes ceuls du pais bas   O wee nederlant isser uv uyet wel aeu

parma   Grannelle   alba   pius V papa

Par or et argeut a duck dalba le   Met gelt ende goet doet hem den pays onder
Pape fait fecours gue le preftre   Stane dat die papen moehten houden
Demorant en leur tours auſi par tiraye   Douerhanc ock met gewele en met brant

2

Allegorical print showing Alva receiving a sword from Pope Pius V, who has a chest and pots full of money lying at his feet. Granvelle and Margaret of Parma are on the left.

billeted in the city's largest quarter, where they caused the residents great inconvenience, not to mention the 2,400 florins the municipal government had to pay weekly for their upkeep. But as the States of Utrecht were still not prepared to change their standpoint, Alva had no choice but to change his tactics. On December 15, 1569, he summoned the States of Utrecht to appear before the Council of Troubles within two weeks. They were officially charged in the summons with not having acted forcibly enough to check the Iconoclastic Fury. But clearly the States' refusal to comply with the Tenth Penny was what prompted the Duke to deal so harshly with the province. In the summons, which was conveniently formulated as a verdict, the city and the province were found guilty of high treason and were, by way of punishment, to be deprived of their charters and attendant privileges, liberties and customs. Furthermore, all their property, both real estate and personal property, was to be forfeited, while all tolls, annuities, excise taxes and other taxes were to be confiscated by the King. Before this provisional sentence was carried out, the States of Utrecht were given the opportunity to reply.

In the six months that followed, lawyers rushed feverishly to and fro, drafting the defense against the charges. On July 14, 1570 the Council of Troubles in Antwerp was finally ready to pronounce judgement in the case. The entire bundle of documents, including a translated version that had only been finished that morning (required for the chairman, Vargas, who could not read or write a word of Dutch), had only been handed over to the Council members that very day. Vargas was evidently intelligent enough to form an opinion of the matter within half an hour! Having first attended mass at St. Goedele's in Brussels with his boots and spurs on, he had made his way posthaste to Antwerp in order to render his verdict. This was identical to the sentence laid down in the summons, with all the dire consequences that entailed.

Utrecht understandably sent a deputation to the King to appeal against the harsh verdict. Philip was not prepared to reconsider the sentence pronounced on Utrecht, but at least he did not have the two envoys thrown into a dungeon and strangled, as he had done with Montigny when he was sent to Spain by the States-General in 1566. Their heads still squarely on their shoulders, the Utrecht envoys set off for their fatherland. Utrecht's sentence was not reviewed until April 14, 1574 by Don Luis de Requesens, Alva's successor. All its charters, privileges and liberties were then returned to the city, and Utrecht's States and City Council were reinstated with all their powers.

The adoption of Alva's tax program

The Hundredth Penny was undoubtedly the simplest of Alva's three pennies. The provinces adopted this one-time tax almost without protest, and there was very little difficulty with its collection. When the revenues from this tax, which had to be paid in three installments, began to flow into his coffers, Alva decided that he rather liked the taste of his own medicine. He therefore ordered another Hundredth Penny, to be collected several years hence in the case of an emergency, such as a domestic rebellion or a foreign invasion. The States violently opposed this second Hundredth Penny. Although it was adopted in principle, it was never effectively levied. Materially speaking, the most important provision in the Hundredth Penny involved the method of appraising real estate (still the most important form of ownership). The starting point was the rent, or in the case of owner-occupation, a commensurate rental value. The market value of the residence was obtained by multiplying the rent (or rental value) by the sixteenth penny and the land revenues, including any residences on that land, by the twenty-second penny. This method ensured that the tax liability would more or less reflect the market value of the real estate. At the urging of the States — whose members often belonged to the property-owning class — the leaseholder or tenant (contrary to the initial intent of the proposition) was included in the tax. They were expected to contribute a sixth of the tax, which somewhat transformed the character of the Hundredth Penny.

Personal property appears to have been assessed "arbitrarily." This is probably one of the reasons why Alva, doubtless alerted to the danger by his spies, ordered the tax registers to be audited in 1570. Today, we would say that he investigated whether there was reason to make additional assessments, and if so, in what cases. For that matter, any taxpayer could avoid having his movable goods assessed by declaring 1,000 florins, which was the maximum taxable amount for this type of ownership. It was determined that tax debts of 200 florins or more could be settled by means of IOU's, with the interest rate determined on the basis of the fourteenth penny. A mortgage was then placed on the taxpayer's property. This was important in a society in which the circulation of money was fairly limited.

It took considerably more effort to get the Tenth and Twentieth Pennies off the ground. The States of Holland convened on April 5, 1569 to discuss Alva's proposal. A series of arguments against the Tenth and Twentieth Pennies was put forward. The States reasoned that sales transactions were not always profit-making and, in fact, often led to losses on account of leakages, short measures, trade developments, etc. The merchant often had no option but to sell his goods at a loss in order to recoup some of his money. Or, faced with such setbacks, he had to enter into other business transactions in order to maintain his credit. A tax on top of these tribulations would inflict unbearable hardship on the merchant.

The Tenth Penny, so the States argued, would lead to a decline in the textile industry, which would be unable to stand the pressure of price hikes. This would, in turn, threaten the living of the thousands of people employed in the industry. In addition, the Tenth Penny would adversely affect the poor, who could only buy their commodities in small quantities. The States clearly felt that the Tenth Penny would undermine the livelihood of the residents of cities in Holland where trade goods were imported from abroad and subsequently re-sold and transported to neighboring cities and countries. Since the first sale was exempted from the tax, they feared that people would start buying goods directly from foreign merchants. Up to this point, additional tax levies had ignored the principle of equality. So Gelre, Overijssel, Friesland and Groningen paid paltry sums compared to Holland. The States feared that the mild tax climate would give traders an incentive to move their businesses to these provinces.

The herring and small-scale fishing industries in Holland flourished, not least thanks to exemptions granted some time earlier. The States were afraid that a Tenth Penny — on top of the high costs incurred before a ship even set sail, the uncertainty of the catch and the risk of calamities at sea — would break the back of this branch of industry. For the same reasons, the Tenth Penny was thought to threaten the survival of the mercantile shipping industry.

In spite of their criticisms, the States of Holland were less negative about the Twentieth Penny than the Tenth Penny. The delegates from Holland to be sent to talk to Alva and his advisers about the tax proposals were to emphasize the hardship Holland was experiencing on account of the economic recession. They were also to underline the massive contribution, amounting to hundreds of thousands of florins, that the province had made to the recent war effort against France. The States of Holland understood that, in light of the large expenses facing the government in Brussels, they could not leave Alva empty-handed. They therefore contemplated substituting an annual aid of 100,000 florins for the Tenth, Twentieth and Hundredth Pennies. The revenues could be obtained by the system customary in Holland, in which the tax was apportioned over the cities and villages, subject to the usual pardons.[10] It was decided to meet again to discuss the matter further on the Wednesday after Easter, April 14th.

This decision marked the end of their initial response to the proposals. For the time being, it served only as a broad outline for the delegates who were to do the negotiating in Brussels.

What is striking about this initial response is that the States were already thinking of replacing the Tenth and Twentieth Pennies by an aid and even stated an exact amount. How they arrived at the figure of 100,000 florins is anybody's guess. As there was no telling how much the Tenth Penny would yield, the most likely explanation is that the States either knew or guessed what the financial needs of the central government were and began the bargaining by putting their opening bid − a low one, of course − on the table.

In the interim, the States busily consulted with each other, so as to be able to assume a provisional position at the next meeting. The nobles and the city of Dordrecht were prepared to grant the Tenth and Twentieth Pennies because the Duke had expressly declared that these taxes were consistent with the King's wishes and objectives. They agreed, even though they dreaded a great loss in trade. However, they trusted that neither His Majesty nor His Excellency intended to drive trade and business out of the country. The speedy acquiescence of the nobles (who had no vested interest in the Tenth Penny and whose social status was greatly enfeebled) was of minor significance; but the fact that Dordrecht, Holland's leading city and long a trading center and storage depot, acceded so readily to Alva's wishes was a great blow to the opposition.

The other cities in Holland adopted a tougher stance, preferring to offer 100,000 florins per year instead. They were confident this amount could be scraped together by doubling the current wine and beer excise taxes, the *morgengeld*[11] and other existing taxes.

10. Discounts.
11. A local real-estate tax, calculated either according to area or produce. The leaseholder usually paid a third of the taxes. As with dike assessments (from which the *morgengeld* was presumably originally derived), there was no exemption for the clergy or the nobility as landowners.

Aided by his Stadtholder in Holland, Alva stepped up his pressure on the States. He alternately cajoled and threatened them, though the latter prevailed in the end. The cities which continued to refuse were driven to the wall by the unremitting and ever-mounting pressure. When they met again on May 17th, Delft and Leiden capitulated, declaring that after due consideration they would accede to the views of the nobles and the city of Dordrecht and thus toe Alva's line. Gouda soon followed suit. Amsterdam had initially decided to stand firm, no matter how many other cities granted their consent.

Die scepen veruallen die sciplieden couden   Par destruction de nauires le nauireurs se
Nyet behelpeu die copman en vercopt geen   Poueut surporter par faulte de marchandise
Waer babels hoer is vrolick met ducdalba   Selou duck dalba aueck babilõ prẽd so solas

babilón alba

Deu cramer sit armelijck neder hy can   Le marchaut son pourrement abasis
Syu Ware nyet vercopeu doer ducdalbas   Ne pouoynt gaigue pour vivre pour
outlyueu schatteu en roueu   Le ranson du duck et se pilieurs

3

Allegorical print depicting the seated Alva embracing the "Whore of Babylon," who has a tiara on her head and is seated on a many-headed monster. A ship's captain and his broken ships are on the left and a despondent merchant is on the right. An exhausted peddler is lying in the foreground.

But amid the crumbling opposition, Amsterdam decided it would be more prudent to give the matter a good night's sleep. Haarlem likewise decided to defer its decision to the following afternoon.

On May 18th, the representatives of Haarlem and Amsterdam consulted with each other. As a result, they decided to move with the tide and join the ranks of Delft, Leiden and Gouda. After only two months, the Duke had managed to persuade the next most important province, Holland, to accept his proposals, though the States of Holland frankly disclosed in the deed of acceptance that the Duke had left them no option but to comply.

After presenting his proposition of March 20th, Alva, unwilling to allow any deliberation among the representatives of the various provinces, called the representatives of Flanders before him the next day and pressed them to come to a quick decision. The four orders were not to wait for Brabant's consent, but were to provide a good example by being the first to accept the proposition. Alva evidently feared (not without some justification) that he would encounter the stiffest opposition from Brabant.

Interminable discussions followed between the representatives of Ghent, Bruges, Ypres and the Bruges *Vrije*. Although they were unanimous in their rejection of Alva's proposed taxes, they failed to agree on alternative ways of funding the government. Their counter proposals all fell a long way short of the government's needs.

Alva's patience was wearing thin. He wrote the States that other provinces had already lent their unconditional approval – a blatant lie – and once again pressed them emphatically for a "fruitful response." Finally, on June 7, 1569, the four orders drafted a deed in which they accepted the Hundredth Penny, but in a severely restricted form. The Tenth and Twentieth Pennies were rejected, after the underlying dangers to the Flemish economy, particularly the weaving industry, had been outlined.

Alva's next tactic was to threaten the four orders in Flanders. If the representatives did not agree within ten days, he told them, Flanders would be punished as an object lesson to the other provinces. Not wishing to be the sole scapegoat, none of the estates dared shoulder the responsibility for a refusal. Without consulting again with their rank and file, the dignitaries in Ghent changed sides and approved the proposed taxes on June 21st. A week later, Flanders granted its final consent. Alva's threats had brought the four orders to their knees almost without a struggle! From now on, this important province could be held up as an example to those provinces which had not yet given their consent.

One by one, the other provinces followed suit. But what would be the reaction of Brabant, the most important province and the least willing to part with money for the sovereign ruler? After months of meetings, discussions, evasions of responsibility, increasing pressure from Alva, etc., the orders in Brussels, Antwerp, Louvain and 's-Hertogenbosch found themselves in the following situation: some flatly refused to approve the taxes while others were completely amenable to them; yet most were prepared to grant their permission if all the orders in the principal cities did the same. In the circumstances, this was tantamount to the entire third estate refusing, for no single city had agreed fully. At the end of July, the Duke had reminded Antwerp of the events of 1566, the Iconoclastic Fury and its repercussions. He pointed out that even if the municipal government were to do its level best to obtain the consent, the city would have to pay dearly for a refusal. His threats were to no avail, for the second and third orders of Antwerp dug in their heels and stood by their refusal.

Consequently, Alva decided that the hour to change tactics had come. He attempted to convince the States that partial permission had to be considered as approval, according to the principle of replacement. In the meantime, he did his best to put the minds of the people of Brabant at rest, repeatedly emphasizing that he wanted to stimulate rather than cripple trade. The guilds in the cities remained unconvinced. On July 28th, Louvain's guilds indicated that they were not prepared to grant the requested consent, and those in Brussels followed a few days later.

The Duke now felt that it was time for sterner action. On August 13th, the States of Brabant were convened at 10:00 a.m. in Brussels' City Hall. Alva announced that he would replace (outvote) the handful of orders who had refused to grant their consent. The representatives from Brussels asked for the conditions under which every order granted its permission to be put on record, but the Chancellor of Brabant recorded the vote as if only the third orders of Brussels and Louvain had refused and even ignored Louvain's fourth order altogether! In less than an hour, the prelates and nobles as well as the majority of the municipal representatives had given their consent. The orders who continued to refuse were given two weeks in which to join in the accord. As had happened earlier elsewhere, the municipal governments of Brussels and Louvain buckled under the pressure and assented within a few days. It should be noted that Louvain caved in only after the Duke had threatened to quarter ten companies of Spanish soldiers in the city.

Alva's victory was officially confirmed on August 31st. He had triumphed on all fronts. Against the tradition and wishes of the States of Brabant, the Duke had persuaded them to sign a proposition that had not been accepted unanimously. It evidently mattered little to him that he had violated the promises that the Emperor had made to Flanders in 1544 and to Brabant in 1554 (the latter was reaffirmed by the King in 1557), never to request another Tenth Penny. Nor did he seem to care that Philip had solemnly declared in September of 1568 that the rights of Brabant's cities would be respected. His success was something of a Pyrrhic victory. He had been obliged to use drastic means to achieve his goal and had applied much more pressure on Brabant than on the other provinces, in the face of its determined opposition. Eventually, he had been forced to resort to the principle of replacement. But he had, to put it mildly, used dubious methods. When the States of Brabant sent a delegation to Philip in the spring of 1572, they stated that the replacement had not been carried out according to regulation, an allegation Alva denied when he left the Low Countries.

In fact, it was blackmail that had broken down the last of the opposition. Louvain's third order had only thrown in the towel after Alva had threatened to billet soldiers there (at the citizens' expense), and Louvain's fourth order had simply been spirited away. In the end, all sides, with the exception of the obstinate province of Utrecht, had signed the document consenting to the tax. But granting the tax and collecting it were two very different matters.

A temporary outright grant of two million florins a year replaces the Tenth and Twentieth Pennies

In hindsight, it seems probable that Alva might even have been able to push through the actual levy of the Tenth Penny in the fall of 1569. By fair means or foul, he had brought all the provinces into line, with the exception of Utrecht, which had been summoned to appear before the Council of Troubles; his army was still supreme; all opposition had been nipped in the bud and nothing stood in his way. Alva doubtless felt he could secure sufficient funds to finance his expensive army and even add reinforcements. This might in turn have prevented the later mutinies in the Spanish army (which could always be traced back to discontent among the soldiers over back pay), and thus might have changed the entire course of events in The Netherlands.

For whatever reason, Alva temporarily let the Tenth Penny rest. Possibly his Councilors managed to convince him that their many serious objections were not unfounded. All sources suggest that Alva felt it advisable during this period to see how the original proposal could be changed or modified to accommodate these objections.

However, Alva needed money and he needed it immediately, particularly to pay his troops. Since he had presented the proposition to the States-General in the spring, he had not received so much as a single penny. For a period of three months, he had lifted the authorization for the tolls, so that the toll revenues flowed into the coffers of the central government, but the stopgap measure had little effect and was only temporary.

This critical financial situation probably gave rise to the practice of having the provinces temporarily buy off their obligation to pay the Tenth Penny with a lump sum. Such a commutation would provide him with ready cash, giving him time to revise and refine his plan. Although he initially had a higher figure in mind, Alva contented himself, after consulting with his Dutch Councilors, with an outright grant of two million florins a year from the combined patrimonial provinces, to be paid over a period of six years, during which time he would suspend the Tenth and Twentieth Pennies. At the end of that period, he intended to request another Hundredth Penny in wealth taxes. The revenues from this second Hundreth Penny were to be deposited in the Treasury as a reserve, to be drawn upon in emergencies that entailed additional expenses, such as rebellions, enemy attacks, etc.

In the course of October 1569, the local Stadtholders presented these new tax schemes to the assemblies of the States. Holland's share of the two million florins was to be 271,000 florins, while Flanders was to pay 650,000 florins and Brabant 542,000 florins. As before, the States were handed a copy of the proposal.

Alva began his proposal by commending the States, in the name of the King, for assenting to the Tenth Penny. He continued by stating that several objections to this levy had arisen, but that he had considered them in advance and had found them wanting. As there appeared to be such a strong aversion to the Tenth Penny and as the States, moreover, feared that this method of taxation, with which they had had little experience, would be harmful to trade and industry, he was prepared to commute the Tenth and Twentieth Pennies for a period of six years

Hy neuipt met gewelt den ryckdom van   Il prend par fortresse le risesse du pais
Het laut ende heeft veel outschuldich   Et par sinesse a respaudu le sang
Bloet laten haugen ende branden   Iuocent par gand triesse

Hy heeff ock egmont ende horn dat leuen   Il a mis a mort egmont et horne et
Genomen ende den heelen edeldom ouder bracht   Tout gentils barons occis par insame que
Dat wort van borger en boeren beclaecht   Bourgoys seu plaint et laboureurs   4

to the above-mentioned sum of two million florins, to be imposed on all the provinces collectively, without any discounts, pardons or cancellations. The States themselves were to determine how to raise the amount. They would have to give him an answer within a month, at which time they would also be required to explain how they proposed to come up with the necessary funds, as he wanted to ascertain for himself whether this would not be detrimental to the welfare of the country. In the meantime, the States would be able to study the Tenth Penny, so that it could be imposed after the six years had passed.

He tacked on to his offer the demand that all of the provinces grant their permission. If the provinces were not unanimous in their consent, he would withdraw his offer and implement the Tenth Penny. There was one more condition. The States were to furnish the two million florins for the outright grant by August 13, 1569. This was the date of the deed of acceptance drawn up by Brabant, the last province to be won over, which meant that as of that moment all of the provinces had granted their permission and, in theory at least, were supposed to have collected the Tenth and Twentieth Pennies. Incidentally, it was quite unreasonable of Alva to make this demand, as the mechanics of imposing and collecting the two levies had not even been regulated yet. As a final injunction, the States were again enjoined to answer as quickly as possible.

Predictably, the provincial States discussed the proposal to buy off their tax obligation at great length. Unanimity over the commutation itself could be reached in most of the provinces, but they were, as usual, hopelessly divided over the question of how each province should raise its share of the two million florins. Vexed by the delay, the Duke unwisely maneuvered himself into an ambiguous position. On the one hand, he attempted to persuade the States to accept the aid of two million florins a year as a temporary replacement for the Tenth Penny. On the other hand, when progress proved slower than he, with one eye pinned on the dire needs of the Treasury, had hoped, Alva started to modify the original Tenth Penny proposition.

This zigzag course led Alva to present a new proposition to the March 1570 meeting of the individual provincial States. He himself denoted his latest proposal as a moderation of the Tenth Penny. Any mercantile goods, food and other wares whose production entailed a series of sales would be exempt from the Tenth Penny until the last sale, i.e. the point at which the merchandise reached the consumer; such goods were only to be subject to the Tenth Penny when sold "to be worn and used." To stimulate industry, the sale of raw materials and materials bound up in the production process was exempted from the Tenth Penny. Both of these exemptions were significant concessions. The Tenth Penny was cut back from a recurring to a one-time cumulative sales tax. The exemption was valid for the entire distribution process and for part of the production process, i.e. for the products manufactured by craftsmen. The Tenth Penny was only to be paid upon the retail sale of the craftsman's finished products. Second-hand goods, however, were to be liable for taxation.

As with the first proposition, the Tenth Penny was to be due on the export of goods, unless it had already been paid when sold to a consumer. This moderate version of the Tenth Penny was to be binding for a period of six years. However, the Twentieth Penny was not to be alleviated in any way.

Philip II (1527-1598).

Having lightened the tax burden to such an extent and anticipating a correspon-
ding drop in revenues, the Duke considered it reasonable to levy an extra Hundreth Penny to set aside in an emergency fund against a war or rebellion. The
States were to grant their consent forthwith, or he would implement the Tenth
Penny in accordance with the first proposition. He also warned that, come what

may, the levy was to be retroactively effective as of August 13, 1569, the date on which all the States had agreed to his proposition. The King, who had to pay his troops, was not to become the victim of the States' prevarication.

At the end of the proposition, the Duke once again made an about-face: if necessary, he would content himself with the payment of two million florins a year instead of the moderate version of the Tenth Penny. The term of the commutation was to be reduced from six to two years, presumably because it was, in practice, impossible to collect the Tenth Penny, moderate or otherwise, retroactively. The entire proposition was designed to force a quick decision, which was urgently needed to replenish the King's exhausted financial resources. On March 22nd, Philip had expressly requested his Governor to settle the issue of the Tenth Penny as soon as possible.

Coupling the second Hundredth Penny to the moderation of the Tenth Penny was a clever move on Alva's part. It allowed him room to maneuver at a later stage to also obtain the States' implicit consent for the second Hundredth Penny, even if they opted for the outright grant.

Even so, Alva's proposal in October of 1569 to replace the Tenth Penny temporarily by an outright grant did get him into hot water. His proposition of March 1570, in which the States were allowed to choose to accept a moderate version of the Tenth Penny instead of the commutation, only made matters worse. His change of course created a great deal of protracted discord among the States in the various provinces. They argued about whether to accept the moderate Tenth Penny or the outright grant or whether, alternatively, to introduce – as Flanders and Brabant wanted – uniform taxation in all provinces. Even if they opted for the outright grant, they were faced with the question of how to raise the money. In Holland as well, these questions led to many differences of opinion and endless discussions.

Fearing the situation was also getting out of hand in the other provinces, the Duke resorted to a fairly drastic measure. In an attempt to force matters to a conclusion, he had deeds of acceptance drawn up at the beginning of June and sent to Artois, Flanders and Zealand, at that moment the provinces opposing him the most. He kept similar documents up his sleeve for Brabant, Holland and Walloon Flanders. These deeds of acceptance were accompanied by the announcement that, unless they were accepted within fourteen days, the Tenth Penny would be implemented in the original form in which it had been accepted a year earlier. Because the provinces continued to hesitate, open letters, containing the announcement of the original Tenth Penny, were shortly afterwards sent to the highest figures of authority in Artois, Flanders and Zealand. Of course, the States in Holland heard of this and, knowing that they would be next in line, complied with Alva's request at the eleventh hour.

And indeed, after great deliberation, the four orders in Flanders reconciled themselves, in principle, to commuting the Tenth and Twentieth Pennies for six years for 650,000 florins per year. The next question was how to raise the money. Once again, the representatives from Ghent, Bruges, Ypres and the Bruges *Vrije* became entangled in endless debates, without ever reaching an agreement. Bruges again dredged up the basic objection that they would not grant the Tenth Penny without knowing the period for which it was binding. After much palaver,

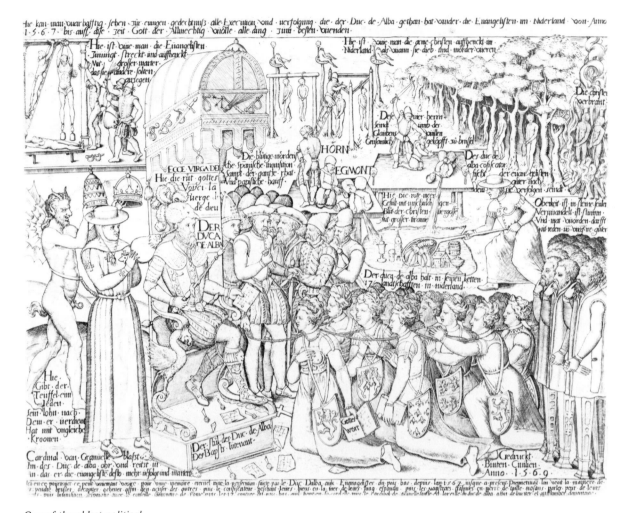

One of the oldest political cartoons of Alva and his policy (1569). Granvelle is using a bellows to blow revenge and murder into Alva (seated on the throne to the left of center). Satan is holding a papal tiara and imperial crown above the Duke's head. The seventeen Dutch provinces are represented as virgins, tied together and kneeling in front of Alva. The representatives of the States are standing on wooden stakes on the far right, with their fingers on their mouths to symbolize their inability to govern. Instruments of torture are depicted on the canopy above Alva's throne. The torture itself is illustrated at the top of the print.

the four orders managed to break the stalemate by suggesting the money be raised by the tried and tested method of apportioning taxes. Thus, Flanders raised the sum of 650,000 florins by the methods used since the days of Charles V, i.e. by levying a twentieth penny on the yearly rental of houses and property as well as a ten-shilling tax on every barrel of imported wine. So Alva finally got his way in Flanders with the temporary commutation of the Tenth Penny, but the struggle had taken longer than in any other province, with the exception, of course, of Brabant.

Let us therefore direct our attention to this province. How did Brabant react to Alva's propositions? As we saw, Brabant's consent had been exacted with greater difficulty and opposition and at a later date than that of any other province. When the States of Brabant were subsequently informed on October 21, 1569 that the Tenth and Twentieth Pennies could be suspended for a period of six years at the price of 542,000 florins a year (Brabant's share), they heaved a sigh of relief and agreed to the commutation at that very session. The next key question was how to raise the 542,000 florins. Differences of opinion arose even before the meeting was over. Prelates and nobles proposed levying taxes on a number of consumer articles such as wine, beer, poultry and game in addition to extra taxes ("surcharges") on excessive opulence in clothes, food, drink and woven fabrics (for horses as well as for people) and on the wearing of jewelry.

They also suggested export duties on spices, sugar, dried fish, herring, butter, cheese, salt, flour, leather, soap, flax, oil-bearing seeds and fruit as well as import and export duties on textiles. Lastly, they proposed having the loser in a trial case turn over the fiftieth or the hundredth penny (in proportion to the amount in question) of the fine or the compensation money imposed.

While opinions in 's-Hertogenbosch were divided, Antwerp, in particular, was sharply opposed to these suggestions. They went through almost every item with a fine-tooth comb to see whether it would damage trade and industry in The Netherlands in general, and Antwerp in particular. Prelates and nobles and the first orders of the cities, representing the upper middle class, shared the same interests and opposed any taxes on wealth and income from property. By contrast, the other orders in the cities vigorously opposed any taxes on consumer goods.

The discussions within Brabant dragged on for months on end, with the result that Alva still did not have the definite consent of the States, although they did accept his commutation proposal. By now at the end of his tether, Alva ordered an ordinance to be issued on August 2, 1570, establishing the outright grant of 542,000 florins. Little did he know that this was just the beginning of his troubles, for there was still no agreement about how the money was to be raised. To start with, the States only convened in Brussels in the beginning of September 1570 after much effort had been expended. The deputation from 's-Hertogenbosch attached greater importance to a meeting with Don Frederick[12] in Bergen op Zoom about the possibility of shutting down the garrison and reestablishing toll exemptions. As a result, the party did not travel to Brussels until September 11th, and only at the express exhortations of the Duke. The delegation from Louvain had not even departed on that date. Threatened with a fine, Louvain's Pensionary,[13] Jan Lievens, set off for Brussels two days later. The day after that, Antwerp's delegation had still not shown up, although it was expected to arrive at any moment.

On September 20th, the cities were finally ready to notify the General Secretary of the States, Cornelis Weellemans, of their views. Antwerp rejected the proposed method out of hand. The third order of 's-Hertogenbosch was not prepared to give its consent in any form until the city was relieved of the garrison stationed there and its toll exemptions were restored. On the other hand, the first and second orders of 's-Hertogenbosch, the first and third orders of Brussels and all four orders of Louvain did give their assent. In short, the cities were still clearly divided. The meeting planned for the next day had to be postponed because not enough prelates and nobles were present. When there was finally a quorum, the prelates and nobles started quarreling over side issues with the cities.

The next serious meeting took place in Antwerp's City Hall on October 9th and continued into the following day. Antwerp proposed waiting one year before introducing new taxes, which would give them the opportunity to see how Flanders fared. The prelates and nobles rejected the proposal, as the province could not possibly raise the 542,000 florins by bond issues within a single year. Alva hoped that his presence in the States of Brabant would compel them to reach a unanimous agreement. Chairing a meeting of the States, he commanded the clergy to suggest a new method of collecting the money and instructed the remaining members of the States to comply with the clergy's proposals. Naturally, this only served to arouse renewed opposition from the third estate.

12. Alva's son, who often acted as his substitute in army matters.
13. A Pensionary was an official charged with providing legal counsel and acting as General Secretary of the municipal or provincial governing bodies.

Portrait of Alva, painted
by William Key in 1568,
just after the Duke's arriva
in the Low Countries.

October passed into November of 1570 and Alva had not progressed an inch nearer his goal. The longer matters dragged on, the greater the pressure he applied. He ordered the first and second estates to continue to convene or pay a fine of 300 florins and dispatched the municipal representatives to obtain the consent of their City Councils. The responses of the cities arrived on November 23rd. Brussels and 's-Hertogenbosch had no objections to the method that the Duke had proposed for collecting the outright grant, Antwerp was opposed and Louvain undecided. Encouraged by their partial approval, Alva persevered and on December 7th issued instructions for the collection of the annual sum of 542,000 florins. This brought the last of the opposition to its knees, and on

Portrait of Alva, painted by an anonymous master, probably in 1574, just after Alva returned to Spain from the Low Countries.

December 14th he issued a placard, which had been accepted by common consent, detailing the collection of the 542,000 florins. By January 1571, he had not received so much as a penny of the aid of 542,000 florins authorized on August 13, 1570 in commutation of the Tenth Penny (which was to have commenced exactly one year prior to that date). Although the States had given their approval to the December 14th placard, they had not yet signed it. The cities, still very much divided over the issue, continued to raise objections. They demanded the withdrawal of the garrisons before they could or would start collecting the taxes.

On January 20, 1571, the prelates and the nobles in the States suggested that Brabant would only be able to raise the sum of 242,000 florins for the first year by issuing an IOU. Because they were farming out the tax collection, the cities would not be able to raise more than 300,000 florins a year, while the first year was already a lost cause. They were prepared to negotiate with the Duke about this matter. The idea of the IOU appealed to Alva, because it would enable him to get his hands on the money immediately.

The deed of acceptance of the IOU for 242,000 florins was read forth in the January 28th meeting; the third orders of Brussels, Antwerp and 's-Hertogenbosch and all four orders of Louvain voted against the motion. Once again, Alva resorted to replacement (outvoting) and demanded a definite answer from the orders that continued to object within thirteen days. When it actually came to confirming the agreement, no more than a few prelates were prepared to sign, and only then on the condition that all the others would sign it too. At that moment, only Antwerp and 's-Hertogenbosch were prepared to do so. Louvain only signed at the Duke's insistence. But Alva's patience had been sorely tried. As he was leaving the meeting, he upbraided Louvain's burgomaster for his persistently obstructive tactics, especially where money was concerned. The burgomaster began an elaborate apology, claiming that he had no control over the opinions of his rank and file, and so on. But the Duke remained indignant.

It seemed as if the troubles with Brabant would never end. Toward the end of March, the States asked permission to include the Spanish soldiers in the tax levy, in order to help them scrape together the aid of 542,000 florins. Undaunted by a negative reply, they repeated the request. Shortly thereafter, the high officials of the Collateral Councils (the Heads and Chairmen of its three Councils, the Councilors themselves, the Committee Members, the Receivers-General, the Secretaries and other personnel) asked to be exempted from Brabant's taxes. Alva responded positively to this request. The States were not prepared to endure all this bargaining and wrote a "firm" letter to the Duke, who responded that they were expected to sympathize with those who placed themselves entirely in the service of the King. The States, dissatisfied with this answer, met in June. But the discussion never progressed beyond the same two points.

At this same meeting, Alva was asked, to no avail, to extend the term for paying the two installments of the 542,000 florins. The reason for this request was that the province would only have 300,000 florins left after the tax farmers took their share, leaving a deficit of 242,000 florins. Alva replied in October that the States of Brabant would have to look for other sources of money. As raising imposts was virtually impossible, Alva advised them to levy an extra property tax. In desperation, the States of Brabant decided to fill the gap by spreading the tax burden over the municipal districts by means of the old-fashioned system of apportionment. And so at long last Brabant managed to raise the amount it owed. The difficulty they encountered is evident from the fact that the city of 's-Hertogenbosch only paid off its arrears in 1575 or 1576. The States of Flanders and especially those of Brabant had driven Alva to extremes by their delaying tactics, bickering and constant retraction of decisions (or unwillingness to implement decisions), all of which looked suspiciously like sabotage. Alva therefore moved the battle to another front.

The placard of July 31, 1571 immediately implementing the Tenth and Twentieth Pennies

In October of 1569, Alva had proposed the temporary commutation of the Tenth and Twentieth Pennies because he was in dire pecuniary straits and hoped that if he dangled this carrot in front of their noses, the States would swiftly part with the money. He also wanted to take a look at possible modifications to the original proposals, as the objections advanced by the States had made an impression on him and his advisers. The modified propositions of March 1570 were the

The title page of the July 31, 1571 placard announcing the imposition of the Tenth and Twentieth Pennies.

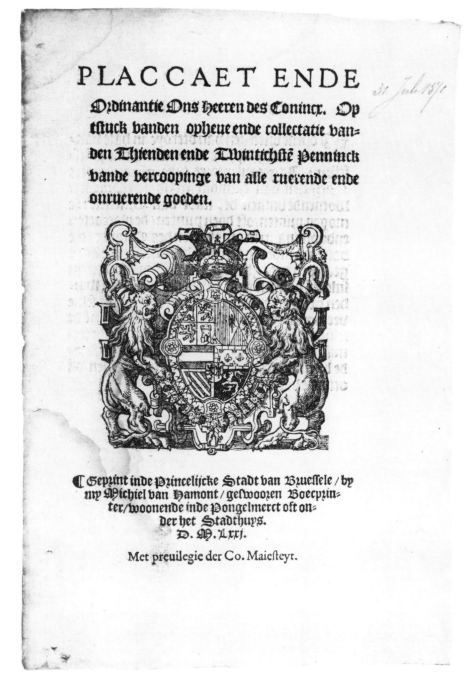

PLACCAET ENDE

Ordinantie Ons Heeren des Conincx. Op tstuck banden opheue ende collectatie van=
den Thienden ende Twintichste Penninck
bande bercoopinge van alle ruerende ende
onruerende goeden.

Gepzint inde Pzincelijcke Stadt van Bzuessele / by
my Michiel van Hamont / gefwoozen Boecpzin=
ter / woonende inde Pongelmerct oft on=
der het Stadthuys.
D. M. Lxxj.

Met preuilegie der Co. Maiesteyt.

fruits of his renewed deliberations. However, he was greatly disappointed by the way the commutation proposal had been handled. He had been obliged to exert himself to the utmost and to endure numerous delays, especially in Flanders and Brabant, in order to get the States to consent to the outright grant and to agree unanimously about how to raise this annual sum. In addition, the States continued to oppose the Tenth and Twentieth Pennies, in spite of the moderations and the fact that they had officially approved them. It is therefore not surprising that Alva contemplated more drastic measures. Even a man less short-tempered and impetuous than Alva would have lost patience with the States. However, in 1571 Alva's position was considerably weaker than it had been two years earlier.

Viglius, his most important Dutch Councilor — who was continually kept up to date on which way the wind was blowing in the Spanish court by his friend Hopperus in Madrid — knew only too well that Alva's flag was no longer flying very high at the court. Although the King still supported his Governor, his heart was apparently no longer in it. In Spanish eyes, the taxation question in the Low Countries was both lamentable and incomprehensible. In addition, Ruy Gómez's faction was constantly stirring up trouble for Alva whenever the opportunity presented itself. In any case, Viglius was so heartened by these signs that he adopted a tougher stance toward Alva.

In anticipation of the expiration of the two-year period for the commutation of the Tenth Penny on August 13, 1571, the Duke began well in advance to consult with his Councilors about future measures. When Berlaymont and other Councilors expressed their doubts as to whether the States were bound to their previous consent to the Tenth and Twentieth Pennies, in view of the fact that these taxes had been commuted for two years, Alva flew into a rage and hurled reproaches at Berlaymont for his spineless attitude. He added that he was sick to death of the commutation measure and was therefore planning to start collecting the Tenth and Twentieth Pennies. Schetz, the Treasurer, was to prepare the necessary measures.

As usual, Alva did not give a single thought to the opposition to his plans; he sent the King a preliminary message, stating that, once the commutation period had expired, he would convert to the Tenth Penny. On July 31, 1571, Alva carried out what was, to all intents and purposes, a financial coup: instead of offering the States a new proposal, he published a placard proclaiming the imposition and collection of the moderate version of the Tenth and Twentieth Pennies as of August 13th. He also issued detailed instructions for its implementation. These included procedural matters, such as appointing a general tax collector for each city or rural district (to be selected from a list of three prominent nominees drawn up by local government officials), appointing special collectors for various goods (such as liquids, poultry, game, fish, dry goods, bread, draper's goods such as cloth and items sold singly or by weight) and regulations concerning bookkeeping, official inspection visits, payment installments, appeal procedures, etc.

This was all to be set in motion two years after the States had granted their definite consent to the Tenth Penny, which was the exact moment the commutation period ended. The Great Council of Mechelen[14] was ordered on August 12, 1571 to act as a watchdog over the new placard. In a burst of candor, Alva reported to the King on August 3rd that, notwithstanding the protests of his financial advisers, he now finally intended to press on with the Tenth Penny.

Looking back after four centuries, the July 31, 1571 placard seems predictable enough. But to Alva's contemporaries it was a bolt from the blue. Such agitation and unrest erupted on all sides that Noircarmes, one of the Finance Councilors, considered it advisable to warn the King that the Tenth Penny would end in disaster. The States of the various provinces rose in protest against a phrase in the placard describing the States as "those who had previously given their general consent [to the Tenth and Twentieth Pennies]." Each of the provinces had its own reasons for considering the accords invalid. According to Brabant, the principle of replacement had not been applied lawfully because, in essence, the entire

14. The Great Council of Mechelen served as a Supreme Court of Justice for certain categories of persons not otherwise covered by the judicial system, such as the Knights of the Golden Fleece, and as a Court of Appeals in civil suits.

This wood and polychrome satirical sculpture (artist unknown) shows how the Duke of Alva had to fight the enemies of his King (Philip II), namely Queen Elizabeth, the Pope and the Electoral Prince of Saxony.

Viglius ab Aytta
Zuichemus, actually
Joachim van Aytta van
Zuychem (1507-1577).
Dutch jurist and chairman
of the Privy Council.

third estate had been outvoted. Two years later, the States protested that no single city had given its total assent, which actually meant that the entire third estate had refused. They considered the replacement of the entire third estate to be so drastic as to be deemed invalid. Hainaut pleaded that the consent of the States had been based on Noircarmes' misrepresentation of the position when he had told them that the acceptance of the proposals should merely be seen as proof of their allegiance to their monarch and that their consent would probably not be implemented.

Further, all of the Councils of the States claimed that their consent was subject to the condition that the Tenth and Twentieth Pennies also be raised in the non-patrimonial provinces. As we have already seen, these provinces were allowed to commute both taxes for a certain sum per year and were also excluded from the placard of July 31st. This placard was intended for only Brabant, Flanders, Artois, Hainaut, Namur, Holland, Zealand, Utrecht, Walloon Flanders, Tournai, Mechelen and Valenciennes.

Up to this point, the Tenth Penny had not assumed any reality in the minds of the populace. It was merely a governmental sleight-of-hand that had created a furor, but for the rest had not affected their everyday lives. Times had now changed. The latest version of the Tenth Penny had been cast in the form of a placard, which was proclaimed everywhere for the edification of the general public, usually by posting it on the front of City Hall as well as having it announced by the town crier. We can well imagine the shock and consternation this notice caused among the general population. Now everyone was able to hear and read what the future held in store. Many municipal governments delayed the proclamation for as long as possible under a variety of pretexts. Here and there, the proclamation was even rejected pointblank, although the Stadtholders usually managed later to force the local administrators to relent. Once again, the ambiguity of Alva's strategy came to light. On the one hand, he published a placard that was, at least in his eyes, legally valid, allowing him to impose and collect the Tenth Penny; on the other hand, he reopened negotiations with the provincial States. One minute butter would not melt in his mouth as he tried to win the States over to his side by promising new and more lenient modifications, and the next minute he was harsh and unapproachable, threatening them with hell and damnation if they did not start imposing and collecting the Tenth Penny at once.

In his missive to Philip dated October 19th, Alva went into the question of the Tenth Penny once again. The King, he said, would be able to draw as much money from it as he wanted. He urged the King to try to imagine the effort he had already put into the affair and the obstacles, put in his path by his Dutch advisers, that he had had to overcome. He added that all the heads that had rolled and the privileges that had been abolished had not aroused as much opposition and hostility as the Tenth Penny!

His letter of a few weeks later, dated November 4th, is even more revealing. He reminded Philip that he had written him several times about the importance of the Tenth Penny and reaffirmed that the King would presently be able to extract as much as he wanted from the country. Up to now, the King had been obliged to relinquish part of his royal privileges in exchange for every florin extracted from the States. Alva felt that the States' resistance was actually motivated by their desire to retain control over the King's actions. The issue was not about protecting the interests of industry or fishing or whatever. The States had tried to intimidate him with prophecies of doom, even in the Council, but now they knew he was made of sterner stuff. Alva added that they would probably try to persuade the King to rescind his decision. The case would be lost, he wrote, if the King were to greet them with his indulgence, as the situation would never be so favorable as the present. If the King were to comply with the States' request, he would lose sway over these countries. Once the tax had been introduced, all their suffering would be forgotten within three months. Lastly, he cautioned the King not to let anyone read his letter.

Alva ignored the general consternation and continued to work assiduously at his preparations for implementing the Tenth Penny. New instructions for the provincial tax collectors appeared on October 16th. They were to set to work immediately, an order that was repeated a few weeks later. The problem was that, so far, no collectors had been appointed anywhere. The first step, therefore, was to arrange these appointments at the local level with all due speed. However, as we shall see, all efforts ran aground on the intransigence of the local magistrates.

In order to take the wind out of the opposition's sails, Alva introduced yet another modification: the Tenth Penny on the export of manufactured products would be reduced to the thirtieth penny. Other modifications followed: the thirtieth penny would also have to be paid on the products of cottage industries and fish destined for export. Liquids, beverages and any merchandise sold by dry measure would be exempt from the Tenth Penny. Such tax relief was intended to help the man in the street, who did not have enough money to buy in bulk and almost literally bought his food by the mouthful. Woven fabrics were also made exempt. Oils and other liquids used in production processes were exempt as raw materials. On November 2nd, the levy was simplified to accommodate small tradesmen, who were often illiterate and unable to keep accounts. They were required to swear under oath that they would put a tenth of what they received from every purchase (or at any rate at the end of the day) in "une caisse," a chest which they were obliged to have on the premises for that purpose. They were not to spend that money but to hand it over to the tax collector. Compulsory lead seals on textile products sold in stores were to be abolished. From now on, the storekeepers were asked to state under oath how much fabric they had in stock. Another important moderation was that liquid and meltable goods employed in the production of other goods were to be tax-exempt. Hardly two weeks had passed before Alva came up with another new and possibly even more important promise. On account of the exorbitant bread prices following the grain harvest failure of 1571, the sale of wheat and rye would be exempt from the Tenth Penny until the next harvest.

The growing opposition to the Tenth Penny

As it turned out, Alva's concessions only served to fan the flames of resistance and obstruction. After the fall of 1571, the opposition to the Tenth Penny grew rapidly, resulting in a surprising denouement in the summer of 1572. In this period of confused and heightened activity, it is extremely difficult to unravel the precise course of events. For this reason, it may be helpful first to look at the situation from the point of view of the various players or groups of players involved in the rapidly escalating conflict.

As King of Spain, Philip had to divide his attention between the Turks in the East – where he had to consolidate his position after his triumph at the Battle of Lepanto on October 3, 1571 – and The Netherlands in the North, where tension was gradually mounting over a complex tangle of political, religious and financial issues. The King had sent Alva to the Low Countries to restore order (and Catholicism!) and impose a permanent tax, but the Duke had clearly failed in his mission. The massive flow of revenue that Alva had promised the King from the Tenth Penny had proved to be a mere trickle. The King, alerted by reports from several sources, was becoming increasingly worried about the situation.

The fiscal dispute had meanwhile become a matter of personal prestige for Alva. Beset on all sides by both internal and external opposition, he recognized that his personal reputation was at stake. The internal opposition came from his Dutch Councilors, led by Viglius. Though in favor of a uniform tax for all provinces, they felt that the Tenth Penny was too high and would be harmful to trade and industry. These Councilors, still unwaveringly loyal to the Crown, would only accept Alva's policies if these had the King's unconditional support. The more Alva tried to persuade them that his policies had Philip's backing, the more

The seventeen Dutch provinces before Alva; an allegory of Alva's tyranny (Bartholomeus van Bassen, c. 1590-1652).

suspicious they became, so much so, in fact, that they eventually developed into an independent party in the conflict. The external opposition was divided into two camps. The first gave voice to its opposition on the streets. Particularly at the beginning of 1572, the atmosphere became charged, and riots and strikes cast a shadow over the daily life of the people, especially in Brussels, where Alva himself resided. The other camp comprised the various assemblies of the States, which constantly frustrated the Duke's plans and took great pains to prevent the implementation of the Tenth Penny. While Alva's military power could conceivably help bring the people to heel, it was ineffectual against the subtle manipulations and overt or covert obstructionism of the States. For this reason, their political and legal opposition was more dangerous to him than the popular resistance on the streets.

The provincial States were at their wits' end. They felt caught between the Duke's increasing pressure to finally set the tax collection in motion and the mob's rage at their having consented two years earlier to levy the Tenth Penny. Realizing that only the King could provide a solution to their problems, the States decided to send deputations to Philip in Spain in order to induce him to withdraw the Tenth Penny. In Alva's eyes, this act was tantamount to civil disobedience. He did his utmost to stop them, but failed to prevent their departure.

The final protagonist in the revolt was the huge mass of common people, plunged into poverty by unemployment, bereft of future prospects because of economic hardship and the threat of war, not free to state their own opinions or religious beliefs, caught in a vice between high grain prices and low wages, oppressed by Alva and his soldiers, neglected by the clergy and betrayed by their City Councils. Their despair and suffering is graphically portrayed in Pieter Breughel the Elder's harrowing painting "The Triumph of Death." These wretched masses focused their wrath on the Tenth Penny, which came to symbolize all the injustice responsible for their misery. Not surprisingly, William of Orange's secret agents fanned the fires of resistance. Having been handed the Tenth Penny issue on a silver platter, they were quick to seize upon this matter as a propaganda tool. Surprisingly, here and there, people actually dared rise up in revolt, despite the iron grip that Alva and his soldiers had on the country.

Increasing resistance to the Tenth Penny

In November of 1571, Alva took several steps to speed up the collection of the Tenth Penny. He organized a general inspection in all provinces in order to investigate the extent to which the placards were being complied with. To carry out the inspection, he appointed special commissioners, usually members of the provincial courts and councils. These commissioners were to convene the municipal councilors and royal officials in their area of inspection in order to establish whether the placards had been published and whether the collection had begun. At the end of November and the beginning of December, the reports from the special commissioners began to trickle in. A revealing picture of the constant obstruction with which Alva had to contend emerges from these reports. Any and all possible pretexts and prevarications were used to avoid imposing the Tenth Penny. Take, for instance, the example of a certain Jehan Macrel, who was appointed as a general collector in Artois. After a long delay, he was ordered by the City Council to finally come take his oath. He replied that he was not feeling well, that he had no knowledge of bookkeeping and that he could not guarantee that he would be able to fulfill his office because he had no friends and relatives. While he was certainly prepared to serve His Majesty and His Excellency, he was too simple-minded to know what to do. It is a moot point whether Arras' Aldermen deliberately appointed such a simple soul as general collector or whether he was a glib talker seizing on any excuse to shirk his duty. A similar case occurred in 's-Hertogenbosch, where the general collector swore up and down that he could not read or write, even though he traded in silk, cloth and horses, as the City Council pointedly remarked.

Things were no different in Zealand. Guillaume Le Normand, member of Middelburg's Council, held an inspection from December 21st to December 24th. A general collector had indeed been appointed for Middelburg, but a grave illness had kept him from taking any action. The collectors in Arnemuiden were willing to go along with the Tenth Penny, but only if Middelburg set an example. In the countryside in Walcheren (one of Zealand's islands), the collector said he could not read the placard "as he is a country person." He made no secret of the fact that he had taken his oath as inspector "under the rigors of torture." He had done nothing further, as the cities in Walcheren had not set an example. The other inspectors questioned by Le Normand also indicated that Middelburg should take the lead. But the authorities in Middelburg, evidently incompetent in such matters, were powerless to act, with their general collector laid up in bed.

Detail of the funeral procession of Charles V, including on the right the Prior Antonio Henriquez de Toledo, Alva's brother-in-law, who kept him informed of events in Madrid during the time Alva was in the Low Countries.

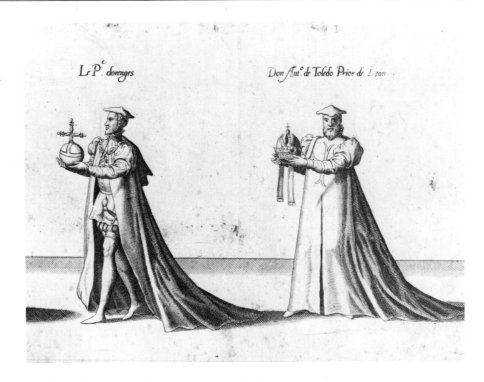

Le P.ᶜ *dorenges*   Don Ant.º de Toledo Prior de Leon

No matter what the City Councilors did to thwart the Tenth Penny, the people's anger did not abate. On the contrary, it assumed a more definite shape after December 1571, especially in Brabant. Anxiety over the popular opposition drove the provincial States to renew their efforts at political intervention, first in Brussels and then, when that made no impression, at a higher level in Spain. The States relied on the hostility of the clergy to the hated tax and the opposition of Alva's Dutch Councilors.

The unrest surfaced first in Antwerp, and quickly spread to other cities. Brussels was hit hard. Its City Council had summoned merchants and small businessmen to City Hall in the beginning of December in order to swear on oath that they would pay the Tenth Penny. The stores of those who refused were to be closed. As few turned up to take the oath, a second order followed, addressed especially to butchers and poultrymen. They did not budge an inch, not even when several leading members of the butchers' guild were thrown into prison. In response, the butchers closed down the meat hall for most of December, preventing any meat from being sold. To break the strike, the City Council temporarily suspended stringent guild regulations, allowing anyone inside or outside the city to function as a butcher. But this action did not bring the municipal authorities any closer to their goal. In the middle of December, they tried to break the impasse by decreeing that the butchers would not have to start paying the Tenth Penny until the New Year. The City Council professed to understand the complaints of the craftsmen and advised them to send a petition to the Duke, stating clearly that they did not reject the Tenth Penny out of defiance, but out of great material necessity.

With this formulation, they had hit the nail on the head. For it was not so much the Tenth Penny itself that had sparked all the protests. The matter was far more complex. Since the beginning of the economic crisis in 1565/1566, the price of grain had continued to plummet, providing some consolation for the drop in

*Portrayal of various
outdoor butcher stores.*

wages which had set in in 1567. In 1571, the crop failure led to a scarcity of grain, which drove prices up considerably. Amsterdam, long the largest staple market for grain, even forbade its export. One of the reasons for the grain harvest failure was the lack of farm laborers, as many had been felled by the plague epidemic in the countryside. As a result, the crops were left to rot in the fields. The plague raged until checked by another calamity, severe frost. The winter of 1571/1572 brought heavy snowfall and freezing temperatures that lasted five weeks, from the middle of February until the end of March. The rivers froze over and most of the fruit trees were damaged by frost and died. This misery came on top of the general economic malaise, which had been caused by the increase in privateering, the war between Denmark and Sweden and the shortage of salt, indispensable for preserving herring and other fish. Add to this the extensive floods which occurred in November of 1570, the heavy costs of billeting the Spanish soldiers and the climate of insecurity resulting from suppression and religious persecution, and it need come as no surprise that popular unrest became centered on the Tenth Penny. In Antwerp no more laborers were hired because of the Tenth Penny. According to Morillon, merchants cited the same reason for wanting to pay only two thirds of the stipulated wages. In Brussels thousands of unemployed were already living off charity. Similar social factors lay behind the strike of Brussels' bakers, brewers and butchers. The striking storekeepers surreptitiously sold their merchandise for extortionate prices. The strike left the poor with only fish to eat, to be washed down with a watery brew that the City Council was trying to pass off as beer.

The tension rose to fever pitch in Brussels in January of 1572. The New Year was just one week old when the Duke forbade the sale of any merchandise whatsoever unless the Tenth Penny had been paid on it. All the stores in Brussels promptly closed their doors that very day. Fresh fish was no longer sold, wool and silk fabrics were nowhere to be had, the brewers stopped working and the grocers, apothecaries and oil and lard dealers closed shop. By way of punishment and to set an example, the goods of a prominent citizen of Brussels, who had refused to pay the Tenth Penny, were confiscated. The impounded merchandise was to be sold by public auction, but no one turned up. And even if the items had been handed out for free, Morillon wrote, the people, rich or poor, still would not have wanted them!

In Alva's eyes, the City Councilors' lack of decisive action was to blame for all the unrest. He showered a hail of abuse upon their heads, telling them there would be hell to pay unless they took suitable measures against the brewers. He evidently reasoned that if the resistance of the powerful brewers' guild could be broken, the others would follow suit. The municipal government attempted to break the deadlock by proposing to pay the Tenth Penny itself, but that was acceptable to neither the brewers nor to Alva. In the meantime, the brewers were spurred on by dire threats to resume their work. They were faced with the prospect of a monetary fine of 100 florins per person and confiscation of their goods. Some sources mention that the brewers were even threatened with the death penalty, but this is doubtful. It is true, however, that the recalcitrant brewers were banished from the city, despite a legal protest drawn up by lawyers and presented to the City Council. When all efforts proved to be in vain, the City Council tried to break the strike by admitting duty-free beer brewed outside the city and by supplying storekeepers with cheap Council-commissioned beer. Free beer was brewed for the poor, although this brew was as thin as the wallets of those who had to drink it.

The City Council, at a complete loss, tried to pour oil on troubled waters by reaching a compromise with the striking brewers. The latter re-opened their breweries on February 13th, following an agreement reached the day before. The text of this agreement shows that the brewers were not prepared to accept any tax liability unless it was ratified by the city's three orders, namely the magistrates, the Large Council and the ''nations'' (i.e. the masters of the crafts guilds). In addition, they were to be free to quit the trade of brewer after Easter, an offer that was also valid if they were taxed with the Tenth Penny or any other tax not approved by the three orders. The latter clause, in particular, indicates that the brewers had come out on top. The stores also opened their doors on February 13th, which suggests that the storekeepers drew support from the brewers' accord. But on March 15th, the butchers stopped working again when it appeared that the Tenth Penny was still being imposed.

Morillon reports that Alva nearly exploded with rage when he heard of the strike and did not leave his room for eight days, but perhaps this was also due to his gout. He had not been idle during the unrest in Brussels, which was, to exacerbate matters, his place of residence. He had threatened to quarter soldiers in the stores that were closed, an efficacious means of scaring the living daylights out of law-abiding citizens. At his command, collectors went from door to door on January 14th and 15th, but came back empty-handed. Alva also put pressure on the City Councilors who, according to Morillon, were in turn incensed when he called them scoundrels. Whatever Alva did only appeared to stiffen the brewers' resistance. It is therefore not difficult to see why he was driven to extremes. On February 24th, yet another placard was issued, ordering the local councils and public officials to assist the collectors of the Tenth Penny in the performance of their duties. This placard outlined how they were to proceed against acts of defiance and also imposed stiffer penalties.

The hatred the recalcitrant populace felt toward Alva was only matched in intensity by their contempt for the first and second estates and their bitterness toward their own City Council for betraying them two years earlier by accepting the Tenth Penny and yielding to the Duke's fiscal policies. Against this background, it is perhaps easier to understand why women in Namur turned their bloodhounds loose on the collectors. Cornet, Dordrecht's Pensionary, feared for his life. The seamen in that city, he said, were so unruly and violent that any attempts to collect the Tenth Penny were bound to provoke a riot. "And in heaven's name please don't tell that to the Duke, for if he were to send soldiers, all hell would break loose," he concluded. The magistrates in Douai did not appoint any collectors, fearing the people would beat them to death. The situation in Lille and Oorschie was no different. Driven by the hostile and restive mood of the people, the provincial States redoubled their attempts to rid themselves of the hated tax. They not only thwarted its actual imposition and collection, but also directed a barrage of petitions at the Duke, offering him outright grants of money in lieu of the tax that would formerly have made his mouth water. And when all their petitions once again proved in vain, they seriously considered sending delegations to Philip in order to persuade him to change his course.

The clergy, from high to low, also gradually began to oppose the new tax. The Flemish bishops asked the Duke to waive the Tenth Penny, and the lower monastic orders also started to speak out against the tax. Jacob Tsantele, the priest of St. Martin's Church in Kortrijk, preached openly against the Tenth Penny, and he was not alone. He vehemently denounced local governments for failing to defend the poor who, in his eyes, would suffer the most from the Tenth Penny. On Christmas Eve of 1571, the rebellious priest refused to give absolution to the members of Kortrijk's City Council and a collector of the Tenth Penny. He had warned previously that those associated with the Tenth Penny (particularly the City Councilors and the collectors) were de facto excommunicated, and that he would therefore refuse them absolution if they came to him for confession. The Duke ordered a thorough judicial inquiry and had the priest put in prison, although he was released some time later. Alva demanded that Tsantele be punished as an example, but the Bishop of Tournai shielded him, and soon afterwards, he was able to resume his duties. He persisted in his defiance and began preaching against the Tenth Penny on February 23rd, although this time less openly. New interrogations followed, but on April 4th, Tsantele was back at his post. Alva's demand that Tsantele be compelled to retract everything he had said about the Tenth Penny was coolly rejected by the Bishop of Tournai on the grounds that without the Pope's permission, the Bishop was not allowed to lapse into such "servitude."

Alva was not only confronted with opposition from the common people, the States and the clergy. The internal opposition from his Dutch advisers was every bit as determined. Admittedly, their influence was waning, owing to the volatile circumstances, the Duke's authoritarian character and his secret exchange of let-

Cartoon of Alva's statue in the castle in Antwerp. The words "Tienden penninck" ("Tenth Penny") are written a little to the right of center.

ters with the King. However, he could hardly run the whole show singlehandedly without consulting them. The local governments sensed that their opposition and obstruction was backed by the Dutch members of the Collateral Councils. Councilor Viglius, in particular, made no secret of his opinion. This is not to imply that the Councilors were a shining example of valor in the face of their Spanish boss. As so often happens in these situations, they expressed their opinions in private rather than to Alva's face.

Alva fails to collect the Tenth Penny

In the meantime, the Duke continued to turn the financial thumbscrews tighter and tighter. He rained down threats on unwilling and dilatory magistrates. The Councils of Flanders, Brabant and Holland as well as Zealand's general steward were urgently requested to proceed with the actual collection forthwith. He warned them that steep fines would be imposed if they failed to assist the collectors. On February 24, 1572, the penalties in the ordinance of July 31, 1571 were stiffened considerably. What was more, any merchants attempting to swindle the treasury by submitting false accounts or by any other means would be punished by having the goods involved in the fraud confiscated. If the fraud were to be repeated, the fine would be quadrupled, while a third-time offender would be brought before a criminal court. Merchants who refused to pay the Tenth Penny or to open their books and confirm their accuracy upon oath could be assessed to maximally a tenth of the value of their stocks at the last inspection.

The placard of February 24th proclaimed even more stringent measures. In the preamble, the City Councilors and local officials as well as the general and special collectors were reproached for neglecting their duty. The placard pointed out that the City Councilors were not only obliged to appoint the collectors, but also to support their tax-collecting efforts. Those in authority were to send for the collectors and to refute the arguments against the Tenth Penny. The collectors, if necessary accompanied by officers and bailiffs, were to start collecting the Tenth Penny immediately. The placard concluded with the warning that failure to follow this order would be punishable by imprisonment!

The storekeepers were supposed to declare how much they had sold since the publication of the placard of July 31st. Anyone who refused to do this would receive a 30 − 60 florin fine. If a storekeeper was prepared to pay the Tenth Penny but did not keep any books, an amicable settlement was to be negotiated. Those who threatened to close their stores on account of the Tenth Penny would be barred from trade for the rest of their lives. If they ignored this ban and continued to trade, they would risk a fine of 100 gold reals and imprisonment.

No ban was pronounced on the trade of brewers, bakers, butchers, fish sellers, dealers in oil and lard, innkeepers and others engaged in the distribution of vital foodstuffs. In fact, they were compelled to continue trading under penalty of imprisonment, fines, seizure of their merchandise and household goods and even lifelong exclusion from their trade.

The punishment for any party to a conspiracy (meaning an agreement among storekeepers to close their stores) would be confiscation of goods and banishment. If storekeepers refused to sell their merchandise with the approval of their guild, all of the guild's privileges would be abolished and its goods permanently confiscated. No lawyers would be allowed in any subsequent trials, and there would be no question of appeal. Special courts were to be set up, to be alternately served by vassals, jurors and aldermen. One third of the fines imposed were to go to the central government, one third to the councilmen, officials and collectors and one third to informers reporting cases of tax evasion and fraud. On the previous day (February 23rd), a special placard had been issued for Antwerp, which announced that no goods were to be exported unless the Tenth Penny had been paid on them. The placard also included various details of penalties for collectors, shipmasters and wagoners.

In spite of the repressive measures decreed in these placards, the collectors were sensible enough not to comply with them. In Antwerp, where the placard was published on February 27th, the masters of the guilds obstinately refused to hand over their membership lists. In Brussels, the collectors, who had fixed up an office in City Hall, waited in vain for the merchants who were to pay the Tenth Penny.

Like the Spring Procession in Echternach,[15] the Duke retreated a step. In his letters of February 26th, he noted that many were averse to the Tenth Penny because they were unaware of the numerous moderations that had been introduced in the meantime. Consequently, a few further modifications were added and the placards were re-issued. The merchants were relieved of their obligation to declare under oath the amount of goods they had in stock or had sold; from now on a simple statement would be sufficient, and the collectors were to trust

15. This refers to the annual procession in Luxembourg, in which five steps are taken forward and three steps backward.

Detail of the title plate of Emanuel van Meteren's "History of The Netherlands and its Neighbors: Wars and History up to the Year 1611," showing the publication of the Tenth Penny.

in the good faith of those making the statement. However, the oath was still required for those opposed to the Tenth Penny. The general and special collectors no longer had to stand guarantee for the revenues. Instead, the government was to rely on the collectors' integrity and accurate bookkeeping. All of these placards had to be published, sufficient reason for resentment and resistance on the part of the general public, even when they only dealt with a moderation.

Opinions are divided as to whether the Tenth Penny was ever actually collected. The sources are virtually silent on this point. There are scattered references to collectors carrying out preparatory work, such as drawing up stock lists, but this is no indication that they actually managed to bring in the tax. Certainly, the repeated publication of placards in the various cities throughout March suggests that nothing had been collected up to that point. This conflicts with the optimistic reports that Alva sent the King about the Tenth Penny's progress. If his reports were true, one would expect to find corroborative evidence in the archives. But reports of successful levies of the Tenth Penny are few and far between. A case in point is Tournai. In his April 2nd missive to the King, Alva wrote that placards had been implemented in Tournai without a struggle from the very first day. He added that this result had been achieved without help from the Spanish soldiers quartered there! The success was all the more striking in view of the fact that Tournai had strong Protestant sympathies.

As stated previously, the general crisis was merely aggravated by the threat of the Tenth Penny. There are sufficient indications that the rental value of real estate plummeted during Alva's administration. Complaints that commercial activity in such ports as Antwerp and Amsterdam melted away like snow before

the sun should be taken seriously. For foreign merchants thought nothing of turning to other harbors such as Hamburg, Emden and London if and when the need arose. Interestingly enough, Hamburg attempted to entice Antwerp's foreign merchants by pointing out that Hamburg had no such thing as a Tenth Penny.

Significantly, the tonnage, a reliable gauge of activity in Antwerp's harbor, dropped drastically, and masses of merchandise remained unsold in the city. Antwerp fell prey to widespread unemployment. In Holland, the situation was no different. There was widespread poverty and discontent in Dordrecht. Ships from Cleves were reputedly impounded because the Tenth Penny had not been paid. For this reason, merchants from the Baltic regions bypassed Holland and transported their goods directly to Portugal. Numerous fishermen and herring packers from Holland and Zealand are said to have left for England.

The last resort: deputations to the King

When it became clear that neither obstructionism nor new petitions addressed to the Duke could hold back the Tenth Penny, various provinces decided to make a last-ditch attempt to stave off the tax by sending deputations to Philip. Rumors that the King was not actually in favor of the Tenth Penny probably inspired the States to undertake such a daring venture.

In the middle of December, the States of Brabant, at the instigation of the prelates and nobles, decided to ask Alva for the last time to suspend the Tenth and Twentieth Pennies. Unless Alva granted this request, a deputation would be sent to the King to explain "the ruination of the country" that would result from the implementation of the Duke's proposals. This request was sent on December 18, 1571. The negative reply received on January 10, 1572 pointed out the futility of their request. While Alva claimed that he was prepared to listen to an explanation of the possible damaging effects of the Tenth Penny, this was a routine concession. Even before Alva's answer had arrived, the States of Brabant had decided that the delegation to the King would consist of one prelate, one nobleman, one representative of the cities and two academics, fluent in Latin, French and Spanish. The General Secretary of the States, Cornelis Weellemans, by now an old hand in such matters, was to prepare the instructions and compile a file with the evidence. It was not easy to find suitable persons for the delegation. A dozen names were put forward, but most declined the honor. While they all supported the plan, they excused themselves on the grounds of poor health or prior commitments. They feared the Duke's wrath at least as much as the perils attendant on the journey to Spain. After much effort, a delegation was finally assembled. Several of the other provinces followed Brabant's example and prepared to send delegations.

Alva tirelessly endeavored to prevent the departure of the delegations from Brabant and the other provinces. But nothing could deter the States from their plan. Neither the moderations of February 26th nor Alva's letters of that and the following day, addressed to the Governor of Antwerp and Louvain's City Council (advising them to start collecting the tax immediately) could stop them. The threats of fines and imprisonment Alva leveled at those who refused to collect the tax had no effect. The States undoubtedly drew comfort from the letter of Sonnius, the Bishop of Antwerp, who stood squarely behind the plan of sending a mission to the King. Ultimately, Alva did not dare bar the delegations from setting off on their journey. A travel ban would have given rise to the suspicion that the Tenth Penny was entirely of Alva's own making and that the King knew nothing of it, or at least was not involved in the matter.

The delegation from Hainaut had departed several weeks earlier, and those from Artois and Walloon Flanders were ready to set sail. The Dean of the Chapter would be traveling for Utrecht. While certain parties in Holland also wanted to send a delegation, the States had not been convened and so could not come to a decision. Flanders was to decide whether to send a deputation at a later date. And so the delegations of the various provinces departed one after another on the long and dangerous journey to Spain.

Meanwhile, back in their homeland, tempestuous events (both literally and figuratively) were taking place. The Sea Beggars,[16] driven out of England by Queen Elizabeth and sailing under the Prince of Orange's flag, had taken the city of Den Briel by surprise on April 1, 1572, an event that created an enormous stir throughout the country. Bossu, the Stadtholder of Holland, and his army arrived on the scene quickly, but the wind prevented him from crossing the Meuse River. When he finally approached the city, he could not reach it because the surrounding land had been flooded. The occupying forces jeeringly asked him from across the water what had taken him and his Tenth Penny so long. As his own military forces were outnumbered, Bossu was forced to retreat to Dordrecht via Rotterdam. His arrival at Dordrecht's city gates created such a stir among the populace, who feared that he had come to collect the Tenth Penny, that the municipal government did not dare let him inside the gates. Offering its apologies, the City Council sent him on his way with foodstuffs and ships. Other cities in Holland and Zealand were also in a state of ferment, but Bossu was generally able to maintain control.

16. The Beggars (initially a derogatory term applied by government officials) were insurgents openly opposed to the King and forming the opposition at the beginning of the Eighty Years' War. The Sea Beggars could be considered the maritime branch.

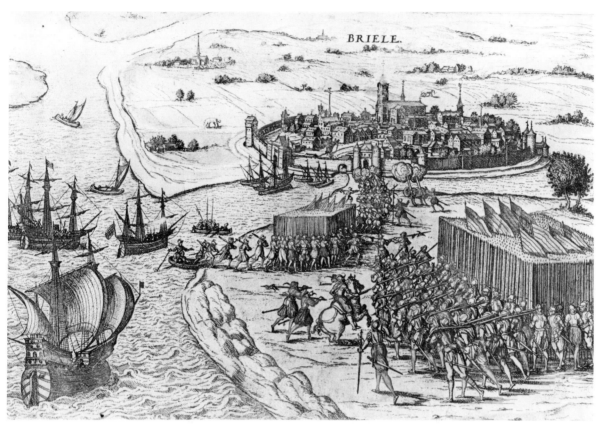

The capture of Den Briel by the Sea Beggars (April 1, 1572).

Flushing, however, was an exception. When Flushing's residents poured out of church on April 6th, Easter Sunday, they saw Spanish quartermasters making their way to City Hall to arrange the billeting of their soldiers. The crowd took up a menacing stance. While they were prepared to accommodate a garrison of Dutch soldiers, Spaniards were on no account to set foot in Flushing. Shortly afterwards, the Walloon garrison was driven out of the city, and on April 22nd, fourteen ships of Sea Beggars were ushered in. This gave the insurgents control over the mouth of the Scheldt, and their position was strengthened when they were joined soon afterwards by the cities of Veere and Arnemuiden.

As a result of the invasion and revolt in Holland and Zealand, opposition against the Tenth Penny intensified. In every city in Holland and Zealand that they entered, the Beggars proclaimed that they had come to save the people from the Tenth Penny.

Suspension and abolition of the Tenth and Twentieth Pennies

In the Netherlands, everyone anxiously awaited the result of the deputations which had been sent to Spain. Alva meanwhile wrote Philip that he should not let the bad news from Holland and Zealand influence his attitude toward the delegations. If the King were to give way, all of the advantages of the new system of taxation would be lost for good. Still, he could no longer deny that matters had taken a turn for the worse. A letter to Cardinal de Espinosa was also intended to prepare the court in Madrid for his upcoming change of course.

The Duke of Alva's top military architect, Don Pedro Pacieco, and two Spanish noblemen, hanged in Flushing in 1572.

The conviction that the Tenth Penny was on the way out had now gained ground on all sides. Amsterdam's Town Council considered asking Alva to withdraw the tax, but the burgomaster felt this was an unnecessary step. A few weeks later, Amsterdam's burgomaster, Joost Buyck, returned from Brussels with the reassuring message that the imposition of the Tenth Penny was no longer matter for concern.

A few months prior to this, the Council of Finance had proposed commuting the tax obligation to an outright grant of money. The Duke now turned this proposal to good account. His son, Don Frederick, was to prompt the States to act without arousing the suspicion that Alva was the instigator. The Council believed that the States would indeed be prepared to grant an aid of two million florins for the year ending on August 13, 1572. Don Frederick would have to play his hand carefully to ensure that the States would make the offer of their own accord, without realizing that Alva and the Council of Finance had concocted the scheme. Alva instructed the Councilors to play their role as agreed and sent them to talk to the States. His scheme was a success, and he was able to write to the King on May 22nd that the Council of Finance proposed suspending the Tenth Penny until August 13th and that in the meantime it would be able to search for other funds.

This series of events would appear to indicate that the Duke was already preparing his retreat. The explosive political and military situation gave him good reason to take these precautions. The signs were that William of Orange's policy of encirclement was finally paying off. Even though England's Queen Elizabeth had bowed out, the Sea Beggar's still posed a substantial threat in the West and mercenary troops stood at the ready in Germany. With the Huguenots in France in the ascendancy, a declaration of war and invasion from the South seemed imminent. On May 23rd, Whit Saturday, Valenciennes fell into the hands of the Huguenots. At four a.m. the next morning, Louis of Nassau took Mons, the capital of Hainaut, by surprise. Mons was initially intended as a defensive outpost on the French border, but its defense had been neglected and its most capable leaders were in Spain, requesting the abolition of the Tenth Penny. Alva, his back against the wall, had other things on his mind besides the Tenth Penny. The impending military action would once again put him at the head of his army, a role which came more naturally to him than that of tax innovator. In the circumstances, abolition or suspension of the Tenth Penny seemed the most obvious course, as it would permit him to replenish his empty coffers immediately and prepare for the approaching military operations. Moreover, abolition would deprive the insurgents of one of their most effective arguments for winning over the cities to their cause.

Madrid also slowly began changing its policy. The delegations were received with extreme coldness by Hopperus, Philip's adviser for affairs in the Low Countries. The deputation from Brabant, which arrived later than the others, received the same treatment. However, the Brabant delegation had one tactical advantage: their "Joyous Entry" had explicitly decreed that the subjects had the right to address the sovereign ruler directly. Philip, startled at the bad news from The Netherlands, was slowly beginning to experience a change of heart. At least, one can conclude as much from the letter he wrote to Alva on May 17th, in which he reported that the representatives from Brabant and Artois had arrived in the capital a short time ago. Significantly, he added that his answer would probably depend on the course of events in The Netherlands.

The news that Valenciennes and Mons had fallen reached Madrid on June 8, 1572 and evidently goaded the otherwise indecisive Philip into action. Alva's May 22nd missive, in which he explained his maneuver of using the Council of Finance to change his financial and political course, was probably also instrumental. It should be emphasized, however, that the initiative for replacing the Tenth Penny by an aid of two million florins did not come from the King. All Philip did was to uphold a decision that Alva had already made, albeit reluctantly. Alva had, in fact, abandoned all attempts to force through the imposition of the Tenth Penny in April, i.e. shortly before the King received the deputations in Madrid.

On June 26th, all the representatives from Hainaut, Artois, Walloon Flanders, Brabant and Flanders were summoned before the King at four o'clock in the afternoon. Philip began by commenting that there should be no need to abolish the new taxes. Next, he praised Alva for his loyal service. However, he felt that it would be in the country's best interests to suspend the new taxes for the time being and replace them by uniform taxes binding on all provinces. Philip said that he would appoint special commissioners, who would confer with the representatives of the States about how to proceed. The Tenth and Twentieth Pennies would be discontinued during the negotiations. Until further notification, the States would have to raise a yearly aid of two million florins and a second Hundredth Penny on the value of personal property, to be put aside for emergencies such as an invasion. In fact, the latter had already been granted a few years ago earlier.

According to the report of the session the King sent to Alva, the representatives appeared to be quite satisfied with the outcome. But Philip was mistaken. Evidently the delegates had not dared show their displeasure in his presence. Afterwards, the Flemish delegates explained to Hopperus that Philip's reply did not satisfy their request to permanently abolish the new tax. Hopperus reassured them that the King meant to abolish the tax for good, but had not used the term "abolish" out of consideration for the Duke's reputation. The Flemish asked for clarification on some other points. One of these was whether the aid that they were to grant His Majesty was "in perpetuity"? Hopperus confirmed this. In short, having bowed and scraped before the King, the delegates were at last freed from the hated Tenth Penny, an important victory over central authority. Not content to leave well enough alone, they immediately began negotiating with Hopperus for more.

Because of the rampant revolt and the threatened invasion of the Huguenots, Alva expanded his military force with all due haste. The greatest danger appeared to come from the South. Consequently, on June 15th, he ordered his troops in Holland to withdraw to the South, and in addition raised 14,000 horsemen in Germany to keep the French at bay with as large an army as he could muster. Although these deployments meant sacrificing Holland and the Northeast, he was confident he would be able to reconquer these provinces without too much difficulty.

In order to be able to concentrate on military matters, he decided to abandon the Tenth Penny entirely. This step was politically expedient as well, for the rebels were still taking advantage of the people's aversion to the tax. He had already cleared this line of retreat with the King, so that he could rightfully claim to be acting in the King's name. On June 27th, i.e. one day after the King had announced the suspension of the Tenth Penny to the delegates in Madrid, Alva wrote a letter to the States, notifying them of his intention to abolish it. He appended the condition that they grant an annual aid of two million florins and summoned the States to discuss how to raise that amount.

The States of Brabant met on July 13th and 16th, and the four orders convened a few weeks later in Bruges. Bossu requested the States of Holland to meet in The Hague on July 5th. They failed to appear, but the rebellious cities assembled in Dordrecht on July 19th; their objective was no longer to confer over how to do business with Alva, but to ensure that Holland, which had risen up in revolt now that the Spanish troops had retreated, toed the administrative line.

One of the most urgent matters was raising the money to finance the revolt. Now that it came to casting off the hated Spanish yoke, Holland quickly and magnanimously opened its pocketbook. On July 23rd, they promised Marnix, William of Orange's agent, taxes amounting to 500,000 florins. When Alva heard of their generosity, he was infuriated. He wrote to the King on February 11, 1573 that Orange had let the cities which recognized his authority pay four times the amount of the Hundredth Penny. "Really, it is beyond my comprehen-

Medal struck in honor of William of Orange. The general resistance against the Tenth Penny glorified ten heroes: the Prince of Orange and nine of his companions, whose heraldic shields are depicted.

sion, when I compare Your Majesty's efforts to extract aids from them with the magnanimity with which they sacrifice their lives and goods for this revolt.'' He repeated this lament a month later. The renegade cities, he stated, paid Orange an eighth to one third of the value of the merchandise they imported and exported. Orange had got them to pay three or four times the Hundredth Penny, but when he himself had asked them for the Tenth Penny in the service of the King they had refused!

Replacing the Tenth Penny with other taxes also fails

Although the States had achieved some success with the Tenth Penny, they were still unsure whether it had been postponed or canceled. The King and his Governor had issued contradictory statements. The provincial Stadtholders summoned the provincial States to discuss taxes to replace the Tenth Penny. Several proposals were put forward, mainly involving taxes on consumer items and export goods. Several of the export duties were even higher than Alva's moderated Tenth Penny, which after all had partially been reduced to a Thirtieth Penny. A kind of Rump States-General met on August 21st, consisting of representatives from Flanders, Brabant, Artois and Hainaut. As the commissioners appointed by the government wanted real estate spared, Councilor of State Charles de Tisnacq offered a compromise, in which mainly foodstuffs and trade goods would be taxed. After only two days, the deputies from Brabant announced that the imposts recommended by the commissioners would be too injurious to the country. Once again, the familiar tug-of-war between the States began. The representatives of the cities opposed the export taxes which the prelates and nobles favored. Tournai and Hainaut rejected the uniform taxes, which they viewed as the Tenth Penny dressed up in a new guise. In Brabant, the third and fourth orders in the cities had still not been able to reach a unified stand on uniform taxation and were as negative as ever. Without any results to show for its pains, the assembly was dissolved, and the representatives again headed home. The attempts in February of 1573 to introduce an export tax foundered on the uncompromising ''no'' of the merchants in Antwerp. One month later, the Chancellor of Brabant earnestly appealed to the States of that province to pay half of the aid of 542,000 florins proposed in July of 1572. Brabant's prelates and nobles agreed in April of 1573 to sell annuities to raise the 271,000 florins, on the condition that the States-General be reconvened within six weeks and the Tenth Penny rescinded for good. The demands were totally unacceptable to Alva, but his refusal gave the States a convenient excuse to delay payment. So far, the Duke had not managed to squeeze so much as a penny out of the States.

Alva, who had meanwhile been victorious at the siege of Mons, had already ruled out the possibility of eliciting funds from the Rump States-General in the short term. Consequently, he decided to await the outcome of events on the military and political front before pursuing his financial activities any further. As matters now stood, it looked as if his term in The Netherlands was drawing to a close and that he would soon be able to hand his function over to his successor. On balance, his stay had hardly been an unqualified success. He would leave behind a rebellious country whose finances were in total ruins, while only shortly before The Netherlands had been peaceful and a potentially rich source of tax revenue. Even though the States of Flanders still had not fathomed how they were to raise their share of the two million florins, they prudently provided the soldiers in their province with financial assistance in order to prevent mutinies and plundering. On April 16th, Alva requested the King to write him a letter reaffirming that the abolition of the Tenth Penny was subject to the provinces' granting an aid of two million florins. He would then be able to show this letter to the Council of Finance in support of his demands. In his missive, Alva lashed out at the States in unprecedentedly bitter terms. He reiterated that what the States objected to was not so much the Tenth Penny itself as the fact that the tax was not subject to a time limit and would therefore deprive them of their hold over the King. Confident that Holland and Zealand would soon be brought to heel by force, the Duke had no desire to reopen the humiliating negotiations with the States.

Alva's letters reveal how difficult his position in The Netherlands had become. His pride in his abilities as an authoritative and competent administrator had received a severe blow. He sorely needed a scapegoat to save his political skin. But Alva was not to remain in The Netherlands much longer. His frequent requests to the King to relieve him of his post were answered at last. His successor, Requesens, arrived in Brussels in the middle of November 1573, and the gout-afflicted Duke departed from the Low Countries on December 18th. His administration, which had looked so promising five years before on the eve of the Tenth Penny proposition, had ended in a debacle. Just in the nick of time, he had been able to save a few of the provinces, including those in the South, for the King, but the revolt in Holland and Zealand had gained momentum and now seemed irreversible. Haarlem had been recaptured at great cost to human life. But the Spanish troops proceeded to massacre the garrison and, contrary to earlier promises, hang several members of the City Council. The bloodbath in Haarlem had merely served to kindle the resistance in the remaining cities in Holland and Zealand. The subsequent sack of Mechelen and Zutphen and the massacre of Naarden were largely responsible for the evil reputation that the people of The Netherlands attribute to Alva even today. But Alva was not a demon. The ostensibly ruthless Governor was really a dutiful and correct Spanish nobleman whose harshness and cruelty did not stem from personal depravity but from a sense of duty. He always put the King's business first (naturally hoping in the process to enhance his own reputation) and had managed to summon a great deal of patience in his dealings with the Dutch representatives over the Tenth Penny, even though he sometimes lost control of his temper. Given his reputation in the Low Countries, it is not surprising that his departure was jubilantly and mockingly celebrated in the numerous and popular Beggar's Songs of the time.

His successor, Requesens, a man from the camp of the recently deceased Ruy Gómez, needed as much money as Alva did to conduct his wars. Much to his surprise, he found that the issue of the Tenth Penny, which he had considered settled after the deputations' visit to Spain, still had not been resolved. The States continued to make the payment of two million florins a year conditional on the permanent abolition of the Tenth Penny. Requesens had understood from Alva that the States had made the concessions voluntarily, but now the States obdurately denied this. They claimed they had acted out of fear of violence and that they had been threatened with the quartering of soldiers. Moreover, they had been told that their consent was only proof of their allegiance to the King and that there was no question of actual imposition and collection. Lastly, their condition – that no province should be excluded – had not been met. Irrespective of the truth of these claims, Requesens saw that the States would suffer any fate rather

Alva's departure from Brussels (December 18, 1573).

than agree to the Tenth Penny. They also refused to accept a permanent tax in lieu of the Tenth Penny, stating that they could not bequeath a burden in perpetuity to their successors. But, they added, His Majesty could, as ever, rely on them whenever he needed financial assistance.

Requesens was of the opinion that the King would do well to make the best of a bad bargain and permanently abolish the Tenth Penny, which he believed to be the chief cause of the rebellion. Two million florins a year was not a trifle by any standards, even if it was not to be levied permanently. The stubborn refusal of the sums offered had put the treasury in an extremely difficult position, for the States now claimed that they could not possibly pay their arrears on account of the depredations of military occupation and the ruin of trade. To make matters worse, Alva had abolished several local taxes in Brabant and Flanders, including those on wine and meat. While this had admittedly been done to alleviate the burden of the Tenth Penny, it made it difficult for the provinces to use local taxes in order to raise its share of the annual aid of two million florins.

It was not until the assembly of the States-General on June 7, 1574, the day after a new "general pardon" was announced, that the abolition of the Council of Troubles and the Tenth and Twentieth Pennies was proclaimed. In lieu of these two levies, the States were obliged to raise an aid of two million florins a year and the second Hundredth Penny that had been granted in 1570 in the case of invasion. The next day, Requesens asked the representatives of the States to deliberate over which taxes should be levied to raise the two million florins. Little did he know what difficulties still lay ahead of him.

NAERDEN.

The massacre of Naarden
by the Spanish army
(November 30, 1572).

The States' failure to furnish the necessary funds recoiled on them when, in April of 1574, Antwerp was pillaged by mutineering Spanish troops who had not been paid in a long time. Requesens sensibly made a virtue of necessity and compelled Antwerp's Large Council to lend him 400,000 florins to pay his mutinous troops and restore the peace.

In July of 1574, he began to experiment with a new system of maintaining his troops. Special officials were appointed in Brabant and Flanders, two provinces which were wealthy enough to afford the contributions but which could no longer collect taxes in the usual way. The officials were to ensure that the municipalities raised certain sums of money every month, which were to be paid to the soldiers directly. This took place under the supervision of the Council of Finance. Few traces of any money collected with the permission of the States can be found in the *Recette générale*. In fact, this scheme was nothing more than government-backed plundering with a legal gloss. Even when combined with the revenues from the regular taxes, the income it produced did not even cover a third of the military needs. The rest had to come from Spain. But Madrid was conducting a war on two fronts, so that shipments of money from Spain were a mere drop in the ocean. A debacle was inevitable and on November 4, 1576 the so-called "Spanish Fury" erupted: mutinous Spanish troops grimly sacked the city of Antwerp. This hastened the Pacification of Ghent, a treaty between the States, in which they took control of all provinces in The Netherlands.

The Union of Utrecht − The Netherlands' most important political response to the Spanish tyranny which spanned almost two centuries − was concluded in

HAERLEM.

Execution of members of the City Council carried out by the Spaniards after the capture of Haarlem (July 13, 1573).

1579. This pact provided for a uniform tax, valid in all member provinces, to be raised for the common defense of the combined provinces. Yet, as we shall see in the last section, these provisions largely remained a dead letter, as the provinces soon reverted to the old system of apportionment. The Tenth Penny as a modern reform of the tax system in The Netherlands had come a few centuries too early.

The significance of the Tenth Penny

What exactly motivated the various parties to rise in revolt against the King? This question became the subject of heated debate shortly after the rebellion broke out in The Netherlands. The various sides in this battle of words, each convinced of its right to oppose and even take up arms against legal authority, can be categorized according to their motives. To begin with, there were the militant Protestants, who championed freedom of religion yet frequently advocated the repression of Catholics; next, there were the well-to-do merchants, who preached free trade and yet unblushingly supplied food and even armaments to the Spanish foe; then there were politicians, like William of Orange, who advocated tolerance and freedom of thought yet often used this as an excuse to play the political chameleon, and lastly, there were the magistrates, who threw themselves in the breach for the centuries-old liberties and privileges of the cities and provinces and yet reacted with jealousy and petulance as a finger was raised against their positions of power.

MECHE LEN.

The sack of Mechelen in 1572.

The voice of the people is barely heard in these debates. Yet we can assume that those who backed the revolution did so in order to alleviate their barren existence by improving their living conditions or finding solace in the new religious beliefs. Few, however, had a choice, for after 1572 numerous cities in Holland and Zealand went over to the rebels. Typically, a small minority of rebels gained control of a City Council and compelled the majority (by either gentle persuasion or brute force) to toe the new leaders' line.

The next question which arises is whether the revolt can be attributed to one cause or to many, and if the latter is the case, whether one cause predominated. This section will discuss the role of the Tenth Penny within the broad framework of this question. A central issue is how the Tenth Penny influenced the revolt, which first broke out in Holland and Zealand and then rapidly spread after April 1572, bringing the rest of The Netherlands into a revolutionary frenzy.

Was the Tenth Penny merely a catalyst which activated latent feelings of bitterness against the violence, patronizing, extortion and other injustices perpetrated by the Spaniards? If so, the new tax was indeed an important propaganda tool for Orange's party and for his alleged allies, the Beggars, which they could use to sway hesitant City Councilors in Holland and Zealand to their side. Or had the tax itself generated such resentment that numerous cities in Holland, Zealand, Flanders and Brabant rose up in opposition and cast off the hated Spanish yoke, in order to escape a tax that in their eyes posed a direct threat to their survival?

Each of the actors in the drama of *The Tenth Penny* interpreted the tax's significance to suit his or her own needs. Alva dismissed the Tenth Penny as a matter of minor importance. The Protestant ministers saw only a sinful profit motive in it. Requesens and Granvelle viewed it as the cause of the revolt and laid the blame at Alva's door. The Beggars merely used it for propaganda. Orange, with the States of Holland and Zealand in his wake, saw it as a license to rebellion. Morillon, a spectator rather than a player, held the Tenth Penny jointly responsible for the decline in prosperity and the suffering of the poor, which formed, according to Viglius (who consistently opposed the Tenth Penny) the underlying cause of the revolt.

All things considered, however, the revolt cannot be traced exclusively to the Tenth Penny. If there was a single cause, it was the widespread and deep-seated discontent with the Spanish regime found in almost all layers of society. Each social group had its own reasons for this discontent. One reason was undoubtedly the Tenth Penny. Other motives included religion, the lack of freedom, poverty, the behavior of the Spanish army, etc. The main contribution of the Tenth Penny to the success of the revolt was that, as a symbol of Spanish tyranny, it provided a common focus for anti-Spanish sentiment.

It would be possible to conclude our examination into the significance of the Tenth Penny at this point. However, it is interesting to speculate on the rescinding of the Tenth Penny and to ask what would have happened if the Tenth Penny had been collected. The discussion will concentrate on the course of the revolt as well as on the sovereign ruler's efforts to achieve greater centralization and more power. But let us first take a look at the pros and cons of the Tenth Penny itself.

Alva was clearly badly in need of hard cash. The flow of funds from Spain threatened to dry up, as Spain justifiably held that The Netherlands should pay for its own defense. Alva obviously continued to hammer on this theme, contending in all his propositions that he needed the money for defense purposes. His opponents, the provincial States, never questioned his right to request funds, knowing full well that by law (particularly the "Joyous Entry") they were required to raise the money.

In fact, they assented without a murmur to one part of his program, the one-time levy of the Hundredth Penny. Although a second Hundredth Penny featured in the Duke's long-range fiscal plans, it was never seriously negotiated. Alva and the provincial States had agreed that the tax would, in principle, only be imposed in emergencies. The Hundredth Penny meant that the wealthy, in particular, would also have to contribute more to public spending than they had ever done before. This tax was evidently perceived as a positive development by contemporaries, as indeed it has been in later times.

This raises the question of how the Tenth Penny (and the Twentieth Penny) was viewed by contemporaries. The salient characteristic of the Tenth Penny was that it was a uniform tax applied to all patrimonial provinces. The system of apportionment had outlived its usefulness. It was too inflexible, failing to respond in time to economic fluctuations. Although uniform taxation would have undoubtedly strengthened the ties between the provinces, it would also have prompted centralization and thus have reinforced royal authority. In any event,

"The Roman Fisherman."
This 16th century cartoon
shows the Pope attempting
to fob off indulgences on
the priests and the faithful,
who reject his offer in no
uncertain terms.

few objections to the a tax levy of this nature were heard. Brabant and Flanders had even repeatedly advocated a similar tax, albeit primarily out of self-interest, or rather their desire to force their fiscal beliefs on the other provinces.

One of the Tenth Penny's other plus points was that it would lead to a more equal division of the tax burden. In his March 20, 1569 proposition, Alva stated emphatically that one of his objectives was to divide the burden between the city and the countryside more evenly. Although he never said it in so many words, he also wanted to introduce a tax that the nobility and the clergy would not be able to evade. He also intended to distribute the tax burden on basic necessities more equitably by simultaneously lowering or even scrapping existing excise taxes. There was very little opposition to these three fiscal and political objectives; Alva's contemporaries evidently also recognized that they were reasonable.

Once Alva had broken all opposition to the Tenth Penny in the summer of 1569 and had pushed through the deed of acceptance – clearly in the face of great reluctance on the part of the States even though they had all (or just about all!) signed it – nothing barred him from persevering in his wishes and proceeding with its imposition and collection. And yet, he decided to accept the well-known proposal of October 1569, in which the Tenth Penny was commuted, initially for a period of six years and later for two years, to an outright grant of two million florins per year.

Let us suppose that after August 13, 1569 he had succeeded in levying a moderated Tenth Penny for a reasonably short period, say six to twelve months, and had at the same time abolished or lowered the local tax on consumer goods. Let us further suppose that this would not have led to "the ruination of the country," as the States constantly claimed in their petitions. Given these assumptions, the Duke would have had a permanent source of money at his command.

Cartoon lampooning Catholic rituals (second half of the 16th century). Two clergymen are chopping away at the trunk of a tree filled with symbols of Catholic devotion, such as a holy-water font, altar bells, a thurible and monstrances. The Pope and a monk are trying to prop up the holy tree to keep it from falling down.

It is interesting to take a close look at later events in the light of these suppositions. Just what was the obstacle that Alva, and in his wake his successors, kept encountering? The answer is: finances. The most striking example of this is shown by the experience of the Governor during the late 1580's, the Duke of Parma. After capturing one city after another and posing a serious threat to Holland and Zealand, Parma had to call a halt to his triumphant campaign in 1589 because he ran out of money. Years earlier, in the summer of 1576, the Spanish soldiers had mutinied because they had not been paid in a very long time; in the beginning of November, these mutinies led to the "Spanish Fury," in which the Spaniards plundered their way through Antwerp for three days, murdering everyone in sight. The present-day British historian Geoffrey Parker impressively describes the vicious circle in which the Spanish army command found itself: the unwritten law of that time prevented them from dismissing soldiers before they had received their back pay, and yet they did not even have enough money to meet the current payroll. The soldiers as a group posed a latent threat because they refused to be dismissed until they had received their pay.

What would have happened if the Duke had gone ahead with the Tenth Penny in 1569, when he was at the height of his power, and had thereby ensured himself of a regular source of funds? Is it too audacious a thought to suppose that he and his army could have acted more forcefully and that he might even have been able to nip the revolt in the bud (assuming, of course, that it would have broken out in the first place)? To establish such a hypothesis, more in-depth research into causes and effects would be required. Nevertheless, it is not unreasonable to postulate that there was a certain connection between the rescinding of the Tenth Penny and the success of the revolt (or at any rate its partial success, namely in the North). Suffice it to say that, as of the middle of 1571, the clashes over the Tenth Penny claimed the full attention of the central government; so much so, in fact, that we are left with the impression that the administrative bodies no longer had time for other work.

Emergency money minted during the siege of Haarlem (1573).

This suggests that the Tenth Penny's significance as a catalyst in the revolt of 1572 is perhaps overshadowed by its negative importance: if Alva had not shelved the Tenth Penny at a crucial moment in the fall of 1569, the revolt (provided it had broken out) might have taken a very different course, and indeed might not even have been successful.

The connection between the Tenth Penny and the formation of a unified state is a second theme. The Burgundian and Hapsburg rulers continually attempted to promote greater unity between the provinces in The Netherlands. Their pursuit of this goal should be viewed in the light of the following successive stages of development, which have been observed in a number of Western European countries in the last few centuries: personal union, confederation, federal state and unified state. Common taxation has undeniably played a role in this process of unification. The last chapter of this book will show how this development also occurred in the United States of America, and how taxation formed one of the most important binding elements in that country as well.

Attempts to achieve common taxation in The Netherlands, long before Alva's time, have been pointed out earlier. Clearly, the Tenth Penny was precisely this type of uniform tax and was therefore wholly in keeping with the movement toward centralization. The hypothesis that the process of unification would have been accelerated if the Tenth Penny had gained a firm foothold on Dutch soil appears to contain more than a grain of truth. The last section of this chapter will further explore the idea that the rebellious provinces were also advocates of common taxation and will describe what remained of this political ideal in practice.

In the part of The Netherlands that had remained loyal to the King or that had been reconquered in his name, royal authority continued to exist in the person of the common sovereign ruler. Although this should theoretically have led to greater unification, these provinces continued to be bound, at least in a legal sense, in nothing more than a confederation. With respect to taxation, the extra aids continued to be subject to the approval of the States, providing them with a weapon with which to oppose the central government's attempts to create greater unity. But at the same time, this could act as a counterweight to the pursuit of royal absolutism. This leads us to the third and probably most important theme of the Tenth Penny, which will be discussed in more detail below.

The failure of the Tenth Penny and the struggle against the reinforcement of absolutist royal authority

The desire of subjects to take part in all discussions regarding the financial burdens imposed upon them and subject them to their final approval has stood at the cradle of democracy, at least in the form in which we know it today in large parts of the world.

A great deal of progress toward such participation had already been made in The Netherlands in the sixteenth century. Similar developments also occurred in other countries, as is evident from the others chapters in this book. In The Netherlands, a ruler who needed money had to request an aid from each of the States of the individual provinces. Even though the States were not free to refuse him funds for the country's defense, in practice a fairly balanced complex of

Emergency money minted during the siege of Leiden (1574).

legal rules had been created, giving the States a great deal of influence not only on the amounts of the aids but also on their expenditure; indeed, up to a certain limit, they themselves were able to spend the sums collected on behalf of the government. Clearly, when negotiating the aid, the central government and the provincial representatives made use of the opportunity to discuss all kinds of other business as well.

One of Alva's instructions was to eradicate these privileges. This was entirely in line with the aim of first the Burgundian and later the Hapsburg sovereign rulers to consolidate their power. It appears from many sources that Alva also believed that this order obliged him to confront the strong position taken by the States with respect to granting the aids. In his April 13, 1568 report to the King on the initial talks with his Dutch Councilors about his new tax schemes, Alva wrote that the Councilors were of the opinion that the States would never agree to a permanent tax. He had replied that without this guarantee of permanence, the King would have to depend for the defense of the country on the citizens of the third order of Brussels and the fourth order of Louvain; if that was the case, it was not the King who was the ruler, but the subjects. The Duke added that the conditions the States imposed on the granting of aids left the King little room to rule. The Duke emphasized that these political obstacles would have to be removed to consolidate the King's power in The Netherlands. Leaving aside the Duke's exaggerations, his goal was clear: the States would have to be deprived of their power to decide on matters affecting their own pocketbooks! The letter he penned to Philip on February 16, 1572 is also telling. There he says in no uncertain terms that if the Tenth Penny were to be implemented, the King would become a *señor assoluto*.

All Alva's letters contain the same line of reasoning: if a permanent source of finance could be found, the King would never again be compelled to humiliate himself by having to ask for money. The power of the States would be broken in three ways. Because the States' permission would no longer be required for each request, they would lose their grip on central government. Since the Tenth Penny, unlike the aids, was not to be collected by the provinces, the States would lose their control over the expenditure of the central government's tax revenues.

Finally, the government would be free to employ the money as it saw fit, not only to defend The Netherlands and maintain law and order, but also to support the power politics of the Spanish-Hapsburg monarchy in other parts of the world. Indeed, Alva repeatedly pointed out to the King how lucrative The Netherlands would be once the Tenth Penny had been introduced.

The States sensed this as well, and feared that their hard-earned ducats would all go to Spain. In the light of Alva's objective, their fear was not unfounded. But as things turned out, the realization was quite different. Between 1567 and 1576, Spain had shipped considerable amounts of money to the Low Countries; in fact, in each of those years the amounts had equaled or even exceeded the sums that the Low Counties had raised for their own defense. Only in 1570 and 1571, the two years in which the revenues from the Hundredth Penny and the outright grant commuting the Tenth Penny began to flow in, did Spain send fewer funds to The Netherlands. There was never any question of bullion shipments from The Netherlands to Spain in this period.

The question is whether contemporaries were sufficiently aware that what was actually at stake in the Tenth Penny issue was who was to have the upper hand, the sovereign ruler or the provincial representatives. In this context, the absence of a time limit on the tax would severely diminish the provincial States' role in the decision-making process, as they would no longer have to be convened in order to grant an aid.

The fact that the issue of the permanence of the Tenth Penny was brought up less frequently than one might expect does not necessarily mean that this point was not understood at the time. There are enough reactions, not only from the States, but also from the general public, to suggest that the man in the street was aware of this cardinal question. For example, a nun from 's-Hertogenbosch wrote that one of the two main arguments advanced against the Tenth Penny was that: "... we don't know how long it will last, as he doesn't tell us any term." If a nun could think in this way (and our attention is drawn to the plural she employs), we can assume that broad sectors of society, and not just local administrators, realized that this was the crux of the matter.

Alva had not spoken openly about the question of permanence. He prudently only touched upon this point in his March 20, 1569 proposition to the States, remarking that he could not continue without being able to count on good and lasting assistance. He then retracted his statement, declaring that the Tenth and Twentieth Pennies would only be requested to provide for the King's most pressing financial needs or until a better method was found.

Even though the States usually did not raise the issue of permanence in their petitions, Alva felt they knew perfectly well that it was the central question. He repeatedly made this clear in his correspondence with the King. He wrote on November 4, 1571 that it was not the interests of industry or fishing that distressed the States, but the fact that if the Tenth Penny were to be approved, they would no longer be able to dictate the law to their King. In his December 30, 1573 letter to Philip, his successor wrote that the States were reluctant to pass on a permanent tax to their successors.

All of this suggests that the entire population, from high to low, was well aware that nothing less than the division of governmental powers was at stake. The political significance of the Tenth Penny is thus illuminated: what was involved was a full-scale struggle for power between the monarch and the estates representation. It was not a struggle between the ruler and his subjects, as the latter (i.e. the masses) had no political influence. It is not too bold to suggest that if the Tenth Penny had come to fruition in 1569, the power of the central government and hence of the sovereign ruler would have been given a tremendous boost, thus laying the foundation for absolutist royal authority.

An attempt has been made in this and the preceding section to give a broad outline of the significance of the Tenth Penny in the history of the Low Countries. We came to the conclusion that the Tenth Penny was not a primary cause of the revolt that broke out in 1572. Instead, the Tenth Penny acted as a bellows, fanning the flames of discontent.

What consequences did Alva's failure to implement his tax program have for developments in The Netherlands? This failure, of course, was by no means the

TIS AL VERLOREN GHEBEDN OFT GHESCHETEN
ICK HEB DE BESTE CANSE GHESTREKEN
1566

LAET ONS WEL BIDDEN SONDER OPHELDEN | LAET ONS RAS KEREN EN WORDEN NIET MOE

OCH DAT ONS HEYLCDOM TE MEER MACH GEIDEN | WANT AELE DEES CREMEKIE HOORT DEN DVYEL TOE

Anti-Catholic cartoon. On the left, the Pope is riding a many-headed monster and is being worshipped by priests, monks and a bishop. On the right, the Beggars are sweeping up Roman Catholic leavings. The Iconoclastic Fury is depicted at the top right.

only reason why the seventeen provinces were not transformed into a unified Catholic state under absolute rule, modeled after Spain.

It is, in fact, impossible to go any further than posing the three questions which have already been formulated above. If the Tenth Penny had been imposed:
– Would the revolt of 1572 have broken out and, if so, would the insurgents have succeeded (or at any rate succeeded as they did in the North)?
– Would this have given the striving toward greater unity and central authority a better foothold on Dutch soil?
– Would the breeze of royal absolutism have been whipped up into an icy gale?

Although there is no sure answer to these questions, they continue to intrigue us!

Convoys and licenses, the only common taxation under the Union of Utrecht

Tired of endless warfare and rebellion, religious persecution and fratricide, the seventeen provinces of The Netherlands concluded a pact in 1576, known as the Pacification of Ghent. Nothing now appeared to stand in the way of the further unification of the provinces.

However, as time went on, their religious differences, honed to a fine point by sharp-tongued literalists in both the Protestant and Catholic camps, increasingly divided the provinces into two. The Southern provinces united themselves on January 6, 1579 into the Union of Arras and a few months later concluded a legitimate peace with Parma, the newly appointed Governor. They wished to remain Catholic and subjects of the King of Spain. Soon afterwards, on January 23, 1579, the Northern provinces entered into a pact known as the "Union of Utrecht," in the name of the "Principality of Gelre and the County of Zutphen, the Counties and Lands of Holland, Zealand, Utrecht, and those Frisian Ommelanden between the Eems and the Lauwerts." They were later joined by the Prince of Orange, Gelderland, the remaining part of Friesland, Overijssel, Groningen, Drenthe and several cities in Flanders and Brabant.

Although not originally intended as such, the Union of Utrecht functioned as a kind of constitution for the Republic of the Seven United Provinces of The Netherlands. The Dutch Republic was a confederation of several miniature republics united by a mutual defense pact. Their undeniable pursuit of greater unity was offset by their equally manifest desire to maintain their independence. This ambiguity was expressed at various points in the document. Thus, Section V decreed that common taxes, binding on all provinces, would be introduced, while Sections VI and IX made unanimity a condition for the introduction of these taxes. Harmony among the member states, difficult enough to find in the best of circumstances, was practically non-existent when it came to common taxation. Except for the part involving convoys and licenses (which will be discussed below), the section dealing with this topic remained a dead letter until the Dutch Republic ceased to exist in 1795. Another fine principle expressing the solidarity of the provinces (Section XVI) stipulated that the provinces could not impose any taxes which would burden the member states more than their own residents. The provinces, involved in mutual vendettas and competition, continuously and repeatedly rode roughshod over this non-discrimination clause. They constantly sought to shift the tax burden to other provinces, while luring trade and commercial shipping to their own regions.

Because of Parma's continual conquests, the Union of Utrecht's territory continued to shrink, until in 1585, the only free provinces were Holland, Zealand, Utrecht and Friesland. While the city of Groningen had again fallen into Spanish hands after being betrayed by Stadtholder Rennenberg, the rebels still had a few bases in the surrounding Ommelanden. Some cities in Gelderland and the greatest part of Drenthe and Overijssel were likewise under Spanish control. Parma had been repeatedly victorious in battle in recent years, and after the fall of Antwerp in 1585, he posed a direct threat to the three provinces at the heart of the rebellion, namely Holland, Zealand and Utrecht.

This menace did not prevent the insurgents from squabbling among themselves. The most striking of the internal disputes were between the coastal provinces and the inland provinces; between the coastal provinces of Holland and Zealand; and between "the Regents"[17] in Holland and "the Democrats" in Utrecht. The inland provinces felt hemmed in by Parma, who had either partially or totally overrun them. They wanted to use the financial resources of the Union of Utrecht, two thirds of which was raised by powerful Holland, mainly for military operations. Holland, the province the least threatened by an overland attack, felt that the inland provinces could use their overdue contributions to the Union to hire

17. Regents were patrician administrators who dominated the municipal political and social scene at the time of the Dutch Republic.

Medallion. One side exalts the nobles willing to wear the beggar's pouch for the Beggar's cause. The other side depicts the struggle against the Tenth Penny: an upright sword with one coin on its point, nine coins on the right and a whistle and spectacles on the left, as symbols of the capture of Den Briel. (A pun on the Dutch word "bril," meaning spectacles.)

18. The cities united in a Hanseatic League to defend their common trade interests.

their own troops. For Holland and Zealand, it was more important to protect the merchant fleet against the attacks of English pirates and the galleons of the Spanish King.

Nor was all roses between the two coastal provinces. Holland and Zealand had been united in a personal union under the same sovereign ruler for centuries. After the revolt, a defensive pact forged an even closer bond. Yet they maintained separate governments and bickered like an old married couple. The Zealanders, the weaker of the two factions, were generally the most fractious, although the Hollanders certainly did not pull their punches either.

In Holland, the merchants reigned supreme. Having made their way into the Regent class, they dominated the political arena. In religious matters, they were free-thinkers. They had accepted the Calvinist form of Protestantism, but were nevertheless prepared to tolerate those with dissident opinions as long as they behaved like decent citizens and practiced their religion in secret. The merchants balked at any form of popular influence. The States of Holland had therefore forbidden the guilds to have any influence on the decision-making process in the cities.

The city of Utrecht, whose influence dominated the province of that name, had undergone an entirely different development. Little by little, the free-thinking Regents had been replaced by more Calvinist-minded Regents. Moreover, the eight militia captains who represented the people as ward superintendents and were fervent Protestants became very powerful. From then on, the city, its population swelled by numerous Protestant refugees from Brabant and Flanders, was dominated by an extremely radical, strongly Calvinist-oriented atmosphere. The tone was set by a few dogmatic ministers who brooked no compromise, not with the Spanish and certainly not with their Dutch brethren, who in their eyes were on shaky doctrinal footing.

At the heart of the matter lay a highly charged political issue: conducting trade with the enemy. The local administrators as well as the government in Brussels had understood that trade was not to be impeded as otherwise, bending like a supple reed, it would turn away from The Netherlands. The rivals of the Dutch, the Hanse[18] and the English, were constantly on the look-out for ways to attract trade. The export of foodstuffs was only banned when famine raged in the country. Moreover, both domestic and foreign merchants were given a free hand and benefitted from all sorts of tax exemptions.

When the provinces of The Netherlands rose in revolt in 1572, both parties were faced with the question of whether trade relations could still be maintained, and if so, to what extent. The rebels' dilemma was that to conduct the war successfully, they had to cut off the enemy's supply of food and war materials such as gunpowder and bullets. On the other hand, this policy clashed with the private interests of the powerful mercantile class, whose money was urgently needed to sustain the war effort.

Zealand had found its own solution to this question. Shortly after Den Briel (April 1, 1572), the cities of Flushing, Veere and Arnemuiden rose in revolt, giving the rebels control over the mouth of the Scheldt and thus the entrance to Antwerp, at that time the most important city in the Low Countries and the largest harbor in Western Europe. Initially, navigation to the Low Countries which had remained Spanish was left unmolested. But soon the cities in Zealand, which were desperately short of funds, began demanding a license and a license fee for this trading privilege. The revenues from these permits, usually referred to as "licenses," were employed to defray the costs of the warships that were being used to close off the Scheldt.

The reasoning behind this system was that if the Dutch did not supply the enemy, the competition would and that the Dutch could use the profits from that trade (fattened by the license fees paid by the enemy) to finance the war. Later, the States of Zealand took over the license system, making it a provincial matter. In the meantime, an increasing number of cities in Holland had joined the rebels, and on July 19, 1572 — the date of the first assembly of the States in Dordrecht — the rebels took the first step toward setting up a government for their province, which was almost entirely in revolt. They decided immediately to prevent the flow of foodstuffs to cities which were still Spanish, such as Delft and Amsterdam, and to divert trade as much as possible to the cities which had not rebelled. Soon afterwards, they issued a general ban on trade with the enemy. However, these embargoes were constantly being circumvented by alternative trade routes via neutral countries. In other words, mounds of butter and cheese still reached the foe.

In 1573, William of Orange, as Stadtholder of Holland and Zealand, effected an arrangement in which all merchants, of whatever nationality, were free to sell any goods to Flanders and Brabant and any other areas in The Netherlands under Spanish administration, on the condition that they pay licenses for trade passports in certain designated cities. Passports could not, however, be obtained for gunpowder, bullets and other strategic materials. Violations would be punished by confiscation of both ship and merchandise. Thus, Zealand's license system was introduced into Holland as well. One year later, the import of goods from the Spanish-dominated parts of The Netherlands was also included in Holland and Zealand's license system.

This last step effectively merged so-called "convoys" with the license system. Since time immemorial, merchant shipping had sailed from Holland in convoys, in order to reduce the risk of falling prey to pirates. Later, the convoys were escorted by naval ships, which were naturally paid for by the shipowners. These payments, initially called "escort fees," simply came to be referred to as "convoys." In time, the organization of the convoys into naval squadrons and the collection of the escort fees (or "convoys") had passed from private into municipal hands, and then in 1572 into provincial hands. The escort fees and the license fees were always coupled together as "convoys and licenses." This phraseology, which refers to the origin of the payments, will also be employed here. Under this fee system — which came into force in 1573 — licenses were levied on goods exported to enemy and neutral countries and convoys on goods imported from neutral areas into Holland and Zealand. Starting in 1574, convoys and licenses were also collected on imported or transit goods originating from the provinces under Spanish rule.

It would be straying too far from our subject to describe the further history of convoys and licenses. Suffice it to say that convoys and licenses developed into a uniform tax levied at a standard rate throughout the provinces and supervised

*Queen Elizabeth of
England (C. Ketel?).*

by the States-General. The nature of these levies thus changed from that of tributes into taxes earmarked for a specific purpose, namely to maintain the war fleet. This process of development was completed in 1582, when taxes became standardized in all provinces. The change from a tribute to a regular tax was of great significance. For while the tribute was basically an individual *quid pro quo* imposed by the government, a regular tax represented a contribution to the common good. This transition therefore signaled a triumph of solidarity over private interest and, as such, marked the development toward a more mature society.

It goes without saying that a great deal of political quibbling was engaged in before the States-General finally enacted the convoys and licenses and agreed to issue a central ban on trade with the enemy. In the years to come, the ban underwent frequent changes (sometimes becoming more strict of more lax). The lists of banned strategic materials and forbidden ports were constantly being modified, as were the tariffs imposed on permissible trade goods.

Trade with the enemy increasingly became a divisive element in the relations between the provinces, particularly between the coastal and the inland provinces, but also between the various groups in the general population. It was difficult for the people to understand why wealthy merchants — who only got wealthier as a result of the trade — were allowed to supply the enemy with all sorts of goods they often lacked themselves. The rather abstract reason that the war could not be financed in any other way and that the foe would get his merchandise anyway, whether the Dutch supplied him or not, cut little ice.

Shortly after the fall of Antwerp (August 1585), the States-General decided once again, at a meeting which the representatives of Holland were unable to attend, to ban all exports of foodstuffs to every destination. As on previous occasions, the States of Holland high-handedly modified the resulting placard, exempting the export of foodstuffs (with the exception of wheat, butter and cheese) to Bremen, Hamburg and the Baltic cities. They did guarantee that no herring or salt would be transported from neutral countries to the enemy, and, as a concession to the trade policies of the States-General, trade with Spain remained out of bounds.

It was at this moment that the Calvinist militia captains of Utrecht, who detested Holland's mercantile policies, entered the lists. They managed to make their way into the joint session of the Council of State and the States-General, where they vociferously upbraided the Hollanders, in general, and the Amsterdammers, in particular, for their avarice. They felt that the export ban on foodstuffs should be strictly upheld. The incensed magistrate from Amsterdam lodged his complaints about the behavior of the militia captains with the government in Utrecht, but to no avail. The States-General temporarily put an end to the dispute. Upon the advice of Holland (to which they were financially tied hand and foot) they issued a new placard, banning all trade with Spain and Portugal. However, Amsterdam continued to resist trade restrictions in any shape or form, and refused to publish the new placard.

A few weeks later, Robert Dudley, the Earl of Leicester and one of Queen Elizabeth's favorites, arrived with an army in The Netherlands. The English Queen, who did not particularly like having her powerful rival Spain ensconced on the other side of the North Sea but was unwilling to support a rebellion, finally stopped wavering and made up her mind to aid the rebellious provinces. Soon after his arrival, Leicester was proclaimed Governor by the States-General. This appointment displeased his mistress, who feared it would drag her deeper into the Low Countries' political quagmire. When Leicester arrived in The Netherlands, the provinces were still deeply divided over the issue of exporting foodstuffs to the enemy. Understandably, they were curious to see how the Earl would tackle this issue. He wasted no time in making it known that his instructions from Queen Elizabeth were to forbid the export of foodstuffs and to mete out harsh punishments to anyone who violated the ban. Leicester, who was the backbone of the ultra-Protestant party in the English court, chose Calvinist Utrecht as his residence. This was a politically imprudent step, and it was not long before he issued a series of measures that further soured his relations with the most important province, Holland.

Robert Dudley, Earl of Leicester (1533-1588).

In April of 1586, Leicester signed a placard rigorously banning trade with the enemy and threatened to punish all violations with severe sanctions. The terms of this placard were more uncompromising and considerably more austere than those of its predecessors. Leicester naturally had the powers to issue such a placard, and large segments of the population very probably welcomed his hard line. However, whether it was politically wise to offend the powerful province of Holland in this way and mercilessly cut off its source of income is a different matter.

Johan van Oldenbarnevelt (1547-1619), Pensionary of Holland and one of the founders of the Dutch Republic.

Leicester also overstepped the mark in other respects. His ban on trade with neutral countries and threat to seize their ships raised the ire of other countries, particularly powerful France, which did not want to become entangled in the Spanish-Netherlands conflict. The French King, Henry III, also complained to Queen Elizabeth about the actions of her favorite. When she asked Leicester to account for his actions, he misrepresented the course of events, suggesting that he had been more or less compelled by the States to issue the placard.

Under the sensible leadership of their Grand Pensionary, Johan van Olden-barnevelt, the States of Holland kept their powder dry for the time being, and, unlike on previous occasions, refrained from modifying the placard on their own authority. However, their recommendations on the matter, drafted by the Grand

Die nae de waerheyt.

PRAGHON

DE MORT VA EARTS

BALTASAR SERA MOR DER VANDE PRINS

VICTE LINVS

SPRING NHAERS

CAPVCHIN

INQVISITION

Doer den tyt meiter waerheyt wort ons gheivont.
Den schadelijcken nest ontdeckt met die brothen ghecroont.

O edele prineffe loftaer die hier reyn bloeme zijt verheuen
Van got vercoeren met uwen maechden feer fchoone
Zijt diijn voerfchtuch oft ghij juft comen in fnewen
Dat fenymich gebroetfel comt hem wt den dop verthone
Die eyeren van antechryft en van belphegors fonen
Staen fchoen gekijpt in des moeders hydich harten
O godt mochten dit ionghe breeken haer moeders crone
So bleuen defe landen t famen wt grooter fmarten
Die gecroonde beeft bedrijft veel boofelijcke parten
Aen den moort van parijs fteeftmen haer fien wencken
Soo menmich chris tenen haer bloet verfmoert
En wilt den prins van oraengens doot gedencken

*In this 1585 Dutch print,
Queen Elizabeth is
portrayed as Diana and
surrounded by allegorical
figures passing judgement
on the Pope. The coats of
arms of the Protestant
allies are depicted on the
shields. The "Inquisition,"
"Dragon," "Capuchins,"
and "Balthasar Gerards"
(William of Orange's
assassin) are crawling out
of the eggs.*

Pensionary himself, were brought to the Governor's notice. These recommendations were a masterly example of the subtle art of reasoning. The arguments for and against a ban on trading with the enemy were systematically and evenhandedly set forth, and yet the reader was eventually forced to conclude that the ban should not be enforced. While admitting that supplying the foe was "contrary to decent behavior" and that watching the merchants grow rich on the war trade was injurious to the morale of the population, van Oldenbarnevelt concluded that if trade were to be banned, others would provide the enemy with goods, and that this would cost them their own prosperity and therefore the war.

After a few weeks, Leicester produced a more moderate version of his placard and thus undermined his own position. To Zealand, Utrecht and Gelderland, any concession was a sign of unforgivable weakness. Even in its more moderate version, the placard was still hard for Holland (and especially Amsterdam) to swallow. Would trade not relocate in neighboring provinces? What did the placard mean if the Earl did not have the power to prevent their rivals from transporting foodstuffs to the enemy? Would neutral shipping not prefer to sail around Scotland and Ireland so as to avoid both the licenses and the Dutch privateers?

As he was sorely in need of money to continue his campaign and the Queen was reluctant to sink English money into the Dutch war efforts, Leicester had to approach the government of Holland with his tail between his legs. The Hollanders were as incensed by the April 14th placard as they were by the arrest in Utrecht of their former Grand Pensionary, Paulus Buys, which could hardly have taken place without the Earl's prior knowledge. Led by van Oldenbarnevelt, who was eminently capable of holding his own against Leicester, the States of Holland saw a favorable opportunity to negotiate several important moderations to the April 14th placard. The outcome was that trade with foreigners was left entirely free, a sop to French interests, and that only residents were forbidden to trade with Spain and Portugal, unless they had previously been granted permission to do so. Goods brought in from Spain or the Spanish Netherlands but originating from neutral countries could henceforth be imported into the Union of Utrecht provinces without running the risk of confiscation.

In keeping with human nature, no sooner had the sting been taken out of the placard and the greatest danger to trade avoided than Holland's merchants started interpreting the placard to mean that they would be allowed to transport butter and cheese to enemy territories provided they paid the licenses. Mercantile pragmatism ultimately prevailed over Calvinist moral rectitude. But we can surely understand the rage felt by the residents of Flushing, who nearly rose in revolt a year later when merchants, in pursuit of their own profit, did not scruple to supply vinegar to the Spanish army that had won the siege of Sluis. This vinegar was used to cool the barrels of their canons, the very same artillery that had subjected the besieged city to constant bombardment. Indeed, Holland had taken little notice of the siege of Sluis and had not suspended its deliveries to the Spanish army. In view of this, it is hardly surprising that there were renewed clashes between Leicester and Holland after Sluis fell in 1587. Leicester's attempts to get control of the cities of Amsterdam and Leiden also came to nothing. About this time, it was made known that Elizabeth and Philip (with Parma at his side) were conducting peace talks. On the Queen's instructions, Leicester participated in these talks. In doing so, he forfeited the little goodwill he still had in radical Calvinist circles. He departed The Netherlands for good at the end of 1587 and was dead within a year.

The conflict over trading with the enemy resurfaced in the later period of the Dutch Republic, when the need to stimulate trade came in conflict with maritime defense strategy. As a result of the Peace of Münster concluded in 1648, Spain ceased to be the enemy and soon even became an ally against France. The convoys and licenses consequently lost their formal meaning as escort fees for the protection of the merchant fleet and as license fees for trading with the enemy, simply becoming normal import and export duties. But they continued to be levied for the specific purpose of maintaining the war fleet. Ever since Leicester's time, these taxes had been imposed and collected by an admiralty specifically set up for that purpose. The applicable tariffs and the means of imposition and collection were regulated by a placard issued in 1597, which was vehemently opposed by Zealand and almost caused a war between Zealand and Holland. Nonetheless, the placard was not thoroughly revised until 1725. It is worth noting that the tariffs were predominantly fiscal and not protectionist in nature.

The fledgling Dutch Republic became embroiled in numerous wars with England and France. Sea battles were fought from the Sont to the Mediterranean. Never-

"The Cow" (anonymous, 1585, English school). There are several known versions of this satirical theme. The cow represents the dissatisfied Low Countries, being ridden by King Philip II. Queen Elizabeth is standing to the left, feeding hay to the animal. Prince William of Orange is lying under the cow, milking her. The Duke of Anjou is standing to the right, pulling on the cow's tail.

theless, the war fleet was often neglected, owing to the fact that the merchants were unwilling to keep it in repair. Commanders bitterly complained that they were sent into battle with unseaworthy vessels. A low point was reached in 1675 when Admiral Michiel de Ruyter pointed out to the States-General that the fleet was in a deplorable condition. But even the words of such a prestigious admiral carried no weight, and he was sent to sea with a handful of ramshackle ships. The Dutch won the battle by the skin of their teeth, but de Ruyter paid for victory with his life. This conjures up the image of a petty Dutch merchant unable to look any further than the end of his nose for business and too tightfisted to spend enough money to maintain the fleet. Though this image is not entirely inaccurate, it needs to be put into sharper perspective.

In the small-scale world of the seventeenth century, the admiralties were intimately acquainted with their fellow citizens and did not shrink from fraudulent practices to give their friends and neighbors preferential treatment. There were even admiralties in the eighteenth century who had not put a ship to sea in decades. They evidently took seriously the injunction "to increase the trade and business of the honest merchant" in the placard of 1597.

Allegorical print depicting Alva's tyranny and William of Orange's aid. Alva is standing on the left with a pair of scissors to "fleece the inhabitants" and reduce them to beggary. The nation of The Netherlands is represented by a naked and bound woman to Alva's left. Alva is being crowned by "Envy" and "Discord." The man in rags lying at his feet symbolizes the "poor people." William of Orange is standing on the right, being crowned with "Honor." The "Peace of Consciousness" is at Orange's right and the "Country's Prosperity" at his left. His fame is being proclaimed from the clouds. The gallows used by Alva is depicted in the background just left of center.

Because of these abuses, the revenues from the convoys and licenses were usually far too small to keep the war fleet in an adequate state of readiness. Consequently, the States-General had to make up the deficits. As the inland provinces were not willing to contribute to the fleet, money had to be borrowed to cover the deficits. Especially in the eighteenth century, the finances became increasingly unmanageable. By the time the Dutch Republic met its demise at the end of that century, the total income of some admiralties was almost entirely absorbed by internal administrative costs, interest payments and loan installments; on more than one occasion, a ships' officers and crew had not been paid for years.

As the payments of the inland provinces were often in arrears, Holland – the Republic's banker – had to grant the Republic its funds and assume liability for its loans. Indeed, at the time of the Batavian Revolution in 1795, Holland's share of the total debts owed by the provinces was 75% and that of Zealand 7.5%. The tax burden, expressed in florins per capita, is also most revealing: Holland 30, Zealand 25, Friesland 21, Utrecht 19, Groningen 13, Gelderland 7 and Overijssel 7. Not surprisingly, Holland wished to make use of the Batavian upheavals of 1795 to implement two basic financial reforms. The first of these, known as the *amalgama*, entailed merging the debts owed by the various provinces and placing them entirely on the Dutch Republic's account. The second reform, known as "tax unification," involved replacing the system of apportionment by a system of uniform taxation, in which the residents would owe taxes directly to the Republic.

Remarkably, in spite of the distinct financial differences between the provinces, they reached agreement fairly rapidly about merging their debts. As early as January 20, 1797, and thus barely two years after the Batavian Revolution, the principle of *amalgama* was accepted in the National Assembly, although several years went by before this was reflected in the legislation.

The integration of the debts was a preliminary condition for tax unification. But unification was a more complex issue, and in the years between 1796 and 1801, no solution to this problem was found. On January 25, 1798, the Constituent Assembly issued a decree permanently abolishing the system of provincial quotas which had been in force for two centuries. However, opinions were divided about the nature of the taxes to be levied under the common tax system, and no practicable solution emerged.

As we shall see in the last chapter, the thirteen newly independent American states were swiftly able to achieve tax unification. The reason why the Dutch Republic was unable in almost two hundred years of existence to accomplish what the Americans did in a few years was that the local Regents were unwilling to relinquish their positions of power. As the Regents wanted to keep a tight rein on fiscal matters, no system of common taxation – the mortar binding the bricks of a unified state – could be created. Further, their fear and envy of rival states and cities prevented the convoys and licenses, the only tax binding in all provinces, from reaching full maturity.

In short, every attempt to create a system of common taxation in the Dutch Republic had been checked, like the Tenth Penny, by internal division. Although the Dutch Republic had, under the Union of Utrecht, become an independent state with a relatively high standard of democracy compared to its neighbors, it failed to achieve unity within its borders and thus make the transition from a confederation to a federal state.

Session of the English House of Commons in Westminster Hall (c. 1640).

4 Westminster

England under James I, the first Stuart king

Ironically enough, in 1603 an old regulation saw to it that Queen Elizabeth of England was succeeded to the throne by the son of the woman whom she had ordered put to death in 1587, her cousin Mary Stuart. Mary had been forced to flee as Queen of Scotland. In her many years of captivity, she had been involved in one plot after another against the English Queen, claiming her alleged right to the English throne. But ultimately her head, so full of fantasies about a Catholic England under her leadership, rolled into the executioner's basket. As a result, James became the first Stuart on the English throne, and in his person Scotland and England were united.[1]

The Tudors had generally succeeded in preserving good relations with Parliament, although the balance of power clearly lay on the side of the sovereign. Elizabeth and Henry VIII, in particular, used their psychological insight and political powers of persuasion to broaden their position until absolute monarchy would only have taken one small step. But they never wished or dared to go that far. The Stuarts, who inherited the practically unassailable political position of the previous dynasty, were willing to take that plunge. The process went moderately under James I, because the King had enough political insight not to force the issue. When he left the somber Holyrood palace in Edinburgh in 1603 to take up residence in London, he was almost forty years old, and had known since early childhood that he was to be King. James could therefore not be said to be lacking in experience.

At that time, England had a population of approximately four million, more than 200,000 of whom lived in London and its suburbs. Although predominantly an agrarian society, England's trade and navigation were making rapid advances. The elite, lords in their manors, justices of the peace (typically gentry), local sheriffs and constables, numbered around twenty thousand. There were approximately nine thousand clergymen scattered throughout the parishes. Unlike sparsely populated Scotland, England played a meaningful role on the stage of the then known world. Money and religion were the principal factors around which English politics revolved. The power of the King to govern, uphold the law, coin money, decide on war and peace and appoint or dismiss local authorities had been limited for centuries not only by the magistrates upholding case law, but also by Parliament. Parliament was composed of the Upper House, or House of Lords, which served as the highest court of law, and the Lower House, or House of Commons, which granted permission for tax levies. Traditionally meeting in Westminster, Parliament was only in session when and for as long as the King wished.

The King's closest advisers were the members of the Privy Council, consisting of about twenty advisers, ministers and high officials, six or seven of whom carried out the day-to-day work. The Privy Councilors, always in the King's vicinity, were also courtiers. Some were also members of the House of Commons or the House of Lords. The Privy Councilors were appointed and dismissed by the

1. Both countries were united politically in 1707, after which they existed jointly as Great Britain.

King rather than by Parliament. When Parliament lost confidence in an official, its only weapon was impeachment. During an impeachment procedure, the Commons functioned as the prosecuting body and the Lords as the judicial body. Impeachment proceedings could be instigated against an individual who had erred in the discharge of his office, but could also be used to charge the accused with a legal violation, criminal behavior or bribery. Parliament could thus use impeachment to have a minister discharged, imprisoned or even sent to the scaffold. Nevertheless, an impeachment decision, like legislative bills, required the King's signature.

In this chapter, the King's advisers and confidants will be referred to as "ministers," regardless of whether they serve on the Privy Council. This word will likewise be used to refer to the Secretaries of State (typically two) charged with the daily implementation of foreign policy, the Chancellor of the Exchequer and high officeholders. Similarly, the term "government" will denote the King and his ministers. Although inappropriate to this period, these terms will be employed here for the sake of simplicity.

The King was responsible for the welfare and continuity of the state. To cover his expenses, he controlled the "fisc," a complex of estates, revenues and rights which he could call his own and where his authority was undivided and absolute. He could employ the proceeds from the fisc as he so chose, as long as it promoted the good of the kingdom. The standard expression was: "The king must live of his own." He could make no further claim on the money and goods of his subjects, except in the cases of necessity specified in the *Magna Carta*.[2] These cases, also known on the Continent, were defined as: the knighthood of his eldest son, the marriage of his eldest daughter and his own ransom from captivity. Parliament could not refuse to finance these cases, provided the amounts requested were reasonable. In time, the concept of "necessity" evolved into that of "national defense" and then into that of "war" (either offensive or defensive). When the need arose, Parliament was required to grant the King's request for a tax known as an "aid". But necessity was often a very elastic concept. A further consideration was that if the King and his ministers commanded the respect of the House of Commons or sympathized with the financial objectives, Parliament was more likely to grant economic assistance. As we shall see, such respect was often lacking between Parliament and Charles I, the leading character in this chapter. When Charles submitted a doubtful request for financial support, the House of Commons used the opportunity to make demands outside the realm of finance and to air its grievances against the government. A prototype of this relationship can be seen in the reign of Charles' father James I, whose position will be briefly described below. At the time James came to power, Parliamentary powers did not extend to foreign policy. However, Parliament did speak up more frequently on religious matters.

Opinions are divided as to the extent to which Parliament had the right to influence the King's policies. Of course, in trying to answer this question, it is important to know the power relations of the participating parties as well as the customs prevailing at that time. During the Tudor period, Parliament's center of gravity had shifted from the House of Lords (whose barons were members for life but no longer maintained their own armies) to the House of Commons, which represented the voice of the country even though its members were almost exclusively recruited from the upper classes. The constituency system, in which

2.   See page 92.

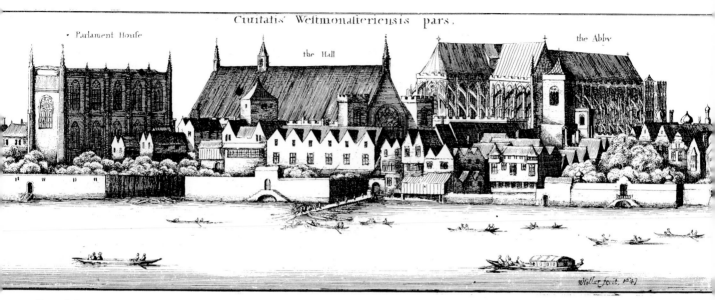

Cuitalis Weltmonaltcriensis pars.

Parlament Houfe · the Hall · the Abby

From left to right: the House of Parliament, Westminster Hall and Westminster Abbey, drawn by W. Hollar in 1647.

every borough[3] and shire[4] sent two representatives to Parliament, ensured that London news could be heard in the farthest reaches of the country. When in session, the House of Commons was therefore able to influence public opinion and, conversely, articulate the public's views. Although what we would refer to today as "ministerial responsibility" did not exist, Parliament insisted that the laws be enacted jointly by the Crown and the Parliament and be binding on the King and the Privy Council. The highest authority in the country ostensibly lay in what has been termed the "King-in-Parliament," but many matters continued to fall solely within royal prerogative.

The great jurist Sir Edward Coke developed the theory that the law, rather than being the instrument of royal authority, delineated the boundaries of the King's power. He also suggested that the magistrates were not "lions under the throne," but intermediaries between the King and his subjects. Such views won him no favor with the King. James relieved him of his post as Privy Councilor and Chief Justice, and the magistrates returned to their role as the Crown's obedient servants. The kernels of wisdom scattered by Coke were avidly picked up by lawyers and others having the public's interest at heart and later bore fruit. James' view of Parliament can be summed up in a remark he made after dissolving the Commons in 1614: "I am surprised that my ancestors should have permitted such an institution to come into existence." James clearly believed in absolute monarchy.

Initially, James' relations with his Parliaments were excellent. Parliament unhesitatingly granted him a lifetime right to the age-old duties known as "tonnage" and "poundage." Originally a form of tribute,[5] tonnage and poundage were paid by a foreign merchant to ensure himself and his merchandise of royal protection. Later, tonnage and poundage evolved into import and export taxes. Since the end of the fifteenth century, Parliament had granted every king the tonnage and poundage as a permanent source of income. The term "tonnage" was derived from a duty levied per ton of wine and "poundage" from the weight of the goods. Incidentally, the tariffs were somewhat differentiated (e.g. sweet wines were taxed double), and foreign and domestic merchants were subject to different tariff rates.

3. A municipal district.
4. A rural district, usually a county.
5. For a definition of this term see pages 69 and 207.

King James I (1566-1625)
(from a painting by Daniel
Mytens, 1621).

During this period, it was not unusual for the imposition and collection of taxes to be contracted out to tax farmers, with the contract being awarded to the highest bidder. Since the government paid the tax farmer a certain amount of money, it did not have to bother further with taxes. Tax farmers usually did a booming business, one of the reasons why tax farming often went hand in hand with corruption. As a result of widespread abuses, tax farming had fallen into disuse under Queen Mary (1553 – 1558) and Queen Elizabeth (1558 – 1603). One of James' first financial acts of government was to reinstate tax farming.

In 1604, the tonnage and poundage were farmed out to a syndicate, a move that did nothing to enhance the popularity of these taxes. Tax farmers, rather nondescript characters living on the fringes of political and commercial life, aroused the unceasing jealousy of the landed gentry, because the King, bound financially hand and foot to the tax farmers, showered them with commissions, export licenses and even titles of nobility. Tax farming was only abolished in 1641, and Charles I's later problems can partly be ascribed to the practice.

The revenues from the tonnage and poundage amounted to 127,000 pounds in 1604, rising to higher levels in subsequent years. Thus, besides his income from the fisc, the King was assured of a sizeable annual income which he could use to meet governmental and household expenses. However, James needed more money to support his luxurious lifestyle. His main budgetary expenses were jewel purchases, gifts and allowances for friends. The court's many ceremonies and festivities also testified to his extravagance. Before long, James was forced to realize that in England, unlike in Scotland, he could not take a single financial step without having to request permission from Parliament. His predecessor Elizabeth had not been similarly troubled. Elizabeth's frugality had made her less dependent on Parliament, which she was able to twist around her little finger. James had difficulty asking Parliament − in the hour-long speeches of which he was so fond − for the money he felt he needed to run his expensive household and conduct his occasional wars.

Even a less dignified monarch would have found it difficult to ask Parliament to levy taxes. Convinced of the divine right of kings, the autocratic James lived by the motto "rex est lex" (the king is the law). Although James had successfully defended this line of reasoning against the fastidious Scottish church, it aroused the suspicions and abhorrence of the English Parliament. Another factor which probably contributed to his difficulties was his total lack of personal charisma. He was an ugly, crude boor with a Scottish accent and nervous, wandering eyes. His manners were so bad that his English subjects could not avoid noticing it. I am not referring to his homosexual leanings, although they were considered an abomination by those who were aware of them. But what are we to think of a king who hunted so avidly that he did not bother to dismount to answer calls of nature, so that at the end of the day, he reeked as he climbed down from his horse? Or one who arranged drunken feasts, in which both male and female guests staggered around the King, spewing food and vomit? Such dissolute behavior was excessive, even given the mores of that day and age.

At the beginning of his reign (1604), James concluded a peace treaty with Spain. All was quiet on the English and Scottish border as well. Relieved of such military expenditures, it seemed that the treasury would need less money. But James' extravagant clothes, jewels and banquets and the financing of his favorites swallowed huge sums of money. Unless he succeeded in tapping his own source of income, James would have to wheedle money from the Commons.

One source of royal income was the purveyance, the right of the Crown to demand foodstuffs and transport at the lowest possible price. However, the amounts were utterly insufficient for his purposes. The purveyance had also fallen into disrepute, being regarded as a highly arbitrary way of allowing the subjects to underwrite the King's expenses. Another source of income dating from the Middle Ages, the wardship, also produced little revenue, especially when measured against the bitterness it generated. The gist of medieval wardship was this: when a vassal left a minor as heir, his liege lord gained custody of his estates until the heir became of age; in return, the liege lord was responsible for raising the children. When the heir was a woman, the liege lord could marry her off, preferably to the highest bidder. As the King was the highest liege lord, wardship developed over the centuries into what we would call "inheritance taxes." In later times, the family was able to buy off the wardship for a lump sum, usually equivalent to the estate's annual income. The minor's ward, usually a member of the family, could also purchase the family estate from the Crown, but the price was frequently steep. Because minors had no legal redress, wardship was frequently exercised arbitrarily and misuses abounded. More and more voices were raised in protest. Another source of discontent was the Crown's supervision of the children's upbringing and fortune.

The right to regulate trade, protect and stimulate certain branches of industry by levying protective import and export duties and grant or sell trade monopolies had long been recognized as one of the powers belonging to the Crown rather than Parliament. It was tacitly assumed that the exercise of these rights was a governmental function, providing little or no revenue for the government. James recognized that, with the growth in trade, a source of income lay ripe for the plucking. The King therefore added import and export levies called "impositions," whose tariffs were listed in the Book of Rates, to the tonnage and poundage on a number of goods. A merchant trading in the Levant protested the new import levy on raisins and currants. But the King's right to levy these duties was upheld by the Barons of the Court of the Exchequer,[6] who argued that the harbors belonged to the King and that he could therefore levy any imposition he wished. Parliament, slow to react, finally realized that there was more to the impositions than met the eye and that its most important power, that over the pocketbook, was at stake. For if the King could establish tariffs arbitrarily, he could also raise them arbitrarily. Two years later, a new Book of Rates was published. This time, luxury items were taxed more heavily and high import tariffs were added to protect domestic industrial products. As this was accompanied by a marked increase in government income, the conflict smoldering between the King and the Commons burst into the open. The conflict was settled by having James relinquish his rights to the purveyance, wardship and impositions in return for a fixed annual sum of 200,000 pounds. However, the Commons argued over how to raise the 200,000 pounds, and the agreement was never implemented. Vexed by this matter as well as by religious disputes, James dissolved this Parliament on February 9, 1611.

Three years later, the King's desperate financial straits obliged him to convene another parliament. Virtually every attempt to raise funds by bypassing the Commons had failed, and the Crown's debts mounted daily. The new House of Commons, even more recalcitrant than the previous one, immediately began debating the King's right to determine import and export levies. James dissolved this Parliament after two months of futile debates and ruled for the next seven years without a parliament. Consequently, James was again forced to look for ways of raising money without having to consult the House of Commons. The most promising options were demanding greater revenues from the crown domains and selling monopolies and offices. In addition, the people were requested to pay "benevolences," which were actually quasi-voluntary gifts the subjects presented to their King. Occasionally, the King had a financial windfall, such as

6. The Court of the Exchequer stems from the time of William the Conqueror and owes its name to a checked (chequered) cloth laid upon the table on which the king's accountants counted out his money and made their calculations. During Henry II's reign (1154 – 1189), it was divided into two rooms: a court of account, in which the counting was monitored and legal questions were handled, and a court of receipt, in which money was weighed, tested and paid out. The officials of this Court were among the king's most important advisers. While the Chancellor was the most important, the Barons of the Exchequer also played a significant role.

the 210,000 pounds that the Republic of the Seven United Provinces of the Netherlands paid to James in 1616 for the return of the cities of Flushing and Den Briel. These two cities, which still housed English garrisons, had been pledged to England to ensure that The Netherlands would abide by treaty agreements. At one stroke, the Dutch Republic was freed of the debts incurred under the government of Queen Elizabeth, who had let it pay dearly for her military assistance. With the exception of the two months mentioned above, James ruled from February of 1611 to January of 1621 without a parliament. If he were to succeed in outmaneuvering Parliament by creating his own sources of income, absolute power would devolve on him.

James never achieved absolute rule. Even though his relations with the Commons progressively deteriorated, he continued to need them from time to time to bail him out of his pecuniary predicaments. James, and in his wake his son Charles, sought to strengthen royal authority, build up a strong army and naval fleet, unite England and Scotland under one government and − to finance it all − improve the system of taxation. In the process, he came into conflict with local authorities and parliamentary rights. The attempts of the first two Stuarts to consolidate their power undoubtedly accorded with the political trends of the time. France, for example, achieved greater national efficiency in the seventeenth century, but the French paid for this with their liberty. The failure of the Stuarts to achieve their goal can be attributed to several factors: the lack of a local bureaucratic machinery, the religious schism, the absence of a standing army and, last but not least, the King's inability to command a greater share of his own monetary resources.

Charles I's continuous clashes with his Parliaments are detailed later in this chapter. Needless to say, finances were usually at the heart of these conflicts. This chapter describes how Parliament repeatedly manipulated the purse strings and how Charles subsequently ruled for years without a parliament. During this time, Charles employed dubious means to raise money and was ultimately compelled to reconvene Parliament. From then on, his hold on power slipped rapidly away.

Foreign relations

In the first half of the seventeenth century, the English government maneuvered cautiously between two continental superpowers: France and the Hapsburg combination of Germany and Spain. France had recovered from the terrible religious wars of the second half of the sixteenth century under the reign of Henry IV and had made rapid strides toward becoming Europe's major power. France's rise, however, was checked by the government's desire to settle accounts with the powerful Huguenot opposition. The Protestant Huguenots had been granted religious freedom by the Edict of Nantes. But in the eyes of France's Catholic leaders, these Protestants continued to pose a threat to national unity. Spain, exhausted by continual clashes with the Turks for the hegemony of the Mediterranean and by futile attempts to reconquer the renegade provinces in the northern part of The Netherlands, slowly degenerated into a second-rate power. Spain's decline was slowed by the strategic strength it derived from its American colonies and territories in Italy. Spain was also able to use the southern part of The Netherlands as a bridgehead in Northwest Europe. If necessary, Spain could command a great deal of money and could therefore finance large armies.

George Villiers, Duke of
Buckingham (1592-1628)
(from a painting by
William Larkin, c. 1616).

England's relations with the rapidly rising Dutch Republic were friendlier than those with the two Catholic superpowers. The Dutch Republic, where the Calvinist form of Protestantism prevailed, was still in the process of shaking off the Spanish yoke. Although the English had supported the Dutch Republic militarily and politically for decades, they could not fail to note regretfully that the Dutch were turning toward the French as new allies. This was mainly prompted by the growing competition in trade and navigation between England and Holland. For the time being, Anglican England and Catholic France considered the Dutch Republic useful, because it kept the Spanish armies tied down.

Further inland, Catholics and Protestants had been engaged in a deadly struggle in the German Empire since 1618. Spain and Sweden were also entangled in the conflict, which was also conducted in Bohemia and the Palatinate, both of which had been ruled by the Electoral Prince Frederick, the husband of James' daughter, Elizabeth. James made various attempts in the last years of his reign to recover the Palatinate, as it was of great dynastic importance to his daughter and son-in-law. However, his feeble support was ineffective. For Charles, who doted on his sister Elizabeth and was on good terms with his brother-in-law, recovering the Palatinate was the only constant in his otherwise fitful foreign policy. England's role was limited to hiring and financing the army of Mansfeld, a condottiere fighting with the Protestant Union against the Catholic Hapsburgs. Charles also occasionally attempted to enlist the support of other countries in the Union cause.

At the beginning of his reign, James had signed a peace treaty with Spain, which recognized England's right to navigate freely on European seas. The English, however, did not relinquish their right to sail the oceans claimed exclusively by Spain and Portugal. James could easily have refrained from war for many years after the treaty was signed. Relieved of having to finance a war, James might even have been able to rule without consulting Parliament after 1611. However, when the Middle European conflict known as the "Thirty Years' War" broke out in 1618, James felt obliged to choose between friendship or enmity with the Hapsburgs. Either way, the long-neglected fleet would have to be refurbished. To obtain the funds for this project, James convened a new parliament on January 3, 1621. The members of the House of Commons were naturally well aware that the King had only grudgingly summoned them to appear and that he did not believe in their constitutional rights. Consequently, they only agreed to approve the requested contribution if the King would concede certain grievances. Their grievances focused primarily on the abuses in the sale of monopolies and offices, whose revenues had allowed the King to rule for a long period without Parliament. The Commons was rightfully vexed by the monopolies. To cite an example, a group of monopolists had assumed the task of maintaining an important lighthouse in Dungeness in return for the right to levy tolls on passing ships. Instead of maintaining the lighthouse properly, they made do with burning a few measly candles. Sailors complained that the lighthouse could only be seen when the ship was close to the coast and in danger of being shipwrecked. The Chancellor, Francis Bacon, became the scapegoat for this unacceptable state of affairs. During his impeachment trial, Bacon confessed to accepting a bribe and was sentenced by Parliament to confiscation of his possessions. He also fell from the King's favor. This was the first occasion since 1459 that the Commons had leveled an impeachment charge against a leading politician. The fact that it was willing to impeach marked its desire to expand its political power.

Dutch GRATITUDE display'd.

See Holland oppress'd by his old Spanish Foe,

To England with cap in hand kneels very low.

The Free-hearted Briton, dispels all its care,

And raises it up from the brink of Despair.

But when three spitefull foes does old England beset,

The Dutchman refuses to pay a Just debt;

With his hands in his pockets he says he'll stand Neuter,

And England his Friend may be D—d for the Future.

4. May.

Publ. accor'g to Act 4 May 1780.

In the 16th, 17th and 18th centuries, Holland and England were clearly caught in a love-hate relationship. Chapter 3 has already described how Queen Elizabeth rushed to the aid of the Dutch against the Catholic Philip II, although in her heart she despised the revolt. Chapter 4 has shown how competition in trade and navigation put the good relationship between both Protestant peoples under pressure during the reign of Charles I. In 1651, Cromwell, the King's greatest opponent, launched the Act of Navigation against the Dutch Republic (not dealt with in the text as it lies beyond the scope of this book). Chapter 5 describes how the British trade and navigation policies were also applied to the American colonies and the Dutch efforts to evade these through smuggling. The enormous profits reaped by the Dutch from the revolt in the American colonies (1775) eventually led to a fourth Anglo-Dutch war (1780-1784). The print on the left shows how the English viewed the Dutch in 1780. The print on the right illustrates what the Dutch felt about their neighbors on the other side of the North Sea, looking back to the 16th and 17th centuries.

In English eyes, Holland was only able to resist the Spanish thanks to English assistance, and now that England was threatened by France, Spain and America, Holland remained neutral. The group on the left represents the situation during the Eighty Years' War. Spain, coming from the left, threatens the kneeling Dutchman with the words: "I am determined Mijnheer you shall never rise more." Holland, hat in hand, laments "the poor distracted states of Holland," and England replies: "I am your friend, Mijnheer. I'll help you up & beat your foes." The group on the right represents the situation in 1780. Spain on the left claims that "Don Diego has vow'd the downfall of England," France adds that "Begar me will have half his possessions," America vows that "It shall never have my Colonies again," and England tells The Netherlands that "Now is the time to pay your debt of gratitude," to which the churlish Dutch man replies that "I am now y'r high and Mighty." The print on the left appeared on May 4, 1780.

V E R K L A A R I N G.

No. 1. Verbeeldende een' Throon, waar op een Man, die door twee goedaartige Amerikaanen ontkleed wordt, roepende, hy die ontkleed wordt, den Lord North ter hulpe.

2. *The king from London*, in de gedaante van Lord North te paard, die langzaam ter hulpe aankomt.

No. 3. Het Afbeeldfel van *Olivier Cromwel*, als Voorftander der Engelfche ondraagelyke Heersch- en Baat-zucht.

Wordende aangebeeden door eenige Engelfche Lords. No. 4. Welke aanbidders, door de Gerechtigheid, No. 5. gewapend met den Blixem, verplet worden.

In the print on the right (likewise from 1780), King George III is seated on his throne on the right. Two young Americans are pulling off his boots. The distressed King is calling for the help of his Prime Minister Lord North, who is approaching on horseback. On the left, English lords are kneeling before the statue of Cromwell, the "Champion of the Thirst for Power and Self-interest," although Cromwell is about to be struck by the lightning of Justice. Like many such political cartoons, this one is clumsy and badly drawn. For example, the cartoonist clearly did not know what the Puritan Cromwell looked like, and so drew him to resemble the humanist Erasmus.

Parliament became increasingly self-confident, so much so that the Commons began to interfere in foreign policy. The Puritan-dominated Commons favored intervention on the Continent on behalf of the Protestant cause. The inexperienced and insular-minded members of the House of Commons believed that the most effective way to achieve this goal would be to send an army to Germany and hamper Spanish involvement there by winning a few decisive naval victories. This was their sole reason for advocating war with Spain. By contrast, the King had no belligerent motives and only wished to deter Spain by building up a strong naval fleet. Indeed, he preferred friendship to enmity with Spain. In pursuit of his dynastic interests, James even went so far as to work secretly with his closest minister and favorite, the Duke of Buckingham, to arrange a marriage between his son Charles and one of the Spanish princesses as a means of setting the seal on his alliance with the Spanish.

A marriage with a princess from the famous Hapsburg dynasty would considerably boost the prestige of the Stuarts, who until recently had been nothing more than the rulers of an obscure group of barbarians in Northern Europe. From an international perspective, England stood to gain from an alliance with mighty Spain. Moreover, it would provide James with an opportunity to use the Spanish to recover the Palatinate for his daughter. Domestically, however, the intended alliance would be fatal, as it would summon up the specter of papism. This is the reason the negotiations were initially conducted in secret.

Informed of the King's plans, Parliament reacted indignantly. James responded that Parliament had no business meddling in foreign affairs. Parliament then drew up a motion, stating in effect that Parliament's liberties, rights and privileges were an ancient and indisputable legacy of English subjects. They added that the difficult and urgent affairs of the king, the state and the English church formed suitable topics of parliamentary discussion. When the King heard that twelve members of Parliament had come to present him with a petition to this effect, he called out in irritation: ''Chairs, chairs, in god's name, twelve kings are coming.'' Justifiably angry at their arrogant behavior, he had the page on which the motion was written torn from the minutes. James then dissolved Parliament and had seven of its members arrested. One of the arrestees was John Pym, who was later to lead Charles I such a merry chase. In this conflict, James had right on his side, in the sense that up until then, foreign policy decisions had indisputably been a royal prerogative. Three years later, Parliament had to be convened again, because funds were needed for the menacing war with Spain.

Because of Spain's prevarications, the marriage negotiations ended in utter fiasco. The resulting chill in the relations between the two countries soon passed into a cold war. The constantly vacillating Buckingham made a complete about-face. Once the most zealous advocate of an alliance with the Spanish, Buckingham now changed his allegiance to the war faction. He enjoyed a short-lived burst of popularity in the newly convened Parliament, which was now calling for war against Spain. In the bellicose mood of the moment, Parliament was prepared to grant three aids, totaling 300,000 pounds. For a short period, harmony reigned between the King and Parliament. Several bills prepared earlier in 1610 and 1614, which were aimed at restricting the King's financial maneuverability, were adopted without difficulty. The most important of these bills became the Monopoly Act, in which granting and selling trade monopolies was made illegal. The Monopoly Act, however, did make an exception for existing monopolies and those temporarily granted to the inventors of new production technologies. The harmony between the King and Parliament did not last long. Irritated because the House of Commons had deprived him of more than he wished, the King fired off such a barrage of abuse in the Commons that its members refused to include the speech in the minutes. In response, the King pointedly ridiculed a Puritan-inspired bill legislating a stricter observance of the Sabbath. Those poor people who work hard all week, can they not relax a little on Sunday, the King asked? He then adjourned the session. This Parliament never convened again, as James died nine months later, on March 27, 1625.

Now that Spain had fallen by the wayside, England was seeking another ally. The most likely candidate was France. Fortunately, France too had a princess to offer: Henrietta Maria, the youngest sister of Louis XIII. Henrietta Maria lacked the religious cynicism of her father Henry IV, typified by his statement "Paris vaut bien une Messe". On the contrary, she had been raised a strict Catholic and was filled with missionary zeal. Her religious fervor contributed considerably to the difficulties soon encountered by her husband Charles.

The leaven of religion

The seventeenth century was dominated by religion and money. The palette of religion contained various shades of opinion. England still housed a small majority of Roman Catholics, mostly in the countryside, who could not reconcile themselves to the Anglican break with Rome. A frequent target of hatred and persecution, the Catholics attempted to remain invisible. They had been stripped not only of their political rights, but also their religious freedom. Only freedom of conscience remained, for it is difficult, as the Bible says, "to fathom the heart and kidneys." They were unable to express their beliefs openly. In spite of (or perhaps because of) their negligible numerical strength, the Roman Catholics were used as lightning rods by the other parties in the political conflicts of the time. The memory of the Gunpowder Plot of 1605, when Guy Fawkes tried in vain to blow up Parliament, was as fresh in their minds as if it had taken place yesterday instead of twenty years ago. "Popery" was associated with dark images and conspiracies against state security. Any king or politician thought to be in league with Rome was sharply denounced by public opinion. The unenviable position of the Catholics in England was even worse than that of the Huguenots in France. The Huguenots were relatively larger in number and enjoyed the protection of the Edict of Nantes, which not only ensured their freedom of religion but also guaranteed a number of rights, including the right to hold public office.

The official church was the Anglican Church. Its clergy, arranged hierarchically under the spiritual guidance of the Archbishops of Canterbury and York, was only allowed to make use of the official Book of Common Prayer and was supposed to profess the Thirty-nine Articles. Many worshippers felt that the Anglican Church had, like the Roman Catholic Church, become a corset, in which the stays of strict religious doctrine were laced tightly by ecclesiastical hierarchy. A certain degree of elasticity in this churchly garment was provided by a moral code. Not surprisingly, many people rebelled against such rigidity. The Puritans, in particular, felt the Anglican Church consisted wholly of a formal worship service and wished to purge it of any leftover Romish practices.

Puritanism was a mentality rather than an ecclesiastical doctrine. Every Puritan clergyman was allowed to decide for himself whether he wished to wear a surplice, make the sign of the cross, kneel before the altar, kiss the ring, etc. Puritans believed lifestyle to be important: they dressed and behaved with sobriety, observed the Sabbath strictly, disliked frivolity and cherished civil liberties. It was said in jest that a cat that chased mice on Sunday would be hung by them on Monday. The Puritans regarded the merry and carefree life in Mediterranean countries with a mixture of wonderment and exasperation. Poetry? Certainly, but that of Psalms and Ecclesiastes rather than that of Shakespeare and Spencer. They baptized their children with Old Testament names and looked upon themselves as God's new people, sent to eradicate the Amelikites in the court. To show their contempt for the long-haired courtiers, the Puritans wore their hair short, earning them the nickname "Roundheads," a name they bore with pride. The French writer André Maurois characterized them in his "History of England" as "somber, decent, insufferable and strong". Some Puritans advocated nothing more than bending the usages of the established church in the direction of fewer ceremonies and more piety. More radical Puritans wished to establish a presbyterian church, modeled after the Scottish church, in which the episcopal hierarchy would be abolished and each local church would be placed under the direction of elders. The Independents viewed the church as a group of Christians bound together solely by free will. The Independents granted total autonomy to local church districts and believed that everyone should be allowed to live according to his or her own religious convictions. The Independents could be divided into two groups. The first group (including the Baptists and the Quakers) believed that every person had the right to arrange his or her own religious life as he or she wished. The second group (including the likes of Oliver Cromwell) felt that this right should be reserved for the Puritans. Because of their tight organization and willingness to make great sacrifices for their convictions, the Puritans managed to prevail over the High Church adherents in the Anglican Church. In time, the Puritans came to dominate commerce and, more importantly, to form the majority in the House of Commons. The Puritans generally had the upper hand in the cities, while the other groups predominated in the countryside. These religious differences had a political impact as well, owing to the intermeshing of church and state (in which the Anglican Church was the state church and the King its Supreme Governor). How did the struggle between public authority and private freedom and between High Church and Puritanism begun under James' administration develop under his son and successor Charles?

The first Parliament under Charles I (1625)

According to a proverb, "Those whom the gods will destroy are struck with blindness." One well-known historical personality to whom this proverb applies is Charles I. Soon after his accession, Charles alienated many subjects from all strata of society. Their antipathy changed in time to deadly hate. The fact that Charles faced death on the scaffold with great dignity was the only virtue to impress future generations. Charles' blindness lay not so much in his misjudgment of the available political options (after all, if France and Spain had strengthened royal authority, why should England not be able to?) as in his inability to place himself in other people's shoes. Lacking imagination, the King regularly misjudged situations and repeatedly made the wrong decisions. He was clearly no match for the increasingly more powerful Parliament.

Charles I as seen by the royalists: a martyr to a holy cause.

Charles was not only blind but also politically unreliable. Though he may have been a gentleman in private, when it came to matters of state, he played people off against each other and hopped from one political bandwagon to another with dazzling speed. The greater the need, the faster he broke his word.

Yet another characteristic was Charles' almost maniacal insistence that he was right. His infrequent admissions of wrong were invariably too late. He regarded those who dared differ with him as criminals and traitors. It did not occur to him that a king, accountable only to God, could err. This high opinion of his kingship caused him to be very reserved, even with his closest advisers. His Scottish accent, falsetto voice, nervous stutter, penetrating eyes, feminine features and melancholia kept everyone at a distance, even though his courtly manners and gentle appearance suggested the opposite. He was modest and devout and sincerely wished to do what was right. But his opinions never wavered — neither when he had been confronted with hard reality nor when the pros and cons of an issue had been pointed out to him.

Charles had no friends, with the possible exception of Buckingham. Charles and Buckingham had journeyed in disguise to the Spanish court in 1623, where both had asked for the hand of the Infanta. After seven months, the two men returned to England empty-handed. All that Charles had to show for his pains was a goatee. Buckingham was a "beau garçon," apparently sufficient reason for James to promote him rapidly from royal cupbearer and chamberlain to minister. Buckingham was the favorite of both James and Charles. Starting as a mere George Villiers, he reached the pinnacle of his career when he was named the Duke of Buckingham. Buckingham's vanity and frivolity were all the more painful because they were accompanied by a total lack of political ability and military insight. His personal courage did little to compensate for these deficiencies. After their futile trip to the Iberian Peninsula, Charles and Buckingham became advocates of war with Spain. Many English subjects shared this war objective, so that they initially accepted the silent and reserved young man, about whom they knew very little, as king after James' death.

Charles was faced in 1625 with three matters needing immediate attention: the imminent war with Spain, his marriage to Henrietta Maria of France and the convening of Parliament to vote money for the war. The fleet was readied with the help of the Dutch Republic, with whom England had a treaty. Maurits, the Stadtholder of five of the seven provinces and virtual ruler of The Netherlands, had just died and been succeeded by his half-brother, Frederick Henry. Although little help could be expected from the Dutch until the new Stadtholder was firmly established, Frederick Henry had promised twenty ships for an expedition against Flemish seaports. The expedition required the tacit approval and/or cooperation of the French government. During the ensuing talks, Charles and Henrietta Maria's forthcoming marriage, which had been postponed owing to James' illness, was arranged. They were married by proxy on May 1, 1625, and the twenty-four year old King met his fifteen year old bride a month or so later. The petite Henrietta Maria, thin as a rail and without feminine curves, had large eyes and buck teeth. Charles was reputedly bitterly disappointed with her appearance. He undoubtedly still pictured the Spanish Infanta, with her voluptuous bust, blond curls, sensual lips and slightly protruding eyes.

Several years lapsed before there was anything resembling affection between the married couple. It was only when Charles had squandered what little political credit he possessed and was living in increasing loneliness with his diminutive Queen in Whitehall that they grew close enough to produce progeny. In the later years of his reign, the Queen's increasing political influence over her husband contributed greatly to his fall. The Queen's advice was not only French-oriented, rash and politically naive, but she became associated with popery, a serious charge in the eyes of English subjects.

But we are getting ahead of our story. In the first years of their marriage, Charles and Henrietta Maria mostly lived apart. There were small problems from the very beginning. Henrietta Maria had been raised under the care of Madame de St. Georges, and she asked not to be separated from her during the journey from Dover to Canterbury. Permission for this was denied, as Madame was not of sufficiently high rank to sit next to the Queen. Her place was taken instead by Buckingham's mother and sister and the Duchess of Arundel. Thus, Henrietta Maria was bereft from the very beginning of her only confidante. This first marital tiff almost escalated into a full-fledged diplomatic conflict. The French ladies who

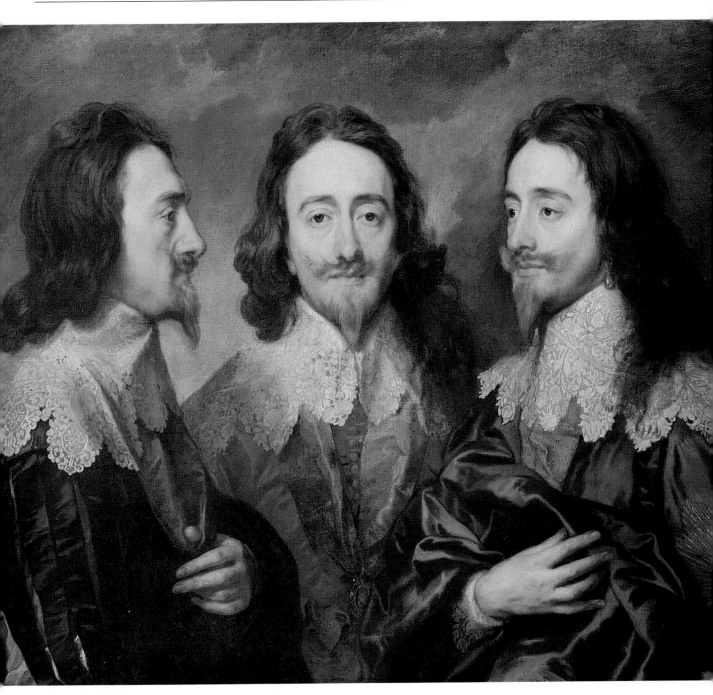

The three portraits of Charles I painted in 1635-1636 by Anthony van Dyck for the Italian sculptor Lorenzo Bernini, who was asked to make a bust of the King. This masterpiece of the art of portraiture reveals the posing monarch's character traits: his stubbornness and unreliability as well as his melancholy and visionary religious convictions.

accompanied the Queen added flames to the fire. They indignantly noted that their mistress had to sleep in an old-fashioned Elizabethan bed and encouraged Henrietta Maria to despise the English. Of course, the French retinue had been carefully screened for their delicate task by France's Prime Minister, Cardinal Richelieu.

This unfortunate beginning cooled relations between the French and the English courts. When the French refused to lend their support to future English-Dutch expeditions against the Spanish Netherlands, the temperature plunged to freezing. Charles needed money.

The King of Denmark (who provided military aid to the German Protestants) had to be kept solvent with 360,000 pounds; Mansfeld's army on the Continent needed 240,000 pounds; the English regiment in The Netherlands required 100,000 pounds; and the naval fleet swallowed 300,000 pounds. This totaled roughly one million pounds sterling, or three times the amount voted in the unprecedently high aids of 1624.

Under the circumstances, Charles was obliged to convene Parliament. In spite of a plague in London, causing some two hundred deaths weekly, Parliament convened in Westminster on June 18th. They were faced with a difficult task. The King had not sought the opinion, let alone approval, of the previous House of Commons for the exorbitant sums he needed to meet his foreign political objectives.

The King and his Councilors committed an initial tactical error. To avoid a debate over war objectives, they asked the Commons for funds without specifying the amounts required. Not one of the King's Councilors who was also a member of the Commons offered a more detailed explanation. Not surprisingly, Parliament felt that Charles had simply thrown the reins around its neck and ordered it to trot in any direction he chose!

During its last session, Parliament had called for war with Spain. But the current House of Commons hesitated to grant the necessary aids, claiming that England was likely to be drawn into a widespread war on the Continent rather than a mere naval battle with Spain. With their limited knowledge of foreign policy, particularly the complex issue of Continental alliances, Parliament assumed that a naval victory over the Spanish fleet would be sufficient to restore the Palatinate to Frederick and Elizabeth's Protestant hands.

To placate the French, Buckingham had promised to provide a few English warships which they could use against the Huguenots in La Rochelle. The Puritan House of Commons opposed this move, but was powerless to stop it. However, opposition to Buckingham grew.

Finances were an additional source of friction. The funds which Parliament had authorized in 1624 had clearly been earmarked for a war with Spain. Instead, the King had given the money to Mansfeld, the mercenary fighting on the side of the German Protestants.

As the new King was requesting money for the first time, the Commons naturally did not want to start off on the wrong foot by offending him. They postponed the moment of decision by first bringing up religious issues. The Commons particularly hoped that the King would speak out firmly against Roman Catholicism, which they perceived as a threat to the kingdom. John Pym, a member of the Commons, drew up a petition, stating that the laws against priests and Jesuits, in particular, should be enforced. The Commons was unaware that soon after his accession, Charles and William Laud, (the Anglican Bishop of Bath and Wells who later faithfully executed the King's ecclesiastical policies) had compiled a list of all clergymen, setting an O (for Orthodox) and a P (for Puritan) next to their names. Had the predominantly Puritan House of Commons known of the list, it would most certainly have adopted a harder stance against the King's religious policies. Instead, the Commons made rather moderate demands, confining itself to an anti-papal motion that could count on support from all sides. Pym's petition was adopted by the Commons and approved by the King. But the Commons was less obliging when it came to finances, as Charles was soon to find out. The Commons initially voted him only one subsidy[7] and one fifteenth,[8] together totaling 100,000 pounds. Later, this was raised to two subsidies, totaling 140,000 pounds. The vote was taken hastily and in the absence of the handful of members who were also the King's ministers (a mere coincidence?). The motion contained the usual clause about subsidies being granted out of their respect for and devotion to the King. But it basically rejected the policies of the Privy Councilors.

Naturally, such meager results were a bitter pill for the King to swallow. An even greater disappointment was in store for him the next day. Since the reign of Henry VI (1422 – 1461), the tonnage and poundage had been granted every new king upon his accession for his entire reign. For the first time, Parliament balked at granting these levies. The Crown's lawyers maintained that the impositions listed in the Book of Rates were part of the tonnage and poundage and therefore belonged to the King. The House of Commons proposed granting Charles the income from the tonnage and poundage for one year, during which time it would examine the Crown's claim further. The House of Lords, unwilling to break with a centuries-old practice, sent the motion back to the House of Commons, where it awaited further action. As a result, the King was more or less compelled to impose tonnage and poundage without the consent of Parliament.

The King's only recourse was to ask the Commons once again to authorize funds, which he did on August 4th in Oxford, where Parliament had retreated because of London's plague. The Commons, faced with the Crown's refusal to discuss the alliance with France and the military intervention in Germany – two political objectives facing tough opposition – was reluctant to grant the funds. As the debates show, the House of Commons only wished to grant a large sum to maintain the naval fleet. Finally, Buckingham himself appeared in Parliament and presented a candid reading of the present situation. His appeal did not achieve the desired results. Parliament, with no knowledge of foreign affairs, saw no advantage in direct involvement with the war on the Continent. Moreover, it was piqued at two clauses in the treaty between France and England: better treatment of English Catholics and support of the French government in its struggle against the Huguenots. Buckingham managed to extricate himself from these two obligations, but the Commons was unimpressed. In Parliament's eyes, it was wrong to contemplate the clauses, much less implement them. Talk of impeaching Buckingham was in the air, but the Commons did not take the step. Instead, Parliament decided not to put the King's request for financial aid to a vote. As one of the members remarked, it would be more painful for the King to appear to be in the minority after a vote than to have the entire House of Commons against him. But the new King had suffered a bruising loss of prestige. This unfortunate denouement stung Charles to the quick. Contrary to Buckingham's insistent advice to pursue the matter to its conclusion, the King immediately dissolved Parliament. The members were only too happy to go home, away from the plague and relieved of the expense of their honorary positions. Charles emerged saddened and disappointed from his first confrontation with the people's representatives. In his eyes, the House of Commons was determined to get the better of his faithful servant, Buckingham. The King was unconcerned that Buckingham had broken his promise to the French. The King was thus placed

7. A "subsidy" was a wealth tax assessed according to a fixed rate. Any subsidy voted by the House of Commons was only valid for the laity. However, it was customary from times of old for the clergy to decide more or less simultaneously to make its own contribution. Problems were rarely encountered, if only because of the time-honored adage: "no king, no bishop."

8. A fifteenth of a penny had raised 39,000 pounds for centuries; every city and county knew exactly how to apportion this among its residents. Because a fifteenth disproportionately burdened the lower classes, it lapsed into disuse under Charles I.

in an unenviable position, for he had lost the confidence of one party without having eliminated the distrust of the other.

Parliament viewed the conflict in an entirely different light. If the King were to recognize Parliament's right to be apprised of current affairs before approving the subsidies, the political authority of those granting the subsidies, i.e. the House of Commons, would be strengthened. The House had not reached a decision about the tonnage and poundage before its sudden dissolution. Undeterred, the King continued to levy these impositions.

In the meantime, Charles' marriage was in the same dire straits as his finances. Charles was totally incapable of understanding the young Queen's predicament. She had left her home for an unknown country, trusting in English promises that the Catholics would be given better treatment, only to discover that these guarantees had been violated when her pillow was still warm from her first lonely night on alien shores. Charles had appointed Buckingham's wife, cousin and sister as the Queen's ladies-in-waiting, although the marriage contract had stipulated that her entourage was to consist of French Catholics and that vacancies were to be filled by Catholics. While packing the retinue with Protestants may not have been against the letter of the law, it was certainly against the spirit of the agreement. The infuriated Henrietta Maria told her retinue that nothing would induce her to allow spies in her private rooms. In the end, of course, she had to concede.

Her revenge was childish. In the houses the King had at his disposal, it was customary for Anglican services to be held. This included Thitchfield, the Queen's residence, even though the King was never present. The Queen protested, considering the Anglican service to be a personal insult. She reasoned that she was mistress of the house in the King's absence, and she objected to the Anglican rites. However, Lady Denbigh, Buckingham's sister and her brand-new lady-in-waiting, would brook no opposition and Anglican services continued to be held. Finally, Henrietta Maria lost her patience. She and her French ladies-in-waiting burst into church in the middle of the sermon and walked up and down in front of the pulpit, talking loudly and making jokes.

Lady Denbigh's husband, who had no maritime experience and only one attribute to his credit, namely that Buckingham was his brother-in-law, was one of the leaders of the combined English-Dutch naval expedition to Cádiz. Buckingham had hoped to win over public opinion with a swift and resounding naval victory abroad. With the public on his side, Parliament was sure to vote the necessary subsidies. However, the venture failed miserably and badly damaged Buckingham's already tarnished reputation. The expedition's failure was not entirely due to the incompetence of its commanders (all of whom were Buckingham's "friends"), but also to fraud on the part of maritime suppliers. There was a desperate lack of provisions, spare parts and fresh drinking water. For example, the fleet was equipped with sails that had been used in 1588 in the confrontation with the Spanish Armada.

The defeated fleet returned to Plymouth. It was a pitiful sight. The canvas-wrapped bodies of sailors and soldiers who had died of exhaustion and disease were thrown overboard. Many sailors collapsed and died in the streets on their way home. One of the witnesses to this wretched scene was Devon's Vice-Admiral Sir John Eliot, a die-hard Puritan. Before long, Eliot was prominent among those in Parliament who tried to lay the blame for the expedition's failure at Buckingham's door. The disaster could be attributed not only to incompetence and fraud, but also to a perpetual lack of funds. It would be incorrect to suggest that the government was entirely responsible for the disaster. After 1624, Parliament had to take its share of the blame, because it was unwilling to vote the necessary resources. Parliament's reluctance to finance the expedition is due in part to its lack of confidence in the government (i.e. in Buckingham). In addition, the members of the Commons, representatives of cities and counties, were too parochial in their thinking. Their narrow perspective hampered the government's attempts to form a strong central government. The government had enough difficulty organizing the country's defense. Assembling and equipping an offensive fleet was an even more difficult task, particularly since the necessary funds had to be approved by a House of Commons that had been left in the dark and was completely unaware of how much money was required.

The second Parliament under Charles I (1626)

In 1626, caught between the devil and the deep blue sea, England began to revive its alliance with France against Spain. This did not serve to improve relations between the English King and his French Queen. Henrietta Maria, not wishing to take part in an Anglican ceremony, had categorically refused to attend the coronation on February 2, 1626.

As a result of the treaty with France, Charles reconvened Parliament for the purpose of voting money for a combined French-English army in Germany. He counted on the Cádiz fiasco being forgotten, if not forgiven. In order to take the wind out of the new Parliament's sails, Charles appointed his fiercest critics in the previous Parliament, including Sir Thomas Wentworth, sheriffs in their own districts. Charles and Buckingham reasoned that these troublemakers would cause fewer problems, as they would be tied to their districts by their sheriff's duties. The new Parliament was convened on February 6, 1626, just a few days after the coronation.

Once again, money was a major issue. The government had tried to raise money by issuing Privy Seals, in a kind of quasi-voluntary bond issue, but the attempt had largely failed. Charles had even considered pawning the crown jewels. Knowing that an Englishman would never agree to pledge these priceless heirlooms, the King sent Buckingham to The Hague to try to interest the wealthy Dutch. But Amsterdam's merchants, worried that the loan would never be repaid, were not eager to use the crown jewels as security on a loan. Charles was compelled to scrape the bottom of the treasury's barrel; at one point, there was hardly enough money to pay the expenses of the royal household.

The first item on the Parliamentary agenda was Charles' request for money. Once a few subsidies had been authorized, the government would be credit-worthy enough to borrow money from wealthy tax farmers. Once again, the government did not candidly discuss its foreign policies with Parliament, despite the fact that it could not implement these policies without Parliamentary-approved funds. Parliament listened impassively to the speeches of the King and his ministers. Charles outlined his plan of persecuting Catholics and reforming the Anglican Church. Although Parliament concurred with this scheme, it did not feel these were strong enough grounds for granting a subsidy. Charles might have won greater support by admitting the errors of the Cádiz expedition, but he was unwilling to make such an admission. He merely filed a request for funds, without alluding to the government's widely known mistakes. He gave no account of the expenditure of past subsidies, although Parliament had insisted on such accounts in 1624. The government refused to accept responsibility for the expenditures or the objectives on which the money had been spent. The House of Commons, speaking through one of its leaders, Sir John Eliot, declared that it would not honor the requested subsidies until the recent setbacks had been investigated and an impeachment procedure had been started against Buckingham.

Buckingham's errors had become exaggerated in the mind of the public and were an obvious target of parliamentary inquiry. Had he not failed to protect the merchants against pirates? Had not his appointment of incompetent commanders caused the Cádiz expedition to fail? Had he not reserved the crown's estates for himself, his family and his friends? Had he not sold titles, honorary offices and judgeships? The King's friend and top adviser had to defend himself against a mixture of political and personal allegations. The conflict revolved primarily around foreign policy, which was indisputably a royal prerogative. Nevertheless, Parliament had to approve the funds needed to implement the King's foreign policy. There was a no-man's land between the two parties where the respective powers had not been delineated. Had Charles been more flexible and prudent enough to realize that the government's policy as a whole was being subject to critical scrutiny, he could have accepted Parliament's offer. Four subsidies lay in Parliament's outstretched hand, but it would only allow Charles to pluck them away after he had conceded a few points of grievance. Unfortunately, Charles was unable to compromise. From his perspective, the criticism leveled at Buckingham was purely personal. As the person ultimately responsible for the state of affairs, the King viewed any other comments as intolerable criticism against his own person.

The impeachment procedure the Commons set in motion against Buckingham was based on malicious talk and hearsay rather than verifiable facts. The incriminating evidence unearthed by the investigative committee was insufficient to lead to a charge of treason or bribery. For example, Buckingham could easily refute the argument that he wore too many administrative hats by demonstrating that the country had benefitted from his activities. Unfortunately, Charles was injudicious enough to appoint Buckingham to fill the recently vacated job of Chancellor of the University of Cambridge while the campaign against him was at its height.

Only a few of the many accusations leveled against Buckingham carried any political weight. These included the unsuccessful Cádiz expedition and the fact that Buckingham had ordered the continued imposition of the tonnage and poundage. The Commons had admittedly agreed to grant the imposition for one year, but Buckingham was not formally empowered to order this imposition. Many of the remaining charges, directed at Buckingham's person rather than his politics, were unjust, a view upheld by later historical research. For example, the Duke was charged with giving away offices, but his behavior was entirely consistent with current practice. Nor was he guilty of enriching himself at the expense of the state. Parliament, which had to learn to deal with the new power it was appropriating for itself, had regrettably mixed the personal with the political. As a result, the King, aware that the personal attacks were ill-conceived, insisted that his friend and protégé be cleared and assumed personal responsibility for any political acts. In fact, every political step taken by Buckingham had either been devised by the King and Buckingham in advance or had been approved by the King after the event. Nor was the King slow to let Parliament know this. In Charles' eyes, the King was accountable only to God, and no mere mortal could call him to account. Parliament, not anxious to sit in judgement on the King, was more interested in letting all its wrath fall on Buckingham.

A long and stormy discussion took place on June 12th as to which topic should be debated first: the subsidies or Buckingham. An overwhelming majority voted to begin with Buckingham's case. Accordingly, the Commons submitted a petition to the King requesting him to dismiss the Duke. The King listened to Parliament's advice, but did not dispense with Buckingham's services, as he had no intention of letting Parliament meddle in his affairs. As far as the subsidies were concerned, Parliament insisted on being allowed to supervise expenditures.

Charles felt he had no recourse but to dissolve Parliament. Thus, in less than a year, the King had gone through two parliaments. The new alliance with France was also foundering. Charles incurred the wrath of the French over a series of insignificant matters. He created ill-feeling by having English Catholics who attended mass in the French embassy arrested. He insisted on mediating the fragile agreement between the French government and the Huguenots, but refused to receive the French ambassador in his court. He put off returning confiscated French ships, even though the French had already returned English ships. Relations between the two royal courts were again dangerously close to freezing. Charles' conduct in such matters was typical. He considered neither his wife's feelings nor the French King's pride and cared little for the consternation aroused by his treatment of the Catholics. He evaluated the situation solely on the basis of his own honor. To Charles, this had nothing to do with keeping his word, let alone fulfilling his royal obligations, but everything to do with demanding what was rightfully his, as a person and as a king.

France's Prime Minister and advocate of the alliance with England, Cardinal Richelieu, was in a difficult position. The Catholic ecclesiastical faction in the French court regarded the Huguenots as their arch-enemies and preferred to join Spain in a war against England rather than align itself with England against Spain. The Catholic faction seized the opportunity to enter into an alliance with Spain and Richelieu was in no position to oppose them. The French alliance with England was thus brought to an end. Would it come to war between the two countries?

In spite of the government's efforts, not so much as a penny had flowed into the treasury. The City of London was asked to lend 100,000 pounds with the crown jewels as security, but the request was denied. The boroughs and shires were then asked to make a voluntary contribution called a "benevolence." The King and his ministers argued that because Parliament had been about to grant four subsidies when it was dissolved, people could reasonably be expected to pay voluntarily the amount they would otherwise have to pay compulsorily. This too was a serious miscalculation. The announcement of the measure in Westminster Hall was drowned out by cries for "a parliament, a parliament." Parochialism and an unwillingness to finance national projects undoubtedly played their role, and the benevolence brought in hardly any revenue.

The government then turned its attention to the tonnage and poundage, the only significant source of income left to the King. The Crown's attorneys maintained that there was no objection to continuing a levy of the tonnage and poundage beyond the one-year term proscribed by Parliament. But tonnage and poundage were insufficient to meet the King's needs. As Charles neither wished to end the war with Spain nor reconvene Parliament, he could only resolve his financial problems by invoking a national emergency. According to precedent, the populace could be asked to waive their local and individual tax rights if the kingdom was endangered. In similar circumstances in the past, the coastal counties had often been asked to supply ships for the naval fleet. Queen Elizabeth had taken this step in 1588 when she assembled the fleet that had successfully repelled the Spanish Armada. Invoking precedent and the great danger menacing the kingdom, the government demanded that the coastal counties and seaports supply sixty-five ships. London was asked to supply twenty ships, more than ever before. When the city demurred, its objections were dismissed with the same arguments.

This print, entitled "Royal and Ecclesiastical Gamesters," shows the Kings of Sweden, Denmark and England playing cards with the representatives of the Roman Catholic Church. The Pope approaches from the right in order to intervene, but the English King, Charles I, tries to stop him. His attempt to grab the Pope's tiara is checked by a cardinal. The print is an allegory of the help offered the Reformation, symbolized by the resistance to the Catholic powers. Charles I's actions refer to the unfortunate expedition under Buckingham's command.

The treasury was so depleted that it did not have the 14,000 pounds needed to dismiss the handful of sailors considered unsuitable for service. By law, servicemen could only be dismissed if they had received overdue back pay. Unable to pay them, the government had to retain their services at a cost of 4,000 a month. Fortunately, the sale of royal silver brought some cash into the coffers.

Various kinds of fund-raising schemes were suggested, only to be rejected, either because they would not raise enough money (one such scheme was increasing the taxes paid by the recusants[9]) or because the government realized the folly and unreasonableness of the plans. The latter category included Buckingham's attempts to clip coins, a dubious practice which had been vigorously and successfully foiled by the City's merchants. Another example was a tax on all "stalls, stools, stairs and other encroachments" on the streets of London.

In the meantime, the Queen's position was becoming more precarious. On one summer day when she was walking with her retinue in St. James' Park, she turned her steps − unconsciously or deliberately? − in the direction of Tyburn, where Catholic martyrs were hanged. She paused in devotion, possibly kneeling and uttering a prayer for the souls of those who had been hanged. The Queen's Tyburn visit was brought to the King's attention two weeks later. The English Queen, it was said, had been on a pilgrimage and had prayed on the spot where traitors had received their just rewards for their crimes. Charles, his patience worn thin, ordered the French retinue, with the exception of two or three personal servants, to leave the country immediately. This was a terrible blow for Henrietta Maria, as she was now deprived of all those who could raise her spirits, talk to her in her own language and sing, dance and make music according to her own customs. The King announced his decision when he was alone with his Queen, and a terrible scene followed. Charles, however, remained resolute. Louis XIII was furious at the injustice done to his sister, and once again, the

9. Catholics who refused to attend the Anglican service of worship and thus paid an annual fine.

alliance hung in the balance. When England and France began to confiscate each other's ships and goods, the relationship between the two countries gradually assumed the shape of undeclared war. As a result of these political imbroglios, France and Spain again fell into each other's arms, not so much in real love as in a "mariage de raison d'état."

Now that war with France was imminent, it became even more imperative to put the kingdom's financial house in order. In September of 1626, the government evolved the concept of a forced loan. This loan was to raise an amount equivalent to five subsidies granted by Parliament. In other words, the lenders would have to lend the same amount of money to the state that they would have contributed by way of the five subsidies. As the government did not know whether the loan would ever be repaid, this was nothing more than a masked form of taxation. Members of special committees rode up and down the country, pressuring citizens of all classes into paying the loan. Those from the lower classes who refused to pay were faced with the prospect of compulsory military service. Others risked banishment to a remote district or even imprisonment. Alternatively, they were harassed to the point that their lives became unbearable.

The government suffered a setback when the magistrates of the Court of the King's Bench[10] refused to sign a declaration legitimizing the forced loan. The magistrates stood firm, even when Charles dismissed the Chief Justice. For the majority of the population, the loan amounted to only a few shillings or at most a couple of pounds. As a result, most succumbed to the temptation to pay the levy rather than risk the consequences. Nonetheless, many persons — young and old, rich and poor, city dwellers and country folk — were unwilling to tolerate this violation of their civil rights. Both sides were locked in bitter combat. In Essex, fifty men who refused to pay were ordered to join the army, but they refused. A heated discussion ensued in the King's Privy Council. Most of the Councilors felt that the men should be hung without delay for violating the laws of military justice. Fortunately, one of the gentlemen was astute enough to note that martial law was not applicable in this case: since the men had refused to be drafted, they were not military personnel and therefore could not be tried under military law.

Another individual unwilling to pay the forced loan was a member of the House of Commons from Buckinghamshire called John Hampden, about whom more will be said later. Hampden was imprisoned for the entire year of 1627, although he was allowed a great deal of freedom. For example, he was sometimes permitted to visit his mother at her house in Downing Street.

Sir John Eliot, the demagogic Puritan leader of the opposition in the previous Parliament, also refused to comply with the forced loan. Because of his constant attempts to thwart the King and Buckingham, Eliot had been imprisoned in the Tower during the last session, but Parliament had successfully pressed for his early release. Eliot had, however, been stripped of the Vice-Admiralty of Devon. He was sent to prison again, but this time for a considerably longer term.

10. The Court of the King's Bench was the supreme court of justice, handling the Crown's lawsuits against its subjects.

Another leading member of the Commons who refused to pay the loan was Sir Thomas Wentworth, a man of an entirely different stamp. Wentworth wanted to have nothing to do with Puritanism and by inclination tended to side with the government. He was banished from Yorkshire to Kent for his refusal to pay.

By July of 1627, the forced loan had raised the tidy sum of 240,000 pounds, and its collection had not been completed. The unsuccessful English naval expedition to the island of Ré, which had been launched in 1627 to relieve the besieged Huguenots in La Rochelle, fanned anew the flames of opposition to the forced loan. Writing from his prison cell, Eliot sent a petition to the King, stating in effect that Parliament's prior consent to a forced loan was needed.

Five knights who were imprisoned for refusing to pay their share of the forced loan used the same argument in an appeal submitted to the Court of the King's Bench. This device was designed to elicit a charge against which they could defend themselves. According to the *Magna Carta*, no one could be imprisoned unless legally sentenced by his peers for having violated the law. The five knights demanded to know what their crime had been. The magistrates decided that they had been imprisoned on the King's special orders and that, while legal proceedings would have to be set in motion at a suitable moment, the King could not be hurried. Although this verdict accorded with contemporary law, it omitted any reference to the point around which the whole matter revolved, namely the legality of the forced loan.

The third Parliament under Charles I (1628 – 1629)

The government's financial situation failed to improve despite the forced loan, an additional loan obtained with great effort from the City of London and the sale of mortgages on crown lands. The only alternative was for Charles and Buckingham to end the war against France that had broken out at the beginning of 1627, but this was a course incompatible with their sense of honor. In the summer of 1627, a large English fleet under Buckingham's command attacked the French on the island of Ré, near La Rochelle. The attack, undertaken to aid the Huguenots, was a complete fiasco. Despite his displays of courage, Buckingham had no experience as a naval commander. His discontented commanding officers often failed to carry out his orders. The starving soldiers and sailors were obstreperous to the point of mutiny. After their return, Buckingham paid them only paltry sums for their service. With hardly any clothes for the winter and without any money to purchase food, the men deserted in droves, and forays into the countryside for food became everyday events. The Lord Treasurer, Sir Richard Weston, had calculated that after the expedition, 251,361 pounds were needed to pay the fleet's debts. His loans on future income amounted to 319,728 pounds, while the absolute minimum required to maintain the soldiers and sailors amounted to 3,862 pounds a week. He joined the ranks of those favoring the end of the war, but the government refused to heed their advice.

On the contrary, the Privy Council decided to ready a fleet of one hundred sailing vessels for the approaching summer of 1628 and mobilize an army of eleven thousand men to be deployed either to help the Huguenots in La Rochelle or the King of Denmark in his struggle in Germany.

The difficulty was clearly to find ways to finance such costly operations: 300,000 pounds were needed for the fleet and 200,000 for the army. The Council discussed at length the possibility of introducing excise duties on beer and wine. The plan had to be scrapped because it was against the law and would lead to legal proceedings in courts hostile to the government. Moreover, no one dared or even thought it possible to use military means to counter the expected opposition to

such a tax. The Councilors debated various other solutions, such as reissuing Privy Seals and having each parish pay to maintain three men in military service. Ultimately, the only remaining solution was to reconvene Parliament. This time, the Council took measures to ensure that the House of Commons would be easier to manage. Apparently the possibility of excluding lawyers from the Commons was briefly discussed. The Council also considered immediately dissolving Parliament if the Commons launched another attack against Buckingham. They reasoned that the King would then be entitled to ignore the laws and customs of the land.

The faulty logic of this suggestion certainly tallied with Charles' philosophy, for his next plan made it appear that he looked upon these laws and customs as a mere hindrance. The King did not even want to give Parliament the opportunity to choose between granting or not granting a subsidy. He preferred instead to present Parliament with a fait accompli by levying taxes even before permission had been obtained. These tax levies were to be raised by invoking national emergency and demanding ships (or a comparable amount of money), as the coastal counties and seaports had been asked to do two years earlier in 1626. In February of 1628, a letter demanding ships or a monetary equivalent was sent to every borough and shire in the country, rather than to merely the coastal counties. The King asked that the money be paid to the Treasury before March 1st, as this was the date the fleet was scheduled to set sail. Charles thus hoped the matter would be concluded before Parliament convened on March 17, 1628.

The letter was soon retracted. Charles' other advisers had convinced him that the demand was unacceptable and reminded him that he had promised after the forced loan not to contravene Parliament's rights. Consequently, the ship money plan was suspended for the time being. Nevertheless, money was needed more urgently than ever. Without financing, the fleet was clearly unable to sail on March 1st. Postponing the sailing date for a month would not solve the problem either, as the minimum of six hundred sailors needed to man the fleet had not yet been recruited (by impressment or other means). Nor could the men be prevented from deserting. It was even worse on land, where the sailors were forced to steal to stay alive.

In the meantime, elections for the new Parliament were in full swing. With only a few exceptions, those elected were critical of the Crown. Many owed their election victory to a rejection of the forced loan. On January 2, 1628, the government, in an attempt to relieve the tension, released the people who had been imprisoned for refusing to pay.

However, the new Parliament was even more intractable than the Parliament of 1626. It was more emphatic about its authority and even more opposed to unlawful measures of any kind.

At the top of the print, Charles I meets with the Privy Council. At the bottom, a session of the House of Commons is depicted.

Parliament got off to a poor start. The King opened the session by noting that he had convened Parliament for the purpose of authorizing subsidies to cope with the dangers menacing the nation. He warned them that failure to do their duty in this respect would compel him — in accordance with his conscience — to employ whatever means God had placed in his hands to raise the money. This was not a threat, for Charles reserved threats for his equals.

It was immediately evident that there would be a struggle over the respective boundaries of royal and parliamentary power and authority. The "opposition leaders" of the Commons – headed by Wentworth and Eliot – had deliberated on their tactics the day before the opening. They had agreed to discontinue the attack on Buckingham, as this would merely irritate the King. They had gradually realized that Charles fully supported his favorite, so that an attack on Buckingham was an indirect attack on the King. The opposition preferred to confront the King directly.

The House of Commons soon made it clear that it was not prepared to discuss the subsidies until their grievances had been aired and satisfactorily answered. Not all of the grievances concerned finances. The predominantly Puritan parliamentarians felt that the Catholics were not being dealt with firmly enough. They were also anxious to have harsh treatment meted out to clergymen with Arminian[11] leanings.

Besides Parliament's religious differences with the government (which supported and was supported by the High Church faction of the Anglican Church), there were two main issues which had aroused wrath and concern in recent years.
The first of these was that the King (i.e. the government) had imprisoned many people without due process of law, for example, those who had refused to "subscribe" to the forced loan. The second issue was that citizens were required to quarter soldiers without payment. The compulsory billeting of soldiers was a frequently employed means of coercion applied to individuals who dared to speak out on an issue. Imprisonment without due process, the quartering of troops without payment and taxation without parliamentary consent were issues included in the Petition of Rights, which will be examined below. Given the framework of this book, the discussion will necessarily emphasize the fiscal side of these matters.

The third Parliament adopted the same standpoint as its two predecessors, which did not make the government's task any easier. The Council of War had calculated that 600,000 pounds were needed in the coming year for the army and the fleet and an additional 700,000 pounds for repairs, spare parts, munitions, etc. This placed the King in the same position as in 1625. If he candidly explained his reason for wanting the money, he ran the risk of having his request denied. If he was too timid in his demands, he would end up with a weak army and a small fleet, his problem in previous years. The King therefore opted for a middle course by specifying the objectives for which the money was needed without stating the amounts.

11. In 1607, the Dutch theologian Arminius had rejected the doctrine of predestination, which stated that man's salvation was predetermined by God. Arminius, on the other hand, taught that man's spiritual salvation depended on what he had done during his lifetime. In England, Arminian adherents believed the state should assume extensive powers in the church.

The members of Parliament also realized that funding was urgently needed and were eager to bring about a reconciliation with the King. Accordingly, voices were heard offering to grant the King five subsidies, an important financial concession. An obstinate Parliament dug in its heels and demanded that existing grievances be attended to first. The King's hope of an immediate financial commitment were thus dashed. While the five subsidies were more than he had expected, he would first have to acquiesce to the demands of the House of Commons, a step he was unwilling to take. The familiar deadlock of previous parliaments was again looming on the horizon.

The Petition of Right

This was the moment Thomas Wentworth chose to present a new idea. On April 7th, he proposed a law explicitly prohibiting the King from imposing forced loans without parliamentary consent and imprisoning people without due process. He added that the passage of this law would remove any obstacles to granting the King the requested subsidies.

Like any new idea, this one had to ripen in the minds of those required to judge it. Several weeks passed before the House of Commons and the House of Lords rallied around this idea of a Bill of Rights.[12] While Parliament was preparing the bill, Charles (imagining he was furthering his cause) sent the House of Commons a message. He urgently requested them to reach a decision, as the authorization of funds could not be delayed any longer. He stated that he would honor the *Magna Carta* and its six additional statutes and would protect his subjects' liberty, according to the laws of the land. The King assured the members of Parliament that they "would find as much sincerity in his Royal word and promise as in the strength of any law they could make." It was characteristic of Charles to think that his word carried the same weight as a formal law. Unfortunately, he had already broken his word countless times in the three years of his rule.

When a draft of the Bill of Rights was submitted for his approval a few weeks later, the King adopted the same position: he would agree to uphold the *Magna Carta* and the six statutes, but his word would have to suffice for the rest. This was another tactical blunder on Charles' part. The present version of the Bill of Rights was couched in fairly moderate terms, from which negative comments on recent events had been omitted. If the King had yielded at this point, he would have obtained his subsidies immediately, and could then have dickered as much as he pleased over the wording of the final text. But Charles refused to give way, and the leadership of the House of Commons slipped out of the hands of the royalist Wentworth and into those of the implacable Eliot.

Thus, the cart of government got mired down in Parliament's mud. Parliament's lenience and patience were exhausted. Sir Nathaniel Rich came up with a new proposal that would lift the veil concealing the real issue, namely whether the King could be trusted. All bills, including the final version of the Bill of Rights, had to be ratified by Parliament at the end of the session, after which they would be submitted for the King's approval. But what was to keep the King from rejecting the Bill of Rights or even dissolving Parliament once the subsidies had been granted? Rich therefore argued that it would be better to draw up a Petition of Right. A petition required an immediate answer and no subsidies would have to be approved before that answer had been given. The motion was approved, and the jurists in the House of Commons drafted a Petition of Right. The Petition was formulated in stronger terms than the Bill of Rights. The King was no longer merely asked to promise to abide by a particular course of action. This time, old wounds were meticulously reopened. The King flew into a rage at not having gotten so much as a penny. But the quibblers in the House of Commons plodded on, using the Petition to pillory the government by summing up the violations of Parliament's former rights.

12. This Bill of Rights should not be confused with the law of that name adopted during the Glorious Revolution of William and Mary in 1689.

On May 28th, the Petition was sent to the House of Lords for approval. While the peers were admittedly greater royalists than the commons − many of them owed their status as Lords to the King — they despised the upstart Buckingham. Moreover, they feared that in the long run the absolute monarchy the King wished to establish would affect their inherited positions. The House of Lords therefore endorsed the Petition of Right.

But how would the King react to the Petition? His position had deteriorated dramatically over the last few weeks. The English commander Morgan had been compelled to surrender Stade to the enemy and the Protestants in Germany were faring much worse than the Pope could have ever dared to hope. More importantly, the English fleet had once more set sail for La Rochelle and been forced to return without having fired a shot and with nothing to show for its pains. To give the Petition his legal fiat, the King merely had to add the French words "Soit droit fait comme est désiré," a holdover from the time of William the Conqueror (1066). But Charles refused this course of action and its implicit acceptance of parliamentary terms. He fired off a barrage of messages to Parliament. He seriously considered dissolving Parliament, but, little by little, he was backed into a tight corner. His own Privy Council, with Buckingham at the fore, clearly saw the hopelessness of the government's position. Finally, at four o'clock on the afternoon of June 7th, the King uttered the liberating words "Soit droit fait comme est désiré" to a session of the House of Commons. The King could admittedly still violate the rights of the citizens, but at least these rights had been cast in clear form in the Petition of Right. One week later, Parliament granted five subsidies.

Next to the *Magna Carta*, the Petition of Right is undoubtedly the most important piece of English constitutional law. As it delineated the King's power with respect to Parliament, the question was now whether Charles would resign himself to it in actuality. Parliament made the first move in the chess game that followed by approving a motion attacking Buckingham. The King ignored the motion as well as Buckingham's urgent requests to be allowed to defend himself. The next move was up to Parliament. One item of unfinished business on its agenda was the passage of a law concerning the tonnage and poundage. On the face of it, there was no reason not to approve these taxes. However, some of the tariffs had to be modified, which meant that it might take two or three months before the final version could be approved. The Commons preferred to pass a provisional bill adopting the tonnage and poundage, leaving a discussion of specific tariffs to a subsequent session. Any enacted bill would be effective as of the date Parliament was first convened, i.e. March 1628. Parliament felt that this bill would eliminate the problem of what it still viewed as the illegal imposition of the tonnage and poundage. The proposal did not seem unreasonable, but Charles felt the Commons was maneuvering to assume for itself the power to impose taxes. On June 23rd, he therefore informed both Houses that they could only stay in session until June 26th.

The heart of the matter was whether the concepts of tonnage and poundage were included in the Petition of Right in the passage "no man hereafter be compelled to make or yield any gift, loan, benevolence, tax, or such like charge, without common consent by Act of Parliament." Today's reader will not find this difficult to judge. Import and export duties — which is all the tonnage and poundage amounted to — come under the header of normal taxes. The seventeenth century was not sure. In 1610, Montague, a member of the House of Commons, had declared: "Tax or tallage only by Parliament. Custom or imposition proceed

Sala Regalis cum Curia Westmonastery. vulgo. Westminster haall.

A print made by W. Hollar (1647), showing the most important buildings in Westminster.

from a regal power and matter of inheritance in the king.'' During subsequent debates, the Crown repeatedly asserted that import duties should be treated differently than other taxes.

In defense of the King's point of view, it can be said that if tonnage and poundage were understood to be included in the impositions listed in the Petition of Right, it would have been easier to have tacked them on to the list, particularly since Parliament knew from the opening session that a tonnage and poundage bill was pending. Another point in the King's favor was that the magistrates considered the previous imposition of the tonnage and poundage to be legal. Even if the Commons might not formally have been in the right, including tonnage and poundage under the term ''tax'' was in keeping with the Petition of Right. In fact, the House's position was a hint to individual merchants to refuse to pay this tax, an interpretation not lost on Charles. Infuriated by this new attack on his rights, the King abruptly adjourned Parliament until October. This time Parliament was not dissolved, but was recessed until it was time to vote more subsidies. Charles had realized too late that it would have been better to accept Wentworth's Bill of Rights. The King then prudently appointed Wentworth to the House of Lords and assigned him important governmental duties, thereby enticing this prominent parliamentarian into the royal camp. From that moment on, many Puritan members of Parliament regarded Wentworth as a renegade and hated him almost as much as they hated Buckingham.

On August 23rd, Buckingham was murdered by a disgruntled officer. There was no question of a conspiracy. The murderer simply blamed the Duke for his being passed over for promotion. Charles had been dealt an appalling blow. He was like David faced with the loss of Jonathan. He was deeply hurt by the exuberant crowds in London and elsewhere, whose drinking, singing and celebrating in honor of the murderer only compounded his grief. Charles knew better than anyone that the hatred directed at Buckingham should actually have been directed at himself. He held Eliot, with his inflammatory speeches in Parliament, particularly responsible for the popular frenzy.

Buckingham had been Charles' only true friend. He looked upon all the rest as servants. A man of action, the Duke had favored attacks on Spain and France, and thereby compensated for Charles' own lack of decisiveness. His death heralded a new policy, in which words took the place of deeds and in which more attention was paid to ambassadorial instructions than to arming the fleet. The King excelled in assiduous attention to detail, poring over his subordinates' memorandums in search of mistakes. He also stifled every attempt at personal initiative. Thus began a period in which the government reacted to domestic and foreign developments rather than attempting to steer them in certain directions.

As the young Queen had been surrounded, very much against her will, by members of Buckingham's family, his death removed an obstacle to improved relations between Charles and Henrietta Maria. She was now resigned to her Protestant household, and Charles sought comfort for the loss of his dear friend in his wife. The Queen was now eighteen years old. She had grown from an innocent, ignorant and undisciplined girl into a gracious and brilliant beauty with fiery eyes and sudden flashes of temperament. Once Charles had cast aside his reserve and superciliousness, she received him with all the smiles, happiness and tenderness attendant on an awakening love. Before long, it was announced that she was expecting a direct heir to the throne.

Charles' political life made less headway. La Rochelle fell to the French after heroic resistance. Contrary to expectation, this was not followed by a mass slaughter of the Huguenots in France. Prime Minister Cardinal Richelieu persuaded King Louis XIII to tolerate Protestantism where it was already being practiced. Further, both Protestants and Catholics alike were allowed to hold public office. The capture of La Rochelle had only been necessitated by the fact that the French government could not tolerate a state within a state.

This was a bitter pill for Charles to swallow. He had cast himself in the role of mediator between the Huguenots and their legitimate government, only to find that he had helped estrange France and England. France's tolerance toward the Huguenots made it clear that his policies had been misguided from the outset. Everything that Charles had fought to achieve for the Huguenots had been handed to them by a magnanimous French government, without the slightest contribution from him. All the past efforts − the forced loan, the expedition to Ré, the numerous arbitrary imprisonments and the press-ganging of unwilling sailors, to name a few − had been made in vain. They were rendered redundant by the political acumen of Richelieu, who realized that internal peace could make France strong externally.

Richelieu's tolerance helped dampen the flames of England's military ambitions. The unsuccessful wars against Spain and France were followed by fruitless attempts to play the superpowers off against each other. This, coupled with England's indifference to events taking place on the Continent (particularly in far-off Germany, with which they had little affinity), caused the King and his people to turn away from foreign politics for the time being and concentrate instead on domestic politics.

The issue of religion, a cauldron of discontent which had only occasionally boiled over in the first years of Charles' reign, would increasingly monopolize the attention and emotions of the King and his people. Charles himself was fairly indifferent to religion. If he believed in anything, it was in the King's superiority to everyone and everything. He supported the High Church faction of the Anglican Church primarily because he could count on the support of its hierarchical network. His opponents, the Puritans and Independents, were consumed with religious fervor and were prepared to do whatever their conviction required, particularly if this meant calling down hell and damnation on anyone with different ideas. Thus, there were two factions ready to fight to the death. The first of these considered Holy Communion and the church service to be the central issue. They also believed that the country was subordinate to the King and the Church subordinate to the clergy. The second faction advocated preaching and conversion, simplicity and religious zeal, Puritanism and purity and were fueled by the desire to dictate how others were to achieve salvation. This dichotomy was one of the most important reasons for the outbreak of the Civil War in the 1640's. But in the decade preceding this, the issue of taxation would drive more and more of a wedge between the King and his people.

Tonnage and poundage: the right to impose taxes

The first storm clouds gathered soon after Parliament had been recessed from June 26, 1628 until October of that year. Merchants, encouraged by the firm language of the House of Commons, refused to pay the tonnage and poundage. Some of the merchants, threatened with compulsory military service, paid the tax as quickly as they could. Others saw the goods on which they had refused to pay the tax confiscated. In the light of this turmoil, the King postponed Parliament's next session until January 20, 1629. The owners of confiscated merchandise reclaimed their goods from the customs office, attempting to elicit a verdict from the magistrates on the question of whether tonnage and poundage were understood to be included in the Petition of Right. The King realized that this was a political rather than a legal issue and that the matter was too important to be decided by a court of law. Aided by his Attorney General, Charles had the question of the ownership of the goods — and the underlying question of the legitimacy of the tonnage and poundage — delegated to the House of Commons. His intention was to get the House to confer with him on ways to resolve this ticklish problem.

13. The Court of the Star Chamber, established by Henry VIII (1485 – 1509), functioned as a higher court. It consisted of the Privy Council and two Chief Justices. Its purpose was to create a central body favoring royal authority which would put an end to the arbitrariness of feudal legal relationships and would counteract the misuse of power by magistrates. Its name was derived from the stars painted on the ceiling of the room where the Court met. In the time of Charles I, the Star Chamber was turned into a political weapon and used to extinguish the voice of the opposition.

It proved to be a bad omen when the King had the entire printing of the Petition of Right ordered by Parliament destroyed. The suppressed version contained the King's final response to the Petition. The version Charles ordered in its place contained an earlier and milder speech as well as his June 26th speech emphasizing that tonnage and poundage did not fall under the Petition of Right.

Pandemonium broke out again at the customs office even before Parliament had convened. Their goods having once again been confiscated, the merchants retaliated with violent protests. They were promptly thrown into prison, where they awaited trial by the Star Chamber.[13] The Privy Council naturally discussed the matter in great detail. It was decided that if the House of Commons were to approve the tonnage and poundage, the King's best tactic would be to try to give these gentlemen satisfaction. Unfortunately, the Council's plans went awry. An overconfident Charles did not deem it necessary to open Parliament with a recital of recent developments. The House of Commons, however, directly declared that the Petition of Right had been violated. It was decided to refer the matter of the tonnage and poundage to a special House committee. The opposition leaders in the Commons then made a major tactical error. One of the merchants whose goods had been seized on October 30, 1628 was John Rolle, who also happened to be a member of the House of Commons. He argued that this seizure contravened the tax privileges enjoyed by the members of the Commons. This was a poor argument, because the parliamentary session had been postponed from October 20, 1628 to January 20, 1629, meaning that it was not in session at the time the goods were seized. What was worse, the opposition abandoned a fundamental political standpoint – namely that taxes should not be imposed without parliamentary approval – for a dubious case concerning one of its members. However, it was not initially apparent that this new position would pose a problem for the House of Commons.

In the meantime, Charles realized that he had to break his silence. His opening bid was played superbly. In a speech before the House of Commons, which was repeatedly interrupted by loud cheers and applause, he acknowledged that he did not have the right to impose tonnage and poundage without Parliament's consent, and then asked them to grant their consent. The matter appeared to be resolved, except that the King and the Commons had not reached a compromise on the question of whether specific impositions were included in the tonnage and poundage.

Unfortunately, the question of religion turned out to be a stumbling block. The House of Commons wanted to debate religious matters before discussing tonnage and poundage. The most important speakers were Pym and Eliot. Their attacks on the government were familiar: it failed to take firm action against the Catholics, it tolerated Arminianism[14] and it appointed bishops whom the Puritan Parliament considered doctrinally unsound. In between the debates on religion, there were occasional discussions of tonnage and poundage. But the favorable atmosphere which had prevailed a few weeks earlier had disappeared. The King was becoming restless. For over one hundred and fifty years every new King had been granted a lifetime right to tonnage and poundage, and Charles felt that any deviation from this custom would unnecessarily strip the monarchy of its sovereignty. Nor were the deliberations over the impositions to be included under the tonnage and poundage making any headway. Clearly, unless the religious questions could be resolved, an agreement about the tonnage and poundage would fail to materialize. Yet it seemed highly unlikely that Eliot, who had become Parliament's most important spokesman, would yield any religious point.

Despite the protests of Pym, who felt that the interests of the House of Commons were secondary to those of the country, Eliot got Parliament to declare that the customs officials had acted improperly in confiscating the goods of the merchant and parliamentarian, John Rolle. This created a full-scale conflict with the King, who stood firmly behind his customs officials. Charles felt he had to support the customs officials, as the House of Commons would otherwise be encouraged to censure the bishops who were unacceptable to them (and that was a majority of the bishops). Charles therefore stood his ground.

Provocations on both sides made matters worse. On the one side, the Commons had a London sheriff sent to the Tower for failing to give satisfactory answers to the questions posed him. On the other side, the Star Chamber instigated a trial against some of the merchants who had resorted to violence when attempting to

14. See footnote 11 on page 246.

*Charles I (1600-1649) (from
a painting by Daniel
Mytens, 1631).*

remove their goods from the customs office. The customs officials who had confiscated John Rolle's merchandise were convicted, and the Commons seized this opportunity to make political capital of this matter. Many members advocated reconciliation and compromise in the tonnage and poundage matter, but Eliot remained intransigent.

A new rift between the King and Parliament seemed inevitable. For the time being, Charles was unwilling to take any action other than briefly recessing Parliament. Eliot, whose implacability only served to escalate the conflict, wanted the Commons to adjourn its own session, although this would be usurping the King's right to convene or dismiss a parliament. Eliot's motion for adjournment stated the reasons for Parliament's actions, as he wanted the entire world to be aware of the conflict between the King of England and his Parliament. To enter his motion, Eliot needed to secure a space of a few minutes just before the Speaker of the House of Commons left the chairman's seat at the end of the session.

On March 2nd, the Speaker, Sir John Finch, declared that it pleased the King to adjourn the session until March 10th. Such statements were normally heard in silence, after which the members each went their own separate ways. On this occasion, cries of ''no, no'' were heard on all sides, and before the Speaker could rise, he was roughly pushed back into his seat by two members of the House. Several members of the government rushed to his rescue, but their way was blocked by a cordon of Commons members. When order was finally restored, Eliot demanded that the House of Commons be granted the right to adjourn itself. Eliot digressed at great length, proclaiming to his listeners that the one true religion was under attack; that Arminianism was preparing the way for papism; that certain authorities disregarded the law and hampered magistrates in their administration of justice; that those in authority had created problems in Parliament by sowing the seeds of panic and the fear of reprisal; and that several Anglican prelates were numbered among the King's bad advisers. Eliot accused Weston (who functioned as a kind of Prime Minister after Buckingham's death) of being the ringleader of the papists and the source of all dangers threatening the true religion. Eliot also charged him with willfully intending to use the tonnage and poundage to cripple trade and prosperity. There was not a grain of truth in this, but in the heat of the moment, such an accusation was effective. The members needed to act quickly, for the Usher of the Black Rod (the Master of Ceremonies in the House of Lords), had come to claim the scepter from the House of Commons and was knocking loudly on the door which one of the members had prudently locked. The agitated members continued to discuss Eliot's speech and their next course of action. But before long, they heard another banging at the door. This time it was a messenger from the King. Charles threatened to force an entry into the House of Commons. They clearly had to take immediate action, with no time for deliberation.

Eliot appended a motion to his speech and had one of the members read it aloud. The motion proposed that any religious reformer advocating Arminianism, papism or any other religious views deviating from the true and orthodox church was to be declared an enemy of the state. The same fate awaited anyone found to be cooperating with the imposition of subsidies and tonnage and poundage without the consent of the Parliament. Any person who voluntarily paid these subsidies would be branded as a traitor to the liberties of the people and an enemy of the kingdom and commonwealth. Parliament voted to support the motion and

The bronze weight depicted here bears several official stamps and was used by the officials charged with collecting the tonnage and poundage to weigh wool.

adjourned itself just in the nick of time, for, at that moment, the door was broken down and the members were driven out. Eleven years would pass before a new parliament was convened.

The Privy Council discussed the events for two days and finally decided to dissolve Parliament, which had been recessed until March 10th. Charles issued a Proclamation on March 27, 1629, outlining the reasons for his actions. While he was prepared to uphold the Petition of Right and did not intend to reform the church, he could not allow the Parliament to appoint itself as a kind of Supreme Court to which all ministers and even courts of law would be accountable. As for the tonnage and poundage, the King reiterated that his predecessors had always been granted a lifetime right to these taxes at the beginning of their reigns and that his father, James, had even collected them a year before they had been authorized by Parliament. In wishing to establish its right to impose these taxes, the House of Commons was attempting to bend the government to its will. Charles was accordingly planning to rule without a parliament for the time being.

Neither party was wise enough to recognize that a balanced government could only be achieved by cooperative effort. Without the check imposed by Parliament, there would be arbitrary rule and, ultimately, despotism. This would become clear in the next eleven years, in which there was a king but no parliament. After the Civil War (1642 – 1649) there was a parliament, but no king. Owing to factionalism and power struggles, the latter situation soon led to the despotism of the Puritans. However, our primary concern here is to demonstrate the dangers of despotism by describing the vicissitudes of taxation.

The King also had Eliot and his most important supporters imprisoned in the Tower. Charles' full wrath was now turned against Eliot, by far his toughest opponent. To the interrogators trying to establish his role in the recent troubles, Eliot had only one response: "I refuse to answer, because I hold that it is against the privilege of the House of Parliament to speak of anything which was done in the House." Ever implacable, he held his ground when a compromise with the Crown lay within reach. A simple prisoner facing a powerful king, Eliot flung himself into the breach for parliamentary independence. He stood firm upon a crucial matter of principle which personally brought him suffering and imprisonment, but which kept the flames of opposition burning bright and ultimately led to one of the great achievements of parliamentary democracy: the freedom of a representative of the people to express his own opinion.

Eliot and his fellow prisoners were tried before the Court of the King's Bench.[15] Charles had not dared to bring their case before the inherently biased Star Chamber. The Court of the King's Bench was a more suitable choice, although the prisoners claimed that this court was subordinate to the Parliament and could therefore not sit in judgement upon its members.

The other prisoners were released one by one for various reasons: bail, a promise of good behavior or on their own entreaty. Eliot rejected these alternatives. Continuing to maintain that he did not need to account for his speech in Parliament, he was left to rot in jail. The Petition of Right did empower the judiciary to rule in disputes between the King and the Parliament, but the judiciary refused to use this power. Unless a new Parliament could regain lost ground, it seemed that the gains made by the Petition of Right would be undone.

15. See footnote 10 on page 242.

Detail of the painting "Apollo and Diana" by Gerard Honthorst (1628). Apollo represents Charles I and Diana Henrietta Maria.

The wretched state of the treasury made it necessary to impose the tonnage and poundage with all due haste. However, the King was unexpectedly faced with opposition from an unlikely corner. Citing one of the three last-minute resolutions adopted by the House of Commons — which stated that anyone who voluntarily paid the tonnage and poundage was a traitor — the merchants refused en masse to conduct their normal trade. Merchants who conducted business as usual were threatened with the same treatment as Dr. Lambe, a rather odd character who had become Buckingham's soothsayer and had been beaten to death on the streets of London by a frenzied mob. The Merchant Adventurers, an organization of textile dealers who controlled the clothing industry, refused to export so much as one scrap of fabric. The government then turned to Dutch merchants with offices in London, but the Dutch were resolute in their refusal. "We shall be much degenerated," they wrote, "if we go about to betray the liberties of the English nation." As several hundred thousand people in England were dependent on the textile and clothing industry, they soon sank into abject poverty. But the merchants could not be deterred from their passive resistance. It was not until 1630, after the peace treaty with Spain had removed any impediments to a revival of trade, that the merchants gradually gave up their opposition, abandoning their political principles for the sake of profit.

In the meantime, the government had devised yet another means of propping up the destitute treasury. For centuries, the King had the right to summon any of his subjects who owned land yielding at least forty pounds a year to be dubbed a knight. The new knight's military obligation could generally be bought off by paying a lump sum to the King. Although no monarch had exercised this right for more than a century, the King was unquestionably entitled not only to demand this right but also to fine any person who refused to respond to the summons. The first summonses were sent off at the beginning of 1630, but some time elapsed before the recipients realized that the King was in deadly earnest and that the magistrates concurred with the government. After the first year, 115,000 pounds in fines and commutations had been collected, and this monetary well had not yet run dry.

A peaceful interlude

The peace treaty signed on April 14, 1629 between England and France also brought an improvement in Henrietta Maria's position. The number of priests in her household was increased, although she was still not allowed to have a bishop. Unfortunately, her premature baby only survived two hours. Nevertheless, the relationship between the two spouses improved steadily. In fact, members of the royal household complained that the King could only be found in his wife's apartments. The profligate Queen was the despair of whoever managed the treasury. Even the painter Rubens, ambassador to London in 1628 and 1629 and certainly no ascetic, was amazed at the amount of money squandered by the English court. Before long, the Queen was expecting another child. The baby, later to become Charles II, was born in 1630, and his birth was followed a year later by that of Mary and two years later by that of a son who was later to become James II. Within a short time after Buckingham's death, the Queen had assumed the role of the King's most trusted and intimate adviser, although religion remained a barrier between them. In time, the Queen had her own "faction" in the Privy Council. Any person bent on power and prominence could not afford to ignore her.

Besides the Queen, two other stars were rising in the royal firmament. The first was William Laud, the Bishop of Bath and Wells, who sat on the Privy Council in 1627. A year later, he was appointed Bishop of London and the year after that, he also became the Chancellor of the University of Oxford. The second star was Wentworth, likewise appointed to the Privy Council and serving as the Lord President of the North. A few years later, he was given the thankless and difficult job of Lord Deputy of Ireland, where he was expected to control what the English regarded as an unruly, barely civilized and divided people.

These two men were to become the King's closest advisers in the coming years. They saw presbyterianism in the church and parliamentarism in the state as two manifestations of the same malady, which either had to be brought under control or eradicated. Wentworth had gradually come to hold the view that Parliament's drive for greater power needed to be curbed and the King's powers expanded. This was a far cry from his original belief in the manifest blessings of the House of Commons. His change of heart might also be attributed to his realization that the Commons was dominated by ambitious lawyers and local gentry defending very parochial interests.

England and France had very different foreign-policy objectives during this period. In the policy outlined by Richelieu, France occupied a central position, and the Hapsburgs in the Southern Netherlands, Spain, Italy, Germany and Austria were to be dealt the greatest possible injury. England pursued a different policy. The only constant in Charles' Continental policy was to restore his sister and brother-in-law to the throne of the Palatinate. However, this was an issue of dynastic, and not English, importance. For the rest, he drifted back and forth between an alliance with Spain and an alliance with France. In a conversation with the English ambassador, the Dutch Stadtholder, Frederick Henry, suggested that the King could swiftly extricate himself from his financial morass by convening Parliament. But Charles himself never contemplated such a step and rejected the Privy Council's tentative suggestion to do so. He also refused to convene Parliament when he urgently needed money to support King Gustave Adolf II of Sweden, who had deeply involved himself in the Thirty Years' War as a champion of the Protestant cause and who now looked to England for military and financial aid.

Charles responded to these pressures by making Eliot's prison regime harsher, transforming the old Puritan in 1631 into an even greater martyr to the liberties of the people. In a cold prison, heated only by a few candles, Eliot's health deteriorated rapidly. In the spring of 1632, he requested permission to recuperate in the countryside. The King rejected Eliot's request, claiming that it had not been formulated in sufficiently humble terms and did not contain an admission of error. Six months later Eliot was dead. He had lived and died for his political creed and remained noble and unbroken to the end. Even after Eliot's death, Charles showed no generosity of spirit to the man he considered a rebel. In the King's eyes, Eliot's words were directly responsible for Buckingham's death. Moreover, he felt that the implacable Puritan would not have hesitated to topple him from the throne. He therefore refused to allow Eliot's remains to be transported to Port Eliot for burial.

The first few years of the 1630's were fairly peaceful. There were no foreign adventures and therefore no extra taxes, so that all was quiet on the domestic

Queen Henrietta Maria's influence on governmental affairs increased as time went by. After Charles I's abortive coup in 1642, she set off for Holland with the Crown Jewels in order to purchase weapons. She succeeded in equipping four ships with guns, armaments and soldiers. On February 22, 1643, she landed safely on the coast of Yorkshire with this small squadron. They did not prevail, and she was forced to flee to the Continent, this time for good. The print shows the Queen in Holland, where she was received by Pensionary Adriaan Pauw at his country estate in Heemstede (September 8, 1644).

front as well. Weston, the Lord Treasurer, kept a tight rein on finances and managed to tap a few unusual sources of income (which will be discussed below) so that Charles did not need to convene Parliament to grant a subsidy. Mainly at Wentworth's instigation, several improvements were made in such diverse areas as the poor relief laws, the road system, the prison system, the coast guard and the stimulation of industry.

Art, protected and promoted by the King, was in its heyday in England during these years. Charles himself built up a fine collection of paintings by sending agents to the Continent to purchase the best available works and bringing famous painters, such as Van Dyck and Honthorst, to England. Thanks to these efforts, we are left with several splendid, albeit flattering, portraits of a sympathetic but melancholy monarch.

Religious disputes were kept under control until 1633. In that year the moderate Archbishop of Canterbury, Abbott, died and was succeeded by Laud, Charles' faithful and devoted servant. Charles and Laud had recently returned from Scotland, where Charles had been crowned in Edinburgh on June 18, 1633. At Laud's insistence, this ceremony had been conducted with more pomp and circumstance than was acceptable to the strongly Protestant Scots, but they and the Scottish Parliament had finally bowed to Laud's pressure.

Laud's predecessor in the episcopal see had been able to subdue the religious disputes. However, Laud's zeal, harshness and lack of empathy (which kept him from understanding dissident opinions, let alone accepting them) ensured that the flock of sheep entrusted to his spiritual care were soon scattered in all directions. Many Puritans fled the country, a number of them heading for the new American colonies. Others no longer felt themselves to be safe or free in England, and braced themselves for the approaching struggle.

Laud endeavored to strengthen the position of the bishops. Bishops once again began to sit on the Privy Council and were ordered by Laud to assert their financial and other privileges before the secular authorities. This reaffirmation of the bishops' status went hand in hand with a religious policy designed to emphasize the outward aspects of religious experience: placing communion tables on the east side of the church and surrounding them with altar rails, installing organs, adding stained glass windows depicting Biblical scenes, requiring the clergy to wear surplices and ordering laymen to kneel at the altar. Viewed in isolation, these measures were relatively insignificant, but they had not been in common use for sixty years. Restoring these customs reeked of popery and candle wax and made the government, which unfailingly supported Laud's reform efforts, immensely unpopular. In addition, statements of opinion, both oral and written, were subject to rigorous control. Only the officially approved view was allowed, and any attack on the church and its bishops was forbidden. Books and pamphlets were strictly censored. Further, the practice of employing domestic chaplains (a favorite with the great lords) was outlawed, and the many Readers among the Puritan congregations were subject to continuous harassment.

Laud's attitude in the case of William Prynne was characteristic. Prynne had published a pamphlet sharply denouncing plays, in general, and women appearing on the stage, in particular. As coincidence would have it, the court had recently put on a play in which the Queen had a small part. Prynne was hauled before the Star Chamber. Laud construed the pamphlet as an accusation that he had encouraged a cesspool of vice in the court. The Archbishop was delighted with the opportunity to strike a heavy blow at an opponent who had attacked him in earlier publications. Prynne was sentenced to lifelong imprisonment, an exorbitant fine and the loss of both ears! But even this exceptionally harsh punishment did not break Prynne's spirit. He wrote a long letter criticizing Laud for his defense of the theater. The following day, the Attorney General appeared in Prynne's cell and asked him if he had written the letter. Under the pretext of taking a closer look at it, Prynne stepped nearer to the window of his cell. Before anyone knew what was happening, he had torn the letter to pieces and thrown the shreds out the window. He presumably reasoned that this was one less piece of evidence that could be used against him.

Four years earlier, Alexander Heighton, a Puritan publicist whose pamphlets criticizing the government's religious policies had fallen into Laud's hands, had also had his ears cut off. Neither his punishment nor Prynne's, both meted out in public, had aroused any general public sympathy. But how long would things remain that way?

The ship money affair

In 1634, Charles secretly carried out serious negotiations with the Spanish government, which had proposed a joint strike against the Dutch. The two governments agreed that if Charles could raise the money for a naval fleet, the

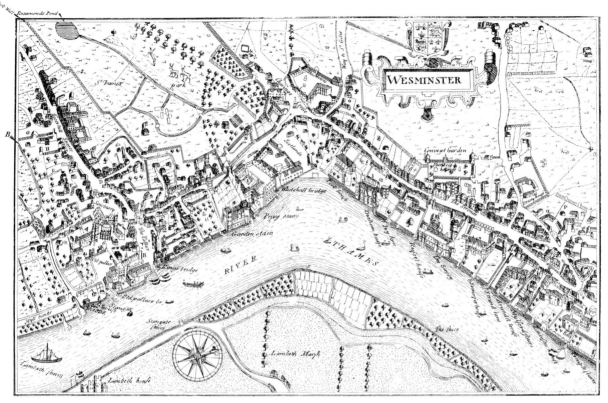

*Map of Westminster,
drawn in 1593.*

Spanish would pay for its upkeep. Charles' problem was that he first needed to find the funds to assemble a fleet.

Over the years, Charles had come to realize that he would need significant financial resources to play a political role on the Continent. A major obstacle was the fact that he could not depend on the House of Commons to grant him money. It was unlikely that Parliament would approve the requisite subsidies for such an unpopular undertaking as a war against the Protestant Dutch. The seven provinces constituting the Dutch Republic were at the height of their power in the seventeenth century. Not only was the Dutch Republic rich and prosperous, but it was prominent in science and art. Although Calvinism was the official religion, the ruling Regent class prudently tolerated dissident opinions. The Catholics were subject to little or no persecution, even though they were sufficient in number to pose a potential threat to the Dutch Republic. The most important province by far was Holland. Its most significant sources of income were from trade and navigation; Holland's ships could be found in every corner of the world. The English Puritans were clearly reluctant to attack kindred souls in The Netherlands, despite the increasing maritime competition between the two countries.

The government considered various fund-making schemes. One of the most inventive when it came to tapping financial resources not subject to parliamentary approval was Sir John Finch, the Speaker of the House who had been pushed back into his seat several years earlier when he was about to dissolve the Commons. In the interim, he had gone over to the government's camp. One of the extra-parliamentary means used by the government to raise money was the re-establishment, on paper, of the former boundaries of the royal forests. As the boundaries were re-drawn to the dimensions of three centuries earlier, many villages and cities suddenly found themselves part of the royal forests. The King now laid claim to these lands. As a result, landowners could be dispossessed unless they redeemed the land by a monetary payment. The payment, sometimes amounting to ten or twenty thousand pounds, was an enormous financial drain for many. Based on long-forgotten boundaries, the royal-forest scheme was an extremely dubious and inequitable measure, but the magistrates — who had to choose between backing the government or being fired — ruled that the government's actions were legal. This plan proved to be an efficacious way of replenishing the royal coffers.

The ship money scheme was concocted by Charles and his Lord Treasurer as they plotted ways to raise money for a fleet. The King had requisitioned ships once before in 1626. There had been an occasional contretemps, but the government had not been unduly concerned. At the time, England had been at war with Spain, so that rigging out a ship could be considered part of a subject's general obligation to defend the kingdom. The current situation was entirely different, for in 1634 England was at peace. The King therefore had to find some way to show that the country was, contrary to appearances, on the brink of war.

Charles explained in detail to the Privy Councilors, the majority of whom were not aware of the scheme, that English merchant ships were frequently attacked by pirates (both Turkish and Dunkirker varieties) and that the Dutch and French navies posed a great threat to English supremacy in the Channel and the North Sea. The King maintained that no foreigners should be allowed to fish or even feed the fish in these waters without his consent. The Privy Councilors swallowed his every word hook, line and sinker.

Throughout the summer of 1634, Charles worked on the secret treaty with Spain, intending to attack the Dutch Republic and divide its territory. Charles had intercepted letters between Frederick Henry and his agent in France, which indicated that they planned to launch a two-pronged attack on the Southern Netherlands and share the spoils.

On October 24, 1634, Charles felt the time was ripe to send out the first ship money writs. On this first occasion, he confined the writs to the seaports and coastal towns. The assessment notices listed the reasons for the writs. Thieves, pirates and privateers (both Turkish and Christian) had harassed English ships in the Channel and the North Sea, stealing both ships and merchandise, and thus posed a threat to trade and navigation. It was therefore necessary to take urgent remedial steps, especially since English kings had always been "masters of the aforesaid sea." The wording of the text, couched only in terms of trade and self-defense, was milder than the language used in the secret treaty with Spain, which was currently awaiting ratification by the government in Madrid. But the terminology aroused Spanish suspicions. Once Charles' fleet was readied, what was to prevent him from attacking the Spanish? The two allies remained locked in such mutual suspicion that their joint plans ultimately came to naught.

Local authorities were assigned the task of raising the money required to equip the ships and keep them afloat for six months. The main question was whether the ship money was a tax. In 1626, the seaports had been exhorted to rig out the ships in their harbors as warships. On the present occasion, the King had indicated that a monetary payment would suffice in lieu of ships. To ensure that money rather than well-equipped ships was contributed, the government requested vessels of specific dimensions, well aware that only London's harbor contained such ships. Many people argued that the ship money was the same as a tax. Sir Robert Heath, Chief Justice of the Court of Common Pleas, concurred with this view, providing the government with a convenient opportunity to dismiss him.

London, required to raise a fifth of the requested sum of roughly one hundred thousand pounds, was the chief source of protest. Its lawyers contested the legitimacy of the ship money imposition, arguing that the tonnage and poundage had been paid for centuries precisely for the purpose of protecting the merchants and their goods. This line of reasoning was dismissed with the specious argument that tonnage and poundage were levied without parliamentary interference and only on the King's orders. After a stormy session in the Privy Council, in which many a reproach was laid at his door, the Lord Mayor of London capitulated. Opposition to the ship money abated, although a general feeling of uneasiness remained.

The embers of this uneasiness were kindled in 1635 when an impressive English fleet crossed the English Channel, although it saw little action. Richelieu was clever enough to ensure that the combined French-Dutch fleet avoided clashes with the English. Nevertheless, these two allies failed to capture the Southern Netherlands. Ultimately, Charles did not dare to go to war against France and the Dutch Republic. The fleet assembled with the help of the ship money was disbanded in October of 1635. When all was said and done, the English fleet had captured one Dutch ship in violation of English waters, escorted a couple of trading vessels and forced passing merchant ships of various nations to lower their sails in recognition of English supremacy on the sea. The ship money was a high price to pay for such paltry results.

In 1635, the revenues from the tonnage and poundage rose steadily to 350,000 pounds. In that same year, the additional proceeds from the new Book of Rates amounted to 70,000 pounds. Nonetheless, the treasury was still chronically short of funds. Some time earlier, the Lord Treasurer had chanced upon a novel remedy for this problem. A new method of manufacturing soap had been developed and the sole production rights bestowed on a private company, on the understanding that it would pay the treasury four pounds for every ton of soap produced. As the company planned to manufacture a minimum of five thousand tons annually, this monopoly would provide the treasury with the tidy sum of at least 20,000 pounds a year. To promote the Westminster Soap Company, the source of this welcome revenue, the government had further decided to bring independent soap manufacturers under the company's supervision. In response to the inevitable objections, the government appointed an independent committee, consisting of the Lord Mayor, the keeper of the Tower and the leading lights of the laundry world, to determine which soap was the best. When the special committee met, two washerwomen were ushered in. One was handed the company's soap, and the other the soap from the independent soap manufacturers. The two women set to work and washed several bundles of dirty clothes in steaming washtubs set up for that purpose. At the end of the show, the committee declared that the clothes washed with the company's soap were whiter and softer than those washed with the other soap. A declaration to this effect was signed by no

Two washerwomen and a man watching them, a chalk drawing made in 1772 from a painting by Philips Wouwerman (1619-1668).

less than eighty persons, ranging from washerwomen to nobles. Backed by these endorsements, the government recommended the company's soap. But the man in the street wanted nothing to do with it. As the soap company was composed of a number of Catholics, the common people referred to it as "popish soap." There were no doubts in their minds that this soap was not only bad for the body, but also for the soul.

The Privy Council plotted a second ship money levy even before the fleet had returned to its winter quarters in October of 1635. This time they intended the inland counties to pay as well. Although formally incorrect, this demand was not unreasonable. It did, however, highlight the probability that the ship money was a normal tax, which, according to the Petition of Right, could not be levied without parliamentary consent. The increased revenues from the tonnage and poundage also made it clear that in times of peace Parliament (should it ever be reconvened) would no longer control the purse strings.

Unfortunately, the King was incapable of learning from the example set by his Lord Deputy in Ireland. Wentworth had swiftly pacified the country. In the process, he supported the lower and middle classes against the abuses of the lords. The Irish Parliament had sufficient freedom of speech, and being convinced of the need to regulate finances, was prepared to grant him subsidies. Wentworth's achievements would have been impossible for Charles, because the King considered the members of the House of Commons as his enemies and either could or would not admit that he had to rely on them to grant subsidies and carry out local administrative tasks. Powerless to change the course he had taken, the King turned a deaf ear to Wentworth's advice to cease levying ship money.

The writs for the second ship money levy were sent out on August 18, 1635. The first imposition of ship money had secretly been intended to allow England to support a Spanish attack on the Dutch Republic (even though the taxpayers were only apprised of the dangers of piracy). When the second levy was imposed, there was no clear military reason for expanding and reinforcing the fleet. But Charles was particularly intent on securing recognition of his rights to the area lying between England and the next coast, i.e. the American colonies. To accomplish this goal, he needed a decent number of ships. The fleet he now assembled was too large merely to be employed in forcing foreign merchant ships to lower their flags or coercing Dutch fishermen into paying for protection against the dreaded Dunkirker pirates, but was too small to exercise any influence over the war on the Continent. Nor did such a large fleet bring Charles any closer to returning the Palatinate to his sister and her husband, an item still on the King's political agenda. One point in England's favor was that the French, anxious to avoid a confrontation, directed their fleet to the Mediterranean.

The ship money currently being requested was around two hundred thousand pounds (roughly the equivalent of three subsides), and therefore almost double the previous levy. To cite an example, the district of Buckinghamshire was asked to deliver to Portsmouth a 450 ton ship, complete with competent officers and a crew of at least 180 men, as well as provisions for 26 weeks and the requisite number of canons, muskets, gunpowder, axes, spears and other armaments. Buckinghamshire was given the option of supplying the ship or depositing 4,500 pounds in the treasury. This approximated the average amount Charles had asked in subsidies during the first four years of his reign, so that it was not unduly

From left to right: Portraits drawn by W. Hollar of the pamphleteers William Prynne (1600-1669), John Bastwick (1593-c. 1650) and Henry Burton (1579-1647), who were sentenced to severe punishments on June 30, 1637 for publishing pamphlets unfavorable to Archbishop Laud (see text).

burdensome, especially when calculated per capita. But the amount of the tax was beside the point. If ship money was a normal tax, the King had neglected to consult the nation as he was required to do. If, on the other hand, it was mainly a service required of the coastal counties in times of need, why were they asked to pay money instead of supplying ships? More particularly, why had the inland counties been drawn into the assessment? The King had launched a new development, but where would it all end?

With even greater meticulousness than usual, the local sheriffs had to convert the amounts demanded in ship money in their districts into tax assessments on the residents. As far as possible, they took into account each individual's wealth and possessions in the form of estates and houses. Of course complaints poured in, but that was no more cause for surprise then than it is today; after all, most taxpayers think they pay too much and their neighbors too little! Nevertheless, the rich paid proportionately less than the middle and lower classes, especially in the countryside; a shortcoming that also characterized the authorized subsidies and fifteenths.

The first opposition based on principle came from Oxfordshire, where the local sheriff could not be persuaded to collect the ship money. The government prudently decided not to make an issue of this case, which might well have kindled resistance elsewhere. The work was proceeding smoothly in other parts of the kingdom, so that three quarters of the required amount had been collected by the spring. However, there was still so much discontent about what many felt to be the illegal nature of the ship money that the Court of the Exchequer Chamber was asked to give its opinion. This was a tribunal of twelve judges, selected from the Court of the King's Bench,[16] the Court of Common Pleas[17] and the Court of the Exchequer.[18] Ten of the twelve judges declared the measure to be legal. They reasoned that the seaports had been required in the past to contribute to the fleet in order to combat piracy. When the entire kingdom was in danger — and the King was the sole judge of that — it was reasonable for the entire kingdom to pay for its defense. The fleet was indispensable to the nation's defense. As the Lord Keeper had said: "The wooden walls are the best walls of

16. See footnote 10 on page 242.
17. The Court of Common Pleas was the civil Supreme Court.
18. See footnote 6 on page 222.

Prynne in the pillory, about to have the letters SL (for Seditious Libeller) branded on his cheeks.

this kingdom.'' This line of reasoning would have been acceptable if the country had been in such imminent danger that there was insufficient time to convene Parliament, but this was not the case. An increasing number of the King's subjects gradually realized that the first ship money assessment in 1634 had set in motion a process that could culminate in despotism.

Finances were not the only contentious issue. Religious matters were also taking a dangerous turn, as Archbishop Laud's actions were alienating English Protestants. Laud's advocacy of High Church practices was of minor importance compared to his strict censorship. It was not until three pamphleteers who had castigated the clergy and church ceremonies and aired dissident views were summoned before the Star Chamber that it became dangerous to express an opinion on religious matters. The three men were sentenced to severe punishment: the loss of both ears, an exorbitantly high fine and solitary confinement in remote castles, far from the comforting power of Puritan sympathy, without even so much as pen and paper. One of the pamphleteers was the above-mentioned William Prynne. As he had already lost both his ears, the irrepressible martyr was sentenced for what, in his eyes, constituted a righteous stand by having the letters SL, for Seditious Libeller, branded on his cheeks. In contrast to the scene three years earlier, Prynne and his two companions in adversity were conducted to the place of punishment by a sympathetic crowd strewing flowers and leaves in their path. It requires little imagination to picture the silent, angry, grim and soberly dressed throng of London Puritans clustered around the scene of justice, observing how punishments intended for obstinate members of the lowest sort were applied to the lawyer Prynne, the clergyman Burton and the physician Bastwick. The spectacle was made even bleaker when the executioner branded Prynne with the wrong letters and had to repeat the process.

Laud, in an attempt to maintain an equilibrium, hounded the Catholics with equal fervor, but with less success. The Queen no longer proselytized on behalf of Catholicism, but always managed to put a stop to the harshest attacks. Her tears obviously influenced the King more than the Archbishop's sermons.

The case of Rex versus Hampden

Upon Laud's advice, William Juxon, the Bishop of London, was appointed to fill the vacancy of Lord Treasurer in March of 1636. He was the first clergyman in recent memory to fill a high governmental post. Nonetheless, the public began associating the official church with the government's unpopular financial policies. Still, Juxon was an efficient administrator who despised corruption (sometimes even personally monitoring bills) and kept a tight hold on the financial reins. He not only reduced the deficits but even turned them into surpluses. Juxon's unimpeachable reputation earned him a myriad of enemies, who expected greater personal gain from a disorganized and chaotic parliament than from an aristocratic technocrat who preferred good administration to freedom and thought himself the best judge of people's needs. It is interesting to contemplate whether Juxon may have indirectly contributed to the King's fall from power. If Juxon had not filled his treasury quite so well, would Charles have been able to go to battle against the Scots at the end of the 1630's, a step which signaled the beginning of the end? A detail worth mentioning here is that Juxon, who by that time had long vacated his high governmental post, was the last to attend to Charles' spiritual needs before the King was beheaded.

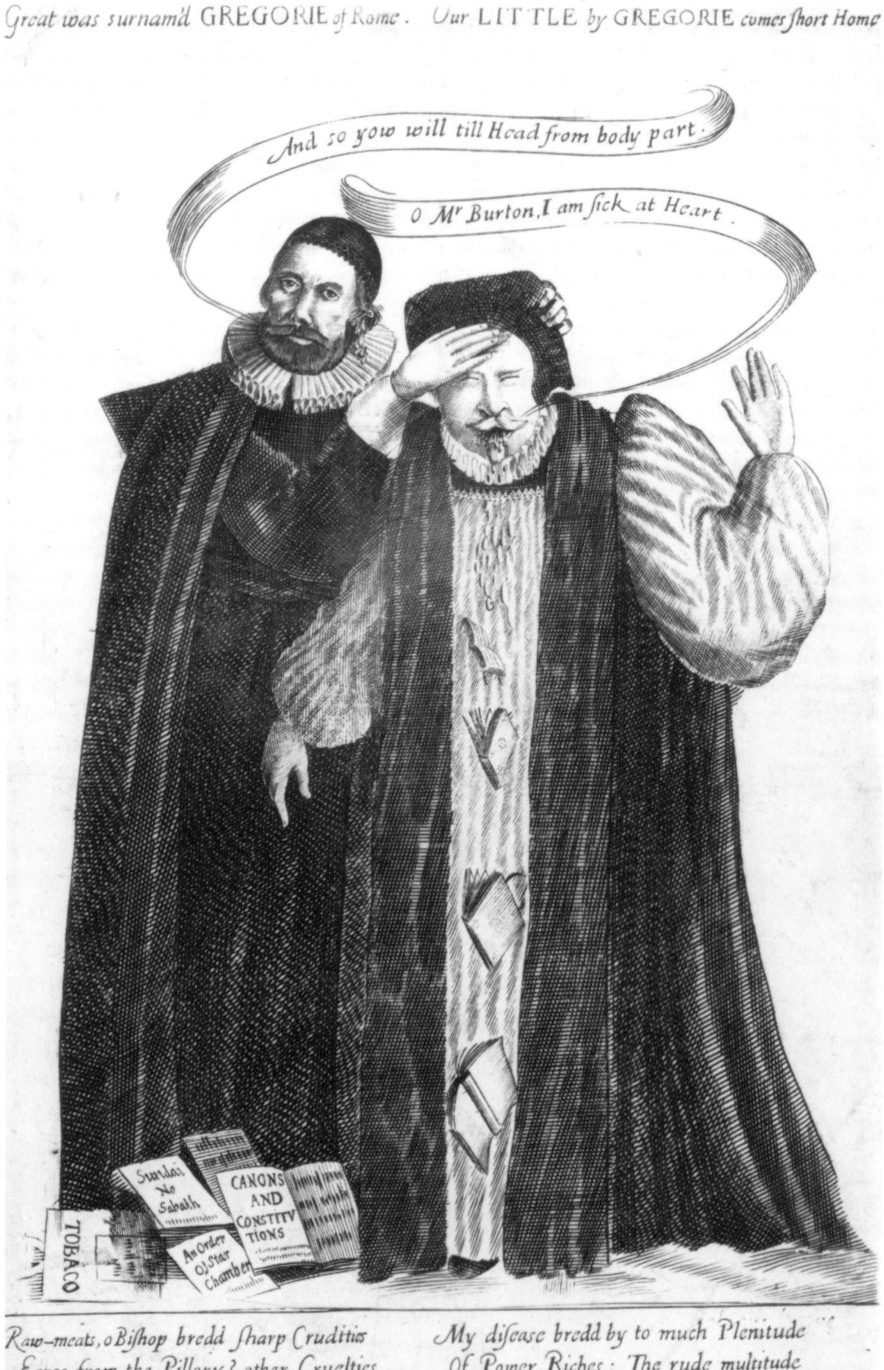

Lying in the foreground are some of the published works vomited up by Archbishop William Laud, seen here in his official garb. The books refer to the Archbishop's alleged role in the tobacco monopoly ("Tobago"), to his essay on the breaking of the Sabbath ("Sundai no Sabath"), to his ecclasiastical regulations ("Canons and Constitutions") and to jurisprudence ("An Order of Star Chamber"). The person with his hand on the Archbishop's forehead is Henry Burton, Rector of St. Matthew's, Friday Street, London, the man who suffered along with Prynne and Bastwick from the Archbishop's censor. Burton's left ear has been torn off and blood is dripping onto his collar, a reference to the punishment meted out by Laud (see text). To understand the caption, it might help you to know that Gregory the Great (590-604) was one of history's most famous popes, that Laud was short and that executioners were referred to as "Gregories." As for the words of the two men, note that the print is dated January 10, 1645, when Laud's trial was in process and it was clear that his head was soon to be severed from his body.

Great was surnam'd GREGORIE of Rome. Our LITTLE by GREGORIE comes short Home

And so yow will till Head from body part.

O Mr Burton, I am sick at Heart.

Raw-meats, o Bishop bredd sharp Crudities
Eares from the Pillory? other Cruelties
As Prisonments, by your high Inquisition
That makes your Vomits have no intermission.

My disease bredd by to much Plenitude
Of Power, Riches: The rude multitude
Did aye invy, and curbing of the zeale
Of lamps, now shyning in the Common weale.

In October of 1636, the government demanded the payment of ship money for the third time, taking it as a matter of course that it would be levied throughout the country. Charle's position appeared to be very strong, since the second ship money levy had almost been paid in full with little protest. But appearances are deceptive. Laud's stringent policies in favor of the High Church had driven the masses into the arms of the Puritans. Discontent over religious matters found a suitable outlet in the ship money issue. Those caring little about religious matters but greatly about money began to fear that they were about to be preyed upon. If the King persevered in his aims, ship money would provide him with an invaluable extra-parliamentary source of income. Once the fleet was in order, another pretext would undoubtedly be found for continuing to impose the ship money, such as the need for a standing army to serve the fleet.

To the King's dismay, there were signs that the third ship money levy would encounter greater opposition from all strata of society. Charles therefore deemed it wise to seek the opinion of the twelve magistrates at an early stage. The magistrates deliberated for five days before returning their verdict. They ruled that when the kingdom was in danger, the King had the right to demand ships, victuals and ammunition from his subjects. Furthermore, the King was the only person allowed to determine when danger threatened. Although a repetition of their earlier standpoint, the ruling had been given more careful consideration and was better formulated. Their pronouncement was published as quickly as possible to discourage lawyers from filing individual suits against the Crown on behalf of clients unwilling to pay the ship money.

Two of the magistrates, Sir George Crooke and Sir Richard Hutton, had noted that they did not consider themselves bound to the ruling when adjudicating individual cases. One of the government's adversaries in the ship money question was Lord Saye. He instigated legal proceedings against the bailiff who had removed from his premises goods of a value equivalent to what he had refused to pay in taxes. The King responded by having him charged with several legal violations supposedly committed against the royal domains. This gave Saye hardly enough time to fulminate against the ship money, let alone instigate proceedings. The King undoubtedly had little desire to cross swords with Saye because he was a peer, which meant that the matter would have to be brought before the House of Lords.

Lord Saye was not the only troublemaker. In February of 1637, John Hampden initiated a highly publicized test case. The amount involved was twenty shillings, which he alledgedly owed on his estates in the parish of Stoke Mandeville, but which he refused to make over to the sheriff of Buckinghamshire. The government was well acquainted with John Hampden: he was a Puritan and former member of the House of Commons, and was both competent and obdurate when he wished to bring a matter dear to his heart to a successful conclusion. He was cut from the same cloth as his good friend Sir John Eliot, with whom he had been imprisoned when they had both refused to contribute to the forced loan.

Sir Thomas Wentworth had likewise refused to pay the forced loan, but he was now clearly in the government's camp. He advised Laud, with whom he was on friendly terms, to attack the Hampden case with his heaviest legal artillery. Wentworth's advice was apparently taken to heart, for on March 5, 1637, the case of "Rex versus Hampden" was brought before the Exchequer Chamber, presided over by highly qualified judges from the various judiciaries. The court began by introducing evidence to show that Hampden had not paid. Then on May 19th, Hampden was asked by the Chancellor of the Exchequer to state his reasons for failing to pay the twenty shillings. Hampden appeared before the court and presented his defense in general terms, stating in effect that he was not legally required to pay. The case was then adjourned until a hearing in the fall, which would be held before the full court.

Hampden used the summer to deliberate tactics with his attorneys. He was clearly directing affairs and largely using the lawyers as his mouthpiece. On November 6th, the twelve judges, decked out in their splendid ermine-trimmed scarlet robes and silver-plated chains of office, took their seats in Westminster Hall. Oliver St. John, Hampden's most important attorney, stepped forward and began his client's defense. St. John had been imprisoned once in 1629 for supposedly passing on to third parties a seditious pamphlet that he had found in a client's library, although he was later released for lack of evidence. A few weeks before the start of the Hampden trial, some of the King's officials searched St. John's office, suspecting him of having drawn up the defense of Bastwick, one of William Prynne's fellow suspects, who had expressed defiance toward Archbishop Laud.

Oliver St. John's address to the court lasted for three days. He wisely left out of consideration the former distinction between the coastal counties which paid ship money and the inland counties such as Buckinghamshire which did not. After all, a defense of this type would have diverted attention from the main point, namely that the King was required to ask for Parliament's consent before imposing taxes. St. John gave a detailed historical survey, beginning with the *Magna Carta* and ending with the Petition of Right. He based his defense on the fact that only Parliament was entitled to ask the citizens for money when the Crown needed more than was forthcoming from its normal sources of income, such as the proceeds from the royal domains and the like. He did not deny the King's right to confiscate the goods of his subjects when immediate danger threatened. But, he asked, could it be said on August 18, 1635, when ship money was requested for ships that did not have to be delivered until seven months later, that the country was in imminent danger? Why had Parliament not been convened at that time to authorize the necessary funds in the customary way? Past kings, he continued, had not levied ship money to defend the country, but they undoubtedly would have done so if they had thought that the imposition of ship money was legal. It was clear beyond a shadow of a doubt, St. John concluded, that without parliamentary consent, past kings would not have imposed taxes on their subjects. Yet this is what had happened in the case of his client.

Sir Edmund Littleton, the Solicitor General, arose on November 11th and spoke for three days. The essence of his argument was that every Parliament since the time of Edward I had recognized the king's right to claim his subject's military obligations and to demand money for the country's defense. Parliament, he added, could not always be convened when danger threatened. For one reason, by law, Parliament could only assemble forty days after the summonses for the election of the members had been sent.

The next to take the floor was Hampden's second attorney, Robert Lincoln. He addressed the court for four days, starting on December 2nd. He also cited historical precedents at great length. His argument revolved around the question of whether the kingdom had been in acute danger. He pointed out that the first demand for ship money had been made to protect merchant ships from pirates and privateers. However, they posed a threat to the merchants rather than to the kingdom. Unlike the first speaker, Lincoln denied that the King should be the sole judge of whether the country was in danger. The King was only allowed to act without consulting Parliament when a sudden crisis arose, and this was not the case in August of 1635. He concluded that while the ship money writ had mentioned the peril to the kingdom, Parliament could easily have been summoned to authorize the necessary funds.

On December 16th, the Attorney General, Sir John Bankes, began his summation of the case to the court. He dwelt at length on the reasonableness and objectivity that had been shown when the ship money was imposed. Against his better judgement (or so one would assume), he brought up the paltry twenty shillings owed by Hampden. It was such a petty sum, he declared, for someone of Hampden's financial standing. If Hampden had disagreed with the amount of the assessment, why had he not approached the sheriff of Buckinghamshire? Bankes then went into the question of whether the King alone should determine whether the country was imperiled. He concluded that not allowing the King to make such a judgement would constitute a fundamental infringement of royal authority, which would lead to government by democracy.[19] As England was a kingdom with an absolute monarch, who had "supreme jurisdiction by land and sea," the King's every order was to be obeyed. After Bankes had finished speaking, the judges adjourned the court until the first quarter of 1638, at which time each magistrate was to pronounce judgement.

In recapitulating the trial, one is struck by the fact that the Crown's defense rested on two incompatible lines of reasoning. On the basis of historical precedents, the King could demand ships and manpower when the safety of the nation was urgently imperiled. However, any ship requisitioned during such a crisis legally remained the possession of those who had "loaned" it to the King. After maximally six months, the requisitioned ship was returned to its owner. The demand was legitimate in this form, except that the King had requested ships of a type that most cities and counties were unable to provide. Failing that, he required money for the fleet, a step he could not take without parliamentary consent. Thus, under the pretext of demanding a service, he had requested a tax.

The magistrates gave their verdict in the course of 1638 with a great deal of ceremony. Each magistrate presented his ruling in turn, beginning with the youngest and ending with the two Chief Justices. Sir Francis Weston, Baron of the Court of the Exchequer, and Sir Francis Crawley, Justice of the Court of Common Pleas, were the first to pronounce judgement. They ruled in favor of the Crown. Before a packed courtroom, the latter lapsed into rhetoric: the King would not request a tax if there was not any danger. Should we then, he asked, sit at home awaiting dire events? No, he replied, we should trust in our just and god-fearing King, protector of the kingdom, etc., etc.

On Saturday, February 10th, Sir Robert Berkeley, Justice of the King's Bench, declaring that the law was the servant of the king, also came out in support of the Crown.

The next in line was Sir George Vernon, Justice of the Court of Common Pleas. He began by noting that this case had far-reaching consequences. He requested a delay of at least a week, citing his poor health. He also wanted more time to read through his extensive pile of notes. His fellow magistrates saw through his ploy and demanded that he give his ruling immediately. Unable to prevaricate any longer, the reluctant judge decided in favor of the Crown on the somewhat unconvincing grounds that a sovereign ruler could set aside any law in times of need.

19. At that time, the word "democratic" was synonymous for many with the word "anarchistic."

The next to speak was Sir Thomas Trevor, Baron of the Court of the Exchequer. He absolutely rejected any notion that the people could supervise the King's actions, stating that England had a monarchy rather than a democratic form of government. He added that the wheels of parliament moved too slowly when actual danger threatened. He pointed out that ships were the King's best defense and that the fleet was now stronger than ever, with more, bigger and better-equipped ships. He concluded with the wish that everyone would pay the ship money with a cheerful heart.

Five magistrates had ruled in the Crown's favor and the King's victory lay within grasp when Sir George Crooke, Justice of the King's Bench, stood up to render his verdict. Like Hampden, he came from Buckinghamshire. More importantly, he was one of two judges the Crown considered unreliable. These two men had made exceptions for individual cases when the King had asked the magistrates to decide on the ship money's legitimacy the previous year. It would be a great triumph for the king if Crooke were to join what was beginning to look like a majority. Friends and relations had urged Sir George to judge solely according to his conscience in this crucial case. He was aware, more than the other judges, of the political and constitutional significance of the case. He therefore began by pointing out that this case was more important than any other case that had been brought before the judges. He was not satisfied, Crooke continued, with the other judges' arguments. Crooke, who was probably a Puritan, stated that in the conflict between royal authority and the liberty of the citizens he was guided by God and his own conscience. He then pronounced judgement in favor of Hampden. The verdict undoubtedly created a commotion in the Exchequer Chamber. Whatever the majority opinion turned out to be, there was now at least one magistrate who had publicly dared to speak out in favor of John Hampden. More excitement was to follow. After Sir William Jones of the King's Bench had hesitantly supported the Crown's case, Sir Richard Hutton, Justice of the Court of Common Pleas and the second voice of doubt in last year's judgement, threw in his lot with Crooke and declared himself for Hampden. Hutton saw no threat to national security. He subtly added that he could still remember a time long ago when twenty shillings that he had "voluntarily" paid to Queen Elizabeth had been returned because the magistrates had determined that this type of contribution was technically illegal.

The two verdicts that followed were completely unexpected. On May 26th, Sir John Denham, Baron of the Court of the Exchequer, declared himself for the plaintiff, although he was too ill to appear before the court. Then, Sir Humphries Davenport, Lord Chief Baron of the Court of the Exchequer, ruled on technical grounds in favor of Hampden. By confining himself to technicalities, he avoided having to rule on the real issue, the dispute between royal authority and the law of the land.

The score was now six rulings in the King's favor and four for Hampden. The penultimate speaker was Sir John Finch, Lord Chief Justice of the Court of Common Pleas. This was none other than the Speaker of the House of Commons who had been pushed back into his seat on March 2, 1629. Since that time, the royal sun had shone brightly on his career, and he had advanced rapidly. As far as Finch was concerned, loyalty to the King was at stake. Parliament, he said, was undoubtedly a worthy institution, but was a mere means of imposing taxes on the subjects and thus defending the kingdom. The Petition of Right, Finch

*Archbishop William Laud
(1573-1645) (from a
painting by Sir Anthony
van Dyck).*

declared, had made no mention of ship money. The King could admittedly make use of the ship money revenues for other purposes besides defense. But the King had stated to the Chief Justices that he had no intention of doing so. The King had even declared that he would sooner eat the money than use it for another purpose (this remark presumably occasioned general merriment). He even went so far as to declare that the laws of Parliament were of no value and that the King was in no way bound by them. In times of need, the King could command his subjects and their money and goods as he saw fit. Finch unequivocally cast his vote for the King.

The last magistrate to speak, Sir John Bramston, Lord Chief Justice of the King's Bench, meticulously examined the wording of the third ship money writ. He concluded that the issue was taxation rather than the granting of a service. He took the same technical line as Davenport, likewise avoiding the constitutional issue involved, and ruled in favor of Hampden.

The Court of the Exchequer formally imparted its verdict to the King on June 12th. The Crown had won, but by the narrowest possible margin.

The memoranda of the oral pleas presented by the two attorneys had been passed from hand to hand at the beginning of the trial. They had provoked comments from all sides and stiffened resistance. The rulings of Sir George Crooke and Sir John Hutton breathed new life into the opposition to the ship money. The protests spread from Buckinghamshire to Essex, Kent, Oxfordshire and Gloucestershire, especially when ship money was demanded for the fourth time in September of 1637. The fourth ship money writ left no one in doubt that the King, without parliamentary consent, had replaced the former subsidies by ship money. A year later, the King asked for ship money for the fifth time, and in November of 1639 for the sixth time. Protest had grown to such an extent that virtually nothing was collected in Buckinghamshire in 1639. Throughout the country, the sheriffs were either passively or actively opposed to the ship money, so that in 1640, no more than one third of the required amount was collected. Even when the sheriff's men confiscated livestock in lieu of monetary payment, there were no buyers at the public auctions. By 1640, the King's power had been thoroughly weakened, owing in no small measure to opposition to the ship money.

The Hampden case did more than encourage the public not to pay the ship money. People realized that even though Hampden had lost on technical and legal grounds, he had emerged as the moral victor in the fundamental issue, namely the conflict over whether taxes could be imposed without the consent of Parliament. After all, this august body functioned as the mouthpiece of the whole populace, from farmers to shopkeepers.

As a result of this trial, the scales also fell from the eyes of those previously unable or unwilling to see that what was at issue was the protection of citizens' property against a grasping state. Lord Chief Justice Sir John Finch's comment that in times of need the King could command the money and goods of his subjects as he pleased spoke volumes. The true significance of the Rex versus Hampden case was that it served as a breeding ground for the later Civil War, though the foremost cause of the war was religion. Nonetheless, the ship money dispute lived on in people's memories as an occasion in which the right of the people to decide on matters affecting their own pockets had been championed. Charles I and his closest advisers (first Buckingham and then Laud and Wentworth) epitomized the spirit of the age: strengthening the ties between church and state, suppressing political and religious dissidence, creating a powerful court and achieving far-reaching financial and military mandates. In short, Charles and his advisers wished to create a basis for royal absolutism on all fronts. Using the tax apparatus as their weapon, they had successfully launched an attack in 1637 on the growing influence of the people. But as we shall soon see, the royal victory was short-lived. Like Alva, who had failed three quarters of a century earlier in The Netherlands to make Philip II into a *señor assoluto*, Charles failed to become an absolute ruler. Thus the seeds of royal absolutism in such countries as neighboring France failed to take root in England. The ship money issue alerted the citizens to the fact that the time had come to block the road to absolute monarchy. The effects of their invaluable service were felt beyond English shores. For the democracy that ultimately ensued became a beacon of light to nations around the world.

Cartoon of a monopolist or patent-holder. He is depicted as a wolf, with hands in the form of fish hooks and screws as legs. The salt, wine, soap and butter, etc., patents are attached to his body.

The Short Parliament

Fortified by the judgement of the magistrates in the Hampden case, Charles proceeded energetically to collect the ship money. But the opposition, bolstered by several other financial grievances, was stronger than ever. There was still a great deal of discontent over the encroachment of the royal forests, the sale of monopolies (on such products as bricks, coal, soap, salt and candles) and the patents on specific production technologies. The government considered creating a malt monopoly, but withdrew the plan in the face of great opposition. The King was formally entitled to grant monopolies. Under the guise of industrial reorganization, however, the monopolies were granted for the sole purpose of replenishing the treasury's coffers.

20. See page 222.

Thomas Wentworth, Earl of Strafford (1593-1641) (from a painting by Anthony van Dyck, 1633).

Another source of dissatisfaction was that the receipts from wardship, the inheritance tax on minors (another tax from the feudal ragbag),[20] had tripled in a short amount of time. The arbitrary application of the wardship led to growing resentment.

Financial grievances were surpassed in intensity by religious grievances, despite the fact that Charles' tax policies had aroused the ire of large segments of the population across the entire religious spectrum. His religious policies went straight to the heart of his fiercest adversaries, the English Puritans and the Scottish Presbyterians. Charles, no match against a Parliament bent on appropriating political rights, banged his head against such a wall of intransigence that it finally bounced right off and into the executioner's basket.

The religious problems assumed their most serious form in Scotland. Charles had always wanted to model the Scottish church after the English example. He was probably inspired by Laud, who abhorred the thought that the Scottish "Kirk" was still organized along presbyterian lines, even though it had been appointed bishops under James I. Laud ordered the Scottish church to introduce Anglican ritual and prayers. A full-scale riot broke out among the faithful on July 23, 1637 when the first Anglican-based service was held. The service had to be prematurely terminated. There were minor riots at St. Giles Cathedral in Edinburgh, where the Scottish bishops escaped by the skin of their teeth. All of Scotland was immediately up in arms. In an agreement known as the "Solemn Covenant," the signatories (primarily minor landed gentry) promised to remain faithful to their church. The Scots had not shaken off the yoke of Rome only to have it replaced by that of Canterbury. An interim government was set up in Edinburgh, and Charles could consider his authority North of the Tweed (the border river between England and Scotland) as good as lost. Despite negotiations, the two parties were unable to reach a compromise. The King felt that his only recourse was to go to war against the Scots.

The badly armed, poorly fed and undisciplined English troops were no match for the excellent Scottish army of twenty thousand men, including many who had fought on the Continent in the armies of the Protestant princes. This first "Bishops' War" would have ended in a rout for Charles, except that negotiations called a halt to the advancing Scottish army. A truce was signed on June 18, 1639.

The King's sole hope was Governor Wentworth in Ireland, the only powerful figure on whom he could still rely. Wentworth's firm action had broken the resistance in Ireland. He had retained a puppet parliament and had managed to raise both money and troops. He had even been able to send the King twenty thousand pounds for the extremely unpopular war in Scotland. Charles was in desperate need of funds, as the general opposition to the ship money had turned this river of income into a mere trickle. Wentworth advised Charles to take forceful measures. To begin with, the King needed to put his finances in order. This could only be achieved by convening another Parliament. To win Parliament's financial support, Wentworth advised him to divulge the intrigues between Richelieu and the Scots, who had sought French support. The King should also renew the war with the Scots. Wentworth, seriously plagued by gout but resolute, hastened to Ireland, recruited eight thousand men and returned to England. Having become the King's most valued adviser, Wentworth was named Earl of Strafford in the beginning of 1640. Strafford and Laud both realized that the convening of Parliament could no longer be avoided.

The Parliament that met on April 13th, the first in eleven years, was burning with its old resentment, in spite of the fact that it was largely composed of new members. Sir John Finch's opening speech on behalf of the government was an immediate failure. He began by arrogantly demanding that the House of Commons first of all grant the King the tonnage and poundage for the duration of his reign, which would neutralize the illegitimate imposition and high tariffs of the last ten years. As a sop to Parliament, the exchange of letters between the Scots and the French was described in detail. Irritated, the House of Commons heard Finch out. The members were well aware that Finch had attempted to dissolve the last parliament on the King's orders. Even worse, he had cast the deciding vote in the case of Rex versus Hampden, in which he had declared Parliament's laws to be utterly worthless. Having Finch open the debate was a bad move on the King's part. The House of Commons, which had not paid the slightest attention to the account of the reputed treachery of the Scots, hastened

The dissolution of Parliament was a highly significant political event. The government naturally wished to encourage public acceptance of this step by publishing an explanation. The title page of the document which appeared after the Short Parliament was dissolved in 1640 (see text) is shown here.

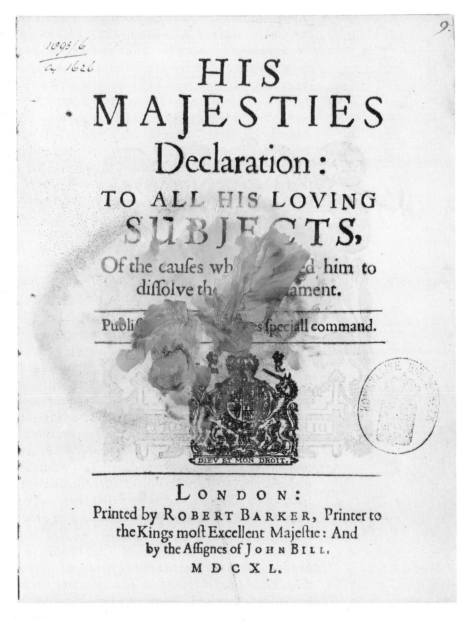

9.

1093/6
a 1626

HIS
· MAJESTIES
Declaration :
TO ALL HIS LOVING
SUBJECTS,
Of the caufes wh...d him to
diffolve th...ament.

Publi...special command.

DIEV ET MON DROIT.

LONDON:
Printed by ROBERT BARKER, Printer to
the Kings moft Excellent Majeftie : And
by the Affignes of JOHN BILL.
MDCXL.

to counterattack. They appointed the experienced Pym, survivor of six parliaments, as their chief spokesman. The Commons then voted to abolish ship money, review the Hampden case and open an investigation into the imprisonment of the members of the previous parliament who had been arrested at the end of the last session (including the late Sir John Eliot). Without a moment's hesitation, they went on to accuse Finch of breaking the law when he attempted to end the previous session against the will of the House of Commons.

Strafford, held up by headwinds, arrived in London a week too late. Nonetheless, he did win the support of the House of Lords (of which he was a member by virtue of his earldom) and successfully played the Lords off against the Commons. He was on the verge of getting both Houses to authorize six subsidies in exchange for abolishing the ship money when his plan collapsed. Because the ship money now brought in little revenue, this exchange would have been a good bargain for the King. The subsidies would also have legitimized the

Crown's income and made it impregnable to attack. But the King refused to settle for anything less than eight subsidies. Charles' inept spokesman started by demanding twelve subsidies and was immediately reprimanded by Pym. In fact, Pym did not wish to reach any kind of agreement and seized upon the opportunity to reject the request. He demanded that the King concede *all* grievances before the discussion of the subsidies could be continued. Thus the two sides arrived at the same deadlock as on previous occasions.

The House of Commons had no intention of giving the King so much as a penny to fight a war against their kindred spirits in Scotland. In the meantime, alarming reports had arrived. These dispatches suggested that the Scots were in contact with the opposition leaders of the House of Commons and wished to resume the war. As his only achievement had been to strengthen and unite the forces of opposition, the King felt himself obliged to dissolve Parliament on May 5th. This Parliament, only in session for eighteen days, has gone down in history as the "Short Parliament" in contrast to the "Long Parliament" convened six months later, on November 3rd, and not formally dissolved until March 16, 1660. The decision to dissolve the Short Parliament was made by the King and a majority of the Privy Council. Strafford and Laud, who had not been notified that the time of the meeting was changed, arrived too late and were unable to reverse the decision. The tide of events could no longer be turned. The situation rapidly deteriorated in the summer of 1640. The Scots again invaded England in what is known as the "Second Bishops' War." Very little ship money was being collected. Riots broke out in London. A frenzied mob beset Laud's palace and threatened to tear him to pieces. One of the ringleaders and an innocent sixteen year old boy were hanged and quartered. The boy's death aroused more public outrage than that of any of the Archbishop's Puritan victims. To divert attention, Laud once again attempted to persecute the Catholics. He begged the King on his knees for permission to do so, but to no avail. The Queen had just given birth on July 8th to a son, and Charles never refused her anything in these circumstances. Laud had to make do with a public burning of Catholic books, an act that impressed no one.

The increasing mood of unrest was hardly dampened when the government had a few members of the Commons put in prison and pressured the sheriffs to collect the ship money. The government attempted to borrow money from Spain, promising in return to remain neutral during Spanish military operations in The Netherlands. They also considered a currency devaluation and even made plans to seize Spanish money that was being stored in the Tower. Charles, lacking money and the loyal, disciplined, well-paid and well-fed soldiers he needed, was defeated by the Scots, who now occupied the Northern Counties and would only relinquish them in return for a guarantee of religious freedom and an indemnity payment. How was Charles to defend himself in the face of such odds? Strafford advised him to take the harshest possible measures. He opined that hanging several of London's Aldermen, who had refused a loan, would bring the others to reason. He could have troops brought from Ireland to fight alongside the English, he said, and together these forces would defeat the Scots within five months. The King ignored his advice. The Lords urged him to convene another Parliament, and Pym collected ten thousand signatures on a petition making the same request. Charles felt obliged to sign a two-month truce with the Scots, even though this cost him 850 pounds a day. He had no other choice but to succumb to the pressure for a new Parliament.

Archbishop Laud published the "Canons and Institutions Eccleciastical" on May 6, 1640, which was supposed to be accepted by the clergy on oath. After roughly seven months, on December 16, 1640, the roles were reversed, for Parliament declared that the "Canons" were illegal and were designed to foster factionalism and insurrection. Laud is shown firing a canon in the middle of several clergymen, with the ball denoted as an "oath."

The Long Parliament

The country breathed a huge sigh of relief. As hopes that the King and the Parliament would come to a settlement were running high, the elections were the subject of greater interest than ever before. Pym and Hampden (both of whom enjoyed great authority) wished only pure, unadulterated Puritans willing to wage a battle against absolutism to be elected. For the most part, their wishes were fulfilled. The City of London, for example, elected four militant opponents of the court, including one who had spent several years in prison for refusing to pay taxes not approved by the House of Commons. The City, whose Council now consisted entirely of Charles' adversaries, refused to grant the King a loan unless Parliament was convened. They reasoned that if they did not take this approach, the King would become independent of the Parliament. The representatives to the Long Parliament were inspired by a militant spirit. They were landowners – serious, devout and educated men – who wanted to return to their family estates as soon as possible. They were certainly not antagonistic to the monarchy; on the contrary, they could conceive of no other form of government. But their task was to solve, together with Charles, the political and religious conflicts that were poisoning English life more and more as time went on.

The Long Parliament met for the first time on November 3rd. The King had asked Strafford, who was in the North, to return to London, as Strafford knew how to handle Parliament and was the only servant Charles trusted. Strafford did as he was bid, even though he was aware that this could mean his impeachment or death. He arrived in London on the evening of November 9th. Pym, still leading the House of Commons, had counted on Strafford's staying in the North or going to Ireland. He considered the King and Strafford fully capable of arresting opposition members of Parliament in an attempt to swing the balance in their favor. Pym therefore needed to act quickly. Consequently, on November 11th, he stood before a packed House of Commons (whose doors had been locked) and proposed that Strafford be impeached by the House of Lords for high treason. Strafford was well aware that all would be lost if he went to Parliament, and he informed the King of this. Charles responded that, as King of England, he could protect Strafford against any danger and that Parliament would not harm a hair on his head. Strafford therefore proceeded toward the House of Lords at the very moment that Pym, head of a delegation from the Commons, came to demand his arrest. Strafford, entering with his head held high, was made to kneel before the bar to hear the charge. He left the building as a prisoner. He could have been saved if reason had prevailed, for who could seriously accuse the King's most loyal servant of high treason, and thus of an offense against the King? If only the impeachment change had been "misconduct in office," the King could have dismissed his minister. But this time the Commons took matters a step further than it had with the case against Buckingham. He had "merely" been accused of criminal behavior, while Strafford had to face the charge of high treason. By definition, high treason was an act committed against the King. But Strafford was his most faithful servant! The King still supported Strafford, even though he had allowed him to be carried off to prison.

Soon after Strafford's impeachment, the Commons set about turning the tables, which included a "purge." Laud's freedom of movement was limited and then, on March 1st, he was thrown into the Tower. Sir John Finch managed to flee to The Netherlands. Impeachment procedures were instigated against the five other judges who had ruled in the King's favor in the ship money case. The books of the jurist Sir Edward Coke, who had been dismissed decades earlier by James I for propounding the theory that the King's authority was demarcated by law and justice, were published in full. The three pamphleteers, Prynne, Burton and Bastwick, were released from prison and carried to London in triumph. All holders of monopolies were turned out of the House of Commons, reducing the handful of members on the King's side by twelve persons at a stroke. The Westminster Soap Company's monopoly was withdrawn. After auditing the tax collectors' books, the Commons forbade further money to be sent to the treasury, except to cover the court's daily expenses. The King had no choice but to submit to this unprecedented violation of his rights. In making fiscal decisions about spending tax revenues, the House of Commons had abrogated one of the King's powers. Strafford's most important witness, his nephew and confidant George Radcliffe, was in Ireland. Legal proceedings were immediately instigated against Radcliffe to keep his voice from being heard.

Charles had been forced into a tight corner by these setbacks, but was not yet defeated. He feverishly attempted to find new friends to help him out of his present difficulties. As friends were few and far between on the home front, he cast his eyes abroad. Henrietta Maria, now a politically significant factor in her own right, negotiated with the Pope via a papal nuncio. Would he be prepared to provide her husband with financial support to enable him to be less dependent on Parliament? The Pope was rather taken with the idea, but was only willing to offer help if Charles would convert to Roman Catholicism. At this point, negotiations broke down.

In Holland, Frederick Henry of the powerful and wealthy House of Orange had become Stadtholder. A marriage between Frederick Henry's son and the daughter of an English king would be a considerable step up the royal ladder. Charles, who looked upon Frederick Henry as a parvenu, considered the marriage to be merely a means of gaining Dutch financial support. Therefore, the engagement of the fifteen year old William of Orange to the nine year old Mary Stuart was announced at the beginning of 1641. This engagement was presented to Parliament as a change in foreign policy: the alliance with Spain was traded for one with the Dutch Republic. But against the financial background, the motive was crystal clear.

After some months of preparation, Strafford's impeachment trial began on March 22nd in Westminster Hall. The throne placed there for the King remained empty, for Charles, accompanied by the Queen, the Crown Prince and Princess Mary, sat to the side in a box. According to an eyewitness, very little attention was paid to the royal party; it was as if they did not exist. The gallery was full of ladies who would not have missed the spectacle for all the money in the world. The atmosphere was far from grave. Lords and Commoners walked around during the breaks, gesticulating and talking excitedly. Picnics were held throughout the building, or as the same eyewitness describes it, there was "much public eating not only of confections, but of flesh and bread, bottles of beer and wine going thick from mouth to mouth without cups."

The leaders of the Commons, who served as the prosecuting attorneys, were Pym and Oliver St. John, who had been John Hampden's most important attorney in the ship-money case. They attempted to compromise Strafford by citing speeches he had made before the Privy Council. According to the Commons, Strafford had proposed using an Irish army to force England into submission. This charge was patently untrue, as Strafford had intended to use the army against the Scots. Pym and his allies realized to their chagrin that the House of Lords would be unable to summon a majority to condemn Strafford, who defended himself eloquently and courageously even though enfeebled by illness. After fourteen days, the prosecuting attorneys realized that with every moment that passed, they were losing ground. It appeared increasingly unlikely that a majority could be found in the House of Lords to find Strafford guilty of a capital offense. This would be an enormous blow to Pym and the Puritans and would frustrate their attempt to change the power relations between the King and the Parliament. Therefore, they suddenly dropped the impeachment charge and took refuge in a simpler and cruder procedure: a Bill of Attainder. This was a parliamentary bill demanding Strafford's death for the security of the country. If the majority found a strong enough suspicion of guilt, it could pass a Bill of Attainder without further evidence. This procedure provided the accused with none of the safeguards of a normal trial. It is not possible to justify the behavior of the majority of the members of the House of Commons on the grounds of legally obtained evidence. Pym and his political friends murdered Strafford on the basis of a legal sleight of hand. Still, if Strafford had lived and regained his freedom, he would not have hesitated to bring his accusers to the scaffold. Lord Digby, in a speech greatly to his credit, declared that he could not approve the Bill of Attainder. He argued that a man should not be sentenced to death on the

Master **PYM**
HIS SPEECH
In *Parliament*, on *Wednesday*, the fifth of *January*, 1641,

Concerning the Vote of the House of *Commons*, for his discharge upon the Accusation of High Treason, exhibited against himselfe, and the Lord *Kimbolton*, Mr. *Iohn Hampden*, Sr. *Arthur Haslerig*, Mr. *Strowd*, M. Hollis, by his Maiesty.

The true Effigies of Mr. *Iohn Pym*, Esquire

London Printed for I. W, 1641.

basis of a law enacted retroactively. The vehemence of the emotions of that period is evidenced by the fact that the House of Commons ordered Digby's courageous speech to be burned and requested the King to refrain from according him any titles or functions.

The House of Commons passed the Bill of Attainder on April 21st with 204 voting for and 59 voting against the motion (note that almost 200 members were absent). Those voting against the motion were labeled "Straffordians and enemies of the country," and their names were posted in the City, in contravention of the law. The City's stores closed their doors. Masters and journeymen came to Westminster and threatened the Straffordians. The country was in a state of upheaval. Henrietta Maria did everything in her power to dissuade the peers from convicting Strafford. She reputedly conspired to form an army in the North to come to the King's rescue. As it turned out, nothing came of the venture, except the further hardening of Pym's heart. In his view, Strafford's execution would remove the last obstacle to parliamentary rule. He believed that the country could then flourish under Parliament's beneficent leadership.

On April 19th, the young William of Orange arrived to marry Mary. He was accompanied by a splendid entourage consisting of four hundred nobles and servants and chests full of money. The marriage took place on May 2nd, in the middle of the turmoil surrounding the Strafford trial. Not surprisingly, the marriage contributed greatly to the feelings of unrest in the hearts of those in the House of Commons dedicated to the Strafford case.

The end was not yet in sight, for although the Commons had passed the Bill of Attainder, it still had to be approved by the House of Lords and signed by the King. In an attempt to save Strafford's life, Charles convened the Lords. He told them he would not sign the Bill of Attainder because he considered Strafford to be innocent. Further, he promised that if Parliament would allow Strafford to resign on the grounds of misconduct, he would dispense with his services entirely. This major tactical error greatly damaged Strafford's case, for it was seen as an attempt to influence the decision of the Lords. Their resolve was further undermined when the King informed them that he would not sign the bill under any circumstances. Using his brother as mediator, Strafford had done all he could to dissuade the King from taking this ill-advised step.

Thousands gathered in Westminster in the early morning of May 3rd. To reach the meeting place, the Lords were obliged to pass through rows of spectators screaming "justice and execution" in their ears. Owing to mob pressure and the sudden illness of his friends, Strafford was sentenced to death by the House of Lords on Saturday, May 8th, by a vote of 37 to 11. Strafford's fate then lay in the hands of the King. Would the King, who had written to Strafford on April 23rd that no ill would befall him "upon the word of a king," sanction the bill?

He first sought the advice of the magistrates, but they were unable to extricate him from his predicament. He then turned to the bishops for advice. The first to be consulted was Ireland's primate, Archbishop Ussher, who happened to be in London at the time. He stated categorically that the King should not sign a bill that did not accord with his conscience. William Juxon, the Bishop of London, offered the same advice. The third visitor was John Williams, the Bishop of Lincoln. His conciliatory attitude towards the Puritans had already involved him in a conflict with Laud. He had rightfully been sentenced to imprisonment in the Tower in 1637 for bribery and perjury. The common people considered Williams to be a friend to the Puritans and a kind of martyr. Confident of Puritan support, Williams refused the King's offer to release him from prison in exchange for relinquishing his episcopal see. Time proved him right, for Laud was imprisoned in one of the Long Parliament's purges, and Williams was able to resume his seat as a peer in the House of Lords. Fearing that the bishops in the Lords would vote against sentencing Strafford, Pym initiated a bill in the Commons to the effect that the exercise of judicial powers by bishops and

A 19th century version of the scene in which Strafford, en route to his execution, passes the cell of Archbishop Laud who blesses him (and then faints; not pictured).

clergymen was inconsistent with their ecclesiastical functions. Williams picked up this thread and proposed that the bishops in the House of Lords abstain from passing judgement on their noble colleague — peer Strafford — in the impeachment case in order not to offend the House of Commons and the people. The bishops agreed, but whether in the interests of the church or out of a desire to save their own skins is a moot point. Williams began his advice to the King by remarking that Charles' refusal to comply with the wishes of the people could have serious consequences. He next explained the ambiguous character of the monarchy. The King had to maintain two consciences: one for his private life and another for his public life. As a private individual, he could not uphold Strafford's death sentence. But as King, he had to take political consequences into account. He was ultimately only accountable to God, from whom he derived his power. Williams' advice brought Charles a certain relief. Was it not actually his duty to sign the Bill of Attainder?

The situation steadily worsened. The day after the verdict in the House of Lords, London's unruly mob made its way to Whitehall. Seriously threatened, the Queen and her Catholic courtiers went to confession, and the bravest military leaders readied themselves to die defending the castle's stairs and corridors. The following Sunday, the tumult grew; at nine o'clock in the evening, the King, fearing for the Queen's safety, signed the bill. "My Lord of Strafford's condition is happier than mine," he said, and those near him could see the tears glistening in his eyes.

A. Doctor Vſher, Lor
te of Ireland,
B the Sherifes of Lou
C the Earle of Straff
D his Kindred and I

The execution of Thomas Wentworth, Earl of Strafford, on May 12, 1641.

Strafford was not permitted to talk to Laud and ask his blessing before his execution, even though both of them were imprisoned in the Tower. He was not even given the opportunity to put his affairs in order, as the execution was to be carried out right away. As Strafford was being led to the scaffold, the old Archbishop came to the window to bless his fellow sufferer from afar, which affected the elderly man so much that he fainted. Strafford died displaying the same courage with which he had lived. The residents of London, their numbers swelled by visitors from far and near, maintained a respectful silence, but after the execution celebrated profusely into the night. This was the end of a man who had once articulated his concept of the king's place in the structure of government as follows: "The authority of the king is the keystone which closeth up the arch of order and government, which containeth each part in relation to the whole, and which, once shaken, infirmed, all the frame falls together in a confused heap of foundation and battlement." His political belief was that Parliament should support, but not dominate, the monarchy. He forfeited his life by remaining loyal, right up to the last, to a king who deserted him at the moment of truth.

Strafford's execution eliminated the only man who would have been capable of turning the English monarchy into an authoritarian form of government, modeled on France and Spain. To permanently rule out the possibility of an absolutist victory, the King had to be forbidden to rule without a parliament, as he and his father had both done for long periods of time. Up to this point, the Achilles' heel of an elected body had been the fact that the King could dissolve it whenever there was a difference of opinion. Parliament's only defense was to lay down fixed rules, stipulating when it was to be convened by the executive branch of government.

Confused by Strafford's death and bereft of any support now that Laud was in prison, the King signed several parliamentary bills curtailing royal power. The driving force behind the changes was Pym, who had clearly defined ideas about a more balanced division of power between king and parliament. From now on, Parliament was to be convened regularly, at least once every three years. It could also meet without a royal summons if the King had not convened it by the end of the third year. It could only be dissolved if it had been in session for at least fifty days, and no session could last longer than three years. Charles was also forced to accept the fact that special courts such as the Star Chamber would have to make way for civil courts. The High Commission, a kind of court to which Laud had had frequent recourse in his attempt to subjugate unwilling clergy (it was once compared to the Catholic Inquisition), was also slated to disappear. The House of Commons and the House of Lords adopted a joint resolution (which did not become a law) to the effect that judges should be appointed for life, as this would make them independent of the executive branch of government. Lastly, the King had to recognize that taxes could no longer be imposed without parliamentary consent. Ship money levies and the unauthorized imposition of tonnage and poundage were strictly forbidden. In one and the same breath, Parliament forbade the farming out of certain taxes and the misuse of royal forests and abolished compulsory knighthood, practices which had brought a great deal of money to the treasury.

These agreements between an enraged Parliament and an enfeebled monarch signified the victory of the law over the king. Indeed, it appeared that the law had become king. It was as if James I's motto "rex est lex" had been turned around. Although some of the changes were subject to temporary reverses, all were ultimately included in the Constitution. Thus, England's parliamentary democracy, such a shining example to many nations, took its first uncertain steps. Parliament first had to learn that one of the prerequisites of a people's liberty and prosperity is the achievement of a subtle balance between the executive, legislative and judicial branches of government. Such insight eluded them in the 1640's. In 1642, Parliament temporarily assumed royal authority, referring to itself as "King-and-Parliament." The reason they gave for their action was that the King, influenced by poor advisers, was unable to govern effectively. This usurpation clearly demonstrates that Parliament still had much to learn about how to handle power. Unfortunately, this learning process was initially accompanied by great bloodshed. The Civil War broke out and split the country into two. Feelings ran high, and many heads rolled.

In 1645, the next in line for the scaffold was Laud. Imprisoned for years, Laud had been forgotten by many, but not by Prynne. The irrepressible Puritan had continued to publish pamphlets, particularly aimed at discrediting his arch-enemy, Archbishop Laud. Prynne made occasional forays into non-religious matters. For example, in 1641 he issued a pamphlet he had written in 1637, entitled "An Humble Remonstrance to His Majesty Against the Tax of Ship Money." In this work he declared that one of the objections to the ship money was that it placed a disproportionate burden on "the middle and poor sort of people."

Endhaupfung deß Konias in Engaeland ño 1649

The execution of Charles I in 1649.

The House of Commons appointed Prynne as prosecuting attorney in Laud's trial. Prynne confiscated the papers Laud had been allowed to take with him to prison in order to prepare his defense and returned only a few of them. Even worse, he had taken excerpts from Laud's personal diary and unscrupulously twisted the text to suit his own purposes, omitting certain points, fabricating others and occasionally maliciously changing entire passages. In short, he shamelessly attempted to reveal Laud in a worse light than he deserved. Laud's trial, which lasted weeks, was conducted before a handful of members still left in the House of Lords, as most had chosen the King's side during the Civil War. In the mornings, the members listened to the charges against Laud. In the afternoons, when it was Laud's turn to present his defense, the court was virtually deserted, except for the chairman. In spite of this, the Archbishop was not impeached. The Rump Parliament (whose name refers to the remnant of a divided Parliament) therefore prepared a Bill of Attainder. The rabble, thirsting for Laud's blood, was mobilized. The House of Lords soon added its agreement to that of the House of Commons, and Laud was sentenced to die. The requisite approval of the King was replaced by a resolution passed by the Commons, a simple enough matter as it already operated as King-and-Parliament.

Barely four years after this judicial murder, it was the King's turn. By that time, he had lost everything: his wife and children (who had fled to the Continent), his power, his army and his servants. In the intervening years, he had scurried

A 1649 royalist print showing how the "Royal Oake of Brittayn" (Charles I) was chopped down. The three persons felling the oak symbolize the army, those pruning the branches the members of the House of Lords and those pulling on the tree with ropes the members of the House of Commons. The pigs being fattened for slaughter represent the common people. Books and statutes, including the Bible and the Magna Carta, are hanging in the oak tree. The figure on the left is Cromwell, standing on the slippery path to hell.

back and forth from one faction to another. He gave his word, only to break it. He antagonized many with his inept attempts to play the various factions against each other. In the process, he threw away the reputation of which he was so proud and lost whatever trust he had inspired. He was escorted to a special court, where one hundred and thirty-five people were to pass judgement on the basis of a law introduced especially for the occasion. On the way to the meeting room, he accidentally let fall his gold-topped cane. Charles waited a moment, accustomed to having a servant hasten to retrieve it. But no one moved. Realizing his position, he bent down and picked up the cane. And so, dignified but utterly devoid of any insight into humanity and the world around him, he laid his head on the block.

The Boston Tea Party (1773) and the subsequent British sanctions were an important reason (possibly the most important one) the thirteen American colonies revolted against England and obtained their independence. The tea was thrown overboard by colonists disguised as Indians because the Americans abhorred the idea of the British government levying a tax on tea without giving the colonists a voice in the decision-making process.

5 Boston

The thirteen American colonies

Adopting the unctuous and even lachrymose tone familiar to us from the second half of the seventeenth century, English parliamentarians and authors of letters to the editor preoccupied with the "American issue" frequently compared the British Parliament to a wise old father, who had always meant well by his children, the American colonists, and who still knew what was best for them. This analogy was inevitably followed by a long list of filial obligations the children owed their father. Proponents of these views demonstrably lacked historical insight, for the thirteen colonies on the other side of the ocean were mainly populated by the descendants of sulky runaways: children like the Pilgrim Fathers and Puritans who left home out of anger and heartbreak at not being able to practice their religion freely, paupers unable to keep their heads above water, deportees arrested for vagrancy, prisoners of war hoping to regain their freedom or younger sons embittered by their inability to get ahead.

England initially took scant notice of its colonies. The Mother Country's interest was only kindled when the colonies began to enjoy some success. The English government responded by weighing the colonists down with trade and navigation regulations, much to England's advantage, I might add. The charters granted to the newly founded colonies allowed each colony to regulate its internal affairs, subject to British supreme control, and provided them with specific forms of popular representation capable of influencing the executive branch of government to a limited extent. England maintained a different standard for the American Colonies than for its conquered territories (e.g. India). Neither standard resembled the founding of Greek colonies known to us from antiquity. A Hellenic city which sent out its residents to establish colonies intervened actively in the government of the colonies and lavished on them its blessings and care. However, the founding of the American colonies did not resemble Hellenic colonization. The initiative for American colonization did not stem from the English government, but from private individuals, motivated by the desire to make a profit or live according to their own religious precepts, and the Mother Country only involved itself to further its own interests.

In the 1580's, a handful of colonists had sojourned briefly on the coast of North America. On the basis of this residence, England claimed possession of a territory it called "Virginia" after the Virgin Queen, Elizabeth. The Virginia territory extended over the entire area later destined to become the Thirteen Colonies. Some twenty years later (in 1606), a group of wealthy Englishmen formed a joint-stock company to develop Virginia, in the hope of finding gold. King James I granted them a letter of patent for their enterprise and also issued a charter regulating the territory's governmental structure and granting the company such royal rights as the right to mint coins, establish laws in the new territory, etc. The shareholders were the highest authority in the company, although to all practical intents and purposes, it was controlled by a Board of Directors residing in England and appointed by the King. In return for the royal rights granted, the King was to receive a fifth of any gold and silver found and a fifteenth of any copper.

Virginia.

It goes without saying that the colonists initially encountered many difficulties. The hundred or so colonists who landed in Chesapeake Bay in May of 1607 found Indians, disease and hardship instead of precious metals. The fact that there were more adventurers, criminals and shiftless workers among them than respectable farmers and artisans was hardly conducive to success. The few nobles in the company preferred fishing and hunting to hard work. In spite of the extremely high mortality rate, Virginia grew steadily, thanks to the regular transport of migrants from England. The cultivation of tobacco, a skill learned from the Indians, brought some relief and kept the colonists going. After a decade, the shareholders, inspired by democratic ideals, were prepared to grant the colonists some measure of self-government. The House of Burgesses, formed in 1619, was comprised of representatives of the various townships. The first type of popularly elected assembly of its kind in the New World, it served as a model for similar institutions in other colonies.

In that same year, a Dutch ship arrived with the first shipload of African slaves. Hundreds of thousands were shipped to the colonies in the years that followed. In about 1775, an insider remarked that roughly one third of Virginia's wealth consisted of slaves. Because of the slave labor, the cultivation of tobacco boomed, bringing more and more prosperity to its owners. Attracted by this wealth, increasing numbers of English nobles and Puritans fleeing the confines of life in the colony of Massachusetts settled in Virginia. By the second half of the seventeenth century, Virginia was dominated by large landowners on vast plantations. Cities and towns were few and far between, and independent tradespeople were a rarity. Virginia was almost exclusively populated by slaves, forced laborers and indentured servants, and its political power lay entirely in the hands of aristocratic plantation owners. It was only further West, across the Allegheny Mountains, that any sounds of protest were heard. These border residents demanded a greater voice in government. They were largely of Scots-Irish stock, having first migrated to Ulster from the Scottish-English border. When the English Parliament denied Presbyterians the right to hold military and civilian office in 1704, many of these Presbyterian Scots emigrated from Ulster to America. Living up to their reputation as intolerant troublemakers, they had another confrontation in Virginia with the Anglican Church. After failing to obtain land development concessions from the established planters, they settled in the less attractive mountainous regions across the Allegheny Mountains.

Virginia was known as a "royal colony," since it had received the charter regulating its government from the King. The English Crown had greater influence in Virginia than some of the other colonies, if only because it appointed Virginia's governor and councilors.

The initiative for founding a colony did not merely stem from joint-stock companies. Several colonies were founded by groups seeking religious freedom. One such group was the Pilgrim Fathers, who fled religious persecution in England in 1608 by moving to Holland. Then, in 1620, they sailed from Delfshaven to America, where they founded the Plymouth Colony, which was annexed in 1691 by Massachusetts. The Massachusetts Bay Colony was created in 1629, when King James I, anxious to be rid of English Puritans, granted them a charter to set up the Massachusetts Bay Company. The company's Board of Directors was also transported to the other side of the ocean in 1630, making Massachusetts the colony least dependent on the Mother Country in the seventeenth century.

Title page of a document from 1619/1620, containing the regulations governing the colony of Virginia.

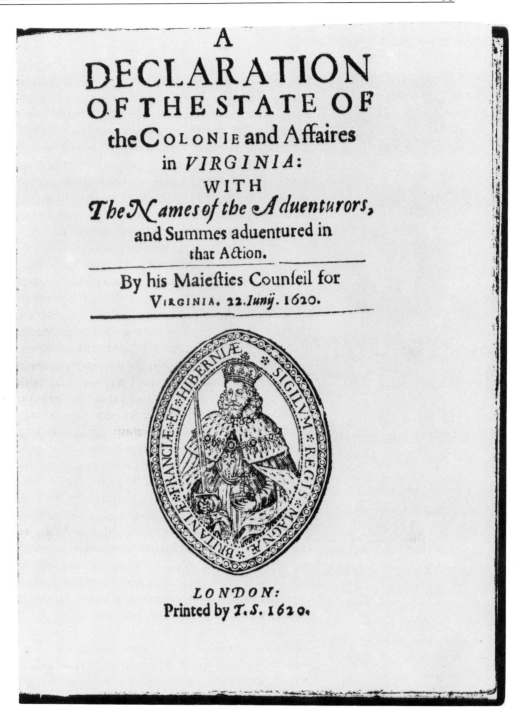

A

DECLARATION
OF THE STATE OF
the COLONIE and Affaires
in *VIRGINIA:*
WITH
The Names of the Adventurors,
and Summes adventured in
that Action.

By his Maiefties Counfeil for
VIRGINIA. 22.*Iunÿ*. 1620.

LONDON:
Printed by *T.S.* 1620.

Unlike Virginia, trade interests had not been the paramount considerations when this colony was founded. The Bay Colony consequently became a tightly knit community with a definite Puritan stamp: the colonists were hard-working, frugal and successful in business, but intolerant and therefore not well liked by the other colonies. Incidentally, the colony's considerable wealth, centered mainly in Boston, was due in part to its booming slave trade.

In 1637, Massachusetts made church membership a prerequisite for such civil rights as the right to vote. For all practical purposes, control of the colony was placed in the hands of church authorities, who could decide on such matters as

Massachusetts.

Rhode Island.

Connecticut.

exile and excommunication. The colonists' lives and beliefs were thus subject to the strict supervision and unrelenting discipline of a theocratic government, supported by a network of church spies. It was not until 1691 that the right to vote was linked to property ownership rather than church membership.

Massachusetts' first leaders were self-educated men who placed a high value on education and training. They believed that everyone should be able to read the Bible and that educational facilities should be established to train ministers. Therefore, an elementary school was promptly set up in 1630. The famous Harvard College and the Latin School of Boston were founded in 1636. Compulsory general education was introduced in 1647. Even before 1700, Boston was the acknowledged intellectual center of the colonies. Significantly, in 1685, Boston had no less than five bookstores.

The unit of local government in Massachusetts was the town: a compact settlement organized around a grassy common, serving simultaneously as meeting place, graveyard and communal pasture. The prayer house doubled as church and arsenal. The town meeting was a political forum for all freeholders having the right to vote. As the town grew, the town meeting became a representative assembly. The town was autonomous in local matters. The voters elected their own local officials, determined taxes and tax assessments, maintained schools and issued city ordinances. Each town had the right to send representatives to the popular assembly in Massachusetts, which was known in the Bay Colony as the "General Court." The Puritans of Massachusetts had therefore organized themselves into a republic. In principle, it was independent of England, as all residents were required to pledge an oath of loyalty and obedience, not to the King, but to the government of the new colony. Seen in this perspective, later events may seem less strange. From the outset, the residents of Massachusetts were determined to achieve full independence. The idea of secession matured more rapidly in Massachusetts than in the other colonies. However, Massachusetts was made a royal colony in 1691, an act that merely intensified their longing for independence.

Just as the founding of Massachusetts resulted from Anglican intolerance toward the Puritans, Puritan intolerance in Massachusetts led to the creation of Rhode Island. When Massachusetts was first founded, the effort required to wrest civilization from the wilderness did not leave much room for dissidence. Later, numerous colonists with dissident opinions were deported from the Bay Colony. One deportee was Roger Williams, an independent thinker and young clergyman mainly preaching tolerance. Although he was scheduled to be deported back to England, he managed to escape in the middle of the winter to the shelter and hospitality of friendly Indians. Williams and several of his followers later founded the colony of Rhode Island.

Connecticut can also be considered an offshoot of Massachusetts, as a group of colonists detached itself from the Bay Colony and emigrated to the fertile Connecticut Valley. They joined forces with colonists sent out by a group of Puritan lords who had received a concession for that territory. An unscrupulous lot, the residents of Connecticut annihilated the local Indian tribe and took their land, breached a treaty and stole Dutch possessions in the surrounding areas. Because of their marginal economic significance, Rhode Island and Connecticut, denoted as "corporate colonies," were the only two virtually autonomous miniature republics in which the English showed little interest.

In 1654, less than twenty-five years after Massachusetts was first colonized, a book dealing with the history of New England up to the year 1652 was published. It included a description of the form of government, etc.

A

HISTORY

OF

New-England.

From the Englifh planting in the Yeere 1628. untill the Yeere 1652.

Declaring the form of their Government,
Civill, Military, and Ecclefiaftique. Their Wars with
the Indians, their Troubles with the Gortonifts,
and other Heretiques. Their manner of gathering
of Churches, the commodities of the Country,
and defcription of the principall Towns
and Havens, with the great encou-
ragements to increafe Trade
betwixt them and Old
ENGLAND.

With the names of all their Governours, Magiftrates,
and eminent Minifters.

PSAL. 107.24.
The righteous fhall fee it and rejoice, and all iniquity fhall ftop her mouth.

PSAL. 111.2.
The works of the Lord are great, and ought to be fought out of all that have pleafure in them.

LONDON,
Printed for NATH: BROOKE at the *Angel*
in *Corn-hill.* 1 6 5 4.

New Hampshire.

Maryland.

Maine and New Hampshire, founded by private individuals, were later partly incorporated by Massachusetts. The Mother Country also left these two colonies pretty much to their own devices because they were economically insignificant. Massachusetts, Rhode Island, Connecticut, Maine and New Hampshire were later referred to collectively as "New England." Massachusetts' local system of government was imitated to some extent by the other New England colonies.

While the colony of Maryland also owed its existence to religion, it developed differently. Maryland was initially the property of a private individual charged with governmental powers in the territory, and was therefore known as a "proprietor colony." Maryland's proprietor was the Catholic Lord Baltimore, who was granted a charter by Charles I in 1632. The charter allowed Baltimore to found a colony north of the Potomac River and stipulated that the King had a right to one fifth of any gold and silver found there. Baltimore lured colonists by promising to cede them land in exchange for settling the colony. His charter awarded him royal rights. While he was the head of government and controlled all executive governmental bodies, Baltimore needed the consent of a representative form of popular government to enact laws. He was also head of the Church, Captain-General of the army and grantor of both ecclesiastical and

North Carolina.

South Carolina.

Georgia.

civilian offices. The primary objective in setting up this colony was to create a territory where freedom of religion prevailed. Consequently, Catholics were also accepted as colonists. Drawn by this religious tolerance, Puritan dissidents from Virginia and Massachusetts also settled in Maryland and eventually became the majority. To afford some protection to the Catholic minority, the Catholic proprietors passed a Toleration Act in 1649. This act guaranteed, in principle, freedom of conscience. Nevertheless, the Toleration Act was soon abolished and replaced by a law prohibiting the civil rights of both Catholics and Episcopalians. The Catholics were thus thrust aside in the colony they had founded. Their rights were restored in 1660, and the Catholics enjoyed thirty years of religious freedom. But King William III, who disliked having a Catholic proprietor in the middle of English colonial territory, canceled the charter of Lord Baltimore's descendants and once again abolished the freedom of religion in 1690. Thus the principle of tolerance that had been planted in Maryland was swiftly uprooted.

Carolina also owed its existence to a transfer of land to a private individual. In this case, Charles II permitted eight nobles to take possession of the Carolina territory and promulgate laws for the settlers. For seven years, Carolina was permitted to export tax-free to England silk, wines, currants, raisins, wax, capers, almonds, oil and olives and to import from England tools and implements of use to planters. In return, the Mother Country expected recognition of its rights to twenty pounds a year plus a quarter of any gold and silver found in Carolina. The territory soon split into a northern and a southern part. North Carolina, more of a border territory, was populated by adventurous, headstrong people, including many Scots-Irish refugees undaunted by the hardships of life in the wilderness. By trading furs and hides with the Indians and dealing in pitch and resin, they were able to eke out a frugal existence. North Carolina had few plantations and therefore few slaves. South Carolina, on the other hand, developed into a plantation area, like Virginia and the West Indies, where blacks and Indians labored while the whites managed the plantations and the sale of the crops, typically rice and indigo. The Carolinas copied the governmental structure of the New England colonies, which meant that towns sprang up everywhere. The most important settlement was Charles Town (Charleston), a well-situated port on the Carolina seaboard. The first wave of colonists came from Barbados and the second wave from England and Ireland, while the third wave consisted of French Huguenots. Numerous merchants from New York joined the ranks of Charleston's traders. The rich planters were lord and masters of their plantations, but many also owned large houses in Charleston, where the climate was cooler and healthier than inland.

When Georgia was founded, profit-making was not a primary objective. Georgia's founder was James Edward Oglethorpe, former officer in the army of Prince Eugene of Savoy and member of the English House of Commons. In the latter capacity, Oglethorpe was chairman of a parliamentary investigative committee looking into conditions in debtor's prisons. What he saw in the English Houses of Detention convinced him that many lives could be saved if the prisoners could start afresh in an agricultural colony, far away from large cities. In 1732, King George II provided Oglethorpe with land to be settled by convicted debtors. The land grant, valid for twenty-one years, lay between the Savannah and Alatamaha Rivers. He christened it "Georgia" and labeled it the "Colony of Benevolence." This new colony soon became a haven of refuge for persecuted Protestants, particularly the Moravian Brothers and the Evangelists of Salzburg,

A sugar and tobacco plantation. In this old print, it is the Indians who are doing the work.

who had been driven out of their city by the Archbishop. The charter guaranteed freedom of religion, except for Catholics. Oglethorpe selected one hundred and twenty men, women and children from the prison population, and shipped them to the South bank of the Savannah River, the site of the later fort and town of Savannah. A few Indians who were to teach the Moravians and Salzburgers the

*Today we would call this
1630 pamphlet, whose title
page is depicted above, a
prospectus. It summarizes
the liberties and advantages
offered the colonists
settling in New Netherland.
For one, the colonists did
not have to pay taxes.*

art of silkworm breeding settled there as well, along with a fair number of Scottish Highlanders and a few Jews. Their numbers were later swelled by an influx of emigrants from the Carolinas. Methodists also got a foothold in Georgia. In the beginning, Georgia had no slaves. But because many white colonists were unequal to the arduous work in Georgia's hot climate, the already-existing pockets of slavery were legitimized, over the protests of the Moravian Brothers, the Scottish Highlanders and the Salzburgers.

New York

New Jersey.

Pennsylvania.

The colony of New York owes its existence to an entirely different set of circumstances. While searching for a Northwest passage in 1609, Henry Hudson, in the service of the Dutch West India Company, discovered the river later named in his honor, the Hudson River. While the Company was not interested in developing the area, a few enterprising merchants from Amsterdam built some log cabins in 1613 and began trading in beaver and otter furs with the Indians. After the States-General granted the West Indian Company a letter of patent, this settlement became the colony of New Netherland. The first group of colonists, mainly Walloon Protestants, arrived in 1623. Further growth was checked by the Company's lack of vision. It offered the colonists too few opportunities for agricultural development, so that their only source of wealth was the fur trade. But the tolerant attitude of the Dutch did allow colonists of all nationalities and denominations to settle there. New Netherland was conquered by the English in 1664, after which Charles II bestowed it on his brother James, the Duke of York, in return for recognition of his right to forty beaver pelts a year. Because James prudently did not interfere in their affairs, the Dutch remained in the colony, keeping away from politics and continuing to speak their own language. More than a hundred years later, at the height of the struggle for independence, myriads of older Dutch people in New York still spoke only Dutch. In fact, Thomas Paine's well-known pamphlet "Common Sense," outlining the theoretical reasons for rebellion and independence, was translated into Dutch for their benefit. In 1683, New York drew up a Charter of Liberties and Privileges. This Charter served as a kind of constitution, establishing freedom of conscience, granting the same civil rights as in England and regulating how representative bodies were to be involved in governing the colony.

In 1664, Sir George Carteret and John, Lord Berkeley, purchased that part of the Duke of York's newly acquired New Netherland lying on the Delaware River. The colony was named New Jersey. Its first colonists were Hollanders from New York and Puritans from Long Island, New Haven and Massachusetts. Because of the Puritan influence, the eastern portion of New Jersey became a miniature New England, adopting not only typical New England features such as town meetings, Congregational Churches and a love of independence, but also religious intolerance and a perennial self-righteousness. New Jersey's western and eastern portions were united into one colony in 1702. In subsequent decades, the main settlers were Scottish Presbyterians, who gave the colony an overwhelmingly Presbyterian stamp. The University of Princeton, founded in 1747, clearly exemplified Presbyterian principles.

Berkeley sold the western portion in 1674 to a London Quaker who shortly thereafter transferred his rights to another Quaker named William Penn and his followers. In 1681, Penn, whose father had served as admiral under the Stuarts and who himself enjoyed the trust and support of Charles II and his brother James, thus came into possession of a fertile territory rich in minerals and good-quality timber. Penn's woods were slated to go down in history as Pennsylvania. The recognition of his rights amounted to two beaver pelts a year plus a fifth of any gold and silver found in the colony. Many Quakers, feeling their influence to be limited in England, emigrated to the colony of Pennsylvania. Penn himself was a nobleman, but his followers were dirt-poor farmers and laborers. Their ideas were extremely radical for that day and age. The Quakers took the fundamental ideas of the Reformation a step further, maintaining that every true believer should seek direct contact with God, without the intervention of the

Delaware.

Church, and thus becoming in effect his or her own priest. Consequently, the Quakers had no ministers and rejected any authority in religious matters. Penn, a wise and noble individual full of high ideals, drew up a highly democratic constitution for the new colony. This constitution attested to a deep respect for human dignity. The key to Penn's actions lies in the statement of principle preceding the constitution, particularly the following sentence: "For liberty without obedience is confusion, and obedience without liberty is slavery." The Quakers, believing more in each person's "internal light" than in the word of the Bible, adhered to a practical kind of Christianity, in which the love of truth and independence, diligence, simplicity, brotherly love and self-awareness were the key characteristics. The new colony grew rapidly with the influx of Quakers from other countries and colonies, followed by Huguenots, Mennonites from the Lower Rhine area, Lutherans and Reformed Protestants from the Rhine Palatinate and Swedish Lutherans. The last of these settled mainly in Delaware, which broke away from Pennsylvania in 1701 and formed a separate colony. Pennsylvania's capital, Philadelphia, thrived, soon becoming one of the most important cities in the American colonies. After 1720, many Scots-Irish immigrants arrived in Pennsylvania. Joining forces with the numerous Germans, they threw themselves into opposition against the liberal Quakers. Generally speaking, the Quakers dominated the cities, where they constituted the wealthiest segment of society. The Germans and the Scots-Irish were primarily farmers and tradespeople. In later years, they would become the fiercest champions of colonial independence.

Rough estimates indicate that in 1689, when a series of wars broke out between England and France (with hegemony over the American colonies being one of the stakes), the thirteen colonies had a population of about 200,000 people. By the time the Treaty of Utrecht was signed in 1713, this number had doubled. In subsequent years, the population doubled every twenty or twenty-five years. No more than four or five percent of the total population of the American colonies lived in the seven largest cities combined. Philadelphia, with a population of more than 30,000, was one of the four or five largest English-speaking cities in the British Empire. New York and Boston followed with approximately 20,000 residents. When the War of Independence broke out in 1775, England had a population of approximately 7.5 million, roughly three times that of the colonies.

The remainder of this chapter will be devoted to the role of taxation in the Colonies' struggle for independence and will show how taxation helped forge greater unity among the thirteen colonies.

Relations with the Mother Country

Not all colonists came from England and Ireland; masses of people seeking better opportunities for themselves — whether economic advancement or political or religious freedom — arrived from other European countries as well. The colonies were sharply divided on the subject of tolerance toward other faiths, but there was no actual religious persecution. The colonies had a reasonable degree of self-government, with the financial upper crust forming, just as in England, the political elite. Voters in the Southern and Middle colonies did nothing more than decide which gentleman was the most suitable to govern the colony. In the New England colonies, where local democracy flourished thanks to the town meetings, the lower and middle classes participated in government to a greater

PENNS TREATY with the INDIANS, made 1681 with out an Oath, and never broken. The foundation of Religious and Civil LIBERTY, in the U.S. of AMERICA.

In 1681, William Penn signed a treaty with the Indians. Naive painting "avant la lettre" from 1843, with a similarly naive caption.

degree. The Governors of the royal colonies were appointed by the British Crown, those of the proprietary colonies by the proprietors and those of the corporate colonies by the local population. The Governors had to work together with the assemblies chosen by free men, although the right to vote was limited in all colonies. Despite the fact that there was no suffrage for women, minors, Catholics, Jews, non-believers, blacks, Indians, mulattoes or indentured servants and the fact that property ownership was usually a precondition for the right to vote, the popularly elected assemblies in most colonies were chosen more democratically than the British House of Commons. In England, a tiny elite still held the reins of power, and the people were irrelevant. But in the American colonies, the freeholder could let his voice be heard on the political level. In some colonies, the Governor had a theoretical veto right over the decisions reached by the assemblies. He rarely made use of this right, if only because the assemblies often determined his salary (and that of the other top officials). The assemblies could therefore use this leverage to exert financial pressure on his conscience. A governor was often in a difficult position, since he sometimes had to serve two masters: he owed his position to one master and the food on his table to the other. Most of the colonies also had a Council, which served as the Governor's advisory organ. In the majority of the colonies, the Councilors were chosen by the King from among the local elite. But in Massachusetts the assembly chose the twenty-eight Councilors with the Governor's approval. Though the Governors could ignore the Council's advice, in practice they usually prudently abided by their counsel, particularly when the Councilors unanimously supported an issue.

In the middle of the seventeenth century, England enacted a series of Trade and Navigation Acts. As the Dutch built ships and transported cargoes faster and cheaper than the English, these acts were intended to counter their superior position. The Trade and Navigation Acts were also intended to turn England into the sole entrepôt for a large number of colonial wares, such as rice, sugar, tobacco, cotton, wool, indigo and copper, and to have the colonies purchase as many English wares as possible. These acts decreed that only English ships or ships coming from the colonies could be used to transport goods to and from the colonies. The Board of Trade, a separate government service, was created to monitor compliance with the Trade and Navigation Acts. For sea-faring New England and later New York and Pennsylvania, the Trade and Navigation Acts stimulated the development of colonial shipping and trade. Shipbuilding also boomed. It has been estimated that one third of the ships sailing the Atlantic Ocean were built in the American colonies. However, the Trade Acts initially disadvantaged the one-crop Southern colonies such as Virginia, whose economy was based solely on tobacco. The Dutch who had been transporting the tobacco were cheaper and more efficient than the English, and it took the latter a long time to take over the transport and sale of tobacco. Colonies exporting raw materials to England found to their advantage that the Trade Acts provided them with a steady market and a position of monopoly. Nevertheless, London retailers did not always pay the best prices, because of the fixed trade pattern. In order to lessen the English navy's dependence on Swedish suppliers, the acts also reserved many products, such as hemp, tar, pitch and other naval stores needed to rig a ship, for the Mother Country. Rice, shipbuilding materials and furs were later enumerated on a list of products that could only be shipped to England. Any merchant wishing to ship the enumerated commodities from the colonies had to offer sufficient guarantee that the goods would be transported to England. If he could or would not provide such security, a heavy tax was levied on the goods.

To discourage the sugar trade from the French West Indies, the British Parliament (seventy-four of whose members had an interest in sugar plantations!) enacted the Molasses Act in 1733. This act imposed high taxes on the import of rum, molasses and sugar to England and the colonies. Strict compliance with the Molasses Act would have dealt the colonies a severe blow, as it would have eliminated one step of a highly profitable trade triangle. In the so-called Triangular Trades, New England exported grain and lumber to the West Indies, receiving in turn sugar and molasses. The colonies then processed the sugar and molasses into rum and used the proceeds from rum sales to purchase African slaves. The colonies generally ignored the Molasses Act, and the sugar trade thrived. The colonists dodged the other Trade Acts on a large scale as well. In the first half of the eighteenth century, the British government was indifferent to this non-compliance. In fact, the minister who had the American colonies in his portfolio usually left the reports on the colonies unread. Prime Minister Walpole himself avoided all constitutional questions and advised the Governors of the American colonies to ignore any constitutional disputes that might arise.

While little political interest was shown the colonies, economic matters were another story. As a result of the inflexible Trade Acts, the colonies started buying fewer English products and manufacturing more of their own. The English lost no time in protecting the country against American colonial competition. In 1699, England forbid the export of yarn and woolen fabrics from the colonies. In 1732, the English hatter's guild successfully lobbied to prohibit the American export of hats. Steel manufacture was limited, sugar refineries were banned and slave labor was forbidden in factories. William Pitt, the British Prime Minister, even threatened to unleash hordes of soldiers on the American colonies if they manufactured so much as one horseshoe or strand of yarn. In 1763, the colonies imported roughly two million pounds of goods from England, and on the eve of the Revolution, this had risen to three million.

The English did not interfere with the colonists' slave trade. After the monopoly of the Royal African Company was lifted, both English and American merchants were allowed to trade in African slaves, provided ten percent of the purchase price of this "imported merchandise" was deposited in the British treasury! As many as five thousand slaves were shipped to the North American continent annually in the middle of the eighteenth century, so that this "transportation tax" brought the British treasury a tidy sum.

The Trade and Navigation Acts helped widen the breach between the American colonies and the Mother Country. Though the Trade Acts were not particularly oppressive, the colonists took pains to evade them. The English were lax in their implementation of the Trade Acts, so that the import and export duties produced relatively little revenue. Nonetheless, the thirteen colonies felt that they were being treated like mere conquered territories. In their eyes, the advantages to the Mother Country far outweighed the sacrifices England had to make to maintain an army in the colonies in order to defend the colonists against the French and the Indians. The colonists believed that there was no reason for the British Parliament to levy a tax as well as reap the revenues from the Trade Acts.

The first and actually quite moderate step in the direction of greater colonial financial participation was taken during the Seven Years' War (1756 – 1763). To facilitate the collection of import duties by customs officials, England issued search warrants called "Writs of Assistance," permitting officials to search private residences, stores and warehouses on the mere suspicion that they contained smuggled goods. Legal protests proved worthless, because the Attorney General in London had decreed that the Writs of Assistance were a legal means of implementing the Navigation Acts. Nevertheless, England paid dearly for the increased revenues from the import duties and fines, as they signaled the beginning of the estrangement between the colonies and the Mother Country. At the end of the Seven Years' War, which had greatly bolstered the colonists' self-confidence, England ordered the customs officials to collect existing taxes strictly according to the book. But this measure only alienated England and the colonies even further. The colonists interpreted the order as a form of taxation for which they had not granted their consent. The more advances the American colonists made on the road to political and economic maturity, the more leaders there were to incite the people to British opposition. These protesters were labeled "Patriots." The term, originally meant to be derogatory, was borne with pride. The leaders of the Patriots, usually drawn from conservative governmental circles, had a powerful tool at their disposal: they were usually able to manipulate the masses at the town meetings. The great masses of American colonists frequently rioted to evince their discontent over, for example, the high cost of living, the corruption of the regents or oppressive taxation. Even so, American

*Samuel Johnson
(1709-1784) (from a
painting by Sir Joshua
Reynolds, 1756).*

society was well on the way toward democracy, in which large segments of the population participated. In this respect, the American colonies were far ahead of the Mother Country. The fact that several British parliamentarians backed the American colonists in 1765 – 1775 reflected their desire to provide England with a more democratic society as well. To the colonists, the economic curbs of the Trade and Navigation Acts were sufficient reason to complain about the English. On the other side of the Atlantic, few in the Mother Country said anything positive about the colonists. Samuel Johnson, the famous literary figure and philosopher, remarked in 1769: "Sir, they are a race of convicts, and ought to be thankful for anything we allow them short of hanging." Less educated Britons even thought that all Americans were black.

To return to the metaphor used at the beginning of this chapter, too few members of Parliament and other policy makers were as wise as the May 14, 1774 author of a letter to the editor of the Middlesex Journal. Characterizing the colonies as Britain's children, he noted: "When the child is become in turn a man, he does not cease for that to be a son, but he is a competent judge of his own actions; he still owes to his father respect and deference, but no longer blind obedience."

*William Pitt, Earl of
Chatham (1708-1778) (from
a painting out of William
Hoare's atelier, c. 1754).*

*William Pitt, Earl of
Chatham (1708-1778) (from
a painting out of William
Hoare's atelier, c. 1754).*

Tea

Tea, an exotic brew from China, was first imported to Europe by the Dutch in 1610. In less than a century, tea had conquered the Western world. The English, in particular, became ardent tea-drinkers. In the eighteenth century, an age dominated by elegant conversation and refined manners, the tea-drinking ceremony developed in the upper classes into a daily ritual of social intercourse. Enthroned behind the tea table, which sported family silver and costly Chinese porcelain, the mistress of the house conducted her guests like an orchestra. Each person was expected to pull his or her conversational weight by contributing with great wit and civility to the general mutual approbation, conversations on the Church, the government or literature and malicious gossip about those absent from the present company.

The middle and working classes also converted en masse to drinking tea. This addiction to tea was articulated by no less than Samuel Johnson, who described himself as "a hardened and shameless Teadrinker, who has for twenty years diluted his meals with only the infusion of this fascinating plant; whose kettle has scarcely time to cool, who with Tea amuses the evening, with Tea solaces the midnight, and with Tea welcomes the morning.''

Tea had an even greater impact on the economy. By the second half of the seventeenth century, the lion's share of the tea imported to Europe had been taken over by the English East India Company. The highest profits were soon reaped by the tea trade. It has been estimated that around the middle of the eighteenth century, the tea trade accounted for no less than ninety percent of the Company's profits. The tea trade's success can also be attributed to the fact that the Company had a monopoly in England. At the beginning of the eighteenth century, it annually imported something short of 100,000 pounds of tea. In 1730, this amount had doubled, and by 1760 a grand total of 4,000,000 pounds of tea were traded a year. Considering that a pound of tea was sold for an average of a shilling a pound in Canton and five times that in London, the profit margin was enormous, even after transport and other costs (including the largest budgetary item, taxes) were deducted. The English government had concluded fairly quickly that tea was a pure-bred milch cow. Around 1760, the tax on tea amounted to as much as 100 percent *ad valorem*.[1] The tax was calculated as follows: tea imported into England was subject to a 25 percent tax on the import value; in addition, an excise tax or inland duty of an extra 25 percent plus one shilling per pound was levied on domestic consumption.

The English East India Company, its Board of Directors and shareholders and the English government were not the only groups to profit from the tea trade. Entire branches of industry revolved around the seemingly unquenchable thirst of the English public for tea: potters, sugar planters, retailers and owners of tea houses and bars all profited from the brew. Another branch of industry was reanimated, namely smuggling. The high taxes turned the illicit importation of tea into England into a highly profitable business. The Dutch did not levy an import tax on the tea the Dutch West India Company imported to Holland. Hundreds of English merchants therefore purchased tea in Holland and, via the Channel Islands of Jersey and Guernsey, brought it ashore in the numerous isolated bays of Cornwall and Sussex. According to the estimate of a government official, during the 1770's, the English drank about 13 million pounds of tea annually, which works out to a formidable 2 pounds or 300 cups of tea per capita. More than half of that amount was allegedly smuggled.

Tea-drinking got off to a later start in the American colonies. Still, it gained rapidly in popularity until the per capita amount consumed was only slightly less than in England. After 1721, the colonists were only allowed to import tea from England. The English East India Company was not permitted to supply tea purchased in Canton directly to the colonies. Instead, the tea first had to be imported to England, where it was then auctioned. English merchants specialized in the tea trade with the American colonies bought up consignments in London, which were then shipped by American importers. A relatively small number of American merchants, with offices in Boston, New York and Philadelphia, controlled 90 percent of the market, and a limited amount of tea was also imported to Charleston. As we have seen, this tea was subject to a 25 percent tax when it was imported into England, and the tax was not refunded upon export, since the English government feared that the very same tea would be smuggled back into England. However, the 25 percent inland duty plus one shilling per pound was refunded, provided the exported article was still wrapped in the same packing as

1. *Ad valorem* refers to a tax (in this case a consumption tax) imposed at a rate proportional to the estimated value of the product. In contrast, the so-called specific taxes are imposed according to the contents or weight of the product.

when it was imported. The merchants were also required to pay a deposit that was only refunded upon receipt of a certificate stating that the tea had actually been imported into the American colonies.

To avoid the 25 percent import tax, Dutch and English merchants avidly smuggled tea from Holland to the colonies. A significant number of American merchants, including some very illustrious names, was engaged in smuggling, either as a main source of income or an avocation. Illegal tea imports in the colonies were so frequent that forged documents could be obtained to indicate that the tea had been imported from England. The tea was often secretly transferred to smaller boats off the coast and clandestinely brought ashore. Once the cargo had been brought on land and uncrated, it was impossible to tell whether the tea had been smuggled in or imported legally. Everyone, including the authorities, knew of the large-scale smuggling operations and that even established merchant houses engaged in smuggling. Much to the delight of a smirking public, customs officials could rely on fierce opposition if they chanced upon a smuggling operation. This state of affairs was damaging to the authorities in the three largest American harbors, and it germinated the first seeds of the later rebellion.

The smuggling activities in both England and the colonies drastically reduced the English East India Company's own tea sales. Consequently, in 1767, the Company proposed that Parliament lower the tax on tea in order to improve the Company's competitive position with respect to the contraband tea from Holland and other countries. The Company reasoned that a tax reduction might increase the legitimate tea trade, in which case the treasury would either suffer no losses or would be enriched by even higher tax revenues. Parliament adopted the proposal for a five-year trial period by passing the Indemnity Act, in which the inland duty on tea consumed in England was lowered and the 25 percent import tax on tea imported into the American colonies was made refundable.

The effects of the Indemnity Act on the tea legally imported from England were immediately discernible. In the first eighteen months after the new law went into effect, the legal import of tea soared 42 percent in New York and 100 percent in Philadelphia. To the non-smuggling American tea importer, the future seemed to be paved with streets of tea now that the import price was close to the price of the contraband. Nevertheless, one small cloud on the horizon would soon darken the entire sky: close on the heels of the Indemnity Act, Parliament adopted the Townshend Revenue Act, imposing a tax of three pence per pound (i.e. 2 ½ percent) on several products imported into the American colonies: glass, paper, lead, dyes and.... tea.

The Stamp Act

The Townshend Revenue Act cannot be explained without a discussion of the Stamp Act. Before discoursing upon the Stamp Act, however, it is necessary to describe England's attempts to force the colonies into assuming a greater financial share of the costs of colonial defense and government.

Thanks to the unceasing efforts of Prime Minister William Pitt, England emerged in 1763 as one of the victors of the Seven Years' War, having finally defeated France as a colonial superpower on the American continent. Although the war had been waged in defense of the thirteen colonies, the colonies had offered only partial assistance. Some colonial governments had vigorously supported the British, while others had acted as if the war had taken place on another planet. England had stood by helplessly while the colonies engaged in large-scale trade with the enemy; in fact, the French army was largely supplied by American tradesmen. Yet England had achieved a Pyrrhic victory, for the war had drained its financial resources. The national debt had nearly doubled, from 72 to 130 million pounds, and its budget had increased tenfold from 14.5 to 145 million pounds. Faced with sky-high debts as well as the obligation to maintain an army in the American colonies and pay the salaries of a sizeable number of government officials, the Mother Country tackled the Americans about assuming a greater portion of the financial burden. The idea of taxing the American colonies had been raised earlier, when Sir Robert Walpole was Prime Minister. This wise and cautious statesman had replied ''that it was a measure too hazardous for him to venture on; he should therefore leave it to a more daring successor in office to make the experiment!''

Up to this point, import and export duties had been levied in the American colonies, but as part of trade regulation. No one had imagined that these duties would ever be cited as an example to justify direct taxation of the American colonists, with the revenues being used to benefit the British treasury.

England's constitutional authority over the American colonies had never been brought up for discussion. English authority had never even been defined, much less analyzed. Basically, the colonies were generally allowed to govern themselves under British supervision. England could establish trade regulations and was responsible for the colonies' defense. Imposing taxes on the Americans was a novel concept that did not fit into traditional patterns of thought. The tax issue sparked off questions about the relationship between the Mother Country and the colonies. As explained earlier, the colonies already indirectly shared the economic burden, because the Trade and Navigation Acts brought sizeable revenues to the English treasury (in spite of frequent non-compliance). The colonies thus contributed to England's economic welfare. In addition to the levies imposed under the Trade and Navigation Acts, a duty had been imposed since 1733 on sugar and molasses imported to the American colonies. These revenues had also gone into English coffers.

During the Seven Years' War, the government in London had attempted to curb contraband operations by allowing customs officials who suspected smuggling operations to invoke police assistance. Immediately after the war ended, the British Parliament passed a law allowing British warships to be stationed in American waters, even in times of peace. To help curtail smuggling activities, naval officers were empowered to function as customs officials. England had already passed a similar law with respect to its own territorial waters. The Sugar Act of 1764 tightened the thumbscrews. Its provisions covered much more than sugar, as it was the first in a series of measures reorganizing the colonial system. While the Sugar Act admittedly sharply reduced the import tariffs on raw sugar and molasses, it raised the tariffs on refined sugar. Indigo, coffee, wine and textiles were subject to import duties, and the import of rum — essential for the Triangular Trades — was prohibited. Lumber, iron, potash, hides and pelts were placed on the list of enumerated commodities that were not allowed to be exported to Europe. The customs officials were granted more extensive powers,

England lampooned as an old man on a wooden leg and crutches, standing on one side of the Atlantic Ocean and threatening five American colonists on the other side. The Englishman leads them with a rope attached to hooks in the noses of four of the colonists.

and special courts of law were set up to more effectively enforce the Trade Act regulations. These steps were primarily intended to increase the revenue flowing into the English treasury.

The Americans were appalled by the Sugar Act because their profitable Triangular Trades (which they continued to operate via smuggling and evasion) would now be tightly controlled by the British. The Sugar Act set off a chain of fiery protests and the publication of pamphlets denouncing the British measures. From the beginning, the colonists had propounded the theory that a citizen was deprived of his liberty if he was taxed without the consent of his representative body. Without such representation, the colonists believed that citizens were mere slaves. For the first time, the colonists demanded that Parliament make an exception of the Americans in its tax legislation. Despite the far-reaching financial and economic impact of the Sugar Act, the opposition was limited to written protests, because the act did not break the pattern of British control over and regulation of American trade and industry.

The difficulties of implementing the stricter customs regulations were discovered by John Robinson, who owed his 1764 appointment as revenue agent in Newport, Rhode Island, to the reform of the customs system. The local merchants began by promising him a tidy annual sum if he would agree to look the other way when illicit shipments were brought ashore. But Robinson was an honest man and did not intend to succumb to the customary bribery. He set to work, but soon discovered that the local law court often failed to sentence the merchants he or his men had caught smuggling. The judge and the prosecuting attorney appeared to have scores of friends, including many of the merchants. When Robinson was temporarily out of town, the judge would quickly call up a smuggling case. When the prosecutor failed to appear in court, the merchant charged with smuggling was released for lack of evidence. If all members of the court happened to be present and a ship was actually impounded, its owner was able to buy it back cheaply at the auction, since no bids were forthcoming from the other merchants.

In April of 1765, Robinson confiscated the sloop *Polly*, which had failed to report its load of molasses, in Dighton, Massachusetts. Robinson left the ship under guard and returned to Newport. He hired a crew to sail the *Polly* from Dighton to Newport, where he could carry out the required confiscation procedures. Robinson's failure to locate willing crew members in Dighton should have alerted him that the *Polly* was loaded with more trouble than molasses. After his departure, the local populace stripped the sails from the masts, destroyed the cables and anchors, unloaded the molasses and then bored holes in the bottom of the ship, so that it sank part way and ran aground. When Robinson and his unsuspecting crew reached Dighton, a mob convinced the newcomers that it might be better to seek other work. Robinson went to inspect the half-ruined ship and was arrested by the police. The owner of the *Polly* had apparently filed charges for the 3,000 pounds worth of damage to the ship and the loss of the stolen cargo. Under police supervision and accompanied by a jeering mob, Robinson was made to walk the eight miles to Taunton, where the owner of the *Polly* lived. As he lacked sufficient bail money and no one was prepared to help him, he had to spend two days in jail. His friends in Newport secured his release when they heard of his arrest, but by that time Robinson had become a disillusioned man.

A year later, Parliament set out on a fundamentally different course by enacting the Stamp Act. This act required the American colonists to buy stamps, varying in price from a half-penny to 10 pounds, from the British government. These stamps were henceforth to be placed on contracts, court documents, appointments to public office, bills of lading, harbor clearance papers, liquor licenses and other legal documents as well as on playing cards, newspaper advertisements and pamphlets. The government in London had done little to accustom the American public to the idea of a stamp tax. George Grenville, the current Prime Minister, had merely arranged a meeting with a few official representatives of the colonies in London, where he informed them that the Americans would have to contribute more heavily to the British treasury. Grenville had been unable or unwilling to state any amounts, but had alluded to the probability of a stamp tax. He had refused to disclose any details, saying he felt sure everyone knew what a stamp tax was. Even though the colonies had an inkling of some kind of plan for a stamp tax, the Stamp Act itself came like a bolt from the blue. The colonies were almost immediately up in arms. Pamphleteers fired off a volley of pamphlets proclaiming that the British Parliament had no right to tax the colonies and that only the colonial assemblies could consent to taxation, in which case the revenues were to be considered a voluntary contribution offered the Crown from its citizens. Some pamphleteers contended that the Parliament could determine the import and export duties to regulate the economy as a form of external (or indirect) taxation, but that internal (or direct) taxation such as the stamp tax, which was only levied with the aim of providing revenue for the British treasury, was absolutely reprehensible. Other opponents considered this distinction to be legal hair-splitting; they felt that any tax whatsoever should first be approved by the colonies and their assemblies. During another meeting between the Prime

Small stamps with a big impact.

The "Pennsylvania Journal" used this device to express its opinion of the stamp tax.

Minister and the colonial agents, the latter acknowledged that it was reasonable to have the colonies share the financial burden, but insisted that the colonies themselves should determine how this was to be accomplished. In the meantime, petitions and protests poured in from the colonies, but these only aroused irritation in London.

The protests were accompanied by numerous riots, instigated by the "Sons of Liberty." This group of patriotic citizens borrowed its name from a speech given by one of the English opposition leaders in the House of Commons, Isaac Barré. During the debate in the British Parliament over the Stamp Act, in which not one of the members, not even those in the opposition, had denied Parliament's right to tax the colonies, Charles Townshend, the minister responsible for the colonies, had accused the Americans of ingratitude, calling them "children planted by our care, [and] nourished by our indulgence." Isaac Barré rebuked him, arguing that English oppression had driven the colonists to wild and uncultivated America and that the only nourishment the Mother Country had provided was to dominate the colonists and reap the profits, thus frequently bringing the blood of these "Sons of Liberty" to the boiling point.

British soldiers roughly clearing the road for the transport of the stamps.

The Sons of Liberty organized acts of violence and terror in an attempt to prevent the introduction of the Stamp Act. One of the more innocent forms of mob protest was for the crowds (usually incited by the leaders and frequently provided with free alcohol) to hang an effigy of some disagreeable character from a tree.

A straw doll is easy enough to make and there are always enough old clothes around, so that the enemies of the people can be hanged without doing violence to their persons.

And so it was in Boston, where Andrew Oliver, a stamp official appointee, and Lord Bute, the British Prime Minister, suffered for their sins by having their effigies dancing in the wind. Alarmed at the sight, the Governor, Sir Francis Bernard, looked to the Council for advice. The Councilors replied that it was nothing more than a childish prank. Bernard subsequently ordered the police to step in and remove the effigies, but they refused. After sundown, the mob set off, with the effigies in tow, for Oliver's newly built house. They ripped off whatever wood they could find and tore down the fence to make a bonfire for the effigies. Nothing was stolen from the house, but Oliver's stock of wine and his hopes were smashed to pieces. The Governor then asked the Colonel of the militia to call his men to arms, but the Colonel replied that it would be useless, as most of his men were part of the mob. The Lieutenant-Governor, Thomas Hutchinson, and the police chief went to view the scene and were driven away with stones. The preservers of law and order were therefore powerless to act. The riot died down around midnight, only because the participants were exhausted after so many hours of uninterrupted activity. Oliver declined to accept his appointment the next day, August 15th. But the rioting flared up again the next evening. Rumors were flying that Hutchinson (about whom we will hear more later) was one of the silent forces behind the idea of a stamp tax. The mob repaired to Hutchinson's house, but he refused to come out. As luck would have it, some gentlemen with well-established reputations were present, and they assured the crowd that the rumor was false. The damage was limited to nothing more than a few broken windows.

Unfortunately, this was not the end of the matter for Hutchinson. He had long been the target of Patriot leaders, who had launched fierce attacks against him in the newspapers and at town meetings. The Patriots were now asserting that while he might not be the author of the Stamp Act, he was its originator and prime advocate. The accusation was far-fetched, but the highly inflammable crowd was so easily stirred that more riots erupted. On the night of August 26th, a huge throng of people advanced on the house of the customs inspector and demolished his furniture. As this failed to assuage their rage, they moved on to Hutchinson's house. To borrow Hutchinson's own words: "the hellish crew fell upon my house with the rage of devils." He never contemplated fleeing his house, as he hoped to appease the mob himself. His daughter, however, refused to leave on her own, and Hutchinson considered it his duty to bring her to safety. In his absence, the frenzied hordes worked through the night, leaving little intact besides the walls and floors. Doors were battered, furniture was smashed to bits and clothes, beds and blankets were flung outside. The books and manuscripts that Hutchinson had collected in the course of thirty years were destroyed and thrown onto the streets. Nine hundreds pounds in gold bars were stolen, and all the silver disappeared. It took the rioters two hours to pull the dome of the roof down, and when daylight arrived, they were tearing off the roof tiles. Boston's Patriot leaders, dreadfully shocked by such an unprecedented outburst of rage and fearing a British reprisal, promised the Governor to maintain order with the help of the militia. The leaders convened a town meeting the next day, in which they expressed their abhorrence of the previous night's events. But no one took this stock statement seriously, least of all Thomas Hutchinson. The police, acting under the orders of the Governor and the Council, arrested the leader of the acts of violence. The actual instigators of the riot, fearing that the arrested ringleader would disclose their role in the affair, had threatened to withdraw the militia if he was not released. One day later, the leader was again walking Boston's streets

Thomas Hutchinson, born in Boston on Sept. 9, 1711. Governor of Massachusetts from 1771 to 1774. Died in London on June 3, 1780.

Governor Hutchinson and the Chief of Police fleeing the rioters.

as a free man. The popular leaders had decided that the attack on Hutchinson's house had been carried out by persons unknown, a view shared by many of Boston's prominent citizens.

After the events in Massachusetts, the stamp tax had become a dead letter. Some of the stamp officials did not even wait for violence to erupt, but resigned from their jobs. Others were made of sterner stuff. One of these was Jared Ingersoll of Connecticut, who had already decided to ignore the protests. He had good reason to hope his job would not be too difficult, for a number of citizens had already asked him to become the assistant stamp official. But Ingersoll was in for a rude awakening. Formerly a popular figure in his colony, he suddenly noticed that the public likened his initials to those of Judas Iscariot. The fact that his effigy was publicly burned in various places in the city was not so bad. Matters became more serious when Ingersoll suddenly found himself encircled and entrapped by a large crowd, which plunked him down under a sturdy tree and demanded to know whether he would relinquish his office. Protesting and refusing, he managed to keep the discussion going for several hours. But the crowd swelled in size and became more menacing. In the end, Ingersoll succumbed to the pressure and was forced to confirm his resignation later. And so Connecticut was delivered of the dreaded stamps.

The crowds in Newport, Rhode Island, carried on like those in Boston. As a result, the stamp official and the customs inspector fled to a British warship. Newport also experienced riots, during which houses were sacked. The leader, a young Irishman, was arrested, but was released under the pressure of the popular leaders, who had first incited the crowd to action and then feared for

*Public burning of the
stamps at the usual place of
justice.*

the consequences. In Virginia, a friendly welcome was extended to the official charged with implementing the Stamp Act, but he was given to understand that it would be in his best interests to leave immediately. He was on a boat for England the next day. In Philadelphia, flags were hung at half-mast and church bells rang continuously throughout the city the day the ships carrying the stamps arrived in the harbor. In New Jersey, the lawyers voted unanimously not to use the stamped paper, and the printers were quick to follow their example.

However, the political battle over the Stamp Act had yet to be waged. In October of 1765, the delegates of nine colonies met in New York at what is known as the "Stamp Act Congress." They drew up a "Declaration of the Rights and Grievances of the Colonists in America," which was sent to King George III and both Houses of the British Parliament. This document expressed their affection for the British Crown, but declared that the stamp tax was a new concept, contravened existing agreements between England and the colonies and constituted an attack on the exclusive right of the colonial governments to impose taxes on their own residents. The delegates rejected the notion that the Parliament in Westminster had the right to tax the Americans. They further declared that the Stamp Act contravened the basic principle laid down in the British Constitution of "no taxation without representation."

Another motive lay behind the protests against the Stamp Act: there was already a critical currency and gold shortage, and the colonists feared the Stamp Act would create an even larger drain to England. A boycott of English goods was set in motion. The merchants in New York, who were quickly joined by colleagues in other seaports, decided that as of January 1, 1766 they would not import any goods from England until the hated Stamp Act had been repealed. When the customary orders began to decline, the merchants in London, Bristol, Liverpool, Lancaster, Hull and Glasgow and manufacturers in numerous English cities realized that the boycott posed a serious threat to their economic well-being. Parliament was besieged with petitions asking for the quick repeal of the act that had so grievously harmed trade relations with the Americans. In the meantime, the colonies continued to rebel against the Stamp Act. The Sons of Liberty, manifesting itself as a political party, kept the fires of protest burning and bombarded the newspapers with an unremitting stream of letters to the editor, which the publishers did not dare refuse to print. From time to time, the Sons of Liberty burned stamps and hung effigies to pacify incited mobs. As a result of these efforts, the Stamp Act was repealed a year after it had been enacted.

The Stamp Act was also rescinded thanks to internal political relationships in the Mother Country. King George III wanted to assume a more active role in English politics than his two predecessors. Soon after he became King in 1760, he replaced the popular William Pitt by one of his favorites, Lord Bute, apparently indifferent to the fact that the country was in the middle of the Seven Years' War. George III was of the opinion that a small elite held too much sway over the Parliament. It was even possible to purchase one's seat in this legislative body. The King endeavored to extend his own influence as well as that of the people. His followers in the House of Commons were referred to as the "King's Friends." In the summer of 1765, supported by only the King's Friends and a handful of members representing mercantile and industrial interests, he appointed a new Cabinet. As was soon obvious, the new government was no match

George III William Frederick (1738-1820). King of Great Britain and Ireland and Electoral Prince of Hannover as of 1760.

THE REPEAL. — or the Funeral Procession, of MISS AMERIC-STAMP.

The "Miss Anne Stamp"
(also referred to as the
"Miss Americ-Stamp")
which is about to be buried
in this print is twelve
months old. Born in 1765,
she died in 1766 and her
casket is being carried to
the grave by the "gentle
mr. Stamper" (Lord
Grenville, fourth from the
left). The warehouses from
which trade can again be
carried out with the
American colonies are
shown in the background.
On the right is a package of
stamps which is being sent
back to England and a
chest with a statue for
Mr. Pitt.

for the insistent pressure of the many people, deeply shocked at the American boycott of English goods, who wished to repeal the Stamp Act.

In the beginning of 1766, Pitt — a good friend to the Americans and rated highly in the colonies — also became embroiled in the parliamentary dispute over the Stamp Act repeal. Serious gout attacks prevented Pitt from leading a physically active life. Despite the fact that he could no longer walk without crutches, eat with a fork or write legibly, he traveled from his home in Bath to Westminster on January 14, 1766, the day of the King's Speech, to recommend repeal of the Stamp Act. Pitt's impassioned speech took the government to task. England, he proclaimed, had absolutely no right to tax the colonies. While he believed the British empire had supreme sovereignty over the colonies, he felt the Americans had the rights provided by the English constitution. They were England's legitimate sons and not its bastards. He added that England, acting as the highest executive and legislative authority, could bind the colonies through its laws, regulations and restrictions on trade, navigation and industry. But the government should not be allowed to extract money from the Americans without their consent. He maintained — and this echoes the Late Middle Ages described in Chapter 2 — that taxation is not part of the executive or legislative powers; instead, taxation is a voluntary contribution from the representatives of the people.

The members were impressed by his eloquence but understandably puzzled as to why Britain should be allowed to bind the Americans through trade and navigation acts but not through taxation. The only person who dared pick up the gauntlet against the mighty Pitt's oratorical blast was George Grenville, who had been Prime Minister when the Stamp Act was enacted and who was strongly opposed to a conciliatory attitude toward the Americans. Grenville responded that the right to impose taxes was an integral part of the sovereign's power and that it applied to many interest groups not represented by the Parliament. Consider, for example, he said, the East India Company, London's merchants, shareholders and large industrial cities. He further argued that the Americans enjoyed the protection of the British government and that they merely had to obey its orders. He pointed out that the British nation had incurred massive debts to provide the colonies with this protection. Moreover, the Navigation Act had been modified on their behalf, and as Prime Minister he had done his utmost to promote American trade. When all was said and done, Grenville concluded, the Americans were simply ungrateful.

Pitt warmed up to his subject after Grenville concluded his speech. He brushed aside the argument that other interest groups were not represented in the Parliament by pointing out that these shareholders, merchants, etc. were landowners or city-dwellers and as such entitled to vote. Pitt considered Grenville's remarks about the ingratitude of the Americans to be much more invidious. While he was Prime Minister, Pitt said, Great Britain realized a profit of two million pounds a year on its trade with the Americans, and the proceeds had risen steadily since then. While the Americans had not always acted judiciously (a reference to their smuggling operations), they had been driven to their deeds by the injustice of the British government. Pitt's opinion was that "the Stamp Act [should] be repealed absolutely, totally and immediately." Not surprisingly, the Americans took his words to heart and erected statues in his honor.

Pitt's intervention set the tone for the debate that followed a few weeks later. A petition demanding the repeal of the Stamp Act was submitted by several merchants from the larger seaports, whose businesses suffered as a result of the boycott on English goods. The unrelenting agitation in the colonies became a frequent topic of discussion. Every ship sailing to England brought new and juicier details. However, the debate was largely devoted to deliberations on Britain's right to impose taxes on the colonies. The opposition denied that right. Referring to the principles of the *Magna Carta* and its later statutes, the opposition contended that British subjects could only be taxed upon their approval. Consent had to be secured either from the subjects themselves or from their representatives, i.e. the House of Commons. British subjects had taken that right with them when they emigrated to the colonies. Lord Camden emphatically expressed this concept in the House of Lords: "My position is this − I repeat it − I will maintain it to my last hour, taxation and representation are inseparable." He cited Locke: "The supreme power cannot take from any man, any part of his property, without his own consent." The government disagreed, declaring that the opposition's appeal to the constitution was too inflexible. After all, the constitution was still evolving, and a fixed system of representation via the House of Commons had only been in effect since Henry VII. The government maintained that it was imperative to consider the relationship between the Mother Country and the colonies as a whole. England offered protection and expected colonial dependence in return. In the government's view, taxation was intended to partially defray the

This cartoon illustrates the role played by William Pitt in the repeal of the Stamp Act. Pitt (on crutches because of his gout) bows to Britain, who is depicted as an old woman almost lying on the ground, while her daughter America, an Indian, stands at her side. "Have you a Mind to turn your Daughter adrift?" asks Pitt, whose statue has been erected along the coast (on the right). The British lion is sitting quietly in the foreground next to goods which have been marked with an arrow to indicate that they have been smuggled.

costs of maintaining the colonies, and was to be considered as a supplement to existing Trade and Navigation Acts, which the colonies had already accepted. The Americans were bound by the laws of Parliament on the basis of a legal construction in which they were considered to have consented to these laws as British subjects.

The British government was fully aware that the law could only be enforced by sending a large army to the other side of the ocean, and they were reluctant to take such a step. After several weeks of debate, the British Parliament voted on March 17th to repeal the Stamp Act by a wide majority. Elated, the colonies celebrated the repeal. The Sons of Liberty organized parties, during which affirmations of loyalty to the King and the Parliament were interspersed with shouts of triumph. Toasts to the King, the royal family, the Parliament and the Mother Country were drunk throughout the colonies, and everyone breathed a sigh of relief and returned to work as if nothing had happened. Very little of the breach between England and the colonies was visible. In a number of areas, the Sons of Liberty even dissolved their groups. Now that the basic rights of the colonies had been recognized, or so they thought, there were no longer any obstacles in the path to American welfare and prosperity.

The Townshend Acts

The repeal of the Stamp Act did not imply that the Parliament had relinquished its right to tax the colonies. At the time the Stamp Act was abolished, Parliament adopted the Declaratory Act. In fact, for many members of the House of Commons, this had been a precondition to the repeal of the Stamp Act. The Declaratory Act stated that the Parliament "had, hath and of right ought to have full power and authority to make laws and statues of sufficient force and validity to bind the colonies and the people of America ... in all cases whatsoever.'' Isaac Barré, assisted by William Pitt, lobbied unsuccessfully for the removal of the last four words. The Parliament viewed the British Empire as one centralized state, in which the Parliament itself possessed the highest authority. It naturally considered the imposition of taxes to be an integral part of that power. The colonies, still in a mood of celebration, had not perceived the catch, perhaps because the word ''tax'' had not appeared anywhere in the Declaratory Act. With the defeat of the Stamp Act, George III felt obliged to appoint William Pitt as the leader of the government. Pitt simultaneously accepted the title of Earl of Chatham and thus entered the House of Lords. This was a major political error. He had served his political apprenticeship in the House of Commons and had emerged as ''The Great Commoner,'' defender of the people against corrupt politicians, a vision he himself encouraged to the hilt. The new Earl of Chatham was not invincible; he suffered a defeat in the Parliament in the area of finances and was confronted with a budget deficit of 500,000 pounds sterling. What could be done? Chatham hoped to acquire some funds from the East India Company. But before he could arrange it, he suffered a severe attack of gout that progressively worsened, so that he was unable to head his Cabinet. Charles Townshend, charged with the financial portfolio, leapt into the vacuum created by Chatham's incapacitating illness. Unlike Chatham, Townshend was of the opinion that the Parliament did have the right to impose taxes on the colonies. His support of taxation was also motivated by the realization that it cost more than 400,000 pounds to maintain an English army in the colonies. Unencumbered by Chatham, Townshend pushed several proposals on the colonies through a protesting Cabinet. To shore up the British treasury in America, Townshend proposed imposing an import duty on glass, paper, lead, dyes and tea. The revenues were estimated to be 27,000 pounds, 20,000 of which would come solely from tea taxes. While the other goods were not crucial to British export to the colonies, tea was included on this list primarily because the Parliament was in the process of enacting the above-mentioned Indemnity Act. Townshend reasoned that this act would make legally imported tea in the colonies less expensive. Why not try to get a portion of this back for the English treasury? Parliament's successive enactment of the Indemnity Act and the Townshend Revenue Act meant that the 25 percent import tax levied in England would be refunded on tea destined for the colonies, and replaced by a 2 ½ percent import duty in America.

To help clamp down on smuggling activities, which might increase as a result of the new tax law, the government also proposed strengthening the customs system in the colonies. Accordingly, Parliament appointed five salaried commissioners (to be paid by the British Crown), one lawyer, various assistants and the necessary administrative personnel to administer and monitor the customs service throughout the colonies. Boston was to be their headquarters, presumably because of the magnitude of its violations of the Trade and Navigation Acts. Or perhaps it had something to do with the fact that the British Governor of Massachusetts, Sir Francis Bernard, had the most uncompromising attitude toward the Patriots, whose leaders he regarded as personal enemies. The Parliament may simply have felt that the despised customs system would be safer in Bernard's hands. As early as 1764, the Governor had proposed to the government in London that the rights in the colonies' charters be drastically curtailed. He deeply regretted the repeal of the Stamp Act, and had even gone so far as to propose abolishing the Massachusetts assembly.

This etching sketches three scenes from the year 1765. Britannia (in the middle), in a state of confusion, is leaning on an angry Indian, representing the American colonies. Lord Grenville, the promotor of the Stamp Act, is shown running on the right with his sword drawn, calling that he will enforce the Stamp Act. He is being checked by William Pitt (the later Lord Chatham), who informs him that he has no rights. Lord Camden is shown on the left, trying to prevent general warrants (writs of assistance) from being issued.

Much to the colonists' distress, the Townshend Acts also required the salaries of the servants of the British Crown in the colonies, starting with that of the Governors, to be paid directly from the import duty revenues. The local assemblies, which had previously determined and paid these salaries, would therefore lose their hold over these officials. Another point that inflamed tempers was that the tax had to be paid in hard cash, which put an additional strain on the already marginal circulation of money. It seemed as though whoever drew up the act had wanted to seize any available means to aggravate the Americans. The crowning blow came when customs officials were permitted to obtain court-ordered Writs of Assistance, giving them the right to unlimited searches on a mere suspicion of smuggled goods.

The colonies were slow to oppose the Townshend Acts, since news of the act only trickled into the colonies. When the Americans finally realized what was happening in the fall of 1767, they launched a series of protests that progressively increased in intensity. The pamphleteers set to work, once again bringing to the fore the fundamental question of whether the English Parliament had the right to levy taxes on the colonies. John Dickinson of Pennsylvania refuted the argument that the taxes in the Townshend Revenue Act were insignificant by remarking: "If they have the right to levy a tax of one penny on us, they have the right to levy a million upon us." He also mentioned the ship money trial of John Hampden.[2] While that case had only involved a few shillings, the whole of England had anxiously followed the case. Dickinson rejected the Townshend Revenue Act, because in his eyes any tax intended to collect American money for the British treasury was repugnant, even when disguised as a trade regulation

2. See pages 267-274.

measure. This reasoning was too subtle for American extremists, who simply believed that the Parliament in London had no right whatsoever to enact laws that were binding on the colonists.

In 1768, the General Court of Massachusetts sent a petition to the British Crown, requesting the repeal of the Townshend Acts. Lord Hillsborough, the newly appointed Secretary of State for the Colonies, was infuriated. He issued a circular to the Governors, ordering them to prevent their respective colonies from endorsing Massachusetts' petition. If that failed, the Governors were to dissolve the assemblies in their colonies, which they were entitled to do according to their charters. Governor Bernard was ordered to demand that the General Court withdraw the petition. If it refused, that legislative body was to be dissolved. This tactic boomeranged. The General Court refused to withdraw the petition by a vote of ninety-two to seventeen. The number "ninety-two" was thereafter venerated throughout the colonies, with many a toast being drunk to the Glorious Ninety-two. As a result of this effective piece of propaganda, the other colonies rallied around Massachusetts. Once again, British policy had achieved the opposite of what it had set out to accomplish.

Boston was again in an uproar. The five customs commissioners arriving in the city in November of 1767 were given a cool reception. Before long, the pinpricks of annoyance between the merchants and the customs officials had evolved into sword thrusts. Establishing the new customs headquarters in such a hotbed as Boston had been a political faux pas, as it was an invitation to trouble. The second anniversary of the repeal of the Stamp Act, celebrated on March 18, 1768, provided a convenient opportunity for the citizens to hang some of the tax officials in effigy from the Liberty Tree. Shortly thereafter, a series of incidents involving ships suspected of smuggling occurred in the harbor. The *Lydia*, owned by John Hancock, arrived in Boston Harbor in April. Customs was on the scene immediately, and two junior officials were sent on board to guard against cargoes being illicitly brought ashore. One of them foolishly ignored instructions and went below deck for an inspection, where he was detained by the crew. John Hancock was summoned, and before they knew what was happening, the two officials found themselves unceremoniously thrown off the ship.

The customs office was understandably intent on getting its revenge. A month later, another of Hancock's ships, the schooner *Liberty*, sailed into the harbor. The suspicions of the customs office were aroused when Hancock only reported a cargo of twenty-five cases of wine, a quantity way below the ship's cargo capacity. What is more, the imprudent Hancock had been boasting that he was going to outwit customs. Upon inspection, the tax officials found no traces of smuggling. The two customs officials who had boarded the ship reported no irregularities in their sworn reports.

John Hancock, painted by John Singleton Copley (1738-1815).

In the meantime, Hancock had the *Liberty* loaded with whale oil and tar, destined for the London market. According to regulation, Hancock, as the ship's owner, should have obtained permission from the customs office to load the cargo. However, the revenue service had never before enforced the regulation because it served no purpose in the execution of their official duties. But they wanted to teach Hancock a lesson, and besides, customs' share of the reward on this valuable cargo was substantial. So the officials blew the technical violation up out of all proportion.

The Patriot goldsmith, Paul Revere, crafted a silver goblet to the memory of the "Glorious NINETY TWO" (see text).

On June 10th, the revenue agent Joseph Harrison, one of the newly appointed officials, boarded the schooner in order to mark it with the sign of an arrow, indicating that the ship had been confiscated. The swelling roar of the onlookers on shore boded ill for the enterprise, so that the accompanying revenue agent Hallowel requested the assistance of the warship *Romney*. Under a hail of stones from the impassioned crowd on shore, the sailors of the *Romney*, in an open boat, succeeded in unmooring the schooner and tying it to the *Romney*, which then towed its prize to a safer location in the harbor. Powerless to halt what they regarded as an unlawful seizure of the *Liberty*, the onlookers vented their rage on the two customs officials, chasing them through the streets, pelting their houses with stones and burning Harrison's private yacht. The next day, four of the five customs commissioners (the fifth had Patriot connections and was left alone) and their families sought refuge on board the *Romney*. They went to live shortly thereafter in Castle William, a fort located in the harbor, carrying out their normal work activities from the fort. They only returned to the city six months later, long after Boston had quieted down. This was not the end of the matter, for the case took a surprising − and fortuitous − turn for the customs officials. The day after the *Liberty* was impounded, one of the two customs officials who had boarded the schooner in May informed the revenue agent that he wanted to amend the report he had filed the night the *Liberty* had arrived in the harbor. He was now prepared to testify that one of Hancock's captains had offered him a bribe, which he had refused, and that he was subsequently locked below deck for three hours. During that time, he had heard cases of wine being unloaded. On the basis of this statement, the case against John Hancock was changed from a petty violation to a serious smuggling charge. Counting the fines, the amount of money involved was more than 50,000 pounds sterling, a share of which would go to the customs officials, including the witness.

Despite the difficulty of proving guilt, the customs office persisted in charging Hancock not only with the violation of a customs formality, but also with wine smuggling. John Hancock had been until that time nothing more than a wealthy merchant unknown beyond the borders of Massachusetts. His name was soon to become a household word throughout the colonies, for the Patriots succeeded in turning the case into a *cause célèbre*. Although the Attorney General dropped the case after a year, the negative publicity inflicted considerable damage on the British cause.

In the aftermath of the riots surrounding the confiscation of the *Liberty*, the British government, fearing a repetition of the disorders two years earlier, dispatched two regiments to Boston. Benjamin Franklin's remark that an infantry regiment could not compel anyone to use stamps or drink tea if he did not want to was lost on the government. His warning that the troops would not find a rebellion but would create one likewise fell on deaf ears. Not surprisingly, the tense situation was only aggravated by the arrival of the troops on October 1, 1768. The city took its revenge by thwarting the soldiers' attempts to locate suitable quarters. The Council pointed to a clause in the charter which provided that the city could not be required to house and feed the soldiers so long as the harbor fort of Castle William was not filled to capacity. But the only reason the British wanted to quarter the troops in the rebellious city was to enable the troops to take immediate action when necessary. The troops were finally allowed to be quartered in old factories throughout the city, providing them with some shelter in the face of the cold New England winter.

A list of merchants who still took no notice of the non-importation agreement.

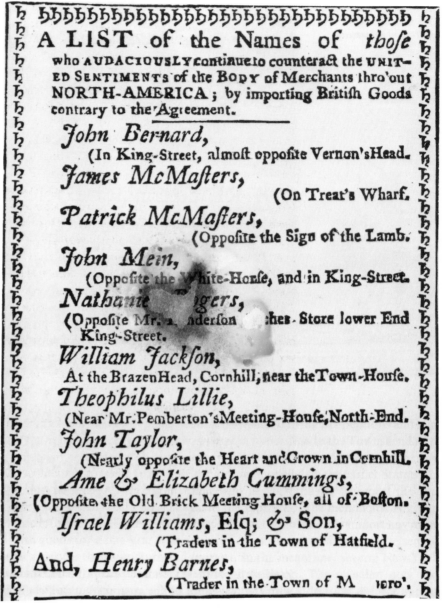

A LIST of the Names of *those* who AUDACIOUSLY continue to counteract the UNITED SENTIMENTS of the BODY of Merchants thro'out NORTH-AMERICA; by importing British Goods contrary to the Agreement.

John Bernard,
(In King-Street, almost opposite Vernon's Head.

James McMasters,
(On Treat's Wharf.

Patrick McMasters,
(Opposite the Sign of the Lamb.

John Mein,
(Opposite the White-House, and in King-Street.

Nathaniel Rogers,
(Opposite Mr. Henderson Inches-Store lower End King-Street.

William Jackson,
At the Brazen Head, Cornhill, near the Town-House.

Theophilus Lillie,
(Near Mr. Pemberton's Meeting-House, North-End.

John Taylor,
(Nearly opposite the Heart and Crown in Cornhill.

Ame & Elizabeth Cummings,
(Opposite the Old Brick Meeting House, all of Boston.

Israel Williams, Esq; & Son,
(Traders in the Town of Hatfield.

And, Henry Barnes,
(Trader in the Town of M   ero'.

English Parliament claiming the right to impose taxes on the colonies as it pleased.

Much had happened in England since the adoption of the Townshend Acts. The man to whom the act owed its name died suddenly in 1767 and was succeeded by Lord North. The Cabinet was still being led by the Duke of Grafton, as Chatham was still incapacitated by gout. When it came to his official duties, Grafton was hardly a model of diligence. He journeyed to London roughly twice a month to sign documents. While his visits to the horse races should have been diversions in his running of the nation, the reverse was usually the case. His most spectacular deed consisted of escorting his mistress, Nancy Parsons, to the opera, in the company of the Queen and the Duchess of Grafton, from whom he was divorced. In the year 1768, this event was the talk of London society, completely overshadowing the troubles with the Americans. The Prime Minister's daring act generated even more interest than the problems with John Wilkes, a radical and rather scatterbrained member of the House of Commons, whose attempts to thwart the government continually thrust him into the limelight. Soon after Townshend's death, the Cabinet took a novel step and created the position of Secretary of State for the Colonies. Lord Hillsborough, one of the King's Friends, was appointed to the post. Although at his wit's end with the Townshend Acts, he refused to amend his position that the acts would not be repealed so long as the Americans doubted Parliament's authority to tax them. Hillsborough's first deed of office consisted of addressing a circular to the colonial Governors, expressing "the high displeasure his majesty had conceived against his American subjects" and denoting American opposition as an open rebellion. This was the circular mentioned above, in which he ordered the Governors to quash any opposition to the Townshend Acts. The opposition in the House of Commons took the American matter very much to heart and emphasized the danger of compelling the colonies to pay the taxes by sending in the army. London merchants also appealed to the government to repeal the Townshend Revenue Act. In the beginning of 1770, the Cabinet devoted hours of debate to the issue. They were not so concerned about abolishing the levy on the other goods. The central question in their minds was what to do about the tea. The Cabinet finally voted, by a narrow five to four margin, to maintain the levy. The King's influence in the decision was apparent. Hillsborough and North, both part of the King's Friends faction, had lobbied heartily to maintain the import tax on tea. The point disputed by the Americans, i.e. whether the Parliament could compel them to pay taxes, was a decisive reason for these two men to maintain at least one imposition, namely that on tea, as a symbol of Parliament's right to impose taxes. To the outside world, in particular to the Governors of the American colonies, Hillsborough created the erroneous impression that the Cabinet had been unanimous in its decision.

In the spring of 1770, the British Parliament occupied itself with the issue of whether to maintain the tea levy. In the meantime, North had succeeded Grafton as Prime Minister. Much more active than his predecessor, North blocked every attempt at repeal. The opposition contended that the Parliament had no right to tax the Americans because they were not represented in the Parliament; that the costs of maintaining the customs service were higher than the revenues derived from the tea tax; that the interests of the East India Company were endangered by the increased smuggling; that the unrest and uneasiness in the colonies would continue; and that there was no need to maintain the tea tax as a symbol of England's right to tax the colonies. However, the opposition encountered North's point-blank refusal to make so much as one concession to the tea tax.

Benjamin Franklin, acting in his capacity as Massachusetts' colonial agent in London, conveyed the news that the Parliament did not wish to abolish the Townshend Acts to his principals in Boston. He stated in his letter that he hoped nothing would happen to undermine colonial loyalty to the King, expressing in several well-turned phrases the colonists' love for the King as well as the friendship and solidarity between the English and the Americans. This same letter was discovered in Boston six years later by a British officer, who forwarded it to the King. In the meantime, the War of Independence had broken out, and much blood had been shed. George III, who congratulated his ministers on their harsh laws against the colonists and who was annoyed at any public personality displaying a modicum of friendliness or tolerance toward the Americans, was able to read with his own eyes the extent of the love and loyalty to his person

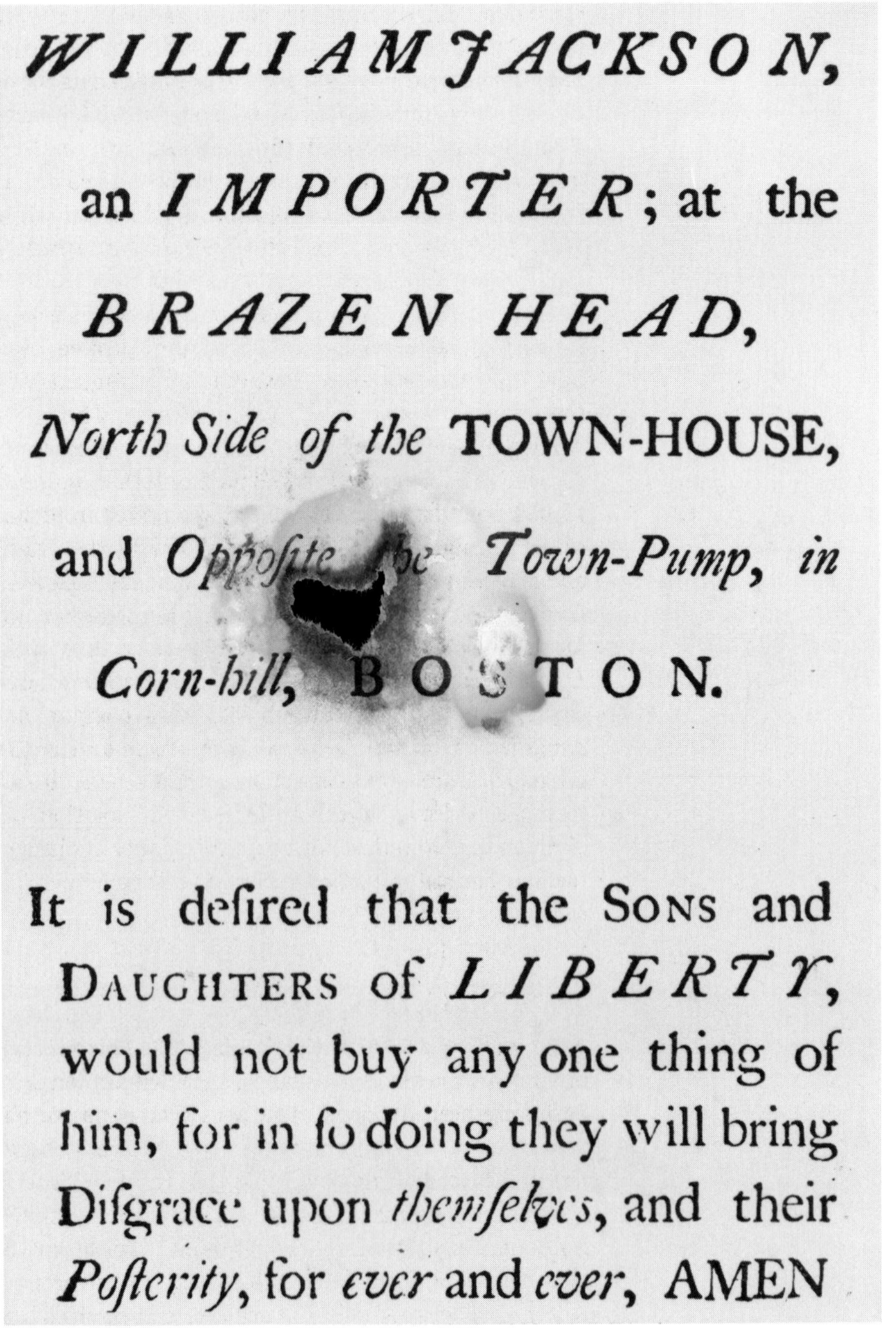

WILLIAM JACKSON,

an *IMPORTER*; at the

BRAZEN HEAD,

North Side of the TOWN-HOUSE,

and *Oppofite the* Town-Pump, *in*

Corn-hill, BOSTON.

It is defired that the Sons and
Daughters of *LIBERTY,*
would not buy any one thing of
him, for in fo doing they will bring
Difgrace upon *themfelves,* and their
Pofterity, for *ever* and *ever,* AMEN

and to England which had existed only a short time before. Now all of that had faded away. Only at this point did the Mother Country ascertain how much money had been siphoned off from the colonies to benefit the British treasury. An astute but anonymous member of the House of Commons asked in 1776 (after the onset of the Revolution) how much revenue the cultivation of tobacco had brought the British treasury before the war. Taking all relevant deductions into account, this was calculated to be 274,000 pounds a year for the years 1761 – 1775, or roughly two thirds of the entire deficit the colonies created for England. This amount had been paid by the tobacco planter, who received too little, and the British consumer, who paid too much. And this was only tobacco.

One is left with the inescapable impression that if the government in London had put its brains to better use or had paid more attention to government bookkeeping, it would have banished all thought of taxing the colonists, as they apparently already contributed enough to the treasury. This was exactly what the Americans thought. Not that the colonists were endowed with more financial insight. They simply intuitively felt that the amount they paid via the Trade and Navigation Acts was sufficient. Thus the lofty ideal of "no taxation without representation" is reduced to a simple matter of dollars and sense.

In May of 1770, the colonies were informed of the partial repeal of the Townshend Revenue Act. This sparked heated discussions about whether the non-importation agreement should be continued. They were loath to stop, since the boycott was now in high gear, and ships whose cargoes had been refused were being sent back to England. John Hancock of Boston offered his ship, the *Lydia*, for this purpose, and it had sailed off for London in May with a cargo worth 15,000 pounds. Ironically, there was no tea in its hold, because re-importation of tea to England was strictly forbidden by the Trade and Navigation Acts, and any offender was able to have his ship confiscated. The New Yorkers were the first to capitulate the import activities, and the Philadelphians followed on th heels. Boston, however, stuck to its guns, partly because sending the *Lydia* back to England had rekindled the flames of patriotic sentiment in that city. But their opposition also broke down, and in the middle of October, all that remained of the massive protest movement against the Townshend Acts was rancor and resentment against the merchants in the three largest harbors. The Bostonians were lectured for their obvious violation of the agreement, the New Yorkers were rebuked for being the first to capitulate after the partial repeal of the Townshend Revenue Act and the Philadelphians were berated for hesitating to sign the agreement.

Incidents

A relatively calm period began in 1770. For one thing, the tax issues had died down. For another, the plan to establish an Anglican episcopal hierarchy had definitely been dropped. The British government had never warmed up to the idea. The mere thought of strict bishops was sufficient to arouse American unrest, and the British had enough troubles with the colonies. Once this specter was removed, the colonies quieted down. The respite would last until 1773. This is not to imply that nothing was going on in the colonies during this period. One well-known incident from 1770 is the Boston Massacre. Day after day, Samuel Adams, one of the leaders of the Patriots, published in his Boston Gazette highly inflammatory stories about the atrocities and rapes committed by the British army of occupation, which had been quartered in the city since October 1768. Any soldier appearing alone on the streets would be beaten up by overgrown youths. A soldier lodging a complaint about the insults, snowballs, garbage and stones hurled at him could rely on the judge siding with the residents. On Thursday, February 22nd, the schools were closed for a day. Several boys, prompted by their parents, passed the time by pestering a storekeeper, a violator of the non-importation agreement, and sticking a caricature of him on the door of his store. His neighbor, Ebenezer Richardson, a known customs informer, ripped the paper from the door, thereby attracting the attention of onlookers. The boys followed him into his house and stones were thrown through the windows. Richardson, his wife and his daughter were struck, and a riot erupted. Richard-

Portrait of Samuel Adams (painted between 1770 and 1772 by John Singleton Copley, 1738-1815).

son grabbed his gun and shot into the crowd. One boy suffered light injuries, while another died eight hours later of severe wounds. Richardson was arrested and sentenced to imprisonment, but was later pardoned by the King. Thousands attended the boy's funeral.

Not surprisingly, an uneasy atmosphere permeated the city, and sporadic incidents occurred. A week later, trouble flared up again, only this time it was much more serious. On March 5, 1770, the same day the Parliament partially repealed the Townshend Revenue Act, there was a heavy clash. The moon had risen early that night and brightly illuminated the city. The temperature was way below freezing, and the snow was a foot deep. Because of the bright moonlight, the British sentry guarding the customs office in King Street could barely see the other side of the street, which had been cast in darkness and shadow. At eight o'clock, a riot broke out between civilians and soldiers: some boys had jeered at the soldiers and pelted them with snowballs and ice. Suddenly the bells began to sound a small alarm, which brought many people outdoors. The taunted soldiers were marshaled back to their barracks by the officers. Seeking a target upon which to vent its anger, the mass of people attracted by the incident headed for the customs office where the British government stored its money. As the sentry was surrounded on all sides by the crowd, the picket officer, Captain Thomas Preston, accompanied by a platoon of soldiers, set off to rescue the sentry. Having forged their way through the layers of people, the soldiers posted themselves in front of the crowd with their bayonets affixed to their rifles. The crowd had meanwhile swollen in size. Preston was taunted: why did he not shoot at the people? While he was explaining his reasons, fate struck. A club thrown through the air hit a soldier, who then fired at random. Or did he slip on the ice, causing the gun to go off accidentally? In any case, Preston called the man to account, demanding an explanation of why he had fired without orders. At that same moment, Preston too was struck by a flying object. The mob then launched a general attack. The soldiers, facing the dark side of King Street, responded by firing six or seven times, although no one had given the order to shoot. The crowd fled, leaving behind five dead and a handful of wounded. The soldiers maintained that they had heard the word "fire." The unfortunate Preston was put in an awkward position, for a number of embittered residents would later swear before the examining magistrate that Preston had given the order to fire, although others denied this. The possibility that someone in the crowd had yelled "fire" cannot be ruled out. One of the wounded, an Irish immigrant, declared before dying: "I have been through a lot of riots in Ireland, but I have never seen English soldiers endure so much as here in Boston without starting to shoot."

Preston emerged from the case with his good name intact, for the judges ruled that he had been on a legitimate mission and that it had not been proved that he had called out the word "fire." Preston also owed his acquittal to the fact that he wisely chose two Patriot lawyers, Josiah Quincy and John Adams, to defend him and the two soldiers accused with him. In spite of intense pressure, these two attorneys managed, with admirable diligence and objectivity, to obtain an acquittal for their clients. Another Patriot leader, Paul Revere (a goldsmith and graphic artist), made a drawing after the event, which was used for propaganda. In his version, the crowd was transformed into a number of exquisitely bewigged gentlemen wearing three-cornered hats, and the one black victim was omitted from the picture. The Boston Massacre, either devised or incited by Samuel Adams, was commemorated annually by the Patriots. More important-

Paul Revere (1735-1818). Patriot leader in Boston and a talented goldsmith (see picture on page 322).

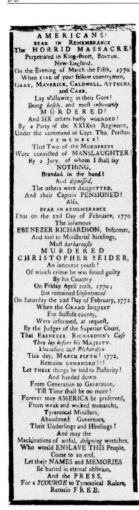

Two years after the event, the Boston Massacre is once again made use of in an inflammatory Patriot handbill.

ly, a few weeks later the British troops were withdrawn from the city and quartered in the fort on Castle William, much to the regret of Governor Hutchinson, who had his hands full maintaining law and order in the rebellious city.

Another incident occurred in June 1772 when two hundred residents of Providence, Rhode Island, carried out a night attack on the schooner *Gaspee*, which had run aground during an ebb tide. The *Gaspee* had been ordered by the revenue service to guard the coast against smugglers. Its captain was wounded in the attack, and the ship was burned to the water line. The people had taken their revenge on the *Gaspee* because its captain performed his task mercilessly and because the crew went on land at will to chop down trees for fuel and steal sheep to supplement their scanty meals. The English government took the case seriously and appointed an investigative committee. The committee did not have an auspicious beginning: when Admiral Montagu arrived in the colony to give his statement, the Governor re_____ _____ _____ _____mary salute, stating – with a deadpan expressio_____ th_____ _____ _____for budgetary reasons to holidays. The admiral deer_____ _____ _____turn the ship around. One of the witnesses then bolted. As th_____ _____ _____so had good reason for not appearing before t_____ c_____ _____ _____oundered. In any case, the committee had pre_____ _____ _____t had been provoked by the objectionable beh_____ of t_____ _____ of t_____ _____pee.

The investigation did, however, have an unforeseen consequence. The investigative committee was authorized to send any of the accused to England to stand trial. The House of Burgesses in Virginia was incensed. Although Virginia was far from Rhode Island and as a purely agrarian colony had little to do with issues of this kind, its citizens were alarmed at what they perceived to be a threat to American society. They therefore took the initiative and created a Committee of Correspondence, whose purpose was to maintain contact with the other colonies about matters of common interest with respect to the relationship between England and the colonies. Other colonies followed suit, and within six months a communication network had developed among the colonies. This network later assumed crucial importance, when the colonies organized an actual resistance movement against the British.

Constant skirmishes took place with customs officials about the smuggling of tea and other goods falling under the Trade Acts. Just as a smoldering fire can suddenly catch flame, these clashes occasionally flared into violence. To cite an example, at the end of November 1771, John Swift, head of the customs service in Philadelphia, sent his customs boat down the river to inspect a pilot boat sailing upstream from Chester. When the officials boarded the boat, they discovered a suspicious cargo of crates containing what appeared to be smuggled tea. The officials seized the ship, intending to take it back to Philadelphia. But as the tide had turned, they had to anchor alongside the boat. During the night, both ships were taken by surprise by a group of people in another pilot boat. The customs officials were attacked with "clubs, cutlasses and guns" and locked in their own cutter, which had been cast from anchor. The cutter washed up onto a mud bank, and the raiders took off in the two pilot boats.

John Swift had previously suffered another unsettling experience. When it was known in London that a ship with a cargo of tea had left the Continent for America, the customs authorities in the colonies were notified as quickly as possi-

Print of the Boston Massacre (March 5, 1770) drawn by Patriot and goldsmith Paul Revere for propaganda purposes. The drawing contrasts sharply with the facts described in this book!

ble. In November of 1770, Swift had received a report stating that the *Speedwell* had left Gothenburg, Sweden, with a cargo of tea and was heading for Philadelphia. The schooner arrived in the harbor the day after Swift received the report. He boarded the *Speedwell* immediately, but only found the hold filled with coal. Suspecting that the tea lay under the coal, he ordered the coal to be unloaded, at the expense of the customs service. Not a trace of tea could be found. As Swift still suspected deception, he ordered the crew to be interrogated, disregarding the captain's demand to be granted clearance as he had to sail his ship immediately to Carolina. The crew members he managed to locate refused to testify, claiming that they were not required to cooperate in what might result in legal proceedings against themselves. Presumably inwardly seething, Swift departed the ship convinced that the captain had employed the usual practice of bringing the tea ashore at the mouth of the Delaware River before sailing the ship upstream. Because the coal had been unloaded and reloaded in vain, with the costs borne by customs, Swift had been taught an expensive lesson. In his report to London, he wrote gloomily: "In this country, an officer of the Customs ought to see his way very clear before he ventures to make a seizure, because he is sure of having every possible difficulty thrown in his way; he is looked upon as an enemy to the community and treated accordingly, and whether he succeeds or not he is sure never to be forgiven, and thinks himself fortunate if his punishment is deferred to a future day...."

The East India Company starts shipping tea to America

Apart from these incidents, all was quiet on the tea front in this period. The extent of the calm can be measured by the number of debates in the House of Commons. In the years 1771 and 1772, there were no deliberations on American issues. Instead, the House devoted itself to the crisis surrounding the Falkland Islands. In 1773, America did not warrant more than a single column in the "Historical Summary." By contrast, in 1775, no less than 142 out of 158 columns were devoted to American matters!

Even though the British Members of Parliament had not occupied themselves with the topic of taxes in the American colonies since 1773, this does not mean the issue of taxation escaped their attention entirely. In that year, the Irish Parliament considered imposing a tax of two shillings a pound on the produce of estates whose owners did not live in Ireland. The Irish government, hard pressed for money, greedily latched onto the idea. The English government was prepared to accept the tax so long as it was strictly confined to Ireland. English landowners possessing estates in Ireland (several of whom had seats in both Houses of the British Parliament) rose up in protest. A request signed by some of the most illustrious names in England was sent to the Privy Council, urgently requesting that the Irish tax bill not be approved. Chatham turned his back on them. He felt that if the Irish House of Commons viewed the tax as an acceptable solution, it would be contrary to the principles of the constitution for England to forbid it. The bill was finally defeated in the Irish Parliament by a narrow majority. Apparently the English landowners had a greater influence in Dublin than in London. This defeat averted what would have been the shameful spectacle of a complaint being lodged in an English House of Commons − which wanted to impose taxes on the Americans without their consent − about the fact that the Irish Parliament wanted English estate owners to contribute to the expenses of the Irish state.

This period was apparently the calm before the storm. The precipitating cause of the storm in 1773 was the English East India Company. For a variety of reasons, the Company – a mighty bulwark of capitalism but not as reliable as the Bank of England – found itself in financial difficulties and had turned to the English government for assistance. Inevitably, endless discussions ensued about whether help should be offered, and if so, in what form. A certain Robert Herries finally devised a plan that would be the key to the solution. Herries' starting point was the Company's 18 million pounds of surplus tea. If the Company were to dispose of the surplus on the European continent, the state would have to refund all the import duties paid on the tea. While Herries realized that such a large supply of tea would distort the market on the Continent, he expected that the party to suffer from the plan would be the continental merchants. Disposing of the surplus would be a great boon to the Company's liquidity. It would be relieved of interest payments, storage fees and worry over the deteriorating quality of the tea. Under existing laws, the Company could only sell its tea at wholesaler's auctions in London. To implement Herries' plan, it was therefore necessary for the House of Commons to grant permission for the export of the tea and the tax refund. Seeking advice, the Company approached Hope & Co., an Amsterdam-based Anglo-Dutch banking and trading house with an international reputation. Hope & Co. suggested an alternative solution. It concluded that it would be less disruptive to the market to let the English wholesalers in London handle the export. The Company, equally dissatisfied with this proposal, then hit upon the brilliant idea of selling only part of its tea surplus to the Continent and shipping the rest to the American colonies. Parliament's consent was also needed for this plan, including the tax refund. During the debates in the Commons, one of the members of the opposition, William Dowdeswell, brought the House's attention to the delicate question of tea duties imposed in America in accordance with the Townshend Revenue Act. "I tell the noble Lord now," he said prophetically, "if he don't take off the duty, they won't take the tea."

But Prime Minister North remained as obdurate as ever. He had no intention of abolishing the tea duty levied under the Townshend Revenue Act. The idea of simultaneously reducing the tax refund by 2 ½ percent, so that total repeal of the act would cost the treasury nothing, likewise found no favor in his eyes. The proposal of exporting tea to the American colonies was then approved, and on May 10, 1773, the Tea Act of 1773 went into effect.

The next hurdle was to locate merchant houses with sound reputations in the American harbors who would take the tea on consignment and bear the responsibility for sales and payment to the East India Company. The Company would also have to secure the necessary cargo space on America-bound ships. The first problem was easier to solve than the second. Although consignees had been contracted in the three largest harbors, various captains, including James Scott of Hancock's ship *Hayley* and some New Yorkers, refused to carry the cargo. The Company finally found the cargo space it needed. This included the brig *William*, owned by Jonathan Clarke, one of Boston's consignees. Only one obstacle remained. The Company's Board of Directors realized that the payment of the Townshend tax on tea in the colonies might lead to problems. Their solution was to issue bills of exchange in London to cover the amount of the tax. It consequently appeared as if the duty had been paid in England. Lord North approved this method of payment, thereby in his eyes disposing of the problem.

Around the end of September, the tea ships the *Dartmouth*, the *Eleanor*, the *Beaver* and the *William* sailed down the Thames toward Boston; the *London* was bound for Charleston and the *Polly* for Philadelphia. They were later joined by the *Nancy*, bound for New York. The ships carried a total of more than 2,000 crates in their holds, good for almost 600,000 pounds of tea. On October 18th, when the wind had turned in a favorable direction, they sailed into the English Channel en route to America.

Vague reports of the East India Company's plans to ship tea to America only began to trickle back to the colonies at the end of August 1773. The details were disclosed a month later. New York, the first to oppose the plans, issued a series of pamphlets. The first of these, entitled *Alarm*, no. 1, was signed by the meaningful nom de plume of "Hampden"! The first issue covered two points. First, if the tea tax was not abolished, other taxes were sure to follow. Second, if the East India Company succeeded in obtaining a monopoly on a certain product, it would soon monopolize America's entire foreign trade. Subsequent issues of *Alarm* declared that these two points were part and parcel of a wicked conspiracy between the East India Company and the British Crown, designed to subjugate the colonies and bleed them dry through trade monopolies and taxes.

The colonists immediately saw through the shabby ruse in which the tax money was paid in London rather than in the colonies. One New Yorker ridiculed the practice by asking: "Are Americans such blockheads as to care whether it be a hot red poker or a red hot poker?". It was not long before there was public uneasiness about the Company's plans in all layers of society. The flames of unrest were further fanned by commentaries and letters to the editor printed in the newspapers. The letters contained an increasing number of thinly veiled threats. The consignees, some of whom were New York's most respected citizens, gradually began to feel the heat.

New York's consignees first pressed for a compromise, proposing to store the tea until they had received further instructions from the Company. The Company was to be informed that the shipment of tea had led to great unrest among the New Yorkers. The crafty consignees reasoned that once the tea from the smuggling trade was sold out in the spring, the Company would be able to sell its tea with ease. The proposal found no favor in the eyes of the Patriot leaders. Bringing the tea ashore was akin to accepting the tax, and that meant virtual slavery. The plan evidently leaked out, for a letter appeared two days later, warning that anyone helping to bring the tea ashore would get what he deserved. This meant tar and feathering at the very least.

As the end of November approached, the New York consignees began to realize that it might not be wise to bring the tea ashore against the will of the people. After all, unloading the tea would automatically imply that the tax would have to be paid. Like it or not, the consignees agreed not to implement the Company's order so long as that meant a de facto payment of the tax.

On December 1st, the consignees petitioned the Governor and the Council (one of the consignees was actually a Councilor), requesting them to assume responsibility for the tea and order the warship the *Swan* to escort the tea ship into the harbor. In a letter simultaneously addressed to the Company, they asked to be discharged from their duties as consignees. If the Company could somehow get the tea tax removed, they would be able to sell 1,500 to 2,000 cases of tea a year in New York. The argument that the Company was busy trying to create a tea monopoly was apparently less objectionable, at any rate in the eyes of the consignees.

Philadelphia raised the same objections to the tea shipment, and Philadelphia's consignees were soon forced to give way. Their decision to capitulate was hastened by the fact that the Patriot leaders had arranged a successful mass meeting, during which the consignees were asked to renounce their commissions.

Monday Morning, December 27, 1773.
THE TEA-SHIP being arrived, every Inhabitant, who wifhes to preferve the Liberty of America, is defired to meet at the STATE-HOUSE, This Morning, precifely at TEN o'Clock, to advife what is beft to be done on this alarming Crifis.

Philadelphia also digs in its heels against the tea shipments!

The situation in Boston

How would the situation develop in Boston? Before going into the events which took place in that city, let me introduce the persons who were to play leading roles in the Boston Tea Party by outlining the positions and motives of the Governor, the consignees and the Patriots.

The highest English authority in Massachusetts was the American-born Governor, Thomas Hutchinson. After a successful mercantile career, he became Supreme Court Judge and then Lieutenant-Governor. Hutchinson was a wealthy and well-educated man, who as author of "The History of Massachusetts" had also earned a reputation as a historian. He was appointed Governor in 1769, as successor to Sir Francis Bernard, whose position had gradually become untenable. The new Governor's salary was fifteen hundred pounds a year, and that of his Lieutenant-Governor and brother-in-law, Andrew Oliver, three hundred pounds. Both salaries were to be paid from the tea duty revenues. Although the Patriots considered Hutchinson a tyrant and claimed that he had been a proponent of such repressive measures as the Stamp Act and the Townshend Acts, he had never supported the idea of the English Parliament taxing the American colonies. In the summer of 1773, he had even written to Lord Dartmouth – the more moderate Secretary of State for the Colonies, who had replaced Hillsborough and who maintained excellent personal relations with several prominent Americans – that in his view the benefits the colonies had offered the Empire should spring from well-regulated trade relations and not from taxation. Despite this moderate tone, Hutchinson believed that there was too much popular influence in Boston, as manifested in the General Court and the town meetings. Worse still, he had to contend with the fact that the influence of the people of Massachusetts made itself felt not only through legal channels, but also through riots and disorders. The fact that the mob had sacked his house during

*Benjamin Franklin
(1706-1790) (from a
painting by Joseph Siffred
Duplessis).*

the Stamp Act crisis and that the Patriot leaders tried to frustrate his every plan clearly did not make the Governor any more charitable toward the desires of the people.

The Patriots were provided with a splendid opportunity to thwart Hutchinson and Oliver when private letters the two men had written to the deceased Thomas Wateley were made public. These letters contained unflattering remarks about the Patriot leaders and intimated that it was high time for this far-reaching popular influence in Boston to be curtailed. Samuel Adams made clever use of the letters: they were read aloud in the General Court. The assembly then requested the government in London to remove Hutchinson and Oliver from office, but the English were affronted by the impudence of this unprecedented request.

For Benjamin Franklin, this matter carried a sting in its tail. It was Franklin who had actually been handed the letters and who had passed them on to the Chairman of the General Court of Massachusetts, later requesting that the letters not be copied or made public. The publication of the letters had also created a stir in London. Franklin, fearing that his role in the matter would be revealed, maintained a low profile. But when Wateley's brother and executor arranged a duel with pistol and swords in Hyde Park with the person he suspected of purloining the letters, Franklin felt obliged to break his silence. He took out an advertisement, in which he admitted his role in the affair. Franklin's admission provided the English government with a splendid opportunity to cut the offending colony's agent down to size. They were all the more inclined because the news of the Boston Tea Party had just crossed the Atlantic. In a public session of the Privy Council, in which all members were present and the rooms and antechambers were bulging with spectators, the riots in Massachusetts were expatiated upon and the Attorney-General censured Franklin for his indiscretion. For good measure, Franklin was chastised for the impudence of his American principals. The sixty-eight year old Franklin heard this torrent of abuse in stoic silence. The next day, he was dismissed from his post as Deputy Postmaster-General for America. After this humiliation, Franklin relinquished his other colonial positions and returned to the colonies. No one, least of all Franklin, could have suspected that the pinnacle of his career was yet to be reached.

Back in Boston, Hutchinson had asked to be relieved of his post even before the problems with the tea ships arose. Nonetheless, he was determined not to give an inch. He backed his resolve with what he felt were sufficient soldiers, warships and government officials to prevent any acts of mass violence. The naval fleet was under the command of Admiral John Montagu, a notoriously loud-mouthed bully. Montagu was able to monitor all incoming and outgoing ships from the fortress on Castle William in Boston Harbor, where the British troops were stationed. When necessary, he could compel ships to turn around or even send them to the bottom of the bay with a few well-aimed volleys from his cannons. Hutchinson's greatest supporter among the government officials was the revenue agent, Richard Harrison. Harrison had already experienced some nasty treatment at the hands of Boston's Patriots. In June of 1768, he had accompanied his father, at that time the revenue agent, in the previously described mission to seize John Hancock's sloop the *Liberty* for a technical violation of the Trade Acts. The crowd had chased the young Harrison through the streets and pelted him with stones and garbage, until he was rescued by a handful of friends. Even if he had not suffered this unfortunate experience, Harrison would not have been a man to quickly make concessions. Once he had reached a position, he refused to abandon it.

In Massachusetts, unlike in Philadelphia and New York, the Governor and the consignees pursued the same course. This may have had something to do with the fact that the Governor's two sons were consignees. They had hinted to their father in the summer of 1773 that he should try to persuade the Company to appoint him as consignee. Thomas Jr. and Elisha Hutchinson, known popularly as "the children," were not the only consignees. They shared this distinction with the Clarkes and a couple of less prominent merchants.

Richard Clarke, whose daughter was married to Thomas Hutchinson, Jr., had been active in the American tea trade for decades, together with his sons Isaac and Jonathan, who traveled regularly to London on business. The Clarkes and the Hutchinsons had been the last to sign the non-importation agreement in 1769. They were also responsible for the bulk of the 2 ½ percent taxed tea that had arrived in Boston after the boycott ended in 1770. The array of local Patriots had long been a thorn in their sides. If the Bostonians had known that Lord North had preserved the tea tax because he found the importation of tea to Boston to be so encouraging, they would have been even angrier than they already were!

The owner of the first tea ship to sail into Boston Harbor, the *Dartmouth*, was Joseph Rotch, although his twenty-three year old son, Francis, generally deputized for his father. In the events to follow, Francis was forced to steer a delicate course between the demands of the Patriots and his obligations as shipowner.

The Patriot leaders in Boston had always vehemently opposed Parliament's alleged right to levy taxes. They considered the greatest danger of the tea ships to lie in the Townshend Revenue Act rather than in the monopolistic tendencies of the East India Company. If the tea operation succeeded, the Townshend Acts could be extended to include other articles. However, the Patriots had tarnished their reputations by the published violations of the non-importation agreement by Boston's merchants and now wished to make amends. Their strength lay in the fact that they were well organized, knew how to play on public sentiment and could assemble large masses of people at will. Their leaders were Samuel Adams, John Hancock, Joseph Warren, Paul Revere, William Molineux and Thomas Young. The driving force behind them all was Sam Adams. Born in Boston in 1722, the son of a brewer, he was sent at an early age to Harvard, where he received a degree. He had worked for some time in Boston as a revenue agent, where it was noted that his ledgers were always hopelessly in arrear. Making an early start in local politics, Adams had climbed to great heights by always throwing himself into the breach for the liberty of the people and thus winning the trust of both the merchants and the lower classes. Adams was devout, with the moral and religious zeal of a Puritan. More importantly, he was a gifted orator, who knew how to manipulate the masses to his advantage. In addition to writing fiery and passionate pamphlets, Adams organized parades and semi-military meetings, during which the attendees were regaled with oratory and generous amounts of food, drink and music. Hutchinson once called Adams "the great incendiary leader." Those Americans wishing to remain loyal to British authority later called the Revolution "Adams' conspiracy," and Lord North disparagingly referred to the Patriots as "Sam Adams' crew." King George III himself ordered Adams to be hanged the moment he was captured. Adams was also deliberately excluded from the general amnesty offered to break the stalemate just prior the war. At the very least, it could be said that Adams did not always use the most savory methods to attain his goals. His enemies were harsher in their judgments and looked upon him as a brilliant student of Machiavelli. Adams was a rugged Puritan, like his opponent, Thomas Hutchinson. Hutchinson, however, was driven by thoughts of money and his career. Adams had no such motives.

The vehement opposition to the East India Company tea may seem out of proportion at first glance, as the duty on tea imported to the American colonies since the 1767 Townshend Revenue Act amounted to a mere 2 ½ percent. In the years following the act, the revenues from the tax had been marginal as a result of the non-importation agreement, the boycott on tea and the prodigious growth in tea smuggling. Dowdeswell, the member of the Commons who had unsuccessfully pressed for abolition of the tea tax, had calculated that the revenues amounted to only 400 pounds annually, and Lord North had not challenged this assertion.

Knowing that the East India Company was anxious to be rid of its excess tea, the Patriot leaders feared the Company would flood the colonies with cheap tea. The smuggled tea would be no match for low-priced Company tea, and the Americans might thus be induced to pay the 2 ½ percent import duty.

The Boston Tea Party

It was not until the middle of October of 1773 (and therefore later than in New York and Philadelphia) that Boston began opposing the tea shipments and pressuring the consignees. On November 2nd, Richard Clarke was awakened at one in the morning by a loud knocking on his front door. He saw two men standing in the moonlight in his front yard. They called out that they had a summons for him to appear the next day at twelve o'clock at the Liberty Tree to publicly withdraw as consignee. Similar letters had been distributed in the night to his fellow consignees. The next day, the residents of Boston were invited by means of fliers posted throughout the city to witness the consignees' resignations. A large crowd gathered under the Liberty Tree on Wednesday, November 3rd, but Clarke and his colleagues were nowhere to be seen. In fact, at that precise moment, they were a few blocks away at Clarke's place of business, trying to decide what to do. Before long, William Molineux appeared on the doorstep with the message that the populace demanded their resignations from their commissions. The consignees yelled through the open door that they wanted to have nothing to do with the demands of the people. Part of the crowd which had followed on Molineux's heels then retreated, but another group stormed the store before the doors could be bolted and threw stones and garbage. The consignees barely escaped by fleeing to the attic, where they were protected by a strong door. Discouraged, the crowd withdrew. The consignees were able to proceed to their homes without further hindrance, but they were shaken by the incident.

The pressure on the consignees was increased that same evening when another of their number received an intimidating letter containing thinly disguised threats of bloodshed. On Friday, November 5th, an official town meeting was convened by the selectmen,[3] and John Hancock chaired the assembly. A committee was formed to request the consignees to abandon their plans, but they again refused. They pleaded that they could do nothing about the tea since they had not received any further instructions from the Company. Earlier, the consignees had spurned the demands of the spontaneously organized mass meeting. They now took matters a step further by ignoring the wishes of a legitimately convened town meeting. At this point, the consignees decided it was no longer advisable to remain in the city at night, and they sought safer accommodations in the surrounding area.

Thomas Hutchinson was now faced with a likely deterioration of the situation. As Governor, he was also Captain-General of the colonial army. In this capacity, he ordered the Commander of the Cadet Corps, John Hancock, to summon the company to arms. For the time being, Hancock ignored the order.

On Wednesday, November 17th, Hancock's ship, the *Hayley*, arrived in Boston Harbor. Captain James Scott, who had refused on this occasion to transport tea for the Company, brought a passenger with him. His passenger was Jonathan Clarke, a man who had done everything in his power to get his firm appointed as consignee.

3. The selectmen were charged with the organization of the town meetings.

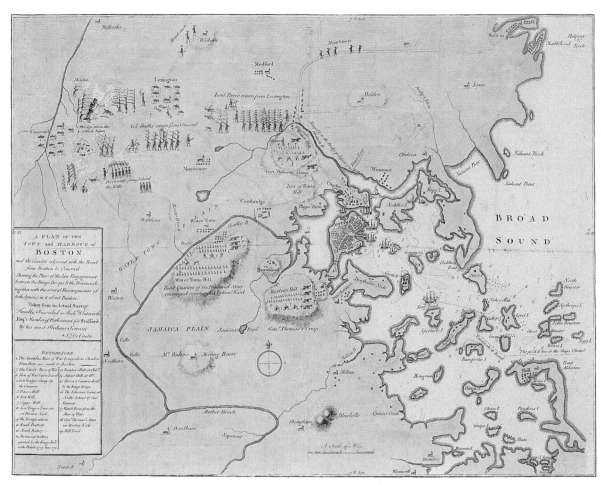

Map and detailed view of the city of Boston and its harbor in 1775, drawn by J. De Costa, in which Castle William and the fort can clearly be seen in the detailed view. Griffin's Wharf is located just to the south of Fort Hill (denoted by a "6"). Some ships are anchored in the naval area (denoted by a "3").

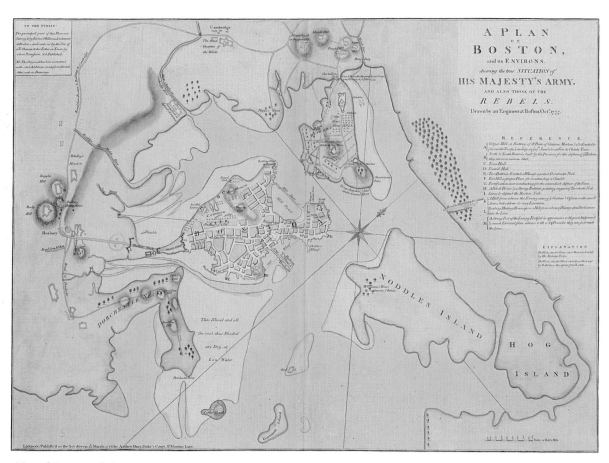

Map of Boston and the surrounding area, drawn in October of 1775, "designing the true situation of his Majesty's Army and also those of the Rebels."

The Clarkes held a party at their house that evening, probably to celebrate Jonathan's safe arrival. The party was interrupted by a large crowd, ranting and raving and pounding on doors and windows. The ladies were quickly escorted to the highest floor. One of the sons, presumably Jonathan, fresh from London and not accustomed to Boston's rabble, grabbed his pistol, opened one of the bedroom windows and threatened to shoot if the crowd did not disperse. A shot was fired, although no one was hit. This prompted the people to hurl themselves at the house, tearing off doors and windows and throwing stones before dispersing.

The following day, the consignees again refused to withdraw. Aware that they could not prevaricate much longer, the consignees turned to the Governor and the Council "as the guardians and protectors of the people," requesting that they assume responsibility for the tea until the consignees could freely take charge of it in accordance with the instructions of the East India Company. The Governor and the Council received the consignees' petition during their November 19th meeting. The ensuing debates were continued on November 23rd and November 27th. But the Council refused to proceed as requested in the petition. The Governor thus remained the sole champion of the consignees. He became increasingly worried that matters would escalate out of control. As the Council neither undertook nor approved any action, the consignees turned to the city's selectmen, in the hope that they could bring about a compromise. Jonathan Clarke claimed that he had never even wanted the consignment, because it was so distasteful to his firm. This was a blatant lie, but he was desperate. Clarke declared that he

BOSTON

> ### BOSTON, December 2, 1773.
>
> WHEREAS it has been reported that a Permit will be given by the Custom-House for Landing the Tea now on Board a Vessel laying in this Harbour, commanded by Capt. HALL : THIS is to Remind the Publick, That it was solemnly voted by the Body of the People of this and the neighbouring Towns assembled at the Old-South Meeting-House on Tuesday the 30th Day of *November*, that the said Tea never should be landed in this Province, or pay one Farthing of Duty : And as the aiding or assisting in procuring or granting any such Permit for landing the said Tea or any other Tea so circumstanced, or in offering any Permit when obtained to the-Master or Commander of the said Ship, or any other Ship in the same Situation, must betray an inhuman Thirst for Blood, and will also in a great Measure accelerate Confusion and Civil War : This is to assure such public Enemies of this Country, that they will be considered and treated as Wretches unworthy to live, and will be made the first Victims of our just Resentment.
>
>
>
> ### *The* PEOPLE.
>
>
>
> N. B. Captain *Bruce* is arrived laden with the same detestable Commodity : and 'tis peremptorily demanded of him, and all concerned, that they comply with the same Requisitions.

Bloodthirsty language directed at anyone daring to help bring the tea ashore.

was prepared to do anything within reason. However, sending the tea back to England as the selectmen proposed was out of the question, because both the tea and the ship would be confiscated in accordance with a 1721 act prohibiting the re-importation of tea into England. After hours of discussion, Clarke finally declared that he would bring the tea ashore, but promised to do this in full view rather than surreptitiously.

The next day, Sunday, November 28th, the *Dartmouth* wound its way through the islands near Boston and anchored in the protective waters of the harbor. News of the ship's arrival spread like wildfire through the city. As far as was known, this was the first tea ship to arrive in America. The Bostonians were sure of only one thing: the tea had to be sent back to England, in spite of the legal problems Jonathan Clarke had outlined to the selectmen. It behooved them to be quick about sending the ship back, for according to an old regulation, customs officials could impound the goods on which import duty was due if no payment had been received within twenty days. The deadline for the *Dartmouth's* cargo was December 17th.

Castle William and the fort
in Boston Harbor.

That Sunday, Boston was buzzing with activity. The selectmen deliberated on how they might keep the next day's town meeting under control and prevent violence. The selectmen were also curious to know what the new proposals of the consignees would be once they had received instructions from the Company. The Patriots were also active. They exhorted Francis Rotch, as owner of the *Dartmouth*, to see to it that the ship remained offshore, so that it could be sent back to England without having to put into port. Molineux also asked Rotch to ensure that the customs authorities did not clear the ship before Tuesday in order to give them time to mobilize the masses. The young Rotch answered that the Townshend Acts required him, as shipowner, to clear customs immediately after arrival and that he could not wait any longer than forty-eight hours, the customary period of respite.

The residents were greeted Monday morning with posters plastered throughout the city, summoning them to a meeting. This was not to be a regular town meeting, as special rules (residency requirements, the payment of a minimum amount of tax, etc.) regulated attendance at town meetings. Instead, it was an open meeting to which everyone was invited. Since it was not a legitimately convened town meeting, it was called "the Body." Despite the flood of spectators, including numerous residents of other areas, the discussions proceeded in a very orderly fashion. The five thousand people who met that morning unanimously resolved to send the tea back to England. The consignees were given until three o'clock that afternoon to comply. Francis Rotch and James Hall, the Captain of the *Dartmouth*, who were both present at the meeting, were asked not to clear the ship through customs. Unwilling to do this, Rotch responded that he would have his objection notarized. The meeting then appointed a twenty-five man guard to protect the cargo and the ship, which had meanwhile been anchored at Griffin's Wharf, closer to the city.

The consignees sent word that they needed more time, and the Body granted them another day in which to revise their opinions. During this interval, the Governor and the Council met to discuss the consignees' proposal that they assume responsibility for the tea and its customs clearance. The Council was unwilling to do any more than provide instructions for maintaining law and order.

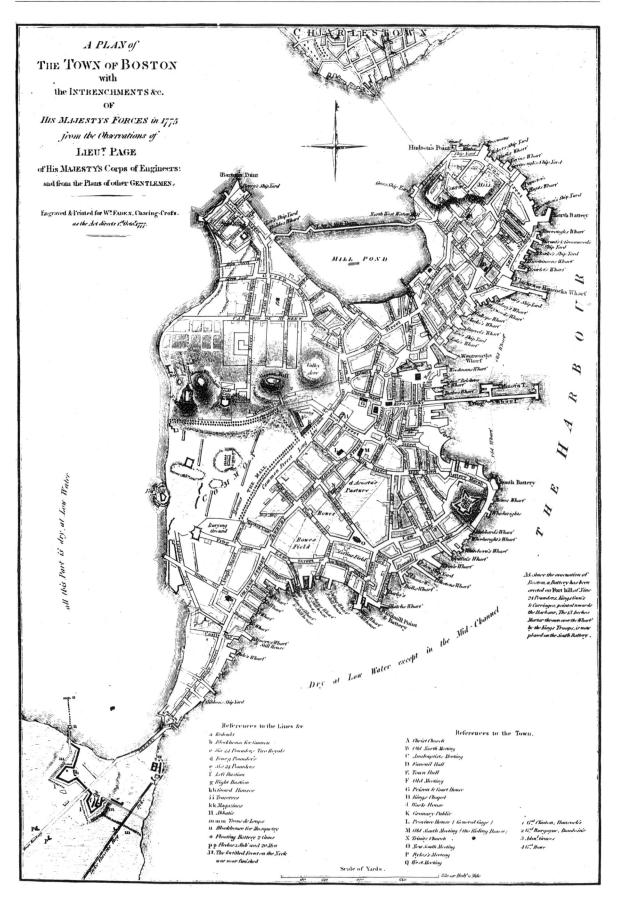

A PLAN of
THE TOWN OF BOSTON
with
the INTRENCHMENTS &c.
OF
HIS MAJESTYS FORCES in 1775
from the Observations of
LIEUT. PAGE
of His MAJESTYS Corps of Engineers:
and from the Plans of other GENTLEMEN.

Engraved & Printed for Wm. FADEN, Charing-Cross.
as the Act directs 1st Octr. 1777.

References to the Lines &c
a   Redoubt
b   Blockhouse for Cannon
c   Six 24 Pounders Two Royals
d   Four 9 Pounders
e   Six 24 Pounders
f   Left Bastion
g   Right Bastion
h h Guard Houses
i i Traverse
k k Magazines
l l Abbatis
m m Trous de Loups
n   Blockhouse for Musquetry
o   Floating Battery 2 Guns
p p Fleches 1 Mob' and 2d Men
A A The fortified Front on the Neck
    was near finished

References to the Town.
A   Christ Church
B   Old North Meeting
C   Anabaptists Meeting
D   Faneuil Hall
E   Town Hall
F   Old Meeting
G   Prison & Court House
H   Kings Chapel
I   Work House
K   Granary Public
L   Province House (General Gage)
M   Old South Meeting (the Riding House)
N   Trinity Church
O   New South Meeting
P   Pyles's Meeting
Q   West Meeting

1   Gl. Clinton, Hancock's
2   Gl. Burgoyne, Bowdoin's
3   Admrs. Graves
4   Gl. Howe

Scale of Yards.

The Governor and the consignees, thus left to their fate, felt the time had come to seek safety in the countryside. The two Clarke sons and Thomas Hutchinson Jr. fled to Castle William and the others dispersed to various places in the surrounding area. After November 29th, the Governor stayed whenever possible on his country estate, Milton.

The consignees continued to refuse to appear before the Body. Supported by the Governor, they saw no reason to submit to public pressure. Although the consignees in the other harbors were brought to their knees at the beginning of December, those in Boston stood firm. This was a clear sign to the Patriots that Boston was the place to tackle the issue.

However, shipping the tea back to England was not as simple as the Patriots seemed to think. It would take more than an order from the owner, Francis Rotch, to get the ship out of Boston Harbor, as there were far-reaching legal ramifications. According to the Townshend Revenue Act, the tax had to be paid when the tea was imported. But what exactly did that mean? Did importation refer to the ship's arrival in the harbor, its customs clearance or its tying up at a wharf? If the mere act of the ship's arrival was not tantamount to import, then the customs clearance presumably was. A shipowner (or his representative) was required to report for customs clearance directly after the ship's arrival or pay a fine, although a forty-eight hour respite was customarily granted. After a ship put into port, the customs officials could, according to an act dating from 1662 and valid for the colonies since 1696, confiscate any transported goods for which no import duties had been paid within twenty days.

Let us take a moment to trace the movements of the ship the *Dartmouth*. The *Dartmouth* arrived at the lighthouse at sunset on November 27th and anchored outside Boston Harbor. It entered the harbor the following day at six a.m., anchoring at King's Road. According to J. De Costa's 1775 map of Boston Harbor, this is the area between Deer Island (north of Spectacle Island) and Castle William. As this maneuver brought the *Dartmouth* within the confines of Boston Harbor, the ship could be said to have arrived in the harbor. The Patriots' request to Francis Rotch to keep his ship outside the harbor was therefore made in vain. Three hours later, the ship sailed away and anchored near the admiralty, a few hundred yards from Long Wharf. That same evening, two tax officials boarded the ship, a rare event in Boston Harbor. They had evidently been sent by Harrison to keep an eye on things.

It was not until November 29th that Captain Hill first went ashore. That evening, the Patriots sent twenty-five men to guard the ship. On Tuesday, November 30th, the captain reported the ship's arrival to the customs authorities. As the Patriot leaders feared that the soldiers from nearby Castle William would be able to overpower the twenty-five man guard and order the tea to be unloaded, they asked the captain to bring the ship closer to the city. The advantage to the Patriots of having the ship closer was that they controlled Boston's streets and waterfront, which they patrolled with armed militias. With the city so near, it would be easier to organize a crowd to prevent the tea from being compulsorily unloaded. One of the drawbacks of this tactic was that the ship could no longer sail past Castle William without coming within range of the army cannons. Francis Rotch agreed to move the ship to the city, near Griffin's Wharf, because the remainder of the cargo could be unloaded and taken to its destination. Rotch was interested in having his ship released as quickly as possible so that it could set off with a return cargo. Consequently, the ship was anchored on the evening of November 30th near Griffin's Wharf and moored with cables to the embankment, where all the cargo except the tea was unloaded. And so the first round in the cat-and-mouse game between the American Patriots and the English Redcoats was ready to begin.

The Governor and the consignees were fairly satisfied with the turn of events. The ship lay safely in Boston Harbor, and they only had to wait until the twenty days were up, after which time the revenue agent could impound the tea cargo under military protection. The ship could no longer move offshore, because the Governor had ordered Admiral Montagu not to allow any ship to pass by Castle William without customs clearance and a legitimate pass. Montagu was also charged with tightening the guard on less frequently used exits from the harbor.

When the second tea ship, the *Eleanor* sailed into the harbor on December 2nd, it was directed as a matter of course to Griffin's Wharf. A third ship, the brig *Beaver*, conveyed smallpox as well as tea, and was therefore put in quarantine; it only joined the other two ships on December 15th. A fourth ship, the *William*, ran up against some rocks in a storm. The ship was lost, and although its cargo could be salvaged, it played no further role in Boston's drama.

Francis Rotch, impatient at not being in control of his own ship, was the first to attempt to break the stalemate. On December 7th, he arrived at Castle William in the company of Captain Hill and a notary to demand that the consignees unload the tea and release his ship. The consignees replied that they were prevented from doing this by circumstances beyond their control. The consignees also refused to pay the bill for the cargo and to release him from his responsibility for the tea cargo, so that Rotch was forced to return empty-handed. Four days later, Captain Bruce of the *Eleanor* made a similarly futile trip to Castle William. But Rotch and Bruce could at least declare to the outside world that they had done their utmost to deliver their ships of their cargo.

The young Rotch had to contend with yet another obstacle. At a second mass meeting on November 30th, he had promised to send his ship and its tea back to England. On Monday, December 13th, a meeting of the Patriot committees of Boston and five other cities reminded him of this promise. In the interim, he had prudently sought legal counsel. Rotch pointed out to those present at the meeting that he had made the promise under duress and that shipping the tea back to England would result in confiscation of both his ship and its cargo. Moreover, his ship could not leave the harbor, because it first had to be cleared by customs before it could pass Castle William. The Patriots responded by organizing another mass meeting for the next day. On Tuesday, December 14th, thousands poured in from Boston and the surrounding areas to attend. They demanded that Rotch ask the revenue agent for customs clearance. Dozens of people accompanied Rotch to Harrison's office. Harrison responded that he wanted to give the matter a good night's sleep. The next day, he declared that granting such a clearance would be contrary to his official duty. Harrison refused to expound on his statement. The idea of doing Sam Adams and the Patriots a good turn evidently did not appeal to him. And so one more door to a peaceful solution had been resolutely slammed shut.

The Boston Tea Party.

In Boston itself, the unrest grew ominous as the end of the twenty-day waiting period approached. The last day before the fatal deadline was a melancholy and wintry December 16th. The tension in the city had risen to fever pitch. More than five thousand people from the Boston area met that morning at ten o'clock in the Old South Meeting House, which was hardly large enough to accommodate them. Outside, a cold rain fell throughout the day. The meeting had hardly begun before Rotch was again asked to sail his ship out of the harbor without customs clearance. Once again, Rotch explained that this was impossible. The only remaining peaceful way to break the deadlock was to ask Governor Hutchinson to issue a pass allowing the ship to leave the harbor. Rotch set off on another quest, this time to the Governor. As Hutchinson was located seven miles away at his estate in Milton, the meeting was adjourned until three thirty, giving Rotch enough time to journey back and forth. The Governor was fully aware of the seventy year old law requiring him to issue a pass only if a ship had been cleared through customs. He and Rotch therefore discussed the possibility of allowing the ship to sail out with a pass as far as Castle William, where it would be intercepted by the British fleet. Rotch realized that such an act of treachery would cost him dearly and refused to embark on the plan. For the second time, he returned empty-handed to the Body.

In the meantime, the meeting had been reopened at the appointed hour. While awaiting Rotch's arrival, the people had adopted several resolutions, such as one in which the shipping of tea was declared to be "improper and pernicious." When Rotch had not returned by five o'clock, many wanted to abandon the meeting in favor of action, but were persuaded to hold off for another hour.

A 19th century biased version of the Boston Tea Party (note the American flag!).

Rotch finally returned at a quarter to six, just as darkness was falling. He reported that the Governor had refused to issue a pass, and for a moment it looked as if the crowd would tear him to pieces. But order was restored, and Rotch was asked two final questions: whether he wished to send his ship and its tea back to England or whether he was planning to unload the tea. Rotch replied that he could not send the ship back, as that would ensure his own ruin, and that he would only unload the tea if forced to do so by the authorities, and only then in self-defense.

Sam Adams chose this moment to stand up and protest that he could not imagine what more the people could do to save their country. Adams' words were probably a prearranged signal, because the balconies suddenly rang with a battle cry that was answered by a small cluster of people standing by the entrance, disguised as Mohawk Indians. Shouts and cries such as ''Boston Harbor a teapot tonight,'' ''Hurrah for Griffin's Wharf,'' ''Every man to his tent'' and ''The Mohawks are coming'' resounded through the hall. The masses streamed outside and headed for the harbor, where the *Dartmouth* and the *Eleanor* lay side by side, each with one hundred and fourteen crates of tea in its hold. The brig *Beaver*, with its one hundred and twelve crates, was moored nearby. In total, these ships were carrying more than 90,000 pounds of tea, worth 9,000 pounds sterling. In a flash, several gangs of people scrambled on board. Some were dressed as Indians to avoid recognition; a dab of paint and an old blanket served the purpose. While

*A romanticized version of
the Boston Tea Party.*

one group chopped open crates with axes, another group briskly hoisted the tea from the holds with a block and tackle. The rain had stopped, and the moon occasionally peeped through the clouds. The scene was further illuminated by lanterns held by onlookers on the embankment. A hushed but assenting crowd watched from a distance. It was so quiet that the only audible sound was the chopping of axes and the splash of tea bales striking the water. They completed their task around nine o'clock, roughly three hours after the first tea bale had been thrown overboard. They checked to make sure that no one took any of the tea home. One man foolish enough to attempt it was caught and beaten by the crowd.

A few dozen men, not more than sixty all told, participated in the Boston Tea Party. Their identity was understandably concealed for a long time. The authorities never succeeded in bringing even one participant before a civil or criminal court. When their identities were finally disclosed, the participants turned out to be from all walks of life. While the list included young merchants, such as Thomas Melvill, a Harvard and Princeton graduate, and Lendall Pitts, they were largely craftsmen. The bricklayer James Brewer had offered his house as an assembly point, and Mrs. Brewer had blackened the faces of her husband and his cohorts with burned cork. Builders such as John Crane, Thomas Bolter and Samuel Fenno had used Crane's house as their assembly point. Young carpenters, such as Peter Slater and Robert Sessions, had also taken part. The majority hailed from Boston itself, but some came from surrounding areas. The most famous participants were the Patriot leaders William Molineux, Thomas Young and Paul Revere. John Hancock, Joseph Warren and Sam Adams had not gone on board: their task had already been accomplished. The plan of throwing the tea overboard had presumably been devised at the November 29th and

30th meeting. It is likely that the Patriot leaders had agreed to implement the "tea party" plan only as a last resort. Their primary motivation was probably the desire to see Boston regain the trust of the other colonies, which it had forfeited by its countless violations of the non-importation agreement. They undoubtedly also realized that the growing unity between the colonies would have been dealt a severe blow if the tea had been brought ashore.

During the evening, governmental authorities made no attempts to intervene. Admiral John Montagu witnessed the spectacle from a house not far from Griffin's Wharf. Had he ordered his troops to interfere, there would probably have been a bloodbath, one which would have made the Boston Massacre pale in comparison.

The day after the event, John Adams wrote in his diary: "This is the most magnificent Movement of all. There is a Dignity, a Majesty, a Sublimity in this last Effort of the Patriots that I greatly admire. This Destruction of the Tea, is so bold, so daring, so firm, intrepid, inflexible and it must have so important consequences and so lasting, that I can not but consider it as an Epocha in History." The truth of these words would soon be made manifest.

En route to destroying the tea.

*The tea crates are hoisted
from the hold and pried
open, and their contents
are dumped in the water.*

British sanctions

Governor Hutchinson's initial reaction was one of surprise. Like the consignees,
he had expected that the tea would ultimately be unloaded. It apparently had
never occurred to him that the Patriots would resort to violent tactics when they
failed to have the tea returned to England. His next reaction was to convene the
Council to punish the guilty. However, the meeting was repeatedly postponed for
lack of a quorum. When the Council finally met, it refused to support any action
beyond ordering the Attorney General to investigate the matter and submit its
findings to the Grand Jury for possible prosecution. However, nothing came of
the investigation.

While Boston was still basking in the glow of victory, the Patriots convened a
meeting and notified New York and Philadelphia of the latest development.
Before the year was out, everyone in the colonies knew of the Boston Tea Party.

The tea ship the *Nancy*, bound for New York, encountered a heavy storm and
never reached its destination. The tea ship the *Polly* reached Chester (a town at
the mouth of the river leading to Philadelphia) on Christmas Eve. On December
27th, roughly eight thousand Philadelphians held a mass meeting, in which Captain Ayres was asked not to clear customs, but to return with his cargo to London. The captain agreed and anchored his ship beyond the reach of the customs
officials. His next step was to formally ask the consignees to accept the tea. The
consignees had declared earlier in public that they would refuse the tea, and they
kept their word. As a result, the *Polly* raised anchor that same evening and sailed
down the Delaware, the first leg of a long journey back to England, with the East

Copper engraving of John Adams (1735-1826), one of Boston's Patriot leaders. Captain Prescot's defense lawyer during the "Boston Massacre" trial. He conducted peace negotiations with the English in Paris in 1793, was the first U.S. Ambassador to the Dutch Republic and later became the second president of the U.S. (1797-1801).

India Company tea and other goods on board. No further mention is made of the subsequent fate of the *Polly* and its cargo.

The Boston Tea Party revived resistance throughout the colonies to tea on which duty was levied. A veritable anti-tea hysteria took hold of the colonists. The air was filled with outrageous rumors, such as the tale that the Chinese in Canton pounded the tea into the crates with their dirty bare feet. A British loyalist scoffed that Bostonians would not eat the fish from their own harbor because the fish had drunk the tea. In the beginning of March 1774, the Bostonians were once again put to the test. The brig the *Fortune* arrived with twenty-eight crates of tea, much to the surprise of the owners, who were prepared to send it directly back. Revenue agent Harrison, however, demanded immediate customs clearance and payment of the tax. Two days later, a group of sixty men disguised as Indians boarded the *Fortune* and threw the tea overboard, Boston's second Tea Party. The mood in the colonies after the Boston Tea Party can be illustrated by a resident of Philadelphia, who wrote to an English friend: "I love Great Britain and revere the King; but it is my duty to hand down Freedom to my posterity, compatible with the right of Englishmen; therefore no tea duty, nor any unconstitutional tax whatever."

What were the reactions in the Mother Country? News of the Boston Tea Party reached England on January 20, 1774. Public opinion was quick to form a negative judgement. America's friends in the Parliament also condemned the operation. Even Benjamin Franklin, Massachusetts' agent in London, was unhappy with the Boston Tea Party. The reaction of the Board of Directors of the East India Company, which merely requested compensation for the damages, was fairly matter-of-fact, unlike that of the British government, which considered it high treason. Beginning on January 29th, the Cabinet convened a series of meetings to consider what measures to take against Boston and its residents. Lord Dartmouth, the Secretary of State for the Colonies, was the only pro-American member of the Cabinet. He was prepared to react moderately, but was unable to swim against the tide.

The government soon had to abandon the plan of prosecuting individuals because several of those involved in the case, such as Rotch and Captain Hall, could or would not attribute the action to particular persons in their statements to the Privy Council. Consequently, the government confined itself to punishing the city of Boston. The city had long been a hotbed of colonial resistance, and the government felt it was high time Boston was taught a lesson. Even at the time of the Stamp Act riots, Boston had been considered the worst offender in the colonies. In the government's view, Boston had constantly sought ways to undermine British authority and had even dared to request Governor Hutchinson's dismissal because he had expressed a negative opinion of the Patriot leaders, an act the British regarded as injudicious but justified.

To retaliate against Boston, the government proposed two measures, which were drawn up in two separate bills and presented to the Parliament for approval. The first bill proposed moving the seat of the government to another city. The second required Boston's customs office to be relocated to another harbor. Boston Harbor would only be reopened when the East India Company had received total compensation for the damages (the tea floating in Boston Harbor was estimated to have cost 9,659 pounds) and the Bostonians had shown remorse for the incident.

A bitter potion, the Boston Port bill, is poured down the throat of the American colonies from a teapot. A soldier with his drawn sword bearing the words "Military Law" is shown on the right. The "Boston Petition" requesting Governor Hutchinson's recall lies trampled on the ground.

These sanctions lay well within the Crown's jurisdiction. Nevertheless, it was decided to leave the King in the role of benevolent monarch and to make the Parliament responsible for the Boston Port Act and other punitive measures. The reasons cited in the bill for closing the harbor were that trade could not be carried out safely in Boston Harbor and that the customs office was hampered in its efforts to collect import duties.

The bill came up for discussion in the Parliament on March 14th. Lord North declared that the customs officials had been forced to flee the city three times since 1768, which was in itself sufficient grounds to move the customs office elsewhere. He added that Boston needed to be punished as a lesson to other cities contemplating rebellion. The opposition protested mildly, reproaching the government for its decision to discipline the city rather than the perpetrators, since the non-rioters would suffer as well. The government replied that these good citizens should have taken steps to prevent the riots, a viewpoint Edmund Burke termed a "devilish doctrine." Burke feared that the disciplinary action could have dire consequences. He asked for a general policy discussion on the American colonies, but the government denied his request. Instead, the Boston Port Act was adopted by a wide majority in both houses.

In reply to the opposition's question of whether the Cabinet was considering other disciplinary measures against Boston, Lord North replied in the affirmative, but declined to go into the matter further. The truth was finally disclosed a month later. The government put forward a proposal it had discarded earlier in 1768 and 1770, namely altering Massachusetts' charter. Governors Bernard and Hutchinson had both advocated such a measure. The fact that the Council was directly chosen by the people had always been a thorn in the side of the English government. They considered the time ripe to get a better grip on this rebellious colony. The proposed Massachusetts Bay Government Act was accordingly sent to the Parliament soon after the passage of the Boston Port Act. This new act would allow the King to appoint the Councilors. The Governor would be able to appoint the judges, and − a crucial point − the town meeting would only be allowed to convene a few times a year, to decide on official appointments and draw up local government regulations.

Shortly thereafter, two more bills were submitted for Parliamentary approval. The first was the Administration of Justice Bill, which would ensure that British government officials accused of misconduct in office would be returned to England to stand trial. The second was the Quartering Bill, which would allow British troops in the colonies to be quartered not just in barracks but in empty buildings as well. Although the latter bill was applicable to all colonies, it was clearly inspired by the events in Boston. Stationed on the island of Castle William, the troops were unable to intervene quickly during the recent disorders. Lastly, General Gage was named as both Commander-in-Chief of all British troops in the American colonies and Governor of Massachusetts, as a replacement to Hutchinson.

The opposition in "good old England" was taken unawares by these new sanctions, which went way beyond the government's initial plan to close the Boston Harbor. By endorsing the Boston Port Act, the first of the so-called Intolerable (or Coercive) Acts, or at any rate not actively opposing it, the opposition had been rendered powerless by the government. The debates on the subsequent Intolerable Acts were conducted on the basis of principle. Although the speakers presumed that Great Britain exercised supreme rule over the American colonies, they differed over the questions of whether this authority was derived from the Crown or the Parliament and whether it was better to use gentle persuasion or brute force to maintain this authority. The opposition urged moderation, pointing to the acquittal of Captain Preston in the Boston Massacre case. The populace had accepted the verdict calmly, which the opposition considered proof of Massachusetts' desire to exercise restraint. Although this tack failed, the opposition did succeed in steering the Parliament into an extensive policy debate over the American colonies, combining it with a plea for the repeal of the Townshend Revenue Act. The debate went right to the heart of the matter, namely whether Parliament had the right to tax the colonies. The speech most-admired on the government side was delivered by young Lord Carmarthen. He asked wonderingly what the Americans had to complain about. After all, a city such as Manchester (and he might as well have added Leeds, Sheffield and Birmingham) was likewise not represented by a seat in the Parliament!

Remarkably, the Parliament never seriously discussed the possibility of reserving a number of seats in the House of Commons for the American colonies. Perhaps the British system, with its cliques and its oligarchic and undemocratic exercise of power by a small group of nobles, was too rigid to accommodate such a large-scale reform. Still, the Americans themselves never really demanded representation in the British House of Commons, perhaps out of fear that they would have to start paying British taxes!

The British had devised the theory of virtual representation to cover the masses having no vote or representation in the Parliament. The crux of the theory, articulated by Lord Carmarthen during the debate, was that every member of the House of Commons represented the entire population, and not just a particular district. While the theory was essentially correct, it did not explain why the above-mentioned cities were without representation, while thinly populated Cornwall and Devon had no less than seventy representatives.

On April 19th, Edmund Burke delivered to the House of Commons his celebrated speech, which was later published under the title "On American Taxation." In his eloquent plea, Burke stated that since the first Navigation Acts, the heart of England's financial policy with respect to the American colonies had been for the Americans to contribute to the British Empire through trade. Adding taxation to this contribution, as the Stamp Act had done in 1765, was tantamount to enslaving the American colonies. Burke rebuked Lord Carmarthen,

Edmund Burke (1729-1797) (from a painting by J. Barry).

BOSTON

who had called the Americans "our children" and had asked in astonishment how they could rebel against their parents, as follows: "They are 'our children,' but when children ask for bread, we are not to give a stone." Burke added that even if the British government had the right to involve the colonies in its taxation, such a policy was neither prudent nor fair, for the benefits of regulated colonial trade greatly exceeded the costs of maintaining the colonies.

The next speaker was Charles Fox, the opposition leader. He noted succinctly that there were three reasons for imposing taxes: to regulate trade and industry, to acquire money for the treasury and to explicitly establish the right to impose tax. In this case, the government denied its interest in the first two reasons, so that it had to be aiming at the third. Yet that meant, Fox concluded, that the British government intended to maintain its so-called right to impose taxes by armed intervention. The inevitable result of such a course of action would be to goad the Americans into open rebellion. Rose Fuller's motion to abolish the tea duty was rejected by a vote of 182 to 49. Parliament thus deprived itself of the opportunity to keep the door of reconciliation open in Massachusetts while applying tough measures. As Fox aptly expressed it: "We must treat the Americans either as subjects or as rebels; in the former case, the punitive measures go too far, and in the latter case, not far enough." Despite the pleas of the opposition, all of the proposed Intolerable Acts were adopted by a very strong majority.

In the spring of 1774, almost all of England supported the idea of punishing Boston and its residents in exemplary fashion. But how did the American colonists react?

The colonies join forces and rise in revolt

Boston initially reacted rather casually to the news of the measures proposed by the Mother Country. But in April of 1774, grim reports began to cross the Atlantic, and on May 2nd, the news of the Boston Port Act made it clear that the British meant business. General Gage arrived in Boston on May 17th. By June 2nd, the harbor was closed, the customs office had been transferred to Plymouth and the government seat had been moved to Salem, twenty miles away. Before long, a regiment of English soldiers had made camp on Boston Common. To bring Boston to its knees quickly, the harbor blockade was strictly enforced. The city that had been tightly bound together by water was thus divided into a number of isolated neighborhoods. Those earning a living from building, sailing, loading and unloading ships saw their activities come to a sudden standstill. Not so much as one ox, cow or bale of hay could be brought ashore from the islands. All maritime traffic between the piers was prohibited, forcing the fishermen to detour thirty miles via an inland route to supply the city with fish.

If the British had believed that the other colonies had such little liking for Bostonians that they would be abandoned to their fate, they were in for a rude awakening. The colonists' dislike for Puritan Boston paled in comparison to the loathing the British had brought upon themselves. A general rage took hold of the colonists. The news spread throughout the colonies via a sophisticated use of dramatic devices: black-bordered posters, flags flown at half-mast, tolling church bells, ritual burnings of English acts, public prayers and fasts. Boston was also furnished with material assistance from all sides. Rice, sheep, fish and other goods were transported overland free of charge by volunteers or professionals.

The inconvenience that the 1774 blockade of Boston Harbor caused the Bostonians is vividly illustrated in this cartoon.

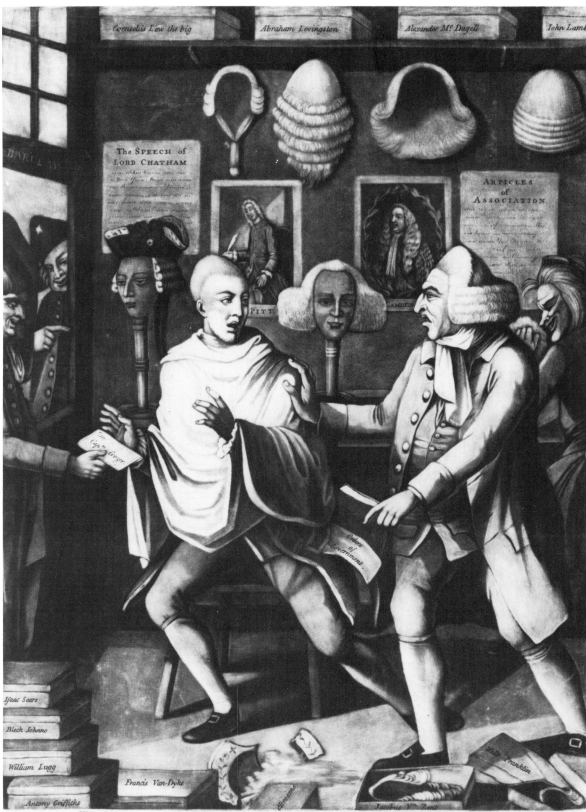

The PATRIOTICK BARBER of NEW YORK, or the CAPTAIN in the SUDS.

Then Patriot grand, maintain thy Stand,　　　　　　　Forbid the Captains there to roam,
And whilst thou sav'st America's Land,　　　　　　　　Half shave them first, then send em home
　　Preserve the Golden Rule:　　　　　　　　　　　　　　Objects of ridicule.

Pl. III　　　　　　London Printed for R. Sayer & J. Bennett, No 53 Fleet Street, as the Act directs 14 Feb. 1775.

The patriotic barber in this print is Jacob Vredenburgh (presumably of Dutch origin). Halfway through the job, he discovered the identity of Captain John Crozer, the Commander of the British transport ship the "Empress of Russia," and immediately showed him the door. The Sons of Liberty in New York seized the opportunity to make a print of the event to be used for propaganda purposes. It includes portraits of William Pitt (later Lord Chatham) and Lord Camden, proponents of the repeal of the stamp tax. The "speech of Lord Chatham" refers to Pitt's impassioned defense of repeal in the Parliament. The "Articles of Association" refer to the agreement reached by the Continental Congress on October 20, 1774, in which it was agreed to cut off all trade with England.

As a result of the Boston Port Act, the rebellion burgeoned from a regional matter involving a coastal community to an issue of national interest.

For Sam Adams and his fellow Patriots, the next step was to steer the assistance from the other colonies into useful political channels. On May 5th, they drew up a Solemn League and Covenant, which was deposited in Boston and other cities in Massachusetts, awaiting signatures. Signatories to the Covenant promised not to import any English goods after August 31st and to boycott any individual who refused to sign the Covenant. The Patriots initially had difficulty persuading even Bostonians to sign the document. Luckily, Governor/General Gage committed a tactical error by issuing a proclamation warning the public that anyone signing the Covenant risked arrest. Gage's warning came only two days after Boston's town meeting had voted, after hours of heated debate, to adopt the Covenant, by a majority of four to one. Once the proclamation had been issued, the Covenant really took hold. Soon the entire colony of Massachusetts had adopted the Covenant, and similar agreements were approved in New Hampshire and Connecticut.

More importantly, New York and Philadelphia had to be persuaded to sign the Covenant. The various factions in New York were too divided to reach a decision. In Philadelphia, the conservatives and the Patriots waged a bitter struggle over the city's position. It was then suggested that the decision be postponed until after a congress of all thirteen colonies could be convened. Sam Adams, for one, had long nurtured the idea of a Continental Congress and had been openly advocating it for the last year and a half. Philadelphia had agreed to the proposal and New York was still debating the issue when the colonies received the news that Parliament had enacted the remaining Intolerable Acts. The issue was now not so much whether the Parliament had the right to tax the American colonies, but whether it could alter their charters. A new wave of resistance swept through the colonies, and many voices were raised in support of a Continental Congress.

Developments now followed each other in rapid tempo. Embracing the idea of a Continental Congress, each of the colonies began appointing delegations and issuing instructions. With surprising rapidity, they reached agreement on such thorny issues as the agenda, voting protocols, etc. The organizational issues surrounding a gathering of this size were solved almost without a murmur. Appointing delegates in Boston turned out to be a touch and go situation. A committee from the General Court met on June 17th to discuss the Continental Congress and elect delegates. One of the participants feigned illness and left. He then hurried to inform the new Governor of the latest development. Governor Gage issued an immediate proclamation dissolving the General Court, and sent his secretary to the meeting with the decree. Encountering a bolted door, the secretary read the proclamation in front of the closed door. Thus, at the eleventh hour, the five delegates from Massachusetts, including Sam and John Adams, were appointed as representatives to the Continental Congress.

The delegates from twelve of the American colonies (Georgia, with its fifty thousand white inhabitants was powerless to join in) met in Carpenter's Hall in Philadelphia on September 6, 1774 in what was to be known as the "First Continental Congress." It was the first time that most of the delegates had left hearth and home on such a long journey. As Sam Adams was virtually penniless, his neighbors had chipped in to buy him new clothes for this grand occasion.

Although most of the delegates were moderates, once the First Continental Congress was underway, they began to veer off in a radical direction. Halting imports to and exports from Great Britain was only the first step. The First Continental Congress adopted a series of resolutions know as the "Declaration of Colonial Rights and Grievances," demanding the right of the colonists to self-government with respect to both taxation and domestic legislation. The British Parliament could no longer claim the right to regulate colonial trade for the Empire, but could only control trade with colonial approval. Likewise, the First Continental Congress also denied England's right to levy taxes to benefit its own treasury. Suffice it to say that the Townshend Acts and the punitive measures taken against Boston and Massachusetts were also rejected in the same resolution. During its last session, the First Continental Congress agreed to convene again in May of the following year. But before that time, the first shots had already rung out on April 19, 1775 in Concord, twenty miles from Boston. This act signaled the beginning of the American Revolution. Chatham and Burkes' attempts at reconciliation failed miserably.

THE ARTICLES OF CONFEDERATION

The resolutions adopted by the Continental Congress in October of 1774 with respect to self-government, taxation and the cessation of trade with England was a source of resentment and tumult. In this print, two English politicians are seated in an outhouse (the "necessary house"). One is ripping up Congressional resolutions, while the other is raptly reading Samuel Johnson's pamphlet entitled "Taxation No Tyranny," which articulated the English position.

The Articles of Confederation

Years of heroic battle followed the signing of the Declaration of Independence, in which the colonies declared themselves to be independent states. Some countries on the European continent, with France in the fore, joined in the melee, glad to oblige when it came to teaching the British lion a lesson. In fact, France's military aid to the young nation was of decisive importance. The Dutch Republic, reduced to the position of a third-rate political and military power, was pleased with the opportunity to engage in trade with the rebels. Dutch support can be dated from 1780, when the Caribbean island of St. Eustatius, a Dutch stepping stone (known familiarly as "The Golden Rock") in the smuggling trade between the Hollanders and the rebels, fired the first salute to an American warship. The Netherlands was thus the first independent nation to recognize the American flag on the open seas. Indeed, the loans the Americans received from Dutch merchants were no less welcome than the military and financial aid supplied by the French.

The War of Independence ultimately led to a peace treaty with England, signed in Paris in 1783. This brief report of the American Revolution will have to suffice here. Although there is clearly a great deal more to be said on the subject, the scope of this book is limited to financial and fiscal matters confronting the rebels and later the Confederation of the thirteen states.

One of the most serious difficulties facing the new nation was its shaky financial foundation. The Confederation was governed by the Second Continental Congress, consisting of a handful of delegates from each state. The Confederation Congress was not much more than a debating club moving from city to city. It was comprised of part-time Congressmen without any experience in joint government and lacking the necessary instruments of government. These instruments had to be fashioned piece by piece. Consider, for example, the difficulty of transforming the local militias into a standing army. The new Commander-in-Chief, George Washington, devoted considerable energy to this task and ultimately succeeded.

The need to maintain a standing army coupled with the other burdens of war consumed vast sums of money. Allowing the Confederation Congress to go over the heads of local governments and levy direct taxes on the citizens to finance the nation was inconceivable. After all, the thirteen colonies had fought the Revolution to achieve self-government. They had rebelled against a central government wanting to curb local ambitions. Human rights, government by the consent of the governed and the concept of "no taxation without representation" were principles imbued in every American. As their horizons extended no further than the borders of their own colony, the former colonists were unable to translate these principles to the level of the Confederation. The first constitution of the United States, the Articles of Confederation, was adopted by the Second Continental Congress early in the war, but only became effective in 1781. While the Articles of Confederation admittedly contained many high-flown statements about cooperation, it left the Congress – the only body exercising power in the Confederation – in an extremely weak position. Several crucial governmental responsibilities had been delegated to the individual states rather than the Congress. The Americans recognized that taxation was the key to the exercise of power, but they preferred to delegate the right to levy taxes to the individual

A Massachusetts treasury note.

Paper money printed by the insurgents.

One of the very first dollars in circulation.

states. To raise the funds necessary to wage the war, the Confederation Congress was forced to turn to the individual states. While each state was obliged to contribute its share, it could determine for itself what taxes were needed to raise its portion.

The key question in this system was obviously what criteria to use to apportion the shares among the states. The first draft of the Articles of Confederation, drawn up by John Dickinson of Pennsylvania, used the number of inhabitants per state as the norm for apportionment. This proposition was vehemently opposed by states having a large black population. If the slaves were counted as inhabitants, the Southern states would pay a relatively larger share. The representative of Maryland therefore proposed only taking white inhabitants into account for the tax quota, because slaves could be considered as the owner's "chattel." Maryland's proposal was rejected by a narrow majority. Months of debate on the apportionment issue followed, starting in the summer and continuing into October of 1777. Three alternative tax-quota plans were proposed: basing the apportionment on the number of inhabitants (i.e. the original proposition), on land values or on general wealth. Despite the strong opposition of the New England states, it was decided to use the land value per state as the criterion for apportioning taxes. This method adversely affected the Northern states because they were more densely populated and land values were higher than in the South. Still, the Northerners resigned themselves to the decision for the sake of the common good.

Given the choice between a strong government that could pose a threat to liberty but could take effective action (particularly in war) and a weak government that offered greater guarantees of freedom but operated less effectively, the states unconditionally opted for the latter. As a Revolutionary contemporary pointed out, it was "a struggle for liberty, not for power."

In the meantime, the Confederation's daily governmental tasks were carried out by permanent Congressional committees. The Confederation Congress was chiefly faced with the problem of financing the war. On the one hand, it could drift on the wave of patriotic sentiment that prompted the states to make their contributions. On the other hand, it had to devise methods to float foreign loans. The Confederation Congress issued its own paper currency, and the presses were forced to roll faster and faster to keep pace with demand. The result was gigantic inflation: the dollar plummeted within a few years to two or three percent of its original value. In the spring of 1781, it was even removed from circulation. The costs of the war therefore had to be defrayed by other means. One method, similar to that used a thousand years earlier, was to pay the soldiers with land; in this case, the land grants lay between the Allegheny Mountains and the Mississippi. The army was frequently obliged to requisition food and supplies and commandeer transport. As was to be expected, this highly arbitrary form of taxation in kind led to bitterness and discord. In addition, a significant number of Americans did not believe in the necessity of the Revolution. Occasional minor civil wars broke out locally between proponents and opponents of independence.

In these chaotic circumstances, many sank into abject poverty. But as is always the case, others made a substantial profit, particularly merchants not averse to trading with the enemy. This had always been standard practice in the colonies, and the War of Independence brought surprisingly little change in the practice.

An English cartoon from 1780. The English bull is tossing a Spaniard into the air, while a shocked American and Frenchman watch. The Dutch farmer, watching from his neutral position behind the fence, is sitting on a barrel of gin, indicating the profits from his smuggling operations during the war.

The British had the advantage of being able to pay with hard cash; the American army had only constantly devalued paper money to offer. The Confederation Congress issued 6 million dollars of paper money in 1775. The next year this jumped to 25 million, and by the end of 1779, there were more than 200 million dollars in circulation. The dollar had been worth 25 cents in 1778, but it had dropped a year later to 12 cents, and the year after that to 2 or 3 cents. Washington's soldiers were starving to death in Valley Forge, but wagonloads of food were flowing into nearby Philadelphia, which was occupied by the English. Trade with the enemy was usually conducted via foreign ports, with American merchants traveling to London to organize their transactions. Their English colleagues were all to willing to grant them loans on easy terms. War profiteering reached such proportions that Washington rightly declared that he feared monopolists and war profiteers more than the enemy.

The Confederation and the individual states naturally attempted to clamp down on such practices. They enacted laws stabilizing the dollar, regulating wages and prices, preventing monopolies and placing embargoes on certain goods needed by the army, but to little avail. It seemed as if the citizens of America had joined together in a pact to evade the laws. Moreover, the various governments lacked the necessary powers to control the economy.

Some relief was provided when the Confederation appointed merchants with good business sense and commercial contacts to ensure a regular transport of certain items, such as grain. Still, this complicated matters, as it mixed personal and public interests. The merchants were frequently tempted to put their know-how and know-who to use for their own speculative transactions.

The former Patriot leaders, of whom Sam Adams was a prototype, were accustomed to using the town meetings to thwart the British. The former rebels were now forced to rule under the pressure of the same crowd, but with fewer results. In their propaganda, the economic legislation was packaged as an effective means of protecting the man in the street from profiteers. This was interpreted by the propertied class as an attempt to play off the rich against the poor. The upper classes, exemplified by Samuel Lee of Virginia, increasingly felt that if given the choice between British tyranny and mob rule they would ultimately opt for the former. The gap between the radicals and the conservatives widened. The radicals expected independence to bring about a domestic revolution that would give the large mass of farmers and artisans a voice in government. The voice of the masses had not been heard in many states, where the right to vote was coupled to property ownership, the so-called poll tax. When Virginia and Maryland were founded, every free man was entitled to vote, but by the end of the seventeenth century, both states had the same property requirement as the other colonies. These requirements were gradually made more stringent in the eighteenth century, until the colonies were being governed by a planter oligarchy in the South and a merchant oligarchy in the North. Their political creed can be summarized as follows: "the people who own the country ought to govern it." Like it or not, these conservative groups were swept along in the struggle for independence. But they believed that once independence had been achieved, they should be the ones to govern the country, all the more so because the Patriot leaders were in no position to rule. Something clearly had to be done, because otherwise the Americans would win the war but lose the Revolution!

Something did happen. Starting in 1780, countermovements, often referred to as the "Counterrevolution," sprang up in various states. This process was accelerated by the military defeat of one of Washington's commanders, General Horatio Gates, in Camden, South Carolina. The more conservative-minded inhabitants had managed to reverse the course of events with their program of heavy taxation, sound money and free enterprise. They attached little value to Thomas Paine's statement that property was safe in the hands of the people. On the contrary, in the eyes of the conservatives, the unequal division of wealth was the most significant source of human conflict. But they wished to maintain this inequality since it brought wealth in general, and to themselves in particular. It served their interests to have a government powerful enough to prevent disadvantaged social groups from threatening the lives and property of the conservatives. This viewpoint prevailed in the Confederation Congress from 1781 to the end of the war. Its adherents discarded the laws designed to stabilize the currency and regulate prices, which they believed would be of no use.

The conservative faction felt that only a sound financial basis and free enterprise could win the war. They began by reorganizing the army into a permanent fighting force and then reformed the central government to increase efficiency. They set up new departments (Treasury, War, Foreign Affairs and Navigation), headed by one person per department instead of by Congressional committees. In fact, the department heads were not even Congressmen. The discredited former Patriot leaders were powerless to resist the new wave of enthusiasm for the innovations sweeping the country. The merchants were even moved to voluntarily procure some funds to support the government. Representatives of the New England states and the state of New York met in Hartford, Connecticut, in 1780. The resulting resolutions were characteristic of the new mood. In former

A 1779 print showing the horse America throwing his master, George III. The King's riding crop is equipped with a sword, a saber, a bayonet, a scalping knife and an ax. In the background, a French officer is rushing to the rescue.

times, a similar gathering would have been occupied with setting prices and laying down trade regulations to curb the activities of the war profiteers. The present resolutions demanded a stronger central government, empowered Commander-in-Chief George Washington to use force, if necessary, to compel reluctant states to pay their share of the war effort and urged that the Confederation Congress be granted the right to impose import duties. The last resolution, in particular, was quite extreme. The Confederation Congress had meanwhile become more conservative and adopted the last resolution. In 1781, it proposed a five percent import tax, to be collected by officials of the federal government. The revenue from the tax was primarily to be used to meet the interest payments on debts incurred by the central government. This proposal contradicted the Articles of Confederation, which had granted the individual states the exclusive right to impose taxes. The tax proposal thus required an amendment to the Articles of Confederation, which had to be ratified by all thirteen states.

The proposal was basically accepted by several important groups striving to strengthen the government at a national level. The new conservatives, advocates of a stronger Confederation, were supported by many wealthy merchants, who considered an effective central government to be the only bulwark against the rule of the radical-manipulated mobs. Moreover, when the government began issuing public bonds instead of paper money, these merchants had bought up the bonds at steadily decreasing rates. If the central government were strong enough to impose taxes, the Congress would in due course be able to pay off its debts, and the merchants would be able to scoop up the profits on their speculations. The new conservatives abhorred paper money, trade restrictions and inefficient government. They realized that the creation of a new nation offered a host of economic opportunities, especially now that the shackles of the English Trade

Robert Morris (1734-1806).

Acts, which had hampered colonial industry, were no longer in force. But they also saw that the government had to be strong enough to finance itself by levying taxes and open enough to stimulate rather than curb trade and industry. They realized that commercial banks, insurance companies and large businesses, which had not existed in colonial America, were essential. This new group of conservatives was bound together by monetary interest, unlike the former − still important − conservatives, who had been tied together by land ownership, birth and education.

The leader of the new conservatives was a Philadelphia merchant named Robert Morris. He was to become the most prominent politician in the later years of the war. One of the most successful merchants in Philadelphia, Morris had enlarged his already considerable fortune by awarding numerous government contracts to his own partners and business associates. His commercial success earned him the reputation of being America's leading merchant. He was as admired as he was hated and envied.

In 1781, Morris was appointed as Superintendent of Finance. Still, his influence extended to more than the field of finance. With the assistance of his faithful flock of followers, he succeeded in formulating a new policy for both the central government and the states. Facing little opposition, Morris' policy was adopted by the Confederation Congress. Circumstances were favorable at that time: since the victory at Yorktown, the war was virtually finished, causing military expenditures to drop considerably. Foreign loans also provided the economy with some breathing space. Morris slashed the budget, fired personnel, cut costs and eliminated various government functions, and therefore helped restore the credit of the central government. Morris' next step was to set up a bank, the "Bank of North America," in order "to unite the several states more closely together in one central money connection." This plan ultimately failed, because the bank, far from being the "principal pillar of American credit," merely became Philadelphia's private bank. The merchants were left with a mishmash of coins minted by a dozen different states. Many coins were badly damaged, too light or counterfeit. In addition, there was a disturbing variety of state and national banknotes, which greatly undermined their monetary value.

Morris' most important objective was to free the Congress from the financial whims of the states. This could be achieved if the central government were allowed to impose taxes to cover its own expenses and if the tax revenues offered enough security to meet the interest payments and repay the country's debts. Morris viewed the debts incurred during the Revolution as a blessing in disguise and a possible "cement to the union"; after all, they justified federal taxes.

Morris fully backed the movement following on the footsteps of the Hartford meeting, which had proposed amending the Articles of Confederation so that the central government could impose taxes. He threw his considerable influence into the campaign: he pressured local authorities, wrote pamphlets and newspaper articles and tapped any conceivable form of publicity. But all his efforts were in vain. An amendment to the Articles of Confederation required the ratification of all thirteen states. The smallest state, Rhode Island, refused to ratify the amendment. No changes were made in the tax structure, and the attempt to mold a confederation into a unified state had failed.

A New Method of MACARONY MAKING, as practised at BOSTON in NORTH AMERICA.

217

Printed for Carington Bowles, N°.69 in S.ᵗPauls Church Yard, London. Published 12 Octᵣ 1774.

The tarring and feathering of an English loyalist. To add insult to injury, he is forced to drink tea.

Just as there were opponents and proponents of the War of Independence in America, opinions in the Mother Country were also divided. The above satire entitled "Six-Pence A Day" was aimed against the recruitment of soldiers to fight in America. It shows the miseries facing the soldier, while his pregnant wife and wretched children beg for money. On the right, he is under attack from two Americans, while skeletal Famine watches. On the left, a well-dressed and well-fed coachman and chair-bearer (representing the lower classes) watch the spectacle with pleasure.

Morris' failure to achieve the most important point in his program is also due to the fact that his ideas gained insufficient support among broad layers of society. While the large landowners and wealthy merchants supported Morris' ideas, the farmers, artisans and middle and professional classes regarded a strong central government as a potential source of tyranny. Many people also feared that the ideas of Morris and his supporters were primarily directed at the Middle states, to the detriment of New England and the Southern states. The time was not yet ripe for putting taxation under the control of the central government. Morris and his adherents would have to wait until all strata of society had accepted the movement toward a stronger Confederation and the constitution had ensured a better balance of powers in the country. Taxation would then become the key to a door opening the way to a splendid, self-confident nation.

The new Constitution

That moment arrived sooner than expected. The end of the War of Independence opened up new perspectives for the resumption of America's trade with England. France and Holland also eventually became important trading partners. American trade got off to a slower start than anticipated because of its lack of credit and export products, the necessity of operating in foreign markets and low tobacco prices. Business picked up in time and set off a much-needed economic recovery, although it was too late to save the Articles of Confederation. Criticism of the central government's lack of decisiveness was heard from all sides. Holders of treasury IOU's, manufacturers and merchants were not the only groups advocating a powerful central government. More nationalistic-minded citizens also had to wait impatiently for the day the United States would assume its place among the powerful nations of the world.

Although there were no trade barriers between the states, each state did impose its own import duties to swell the state treasury. These duties inevitably led to friction and tariff battles between the states. European goods destined for New Jersey had to be imported via harbors in New York and Pennsylvania. When New York refused to refund the tax to New Jersey, the latter imposed a high tax assessment on a lighthouse belonging to New York but located in New Jersey. While this kind of "harassment" occurred infrequently, it does illustrate the shortcomings which prevented the Articles of Confederation from regulating interstate commerce.

The weakness of the central government was also clear on the Western borders, where sporadic fighting broke out with the Indians and where the Spanish could impede trade because they held the mouth of the Mississippi. An additional problem was created by the huge war debts incurred by individual states. Some states attempted to reduce the debts unilaterally, arguing that the debts had been incurred during a time of high prices and paper money, and that it would be improper to repay the same nominal amount with hard cash, because prices had dropped in the interim. Massachusetts' debt had reached such great proportions that high taxes had been imposed to acquire the necessary funds to repay the debt. These oppressive taxes ultimately resulted in an uprising known as "Shays' Rebellion," led by war veteran Daniel Shays. Thousands of farmers, armed with pitchforks, rose up in revolt. While the rebellion was swiftly quelled by the militia, the writing was on the wall. The events in Massachusetts spurred the adherents of stronger central government to greater effort.

Sparked by disputes between Virginia and Maryland over navigation on the Potomac River, a convention was held in Annapolis, Maryland, in September of 1786 to deal with the problems of interstate commerce. The initiative for the convention had come from Alexander Hamilton, a New York lawyer and fervent advocate of a powerful central government. During the Revolution, he had served as Washington's adjutant, enabling him to get a firsthand view of the drawbacks of weak central government. Only five states were represented at the convention. The delegates were unable to break the stalemate between central and local interests. Hamilton then broached the idea of asking the Confederation Congress to organize a new meeting "for the sole and express purpose of revising the Articles of Confederation." The Confederation Congress, wrestling with its own impotence, was well aware that it could only be strengthened if it were em-

Lighthouse on the American Eastern seaboard (1790).

powered to levy taxes. With the thought of Shays' Rebellion still fresh in its mind, the Confederation Congress agreed to the proposal. And so, on May 25, 1787, the constitutional assembly, meeting in Philadelphia, began its first session.

The fifty-five delegates, under the chairmanship of George Washington, realized that patching up the Articles of Confederation would be an exercise in futility. They therefore began the difficult task of framing a new Constitution. All states were represented, with the exception of tiny Rhode Island; it would also be the last state to ratify the new Constitution. The delegates included James Madison, Benjamin Franklin, Alexander Hamilton and other Revolutionary heavyweights; only the old radicals were missing. It was an elite group, encompassing eighteen planters, nineteen slave owners, seven merchants and eight lawyers with commercial backgrounds. The Founding Fathers were children of The Enlightenment, embracing the principles of liberty and human rights and yet convinced that they had the corner on enlightenment. This conviction was borne out in their preoccupation with such subjects as stability, order and the protection of property against the rebellious lower classes! They felt that control of the national government should be in the hands of society's upper class, characterized by Hamilton as "the rich, the well-born and the able." The doctrine of the separation of powers, as propounded by the French political philosopher Montesquieu, formed the basis of the Constitution.

Nevertheless, it would be wrong to discount the Constitution as merely the product of a group of conservatives protecting their own interests. The Constitution was markedly influenced by the theory of checks and balances. Contrary to previous political wisdom, James Madison argued that this theory should be applied to a large and spacious country rather than a small one. According to Madison, freedom in a small country would lead to a tyranny of the majority and irreconcilable differences. On the contrary, in a large country the differences between rich and poor, agriculture and commerce, religion and politics could be maintained in better balance and act as a check on each other. The Constitution was therefore endowed with numerous checks and balances.

Taxation was one of the key issues tackled by the Philadelphia Convention. Hamilton was an ardent supporter of federal taxation. In his view, it was vital for the central government to have the power to tax its citizens directly. He believed that federal taxes should be levied in addition to state taxes, which were designed to raise revenues for state expenditures. The government needed federal tax revenues to carry out the responsibilities of the central government, such as providing for national defense, formulating foreign policy, stimulating trade and administering justice.

The issue of taxation was naturally not the only topic of discussion at the Philadelphia Convention. Another major issue was the formation of the central government. On this point as well as in the area of trade, a wide gap separated the North and the South. The breach would ultimately cleave them in two in the nineteenth century.

The more agriculturally oriented South was interested in exporting such staples as tobacco and obtaining low-priced import goods. The interests of the North, however, lay in promoting navigation and protective tariffs to boost its own industry. A compromise was reached between the two opposing interests. As a concession to the South, the Constitution forbid export taxes. In addition, restrictions on the slave trade were prohibited for at least twenty years. Freedom thus remained a right reserved for the whites. The North was accommodated by allowing navigation laws to be enacted and import taxes imposed. Another compromise allowed states to take slaves into account when deciding the number of representatives to the House of Representatives. Likewise, the number of inhabitants in each state was to be used as the criterion for apportioning direct taxes. The Northerners considered it logical to count the slaves as property rather than as persons, at least when determining the number of Congressmen to which each state was entitled. Elbridge Gerry, a representative from Massachusetts, articulated this viewpoint as follows: "Why then should the blacks, who were property in the South, be in the rule of representation more than the cattle and horses of the North?" Nevertheless, when it came time to apportion the taxes, the Northerners wanted to count the slaves as part of the population. The Southerners defended the opposite point of view: slaves should count for the representation, but not for taxation. The resulting Three-Fifths Compromise was practical but illogical. Five blacks were to be counted as three whites for both representation and taxation purposes.

The delegates, who had kept a sharp eye on their own economic interests, agreed that the central government should be empowered to levy taxes, borrow money, impose uniform import duties, mint coins, determine weights and measures,

*George Washington
(1732-1799).*

*Alexander Hamilton
(1755-1804).*

*James Madison
(1751-1836).*

grant patents and copyrights, create a postal system, maintain an army and a navy, regulate interstate commerce, manage Indian affairs, naturalize foreigners, admit new states to the union, etc.

On September 17th, four months after its opening, the Philadelphia Convention held its last session. The next step was to obtain the ratification of the Constitution by at least nine of the thirteen states, according to an agreement made at the beginning of the convention. Only then would the United States exist in actual fact. It was necessary to mobilize public opinion to rally around ratification. Madison and Hamilton therefore published a magazine entitled "The Federalist," in which their ideas (including taxation) were discussed in detail. The name was slightly misleading because Hamilton favored a strong confederation rather than a loose federation. Hamilton's supporters were quickly dubbed the "Federalists," giving them an advantage in public opinion, because his opponents were automatically labeled "Anti-Federalists." The three states in which the fiercest fight was waged were Massachusetts, which approved ratification by a vote of 187 to 168, and Virginia and New York, which only ratified the Constitution in respectively June and July of 1788. The relatively unimportant states of North Carolina and Rhode Island added their ratification long after the United States had become a nation.

The first Congress of the United States met in 1789 according to the guidelines set out in the Constitution. George Washington was unanimously chosen as the first President, with Alexander Hamilton as Secretary of the Treasury. One of the first acts of the new Congress was to promulgate a Navigation Act to protect American products against foreign competition. The Congress levied a moderate eight percent import duty. This was not intended to protect domestic industry, but to raise income for the national treasury. In addition, Hamilton pushed through a bill imposing an excise tax on distilled liquor. These measures provided the federal government with a solid financial basis. As a necessary supplement, Hamilton created a national monetary system and established a bank of circulation.

The debt problem, however, needed immediate attention. All factions agreed that the twelve million dollar foreign debt should be paid as a matter of honor. But there were differences of opinion with respect to the government's domestic debts, which had mounted, with interest, to roughly forty million dollars. These debts, incurred in a time of high prices and inflated dollars, were concentrated in the hands of a few speculators. Nearly six months of heated debates followed. The issue was whether it was necessary and desirable to repay these debts completely. Hamilton, with an eye to the future financial standing of the United States, advocated integral repayment. Hamilton's view ultimately prevailed.

The debts incurred by the individual states to finance the war were a greater source of disagreement. Some states, such as Virginia, had resorted to rigorous taxation and had paid off most of its debts; other states had done nothing to resolve their debt problem. One of these, Massachusetts, was in dire financial straits, because under the new Constitution, it had lost its right to impose import duties. Hamilton believed that the only possible solution was for the United States to assume the war debts of the individual states. However, this step meant that several Southern states, most importantly Virginia, would have to help pay off the debts of the other states. This problem was resolved by a typical bit of horse trading: in return for agreeing to let the federal government assume the debts, the Southern states, the fiercest opponents, were promised that the new capital would be built in the South. Eventually constructed along the Potomac River, this capital was christened "Washington."

The Founding Fathers were therefore able to devise practical solutions to problems not encountered by the Old Revolutionaries. To the latter, including such men as Samuel Adams, Thomas Young and Patrick Henry, the primary objective had been to cast off Britain's crushing yoke. British taxes had been more than a symbol of this yoke: they had constituted the very yoke itself. And so it can be said that in America as well, taxation sparked off the struggle for independence. Once independence had been obtained, unification of the states followed. Having achieved unification, the country strove to preserve that unity and to use it to build a strong nation. Taxation was therefore a binding force in the country we still recognize as the United States of America. Might this be a hint to the countries in Western Europe groping their way two hundred years later toward greater unity?

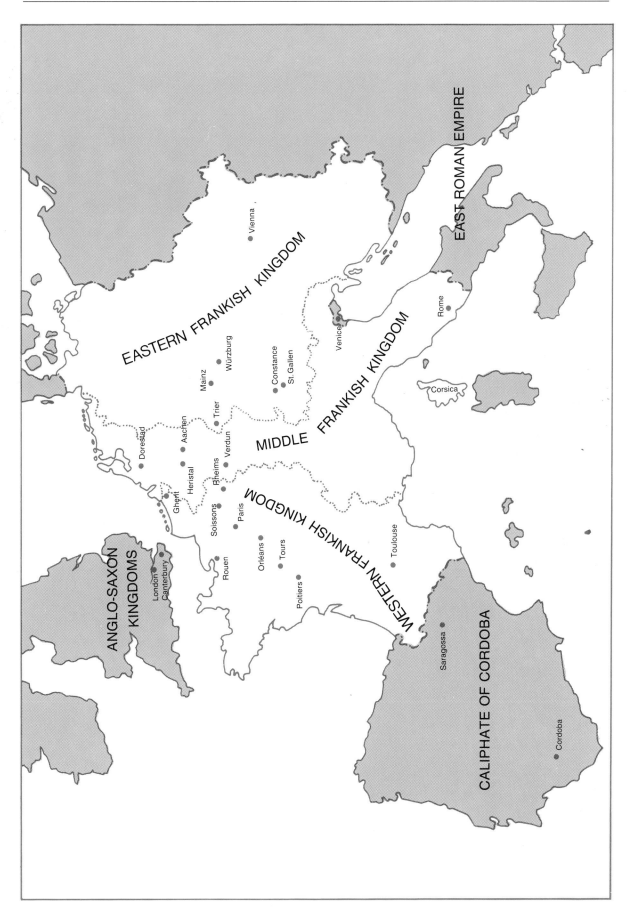

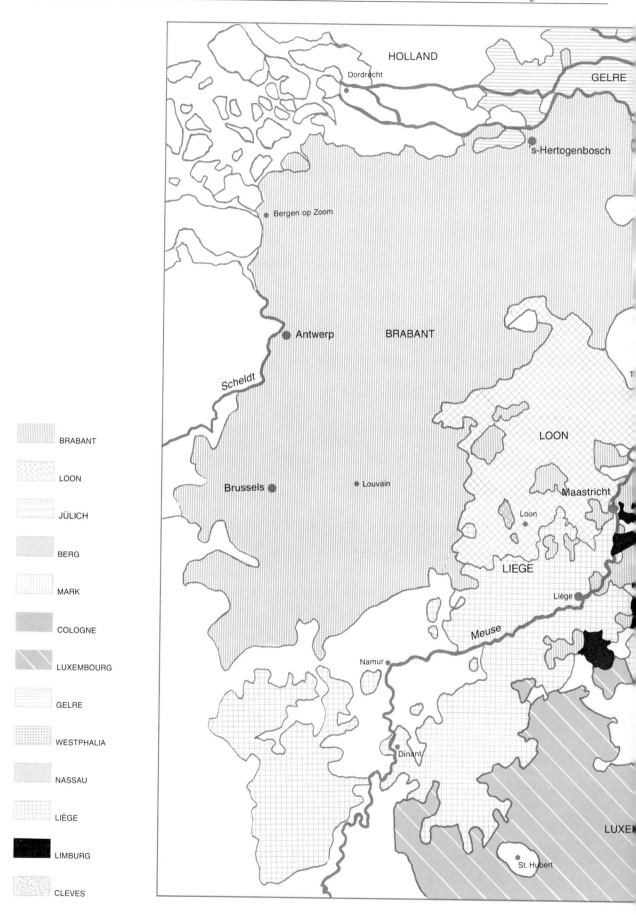

BRABANT

LOON

JÜLICH

BERG

MARK

COLOGNE

LUXEMBOURG

GELRE

WESTPHALIA

NASSAU

LIÈGE

LIMBURG

CLEVES

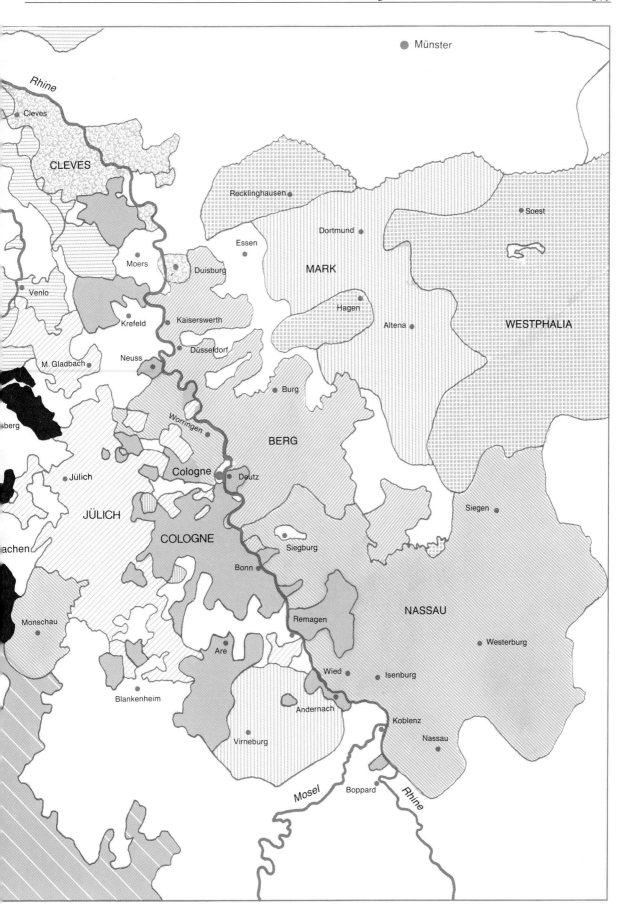

Rhine

Münster

Cleves

CLEVES

Recklinghausen

Soest

Dortmund

Essen

MARK

Moers

Duisburg

Venlo

Hagen

Krefeld

Kaiserswerth

Altena

WESTPHALIA

M. Gladbach

Neuss

Düsseldorf

...berg

Burg

Worringen

BERG

Jülich

Cologne

Deutz

Siegen

JÜLICH

COLOGNE

Siegburg

...achen

Bonn

NASSAU

Monschau

Remagen

Westerburg

Are

Wied

Isenburg

Blankenheim

Andernach

Koblenz

Virneburg

Nassau

Mosel

Boppard

Rhine

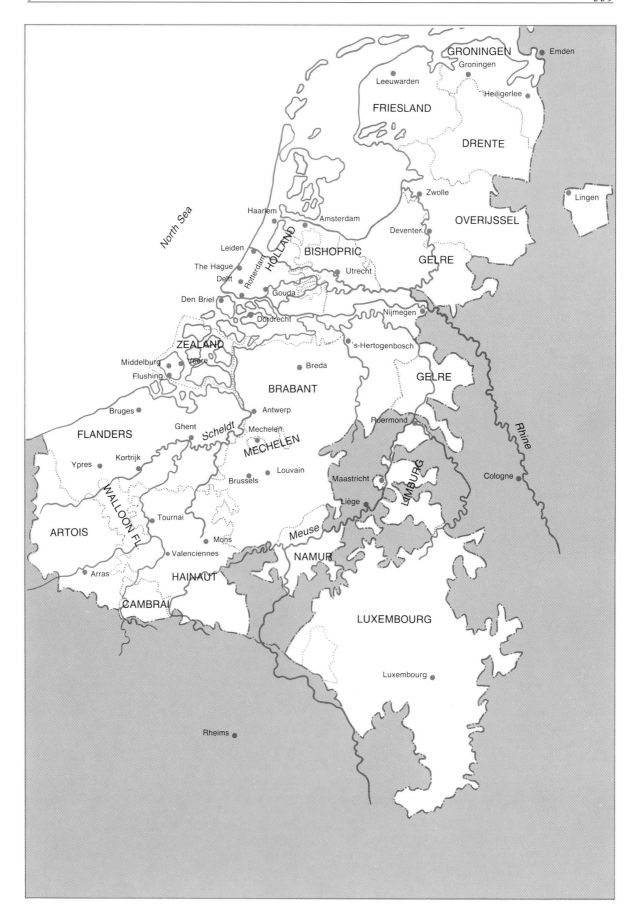

North Sea

GRONINGEN

Emden

Groningen

Leeuwarden

Heiligerlee

FRIESLAND

DRENTE

Lingen

Zwolle

OVERIJSSEL

Haarlem

Amsterdam

Deventer

Leiden

HOLLAND

BISHOPRIC

GELRE

The Hague

Delft

Rotterdam

Utrecht

Den Briel

Gouda

Dordrecht

Nijmegen

's-Hertogenbosch

ZEALAND

GELRE

Middelburg

Veere

Breda

Flushing

BRABANT

Bruges

Antwerp

Roermond

Rhine

FLANDERS

Ghent

Scheldt

Mechelen

MECHELEN

Ypres

Kortrijk

Louvain

LIMBURG

Cologne

Brussels

Maastricht

WALLOON FL.

Liège

Meuse

Tournai

ARTOIS

Mons

NAMUR

Valenciennes

Arras

HAINAUT

CAMBRAI

LUXEMBOURG

Luxembourg

Rheims

Taxes and tithes were paid in kind in the Middle Ages for a very long time. The dates the goods were due were sometimes set according to the time of the harvest, the butchering, etc. and sometimes according to the time in which nature could further ripen the fruits, without any significant human intervention.

In the accompanying pictures, the artist has depicted the due dates in the form of a farmer's almanac. The top picture is a reminder of the so-called lamb tithe. The lambs had to be handed over on May 1st, the feast of St. Walburga. The May tree on the right was frequently planted around the house on that date.

On May 25th, the feast of St. Urbanus, the rightful claimant could be said to have "earned" his future share of the fruit and the vineyard produce, since this marked the end of the spring period of work, represented by the empty work basket on the right. The meat tithe could be demanded on June 24th, the feast of St. John the Baptist, which is illustrated by cows, a goat and a chicken. St. John's crown is presumably depicted on the right.

The grain tithe follows on July 13th, the feast of St. Margaret. According to legend, Margaret put the devil in chains, shown to the right, with sheaves of grain behind her.

The bundle of herbs on the right in the next picture, which is used to prepare the geese on the left, refers to the Herb Mass on August 15th, the feast of Mary's

Ascension, when the geese tithe could be demanded. The remaining tithes could be called in on the feast of St. Bartholomew. As legend has it that Bartholomew was flayed, he is shown carrying his skin on a pole. The various goods to be handed over are stacked on and around the table on the left.

The illustrations have been taken from the Heidelberg Manuscript of the Sachsenspiegel, dating from the beginning of the fourteenth century. The latter is a German lawbook, written between approximately 1220 and 1224, by the knight Eike of Repgow, who delineated Saxon law as handed down from his forefathers.

Index of Persons

Abbot, George (1562-1633). Archbishop of Canterbury as of 1611. Generally considered to be the leader of the Calvinists in the early 17th century. Predecessor of William Laud. **Chap. 4** 259

Adalbert (c. 1000-1072). Archbishop of Bremen as of 1043. Rival of Archbishop Anno of Cologne. **Chap. 2** 81

Adams, John (1735-1826). Patriot leader in Boston. Defense Attorney for Captain Preston in the "Boston Massacre" trial. Later became second President of the United States. **Chap. 5** 331, 351, 352, 361

Adams, Samuel (1722-1803). Patriot leader in Boston. **Chap. 5** 329, 331, 338, 340, 348, 350, 351, 361, 366, 375

Adolf I of Altena (d. 1205). Archbishop of Cologne as of 1193. **Chap. 2** 89, 92, 93

Adrevald. Monk of the Abbey of Fleury. **Chap. 1** 56

Aegidius (d. 464). Roman Commander of the Franks. **Chap. 1** 42

Aethelbert (d. 616). King of Kent as of 560. Converted to Christianity in 598 by Augustine of Canterbury. Married to Bertha, daughter of Charibert I. **Chap. 1** 29

Albertus Magnus, also called Albert the Great (c. 1206-1280). Saint. Doctor of the Church. Greatest German scholar in the Middle Ages. **Chap. 2** 68, 98, 101

Altena and Isenburg, Frederick of. Opponent of Archbishop Engelbrecht of Berg, whom he had murdered in 1225. **Chap. 2** 94

Alva, Fernando Alvarez de Toledo, Duke of (1507-1582). Spanish statesman and general. Governor of the Low Countries from 1567 to 1573. **Preface** 10, 12, **Chap. 3** 134, 142, 143, 144, 145, 146 ff, **Chap. 4** 274

Amandus. Saint, founder of the St. Baafs Abbey in Ghent. **Chap. 1** 45

Anno II (c. 1010-1075). Archbishop of Cologne as of 1056. **Chap. 2** 63, 64, 80, 81, 82, 84

Aquinas, Thomas (1225-1274). Doctor of the Church. **Chap. 2** 67

Armentarius. Tax farmer. **Chap. 1** 31

Arminius, James (1560-1609). Dutch Protestant theologian. **Chap. 4** 246

Arnold II of Wied (d. 1156). Archbishop of Cologne as of 1151. **Chap. 2** 77

Arundel, Duchess of. Lady-in-Waiting to Queen Henrietta Maria. **Chap. 4** 232

Athanagild (d. 567). King of the Visigoths. Father of Brunhild and Galswinth. **Chap. 1** 22

Audinus. Tax official. **Chap. 1** 41

Audo. Count, trusted representative of Fredegund. **Chap. 1** 34

Ayres. Sea Captain. **Chap. 5** 353

Bacon, Francis, Baron Verulam, Viscount St. Albans (1561-1626). English scholar, later Chancellor under James I. Impeached in 1621 by the House of Commons for misconduct in office. **Chap. 4** 225

Bakkerzeel. Egmond's Secretary. **Chap. 3** 146

Baltimore, George Calvert, Baron of (1580-1632). English nobleman. Colonizer of Maryland. **Chap. 4** 295, 296

Bankes, Sir John (1589-1644). Attorney General. **Chap. 4** 271

Barré, Issac (1726-1802). English Member of Parliament. **Chap. 5** 311, 319

Bastwick, John (1593-1654). Puritan pamphleteer. **Chap. 4** 267, 270, 281

Benedict of Nursia (c. 480-c. 547). Saint, Patriarch of Western monasticism. **Chap. 1** 56

Berg, Adolf, Count of. **Chap. 2** 102

Berg, Gerard of. Son of William of Berg. **Chap. 2** 118

Berg, William of. Bishop-elect of Paderborn. Rival candidate of Diedrich of Moers. Married to Adelheid of Tecklenburg. **Chap. 2** 114, 115, 116, 118

Berkeley, Lord John. English nobleman. Colonizer of Carolina and New Jersey. **Chap. 5** 299

Berkeley, Sir Robert. Justice of the King's Bench. **Chap. 4** 271

Berlaymont, Charles, Count of (1510-1578). Head of the Council of Finance and member of the Council of State. **Chap. 3** 138, 170

Bernard, Sir Francis (1712-1779). Governor of Massachusetts. Zealous anti-patriot. **Chap. 5** 312, 319, 321, 337, 355

Bertha. Daughter of Charibert I. Married to Aethelbert. **Chap. 1** 29

Berthold. Mayor of the Palace. **Chap. 1** 35

Bingen, Hildegard of (1098-1179). Saint, visionary, German Abbess of a Benedictine monastery. **Chap. 2** 63

Birkelin, Edmund. Knight. **Chap. 2** 106

Bolter, Thomas. Boston Tea Party participant. **Chap. 5** 351

Bossu, Maximilien de Hénin, Count of (1542-1578). Stadtholder of Holland, Zealand and Utrecht. **Chap. 3** 186, 190

Bramston, Sir John. Lord Chief Justice of the King's Bench. **Chap. 4** 273

Brewer, James. Boston Tea Party participant. **Chap. 5** 351

Bruce. Sea Captain. **Chap. 5** 348

Brueghel, Pieter the Elder (c. 1528-1569). Flemish painter. **Chap. 3** 176

Brunhild (c. 534-613). Daughter of Athanagild. Married to Sigibert I. **Chap. 1** 22-25, 27, 29, 34, 35, 37, 38, 45

Bruno I of Saxony (925-965). Saint, Archbishop of Cologne as of 953. Brother of Emperor Otto I. **Chap. 1** 61, 63, 64, 75, 77, 80

Bruno of Sayn (d. 1208). Archbishop of Cologne since 1205. **Chap. 2** 89, 93

Buckingham, George Villiers, Duke of (1592-1628). Confidant of James I and Charles I. Climbed his way up to the position of Charles' most important minister. **Chap. 4** 228, 232-250, 257, 258, 274, 281

Burke, Edmund (1729-1797). English Member of Parliament and political publicist. **Chap. 5** 355, 357, 358, 362

Burton, Henry (1579-1647). Puritan pamphleteer. **Chap. 4** 267, 281

Bute, John Stuart, Earl of (1713-1792). Confidant of George III. Served at one time as his Prime Minister. **Chap. 5** 312, 315

Buyck, Joost Sybrandsz. (1505-1578). Mayor of Amsterdam. **Chap. 3** 188

Buys, Paulus (1531-1594). Holland's Government Attorney from 1572 to 1585. **Chap. 3** 212

Caesar, Gaius Julius (100 B.C.-44 B.C.). Roman General and statesman. **Chap. 1** 15

Camden, Lord. English member of Parliament. **Chap. 5** 317

Capet, Hugh (d. 996). French King as of 987. Also Duke of the region now known as Île de France. Founder of the Capetian dynasty. **Chap. 1** 57

Capocci, Petrus. Papal legate. **Chap. 2** 96

Carmarthen, Francis Osborne, Marquis of, Duke of Leeds (1751-1799). English politician. **Chap. 5** 356, 357

Carteret, Sir George (c. 1610-1680). Colonizer of New Jersey. **Chap. 5** 299

Charibert I (d. 567). Frankish King as of 561. Oldest son of Lothar I. **Chap. 1** 18, 24, 25, 29, 41

Charlemagne (742-814). King of the Franks as of 768. King of the Lombards as of 774. Roman Emperor from 800 to 814. **Chap. 1** 20, 49, 51, 53, 54

Charles I (1600-1649). King of England, Ireland and Scotland as of 1625. **Preface** 10, 12, **Chap. 2** 73, **Chap. 4** 218, 221, 223 ff, **Chap. 5** 295

Charles II (1630-1685). King of England, Ireland and Scotland as of 1660. **Chap. 4** 257, **Chap. 5** 296, 299

Charles IV (1316-1378). German King as of 1346. German Emperor from 1355 to 1378. **Chap. 2** 87

Charles V (1500-1558). Emperor of the Holy Roman Empire since 1519. King of Spain, etc. **Chap. 3** 130, 131, 132, 133, 136, 137, 149, 151, 164

Charles the Bald (823-877). King of the Western Frankish Kingdom as of 840. Roman Emperor as of 875. **Chap. 1** 20, 46, 57

Charles the Bold, Duke of Burgundy (1433-1477). Sovereign ruler of several Dutch provinces. **Chap. 3** 129, 133

Charles Martel (689-741). Frankish Mayor of the Palace. Illegitimate son of Pepin II of Heristal. **Chap. 1** 19, 51, 52, 53

Chatham, Earl of. See Pitt, William.

Childebert I (d. 558). Frankish King as of 511. Son of Clovis I. **Chap. 1** 17, 18, 45

Childebert II (570-595). Frankish King as of 587. Son of Sigibert I and Brunhild. **Chap. 1** 22, 25, 32, 34, 40, 41, 42

Childeric I (d. 481). Frankish King as of 457. Succeeded by his son Clovis I. **Chap. 1** 17, 45

Chilperic I (d. 584). Frankish King as of 561. Son of Lothar I. Married first to Galswinth and then to Fredegund. **Chap. 1** 18, 22-27, 29, 30, 34, 40, 44, 45, 47

Chloderic. King of the Frankish tribe in Cologne. Son of Sigibert. Contemporary of Clovis I. **Chap. 1** 15, 44

Chlodomer (d. 524). Son of Clovis I. **Chap. 1** 17, 18, 44

Clarke, Isaac. Boston tea merchant. Son of Richard Clarke. **Chap. 5** 339, 347

Clarke, Jonathan. Boston tea merchant. Son of Richard Clarke. **Chap. 5** 335, 339, 341, 343, 344, 347

Clarke, Richard. Boston tea merchant. **Chap. 5** 339, 341

Cleves, Adolf, Duke of. **Chap. 2** 117

Clotild (474-545). Saint. Wife of Clovis I, who converted to Christianity partly due to her influence. **Chap. 1** 16, 17, 18

Clovis. Son of Chilperic I. Murdered on Fredegund's orders. **Chap. 1** 34

Clovis I (466-511). King of the Salian Franks since 481. Married to Clotild of Burgundy. Conquered a large portion of Gaul. Converted to Christianity in 496. **Chap. 1** 15, 16, 17, 58, **Chap. 2** 77

Clovis II (635-657). King of Burgundy and Neustria as of 639. Son of Dagobert I. **Chap. 1** 47

Coke, Sir Edward (1552-1634). English jurist who posed the question of royal prerogatives. **Chap. 4** 219, 281

Conrad III (c. 1093-1152). German King as of 1138, the first from the Staufer dynasty. **Chap. 2** 77

Conrad of Hochstadt (d. 1261). Archbishop of Cologne as of 1239. **Chap. 2** 64, 73, 88, 96-101, 106

Conrad the Red. Duke of Lorraine, married to one of the daughters of Otto I. **Chap. 2** 61

Cornet. Pensionary of Dordrecht. **Chap. 3** 180

Crane, John. Boston Tea Party participant. **Chap. 5** 351

Crawley, Sir Francis. Justice of the Court of Common Pleas. **Chap. 4** 271

Cromwell, Oliver (1599-1658). English Commander and politician. Ended the Civil War and established his own reign. **Chap. 4** 230

Crooke, Sir George. Justice of the King's Bench. **Chap. 4** 269, 272, 274

Dagobert I (602-639). Frankish King from 623 to 639. Son of Lothar II. **Chap. 1** 19, 45, 47

Dartmouth, William Legge, Earl of (1731-1801). English Secretary of State for the Colonies. **Chap. 5** 337, 354

Davenport, Sir Humphries. Lord Chief Baron of the Exchequer. **Chap. 4** 272, 273

Denbigh, Lady. Sister of Buckingham. Lady-in-Waiting to Queen Henrietta Maria. **Chap. 4** 237

Denham, Sir John (1615-1669). Baron of the Court of the Exchequer. **Chap. 4** 272

Dickinson, John (1732-1808). Delegate to the Continental Congress from Pennsylvania. Known as the "penman of the Revolution." **Chap. 5** 320, 364

Diedrich II of Moers (d. 1463). Archbishop of Cologne as of 1414. **Chap. 2** 64, 69, 74, 113-126

Diepholt, Rudolf, Count of (1400-1455). Bishop of Utrecht as of 1423. **Chap. 2** 116

Digby, Lord George, 2nd Earl of Bristol (1580-1654). **Chap. 4** 282, 283

Dowdeswell, William (1721-1801). English Member of Parliament. **Chap. 5** 335, 340

Droege, Georg. German historian. **Chap. 2** 72

Dudley, Robert. See Leicester.

Dyck, Anthony van (1599-1641). Flemish painter. Knighted by the English in 1632. **Chap. 4** 259

Ebargisilus. Clerk. **Chap. 1** 47

Eboli, Prince of. See Ruy Gómez.

Edward I (1239-1307). King of England as of 1272. **Chap. 4** 270

Egmond, Lamoraal, Count of (1522-1568). Member of the Council of State and Governor of Flanders. Beheaded after a show trial held by the Council of Troubles. **Chap. 3** 138, 142, 144, 145, 146

Einhard. Lay-abbot of the St. Baafs Abbey in Ghent. **Chap. 1** 57

Eliot, Sir John (1592-1632). Leader of the Puritan Members of Parliament. Died in prison. **Chap. 4** 237, 238, 242, 243, 246, 247, 249, 252, 254, 255, 258, 269, 278

Elizabeth Stuart (1596-1662). Daughter of James I. Married to Frederick of the Palatinate. **Chap. 4** 225, 234

Elizabeth I Tudor (1553-1603). Queen of England as of 1558. Daughter of Henry VIII and Anne Boleyn. **Chap. 3** 145, 186, 189, 208, 210, 212, **Chap. 4** 217, 220, 221, 223, 240, 272, **Chap. 5** 290

Engelbrecht I of Berg (1185-1225). Also called "St. Engelbrecht." Archbishop of Cologne as of 1216. **Chap. 2** 64, 88, 92-95, 98, 101, 102, 105, 124

Engelbrecht II of Valkenburg (d. 1274). Archbishop of Cologne as of 1261. **Chap. 2** 101

Espinosa, Diego de. Chairman of the Spanish Council of State. Cardinal since 1568. **Chap. 3** 188

Eufronius. Bishop. **Chap. 1** 41

Eugenius IV (c. 1383-1447). Pope since 1431. **Chap. 2** 116, 124

Eugene, Franz, Prince of Savoy-Carignan (1663-1736). Austrian General and statesman. **Chap. 5** 296

Eunonius. Count. **Chap. 1** 31

Faileuba. Queen. Earlier wife of Childebert I. **Chap. 1** 35

Fawkes, Guy (1570-1606). English soldier involved in the Gunpowder Plot. **Chap. 4** 229

Fenno, Samuel. Boston Tea Party participant. **Chap. 5** 351

Ferreolus. Bishop in the time of Chilperic I. **Chap. 1** 29

Finch, Sir John (1588-1653). Speaker of the House of Commons. Later Lord Chief Justice of the Court of Common Pleas. **Chap. 4** 254, 261, 272, 273, 274, 277, 278, 281

Florentianus. Mayor of the Palace and Tax collector. **Chap. 1** 40

Fox, Charles James (1749-1806). English Member of Parliament. **Chap. 5** 358

Franklin, Benjamin (1706-1790). American Patriot, writer and inventor. **Chap. 5** 323, 327, 338, 339, 354, 372

Fredegund (d. 597). Frankish slave. Later Queen and wife of Chilperic I. Brunhild's rival.   **Chap. 1** 23, 24, 25, 27, 28, 29, 32, 34, 37, 40, 41, 44

Frederick I of Hohenstaufen, called Barbarossa (c. 1123-1190). German King as of 1152. Emperor from 1155 to 1190.   **Chap. 2** 77

Frederick II (1194-1250). German King as of 1211. Emperor from 1221 to 1250.   **Chap. 2** 92, 93, 97

Frederick III of Hapsburg (1415-1493). German Emperor as of 1452.   **Chap. 2** 104, 118

Frederick, Don. See Toledo.

Frederick Henry, Count of Nassau (1584-1674). Prince of Orange. Stadtholder of five provinces in the Dutch Republic.   **Chap. 4** 232, 258, 262, 282

Frederick of the Palatinate (1596-1632). King of Bohemia from 1619 to 1620.   **Chap. 4** 225, 234

Gage, Thomas (1721-1787). English General in the American colonies.   **Chap. 5** 356, 358, 361

Gaiso. Count.   **Chap. 1** 41

Galswinth. Sister of Brunhild. Wife of Chilperic I, who had her murdered.   **Chap. 1** 23, 24, 32

Gates, Horatio (1728-1806). American General at the Battle of Saratoga (1777), which turned the tide in favor of the rebels.   **Chap. 5** 366

George II Augustus (1683-1760). King of Great Britain and Ireland and Electoral Prince of Hanover since 1727.   **Chap. 5** 296

George III William Frederick (1738-1820). King of Great Britain and Ireland, Electoral Prince of Hanover since 1760 and King of Hanover since 1814.   **Chap. 5** 315, 319, 327, 340

Gerry, Elbridge (1744-1814). Governor of Massachusetts, after whom the term "gerrymandering" is named. Gerrymandering refers to the practice of dividing electoral districts so as to influence the election outcome.   **Chap. 5** 373

Gerson, Johannes. Writer of the "Bishop's Mirror."   **Chap. 2** 64

Grafton, Augustus Henry Fitzroy, Duke of (1735-1811). English Prime Minister.   **Chap. 5** 326, 327

Granvelle, Antoine de (1517-1586). Bishop of Arras. Councilor under Charles V and Philip II. Cardinal as of 1561.   **Chap. 3** 138, 139, 146, 197

Gregory VII (d. 1085). Pope as of 1073. Also known as the monk "Hildebrand."   **Chap. 2** 62

Grenville, George (1712-1770). English Prime Minister. Wished to tax the American colonies via the Sugar Act of 1764 and the Stamp Act of 1765.   **Chap. 5** 310, 317

Grin, Rutger Hirzelin von. Head of Cologne's Annuity Board.   **Chap. 2** 106

Gundovald. Duke.   **Chap. 1** 25

Guntram (d. 593). Frankish King as of 561. Son of Lothar I.   **Chap. 1** 18, 24, 27, 28, 32, 34, 44

Gustave Adolf II (1594-1632). King of Sweden as of 1611.   **Chap. 4** 258

Hagen, Godefrit. 13th century chronicler.   **Chap. 2** 98

Hall, James. Sea Captain.   **Chap. 5** 345, 347, 348, 354

Hallowel. Revenue Agent.   **Chap. 5** 323

Hamilton, Alexander (1755-1804). American politician and ardent supporter of a strong central government, which he helped shape as Secretary of the Treasury.   **Chap. 5** 371-374

Hampden, John (c. 1594-1643). English Puritan Member of Parliament. His refusal to pay ship money led to the famous trial of Rex versus Hampden.   **Preface** 10,   **Chap. 4** 242, 269-274, 280, 282,   **Chap. 5** 320

Hancock, John (1737-1793). Patriot leader in Boston.   **Chap. 5** 321, 323, 329, 339, 340, 341, 351

Harrison, John. Revenue Agent.   **Chap. 5** 323

Harrison, Richard. Revenue Agent. Son of John Harrison.   **Chap. 5** 339, 347, 348, 354

Heath, Sir Robert. Chief Justice of the Court of Common Pleas.   **Chap. 4** 263

Heelu, Jan van. Chronicler of Duke John of Brabant.   **Chap. 2** 104

Heighton, Alexander. Puritan pamphleteer.   **Chap. 4** 260

Heisterbach, Cesarius of (c. 1180-c. 1240). Chronicler, scholar.   **Chap. 2** 94, 95

Henrietta Maria of France (1609-1669). Married to Charles I of England.   **Chap. 4** 229, 232, 233, 234, 237, 238, 241, 250, 257, 281, 284

Henry I of Molenark (d. 1238). Archbishop of Cologne as of 1225.   **Chap. 2** 64, 95

Henry III (1551-1589). King of France since 1574.   **Chap. 3** 210

Henry III (1017-1056). German King as of 1039. Emperor from 1046 to 1056.   **Chap. 2** 80

Henry IV (1553-1610). King of France since 1589.   **Chap. 4** 223, 229

Henry IV (1050-1106). German King as of 1056. Emperor from 1084 to 1105. Son of Henry III.   **Chap. 2** 80, 84

Henry V (1081-1125). German King as of 1098. Emperor from 1111 to 1125. Son of Henry IV.   **Chap. 2** 84

Henry VI (1421-1471). King of England from 1422 to 1461 and from 1470 to 1471.   **Chap. 4** 235.

Henry VII (1457-1509). First Tudor King of England as of 1485.   **Chap. 4** 251,   **Chap. 5** 317

Henry VIII (1491-1547). King of England and Ireland as of 1509.   **Chap. 4** 217

Henry the Fowler, Stem Duke of Saxony (876-936). German King as of 919.   **Chap. 2** 61

Henry the Lion (1129-1195). Duke of Saxony and Bavaria. Rebelled against Frederick Barbarossa and all his fiefs were declared invalid. **Chap. 2** 77

Henry Raspe (1203-1247). German anti-king from 1246 to 1247. **Chap. 2** 96

Henry, Patrick (1736-1799). Patriot leader in Virginia. Driving force behind including the Bill of Rights in the Constitution of 1787. **Chap. 5** 375

Heribert (d. 1021). Saint, Archbishop of Cologne as of 999. **Chap. 2** 63

Herries, Robert. English Member of Parliament. **Chap. 5** 335

Hersfeld, Lambert of. Medieval historian. **Chap. 2** 81

Hildebrand. See Gregory VII.

Hillsborough, William Hill, Marquis of (1718-1793). English Secretary of State for the Colonies. **Chap. 5** 321, 327, 337

Honorius III (c. 1150-1227). Pope as of 1216. **Chap. 2** 94

Honthorst, Gerard van (1590-1656). Dutch painter. **Chap. 4** 259

Hoogstraten, Antoine de Lalaing, Count of (d. 1568). Dutch nobleman. Cousin of Rennenberg. **Chap. 3** 144

Hopperus, Joachim (1523-1576). Frisian jurist. Came from the same region and was the protégé of Viglius. Member of the Spanish Council of State from 1569 to 1576 and Keeper of the Seal for Dutch affairs. **Chap. 3** 170, 189, 190, 197

Horne, Philippe de Montmorency, Count of (1524-1568). Stadtholder of Gelderland, member of the Council of State. Beheaded in 1568 after a show trial held by the Council of Troubles. **Chap. 3** 142, 144, 145

Hoya, Eric, Count of. Bishop of Münster. **Chap. 2** 116

Hudson, Henry (c. 1565-1611). English explorer. **Chap. 5** 299

Hus, John (c. 1370-1415). Czech reformer. **Chap. 2** 124

Hutchinson, Elisha. Boston tea merchant. Son of Thomas Hutchinson. **Chap. 5** 339

Hutchinson, Thomas (1711-1780). Governor of Massachusetts. **Chap. 5** 312, 332, 337-341, 349, 353-356

Hutchinson, Thomas Jr. Boston tea merchant. Son of Thomas Hutchinson. **Chap. 5** 339, 347

Hutton, Sir Richard. Justice of the Court of Common Pleas. **Chap. 4** 269, 272, 274

Ingersoll, Jared. Stamp official appointee. **Chap. 5** 313

Injuriosus. Vice-count. **Chap. 1** 31

Injuriosus. Bishop of Tours. **Chap. 1** 39

James I (1566-1625). King of England and Ireland since 1603 and of Scotland since 1567. **Chap. 4** 217-223, 225, 228, 229, 230, 232, 255, 277, 287, **Chap. 5** 290, 292

James II (1633-1701). King of England, Ireland and Scotland from 1685 to 1688. Succeeded his brother Charles II, but was ousted by the Glorious Revolution. **Chap. 4** 257, 299

John I (c. 1254-1294). Duke of Brabant as of 1268 and of Limburg as of 1288. **Chap. 2** 102, 104

John I (1167-1216). King of England as of 1199. **Chap. 1** 37, **Chap. 2** 92

Johnson, Samuel (1709-1784). English lexicographer and philosopher. **Chap. 5** 304, 305

Jones, Sir William. Justice of the King's Bench. **Chap. 4** 272

Jülich, William, Count of (d. 1278). **Chap. 2** 102

Justinian I (483-565). Byzantine Emperor as of 527. **Chap. 1** 29

Juxon, William (1582-1663). Bishop of London and Archbishop of Canterbury. **Chap. 4** 267, 284

Kriekenbeke, Johan of. Knight. **Chap. 2** 124

Lallon. Tax collector. **Chap. 1** 47

Lambe, Dr. Buckingham's soothsayer. **Chap. 4** 257

Laud, William (1573-1645). Archbishop of Canterbury from 1633 to 1645. Beheaded after a trial held under the auspices of the Long Parliament. **Chap. 4** 234, 258-260, 267-269, 274, 276, 277, 279, 281, 284-287, 288

Lee, Samuel. Patriot leader in Virginia. **Chap. 5** 366

Leicester, Robert Dudley, Earl of (1533-1588). English militarist and statesman. **Chap. 3** 208-212

Leo III (d. 816). Pope as of 795. **Chap. 1** 20

Lievens, Jan (1515-1578). Municipal Pensionary of Louvain. **Chap. 3** 165

Lincoln, Robert. John Hampden's lawyer. **Chap. 4** 270

Littleton, Sir Edmund. Solicitor General. **Chap. 4** 270

Liudhard. Chaplain forming part of the retinue of Bertha of Kent. **Chap. 1** 29

Locke, John (1632-1704). English philosopher. **Chap. 5** 317

Lothair I (795-855). King of the Middle Frankish Kingdom as of 833. Emperor as of 840. Oldest son of Louis the Pious. **Chap. 1** 20, 57

Lothar I (d. 561). Frankish King as of 511. Youngest son of Clovis I. **Chap. 1** 17, 18, 22, 30, 39, 40, 41

Lothar II (d. 628). Frankish King as of 584. Youngest son of Chilperic I.   **Chap. 1** 19, 28, 34, 35, 37, 38, 46

Louis I the Pious (778-840). Third son of Charlemagne. Emperor as of August 813.   **Chap. 1** 20, 46, 49

Louis XI (1423-1483). King of France since 1461.   **Chap. 3** 129

Louis XIII (1601-1643). King of France since 1610.   **Chap. 4** 229, 241, 250

Louis the German (806-876). King of the Eastern Frankish Kingdom as of 833.   **Chap. 1** 20

Macrel, Jehan. Appointed as tax collector in Artois.   **Chap. 3** 176

Madison, James (1751-1836). American statesman. Fourth president of the United States.   **Chap. 5** 372-374

Mansfeld, Ernst, Count of (c. 1580-1626). Leader of the expedition to the Palatinate.   **Chap. 4** 225, 234

Mark. Tax collector.   **Chap. 1** 29

Mark, Gerard, Count of.   **Chap. 2** 117

Marnix, Philip, Lord of St. Aldegonde (1540-1598). William of Orange's agent.   **Chap. 3** 190

Maroveus. Bishop of Poitiers.   **Chap. 1** 40

Mary, Duchess of Burgundy. (1457-1482). Daughter of Charles the Bold. Married to Maximilian of Austria.   **Chap. 3** 129, 130

Mary of Hungary, actually Mary of Hapsburg (1505-1558). Governor of the Low Countries. Queen of Hungary.   **Chap. 3** 130

Mary Stuart (1542-1587). Queen of Scotland from 1542 to 1567.   **Chap. 4** 217

Mary Stuart (1631-1661). Married William II of Orange in 1641.   **Chap. 4** 257, 282, 284

Mary Stuart (1662-1694). Married to William III of Orange. Queen of England, Ireland and Scotland after the Glorious Revolution of 1688.   **Chap. 4** 247

Mary Tudor, nicknamed "Bloody Mary" (1516-1558). Queen of England as of 1553.   **Chap. 4** 220

Maurice (c. 539-602). Byzantine Emperor as of 582.   **Chap. 1** 45

Maurits, Count of Nassau (1567-1625). Prince of Orange since 1618. Stadtholder of five provinces in the Dutch Republic.   **Chap. 4** 232

Maurois, André. Pseudonym and after 1947 the official name of Emile Salomon Wilhelm Herzog (1885-1967). French writer.   **Chap. 4** 230

Maximilian I (1459-1519). German Emperor as of 1493. Married to Mary of Burgundy.   **Chap. 3** 130

Maximilian II (1527-1576). German Emperor as of 1564.   **Chap. 3** 145

Medard. Assistant to Vice-Count Injuriosus.   **Chap. 1** 32

Melvill, Thomas. Boston Tea Party participant.   **Chap. 5** 351

Merovech. King of the Salian tribe. Founder of the Merovingian dynasty.   **Chap. 1** 15

Merovech. Son of Chilperic I. Switched to the camp of his aunt Brunhild, whom he married.   **Chap. 1** 25, 27

Moers, Henry of. Bishop of Münster. Brother of Diedrich II of Moers.   **Chap. 2** 113, 116, 119

Moers, Walram of. Brother of Diedrich II of Moers.   **Chap. 2** 113, 116, 119

Molineux, William. Patriot leader in Boston.   **Chap. 5** 340, 341, 345, 351

Montagu. See Sandwich.

Montague. English Member of Parliament.   **Chap. 4** 248

Montesquieu, Charles-Louis de Secondat, Baron de la Brède et de (1689-1755). French jurist and political philosopher. Originator of the theory of the *trias politica*.   **Chap. 1** 38,   **Chap. 5** 372

Montigny, Floris de Montmorency, Baron of (1527-1570). Stadtholder of Tournai. Was sent by Governor Margaret of Parma to inform Philip II of the situation in The Netherlands. Secretly murdered on Philip's orders in 1570.   **Chap. 3** 153

Morgan. English commander.   **Chap. 4** 248

Morillon, Maximilian (1517-1586). Vicar-General of the Archbishopric of Mechelen. Granvelle's most important source of information about the situation in The Netherlands.   **Chap. 3** 146, 178, 179, 197

Morris, Robert (1734-1806). American politician. "Financier of the Revolution."   **Chap. 5** 368, 370

Mummolus. Gallo-Roman prefect.   **Chap. 1** 32, 45

Nassau, Louis, Count of (1538-1574). Brother of William of Orange.   **Chap. 3** 146, 189

Noircarmes, Philip of St. Aldegonde, Baron of (d. 1574). Stadtholder of Hainaut. Member of the Council of Finance and Council of State.   **Chap. 3** 172

Normand, Guillaume Le. Member of Middelburg's Council.   **Chap. 3** 176

North, Frederick, Earl of Guilford (1733-1792). English Chancellor of the Exchequer.   **Chap. 5** 326, 327, 335, 340, 355

Odoacer (c. 434-493). Commander of the Germanic tribes.   **Chap. 1** 15

Oglethorpe, James Edward (1696-1785). English officer. American colonizer of Georgia. **Chap. 5** 296, 297

Oldenbarnevelt, Johan van (1547-1619). Dutch statesman. Advocate of the States of Holland. **Chap. 3** 210, 211, 212

Oliver, Andrew. Stamp official appointee. Later Lieutenant-Governor of Massachusetts. **Chap. 5** 312, 337, 338

Orange, William of. See William I, Count of Nassau.

Otto I the Great (912-973). German King as of 936. Emperor from 962 to 973. **Chap. 2** 61, 75

Otto II (955-983). German King and Emperor as of 973. **Chap. 2** 75

Otto IV of Brunswick (c. 1175-1218). German King as of 1198. German Emperor from 1209 to 1218. **Chap. 2** 89, 90, 93

Paine, Thomas (1737-1809). American politician and publicist. **Chap. 5** 299, 366

Parker, Geoffrey. British historian. **Chap. 3** 199

Parma, Alexander Farnese, Duke of (1545-1592). Governor of the Low Countries. **Chap. 3** 199, 204, 212

Parma, Margaret, Duchess of (1522-1586). Governor of the Low Countries. Illegitimate daughter of Charles V and Johanna van der Gheynst. **Chap. 3** 138, 139, 140, 142, 143, 144, 147

Parsons, Nancy. Mistress of the Duke of Grafton. **Chap. 5** 326

Parthenius. Tax collector. **Chap. 1** 30

Penn, William (1644-1718). Quaker leader. The state of Pennsylvania was founded by him and named in his honor. **Chap. 5** 299, 300

Pepin II of Heristal (c. 635-714). Mayor of the Palace. **Chap. 1** 19, 52

Pepin III the Short (c. 715-768). Mayor of the Palace. King of the Franks since 754. Son of Charles Martel. **Chap. 1** 19, 49, 51, 52, **Chap. 2** 61

Philip I of Heinsberg (d. 1191). Archbishop of Cologne as of 1167. **Chap. 2** 77, 78, 88

Philip II (1527-1598). Sovereign ruler of the Low Countries as of 1555. King of Spain as of 1556. **Preface** 10, **Chap. 3** 129, 130, 133, 137-144, 146, 147, 149, 153, 158, 163, 173-175, 180-193, 201, 202, 212, **Chap. 4** 274

Philip II Augustus (1165-1223). King of France as of 1180. **Chap. 2** 90

Philip the Good, Duke of Burgundy (1396-1467). Sovereign ruler of several Dutch provinces. **Chap. 2** 120, **Chap. 3** 129

Philip the Handsome, Duke of Burgundy (1478-1506). Sovereign ruler of several Dutch provinces. **Chap. 3** 130

Philip of Swabia (c. 1180-1208). German King since 1198, from the Staufer dynasty. **Chap. 2** 89, 90, 93

Pitt, William, Earl of Chatham (1708-1778). English statesman. **Preface** 12, **Chap. 5** 303, 307, 315, 316, 317, 319, 326, 334, 362

Pitts, Lendall. Boston Tea Party participant. **Chap. 5** 351

Poitou, Agnes of (1024/1025-1077). Wife of Henry III. **Chap. 2** 80

Preston, Thomas. Army officer during the "Boston Massacre." **Chap. 5** 331, 356

Protadius. Trusted representative of Brunhild. **Chap. 1** 46

Prynne, William (1600-1669). English Puritan publicist. Zealous opponent of William Laud, Archbishop of Canterbury, who had Prynne's ears cut off and his cheeks branded with the letters "S.L." (Seditious Libeller). Later, the tables were turned, and Prynne was one of the driving forces behind the Archbishop's beheading. **Chap. 4** 260, 267, 270, 281, 287, 288

Pym, John (1584-1643). English leader of the Puritan faction in Parliament. **Chap. 4** 228, 234, 235, 252, 278-282, 284, 287

Quincy, Josiah (1744-1775). American lawyer. Together with John Adams, defended Captain Preston in the "Boston Massacre" trial. **Chap. 5** 331

Radcliffe, Sir George (1593-1667). Nephew and confidant of Strafford. **Chap. 4** 281

Raho. Carolingian count. **Chap. 1** 56

Rennenberg, Georges de Lalaing, Count of (c. 1550-1581). Stadtholder of Friesland, Groningen, Drenthe and Overijssel. Defected to the Spanish. **Chap. 3** 204

Requesens y de Zuniga, Don Luis de (1528-1576). Spanish General and Governor of the Low Countries. **Chap. 3** 153, 192-194, 197

Revere, Paul (1735-1818). Patriot leader in Boston. **Chap. 5** 331, 340, 351

Rich, Sir Nathaniel (d. 1636). English Member of Parliament. **Chap. 4** 247

Richard I the Lion-Hearted (1157-1199). King of England since 1189. **Chap. 2** 90

Richardson, Ebenezer. American storekeeper. **Chap. 5** 329, 331

Richelieu, Armand Jean Duplessis, Duke of (1585-1642). French Prime Minister. Cardinal as of 1622. **Chap. 4** 233, 240, 250, 258, 263, 277

Rio, Luis del (d. 1578). Member of the Council of Troubles. **Chap. 3** 146

Robinson, John. Revenue agent. **Chap. 5** 309, 310

Rolle, John. Member of the English House of Commons and merchant. **Chap. 4** 252, 254

Romulf, Count. Tax collector. **Chap. 1** 40

Romulus Augustulus. Last Emperor of the West Roman Empire. **Chap. 1** 15

Rose Fuller. English Member of Parliament. **Chap. 5** 358

Rotch, Francis. American merchant and shipowner. **Chap. 5** 340, 345, 347-350, 354

Rubens, Peter Paul (1577-1640). Flemish painter and diplomat. **Chap. 4** 257

Rudolf I of Hapsburg (1218-1291). German King since October 24, 1273. **Chap. 2** 101

Runkel, Siegfried of. Nephew of Siegfried of Westerburg. **Chap. 2** 102

Ruprecht of the Palatinate. Archbishop of Cologne from 1463 to 1478. **Chap. 2** 126

Ruy Gómez da Silva, Prince of Eboli (1517-1573). Member of the Spanish Council of State and confidant of Philip II. **Chap. 3** 142, 170, 192

Ruyter, Michiel Adriaansz. de (1607-1676). Greatest Admiral in Dutch history. **Chap. 3** 213

St. Georges, Madame de. Governess to Henrietta Maria. **Chap. 4** 232

St. John, Oliver (1598-1673). John Hampden's lawyer and later Strafford's prosecutor. **Chap. 4** 270, 282

St. Sabina, Hugo of. Cardinal legate. **Chap. 2** 98

Saint Martin. See Tours, Martin of.

Sandwich, John Montagu, Earl of (1718-1792). English Admiral commanding the fleet at the time of the Boston Tea Party in the American colonies. The term "sandwich" was named after the food he had prepared to sustain him during his all-night gambling sessions. **Chap. 5** 332, 339, 348, 352

Saye and Sele, William Fiennes, Viscount of (1582-1662). Self-proclaimed opponent of James I and Charles I. **Chap. 4** 269

Schetz, Gaspar, Baron of Grobbendonk (1513-1580). Treasurer in the Council of Finance since 1564. **Chap. 3** 170

Scott, James. Sea Captain. **Chap. 5** 335, 341

Sessions, Robert. Boston Tea Party participant. **Chap. 5** 351

Shakespeare, William (1564-1616). English poet and playwright. **Chap. 4** 230

Shays, Daniel. Rebel leader in Massachusetts during "Shays' Rebellion" (1786). **Chap. 5** 371

Siegfried of Westerburg (d. 1297). Archbishop of Cologne since 1275. **Chap. 2** 64, 88, 101, 102, 104

Sigibert. Frankish King over the area to the left of the Rhine. Contemporary of Clovis I. **Chap. 1** 15, 44, **Chap. 2** 77

Sigibert I (c. 537-575). Frankish King as of 561. Son of Lothar I. Married to Brunhild. **Chap. 1** 18, 22-24, 27, 29, 32, 40, 41, 47

Sigismund (1367-1437). German King as of 1410. German Emperor from 1433 to 1437. **Chap. 2** 114

Slater, Peter. Boston Tea Party participant. **Chap. 5** 351

Sonnius, Franciscus (1507-1576). Theologian. Bishop of Antwerp since 1570. **Chap. 3** 186

Spenser, Edmund (1552/1553-1599). English poet. **Chap. 4** 230

Straelen, Antoon van, Baron of Merksem and Dambrugge (1521-1568). Mayor of Antwerp. **Chap. 3** 145, 146

Strafford, Thomas Wentworth, Earl of (London, 1593-1641). England's Prime Minister under Charles I. Beheaded at the instigation of the Long Parliament. **Chap. 4** 238, 242, 246, 247, 249, 258, 259, 264, 269, 274, 277, 278-287

Sulpicius. Saint. Bishop of Bourges. **Chap. 1** 47

Swift, John. American customs official. **Chap. 5** 332, 334

Tecklenburg, Adelheid of. Married to William of Berg. Niece of Diedrich of Moers. **Chap. 2** 114, 118

Theudebert I (d. 548). Frankish King. Son of Theuderic I. **Chap. 1** 45

Theudebert II (d. 612). King of Austrasia from 596 to 612, when Theuderic II took his kingdom. **Chap. 1** 29, 35, 37

Theuderic I (d. 534). Illegitimate son of Clovis I. Ruled as of 511. **Chap. 1** 17, 18

Theuderic II (587-613). King of Burgundy as of 596. Son of Childebert II and Faileuba. **Chap. 1** 29, 35, 37, 46

Tiberius Constantine. Emperor of the East Roman Empire from 578 to 582. **Chap. 1** 45

Tisnacq, Charles de (c. 1500-1573). Chairman of the Privy Council and member of the Council of State. **Chap. 3** 191

Toledo, Don Fadrique Alvarez de (1529-1583). Spanish commander. Son of Governor Alva. **Chap. 3** 165, 188

Torre, Jacob De La (c. 1500-1581). Secretary of the Privy Council as of 1544. **Chap. 3** 151

Tours, Gregory of (538/539-594). Frankish Church Prelate. Chronicler. Bishop of Tours as of 573. **Chap. 1** 20, 22, 27, 29-34, 39-43

Tours, Martin of (316/317-397). Saint, Bishop of Tours. Sometimes referred to as Saint Martin.   **Chap. 1** 39-41,   **Chap. 2** 122

Townshend, Charles, Viscount of (1674-1738). English Secretary of State for the Colonies.   **Chap. 5** 311, 319, 326

Trevor, Sir Thomas. Baron of the Court of the Exchequer.   **Chap. 4** 272

Tsantele, Jacob. Priest of St. Martin's Church in Kortrijk.   **Chap. 3** 180

Ussher, James (1580-1656). Irish Anglican Bishop.   **Chap. 4** 284

Vargas, Juan de. Chairman of the Council of Troubles.   **Chap. 3** 146, 153

Venantius Fortunatus (c. 535-c. 610). Late-Roman Christian poet. Bishop of Poitiers since 600.   **Chap. 1** 27

Verdun, Nicholas of. Artist who created the Anno Shrine in the Abbey of Siegburg.   **Chap. 2** 84

Vernon, Sir George. Justice of the Court of Common Pleas.   **Chap. 4** 271

Viglius ab Aytta, Zuichemus, actually Joachim van Aytta van Zuychem (1507-1577). Dutch jurist. Chairman of the Privy Council.   **Chap. 3** 138, 151, 170, 174, 181, 197

Walpole, Robert, Earl of Oxford as of 1762 (1676-1745). English Prime Minister.   **Chap. 5** 302, 308

Walram of Jülich (d. 1349). Archbishop of Cologne as of 1332.   **Chap. 2** 120

Warren, Joseph (1741-1775). Patriot leader in Massachusetts. Died in the Battle of Bunker Hill.   **Chap. 5** 340, 351

Washington, George (1732-1799). Commander-in-Chief of the American forces during the American Revolution. First President of the United States.   **Chap. 5** 363, 365, 367, 372, 374

Wateley, Thomas.   **Chap. 5** 338, 339

Weellemans, Cornelis (d. 1585). General Secretary of the States of Brabant.   **Chap. 3** 165, 186

Wentworth, Sir Thomas. See Strafford.

Weston, Sir Francis. Baron of the Court of the Exchequer.   **Chap. 4** 271

Weston, Sir Richard, Earl of Portland (1577-1635). Lord Treasurer.   **Chap. 4** 243, 254, 259

White Jr., Lynn. American historian.   **Chap. 1** 53, 54, 55

Wilkes, John (1725-1797). English Member of Parliament and publicist.   **Chap. 5** 326

William I the Conqueror (1027/1028-1087). Duke of Normandy as of 1035. King of England as of 1066.   **Chap. 1** 54,   **Chap. 4** 248

William I, Count of Nassau, nicknamed "The Silent" (1533 1584). Prince of Orange as of 1544. Founding Father of Dutch independence. Philip II's most important opponent.   **Chap. 3** 138, 139, 142, 144, 145, 146, 176, 186, 189, 190, 195, 196, 197, 204, 206

William II (1228-1256). Count of Holland and Zealand. King of the Holy Roman Empire as of 1248.   **Chap. 2** 96

William II, Prince of Orange (1626-1650). Stadtholder and Captain-General in the Dutch Republic. Married Mary Stuart, the daughter of Charles I, in 1641.   **Chap. 4** 282, 284

William III Henry, Prince of Orange (1650-1702). Stadtholder of five provinces in the Dutch Republic. King of England, Ireland and Scotland together with his wife, Mary Stuart, as of 1688.   **Chap. 4** 247,   **Chap. 5** 296

Williams, John. Anglican Bishop of Lincoln.   **Chap. 4** 284, 285

Williams, Roger (d. 1684). American founder of Rhode Island.   **Chap. 5** 294

Wiomad. Friend of Childeric I.   **Chap. 1** 42

Wisigard. Wife of Theudebert I.   **Chap. 1** 45

York, James, Duke of. See James II.

Young, Thomas. American freedom fighter from Pennsylvania.   **Chap. 5** 340, 351, 375

In the later Middle Ages, taxes in Western Europe once again became facts of everyday life. The accompanying prints (15th century) depict the following:
– Officials charged with levying the municipal excise taxes on wine, who are checking the measured amount of wine in a barrel.
– Four municipal or village notables charged with apportioning the tax over the residents and collecting it, who are handing over their bookkeeping to the mayor.
– The mayor and the notables receiving the tax monies. Writing implements, money bags and coins are lying on the table.

Bibliography

Chapter 1

Autewrieth, J., *Ingelheim am Rhein. Forschungen und Studien zur Geschichte Ingelheim*, Stuttgart, 1964

Barraclough, Geoffrey, *The Medieval Papacy*, London, 1968

Bosl, Karl, "Staat, Gesellschaft, Wirtschaft im deutschen Mittelalter". In: *Handbuch der deutschen Geschichte*, vol. 7, 8th printing, Munich, 1985

Braunfels, Wolfgang, *Karl der Grosse, in Selbstzeugnissen und Bilddokumenten*

Braunfels, Wolfgang, et al. (ed.), *Karl der Grosse, Lebenswerk und Nachleben*, 5 volumes, Düsseldorf, 1966-1968

Brunner, H., *Deutsche Rechtsgeschichte*, 2 volumes, 2nd printing, Leipzig, 1906-1928, edited by Claudius von Schwerin

Buchner, Rudolf, *Gregor von Tours. Zehn Bücher Geschichten*, 2 volumes, Darmstadt, 1967

Catalogue of the exposition "La Picardie, berceau de la France. Clovis et les Derniers Romains", Soissons, 1986

Dahn, Felix, "Zum merovingischen Finanzen". In: *Germanistische Abhandlungen zum LXX Geburtstag Konrad von Maurer*, Göttingen, 1893

Daunenbauer, Heinrich, *Grundlager der mittelalterlichen Welt, Skizzen und Studien*, 2 volumes, Stuttgart, 1958

Daunenbauer, Heinrich, *Die Entstehung Europas. Von der Spätantike zum Mittelalter*, 2 volumes, Stuttgart, 1962

Die vier Bücher der Chroniken des sogenannten Fredegar. Quellen zur Geschichte des 7. und 8. Jahrhunderts, Darmstadt, 1982

Doppelfeld, O. and Priling, R., *Frankische Fürsten im Rheinland*, Düsseldorf, 1966

Duby, G., *Krieger und Bauern. Die Entwicklung von Wirtschaft und Gesellschaft im frühen Mittelalter*, Frankfurt am Main, 1977

Duby, G., *The early growth of the European economy. Warriors and peasants from the seventh to the twelfth century*, London, 1974

Ewig, Eugen, "Das merowingische Frankenreich (561-687)". In: *Handbuch der europäischen Geschichte*, reissued by Theodor Schieder, vol. 1, Stuttgart, 1976

Fichtenau, Heinrich, *The Carolingian Empire*, (translated by Peter Munz), Oxford, 1957

Ganshof, F.G.F.L., *Was ist das Lehnwesen*, Darmstadt, 1961

Ganshof, F.L., *Het tolwezen in het Frankische rijk onder de Merovingen*, Mededelingen van de Koninklijke Vlaamse Academie voor Wetenschappen, Letteren en Schone Kunsten van België, Klasse der Letteren, vol. XX, no. 4, 1958

Ganshof, F.L., *Het tolwezen in het Frankische rijk onder de Karolingen*, Mededelingen van de Koninklijke Vlaamse Academie voor Wetenschappen, Letteren en Schone Kunsten van België, Klasse der Letteren, vol. XXI, no. 1, 1959

Ganshof, F.L., *Een historicus uit de zesde eeuw, Gregorius van Tours*, Mededelingen van de Koninklijke Vlaamse Academie voor Wetenschappen, Letteren en Schone Kunsten van België, Klasse der Letteren, vol. XXVIII, no. 5, 1966

Ganshof, F.L., *Een historicus uit de zevende eeuw, Fredegarius*, Mededelingen van de Koninklijke Vlaamse Academie voor Wetenschappen, Letteren en Schone Kunsten van België, Klasse der Letteren, vol. XXXII, no. 5, 1970

Goffart, Walter, *Barbarians and Romans*, Princeton, New Jersey, 1980

Goffart, Walter, "From Roman Taxation to Medieval Seigneurie: Three Notes". In: *Speculum*, 1972, pp. 165-187 and 373-394

Grahn-Hoek, Heike, *Die fränkische Oberschicht im 6. Jahrhundert. Studien zur ihrer rechtlichen und politischen Stellung*, Sigmaringen, 1976

Haenens, A. d', "De Merovingische periode". In: *Winkler Prins Geschiedenis der Nederlanden*, vol. 1, 1977, pp. 79-98

Haenens, A. d', "De Karolingische periode". In: *Winkler Prins Geschiedenis der Nederlanden*, vol. 1, 1977, pp. 99-118

Haenens, A. d', "De post-Karolingische periode". In: *Winkler Prins Geschiedenis der Nederlanden*, vol. 1, 1977, pp. 119-130

Halphen, Louis, *Charlemagne et l'empire Carolingien*, 2nd printing, Paris, 1960

Hlawitska, Eduard, *Vom Frankenreich zur Formierung der europäischen Staaten- und Völkergemeinschaft 840-1046*, Darmstadt, 1986

Kurth, Godefroi, *La reine Brunehaut*, Paris, 1891

Lot, Ferdinand, *L'impôt foncier et la capitation personnelle sous le bas-empire et à l'époque fran-que*, Bibliothèque de l'école des hautes études, no. 253, Paris, 1928

Lot, Ferdinand, *Nouvelles recherches sur l'impôt foncier et la capitation personnelle sous le bas-empire*, Paris, 1955

Lot, Ferdinand, *De Germaansche invasies. De versmelting van de Barbaarsche en Romeinse wereld*, translated by J. Brouwer, The Hague, 1939

Lyon, Bryce, "Het historisch debat over het einde van de klassieke oudheid en het begin van de mid-deleeuwen". In: *De geboorte van Europa*, Mercator Foundation edition, Antwerp, 1987

McKitterick, Rosamond, *The Frankish Kingdoms under the Carolingians (751-987)*, London/New York, 1973

Meyer, Wilhelm, "Der Gelegenheitsdichter Venantius Fortunatus". In: *Abhandlungen der Königli-chen Gesellschaft der Wissenschaften zu Göttingen*, Philologisch-Historische Klasse, Neue Folge, vol. IV, 1900-1901

Nie, Giselle de, *Views from a Many-windowed Tower: Studies of Imagination in the Works of Gregory of Tours*, doctoral dissertation, Utrecht, 1987

Nie, Giselle de, "Is een vrouw een mens? Het beeld van de vrouw in de verhalen van Gregorius van Tours". In: *Convivium*, presented to Prof.dr. J.M. van Winter upon her departure from the State University of Utrecht, Hilversum, 1988

Orth, Elsbeth, "Vom Königsschatz und Kataster". In: *Mit dem Zehnten fing es an, eine Kulturge-schichte der Steuer*, Munich, 1986

Pirenne, Henri, "Mohammed en Karel de Grote', 1937. Reprinted in: *De geboorte van Europa*, Mer-cator Foundation edition, Antwerp, 1987

Prinz, F. (ed.), *Mönchtum und Gesellschaft im Mittelalter, Wege der Forschung*, vol. 312, Darmstadt, 1976

Riché, Pierre, *Die Welt der Karolinger*, Stuttgart, 1981

Riché, Pierre, *La vie quotidienne dans l'empire Carolingien*, Paris, 1973

Richter, G. and Kohl, H., "Annalen der Deutschen Geschichten im Mittelalter". In: *Annalen des fränkischen Reiches im Zeitalter der Merowinger*, 4 volumes, vol. I, Halle, 1873-1989

Schieffer, Theodor, "Die wirtschaftlich-soziale Grundstruktur des frühen Europas". In: *Handbuch der europäischen Geschichte*, reissued by Theodor Schieder, vol. 1, Stuttgart, 1976

Schieffer, Theodor, "Das karolingische Groszreich (751-843)". In: *Handbuch der europäischen Ge-schichte*, reissued by Theodor Schieder, vol. 1, Stuttgart, 1976

Schneider, Reinhard, *Das Frankenreich*, Munich/Vienna, 1982

Sieder, Th. (ed.), "Europa im Wandel von der Antike zum Mittelalter". In: *Handbuch der europäi-schen Geschichte*, vol. I, Stuttgart, 1979

Slicher von Bath, Bernard, *De agrarische geschiedenis van West-Europa 500-1850*, Aula Paperback, 6th printing, Utrecht, 1987

Stephenson, Carl, *Medieval Feudalism*, Ithaca (N.Y.), 1954

Steuer, Heiko, *Die Franken in Köln*, Cologne, 1980

Steuer, Heiko, "Van Theoderik de Grote tot Karel de Grote". In: *De geboorte van Europa*, Mercator Foundation edition, Antwerp, 1987

Thompson, E.A., *The Early Germans*, Oxford, 1965

Tours, Gregory of, *The History of the Franks*, translation with an introduction by Lewis Thorpe, London, 1977

Verhulst, A., *Der Handel im Merowingerreich*, Antikvarisk Arkiv 39, Stockholm, 1970, pp. 2-54

Waitz, G., *Deutsche Verfassungsgeschichte*, 8 volumes, 2nd printing, Kiel, 1865-1878

Wallace-Hadrill, J.M., *Early Mediaeval History*, Oxford, 1975

Wallace-Hadrill, J.M., *Early Germanic Kingship in England and on the Continent*, Oxford, 1971

Wallace-Hadrill, J.M., *The Long-haired Kings*, London, 1962

Wattenbach, Wilhelm en Levison, Wilhelm, *Deutschlands Geschichtquellen im Mittelalter*, vol. I "Die Vorzeit von den Anfängen bis zur Herrschaft der Karolinger", edited by W. Levison, 1952 and vol. II "Die Karolingen vom Anfang des 8. Jahrhunderts bis zum Tod Karls des Grossen", edited by W. Levison/H. Löwe, Weimar, 1953

Werner, J., *Frankisk Royal Tombs in the Cathedrals of Cologne and Saint-Denis*, Antiquity 38, 1964, pp. 201-216

White Jr., Lynn T., *Mediaeval Technology and Social Change*, Oxford, 1962

Whitelock, Dorothy, *The Beginnings of English Society*, The Pelican History of England, London, reprint 1987

Zöllner, Erich, *Geschichte der Franken bis zur Mitte des sechsten Jahrhundert*, Munich, 1970

Chapter 2

Ardant, Gabriel, *Histoire de l'impôt*, 2 volumes, Paris, 1971

Behr, Hans-Joachim, "Die Landstände". In: *Köln Westfalen 1180-1980, Landesgeschichte zwischen Rhein und Weser*, vol. I, Kölnisches Stadtmuseum, 1981, pp. 136 *ff*

Below, George von, *Probleme der Wirtschaftsgeschichte*, 2nd printing, undated

Below, George von, *Der deutsche Staat des Mittelalters*, vol. 1, Leipzig, 1914

Bender, Franz, *Illustrierte Geschichte der Stadt Köln*, Cologne, 1912

Boshof, Egon, "Ottonen und frühe Salierzeit (919-1056)". In: *Rheinische Geschichte*, published by F. Petri and G. Droege, volumes 1 and 3, Düsseldorf, 1983, pp. 1-120

Bosl, Karl, "Staat, Gesellschaft, Wirtschaft im deutschen Mittelalter". In: *Handbuch der deutschen Geschichte*, vol. 7, paperback edition, 1986

Bos-Rops, J.A.M.Y., "Van incidentele gunst tot jaarlijkse belasting; de bede in het vijftiende eeuwse Holland". In: *Fiscaliteit in Nederland*, Zutphen/Deventer, 1987

Diederich, Toni, "Köln im Hochmittelalter". In: *Ornamenta Ecclesiae, Kunst und Künstler der Romanik in Köln*, Cologne, 1985

Diederich, Toni, "Der Stadtherr". In: *Monumenta Annonis*, Cologne, 1975, pp. 30-31

Droege, Georg, *Verfassung und Wirtschaft in Kurköln unter Dietrich von Moers (1414-1463)*, Bonn, 1957

Droege, Georg, "Die Herzogsgewalt in Westfalen". In: *Köln Westfalen 1180-1980, Landesgeschichte zwischen Rhein und Weser*, vol. I, Kölnisches Stadtmuseum, 1981, pp. 220 *ff*

Droege, Georg, "Lehnrecht und Landrecht am Niederrhein und das Problem der Territorialbildung in 12. und 13. Jahrhundert". In: *Festschrift Franz Steinbach*, Bonn, 1960, pp. 278 *ff*

Droege, Georg, "Die finanziellen Grundlagen des Territorialstaates in West- und Ostdeutschland an der Wende vom Mittelalter zur Neuzeit". In: *Vierteljahrschrift für Sozial- und Wirtschaftsgeschichte*, no. 53, 1966, pp. 149-167

Droege, Georg, *Landrecht und Lehnrecht im hohen Mittelalter*, Bonn, 1969

Engelbrecht, Wilfried, "Ziele kölnischer Städtepolitik bis zum Tode Erzbischof Engelberts von Berg". In: *Köln Westfalen 1180-1980, Landesgeschichte zwischen Rhein und Weser*, vol. I, Kölnisches Stadtmuseum, 1981

Engels, Odilo, "Het Duitse rijk ten tijde van de slag van Woeringen". In: *Der Name der Freiheit 1288-1988*, Aspekten van de Keulse geschiedenis van Woeringen tot heden (manual), Cologne, 1988, pp. 35 *ff*

Engels, Odilo, "Die Stauferzeit". In: *Rheinische Geschichte*, published by F. Petri and G. Droege, volumes 1 and 3, Düsseldorf, 1983, pp. 199-275

Engels, Odilo, "Der Rechtsbischof (10. und 11. Jahrhundert)". In: *Der Bischof in seiner Zeit*, Festgabe für Joseph Kardinal Höffner, Cologne, 1986, pp. 41-95

Ennen, Edith, "Stadtluft macht frei". In: *Der Name der Freiheit 1288-1988*, Aspekten van de Keulse geschiedenis van Woeringen tot heden (manual), Cologne, 1988, p. 35

Ennen, Leonhardt en Echertz, Gottfried, *Quellen zur Geschichte der Stadt Köln*, 6 volumes, Cologne, 1863-1879

Ewig, Eugen, "Zum Lothringischen Dukat der Kölner Erzbischöfe". In: *Festschrift Franz Steinbach*, Bonn, 1960, pp. 238 *ff*

Zur Geschichte und Kunst im Erzbistum Köln, Studien zur Kölner Kirchengeschichte, Festschrift für Wilhelm Neuss, vol. 5, Düsseldorf, undated

Ficker, Julius, *Engelbert der Heilige, Erzbisschof von Köln und Reichsverweser*, Cologne, 1853

Fleckenstein, Josef Horst, *Fuhrmann, Joachim Leuschner*, Deutsche Geschichte, vol. 1, Mittelalter, Göttingen, 1985

Fried, Johannes, "Die Kölner Stadtgemeinde und der europäische Freiheitsgedanke im Hochmittelalter". In: *Der Name der Freiheit 1288-1988*, Aspekten van de Keulse geschiedenis van Woeringen tot heden (supplementary volume), Cologne, 1988, pp. 23 *ff*

Fuhrmann, Horst, *Germany in the High Middle Ages 1050-1200*, Cambridge, 1987

Ganshof, F.L., *Brabant, Rheinland und Reich im 12., 13. und 14. Jahrhundert*, Gesellschaft für Rheinische Geschichtskunde, Cologne, 1938

Grapperhaus, F.H.M., "Functies van belastingen in verleden en heden". In: *Liber Amicorum Albert Thibergien*, Brussels, 1983

Heelu, Jan van, "Die Schlacht von Worringen". In: *Der Name der Freiheit 1288-1988*, Aspekten van de Keulse geschiedenis van Woeringen tot heden (supplementary volume), Cologne, 1988, pp. 105 *ff*

Henning, J.G.A., *Geschichte der Steuer in Köln bis 1370*, Leipzig, 1895

Herborn, Wolfgang, *Die politische Führungsschicht der Stadt Köln im Spätmittelalter*, Rheinisches Archiv, no. 100, Bonn, 1977

Herborn, Wolfgang, "Die Stadt Köln und die Schlacht von Wörringen". In: *Der Name der Freiheit 1288-1988*. Aspekten van de Keulse geschiedenis van Woeringen tot heden (manual), Cologne, 1988, pp. 289 *ff*

Hlawitschka, Eduard, *Vom Frankenreich zur Formierung der europäischen Staaten- und Völkergemeinschaft 840-1046*, Darmstadt, 1986

Janssen, Wilhelm, "Das Erzstift Köln in Westfalen". In: *Köln Westfalen 1180-1980, Landesgeschichte zwischen Rhein und Weser*, vol. I, Kölnisches Stadtmuseum, 1981, pp. 136 *ff*

Janssen, Wilhelm, "Eine landständische Einung kurkölnischer Städte aus den Jahren 1362/63". In: *Festschrift Edith Ennen*, Bonn, 1972, pp. 391 *ff*

Janssen, Wilhelm, "Der Bischof, Reichsfürst und Landesherr (14. und 15. Jahrhundert)". In: *Der Bischof in seiner Zeit,* Festgabe für Joseph Kardinal Höffner, Cologne, 1986, pp. 41-95

Jappe Alberts, W., "Zur Entstehung der Stände in den weltlichen Territorien am Niederrhein". In: *Festschrift Franz Steinbach*, Bonn, 1960, pp. 333 *ff*

Jones, J.A.P., *King John and Magna Carta: Seminar Studies in History*, 4th printing, Harlow, 1983

Kamptz, Staats-Minister von, *Fragmente über das Besteuerungsrecht deutscher Landesherren*, Berlin, 1847

Klersch, Joseph, *Volkstum und Volksleben in Köln*, Cologne, 1979

Klinkenberg, H.M., *Zur Interpretation des Groszen Schied*, Jahrbücher des Kölner Geschiedvereins, no. 25, 1950, pp. 101 *ff*

Kluger, Helmuth, "Die Entfaltung des kommerzialen Lebens in Köln". In: *Der Name der Freiheit 1288-1988*, Aspekten van de Keulse geschiedenis van Woeringen tot heden (manual), Cologne, 1988, pp. 13 *ff*

Knipping, Richard, "Ein mittelalterlicher Jahreshaushalt der Stadt Köln (1379)".

Linssen, C.A.A., "Lotharingen 880-1106". In: *Algemene Geschiedenis der Nederlanden*, vol. 1, pp. 305 *ff*

Lück, D., "Anno II von Köln (ca 1010-1075)". In: *Rheinische Lebensbilder VII*, published by B. Poll, 1977

Mayer, E., "Zoll, Kaufmannschaft und Markt zwischen Rhein und Loire bis in das 13. Jahrhundert". In: *Germanistische Abhandlungen zum LXX Geburtstag Konrad von Maurer*, Göttingen, 1893

Mayer, Theodor, "Geschichte der Finanzwirtschaft vom Mittelalter bis zum Ende des 18. Jahrhunderts". In: *Handbuch der Finanzwissenschaft*, vol. 1, 1952, pp. 236 *ff*

Militzer, Klaus, *Ursachen und Folgen der innerstädtischen Auseinandersetzungen in Köln in der zweiten Hälfte des 14. Jahrhunderts*, Cologne, 1981

Militzer, Klaus, *Die vermögenden Kölner*, Cologne/Vienna, 1981

Müller, Achatz von, "Zwischen Verschuldung und Steuerrebellion. Die mittelalterliche Stadt an den Beispielen Florenz und Köln". In: *Mit dem Zehnten fing es an, Eine Kulturgeschichte der Steuer*, Munich, 1986, pp. 100 *ff*

Müller-Jerina, Alwina, "Zwischen Befreiung und Vernichtung-Juden in Köln". In: *Der Name der Freiheit 1288-1988*, Aspekten van de Keulse geschiedenis van Woeringen tot heden (supplementary volume), Cologne, 1988, pp. 61 *ff*

Penning, Wolf-Dietrich, "Die weltlichen Zentralbehörden im Erzstift Köln von der ersten Hälfte des 15. bis zum Beginn des 17. Jahrhunderts". In: *Veröffentlichungen des Historischen Vereins für den Niederrhein, insbesondere das alte Erzbistum Köln*, Bonn, 1977

Pirenne, Henri, *Geschichte Europas von der Völkerwanderung bis zur Reformation*, paperback edition, 1961

Rathofer, Johannes, "Das Annolied und Denkmäler der Dichtkunst". In: *Monumenta Annonis*, Cologne, 1975, pp. 75-87

Schieffer, Rudolf, "Die Zeit der späten Salier". In: *Rheinische Geschichte*, published by F. Petri and G. Droege, volumes 1 and 3, Düsseldorf, 1983, pp. 121-198

Schieffer, Theodor, "Anno als Erzbischof und Reichspolitiker". In: *Monumenta Annonis*, Cologne, 1975, pp. 24-26

Schmitz, Alphons, *Die Bede in Kur-Köln*, Freiburg i.B., 1912

Stehkämper, Hugo, "Die rechtliche Absicherung der Stadt Köln vor 1288". In: *Festschrift Edith Ennen*, Bonn, 1972, pp. 341 *ff*

Stehkämper, Hugo, "Der Reichsbischof und Territorialfürst (12. und 13. Jahrhundert)". In: *Der Bischof in seiner Zeit, Festgabe für Joseph Kardinal Höffner*, Cologne, 1986, pp. 41-95

Stehkämper, Hugo, "Treubuch wegen des Landfrieden. Die Stadt Köln und die Schlacht bei Worringen". In: *Geschichte in Köln, Studentische Zeitschrift am Historischen Semimar*, vol. 24, December 1988, pp. 5-23

Stelzmann, Arnold, *Illustrierte Geschichte der Stadt Köln*, ed. Robert Frohn, 10th printing, Cologne, 1984

Stern, Leo und Voigt, Erhard, *Deutschland in der Epoche des vollentfalteten Feudalismus von der Mitte des 13. bis zum ausgehenden 15. Jahrhundert*, ed. Johannes Schildhauer, 2nd printing, Berlin, 1976

Strait, Paul, *Cologne in the Twelfth Century*, Gainesville, Florida State University, 1974

Suchy, Barbara, "Vom Güldenen Opferpfennig bis zur Judenvermögensabgabe, Tausend Jahre Judensteuern". In: *Mit dem Zehnten fing es an. Eine Kulturgeschichte der Steuern*, Munich, 1986, pp. 114 *ff*

Verhulst, Adriaan, *De zogenaamde agrarische revolutie van de Middeleeuwen*, Spiegel Historiael, vol. 23, no. 4, April 1988, pp. 239 *ff*

Waas, *Vogtei und Bede*, vol. 2, 1923

Water, R.L. van de, *De landsheerlijke inkomsten van de bisschoppen gedurende hun gezag in Twente*, doctoral dissertation, Enschede, 1965

Welters, Hans und Lobeck, Helmut, *Kleine Illustrierte Geschichte der Stadt Köln*, 7th printing, Cologne, 1986

Wisplinghoff, Erich, "Konrad von Hochstaden". In: *Rheinische Lebensbilder*, vol. II, Düsseldorf, 1966, pp 7 *ff*

Wolf, Gustav, *Aus Kurköln im 16. Jahrhundert*, Berlin, 1905 (reprint Vadus, 1965)

Wrede, Adam, *Neuer Kölner Sprachschatz*, vol. I, A - J, Cologne, 1956

Chapter 3

Arnould, M.A., "L'impôt sur le capital en Belgique au XVIe siècle". In: *Le Hainaut économique*, vol. I, 1946, pp. 17-45

Baelde, M., *De domeingoederen van de vorst in de Nederlanden omstreeks het midden van de zestiende eeuw (1551-1559)*, Brussels, 1971

Bakhuizen van den Brink, R.S., "Over den Tienden Penning". In: *Studiën en Schetsen*, vol. I, 1863, pp. 384-483 (reprinted in: Cartons voor de geschiedenis van den Nederlandschen Vrijheidsoorlog, 3th printing, 1891, pp. 186-289; the latter edition is used for this book)

Berwick and Alba, The Duke of D.C.L., *The Great Duke of Alba as a Public Servant*, 1947

Bigwood, G., *Les impôts généraux dans les Pays-Bas Autrichiens*, Louvain, 1900

Blok, P.J., "De financiën van de graafschap Holland". In: *Bijdragen voor Vaderlandsche Geschiedenis en Oudheidkunde*, vol. III, 1886

Bodin, Jean, *Six livres de la république*, Paris, 1583 (reprint 1977)

Brouwers, D.D., *Les aides et subsides dans le comté de Namur au XVIe siècle*, Namur, 1934

Cadoux, C.J., *Philip of Spain and the Netherlands*, London, 1947

Caldecott-Baird, D., *The Expedition in Holland 1572-1574 from the Manuscript of Walter Morgan*, London, 1976

Cauwenberghe, E. van, "De economische ontwikkeling in de Nederlanden vanaf de tweede helft van de vijftiende eeuw tot omstreeks 1576". In: *Opstand en pacificatie in de Lage Landen*, Ghent, 1976

Clamageran, J.J., *Histoire de l'impôt en France*, Paris, 1868

Craeybeckx, J., *Aperçu sur l'histoire des impôts en Flandre et au Brabant, 1569-1572*, unpublished master's thesis, rewritten for the "Reisbeurzenwedstrijd 1948"

Craeybeckx, J., *De tiende penning van Alva in Vlaanderen en Brabant, 1569-1572*, unpublished master's thesis, rewritten for the "Reisbeurzenwedstrijd 1948"

Craeybeckx, J., "De Staten van Vlaanderen en de gewestelijke financiën in de XVIe eeuw". In: *Handelingen van de Maatschappij voor Geschiedenis en Oudheidkunde te Gent*, no. 4, 1950, pp. 78-119

Craeybeckx, J., "Alva's tiende penning een mythe". In: *Bijdragen en Mededelingen van het Historisch Genootschap*, vol. 76, 1962, pp. 10-42 (rewritten and reprinted as: Vaderland's Verleden in Veelvoud, no. 10, 1975, pp. 182-208)

Craeybeckx, J., "La portée fiscale et politique du 100e denier du duc d'Albe". In: *Acta Historica Bruxellensie, Recherches sur l'Histoire des finances publiques*, vol. I, 1967, pp. 343-374

Craeybeckx, J., "De moeizame definitieve afschaffing van Alva's tiende penning". In: *Album Ch. Verlinden*, pp. 63-94

Deursen, A.Th. van, "Staatsinstellingen in de Noordelijke Nederlanden 1579-1780". In: *Nieuwe Algemene Geschiedenis der Nederlanden*, vol. 5, pp. 196-251

Deursen, A.Th. van, "Tussen eenheid en zelfstandigheid". In: *De Unie van Utrecht, Wording en werking van een verbond en een verbondsacte*, The Hague, 1979

Devavele, J., *Eenheid en scheiding in de Nederlanden 1555-1585*, Ghent, 1976

Dhondt, J., "Bijdrage tot de kennis van het financiewezen der Staten van Vlaanderen (XVIe en XVIIe eeuw)". Reprinted in: *SL*, vol. LXIX, Heule, 1977

Dierickx, M., "Nieuwe gegevens over het bestuur van de Hertog van Alva in de Nederlanden". In: *Bijdragen tot de Geschiedenis der Nederlanden*, vol. 18, 1963, pp. 167 *ff*

Diferee, Henri C., *De geschiedenis van den Nederlandschen handel tot den val der Republiek*, Amsterdam, 1908

Durme, M. van, *Antoon Perrenot, Bisschop van Atrecht, Kardinaal van Granvelle, Minister van Karel V en van Filips II (1517-1586)*, KVA, vol. XV, no. 18, Brussels, 1953

Durme, M. van, "Herziening van het proces van de Hertog van Alva (1507-1582)". In: *Streven, Maandblad voor geestesleven en cultuur*, p. IX, vol. 1, m 2, November 1955

Elias, B.G.J., *Tachtigjarige Oorlog*, Haarlem, 1977

Engels, P.H., *De belastingen en de geldmiddelen van den aanvang der republiek tot op heden*, Utrecht, 1862

Enno van Gelder, H.A., "De Tiende Penning". In: *Tijdschrift voor Geschiedenis*, no. 48, pp. 1-36 and 120-144 (rewritten and reprinted as: Van Beeldenstorm tot pacificatie, 1964, pp. 170-209)

Enno van Gelder, H.A., "De reactie op de Beeldenstorm 1567-1572". In: *Algemene Geschiedenis der Nederlanden*, vol. V, pp. 1-29

Fritschy, W., *De patriotten en de financiën van de Bataafse Republiek*, doctoral dissertation, State University of Leiden, 1988

Fruin, R., "De zeventien provinciën en haar vertegenwoordigingen in de Staten-Generaal (1893)". In: *Verspreide Geschriften*, vol. IX, pp. 1-28

Fruin, R., *Het voorspel van de 80-jarige oorlog*, Aula Books, Utrecht/Antwerp, undated

Gaastra, F.S., *De geschiedenis van de V.O.C.*, Haarlem, 1982

Gielens, A., "Notice sur le large conseil d'Anvers, suivi d'un inventaire sommaire de ses archives conservées au dépôt de l'Etat d'Anvers". In: *Bijdragen tot de Geschiedenis der Nederlanden*, vol. 10, 1911, pp. 455-464

Gilliodts-Van Severen, L., "Un épisode de la levée du dixième denier, 1569-1572". In: *Bulletin de la Commission Royale d'Histoire*, vol. 4, XI, 1883

Gilliodts-Van Severen, L., *La levée du dixième et du vingtième denier à Bruges*, Annales de la société d'émulation de Bruges, 1910

Grapperhaus, Ferdinand H.M., *Alva en de tiende penning*, 2nd printing, Zutphen, 1984

Grapperhaus, F.H.M., *Convoyen en Licenten*, Zutphen/Deventer, 1986

Groenveld, S., "Beeldvorming en realiteit, geschiedschrijving en achtergronden van de Nederlandse opstand tegen Filips II". In: *Men sagh Haerlem bestormen .....*, Haarlem, 1973, pp. 24-39

Groenveld, S., "Natie en nationaal gevoel in de zestiende-eeuwse Nederlanden". In: *Bundel Van der Gouw Nederlands Archievenblad*, 1980, pp. 372-387

Groenveld, S., H.R.Ph. Leeuwenberg, Nicolette Mout and W.M. Zappey, *De kogel door de kerk? De opstand in de Nederlanden en de rol van de Unie van Utrecht 1559-1609*, Zutphen, 1979

Grol, H.G. van, *Het beheer van het Zeeuwsche zeewezen 1577-1587*, Flushing, 1936

Hermesdorf, B.H.D., *Wigle van Aytta van Zwichem*, Leiden, 1949

Heijnsbergen, P. van, "Viglius van Aytta". In: *Verspreide opstellen*, Amsterdam, 1929

Hezemans, J.C.A., "Het gezantschap der Staten van Brabant aan Koning Philips II in 1572". In: *Handelingen van het provinciaal genootschap voor Kunsten en Wetenschappen in Noord-Brabant van het jaar 1879*

Hirschauer, Ch., "L'Artois et le Xe denier". In: *Revue du Nord*, vol. II, 1911, pp. 215-235

Houdoy, J., "L'impôt sur le revenue au XVIe siècle, les états de Lille et le Duc d'Albe". In: *Mémoires de la Société des Sciences de l'agriculture et des arts de Lille*, 3rd series, vol. 10, 1872, pp. 299-383

Houtte, J.A. van, "De zestiende eeuw". In: *De economische geschiedenis van Nederland*, Chapter 2, ed. J.H. van Stuyvenberg, Groningen, 1977, pp. 49-78

Hullu, J. de, *De archieven der admiraliteitscolleges*, The Hague, 1924

Janssens, G., "De eerste jaren van Filips II". In: *Nieuwe Algemene Geschiedenis der Nederlanden*, vol. 6, pp. 186-201

Janssens, G., "Van de komst van Alva tot de Unies". In: *Nieuwe Algemene Geschiedenis der Nederlanden*, vol. 6, pp. 215-243

Janssens, G., "Het oordeel van tijdgenoten en historici over Alva's bestuur in de Nederlanden". In: *Belgisch Tijdschrift voor Filologie en Geschiedenis*, 1976, pp. 474-489

Janssens, G., "Collaboratie en repressie in de Nederlanden vanaf de komst van Alva tot de Pacificatie van Gent (1567-1576)". In: *Handelingen Vlaams Philologen Congres 1977*, vol. 31, pp. 265-271

Janssens, G., *Brabant in het verweer. Absolute monarchie of staatsbewind van Alva tot Farnese, 1567-1578*, doctoral dissertation, Louvain, 1981

Janssens, G., "Brabant in verzet tegen Alva's tiende en twintigste penning". In: *Bijdragen en Mededelingen van het Historisch Genootschap*, no. 89, 1974, pp. 16-31

Janssens, G., "Pastoor J. Tsantele in verzet tegen de 10e penning". In: *De Leiegouw*, SVI, 1974

Janssens, G., "Gezantschap naar Filips II". In: *Spiegel Historiael*, vol. VIII, 1973, pp. 82 *ff*

Jonge, J.C. de, *Geschiedenis van het Nederlandsche Zeewezen*, vol. 1, 2nd printing, Haarlem, 1863

Kernkamp, J.H., *De handel op de vijand 1572-1588*, vol. 1, doctoral dissertation, Utrecht, 1931

Kieft, C. van der, "De Staten-Generaal in het Bourgondisch-Oostenrijks tijdvak, 1464-1555". In: *500 jaren Staten-Generaal in de Nederlanden*, Assen, 1964

Kirchner, W., *Alba, Spaniens eiserner Herzog*, Berlin/Frankfurt am Main, 1963

Klaveren, J. van, *Europäische Wirtschaftsgeschichte Spaniens im 16. und 17. Jahrhundert*, Stuttgart, 1960

Klein, J., *The Mesta: a Study in Spanish Economic History, 1273-1836*, Cambridge, 1926

Klompmaker, H., "Handel, geld- en bankwezen in de Noordelijke Nederlanden". In: *Nieuwe Algemene Geschiedenis der Nederlanden*, vol. 6, pp. 58-74

Kluit, A., *Historie der Hollandsche Staatsregering tot aan het jaar 1795*, vol. 4, Amsterdam, 1804

Korvezee, E.H., "Belastingen in Noord-Brabant vóór 1648". In: *Varia Historica Brabantica*, vol. IV, 1985, pp. 97-163

Kuttner, E., *Het hongerjaar 1566*, 4th printing, Amsterdam, 1979

Lagomarsino, P.D., *Court Factions and the Formulation of Spanish Policy towards the Netherlands (1559-1567)*, doctoral dissertation, Cambridge, 1973 (not published)

Lamens, Hans, "De Unie van Utrecht en de landelijk heffingen". In: *Fiskaal*, vol. 6, no. 11, December 1979

Lefèvre, J., "Les débuts du gouvernment de don Luis de Requesens". In: *Miscellanea historica in honorem Leonis van der Essen*, vol. I, Brussels/Paris, 1947

Lefèvre, J., "La correspondance des gouverneurs-généraux à l'époque espagnole". In: *Archives bibliothèques et musées de Belgique*, vol. XXI, 1950

Linden, H. van der, "Van Straelen, commissaire des Etats-Généraux et l'Union des provinces belges au début du règne de Philippe II". In: *Bulletin Académie Royale de Belgique*, nos. 10-12, 1924, pp. 305-325

Maddens, N., "De beden in het graafschap Vlaanderen tijdens de regering van Keizer Karel V (1515-1550)". In: *Standen en Landen*, vol. LXXII, Heule, 1978

Maddens, N., "De invoering van de 'nieuwe geldmiddelen' in het graafschap Vlaanderen tijdens de regering van Keizer Karel V". In: *Belgisch Tijdschrift voor Filologie en Geschiedenis*, vol. LVII, nos. 2 and 4, 1979

Marx, E., *Studien zur Geschichte des niederländisches Aufstands*, Leipzig, 1902

Mey, J.C.A. de, "De watergeuzen en de Nederlanden 1568-1572". In: *Verhandelingen der Koninklijke Academie van Wetenschappen, afdeling Letterkunde*, Nieuwe reeks, vol. 77

Monté Ver Loren, J.Ph. de and J.E. Spruit, *Hoofdlijnen uit de ontwikkeling der rechterlijke organisatie in de Noordelijke Nederlanden tot de Bataafse omwenteling*, 5th printing, Deventer, 1972

Motley, J.L., *De opkomst van de Nederlandsche republiek*, with an introduction and notes from R.C. Bakhuizen van den Brink, volumes I, II and III, The Hague, 1859 (originally published as: History of the United Netherlands)

Moxo, Salvador de, *La alcabala, sobre sur origenes, concepto y naturalezza*, Madrid, 1963

Noordegraaf, L., "Nijverheid in de Noordelijke Nederlanden". In: *Nieuwe Algemene Geschiedenis der Nederlanden*, vol. 6, pp. 12-26

Parker, G., *Van Beeldenstorm tot bestand*, Haarlem, 1978 (originally published as: The Dutch Revolt)

Parker, G., *Het Spaanse leger in de Lage Landen*, Haarlem, 1978 (originally published as: The Army of Flanders and the Spanish Road)

Parker, G., "The Dutch Revolt and the Polarization of the International Politics". In: *Tijdschrift voor Geschiedenis*, no. 89, 1976, pp. 429-444

Parker, G., *Filips II*, The Hague, 1981

Pierson, P., *Philip II of Spain*, London, 1975

Poel, J. van der, *Het particularisme van Zeeland en de Convoyen en Licenten Archief*, Zeeuwsch Genootschap der Wetenschappen, 1929

Poel, J. van der, "Het 350-jarig bestaan van het Dienstvak der Invoerrechten", Wdb no. 3851, 9 August 1947

Presser, J., *De tachtigjarige oorlog*, 5th printing, 1974

Rachfahl, F., *Wilhelm von Oranien und der niederländische Aufstand*, volumes I, II and III, Halle 1906, The Hague 1924

Read, C., "Queen Elisabeth's Seizure of the Duke of Alva's Payships". In: *The Journal of Modern History*, no. 5, 1933, pp. 443-464

Reekers, B., *Benito Arias Montano*, doctoral dissertation, State University of Amsterdam, 1961

Roelink, J., "De Nederlandse Opstand een Klassenstrijd?". In: *Kritisch Kwintet, Historische opstellen*, Amsterdam, 1964, pp. 49-70

Roosbroeck, R. van, *Willem de Zwijger*, Antwerp, 1975

Roosbroeck, R. van, *Over een anoniem manifest*, 1571

Roover, R. de, "Anvers comme marché monétaire au XVIe siècle". In: *Belgisch Tijdschrift voor Filologie en Geschiedenis*, vol. 31, 1953

Rowdon, M., *The Spanish Terror: Spanish Imperialism in the 16th Century*, London, undated

Rowen, H.H., *The Low Countries in Early Modern Times*, London/New York, 1972

Rowse, A.L., *The Expansion of Elisabethan England*, London, 1955

Rowse, A.L., *The Elisabethan Renaissance*, London, 1971

Schepper, H.C.C. de, "De burgerlijke overheden en hun permanente kaders 1480-1579". In: *Nieuwe Algemene Geschiedenis der Nederlanden*, vol. 5, pp. 388-405

Schepper, H.C.C. de, "De overheidsstructuren in de Koninklijke Nederlanden 1580-1700". In: *Nieuwe Algemene Geschiedenis der Nederlanden*, vol. 5, pp. 388-405

Schepper, H.C.C. de, "De Raad van State in de landsheerlijke Nederlanden en zijn voortgang op gescheiden wegen 1531-1588/1948". In: *Raad van State 450 jaar*, The Hague, 1981, pp. 1-35

Schilling, H., "Der Aufstand der Niederlande: bürgerliche Revolution oder Elitenkonflikt?". In: *200 Jahre amerikanische Revolution und moderne Revolutionsforschung*, ed. H.U. Wekler Geschichte und Gesellschaft, Zeitschrift für historische Sozialwissenschaft, vol. 2, Göttingen, 1976

Schöffer, J., "De opstand in de Nederlanden 1566-1609". In: *Winkler Prins Geschiedenis der Nederlanden*, vol. 2, Amsterdam/Brussels, 1977, pp. 75-118

Sickenga, F.N., *Bijdrage tot de geschiedenis der belastingen in Nederland*, doctoral dissertation, Leiden, 1864

Smit, J.W., "The Present Positions of Studies Regarding the Revolt of the Netherlands". In: *Britain and the Netherlands*, London, 1960, pp. 11-28

Smit, J.W., "The Netherlands Revolution". In: *Vaderland's Verleden in Veelvoud*, no. 8, The Hague, 1975 (first published in: Preconditons of Revolution in Early Modern Europe, ed. R. Forster and J.P. Greene, Baltimore/London, 1970)

Smitskamp, H., "Van Lotwissel en menigerlei geval, 1555-1593". In: *500 Jaren Staten-Generaal in de Nederlanden*, Assen, 1964

Snapper, F., *Oorlogsinvloeden op de overzeese handel van Holland 1551-1719*, doctoral dissertation, University of Amsterdam, 1959

Strong, R. and J.A. van Dorsten, *Leicester's Triumph*, Leiden/London, 1964

Swart, K.W., "The Black Legend During the Eighty Years War". In: *Britain and the Netherlands*, vol. V, pp. 36-57

Terdenge, H., "Zur Geschichte der holländischen Steuer im 15. und 16. Jahrhundert". In: *Vierteljahrschrift für Sozial- und Wirtschaftsgeschichte*, vol. XVIII, 1925

Tex, J. den, *Oldenbarnevelt*, vol. I 1960 and vol. II 1962

Vasquez de Prada, V., *Filips II, heerser van een wereldrijk*, translated from Spanish by G.C. Mohr-Hosman, Bussum, 1975

Verhofstad, K.J.W., *De regering der Nederlanden in de jaren 1555 - 1559*, doctoral dissertation, Nijmegen, 1937

Verlinden, Ch., "Hoe lang duurde de economische crisis in Vlaanderen onder Filips II". In: *Bijdragen tot de geschiedenis der Nederlanden*, vol. IV, no. 1 and 2, 1949

Vrankrijker, A.C.J. de, *De motivering van onzen opstand*, doctoral dissertation, University of Amsterdam, 1933

Vrugt, M. van der, *De criminele ordonnantiën van 1570*, doctoral dissertation, Utrecht, 1978

Wagenaar, J., *Amsterdam, in zyne opkomst, aanwas, geschiedenissen, voorregten, koophandel, gebouwen, kerkenstaat, schoolen, schutterye, gelden, regeringe, beschreeven*, vol. 4, Amsterdam, 1763

Wauters, A., *Levée du dixième denier (épisode de l'histoire de Bruxelles)*, Brussels, 1842

Wee, H. van der, "De economie als factor bij het begin van de opstand in de Zuidelijke Nederlanden". In: *Bijdragen en Mededelingen betreffende de Geschiedenis der Nederlanden*, vol. 83, 1969, pp. 15-32

Wellens, R., "Les Etats-Généraux des Pays-Bas des origines à la fin du règne de Philippe de Beau 1440-1506". In: *Standen en Landen*, vol. LXIV, 1974

Wernham, R.B., "English Policy and the Revolt of the Netherlands". In: *Britain and the Netherlands*, London, 1960, pp. 29-40

Williams, Neville, *The Life and Time of Elisabeth I*, London, 1972

Woltjer, J.J., "Inleiding op catalogus: Opstand en onafhankelijkheid. Eerste Vrije Statenvergadering, Dordrecht 1572", Dordrecht, 1972

Woltjer, J.J., "De vredemakers. De positie en uiteindelijke uitschakeling van een gematigde 'middengroep' in de periode van de zestiger jaren tot omstreeks 1580". In: *Tijdschrift voor Geschiedenis*, no. 89, 1976, pp. 292-321

Woltjer, J.J., "De vredemakers". In: *De Unie van Utrecht. Wording en werking van een verbond en een verbondsacte*, The Hague, 1979

Woude, A.M. van der, "De Staten, Leicester en Elisabeth in financiële verwikkelingen". In: *Tijdschrift voor Geschiedenis*, vol. 74, p. 64

Chapter 4

Adair, John, *A Life of John Hampden*, London, 1976

Adams, George Burton, *Constitutional History of England*, revised by Robert L. Schuyler, London, 1971

Adams, S.L., "Foreign Policy and the Parliaments of 1621 and 1624". In: *Faction and Parliament: Essays on Early Stuart History*, ed. Kevin Sharpe, Oxford, 1977

Ardant, Gabriel, "Financial Policy and Economic Infrastructure of Modern States and Nations". In: *The Formation of National States in Western Europe*, ed. Charles Tilly, Princeton, New Jersey, 1975, pp. 164-242

Ashley, Maurice, *England in the Seventeenth Century*, Pelican Book, reprint 1986

Ashton, Robert, "Tradition and Innovation and the Great Rebellion". In: *Three British Revolutions: 1641, 1688, 1776*, ed. J.G.A. Pocock, New Jersey, 1980

Ashton, Robert, *The English Civil War: Conservatism and Revolution 1603-1649*, London, 1978

Aylmer, G.E., "Crisis and Regrouping in the Political Elites: England from the 1630's to the 1660's". In: *Three British Revolutions: 1641, 1688, 1776*, ed. J.G.A. Pocock, New Jersey, 1980

Ball, J.N., *Sir John Eliot and Parliament 1624-1629*, London, 1977

Carlton, Charles, "Three British Revolutions and the Personality of Kingship". In: *Three British Revolutions: 1641, 1688, 1776*, ed. J.G.A. Pocock, New Jersey, 1980

Braun, Rudolf, "Taxation, Sociopolitical Structure and State-Building: Great Britain and Brandenburg-Prussia". In: *The Formation of National States in Western Europe*, Princeton, New Jersey, 1975, pp. 243-327

Dicey, A.V., *Introduction to the Study of the Law of the Constitution*, 8th printing, London, 1927

Dietz, Frederick C., *English Public Finance 1558-1641*, New York/London, 1932 (reprinted 1964)

Dowell, Stephen, *History of Taxation and Taxes in England*, 4 volumes, London, 1884

Freund, Michael, *Die grosse Revolution in England. Anatomie eines Umsturzes*, Hamburg, 1951

Fletcher, Anthony, *The Outbreak of the English Civil War*, London, 1981

Gardiner, S.R., *History of England from the Accession of James I to the Outbreak of the Civil War*, 10 volumes, London, 1883-1884

Gardiner, S.R., *The Constitutional Documents of the Puritan Revolution*, 3rd printing, Oxford, 1906, reprinted 1962

Gordon, M.D., *The collection of Ship Money in the Reign of Charles I*, Royal Hist.Trans, 3rd, series IV, 1910, pp. 141-162

Harris, G.R., "Medieval Doctrines in the Debates on Supply 1610-1629". In: *Faction and Parliament: Essays on Early Stuart History*, ed. Kevin Sharpe, Oxford, 1977

Hawkins, Michael, "The Government: Its Role and Its Aims". In: *The Origins of the English Civil War*, ed. Conrad Russell, Macmillan, 1975

Hill, Christopher, "A Bourgeous Revolution?". In: *Three British Revolutions: 1641, 1688, 1776*, ed. J.G.A. Pocock, New Jersey, 1980

Hill, L.M., "County Government in Caroline England 1625-1640". In: *The Origins of the English Civil War*, ed. Conrad Russell, Macmillan, 1975

Hirst, Derek, "Court, Country and Politics Before 1629". In: *Faction and Parliament, Essays on Early Stuart History*, ed. Kevin Sharpe, Oxford, 1977

Jones, J.A.P., *King John and Magna Carta*, Harlow, 1983

Jones, W.J., *Politics and the Bench: The Judges and the Origins of the English Civil War*, London, 1971

Judson, Margaret Atwood, *The Crisis of the Constitution: An Essay in Constitutional and Political Thought in England 1603-1645*, New Brunswick, New Jersey, 1949

Keir, D.L., *The Case of Ship Money*, LQR, pp. 546-574

Kenyon, J.P., *The Stuarts*, London, 1958

Kenyon, J.P., *The Stuart Constitution*, 2nd printing, Cambridge, 1986

Kossmann, E.H., "Over de koning die geen kwaad kon doen". In: *Historie en metahistorie. "Robert Fruin" lustrumbundel*, Leiden, 1952, pp. 19-29

Longford, Lord, *A History of the House of Lords*, London, 1988

Manning, Brian, *The English People and the English Revolution 1640-1641*, London, 1976

Marriott, Sir John A.R., *The Crisis of English Liberty: A History of the Stuart Monarchy and the Puritan Revolution*, Oxford, 1930

Maurois, André, *Histoire d'Angleterre*. Dutch translation: Geschiedenis van Engeland, Amsterdam, 1971

National Biography: Eliot, Henrietta Maria, Pym, Villiers, Hampden, Wentworth, Laud, etc.

Ollard, Richard, *The Image of the King*, London, 1979

Prynne, W., *An Humble Remonstrance to his Maiesty against the Tax of Ship Money*, 1641

Richardson, R.C., *The Debate on the English Revolution*, London, 1977

Russell, Conrad, *Parliaments and English Politics 1621-1629*, Oxford, 1979

Russell, Conrad, "Parliaments and the King's Finances". In: *The Origins of the English Civil War*, ed. Conrad Russell, Macmillan, 1975

Sharpe, Kevin, "Parliamentary History 1603-1629: In or Out of Perspective". In: *Faction and Parliament: Essays on Early Stuart History*, ed. Kevin Sharpe, Oxford, 1977

Skelton, Sir John, *Charles I*, London, Paris, Edinburgh, 1898

Stone, Lawrence, *The Causes of the English Revolution 1629-1642*, London, 1986

Stone, Lawrence, "The Results of the English Revolution of the Seventeenth Century". In: *Three British revolutions: 1641, 1688, 1776*, ed. J.G.A. Pocock, New Jersey, 1980

Swart, K.W., *Sale of Offices in the Seventeenth Century*, doctoral dissertation, State University of Leiden, The Hague, 1949

Thomas, P.W., "Two Cultures? Court and Country under Charles I". In: *The origins of the English civil war*, ed. Conrad Russell, Macmillan, 1975

Trevelyan, G.M., *England under the Stuarts*, Pelican Books, 1960

Trevor-Roper, *Archbishop Laud 1573-1645*, London, 1940

Wedgwood, C.V., *Strafford 1593-1641*, Greenwood Reprinting, 1970
Wedgwood, C.V., *The King's Peace 1637-1641*, London, 1955
Woodward, E.L., *Geschiedenis van Engeland*, Prisma Books, 1965

Chapter 5

Adair, Douglass and John A. Schutz, *Peter Oliver's Origin & Progress of the American Rebellion*, Stanford, California, 1967
An Impartial History of England from the Coronation of George I to The Middle of the Year 1799, Blackburn, undated
Andrews, Allen, *The King Who Lost America*, London, 1976
Beloff, Man (ed.), *The Debate on the American Revolution 1761-1783: A Sourcebook*, New York, 1965
Bemis, Samual Flagg, *The Diplomacy of the American Revolution*, Indiana, 1957
Boatner III, Mark Mayo, *Encyclopedia of the American Revolution*, New York, 1966
Buuren, H. van, *De consolidatie van de onafhankelijkheid der Verenigde Staten van Amerika (1763-1795)*, The Hague, 1949
Cappon, Lester Y., *Atlas of Early American History: The Revolutionary Era 1760-1790*, Princeton, 1976
Christie, Ian R. and Benjamin W. Labaree, *Empire or Independence 760-1776: A British-American Dialogue on the Coming of the American Revolution*, Oxford, 1976
Dickerson, Oliver M., *The Navigation Acts and the American Revolution*, Philadelphia, 1951
Dupuy, Trevor N. and Gay M. Hammerman, *People & Events of the American Revolution*, New York, London, 1974
Elliot Griffis, Win, *The Influence of the Netherlands in the Making of the English Commonwealth and the American Republic*, Boston, 1891
Gewehr, Wesley M., Donald C. Gordon, David S. Sparks and Roland N. Stromberg, *American Civilization: A History of the United States*, New York, 1957
Gipson, Lawrence Henry, *The Coming of the Revolution*, New York, 1962
Greene, Jack. P., Charles F. Mulett, Edward C. Papenfuse Jr. (ed.), *Magna Charta for America: James Abercromby's "An Examination of the Acts of Parliament Relative to the Trade and the Government of our American Colonies" (1752) and "De Jure et Gubernatore Coloniarum, or An Inquiry into the Nature and the Rights of Colonies, Ancient and Modern" (1774)*, Philadelphia, 1986
Hermans, Johannes Leonardus, *Het aandeel van Engeland aan de vorming van het staatswezen der Noordamerikaanse Unie*, doctoral dissertation, University of Tilburg, 1941
Hofstadter, Richard, William Miller en William Aaron, *The American Republic, volume 1 to 1865*, 3rd printing, New Jersey, 1961
Imberg, Kurt Ed., "Studien zur Geschichte der englischen Besteuerung in den nordamerikanischen Kolonien im 17. und 18. Jahrhundert". In: *Vierteljahrschrift für Sozial- und Wirtschaftsgeschichte*, vol. XIII, pp. 361-416
Jensen, Merrill, *Tracts of the American Revolution*, Indianapolis, New York, 1967
Jensen, Merrill, *The Founding of a Nation: A History of the American Revolution 1763-1776*, New York, 1968
Jensen, Merill, *The Articles of Confederation: An interpretation of the Social-constitutional History of the American Revolution 1774-1781*, 8th printing, Wisconsin, 1976
Kaplan, Laurence S. (ed.), *The American Revoluton and "A Candid World"*, Kent State University, 1977
Kaspi, André, *Geschiedenis van de Verenigde Staten van Amerika*, volume I, 1607-1945, Utrecht, 1988
Knollenberg, Bernhard, *Growth of the American Revolution 1766-1775*, New York, London, 1975
Koenig, W.J. and S.L. Mayer, *European Manuscript Sources of the American Revolution*, London, New York, 1974
Lewis, John D., *Anti-federalists versus Federalists: Selected Documents*, Scranton, 1967
McDonald, Forrest, *We the People: The Economic Origins of the Constitution*, Chicago, 1958
McDowell, Bart, *The Revolutionary War*, 2nd printing, Washington, 1970
McLean Andrews, Charles, *Colonial Self-Government 1652-1689*, New York, London, 1904
Maier, Pauline, *From Resistance to Revolution: Colonial Radicals and the Development of American Oppositon to Britain, 1765-1776*, New York, 1973
Maier, Pauline, *The Old Revolutionaries: Political Lives in The Age of Samuel Adams*, New York, 1982
Middlekauf, Robert, *The Glorious Cause: The American Revolution 1763-1789*, New York, Oxford, 1982
Morris, Richard B., *The Peacemakers: The Great Powers and American Independence*, New York, 1965

Morris, Richard B., *Encyclopedia of American History*, New York, 1961

Nevins, Allan and Henry Steele Commager, *Amerika, De geschiedenis van een vrij volk*, 2nd printing, Utrecht, Antwerp, undated

Plumb, J.H., *England in the Eighteenth Century*, Pelican, reprinted 1973

Plumb, J.H., *The First Four Georges*, 10th printing, Fontana, Collins, 1976

Pole, J.R., *The Gift of Government: Political Responsibility from the English Restoration to American Independence*, Athens, Georgia, 1983

Pole, J.R., *Foundations of American Independence 1763-1815*, Fontana, Collins, 1973

Rossiter, Clinton, *Seedtime of the Republic: The Origin of the American Tradition of Political Liberty*, New York, 1952

Schlesinger, Arthur M., *The Birth of the Nation: A Portrait of the American People on the Eve of Independence*, London, 1969

Schlesinger, Arthur M., *Prelude to Independence: The Newspaper War on Britain, 1764-1776*, New York, 1965

Schulte Nordholt, J.W., *Voorbeeld in de verte. De invloed van de Amerikaanse revolutie in Nederland*, Baarn, 1979

Schulte Nordholt, J.W., *Triomf en tragiek van de vrijheid. De geschiedenis van de Verenigde Staten van Amerika*, Amsterdam, 1985

Shaw, Peter, *American Patriots and the Rituals of Revolution*, Cambridge, Massachusetts, 1981

Solberg, Winton U. (ed.), *The Federal Convention and the Formation of the Union of the American States*, Indianapolis, New York, 1958

Stark, James H., *The Loyalists of Massachusetts and the Other Side of the American Revolution*, Boston, 1910 (reprinted 1972)

Stark, M.A.W., *America, Ideal and Reality: The United States of 1776 in Contemporary European Philosophy*, London, 1947

Thomas, P.D.G., *British Politics and the Stamp Act Crisis: The First Phase of the American Revolution 1763-1767*, Oxford, 1975

Trevelyan, George Otto, *The American Revolution*, concise edition by Richard B. Morris, New York, 1957

Tuchman, Barbara W., *Het eerste saluutschot. De Amerikaanse vrijheidsstrijd en de Republiek*, Houten, 1988 (translation of: The first Salute)

Tuchman, Barbara W., *De Mars der Dwaasheid. Bestuurlijk onvermogen van Troje tot Vietnam*, 2nd printing, Amsterdam, Brussels, 1984 (translation of: The March of Folly)

Vidal, Gore, "The Four Generations of the Adams Family". In: *Matters of Fact and of Fiction: Essays*, 1973-1976

Warden, G.B., *Boston 1689-1776*, Boston, Toronto, 1970

Winsor, Justin, *The Memorial History of Boston 1630-1880*, Boston, 1881

White, Morton, *The Philosophy of the American Revolution*, Oxford, 1981

Winsor, Justin, *The Memorial History of Boston 1630-1880*, Boston, 1881

Woods Labaree, Benjamin, *The Boston Tea Party*, London, Oxford, New York, 1968

Zee, Henri van der, *Het edelste gewest. De geschiedenis van Nieuw-Nederland 1609-1674*, Amsterdam, 1982

Allegorical print depicting the repression under Alva's regime. The Dutch lion is clamped in a huge hand press, being turned tighter by Alva and Margaret of Parma. The bystanders include the Pope and Philip II.

List of illustrations

Abbey Saint Maurice, Saint Maurice, p. 44

Antiquarian Bookshop Nico Israël, Amsterdam, pp. 293, 295

Atlas van Stolk, Rotterdam, pp. 140, 141, 142, 143, 144, 145, 148, 152, 156, 160, 164, 177, 178, 183, 184, 185, 187, 188, 193, 194, 195, 196, 199, 214, 383

Bibliotheca Philosophica Hermetica, Amsterdam, pp. 2, 49, 97, 118, 119

Bibliothèque Ingiumbertine, p. 37

Bibliothèque Municipal, Laon, pp. 20, 28, 51

Bibliothèque Nationale, Paris, pp. 45, 49

Erzbischöfliches Diözesan- und Dombibliothek, Cologne, p. 79

Erzbischöfliches Diözesan Museum, Cologne, pp. 19, 45

Hessische Landes- und Hochschulbibliothek, Darmstadt, p. 78

Iconographisch Bureau, The Hague, p. 354

Castle Burg, Burg, p. 95

Koninklijke Bibliotheek, Brussels, pp. 23, 100, 131

Koninklijke Bibliotheek, The Hague, pp. 66, 67, 169, 278, 297

Koninklijk Huisarchief, The Hague, p. 210

Kunstmuseum der Stadt Düsseldorf, p. 172

Laurentius, Th., Duivenvoorde, p. 263

Mary Evans Collection, London, pp. 25, 81, 219, 249, 261, 290, 301, 311, 349, 350, 352, 353

Musée des Antiquités Nationales, St. Germain-en-Laye, pp. 27, 31

Musée Condé, Chantilly, p. 36

Musée Goya, Castres, pp. 14, 21, 24

Museum of Fine Arts, Boston, Massachusetts, pp. 321, 322, 330

Museum Plantin-Moretus, Antwerp, p. 135

National Portrait Gallery, London, pp. 162, 209, 220, 224, 236, 253, 273, 276, 283, 288, 304, 305, 338, 357

Oesterreichische Nationalbibliothek, Vienna, p. 48

Palacio de Liria, Madrid, pp. 166, 167, 171

Pinacoteca Nazionale, Siena, p. 207

Print Collection of the Rijksmuseum, Amsterdam, pp. 138, 181, 203, 213

Print and Drawing Room of The British Museum, London, pp. 8, 211, 216, 226, 227, 231, 241, 244, 259, 265, 268, 275, 280, 285, 286, 289, 309, 316, 318, 320, 333, 355, 359, 360, 362, 365, 367, 370, 372, 375

The main figures in this May 1782 print are Britannia, who has set down her shield bearing the words "George for Ever" in order to embrace her daughter America, an Indian, armed with two spears, one of which is marked "Liberty." The friendliness of the two ladies is underscored by their words. Mama says "Be a good Girl and give me a Buss," and daughter answers obediently: "Dear Mama, say no more about it." The other players in this drama have quite a different opinion. France, aided by ally Spain, has tied a scarf around the Indian beauty and is trying to prevent the reconciliation. Inevitably, the Dutchman on the left smokes his pipe and leans on a barrel of Dutch herring, next to a cask of "Holland's gin." He says: "I'll deliberate a little to see which is weakest, then I'll give you a direct answer Kate Russia," a clear reference to Catherine the Great of Russia who tried in vain to mediate a peace between England and the Dutch Republic. On the right, English politicians watch angrily from the sidelines. The print aims to show that the parties starting the War of Independence, namely England and America, wish to make peace, but are held back by their allies. Seen in a broader perspective, the print can be viewed as a call for peace and unity, thereby forming a companion picture to the print facing the Preface and serving as a suitable ending to the book.